SUBSTANCE DEPENDENCE AND CO-OCCURRING PSYCHIATRIC DISORDERS

Best Practices for Diagnosis and Clinical Treatment

Edited by
Edward V. Nunes, M.D.
Jeffrey Selzer, M.D.
Petros Levounis, M.D., M.A.
Carrie A. Davies, B.S.

Civic Research Institute

4478 U.S. Route 27 • P.O. Box 585 • Kingston, NJ 08528

Library of Congress Cataloging in Publication Data
Substance Dependence and Co-Occurring Psychiatric Disorders: Best Practices for Diagnosis and Clinical Treatment / Edward V. Nunes, M.D., Jeffrey Selzer, M.D., Petros Levounis, M.D., M.A., and Carrie A. Davies, B.S.

ISBN 978-1-887554-66-4 (Hardcover)
ISBN 978-1-887554-91-6 (Paperback)
Library of Congress Control Number: 2009942037

To our mentor, Frederic M. Quitkin, M.D.

Table of Contents

Chapter 2: Bipolar Disorder in Patients With Substance Use Disorders
*Timothy G. Benson, M.D., Rachel E. Bender, M.A., Patrice M. Muchowski, Sc.D.,
and Roger D. Weiss, M.D.*

Chapter 3: Posttraumatic Stress Disorder in Patients With Substance Use Disorders
*Kathleen Brady, M.D., Ph.D., Denise Hien, Ph.D., Louise Haynes, M.S.W.,
and Therese Killeen, Ph.D., A.P.R.N., B.C.*

Chapter 4: Other Anxiety Disorders in Patients With Substance Use Disorders: Panic Disorder, Agoraphobia, Social Anxiety Disorder, and Generalized Anxiety Disorder
Carlos Blanco, M.D., Ph.D., Carrie A. Davies, B.S., and Edward V. Nunes, M.D.

PART 3: DISORDERS OF ATTENTION AND COGNITIVE FUNCTIONING AND CHRONIC MENTAL ILLNESS P3-1

Chapter 5: Adult Attention Deficit Hyperactivity Disorder in Patients With Substance Use Disorders
John J. Mariani, M.D., and Frances R. Levin, M.D.

Chapter 6: Delirium, Dementia, and Other Cognitive Disorders in Patients With Substance Use Disorders
Petros Levounis, M.D., M.A., and Efrat Aharonovich, Ph.D.

**Chapter 7: Schizophrenia and Schizoaffective Illness in Patients
With Substance Use Disorders**
Serge Sevy, M.D., M.B.A., Rachel Miller, Ph.D., and Joanne McCormack, L.C.S.W.

**Chapter 8: Antisocial Personality Disorder in Patients With
Substance Use Disorders**
*Robert K. Brooner, Ph.D., Elizabeth R. Disney, Ph.D., Karin J. Neufeld, M.D.,
M.P.H., Van L. King, M.D., Michael Kidorf, Ph.D., and Kenneth B. Stoller, M.D.*

**Chapter 9: Borderline Personality Disorder in Patients With
Substance Use Disorders**
Andrew Ekblad, M.A., Alexander L. Chapman, Ph.D., and Thomas R. Lynch, Ph.D.

**PART 5: IMPULSE CONTROL DISORDERS AND
EATING DISORDERS**

**Chapter 10: Pathological Gambling Among Patients With
Substance Use Disorders**
*Carlos Blanco, M.D., Ph.D., Oshra Cohen, Ph.D., Juan José Luján, M.D., and
Edelgard Wulfert, Ph.D.*

Chapter 11: Intermittent Explosive Disorder and Impulsive Aggression in Patients With Substance Use Disorders
Stephen J. Donovan, M.D.

Chapter 12: Eating Disorders in Patients With Substance Use Disorders: Bulimia, Anorexia, Overeating Disorder, and Obesity
Shelly F. Greenfield, M.D., M.P.H., Susan M. Gordon, Ph.D., Lisa Cohen, Ph.D., and Elisa Trucco, B.A.

Chapter 13: Cigarette Smoking Among Patients With Substance Use Disorders
Eric Schindler, Ph.D., Patricia Penn, Ph.D., and Malcolm S. Reid, Ph.D.

Chapter 14: Common Medical Illnesses in Patients With Substance Use and Psychiatric Disorders
Jeanne Manubay, M.D., and Terry Horton, M.D.

Chapter 15: Substance Abuse During Adolescence
Jeffrey J. Wilson, M.D.

Chapter 16: Pain in Patients With Substance Use Disorders
Deborah L. Haller, Ph.D., A.B.P.P., and Sidney H. Schnoll, M.D., Ph.D.

Chapter 17: Suicide and Substance Abuse
Richard K. Ries, M.D.

**Chapter 18: Drug Interactions in the Pharmacological Treatment
of Substance Use Disorders**
Elinore F. McCance-Katz, M.D., Ph.D.

Chapter 20: Directions for Future Research on Treating Co-Occurring Substance Use and Psychiatric Disorders

Jennifer P. Wisdom, Ph.D., M.P.H., Christiane Farentinos, M.D., M.P.H., C.A.D.C.-II, N.C.D.C.-II, Tim Hartnett, M.S.W., M.H.A., Lucy Zammarelli, M.A., N.C.A.C.-II, and Dennis McCarty, Ph.D.

Acknowledgements

This book is a collaborative effort between clinicians and researchers. In addition to the chapter authors, who hail from both clinical and research backgrounds, many people helped to make publication of this book possible. We would like to thank all the members of the Co-Occurring Disorders Special Interest Group of the National Institute on Drug Abuse (NIDA) Clinical Trials Network (CTN), who provided inspiration and encouragement. We would like to acknowledge NIDA for funding of the CTN, including grant U10 DA13035 of the CTN Long Island Node (where the editors are based), as well as the researchers, community treatment program directors, and NIDA staff members who created the CTN. A debt of gratitude is owed to Deborah S. Hasin, Ph.D., for permitting us to print interview questions from the Psychiatric Research Interview for Substance and Mental Disorders (PRISM) and to Michael B. First, M.D., for permitting us to print interview questions from the Structured Clinical Interview for DSM-IV-TR Axis I Disorders (SCID-I) and the Structured Clinical Interview for DSM-IV-TR Impulse Control Disorders Not Elsewhere Classified (SCID-ICD). We thank Sharon Samet, Ph.D., for help in reviewing and editing many tables in the textbook, Valerie Richmond for assistance with formatting and final editing of many chapters, and Maxine Idakus for careful line editing. We thank the resident physicians at St. Luke's and Roosevelt Hospitals who offered insightful comments during "test-piloting" of the sixty-question Continuing Education and Clinical Skills Examination. Finally, we would like to thank our publisher, especially Deborah Launer, who encouraged us to launch this effort and provided us with continuous encouragement.

Introduction and Overview

by Edward V. Nunes, M.D., Jeffrey Selzer, M.D., Petros Levounis, M.D., M.A., and Carrie A. Davies, B.S.

CALL TO CLINICIANS TREATING SUBSTANCE-DEPENDENT PATIENTS TO LEARN ABOUT PSYCHIATRIC COMORBIDITY

This book was written to teach clinicians who treat patients with alcohol and drug dependence about the psychiatric disorders that commonly co-occur with addictive disorders. Potential readers include anyone working in alcohol and drug treatment programs or specializing in treatment of addictive disorders—from counselors and medical staff to supervisors and program directors—including clinicians and managers with little or no prior training in psychopathology or psychiatric diagnosis and treatment. This book was written to serve as a primer that will stimulate interest in co-occurring psychopathologies and inspire confidence that achievement of a working knowledge of this topic is within the grasp of any clinician and will yield more effective clinicians. We also hope that clinicians from mental health care settings, psychiatrists, psychologists, and social workers will refer to this book as they seek to broaden their knowledge of the special issues involved in psychiatric diagnosis and treatment planning for patients with co-occurring mental disorders and addictive disorders.

As readers learn more about psychiatric disorders, we hope that they not only gain familiarity with the academic literature and broaden their knowledge base, but also acquire skills necessary for screening and treating psychiatric disorders including mastery of the skills required for conducting a psychiatric diagnostic interview, making tentative diagnoses, and identifying patients who should be referred for specialty care. One does not need to become a specialist in treating psychiatric disorders to be able to tailor a treatment plan to the unique needs of dually diagnosed patients. Clinicians can better serve their patients simply by becoming familiar with the treatment options for psychiatric disorders in order to facilitate proper referral of patients to specialty care (e.g., psychotherapy, medication treatment), monitor patients, and provide follow-up.

We believe that any motivated clinician can learn to conduct a basic psychiatric diagnostic interview, understand how psychiatric disorders may impact treatment of addictions, and successfully refer patients to specialty care. By acquiring the skills to diagnose and treat patients with co-occurring psychiatric and substance use disorders, clinicians can improve their treatment alliance with their patients and the overall outcome of their patients' treatment.

IMPORTANCE OF ADDRESSING PSYCHIATRIC COMORBIDITY

Psychiatric comorbidity, most notably the co-occurrence of a psychiatric disorder and substance use disorder, is a common condition that results in tremendous suffering and costs. The presence of a psychiatric disorder increases the risk for the presence of an addictive disorder and vice versa. Much evidence suggests that when these disorders occur together, a patient's prognosis is worse than when the disorders occur alone; evidence also suggests that treatment of both disorders simultaneously in one facility or in a coordinated effort with another facility results in better treatment outcome.

While the caseloads of clinicians in substance abuse treatment programs often contain numerous patients who suffer from one or more psychiatric disorders in addition to a substance use disorder, few of these clinicians have substantial training in diagnosis and treatment of psychiatric disorders. Thus, this book aims to teach clinicians about the diagnosis and treatment of co-occurring psychiatric and substance use disorders. With this knowledge clinicians should be able to more effectively screen dually diagnosed patients, collaborate with mental health care specialists, and improve quality of care for patients with both addictions and other psychiatric disorders.

BRIEF HISTORY OF RESEARCH ON PSYCHIATRIC COMORBIDITY

Attention to co-occurring psychiatric disorders (i.e., a substance use disorder plus another psychiatric disorder) represents a sea change in the mental health field that has occurred over the last decade or two. Historically, the treatment systems for psychiatric disorders and substance use disorders have operated (and largely continue to operate) separately from one another. These two treatment systems have been operated by different state agencies, have offered different treatment programs, have employed different clinicians with different backgrounds in education and training, and have received funding from different sources. Psychiatric clinicians, including psychiatrists, psychologists, and clinical social workers, historically have received little training in diagnosis and management of substance use disorders; similarly, clinicians who treat substance use disorders historically have received training that has focused mainly on diagnosis and treatment of substance use disorders (with little attention to other co-occurring disorders). Dually diagnosed patients have been required to navigate the two separate treatment systems with little assistance from treatment professionals and often receive inadequate treatment for either or both of their disorders.

Increased interest in co-occurring psychiatric disorders began to emerge in the 1980s. A series of large surveys of the general population documented a high prevalence of psychiatric disorders in the general population and a high rate of co-occurring psychiatric disorders, particularly a combination of substance use disorders and other mental disorders, such as mood and anxiety disorders (Grant, 1995; Grant et al., 2004; Kessler, 1995; Kessler et al., 1994; Regier et al., 1990). The presence of alcoholism or another substance dependence disorder was found to increase a patient's risk of having other psychiatric disorders by a factor of two or more. These findings echoed results from studies that documented high rates of co-occurring psychiatric disorders in samples of patients in treatment for substance use disorders (for a review, see Hasin & Nunes, 1998). Studies also indicated that the presence of co-occurring psychiatric disorders often predicted poor outcome and, interestingly, that psychiatric disorders might play a role in motivating patients to enter treatment for problems with addictions. Later studies suggested that treatment that integrates psychiatric and substance abuse treatment modalities leads to better outcomes for patients with both a psychiatric disorder and substance use disorders (Drake & Mueser, 2001; Hellerstein, Rosenthal, & Miner, 2001; Nunes & Levin, 2004; Weiss, 2004). Over the past decade treatment programs that had focused exclusively on substance use disorders have begun to routinely involve psychiatric consultants in patients' care and to set up services for patients with co-occurring disorders.

GENESIS OF THIS BOOK

The inspiration for this book grew out of our participation in the National Institute on Drug Abuse (NIDA) Clinical Trials Network (CTN). The CTN, which was spearheaded by NIDA director Dr. Alan Leshner to "improv[e] the quality of drug abuse treatment throughout the nation using science as the vehicle" (A. Leshner, personal communication, March 14, 2001), was a bold step in addictions treatment research. Funded by the National Institutes of Health/National Institute on Drug Abuse, the CTN is a nationwide network of research centers and community-based substance abuse treatment programs; the CTN was established in response to a landmark study by the Institute of Medicine (1998) that showed that new innovations in treatment for addictions were not being adopted by treatment providers in routine clinical care of patients with alcohol and drug dependence. New treatment approaches had been developed and rigorously tested in clinical trials, which were funded by the National Institutes of Health and were expensive and painstaking to conduct, but these approaches were rarely used in clinical practice. The CTN conducts rigorous research to test the effectiveness of new treatments for substance dependence in real-world treatment settings (e.g., inner-city methadone clinics). The CTN consists of researchers, clinicians, and program directors from across the United States who are interested in conducting research to improve the quality of care of their patients. The diagnosis and treatment of co-occurring disorders has been an abiding theme in the CTN, which aims to integrate psychiatric treatment into substance abuse treatment (and vice versa) and to ensure that treatment approaches that have proven effective in clinical trials are disseminated to the substance use treatment community.

Inspiration for this book arose from discussions by the editors and many of the contributors during meetings of a working group of the CTN: the Co-Occurring

Disorders Special Interest Group. The Co-Occurring Disorders Special Interest Group was formed within the CTN to identify important problems related to comorbidity that were confronting clinicians and treatment programs in the field and that should be addressed with research. Members of the Co-Occurring Disorders Special Interest Group included individuals whose careers had been devoted to clinical research and many program directors and clinicians from community-based substance abuse treatment programs. One issue that emerged repeatedly during discussions was the need to help clinicians who work in substance abuse treatment settings to learn more about co-occurring psychiatric disorders. Members agreed that while there already was a wealth of evidence suggesting that co-occurring disorders are prevalent among substance-dependent patients and are associated with worse outcome and that integrated treatment approaches (i.e., treatment approaches that address substance abuse and other psychiatric disorders in a coordinated fashion) are effective, further research was needed. This book, which represents the first step in addressing the burning need in the field to make coordinated treatment efforts standard practice, should serve as a practical resource for clinicians who wish to learn about diagnosis and treatment of co-occurring disorders.

ROLE OF SPECIALISTS AND CONSULTANTS AND RISING NEED FOR GENERALISTS

In their book *Freakonomics: A Rogue Economist Explores the Hidden Side of Everything,* Levitt and Dubner (2005) present an iconoclastic view of American society through the lens of economic theory, and they challenge Americans' tendency to rely on experts in a range of fields from real estate sales to parenting. The authors argue that the services that experts provide may not always match the needs of their clients and that often the information that experts provide is accessible to anyone who is willing to spend time seeking it. Similarly, we believe that knowledge of psychiatric disorders that co-occur with substance use disorders is easily obtainable and that clinicians can better serve their substance-dependent patients by undertaking the psychiatric diagnosis and treatment planning process that might otherwise be delegated to mental health experts. Clinicians and treatment programs that serve substance-dependent patients should not rely solely on psychiatric consultants and specialists for the treatment of patients with psychiatric disorders, and clinicians who work in substance abuse treatment programs should not limit themselves as specialists in only addiction treatment. Instead, clinicians from substance abuse treatment programs should become generalists and acquire a working knowledge of psychiatric diagnosis and treatment that allows them to recognize psychiatric disorders in their patients, adapt their treatment approaches accordingly, and make appropriate referrals for specialized treatment.

We do not intend to dismiss the role of specialists. Indeed, a specialist's skill in treatment and in the fine points of diagnosis results from study, repetition of tasks (e.g., performing numerous psychiatric evaluations), and specialization. Instead, we simply wish to encourage clinicians in substance abuse treatment programs to expand the boundaries of their competencies, become informed about psychiatric disorders, and become more discriminating in referring patients to specialists.

ORGANIZATION OF THIS BOOK

Chapters on Psychiatric Disorders

Chapters 1 through 12 provide a primer on the diagnosis and treatment of psychiatric disorders that most commonly co-occur in patients with substance abuse problems, including depression, bipolar disorder, anxiety disorders, schizophrenia, attention deficit hyperactivity disorder, and other disorders of cognition, personality disorders, impulse control disorders, and eating disorders. Each chapter follows the following structure:

- *Case Examples:* These descriptions of cases, which are drawn from the authors' clinical experiences, introduce the psychiatric disorder covered in the chapter and illustrate how the disorder manifests itself in substance-dependent patients.

- *Diagnostic Criteria:* This section describes the *Diagnostic and Statistical Manual of Mental Disorders,* 4th edition (*DSM-IV*) criteria (American Psychiatric Association, 1994) for the disorder that is covered in the chapter and discusses difficulties and special issues that arise in making a diagnosis in substance-dependent patients. Substance abuse can cause psychiatric symptoms, thereby making an accurate diagnosis of some psychiatric disorders in substance-dependent patients difficult. This section also contains tables that summarize the *DSM-IV* criteria, briefly discusses issues that complicate the evaluation of each criterion among substance-dependent patients, and suggests interview questions for each criterion from semistructured interviews, namely the Psychiatric Research Interview for Substance and Mental Disorders (PRISM; Hasin, Samet, Nunes, Meydan, Matseoane, & Waxman, 2006) or the Structured Clinical Interview for DSM-IV-TR Axis I Disorders (SCID-I; First, Spitzer, Gibbon, & Williams, 2002).

- *Natural History and Etiology:* This section discusses the course of the psychiatric illness covered in the chapter (both the course of the illness when it occurs alone and the course of the illness when it occurs in the presence of a substance use disorder), as well as presumed causes of the psychiatric disorder and risk factors for developing the disorder.

- *Issues Involved in Making a Diagnosis in Substance-Dependent Patients:* This section examines the potential for confusing symptoms of substance toxicity or withdrawal with symptoms of a psychiatric syndrome.

- *Instruments and Methods for Screening and Diagnosis:* This section provides descriptions of screening and diagnostic instruments, with suggestions on how they might be used by clinicians in substance use treatment programs. The book highlights use of one of the most sophisticated diagnostic instruments for application in dually diagnosed populations–the PRISM. The PRISM quotes *DSM-IV* criteria for twenty Axis I disorders and two Axis II disorders, and it includes interview questions that help clinicians to elicit information from patients about their symptoms and to evaluate each symptom separately in terms of its relationship to substance abuse. For each psychiatric disorder, the PRISM provides a list of substances with intoxication or withdrawal symptoms that mimic the psychiatric disorder. The PRISM may be administered by interviewers with different professional backgrounds (e.g., degree in nursing, bachelor's degree in psychology) and typically requires approximately 120 minutes to administer. Hasin and colleagues began development of the PRISM in 1990 and have revised it several times in order to improve reliability and usability; studies have shown that the PRISM is reliable in making a *DSM-IV* diagnosis in research participants who have substance use disorders (Hasin et al., 1996). Although the PRISM, to date, has been used primarily in research settings, clinicians are encouraged to obtain the instrument and practice using it in order to become familiar with *DSM-IV* diagnostic criteria and the procedure for evaluating comorbid symptoms and syndromes. Information on the PRISM, including instructions on how to obtain copies of it, a review of its uses, and a copy of the *PRISM Training Manual,* is available at http://www.columbia.edu/~dsh2/prism. A computerized version of the PRISM is under development.

- *Differential Diagnosis and Overlapping Disorders:* This section briefly discusses the frequency with which the psychiatric disorder covered in the chapter co-occurs with other psychiatric disorders (e.g., panic disorder with major depression or bipolar disorder), medical problems, or substance use disorders.

- *Treatment Options:* This section provides a brief overview of options for treatment of the psychiatric disorder covered in the chapter and offers hints on how clinicians might tailor a treatment plan to simultaneously treat the psychiatric disorder and a substance use disorder, including suggestions on when to elicit the help of a mental health specialist or consultant. This section also discusses what response can be expected from treatment and how to tell if patients are responding well to treatment or are not responding.

Chapters on Special Issues and Directions for Future Research

Chapters 13 through 20 are devoted to issues that are important for clinicians to consider in the management of substance-dependent patients with co-occurring psychiatric disorders, including nicotine dependence, common medical problems, adolescents and children, pain, suicide, and drug interactions. The last two chapters—Chapters 19 and 20—cover future directions for the field, including organization of treatment services and areas of further research.

Self-Exam

A sixty-question Continuing Education and Clinical Skills Examination (CECSE) appears at the end of the book as a tool for assessing reading comprehension and the ability to apply and synthesize the information provided in the chapters. Questions were designed to query readers about clinically relevant aspects of diagnosis and treatment of co-occurring psychiatric and substance use disorders, not esoteric details or DSM trivia.

The CECSE consists of three multiple-choice questions for each chapter (Chapters 1 through 20) about information presented in the book. The sixty-question CECSE was "test-piloted" on a group of resident physicians in training in the psychiatry residency program at St. Luke's and Roosevelt Hospitals in New York City. The "correct answers" to questions reflect the editors' collective recommendation rather than the definitive word on diagnosis and treatment. At least one question for each chapter includes a clinical vignette that is based upon a case from our clinical experiences and that tests the reader's ability to apply the clinical skills discussed in the book. Questions assess competence in the following ten clinical areas:

1. *Epidemiology*—for example, which disorders commonly co-occur with post-traumatic stress disorder?

2. *Assessment*—for example, which questions are most likely to elicit an accurate answer when assessing a patient for anorexia nervosa?

3. *Psychiatric Symptoms*—for example, what are the vegetative symptoms of depression?

4. *Substance Abuse Symptoms*—for example, is there such a diagnosis as nicotine withdrawal?

5. *Medical Symptoms*—for example, can heroin intoxication or cocaine intoxication result in seizures?

6. *DSM-IV Terminology*—for example, is pathological gambling classified as an addiction, an impulse control disorder, a variant of obsessive compulsive disorder, or a mood disorder?

7. *Differential Diagnosis*—for example, how does one distinguish between substance-induced anxiety and social anxiety disorder (formerly called social phobia)?

8. *Pharmacotherapy*—for example, antipsychotic medications are best for the relief of (a) cognitive symptoms, (b) positive symptoms, or (c) negative symptoms of schizophrenia?

9. *Psychotherapy*—for example, what is the primary dialectic in Dialectical Behavior Therapy (DBT) for borderline personality disorder?

10. *Twelve-Step Programs*—for example, what is the relationship between mutual help groups like Alcoholics Anonymous (AA) and the use of psychiatric medications?

In order to permit readers to receive continuing education credits, an answer key to the CECSE has not been included with the book. Readers may obtain the answer key free of charge by contacting The Addiction Institute of New York by e-mail or snail mail:

The Addiction Institute of New York
St. Luke's and Roosevelt Hospitals
Attention: CECSE
1000 Tenth Avenue
New York, New York 10019
e-mail: CECSE@AddictionInstituteNY.org

The New York State Office of Alcoholism and Substance Abuse Services and other national and state accreditation organizations that certify addiction counselors, rehabilitation counselors, and social workers will award continuing education credits for studying this textbook and successfully passing the CECSE (more information about obtaining continuing education credits can be found on the Web site of The Addiction Institute of New York: http://www.AddictionInstituteNY.org/CECSE). Readers who answer 75 percent of the questions correctly are eligible to receive free of charge a certificate of completion. To receive a certificate of completion (and a copy of the answer key) mail the answer sheet to The Addiction Institute of New York at the address listed above; note that only an original answer sheet (i.e., the sheet found in the back of this book, not a photocopy) can be accepted.

APPLICATION OF ACQUIRED SKILLS AND CONTINUED STUDY

Benefits of Practice in Using Structured Diagnostic Interviews

Study of the chapters included in this book should allow readers to improve their knowledge of psychiatric disorders and their treatment among substance-dependent patients. Since knowledge must be reinforced with practice, we encourage readers to obtain training in use of one of the standard semistructured psychiatric interviews, particularly the PRISM. Through the process of learning to use this instrument, readers will increase their familiarity with *DSM-IV* criteria and can become skilled in psychiatric evaluation.

Benefits of Clinical Practice

Clinicians and treatment programs should take steps to expand the scope of their practice by learning to evaluate and provide treatment for dually diagnosed patients. This book may be used as a resource. Clinical skill improves with practice and is guided by supervision and feedback on one's clinical work. Clinicians and treatment programs should consider engaging a consultant who is an expert in diagnosis and treatment of dually diagnosed patients and who is willing to see specific patients with co-occurring disorders, provide guidance on diagnosis and treatment planning, participate in case conferences, or help to provide services to specific cases. Clinicians and treatment programs should also consider looking for opportunities to develop formal liaisons between substance abuse treatment services and psychiatric treatment services, to expand services, or to open new services that are tailored to the treatment needs of patients with co-occurring disorders. Through these services, substance abuse treatment staff members can work side-by-side with psychiatrists and psychologists, and staff members may learn from each other. Patients will benefit from these expanded efforts to address their problems with substance abuse and psychiatric disorders.

Authors' Note

The research in this chapter was supported in part by NIH grants K02 DA00288 (Dr. Nunes), K24 DA022412 (Dr. Nunes), and U10 DA13035 (Dr. Nunes) and the New York State Psychiatric Institute.

References

American Psychiatric Association. (1994). *Diagnostic and statistical manual of mental disorders* (4th ed.). Washington, DC: Author.

Drake, R. E., & Mueser, K. T. (2001). Managing comorbid schizophrenia and substance abuse. *Current Psychiatry Reports, 3*, 418-422.

First, M. B., Spitzer, R. L., Gibbon, M., & Williams, J. B. W. (November 2002). Structured Clinical Interview for DSM-IV-TR Axis I Disorders Patient Edition (SCID-I/P). New York: Biometrics Research Department, New York State Psychiatric Institute.

Grant, B. F. (1995). Comorbidity between DSM-IV drug use disorders and major depression: Results of a national survey of adults. *Journal of Substance Abuse, 7*, 481-497.

Grant, B. F., Stinson, F. S., Dawson, D. A., Chou, S. P., Dufour, M. C., Compton, W., et al. (2004). Prevalence and co-occurrence of substance use disorders and independent mood and anxiety disorders: Results from the National Epidemiologic Survey on Alcohol and Related Conditions. *Archives of General Psychiatry, 61*, 807-816.

Hasin, D. S., & Nunes, E. V. (1998). Comorbidity of alcohol, drug, and psychiatric disorders: Epidemiology. In H. R. Kranzler & B. J. Rounsaville (Eds.), *Dual diagnosis and treatment: Substance abuse and comorbid medical and psychiatric disorders* (pp. 1-30). New York: Marcel Dekker, Inc.

Hasin, D. S., Samet, S., Nunes, E., Meydan, J., Matseoane, K., & Waxman, R. (2006). Diagnosis of comorbid psychiatric disorders in substance users assessed with the Psychiatric Research Interview for Substance and Mental Disorders for DSM-IV. *American Journal of Psychiatry, 163*, 689-696.

Hasin, D. S., Trautman, K. D., Miele, G. M., Samet, S., Smith, M., & Endicott, J. (1996). Psychiatric Research Interview for Substance and Mental Disorders (PRISM): Reliability for substance abusers. *American Journal of Psychiatry, 153*, 1195-1201.

Hellerstein, D. J., Rosenthal, R. N., & Miner, C. R. (2001). Integrating services for schizophrenia and substance abuse. *Psychiatric Quarterly, 72*, 291-306.

Institute of Medicine. (1998). *Bridging the gap between practice and research: Forging partnerships with community-based drug and alcohol treatment.* Washington, DC: National Academy Press.

Kessler, R. C. (1995). Epidemiology of psychiatric comorbidity. In M. T. Tsuang, M. Tohen, G. E. P. Zahner (Eds.), *Textbook in psychiatric epidemiology* (pp. 179-197). New York: Wiley-Liss.

Kessler, R. C., McGonagle, K. A., Zhao, S., Nelson, C. B., Hughes, M., Eshleman, S., et al. (1994). Lifetime and 12-month prevalence of DSM-III-R psychiatric disorders in the United States: Results from the National Comorbidity Survey. *Archives of General Psychiatry, 51*, 8-19.

Levitt, S. D., & Dubner, S. J. (2005). *Freakonomics: A rogue economist explores the hidden side of everything*. New York: HarperCollins Publishers.

Nunes, E. V., & Levin, F. R. (2004). Treatment of depression in patients with alcohol or other drug dependence: A meta-analysis. *Journal of the American Medical Association, 291,* 1887-1896.

Regier, D. A., Farmer, M E., Rae, D. S., Locke, B. Z., Keith, S. J., Judd, L. L., et al. (1990). Comorbidity of mental disorders with alcohol and other drug abuse: Results from the Epidemiological Catchment Area (ECA) study. *Journal of the American Medical Association, 264,* 2511-2518.

Weiss, R. D. (2004). Treating patients with bipolar disorder and substance dependence: Lessons learned. *Journal of Substance Abuse Treatment, 27,* 307-312.

About the Editors and Authors

Edward V. Nunes, M.D., is a Professor of Clinical Psychiatry at Columbia University College of Physicians and Surgeons. He received his bachelor's degree in psychology and chemistry from Dartmouth College and a degree in medicine from the University of Connecticut School of Medicine; he completed his residency in psychiatry and a research fellowship in clinical psychopharmacology at the New York State Psychiatric Institute at Columbia Presbyterian Medical Center. In addition to coediting *Substance Dependence and Co-Occurring Psychiatric Disorders: Best Practices for Diagnosis and Clinical Treatment,* he has authored over 150 book chapters and peer-reviewed articles on the co-occurrence of substance use disorders and psychiatric disorders. He is Principal Investigator of the Long Island Node of the National Institute on Drug Abuse Clinical Trials Network and Principal Investigator and a mentor/consultant on multiple grants from the National Institute on Drug Abuse to examine treatments for substance dependence and psychiatric disorders. Dr. Nunes is a vice chairman of the New York State Psychiatric Institute Institutional Review Board and served as chairman of the Treatment Research Review Committee at the National Institute on Drug Abuse.

Jeffrey Selzer, M.D., is Medical Director for the Committee for Physician Health, the physician health program for New York State. He served as Medical Director for the Zucker Hillside Hospital and Director of Addiction Treatment Services for the North Shore Long Island Jewish Health System. He is an Associate Professor of Clinical Psychiatry and Behavioral Sciences at the Albert Einstein College of Medicine, a Fellow of the American Society of Addiction Medicine, and a Distinguished Fellow of the American Psychiatric Association. He received a degree in medicine from the University of Michigan Medical School and completed a residency in psychiatry at the University of California at Los Angeles. Since completion of his residency, he has worked in addiction medicine and in general psychiatric settings. In addition to coediting *Substance Dependence and Co-Occurring Psychiatric Disorders: Best Practices for Diagnosis and Clinical Treatment,* he has written and spoken on topics in general psychiatry and addiction medicine, including co-occurring disorders and implementation of evidence-based practices. He coordinates the curriculum on addictions for medical students at the Albert Einstein College of Medicine.

Petros Levounis, M.D., M.A., is Director of The Addiction Institute of New York, Chief of the Division of Addiction Psychiatry at St. Luke's-Roosevelt Hospital, and an Associate Professor of Clinical Psychiatry at Columbia University College of Physicians and Surgeons. He teaches at Columbia University College of Physicians and Surgeons, New York University School of Nursing, and John Jay College of Criminal Justice in New York. Dr. Levounis received a bachelor of science in chemistry and biological sciences and a master of science in biological sciences and biophysics from Stanford University, a master of arts in sociology and social psychology from Stanford University, and a degree in medicine from the Medical College of Pennsylvania. He completed an internship in internal medicine at the New York State Psychiatric Institute at Columbia Presbyterian Medical Center, a residency in psychiatry at the New York State Psychiatric Institute, and a clinical and research fellowship in addiction psychiatry at New York University. As the recipient of the American Psychiatric Association/Center for Mental Health Services Minority Fellowship, he studied HIV risk factors in homeless men with severe mental illness and substance use disorders. His research interests include psychotherapy and psychopharmacological treatments of substance use disorders, gay and lesbian mental health, and crystal methamphetamine. In addition to coediting *Substance Dependence and Co-Occurring Psychiatric Disorders: Best Practices for Diagnosis and Clinical Treatment*, he has written and spoken extensively on addictions and is coauthor of a book entitled *Sober Siblings: How to Help Your Alcoholic Brother or Sister and Not Lose Yourself*, published by Da Capo Press in 2008. He is board-certified in addiction psychiatry, a Betty Ford Scholar, a member and Laughlin Fellow of the American College of Psychiatrists, a Distinguished Fellow of the American Psychiatric Association, and the recipient of several awards for teaching.

Carrie A. Davies, B.S., is a Research Administrator at the New York State Psychiatric Institute at Columbia Presbyterian Medical Center. In addition to coediting *Substance Dependence and Co-Occurring Psychiatric Disorders: Best Practices for Diagnosis and Clinical Treatment*, she has coauthored several articles on treatment of depression. Ms. Davies received a bachelor's degree in human development from Cornell University in 2002 and has worked since graduation at the New York State Psychiatric Institute in research on treatment of depression, anxiety, and substance abuse in preparation for further study in psychology and medicine.

Efrat Aharonovich, Ph.D., is an Assistant Professor of Clinical Psychology in Psychiatry at Columbia University College of Physicians and Surgeons and Director of the Clinical Cognitive Laboratory in the Division of Substance Abuse at the New York State Psychiatric Institute. She serves as Principal Investigator on projects funded by the National Institute on Drug Abuse and is the recipient of a K23 award from the National Institute on Drug Abuse to develop a programmatic line for research on the relationship between cognitive functioning and persistence of substance dependence in patients who have received treatment for substance dependence. She has a private practice in New York City.

Gustavo Angarita, M.D., is a Psychiatry Resident at Yale University School of Medicine. He received a degree in medicine from Universidad Militar Nueva Granada in Bogotá, Columbia, where he worked as an instructor in medicine in 2003. He has worked as a Research Fellow in the Addiction Research Program at Massachusetts General Hospital, where he assisted in administration of clinical trials and MRI trials with cocaine-dependent patients. Dr. Angarita has spoken and written on analyses of the American Society of Addiction Medicine Patient Placement Criteria.

Bachaar Arnaout, M.D., is an Addiction Psychiatry Fellow at Yale University School of Medicine. He received a degree in medicine from Jegiellonian University in Krakow, Poland, and completed a residency in psychiatry at St. Luke's-Roosevelt Hospital Center, where he served as chief resident. He is a graduate of the Intensive Psychoanalytic Psychotherapy Program at the William Alanson White Institute in New York. Dr. Arnaout has taught at John Jay College of Criminal Justice and has spoken on addiction research at several regional and national conferences.

Rachel E. Bender, M.A., previously worked as a Project Manager at the Alcohol and Drug Abuse Treatment Program at McLean Hospital for a study of group treatment for patients with substance use disorders and bipolar disorder. She is a graduate student in the doctoral program in clinical psychology at Temple University, where she continues her work in mood disorders research.

Timothy G. Benson, M.D., is Medical Director of the McLean Center at Fernside, part of McLean Hospital's Alcohol and Drug Abuse Treatment Program at Harvard Medical School, and an Instructor in Psychiatry at Harvard Medical School. He completed a residency in adult psychiatry at Massachusetts General Hospital/McLean Hospital, where he served as chief resident of addictions and then completed a clinical research fellowship with the National Institute on Drug Abuse Clinical Trials Network.

Carlos Blanco, M.D., Ph.D., is an Associate Professor of Clinical Psychiatry at Columbia University College of Physicians and Surgeons and Director of the Gambling Disorders Clinic at the New York State Psychiatric Institute. He received a degree in medicine from the Universidad Autónoma de Madrid, completed a residency in psychiatry at Hospital Ramón y Cajal in Madrid, Spain, and a residency in psychiatry at St. Vincent's Hospital and Columbia University, and completed a National Institute of Mental Health fellowship at Columbia University. His research, which focuses on behavioral addictions (e.g., pathological gambling), mood and anxiety disorders, and treatment of substance-dependent patients with and without co-occurring psychiatric disorders, has been funded by the National Institute on Drug Abuse, the New York State Office of Alcohol and Substance Abuse Services, and several private foundations.

Kathleen Brady, M.D., Ph.D., is a Professor of Psychiatry at the Medical University of South Carolina, Director of the Clinical Neuroscience Division, Director of the Women's Research Center, Director of the General Clinical Research Center, Director of the Southern Consortium of the National Institute on Drug Abuse Clinical Trials Network, and Associate Dean for Clinical Research. As a board-certified psychiatrist specializing in addiction psychiatry, she conducts research on drug and alcohol abuse and comorbid conditions, such as posttraumatic stress disorder and other anxiety disorders. She has served as Principal Investigator, Co-Principal Investigator, and a mentor on numerous research projects and is the recipient of a K24 Mid-Career Investigator Award in Patient-Oriented Research from the National Institute on Drug Abuse. She has received awards for her research, teaching, and clinical work and has been listed in *Best Doctors in America* each year since 1998. She has been President of the Association for Medical Education and Research in Substance Abuse and President of the American Academy of Addiction Psychiatry, has served on the Scientific Advisory Council of the National Institute on Drug Abuse and the Committee on Community-Based Treatment of the Institute of Medicine, and has served on the Board of Directors of the College on Problems of Drug Dependence.

Robert K. Brooner, Ph.D., is a Professor of Medical Psychology and Psychiatry in the Department of Psychiatry and Behavioral Sciences at the Johns Hopkins University School of Medicine and Director of Addiction Treatment Services at the Johns Hopkins Bayview Medical Center. He received a Ph.D. in clinical psychology and completed predoctoral and postdoctoral training in medical psychology at the Johns Hopkins University School of Medicine. Dr. Brooner has published over 150 articles and related reports on psychiatric comorbidity, development and testing of adaptive treatment approaches, and development and testing of service delivery platforms that improve patient adherence to therapies. He received the Ernest Amory Codman Award from the Joint Commission on Health Care Organizations for his work on developing and testing an adaptive treatment model for opioid use disorders and other substance use disorders. Dr. Brooner was selected as a 2009 recipient of the Marie Nyswander/ Vincent Dole Award for his contributions to the treatment of opioid dependence.

Alexander L. Chapman, Ph.D., is an Assistant Professor in the Department of Psychology at Simon Fraser University. He received a bachelor's degree in psychology from the University of British Columbia in Vancouver and a master of science and Ph.D. in clinical psychology from Idaho State University. He completed internship training on dialectical behavior therapy and other evidence-based cognitive-behavioral treatments at Duke University Medical Center and a postdoctoral fellowship with Marsha Linehan at the University of Washington, where he received training in dialectical behavior therapy. He has published empirical and theoretical articles on self-harm, borderline personality disorder, suicidal behavior, dialectical behavior therapy, and impulsive behavior. He regularly gives workshops on dialectical behavior therapy, supervises students' clinical work with dual diagnosis patients, and he cofounded the DBT Centre of Vancouver.

Lisa Cohen, Ph.D., is a Research Scientist at the New York State Psychiatric Institute at Columbia Presbyterian Medical Center and at the City College of New York. She received a bachelor's degree from the University of Pennsylvania and a Ph.D. in clinical psychology from Yale University. She completed a postdoctoral fellowship at the Payne Whitney Clinic of New York Hospital-Cornell Medical Center, where she received training in treatment of anxiety and traumatic stress disorders. Dr. Cohen has conducted research on eating disorders and has received training in Cognitive Behavioral Therapy and interpersonal psychotherapy for patients with eating disorders at the Yale Center for Eating and Weight Disorders. Her current research focuses on the development and testing of treatments for women with posttraumatic stress disorder and co-occurring disorders, including substance use disorders and eating disorders. She has a private psychotherapy practice in New York City.

Oshra Cohen, Ph.D., is a Research Fellow at the New York State Psychiatric Institute at Columbia Presbyterian Medical Center and a clinician at the Center for Psychological Services. She received a master of arts and a Ph.D. from the Ferkauf Graduate School of Psychology at Yeshiva University. Dr. Cohen is the recipient of a grant from the Ontario Problem Gambling Research Center to develop handouts on pathological gambling for counselors in methadone clinics. She has coauthored several articles on pathological gambling.

Elizabeth R. Disney, Ph.D., is a Program Manager at Chase Brexton Health Services, a community health center in Baltimore, Maryland. She received a Ph.D. in clinical and developmental psychology from the University of Minnesota and completed postdoctoral training at the Behavioral Pharmacology Research Unit of the Johns Hopkins University School of Medicine. She has worked at the National Institute of Mental Health and has been an associate investigator at the National Institute on Drug Abuse. Dr. Disney has published many articles on addictions research.

Stephen J. Donovan, M.D., is an Assistant Professor of Clinical Psychiatry at Columbia University College of Physicians and Surgeons and a Research Psychiatrist at the New York State Psychiatric Institute. He received a degree in medicine from

SUNY Buffalo School of Medicine and completed adult and child psychiatry training at the Albert Einstein College of Medicine. He has served as Physician in Charge at the Child and Adolescent Clinic of Queens General Hospital. He is board-certified in adult, child, and adolescent psychiatry and addiction psychiatry and is the recipient of an Independent Scientist Award and a R01 award from the National Institute on Drug Abuse to study the pharmacology of addiction risk factors and aggression.

Andrew Ekblad, M.A., is a doctoral candidate in clinical psychology in the Department of Psychology and Neuroscience at Duke University. He received a bachelor's degree from Vanderbilt University and completed postbaccalaureate work at the University of Washington, where he worked in the Behavioral Research and Treatment Clinics. His research and clinical interests include mindfulness and experimental assessment of mechanisms of change in empirically validated treatments for psychiatric disorders.

Christiane Farentinos, M.D., M.P.H., C.A.D.C.-II, N.C.D.C.-II, is Research Director and Clinical Director at ChangePoint, Inc., an outpatient drug and alcohol treatment program in Portland, Oregon, and a Clinical Adjunct Faculty Member in the Department of Public Health and Preventive Medicine at Oregon Health and Science University. She is board-certified in psychiatry in Brazil and certified as an addiction counselor. She received a master of public health administration and policy from Portland State University. She has worked on several research projects funded by grants from the National Institute on Drug Abuse and the Center for Substance Abuse Treatment and has published articles on addictions in the United States and Brazil.

David R. Gastfriend, M.D., is an Associate Professor of Psychiatry at Harvard Medical School, Director of the Addiction Research Program at Massachusetts General Hospital, and Vice President of Scientific Communications at Alkermes, Inc. He is certified in addiction medicine by the American Society of Addiction Medicine (ASAM) and in addiction psychiatry by the American Board of Neurology and Psychiatry. Dr. Gastfriend has conducted studies of pharmacological and behavioral treatments for alcohol and substance use disorders. He initiated the first multisite study to validate and refine the American Society of Addiction Medicine Patient Placement Criteria, was Co-Principal Investigator on the National Institute on Drug Abuse's Cocaine Collaborative Psychotherapy Study and the National Institute on Alcohol Abuse and Alcoholism's collaborative study COMBINE, and was the recipient of a Mid-Career Investigator Award for Patient-Oriented Research from the National Institute on Drug Abuse. He has chaired the Treatment Outcome Research Committee of ASAM, has served as Delegate-At-Large on ASAM's board, and serves on the board of the International Society of Addiction Medicine. He serves on the editorial boards for *Journal of Substance Abuse Treatment* and *Journal of Addictive Diseases* and is Associate Editor of the *Journal of Computers in Human Services*. He is a coeditor of *The ASAM Patient Placement Criteria for the Treatment of Substance-Related Disorders* and editor of *Addiction Treatment Matching*, published by Haworth Medical Press.

Susan M. Gordon, Ph.D., is Research Director at Seabrook House, a residential program for treatment of drug and alcohol disorders. She received a Ph.D. in professional psychology and interdisciplinary studies in human development from the University of Pennsylvania Graduate School of Education. She served as Assistant Director of Outpatient Services, Acting Clinical Director, and Clinical Administrator, and as a staff psychologist at the Renfrew Center, a treatment program for women with eating disorders.

Shelly F. Greenfield, M.D., M.P.H., is an Associate Professor of Psychiatry at Harvard Medical School, the Chief Academic Officer at McLean Hospital, and Director of Clinical and Health Services Research and Education in the Division of Alcohol and Drug Abuse at McLean Hospital in Belmont, Massachusetts. She is the former Associate Clinical Director of the Alcohol and Drug Abuse Treatment Program and Director of the Substance Abuse Consultation Service at McLean Hospital. She is the Director of Harvard Medical School/ Partners Addiction Psychiatry Fellowship. She received an Independent Investigator Award from the National Institute on Drug Abuse to investigate the efficacy of a new manual-based group therapy for women with substance use disorders. Dr. Greenfield is the recipient of a Mid-Career Award in Patient-Oriented Research from the National Institute on Drug Abuse. is Co-Principal Investigator of the Northern New England node of the National Institute on Drug Abuse Clinical Trials Network, and is Co-Investigator of a study to evaluate the effectiveness of integrating alcohol treatment into routine tuberculosis care in Tomsk Oblast, Russia. She is Editor-in-Chief of the *Harvard Review in Psychiatry.*

Deborah L. Haller, Ph.D., A.B.P.P., is an Associate Professor of Clinical Psychiatry at Columbia University College of Physicians and Surgeons and Director of Psychiatric Research at St. Luke's-Roosevelt Hospital Center. She is a Diplomate in Clinical Health Psychology (American Board of Professional Psychology) and holds advanced credentials in the treatment of alcohol and other psychoactive substance use disorders (College of Professional Psychology). She was a tenured Associate Professor of Psychiatry, Internal Medicine, and Anesthesiology and Acting Chair of the Division of Addiction Psychiatry at the Medical College of Virginia, Virginia Commonwealth University, where she received a Distinguished Mentoring Award. Her research and clinical interests include medical populations with comorbid substance use disorders (e.g., patients with chronic pain, patients with infectious diseases, pregnant women, and surgical candidates). She is Principal Investigator on two treatment development grants from the National Institute on Drug Abuse. Dr. Haller has directed a Health and Addictions Psychology Fellowship Program for many years and has served on a National Institute on Drug Abuse initial review group. She has written many scientific papers on substance abuse and has served as a peer reviewer for several scientific journals.

Tim Hartnett, M.S.W., M.H.A., is Executive Director of CODA, Inc., an alcohol and drug treatment agency in Portland, Oregon, and an adjunct faculty member at Portland State University Graduate School of Education. He has served as Director of the Division of Alcohol and Drug Abuse Prevention and Recovery for the State of New Hampshire Department of Health and Human Services. He specializes in treatment of hard-to-reach populations (e.g., recalcitrant juvenile delinquents, homeless persons with severe and persistent mental illness and substance use disorders) and has worked as a school teacher, direct-service worker, program manager, research partner, state policy maker, and agency executive.

Louise Haynes, M.S.W., is an Assistant Adjunct Professor at the Medical University of South Carolina and the Community Treatment Representative of the Southern Consortium of the National Institute on Drug Abuse Clinical Trials Network. She has worked as a psychiatric social worker at the Veterans Administration Medical Center in Charleston, South Carolina, Director of Women's Services for the Single State Authority, Director of the Division of Alcohol and Drug Services for the South

Carolina Department of Mental Health, and Chief Executive Officer of Morris Village, a 150-bed addictions treatment center.

Grace Hennessy, M.D., is Director of the Substance Abuse Recovery Program at the New York Veterans Affairs Medical Center. She has served as Medical Director of the Partial Hospital Program for the Alcohol and Drug Abuse Treatment Program at McLean Hospital and as a Research Psychiatrist at the New York State Psychiatric Institute at Columbia Presbyterian Medical Center. She received a degree in medicine from Tufts University School of Medicine and completed a residency in adult psychiatry at McLean Hospital and an addiction psychiatry fellowship through the Partners HealthCare Addiction Psychiatry Fellowship Program. Dr. Hennessy has authored several articles and chapters on 3,4-methylenedioxymethamphetamine (MDMA), psychosocial and psychopharmacologic treatments for substance use disorders, gender differences in substance use disorders, and treatment of patients with co-occurring mood disorders and substance use disorders.

Denise Hien, Ph.D., is a Professor of Clinical Psychology at the City University of New York at CCNY and an Adjunct Senior Research Scientist at Columbia University College of Physicians and Surgeons. She is the recipient of grants from the National Institute on Drug Abuse, National Institute on Alcohol Abuse and Alcoholism, and the National Institutes of Health Office of Research on Women's Health to study predictors and treatment of interpersonal violence, substance use disorders, and posttraumatic stress disorder among urban women. Dr. Hien has published articles in many peer-reviewed medical journals and books. She has a private practice in New York City.

Terry Horton, M.D., is Director of the Consult Service at Wilmington Hospital and an Attending Physician and a member of the teaching faculty of the Department of Medicine in the Christiana Care Health System. He has served as Medical Director and Vice President of Phoenix House Foundation in New York and Chief Physician for Prison Health Services at St. Vincent's Hospital in New York. He has had appointments at New York Presbyterian Hospital, Weill Medical College of Cornell University, and New York Medical College. Dr. Horton has served on the New York State Office of Alcohol and Substance Abuse Services Medical Advisory Panel and Detoxification Taskforce; the New York City Department of Health and Mental Hygiene's Buprenorphine Taskforce; the Executive Committee of the Clinical Trials Network Long Island Node; the New York State Council of HIV Ambulatory Care Clinical Directors; the Council for Alcoholism, Drug Abuse, and Mental Health in Delaware; the New York State Department of Health DRG Clinical Panel on Drugs and Alcohol; the Therapeutic Community Committee of the American Society of Addiction Medicine; and the American College of Physicians Health and Public Policy Committee. He is a national mentor for the Physician Clinical Support System.

Michael Kidorf, Ph.D., is an Associate Professor of Medical Psychology and Psychiatry at the Johns Hopkins University School of Medicine and Associate Director of the Addiction Treatment Services at the Johns Hopkins Bayview Medical Center. He received a bachelor of arts from Emory University and a Ph.D. in clinical psychology from Florida State University; he completed an internship at Brown University and postdoctoral training at the Behavioral Pharmacology Research Unit of the Johns Hopkins University School of Medicine. Dr. Kidorf is a licensed clinical psychologist.

His research interests include the use of motivational interventions to encourage drug abusers to enroll and remain in substance abuse treatment to improve participation in, and adherence to, prescibed therapies.

Therese Killeen, Ph.D., A.P.R.N., B.C., is an Assistant Professor of Psychiatry and Behavioral Sciences at the Medical University of South Carolina. She holds a Ph.D. in nursing and has worked as a clinician and researcher in the addictions field for over fifteen years. She has served as Investigator on pharmacotherapy and behavioral research studies of substance use disorders and post-traumatic stress disorder and is a Co-Investigator in the National Institute on Drug Abuse Clinical Trials Network. She oversees projects to disseminate evidence-based interventions to community substance abuse treatment centers.

Van L. King, M.D., is an Associate Professor in the Department of Psychiatry and Behavioral Sciences at the Johns Hopkins University School of Medicine and Medical Director of the Addiction Treatment Services at the Johns Hopkins Bayview Medical Center. He received a bachelor of science in biochemistry from the University of Wisconsin-Madison and a degree in medicine from the University of Rochester School of Medicine and Dentistry; he completed a residency in general adult psychiatry at Massachusetts General Hospital, where he served as chief resident. His research interests include the impact of psychiatric comorbidities on substance abuse treatment outcome and the assessment and comprehensive rehabilitation treatment of substance abuse patients in long-term outpatient care.

Sang Lee, B.S., is a Clinical Research Associate in the Addiction Research Program at Massachusetts General Hospital. He received a bachelor of science in psychology from Brown University and has worked since graduation with substance-dependent patients at the Addiction Research Program, where he has assisted in administration of several clinical trials of treatments for alcohol dependence and cocaine dependence and in analyses of the American Society of Addiction Medicine Patient Placement Criteria (ASAM PPC). He plans to continue work in the field of addictions in a doctoral program in psychology or neuroscience.

Frances R. Levin, M.D., is Kennedy-Leavy Professor of Clinical Psychiatry at Columbia University College of Physicians and Surgeons, Director of Clinical and Educational Activities for the Division of Substance Abuse at the New York State Psychiatric Institute, and Director of the Addiction Psychiatry Fellowship Program at Columbia University/New York Presbyterian Hospital. She received a degree in medicine from Cornell University Medical College and completed a residency in psychiatry at the New York Hospital-Payne Whitney Clinic. She is Principal Investigator on several federally funded grants and a T32 National Institute on Drug Abuse Substance Abuse Research Fellowship, is Co-Principal Investigator on several grants, and is the recipient of an Independent Scientist Grant from the National Institute on Drug Abuse. Her research interests include pharmacologic treatment interventions for cocaine abuse, psychotherapeutic and pharmacologic interventions for marijuana dependence, and treatment approaches for substance abusers with attention deficit hyperactivity disorder and other psychiatric disorders. She has spoken and written extensively on substance abuse and dual diagnosis. She serves on several advisory panels and has served on a National Institute on Drug Abuse initial review group and consensus panels sponsored by the Center for Substance Abuse Treatment.

Juan José Luján, M.D., is a Surgical Resident at Morristown Memorial Hospital in Morristown, New Jersey. He received a degree in medicine from the National University of Cuyo Faculty of Medical Sciences in Mendoza, Argentina, and served as the Chief Student Practitioner in Central Hospital in Mendoza, Argentina. Dr. Luján has worked as an associate researcher in the Gambling Disorders Clinic at the New York State Psychiatric Institute and in the Experimental Surgery Institute at the National University of Cuyo Faculty of Medical Sciences in Mendoza, Argentina. His work focuses on education and training in psychopharmacology.

Thomas R. Lynch, Ph.D., is a research clinical psychologist and a Professor of Clinical Psychology in the Mood Disorders Centre in the School of Psychology at the University of Exeter. He received a Ph.D. in clinical psychology at Kent State University and completed postdoctoral training at Duke University. He was the Director of the Duke Cognitive Behavioral Research and Treatment Program and a member of the Departments of Psychology and Psychiatry at Duke University from 1998–2007 before relocating to the University of Exeter. He has received five research grants from the National Institutes of Health (NIH), a National Alliance for Research on Schizophrenia and Depression (NARSAD) research award, an American Foundation for Suicide Prevention (AFSP) research award, and a John A. Hartford Foundation award. He serves as a research consultant/adjunct faculty member at Duke University and was the Principal Investigator on two National Institute on Drug Abuse (NIDA) R01 grants at Duke University. He is a recipient of the John M. Rhoades Psychotherapy Research Endowment, is a Beck Institute Scholar, is a Grandfathered Fellow in the Academy of Cognitive Therapy, and has been an international trainer in Dialectical Behavior Therapy since 1996.

Jeanne Manubay, M.D., is an Assistant Clinical Professor of Medicine in the Center for Family Medicine and in Psychiatry at Columbia University College of Physicians and Surgeons and Assistant Medical Director of the Buprenorphine Program at Columbia University College of Physicians and Surgeons. She received a degree in medicine from American University of the Caribbean Medical School; she completed a residency in family practice at Reading Hospital and Medical Center and a post-doctoral clinical fellowship in addiction psychiatry at the New York State Psychiatric Institute.

John J. Mariani, M.D., is an Assistant Professor of Clinical Psychiatry at Columbia University College of Physicians and Surgeons, Associate Director of the Addiction Psychiatry Research Fellowship, and the Medical Director of the Substance Treatment and Research Service at the New York State Psychiatric Institute. He received a degree in medicine from New York University School of Medicine; he completed a residency in psychiatry at Beth Israel Medical Center, where he served as chief resident, and a research fellowship in addiction psychiatry at the New York State Psychiatric Institute. Dr. Mariani is the recipient of a K23 Career Development Award from the National Institute on Drug Abuse to study novel pharmacotherapies for addictive disorders.

Elinore F. McCance-Katz, M.D., Ph.D., is a Professor of Psychiatry at the University of California at San Francisco. She received a degree in medicine from the University of Connecticut and a Ph.D. in infectious disease epidemiology from Yale University. She is Director of Addiction Medicine Research at San Francisco General Hospital and is Medical Director for the California Department of Alcohol and Drug Programs. She has worked as a clinician and researcher in the field of addiction medicine for eighteen years. Her research interests include pharmacotherapy for substance use disorders, clinical pharmacology of drugs of abuse. drug interactions, cocaine and alcohol medication development, and co-occurrence of HIV disease and addictions.

Dennis McCarty, Ph.D., is a Professor in the Department of Public Health and Preventive Medicine at Oregon Health and Science University. He conducts health services research and collaborates with policy makers in state and federal government and with community-based programs to examine the organization, funding, and delivery of publicly supported substance abuse treatment services. He is Principal Investigator of the Oregon/Hawaii Node of the National Institute on Drug Abuse Clinical Trials Network and leads the national evaluation of the Robert Wood Johnson Foundation and Center for Substance Abuse Treatment Network for Improvement of Addiction Treatment initiative to improve access to, and retention in, alcohol and drug abuse treatment. Dr. McCarty directed the Massachusetts Bureau of Substance Abuse Services for the Massachusetts Department of Public Health for six years.

Joanne McCormack L.C.S.W., is a Social Work Program Coordinator and clinical interviewer in the Department of Psychiatry Research at The Zucker Hillside Hospital. She received her master of social work from Adelphi University School of Social Work. She has extensive experience in diagnosis and assessment of schizophrenia and affective disorders and has written and spoken on assessment of cannabis use, treatment response, and religious delusions related to first-episode schizophrenia. Ms. McCormack trains clinicians in the use of psychiatric symptom rating scales and serves as the primary diagnostician for several studies of schizophrenia that are funded by the National Institute of Mental Health.

Rachel Miller, Ph.D., is a Senior Clinical Social Worker in the Research Department at The Zucker Hillside Hospital, where she treats young people with co-occurring schizophrenia and substance abuse. She received her master of social work and Ph.D. from Adelphi University School of Social Work. She serves on the advisory board of *Schizophrenia Digest*, has served as an educational consultant for several pharmaceutical company projects, and has published widely on first-episode schizophrenia, including a book entitled *Diagnosis: Schizophrenia*, published by Columbia University Press.

Patrice M. Muchowski, Sc.D., is Vice President of Clinical Services at AdCare Hospital, a 114-bed alcohol and drug treatment hospital in Worcester, Massachusetts, with six outpatient sites, President of AdCare Educational Institute, a Clinical Instructor in Psychology in the Department of Psychiatry at Harvard Medical School, and an Affiliate in Psychiatry at the University of Massachusetts Medical School. She is a licensed psychologist who has worked in the alcohol and drug treatment field for over twenty-five years. She has managed both inpatient and outpatient programs in the public and private sectors.

Karin J. Neufeld, M.D., M.P.H., is an Assistant Professor of Psychiatry at the Johns Hopkins School of Medicine and Associate Director of the Addiction Treatment

Program at Johns Hopkins University. She received a degree in medicine and a master of public health from Johns Hopkins University; she completed a residency in psychiatry and a postdoctoral fellowship in community psychiatry at the Johns Hopkins School of Medicine. Dr. Neufeld has worked with a mobile treatment program called COSTAR, which targets patients with severe and persistent mental illness, and was a visiting scientist at the All India Institute for Medical Sciences, where she worked with substance-dependent patients. She is a Senior Alcohol Medical Scholar in a national program that aims to improve education on substance use disorders in medical schools. She has lectured on antisocial personality disorder to medical students, has administered a clinical trial of behavioral treatment approaches for opioid-dependent patients with antisocial personality disorder, and has published articles on treatment of antisocial personality disorder and substance use disorders.

Patricia Penn, Ph.D., is Director of Research and Evaluation at La Frontera Center, Inc, a nonprofit community behavioral healthcare organization, and a licensed psychologist. She has served as Principal Investigator on several projects on treatment of co-occurring disorders that were funded by the National Institute on Drug Abuse, Center for Substance Abuse Treatment, Center for Substance Abuse Prevention, Center for Mental Health Services, and the state of Arizona. She is Principal Investigator for La Frontera Center, Inc. in the National Institute on Drug Abuse Clinical Trials Network. Dr. Penn was a member of a workgroup of the American Society of Addiction Medicine to add co-occurring disorders to the American Society of Addiction Medicine Patient Placement Criteria, was a member of the Arizona Integrated Treatment Consensus Panel that was funded by Substance Abuse and Mental Health Services Administration, and served on an expert panel that was sponsored by Substance Abuse and Mental Health Services Administration to examine ways to improve treatment of co-occurring disorders. She led development of ADMIRE Plus, an award-winning treatment program for co-occurring disorders, and has received a leadership award from the Arizona Practice Improvement Collaborative.

Malcolm S. Reid, Ph.D., is an Assistant Professor in the Department of Psychiatry at New York University School of Medicine. He received a bachelor of science in psychology from Brown University and a Ph.D. in pharmacology from Karolinska Institute in Stockholm; he completed a National Institute on Drug Abuse Research Fellowship in Substance Abuse Treatment Research at the University of California at San Francisco. He has directed medication development studies of substance-dependent patients that have been funded by the National Institutes of Health and pharmaceutical companies and a multisite clinical trial in the National Institute on Drug Abuse Clinical Trials Network of smoking cessation treatment for drug-dependent patients. Dr. Reid directs Phase I medication development studies with methamphetamine abusers that are funded by the National Institute on Drug Abuse, Phase II medication treatment studies with cocaine abusers, and studies that examine the neuropharmacology and neurophysiology of drug and alcohol craving and reward using quantitative EEG and MRI.

Richard K. Ries, M.D., is a Professor of Psychiatry at the University of Washington Medical School, Director of Substance Abuse Education for the University of Washington Medical School, Director of the Division of Addictions in the Department of Psychiatry, and Director of Outpatient Psychiatry, Dual Disorder Programs, and the Addictions Programs at Harborview Medical Center. He is board-certified in general psychiatry and in addiction psychiatry by the American Board of Psychiatry and Neurology and certified in addiction medicine by the American Society of Addiction Medicine. He is the recipient of clinical research grants from the National Institute on Drug Abuse to evaluate treatment outcomes of patients with dual disorders and has been Co-Investigator on many grants, including the National Institute on Drug Abuse Clinical Trials Network. He chaired the first national consensus Treatment Improvement Protocol of the Center for Substance Abuse Treatment on assessment and treatment of patients with co-occurring addictions and mental disorders and served as cochair of a Treatment Improvement Protocol update on this topic. Dr. Ries is senior editor of the textbook *Principles of Addiction Medicine*, published by the American Society of Addiction Medicine. He is a founding member of the Washington Physician's Health Program, a leading state program for physicians with substance use problems or psychiatric problems, and is the Northwest psychiatric and addiction specialist for the National Football League. Dr. Ries has received the Nancy Roeske teaching award from the American Psychiatric Association for his work with medical students and has been listed in *Best Doctors in America* each year since 1995.

Eric Schindler, Ph.D., is Chief Executive Officer of Child and Family Resources, Inc., an Arizona community nonprofit organization, and an adjunct faculty member in the Division of Family Studies and Human Development at the University of Arizona. He received a Ph.D. in clinical psychology from the University of Arizona; he completed an internship in child and family psychology at the University of California at Davis and postdoctoral training in pediatric psychology in Chicago. He has worked in community settings in Chicago as an administrator, director, and practitioner and as Senior Clinical Administrator at La Frontera Center Inc., a nonprofit community behavioral healthcare organization, where he oversaw all treatment, prevention, research, and quality improvement operations and administered a study of smoking cessation interventions for patients with serious mental illness and/or co-occurring disorders and studies in the National Institute on Drug Abuse Clinical Trials Network.

Sidney H. Schnoll, M.D., Ph.D., is a Clinical Professor of Internal Medicine and Psychiatry at Medical College of Virginia, Virginia Commonwealth University, a Visiting Professor of Psychiatry at Columbia University College of Physicians and Surgeons, and Vice President of Risk Management at Pinney Associates, Inc. He received a degree in medicine from New Jersey College of Medicine and Dentistry and a Ph.D. in pharmacology from Jefferson Medical College; he completed an internship and residency in neurology at Jefferson Medical College. Dr. Schnoll was the Career Teacher in Addictions at the University of Pennsylvania, Medical Director at the Eagleville Hospital and Rehabilitation Center, an Associate Professor of Psychiatry and Pharmacology and Director of Chemical Dependence Programs at Northwestern University Medical School, and Chairman of the Division of Substance Abuse Medicine at Medical College of Virginia, Virginia Commonwealth University. He has served on the Food and Drug Administration's Drug Abuse Advisory Committee, National Institutes of Health study sections, National Board of Medical Examiners test development committees, and the board of the College on Problems of Drug Dependence. He has been listed in *Best Doctors in America* and is a Fellow of the College on Problems of Drug Dependence and the American Society of Addiction Medicine. With over thirty years in academic medicine, Dr. Schnoll has published over 150 research papers, book chapters, and educational materials on addictions and pain management.

Serge Sevy, M.D., M.B.A., is an Associate Professor of Clinical Psychiatry and Behavioral Sciences at the Albert Einstein College of Medicine. He received a degree in medicine from the Université Libre de Bruxelles in Belgium and a master of business administration in health care administration from the Baruch College and Mount Sinai School of Medicine; he completed a residency in psychiatry at Mount Sinai School of Medicine and received advanced training in biological psychiatry and psychopharmacology from the Albert Einstein College of Medicine. Dr. Sevy, who studies the co-occurrence of substance use disorders and psychosis, is the recipient of a grant from the National Institute on Drug Abuse to study cannabis addiction in patients with schizophrenia. He has authored many book chapters and peer-reviewed articles on diagnosis and treatment of patients with co-occurring substance use disorders and psychiatric disorders.

Kenneth B. Stoller, M.D., is an Assistant Professor in the Department of Psychiatry and Behavioral Sciences at the Johns Hopkins University School of Medicine and Medical Director of Addiction Treatment Services at the Johns Hopkins Bayview Medical Center. He received a degree in medicine from the Johns Hopkins University School of Medicine; he completed a medical internship at the Johns Hopkins Bayview Medical Center, a residency in psychiatry at Johns Hopkins Hospital, and a postdoctoral fellowship in addiction psychiatry at the Behavioral Pharmacology Research Unit at the Johns Hopkins University School of Medicine. His research interests include cost analysis of drug abuse treatment, methods to enhance treatment adherence, and treatment of co-occurring psychiatric disorders and substance use disorders.

Elisa Trucco, B.A., is a doctoral student in clinical psychology at the State University of New York at Buffalo. She received a bachelor's degree in psychology from the University of Pennsylvania and has worked as a Project Manager in the Alcohol and Drug Abuse Treatment Program at McLean Hospital, where she has conducted research on gender differences in substance use disorders.

Roger D. Weiss, M.D., is a Professor of Psychiatry at Harvard Medical School and Chief of the Division of Alcohol and Drug Abuse at McLean Hospital. He is Principal Investigator on two grants from the National Institute on Drug Abuse, including the Northern New England Node of the National Institute on Drug Abuse Clinical Trials Network. He has developed a group therapy for patients with bipolar disorder and substance dependence. Dr. Weiss has authored over 280 articles and book chapters on substance abuse and dual diagnosis, coauthored a book entitled *Cocaine*, published by American Psychiatric Press, and coedited a book entitled *Integrated Treatment for Mood and Substance Use Disorders*, published by Johns Hopkins University Press.

Jeffrey J. Wilson, M.D., is an Assistant Professor of Clinical Psychiatry at Columbia University College of Physicians and Surgeons. He received a degree in medicine from New Jersey Medical School; he completed an internship and residency in psychiatry at Montefiore Medical Center, a residency in child psychiatry at Stanford Hospital and Clinics, and a fellowship at New York Presbyterian Hospital. He is board-certified in psychiatry, child and adolescent psychiatry, and addiction psychiatry. He is the recipient of a grant from the National Institutes of Health to study parent-child interactions during addiction treatment at Columbia Presbyterian Medical Center. He has published articles on adolescent substance abuse and has a private practice in Hackensack, New Jersey.

Jennifer P. Wisdom, Ph.D., M.P.H., is an Assistant Professor of Clinical Psychology in Psychiatry at Columbia University College of Physicians and Surgeons and a Research Scientist in the Department of Mental Health Services and Policy Research at the New York State Psychiatric Institute at Columbia Presbyterian Medical Center. She received a Ph.D. in clinical psychology from George Washington University and a master of public health in epidemiology and biostatistics from Oregon Health and Science University. She is a licensed clinical psychologist. Dr. Wisdom was a Research Assistant Professor in the Department of Public Health and Preventive Medicine and Department of Psychiatry at Oregon Health and Science University and has served as an Investigator with the Oregon/Hawaii Node of the National Institute on Drug Abuse Clinical Trials Network and with the national evaluation of the Robert Wood Johnson Foundation and Center for Substance Abuse Treatment Network for Improvement of Addiction Treatment. She is the recipient of a Career Development Award from the National Institute on Drug Abuse to improve the quality of care for adolescents in drug treatment. Her research interests include organization and evaluation of treatment services for addictions and mental illness.

Edelgard Wulfert, Ph.D., is a Collins Fellow and a Professor of Psychology at the State University of New York at Albany and Chair of the Department of Psychology at the State University of New York at Albany. She received a bachelor's degree in psychology from Instituto Tecnologico in Guadalajara, Mexico, a master's degree in clinical and experimental psychology from the University of North Carolina at Greensboro, and a Ph.D. in clinical psychology from the University of North Carolina at Greensboro. She has served as Director of Clinical Training at the State University of New York at Albany. Her research interests include assessment and treatment of addictive and compulsive behaviors, with an emphasis on pathological gambling.

Lucy Zammarelli, M.A., N.C.A.C.-II, is Director of Adolescent and Research Programs at Williamette Family in Eugene, Oregon, where she manages the agency's adolescent substance abuse treatment programs and mental health treatment programs, and an Adjunct Instructor at the University of Oregon. She received a bachelor of science from Cornell University, a master of arts from Temple University, and an associate degree in chemical dependency counseling from Lane Community College. She specializes in women's health issues, including addictions, psychiatric disorders, healthcare, the sex industry, trauma, and relationships. She has served as Principal Investigator on many projects funded by the National Institute on Drug Abuse, Center for Substance Abuse Treatment, and Center for Mental Health Services. She serves as a consultant to Substance Abuse and Mental Health Services Administration and a grant reviewer and has spoken at regional and national conferences on prevention and treatment of substance use disorders and psychiatric disorders.

Part 1
Mood Disorders

This book covers mood disorders first because they are among the most common co-occurring psychiatric disorders in substance-dependent patients and because, arguably, more research has been conducted on the co-occurrence of mood disorders and substance use disorders than any other form of psychiatric/substance abuse comorbidity.

Since the outset of the modern era of psychiatric diagnosis in the 1960s and 1970s, depression has captured the attention of clinicians and researchers because it is prevalent in patients who enter treatment for alcoholism and drug abuse. In addition, many of the symptoms of depression that are observed in substance-dependent patients are caused by substance intoxication or withdrawal and resolve following abstinence. Confusion about the cause, course, and treatment of depression in substance-dependent patients, whose symptoms have proven to be challenging to diagnose and manage, has helped to stimulate a generation's worth of research on comorbidity, thereby providing a strong foundation of evidence for the chapter on depression.

Patients with bipolar disorder have bouts of depression and bouts of mania or hypomania (periods of euphoric or irritable mood that are accompanied by increased energy, impaired judgment, and, in severe cases, psychosis). When a patient presents with symptoms of depression, clinicians should review carefully the patient's history for evidence of bipolar disorder; a diagnosis of bipolar disorder has different treatment implications than a diagnosis of unipolar depression. In the general population, bipolar disorder is rarer than unipolar depression, but substance use disorders are extremely common in patients with bipolar disorder. The frequent co-occurrence of bipolar disorder and substance use disorders has stimulated a substantial body of research that informs the chapter on bipolar disorder.

Chapter 1

Depression in Patients With Substance Use Disorders

by Edward V. Nunes, M.D., Grace Hennessy, M.D., and Jeffrey Selzer, M.D.

INTRODUCTION

Depression is the first psychiatric disorder covered in this book because, along with antisocial personality disorder, it is the most common co-occurring psychiatric disorder encountered in alcohol-dependent and drug-dependent patients. As such, it has received the most study and has also engendered the most controversy.

Depression is one of the most common mental disorders in the general population. Large surveys of representative samples of the general population have consistently found that depression occurs in 5 to 10 percent or more of the general population. Further, the same surveys have shown that the presence of alcohol or drug dependence increases the prevalence of depression by at least a factor of two. This increase in depression has been repeatedly observed among patients presenting for treatment at a variety of different alcohol and drug dependence treatment programs (see Hasin, Nunes, & Meydan, 2004). These studies typically find that between 20 and 50 percent of patients seeking treatment for addictions have experienced an episode of major depression at some point during their lifetime, and 10 to 20 percent are currently suffering from depression. Thus, practitioners working with patients with addictions will frequently encounter depression.

Further, there is much evidence to suggest that depression functions as a motivator for seeking treatment for addictions and a harbinger of poor treatment outcome (working against the effectiveness of substance abuse treatment).

For example, one study found that opiate-dependent patients who were not seeking treatment had lower rates of depression in comparison to opiate addicts enrolled in treatment programs (Rounsaville & Kleber, 1985). In the Drug Abuse Treatment Outcome Study (DATOS) survey of treatment program effectiveness, the presence of depression at baseline was found to be associated with improved retention in treatment (Joe, Simpson, & Broome, 1999). However, a number of studies have shown that the presence of depression during treatment is associated with poor outcome of substance use disorders. This is particularly true for a major depressive disorder that has been identified by clinical history or structured psychiatric interview. In the absence of a clear depressive disorder, depressive symptoms have a less clear impact on prognosis (see Hasin, Nunes, & Meydan, 2004). This finding highlights the importance of diagnosing psychiatric disorders according to standard diagnostic criteria, such as the *Diagnostic and Statistical Manual of Mental Disorders*, 4th edition (*DSM-IV*) criteria (American Psychiatric Association, 1994), which are a focus of this book.

Depression in substance-dependent patients has engendered controversy and confusion because chronic substance use often causes depressive symptoms as a toxic effect of the substance or as a symptom of substance withdrawal. These symptoms are very common and tend to resolve within a period of days to weeks after abstinence has been achieved, as has been repeatedly observed in studies of hospitalized alcoholics or drug addicts or patients entering powerful abstinence inducing treatments such as methadone maintenance (see Nunes & Raby, 2005). In these studies, depression was identified with scales that measure the severity of current depressive symptoms (i.e., not identified according to a clinical history) and that establish the presence of defined depressive disorders. Thus, hasty or superficial diagnosis in a substance-dependent patient can be misleading. At one time, the field of practitioners was quite polarized into opposing camps on this issue. One camp, consisting largely of clinicians working in substance abuse treatment programs, tended to view all depression in such patients as substance-related and, therefore, of little importance to evaluation or treatment planning; the treatment for depression was simply treatment of the substance abuse. The opposing camp, consisting more commonly of psychiatrists and mental health practitioners, who are more likely to be referred patients with persistent and substantial depressive syndromes, tended to view depression as the primary disorder and substance abuse as a response to it (perhaps as a form of self-medication). This view oversimplifies the relationship between an independent depressive disorder and a substance use disorder and tends to encourage inadequate treatment of the latter. Fortunately, the last two decades have witnessed a sea change in the field, in which there is an increasing appreciation for the complexity of several possible relationships between a substance use disorder and depression, as well as an increasing acceptance of the importance of evaluating both types of disorders when they co-occur.

The purpose of this chapter is to provide a practical guideline for clinicians of all types working with substance-dependent patients in how to recognize depression in substance-dependent patients, in how to understand it, in what treatments are available, and in how to approach treatment planning. The goal is to make recognition and management of depression a routine part of practice for all clinicians, from counselors working on the frontlines, to their supervisors, to designers of treatment systems, to mental health professionals who are called in to consult on cases. Straightforward screening tools, diagnostic methods, and treatment approaches exist. We hope to demystify depression and help disseminate these diagnostic and treatment technologies as widely as possible across the treatment system.

CASE PRESENTATION

The case presented below represents a fairly typical pattern of mood and substance use symptoms encountered by the authors in their clinical work. The presentation is organized in the manner that we recommend for evaluating patients with comorbidity and represents the order in which the information should be elicited from the patient during a diagnostic interview. The interview takes about one hour to conduct and provides the information necessary for a preliminary diagnostic evaluation according to the *DSM-IV*. The case will be referred to throughout the chapter as an illustrative example. After reading the case report, readers might want to formulate the case, make a diagnosis, and synthesize a treatment plan, carrying their ideas into the discussion that follows. A treatment plan for the case example is presented at the end of the chapter (see "Treatment Planning for the Case Example").

Chief Complaint

TR is a 35-year-old waiter and bartender who is working toward completion of his undergraduate degree. He presents at the suggestion of a friend who is concerned about his depression and drinking. The patient is concerned that these issues will result in a separation from his long-standing girlfriend.

Patient History

Alcohol and Other Drug History. The patient says that he began drinking alcohol—large amounts of liquor—at the beginning of high school, around the age of 14 or 15. He later dropped out of high school, enlisted in the army, served a four-year tour of duty, and then moved around to different cities during his 20s. During this time, he continued to have alcohol problems. He regularly drank himself to the point of vomiting and experienced hangovers and mild withdrawal symptoms but never had a seizure or delirium tremens. He was charged with a DWI (driving while intoxicated) offense at the age of 24 and had other kinds of legal problems, including misdemeanors and short stays in jail. His first effort to quit was three to four years prior to this presentation. He was enrolled in several twenty-eight-day in-patient treatment programs, as well as short-term detoxification, followed by referrals to outpatient programs and Alcoholics Anonymous (AA), which he has attended intermittently over the last three to four years. However, he regularly relapsed after each in-patient stay. In the past he has used a variety of other drugs, including marijuana, cocaine, lysergic acid diethylamide (LSD), benzodiazepines, and narcotic painkillers, all in combination with alcohol. He identifies alcohol as the most prominent substance use problem. He also regularly smokes a half pack of cigarettes per day. At present, he is newly sober and is planning to end an outpatient treatment program for alcoholism.

Psychiatric History. The patient recounts an extensive history of depression, both at present and dating back many years, and describes his mood as "constantly down." He dates the onset of a persistently depressed mood to his early teenage years, approximately age 13. In addition, his energy is low and his sleep is poor; he frequently awakens during the night. His thinking is typically pessimistic and very self-critical, and he has thoughts of suicide that wax and wane. He identifies the most severe period of depression as an episode that occurred three years ago, at which time he was drinking alcohol heavily and crying all the time, and he made a suicide attempt (the only suicide attempt during his life).

He also describes considerable social anxiety, which began when he was in elementary school and which has been a problem ever since. He remembers being particularly nervous about going to school, about being called on by the teacher, and about having to give an answer to the class or go to the blackboard. At these times, he felt very nervous, shaky and flushed and "had a knot in my stomach." He continues to feel anxious in groups; this anxiety makes it difficult for him to participate fully in treatment programs and in AA.

He does not describe classic panic attacks, but he fears bridges and heights; he avoids heights whenever possible. He denies any episodes of prolonged high or euphoric mood, unusually high energy, or grandiose thinking.

Developmental History. The patient recalls many "awful" experiences during childhood, including being sexually abused by an uncle. He describes himself as a good student without any problems learning to read, write, or master other basic academic skills; he recalls no problem with attention, concentration, or sitting still in class. He recalls that he tried hard to keep a low profile in class because of his fear of being called on to participate.

Treatment History. The patient recalls having been treated with several medications for depression over the last three years (since becoming involved in treatment for his alcoholism). He recalls bupropion as having been the most helpful; it improved his energy and optimism, although he still felt somewhat down and was still socially anxious. Further, after a while, bupropion seemed to be associated with increasing irritability and was discontinued. He tried several selective serotonin reuptake inhibitors (SSRIs), including paroxetine, which made him feel tired, and he discontinued them after only a few weeks. He was also treated briefly with lithium but does not remember if he had a positive response.

Family History. The patient was adopted and has no contact with, or knowledge of, his biological family. His adopted parents did not suffer from substance abuse or other psychiatric problems.

Medical History. The patient has had no serious medical problems (e.g., seizures, liver disease, or cardiac problems), other than minor alcohol withdrawal symptoms (noted previously).

Social History. The patient describes considerable functional impairment: he has difficulty completing his undergraduate studies and has worked a series of low-level jobs. He ascribes his educational and employment problems to his drinking, his anxiety, and his tendency to become pessimistic and easily discouraged. He describes a number of hobbies and a love of the outdoors and a variety of outdoor sports, although he has made little time for these hobbies in recent years.

Mental Status Examination

This adult male looks his stated age. During the early part of the interview, he shifts around in his seat and plays with his hair. As the interview progresses, he becomes calm. His mood is "down" and his affect is sad. He describes low energy, insomnia, and low self-esteem. He denies difficulty with appetite or concentration. He denies suicidal or homicidal ideation. He denies auditory, visual, and olfactory hallucinations. He is alert and oriented to person, place, and time. Brief cognitive testing reveals no abnormalities. His insight and judgment are good.

DIAGNOSTIC CRITERIA AND TECHNIQUE

DSM-IV Criteria for Depressive Disorders

The *DSM-IV* criteria for major depressive disorder, dysthymic disorder, and substance-induced mood disorder are summarized in Tables 1-1A, 1-1B, and 1-1C, respectively. For a more detailed discussion of subtypes and specifiers (e.g., recurrent, chronic, melancholic features, atypical features, postpartum, seasonal), the reader is referred to the published diagnostic criteria (American Psychiatric Association, 1994) and to the *DSM-IV* casebook (Spitzer, Gibbon, Skodol, Williams, & First, 1994). However, three syndromes listed in Tables 1-1A through 1-1C are the essential ones for an evaluation of depression in the setting of substance abuse. These tables also include questions from the Psychiatric Research Interview for Substance and Mental Disorder (PRISM; Hasin et al., 2006) that are designed to aid clinicians in making diagnostic distinctions.

As can be seen in Tables 1-1A through 1-1C, each of these syndromes has as a core feature persistent depressed mood, and each requires the severity of depression and associated symptoms to be sufficient to create significant impairment in the patient's functioning. For major depression, the core feature may be either depressed mood or persistent anhedonia (i.e., loss of pleasure or interest in most usual activities). Thus, a clinician should start the diagnostic interview by asking the patient about his/her mood. It is useful to ask the patient for a description in his/her own words, as patients describe depressed mood differently (e.g., "down," "blue," "empty," "desperate," "hopeless"). Mood may also be irritable, particularly among adolescents. The distinction between the three syndromes lies in the time course, associated symptoms, and relationship to substance use. Major depression represents a discrete severe episode, in which depressed mood or anhedonia is present almost all the time for at least two weeks and is accompanied by several associated symptoms, including loss of interest in activities, sleep disturbances, change in appetite or weight, decreased energy and concentration, lowered self-esteem, or suicidal ideation. A total of five symptoms are needed to make the diagnosis, including at least one core feature (depression or anhedonia) and associated symptoms. Dysthymia represents a more chronic, low-grade depression that must be present at least half of the time for at least two years. Substance-induced mood disorder requires persistent depressed mood or anhedonia that occurs only during active substance use but with symptoms that exceed what would normally be expected from alcohol intoxication or withdrawal.

As can be seen in Tables 1-1A through 1-1C, associated symptoms of depression can be organized into vegetative or physical symptoms and cognitive symptoms. The vegetative symptoms include disturbed sleep (either insomnia or oversleeping), disturbed appetite (decreased appetite and weight loss or overeating and weight gain), low energy or fatigue, and either agitation or physical slowing of movement (so-called psychomotor retardation). Cognitive symptoms include feelings of worthlessness, excessive guilt, or low self-esteem; difficulty thinking clearly, concentrating, or making decisions; and thoughts of death and/or suicide or hopelessness about life, often expressed as "life does not seem worth living anymore."

The minimum number of associated symptoms necessary to meet the requirements for a diagnosis varies by disorder. Major depression requires at least four associated symptoms and the presence of a core symptom of either anhedonia or depressed mood. Dysthymic disorder requires at least two associated symptoms along with the core symptom of depressed mood. As defined by the *DSM-IV*, substance-induced depression

Table 1-1A

DSM-IV Criteria for Major Depressive Episode

Symptoms	DSM-IV Criteria[a, b, c]	Issues in Substance-Dependent Patients	PRISM Questions to Aid Diagnosis[f, g]
	A. Five (or more) of the following [nine] symptoms have been present during the same 2-week period …; at least one of the symptoms is either (1) depressed mood, or (2) loss of interest or pleasure	Substance intoxication or withdrawal effects are usually more transient; in major depression most symptoms are present most of the day every day for at least 2 weeks	
Core Symptoms	[at least one of these symptoms must be present]		
(1) depressed mood	Depressed mood most of the day, nearly every day, as indicated by either subjective report (e.g., feels sad or empty) or observation made by others (e.g. appears tearful) … In children and adolescents, can be irritable mood	Irritability and anxiety are often associated; dysphoric (down or anxious) mood is often part of substance intoxication[d] and especially withdrawal[d]	Have you ever felt sad, blue, depressed almost all day long, for at least 2 weeks?
(2) anhedonia	Markedly diminished interest or pleasure in all, or almost all, activities most of the day, nearly every day (as indicated by either subjective account or observation made by others)	Anhedonia is often a feature of substance withdrawal[d]	Have you ever felt uninterested in things almost all day long, for at least 2 weeks? … Have you ever felt unable to enjoy things almost all day long, for at least 2 weeks?
Vegetative Symptoms			During this time …
(3) weight/appetite change	Significant weight loss when not dieting or weight gain (e.g., a change of more than 5% of body weight in a month), or decrease or increase in appetite nearly every day … In children, consider failure to make expected weight gains.	May result from chronic substance use (e.g., alcohol and weight gain; stimulants, opiates and weight loss)	… did you lose your appetite compared to usual? … Did you lose any weight without dieting? … Did you find you wanted to eat a lot more than usual? … Did you gain any weight (without trying to)?

(Continued)

Symptoms	DSM-IV Criteria[a, b, c]	Issues in Substance-Dependent Patients	PRISM Questions to Aid Diagnosis[f, g]
(4) sleep disturbance	Insomnia or hypersomnia nearly every day	May be substance intoxication or withdrawal[d]	… did you have trouble sleeping, nearly every day? … Did you sleep more than usual?
(5) agitation or retardation	Psychomotor agitation or retardation [speaking or moving slowly] nearly every day (observable by others, not merely subjective feelings of restlessness or being slowed down)	May be substance intoxication or withdrawal[d]	… were you so fidgety or restless that you couldn't sit still? … Did you move or talk much more slowly than is normal for you?
(6) low energy	Fatigue or loss of energy nearly every day	May be substance intoxication or withdrawal[d]	… were you tired out all the time, so that even small things required a lot of effort?
Cognitive Symptoms			During this time …
(7) worthlessness or guilt	Feelings of worthlessness or excessive or inappropriate guilt (which may be delusional) nearly every day (not merely self-reproach or guilt about being sick)	Not a part of DSM-IV intoxication or withdrawal criteria[d]	… did you feel useless, good for nothing, or worthless? … Did you feel guilty about things you had done or not done?
(8) poor concentration	Diminished ability to think or concentrate, or indecisiveness, nearly every day (either by subjective account or as observed by others)	Often accompanies intoxication or withdrawal[d]	… did you have unusual trouble thinking, concentrating, or keeping your mind on things? … Did you find it harder than usual to make everyday decisions, for instance, what to wear, what to eat, what to watch on TV?
(9) thoughts of death or suicide	Recurrent thoughts of death (not just fear of dying), recurrent suicidal ideation without a specific plan, or a suicide attempt or a specific plan for committing suicide.	Not a part of DSM-IV intoxication or withdrawal criteria[d]	… did you find yourself thinking about death or dying? … Did you have any thoughts about suicide or killing yourself? … Did you think of any specific plan for committing suicide? … Did you do anything to hurt or kill yourself? Did you do anything on purpose you knew could have killed you?

(Continued)

Symptoms	DSM-IV Criteria[a, b, c]	Issues in Substance-Dependent Patients	PRISM Questions to Aid Diagnosis[f, g]
Other Criteria			
Rule out bipolar mixed	B. The symptoms do not meet criteria for a mixed episode [manic and depressive][e]	Important to ask about bipolar illness (see Chapter 2)	
Functional impairment	C. The symptoms cause clinically significant distress or impairment in social, occupational, or other important areas of functioning	A regular feature of substance dependence[d]	During this time … did you avoid seeing or talking to people because you didn't want to be around them as much as usual? Did you depend on others to take care of your everyday responsibilities or to give you a lot of attention or comfort? … Did you get into more arguments than usual? Did you have more trouble with [work/school/household tasks]? … During this time … were you very upset by [symptoms]? Did you think of getting help?
Rule out substance effects, medical illness	D. The symptoms are not due to the direct physiological effects of a substance (e.g., a drug of abuse, a medication) or a general medical condition (e.g., hypothyroidism).	See Table 1-1C regarding DSM-IV criteria for primary depression versus substance-induced depression versus expected effects of substances; it is important to ask about medical problems	When you started to feel [depressed] were you drinking or using [drugs]? … Were you having medical problems around that time? What was wrong? … Just before you began to feel [depressed], were you taking any medications prescribed by a doctor?
Rule out bereavement	E. The symptoms are not better accounted for by bereavement[e] …		Had someone close to you died around that time?

[a] Major depressive episode or syndrome can be part of major depressive disorder (unipolar, single or recurrent major depressive episodes), bipolar disorder (see Chapter 2), or substance-induced mood disorder (see Table 1-1C).
[b] American Psychiatric Association (1994).
[c] Reprinted with permission from the *Diagnostic and Statistical Manual of Mental Disorders*, Fourth Edition (Copyright 1994). American Psychiatric Association.
[d] Consult DSM-IV criteria (American Psychiatric Association, 1994) for substance intoxication and withdrawal syndromes; such symptoms are usually transient.
[e] Consult DSM-IV criteria (American Psychiatric Association, 1994) for bipolar disorder, bereavement.
[f] Hasin et al. (2006).
[g] Reprinted with permission.

Table 1-1B
DSM-IV Criteria for Dysthymic Disorder

Symptoms	DSM-IV Criteria[(a, b)]	Issues in Substance-Dependent Patients	PRISM Questions to Aid Diagnosis[(e, f)]
Core Symptom	Depressed mood for most of the day, for more days than not, as indicated either by subjective account or observation by others, for at least 2 years … In children and adolescents, mood can be irritable and duration must be at least 1 year	Chronic low-grade depression may be difficult to distinguish from effects of long-term, chronic substance use	Was there a time in your life lasting at least 2 years, when more days than not you were in a low mood?
Associated Symptoms	Two or more of the following 6 symptoms are present while depressed:		
Vegetative Symptoms			During that period of low mood … did you often …
	(1) poor appetite or overeating	May be substance intoxication or withdrawal[(c)]	… lose your appetite? … find that you overate?
	(2) insomnia or hypersomnia	May be substance intoxication or withdrawal[(c)]	… have trouble falling asleep? …wake up too early? … wake up frequently during the night? … sleep more than usual?
	(3) low energy or fatigue	May be substance intoxication or withdrawal[(c)]	… feel tired out or feel you didn't have much energy?
Cognitive Symptoms			During that period of low mood…did you often.…
	(4) low self-esteem	Frequently present in substance-dependent patients, especially after failed efforts to get abstinent or bad consequences of substance use	… feel down on yourself? … feel you weren't as good as other people? … feel that you were inadequate or a failure?

(Continued)

Symptoms	DSM-IV Criteria[a, b]	Issues in Substance-Dependent Patients	PRISM Questions to Aid Diagnosis[e, f]
	(5) poor concentration or difficulty making decisions	May be substance intoxication or withdrawal[c]	… have trouble thinking, concentrating, or keeping your mind on things? … have difficulty making everyday decisions?
	(6) feelings of hopelessness.	Frequently present in substance-dependent patients, especially after failed efforts to get abstinent or bad consequences of substance use	… feel that things were bad and would never get better? … feel life would never work out the way you wanted?
Other Criteria			
Chronicity and persistence (no long symptom-free periods)	C. During the 2-year period (1 year for children or adolescents) of the disturbance, the person has never been without the symptoms [core symptoms and associated symptoms] … for more than 2 months at a time.		During those 2 years, did your low mood and all the other experiences we just talked about go away for at least 2 months?
Chronic or partially remitted major depression versus dysthymic disorder	D. No major depressive episode …. during the first 2 years of the disturbance (1 year for children and adolescents); i.e., the disturbance is not better accounted for by chronic major depressive disorder or major depressive disorder, in partial remission.	For simplicity, we prefer to waive this criterion and diagnose both major depressive disorder and dysthymic disorder if criteria for both disorders are otherwise met	During those 2 years, did your low mood ever get much worse, so that you felt very depressed almost all day for at least 2 weeks?
Rule out bipolar disorder	E. There has never been a manic episode …, a mixed episode …, or a hypomanic episode, [or] … cyclothymic disorder[d].	Important to ask about bipolar illness (see Chapter 2)	
Rule out psychotic disorder	F. The disturbance does not occur exclusively during the course of a chronic psychotic disorder such as schizophrenia or delusional disorder[g].		

(Continued)

Symptoms	DSM-IV Criteria[a, b]	Issues in Substance-Dependent Patients	PRISM Questions to Aid Diagnosis[e, f]
Rule out substance effects, medical illness	G. The symptoms are not due to the direct physiological effects of a substance (e.g., a drug of abuse, a medication) or a general medical condition (e.g., hypothyroidism).	See Table 1-1C regarding DSM-IV criteria for primary depression versus substance-induced depression versus expected effects of substances; it is important to ask about medical problems	Were you drinking or using drugs … during that time? …. Were you taking any medicines prescribed by a doctor during the whole time you felt [low]?…Were you having medical problems during the whole time you felt [low]?
Functional impairment	H. The symptoms cause clinically significant distress or impairment in social, occupational, or other important areas of functioning.	A regular feature of substance dependence[c]	During that period of low mood, did you often … … have trouble getting along or dealing with people? … have trouble completing your [work/school/ household] tasks or doing them as well as you used to? … have trouble fulfilling other responsibilities? Were you very troubled by [symptoms]?

[a] American Psychiatric Association (1994).
[b] Reprinted with permission from the *Diagnostic and Statistical Manual of Mental Disorders*, Fourth Edition (Copyright 1994). American Psychiatric Association.
[c] Consult *DSM-IV* criteria (American Psychiatric Association, 1994) for substance intoxication and withdrawal syndromes; note: symptoms are usually transient.
[d] Consult *DSM-IV* criteria (American Psychiatric Association, 1994) for manic episode, mixed episode, hypomanic episode, and cyclothymic disorder; see Chapter 2 of this volume.
[e] Hasin et al. (2006).
[f] Reprinted with permission.
[g] Consult *DSM-IV* criteria (American Psychiatric Association, 1994) for schizophrenia or delusional disorder.

Table 1-1C
DSM-IV **Criteria for Primary Depression Versus Substance-Induced Depression and Suggested Operationalization of the Criteria for Clinical Application**

Symptoms	***DSM-IV*** **Criteria**[a, b]	**Suggested Operationalization for Clinical Application**	**PRISM Questions to Aid Diagnosis**[c, d]
Core Symptoms	A. A prominent and persistent disturbance in mood predominates in the clinical picture and is characterized by:	Require that symptom criteria for either major depression or dysthymia be met (see Tables 1-1A and 1-1B) (i.e., core symptoms and the required number of associated symptoms)	
(1) depressed mood	Depressed mood.	Depressed mood most of the day, nearly every day, for at least a two-week period (major depression core symptom) or depressed mood most of the day, more days than not, for at least 2 years (dysthymia core symptom)	
(2) anhedonia	Markedly diminished interest or pleasure in all, or almost all, activities.	Markedly diminished interest or pleasure in all, or almost all, activities most of the day, nearly every day for at least a two-week period (major depression core symptom)	
Other Criteria	B. There is evidence from the history, physical examination, or laboratory findings ... [that] the symptoms ... developed during, or within a month of, substance intoxication or withdrawal.	Establish by careful history taking that a depression syndrome (core symptom plus associated symptoms) was present; then relate its time of occurrence to that of substance use	Did the [depression] ever start while you were drinking or using [drugs] a lot? By a lot, I mean 4 or more days a week or 3 days straight ... Did you ever start drinking or using [drugs] a lot soon after you became [depressed]? By soon, I mean within a couple of weeks. Did the [depression] ever start within a couple of weeks ... ... after you drank alcohol or used [drugs] continuously for 3 days or more?

(Continued)

Symptoms	DSM-IV Criteria[a, b]	Suggested Operationalization for Clinical Application	PRISM Questions to Aid Diagnosis[c, d]
			… after you stopped drinking alcohol or using [drugs] entirely?
			… after you cut down significantly on your drinking or [drug] use?
			Was there any increase or decrease in your [relevant substances] use around the time you were feeling the worst?
	C. The disturbance is not better accounted for by a mood disorder that is not substance-induced.	A diagnosis of primary major depression or dysthymia cannot be established by history.	
	D. The disturbance does not occur exclusively during the course of a delirium.	See Chapter 6.	
	E. The symptoms cause clinically significant distress or impairment in social, occupational, or other important areas of functioning.	Same requirement as for a diagnosis of major depression or dysthymia.	During that time, did you avoid seeing or talking to people because you didn't want to be around them as much as usual? Did you depend on others to take care of your everyday responsibilities or to give you a lot of attention or comfort? … Did you get into more arguments than usual? Did you have more trouble with [work/school/household tasks]? … Were you very troubled by [symptoms]?

(a) American Psychiatric Association (1994).
(b) Reprinted with permission from the *Diagnostic and Statistical Manual of Mental Disorders*, Fourth Edition (Copyright 1994). American Psychiatric Association.
(c) Hasin et al. (2006).
(d) Reprinted with permission.

is a broad category since this diagnosis does not require any associated symptoms to be present. We recommend that clinicians make a diagnosis of substance-induced major depression or substance-induced dysthymia if the patient meets criteria for major depression or dysthymia (including the requisite number of associated symptoms and duration of symptoms) and if the syndrome is not independent of substance use.

How to Take a History

Outline Substance Abuse History. We recommend first asking the patient about his/her substance abuse history and documenting its major landmarks: (1) the age of onset of substance use, (2) the age that substances were first regularly used (i.e., two or three times per week or more), (3) the substances used, (4) the age of onset and length of any substantial periods of abstinence over the course of the history (i.e., two to three months in duration), and (5) the quantity and types of substances used recently and up to the present. This information provides the historical framework in which the history of depression can then be integrated. It is sometimes useful to plot this information on a timeline: record onset of substance abuse, persistence of use, periods of abstinence, and other events such as a DWI and treatment efforts.

Look for Depressive Syndromes. When we asked the patient in the case example about his mood, we found that the patient was feeling depressed most of the time ("constantly down"), that he remembered first feeling depressed in his early teenage years, and that the course of depression has been fairly chronic and persistent since that time. The associated symptoms of low energy and hopelessness have also been present chronically, and, taken together, this fits the pattern for the diagnosis of dysthymic disorder. In addition, when the depression was at its worst several years ago, it met criteria for major depressive disorder, since associated symptoms included loss of interest and pleasure for most things, significant suicidal thinking and a suicide attempt, insomnia, and low energy. The combination of major depression and dysthymic disorder over the course of a lifetime is sometimes referred to as "double depression" (reflecting the fact that the severity of depression may wax and wane). In fact, depression may be thought of as existing on a continuum from mild symptoms below the threshold for a diagnosis to dysthymic symptoms and finally to major depression.

Determine Whether Depression Should Be Classified as Primary (Independent) or Substance-Induced. *DSM-IV* draws distinctions between three types of depressive symptoms and syndromes in the setting of substance abuse: (1) expected effects of substances, representing depressive symptoms and associated symptoms that are nothing more than what would be expected from toxic or withdrawal effects of the substances that the patient is taking; (2) substance-induced depression, representing a depression that has never occurred independently of active substance abuse, but wherein the symptoms exceed what would be expected from the toxic or withdrawal effects of substances alone; and (3) primary depression, representing a depressive syndrome that persists during a substantial period of abstinence of at least one month or more or that precedes the onset of substance dependence, either having an onset prior to the first onset of substance abuse or persisting during a time of abstinence over the course of the patient's history. The terminology is confusing since the term substance-induced calls to mind toxic and withdrawal effects of substances. *DSM-IV*, however, intends substance-induced depression to be a more substantial clinical syndrome that requires clinical attention in terms of further diagnosis and treatment planning. *DSM-IV* is vague about how to distinguish between symptoms caused by the usual effects of substances and symptoms indicative of a substance-induced depression, although diagnostic instruments such as the PRISM (Hasin et al., 2006), offer systematic techniques for accomplishing this and will be discussed later in the chapter.

In the case example, the depression appears to have had its onset at the age of 13, at least one year prior to the onset of substance abuse at age 14 or 15. This would qualify the patient for a diagnosis of primary depression and not substance-induced depression. However, this case illustrates a fairly common dilemma in evaluating the history of such patients: when depression and substance abuse have their onset relatively close to each other during the early teenage years and when one is evaluating an adult many years later, one must maintain some skepticism about the accuracy of the patient's recall of the relative onset of the problems. For this patient, one would feel more confident in a diagnosis of primary dysthymia or major depression if the patient was able to sustain the period of abstinence entered at the time that the history was taken, so that the depression could be evaluated during a period of one month or more of abstinence. Thus, we would wonder if the patient's depression might be more accurately classified as substance-induced rather than primary. Our first recommendation to this patient and first order of treatment planning would be to institute substance abuse treatment and encourage continued abstinence while observing whether the depression either persists or resolves.

Determine Whether Depression Should Be Classified as Unipolar or Bipolar.
After determining the presence of a depressive disorder (in the case example, current dysthymic disorder with a recent history of an episode of major depression), the clinician should inquire as to whether there is a history of manic or hypomanic episodes that would qualify the patient for a diagnosis of bipolar disorder (see "Instruments and Methods for Screening and Diagnosis" in this chapter and also Chapter 2 of this volume). A diagnosis of bipolar disorder requires sustained periods, days or weeks, of a mood that is the opposite of depression—high and euphoric—accompanied by increased energy, decreased need for sleep, and an unusually high level of activity, and, in the more extreme form of mania, markedly impaired judgment, grandiosity, and, often, grandiose or paranoid psychosis. Given the extraordinarily high rates of addictive disorders in bipolar patients, this diagnosis must always be explored in depressed patients with addictions. The patient in the case example denied any such episodes. However, it can be difficult to elicit such a history from patients with long histories of substance abuse, since they may have experienced such symptoms briefly while intoxicated on drugs (including alcohol), and it may be difficult to distinguish a brief or short-lived drug-related mood disturbance from a more persistent hypomanic syndrome. Full mania is usually more obvious and usually results in marked impairment and hospitalization for control of symptoms. Determining if the patient's mood disorder falls in the bipolar spectrum is very important, since bipolar disorder patients usually need to be treated with a mood stabilizer, such as lithium or an anticonvulsant, and the treatment of such patients with antidepressant medications alone can be harmful or even dangerous, since these medications may actually induce episodes of hypomania or mania. There is one hint in our patient's history that would suggest that we should continue to probe for bipolar history: the patient became irritable after a while when treated with bupropion. The mood disturbance during hypomania or mania is frequently irritability, which could also simply be a side effect of the medication.

Ask About Past Treatments for Depression. With the increased availability of psychiatric consultation and treatment programs, patients increasingly present with a history of previous treatment with antidepressant medications. Information on past treatment with antidepressant medications is valuable, since a substantial improvement during a prior trial of medication would strongly suggest that the medication should be reinstituted as part of the treatment plan. There is no point in repeating a treatment that has failed in the past. If possible, elicit from the patient the following information: names of the medications, maximum doses, the total length of the trials, and extent to which each medication was helpful with depressive symptoms or substance abuse symptoms or both. The patient in the case example did not improve on at least one SSRI (paroxetine), although he only took it for a few weeks. Since antidepressant medications may take four to six weeks or more to begin to take effect, we do not know if he might have benefited had he stayed on the medication longer. Information on side effects is also important to elicit, since a medication or class of medications that was not tolerable to a patient in the past probably should not be repeated. It is tantalizing that the patient in the case example did well in the past on bupropion. Despite the development of irritability, one might be tempted to reinstitute this medication, perhaps at a lower dose, and to proceed cautiously.

Examine Family History. A brief family history that emphasizes first-degree relatives (parents and siblings) is valuable because depression is, to some degree, genetically determined, and a convincing history of depression in a close relative, all other things being equal, increases one's confidence that a depressive syndrome observed in a substance-abusing patient represents more than just expected effects of substances. It is useful to ask the patient if he/she is aware of any relatives with depression, if the depression was treated, and if any other clear markers (e.g., suicide attempts or hospitalizations) were present. Brief inquiry regarding family history of substance dependence disorders and other psychiatric disorders is useful. Because the patient in the case example was adopted and did not have any information about his biological parents, family history is not useful in understanding his depression.

Ask About Suicide and Potential for Violence. Thoughts about death and suicide are common symptoms of depression. The risk posed by these thoughts increases to the extent that patients intend to kill themselves (as opposed to just thinking about it), have plans of how to do it, and have histories of past suicide attempts. Substance abuse increases the risk of suicide, so that patients with comorbid substance use and depressive disorders are at somewhat increased risk for suicide. Family history of suicide also raises the risk of suicide in an individual. Many patients with depression have thoughts of suicide without any intent to act on these thoughts. The presence of these thoughts does not require emergency measures, but they require careful watching over time. However, a small proportion of depressed patients will have significant suicide risk, and suicide is a common cause of death among patients with mood disorders, particularly if accompanied by addictions. Hopelessness and agitation are mental states that have been associated with suicide attempts. Any concern about suicide risk should prompt rapid evaluation by a qualified mental health professional or, if necessary, referral to a psychiatric emergency room. Although the patient in the case example currently denies any intent or plan for suicide and seems positively oriented toward the future, he has a history of one suicide attempt during a severe episode of depression. We would want to know more about that suicide attempt, know whether there were other suicide attempts, and be increasingly vigilant with this patient, particularly if his depression or substance abuse were to worsen.

As noted above, the mood disturbance of depression can include a component of irritability or anger, and depression can be accompanied by violence. It is important to inquire about any history of violent acts (e.g., getting into fights, attacking others). Similarly, patients who express a desire or plan to harm someone or have a history of doing so are at increased risk of violence, and substance intoxication substantially increases this risk.

Ask About Psychosis. Psychosis, although rare, may be a manifestation of severe depression. The delusions that accompany the depression are typically delusions of guilt (e.g., patients believe that they have done terrible things that they have not really done or inflate the significance of past regretted behaviors out of proportion). Hallucinations in depression are usually auditory (i.e., the patient hears voices), and the voices are usually critical of or derogatory to the patient. Particularly alarming are voices that tell the patient what to do (i.e., command hallucinations). Patients may obey the orders of these voices, and command hallucinations to kill oneself or kill someone else indicate a high risk for suicide or homicide.

Ask About Other Psychiatric Disorders. Depression is associated with a number of other psychiatric disorders that are also common in substance-dependent patients, including antisocial personality disorder, anxiety disorders, and conduct disorder in adolescence. The patient in the case example appears to have childhood onset of anxiety, which probably meets criteria for social anxiety disorder (see "Instruments and Methods for Screening and Diagnosis" in this chapter and also Chapter 4 of this volume). Anxiety disorders and depression respond to many of the same treatments (e.g., antidepressant medications, Cognitive Behavioral Therapy (CBT)), and early onset of an anxiety disorder increases confidence that the depressive disorder is significant and warrants attention in treatment planning.

Take a Brief Developmental or Childhood History. Patients with substance dependence frequently have a childhood history of school problems due to disruptive disorder, attention deficit disorder, or learning disabilities. These disorders probably increase the risk of subsequent development of depressive disorder. Additionally, depression may begin in childhood. More commonly, childhood anxiety may be a precursor of adult depression (the patient in the case example has a clear history of childhood social anxiety disorder). Another early pattern that is associated with the development of adult depression is separation anxiety, in which a child is very frightened about attending school in the early preschool and elementary school years.

Ask About Trauma and Abuse. Childhood trauma is alarmingly common in substance-dependent patients, and it is also a risk factor for the development of depression and posttraumatic stress disorder. Current trauma or abuse needs to be addressed immediately as part of the patient's treatment plan because it will interfere with recovery from depression and substance abuse. The patient in the case example has a history of sexual abuse by an older family member during childhood. Although no immediate intervention is necessary for this past abuse, it is important to consider how this trauma will be addressed as part of the patient's long-term treatment plan. A history of abuse should prompt an assessment for the presence of posttraumatic stress disorder (see Chapter 3 of this volume).

NATURAL HISTORY AND ETIOLOGY

Risk Factors and Possible Causative Mechanisms

Like substance use disorders, depression is a complex illness with multiple causal mechanisms, all or only some of which may operate in any given patient. Table 1-2 provides a listing of probable risk factors for depression. Twin and adoption studies have established that there is a genetic contribution to the risk for depression, and a family history of depression is a risk factor for depression in close relatives. It is of interest that some of the twin studies suggest that there are genetic factors that contribute to risk for depression, as well as for substance dependence. This is consistent with the fact that a family history of alcoholism is also a risk factor for depression in close relatives. As seems to be the case with most other psychiatric disorders that have been studied, there are probably multiple genes that contribute to this genetic component so that there is no single gene for depression.

A second major contributor to the causation of depression is psychological stress, particularly in the form of trauma and/or loss. Trauma is best known as the trigger for posttraumatic stress disorder, but it is also associated with the subsequent development of depressive illness. It is of interest that stress is a risk factor for the development or prolongation of addictive disorders.

Depression is highly associated with a number of other psychiatric disorders. Depression may be a response to the functional impairment and adverse circumstances that result from other serious disorders such as conduct disorder or anxiety disorders. Alternatively, the high co-occurrence may represent shared psychophysiologic mechanisms between depression and other disorders. For example, there is some evidence from twin studies that conduct disorder, a heritable illness, predisposes a patient simultaneously to depression and substance abuse, and adolescents with conduct disorder are at increased risk for the development of depression. Anxiety disorders and depression frequently co-occur, and, interestingly, both sets of disorders respond to the same types of antidepressant medication, thereby suggesting common physiologic and pharmacologic underpinnings.

The manifestation of some medical disorders may be major depression. Hypothyroidism, a condition caused by an underactive thyroid gland, is one of the medical disorders most commonly associated with the development of depressive symptoms. Hypothyroidism is detected with a routine blood test, and it is recommended that patients presenting with depressive symptoms have their thyroid functioning tested. Other medical disorders associated with depression include cancer, particularly cerebral tumors, diabetes, acquired immune deficiency syndrome (AIDS), multiple sclerosis (MS), fibromyalgia, lupus, and polycystic ovary syndrome (PCOS). Additionally, medications such as beta-blockers, which are used to treat hypertension, benzodiazepines, steroids, and oral contraceptives may cause symptoms of depression. Most patients who take these medications do not experience depression. However, a causal relationship between medication and depression may be suspected if onset of depression occurs when medication is started or when the dose is increased. Part of the treatment plan for patients presenting for the treatment of depression should include a full medical evaluation to rule out any reversible medical causes of depression.

Finally, substance abuse is a risk factor for the development of depression. Depression often develops in the wake of chronic substance abuse, as reflected in *DSM-IV* criteria for substance-induced depression. Further, alcohol dependence in remission (i.e., alcohol dependence that has been resolved in the past, and the patient is currently in stable sobriety) is associated with increased risk of subsequent development of major depression during abstinence. In a depressed patient with substance abuse or

Table 1-2
Risk Factors Thought to Contribute
to the Development of Depression

Genetic factors

Psychological Stress
    Trauma
    Loss

Other Psychiatric Disorders
    Anxiety Disorders
        Generalized Anxiety Disorder (GAD)
        Obsessive Compulsive Disorder (OCD)
        Panic Disorder
        Posttraumatic Stress Disorder (PTSD)
    Conduct Disorder

Medical Disorders
Substance Abuse

dependence, the substance abuse should probably be the first causal mechanism that is considered. Thus, treatment for substance abuse always remains the first priority and a constant component in the treatment of dually diagnosed patients.

Course of Depression in Relation to Course of Substance Use Over the Lifetime

Depression may have its onset at any age, from childhood into old age, although its onset is typically later than that of substance abuse, which often begins in the early teenage years. The case example (See "Case Example") represents early onset of depression, which is associated with childhood onset of an anxiety disorder. Such early onset depressions, as some evidence suggests (Weissman et al., 1984; Weissman et al., 1987; Wickramaratne, Greenwald, & Weissman, 2000), have particularly high genetic loading. The patient in the case example suffered from early onset of trauma in the form of childhood sexual abuse, which could have also engendered early depression.

Most studies of the relative onset and course of depression with respect to substance use disorders have been cross-sectional in nature (i.e., patients or individuals are interviewed at one point in time and are asked to remember the time course of both disorders). Such studies have yielded a variety of results among adults. Some studies show that substance dependence precedes the onset of depression, while other studies show that the population is more evenly split between patients who exhibit symptoms of substance abuse before symptoms of depression and patients who exhibit symptoms of depression before symptoms of substance dependence. Retrospective recall of events is obviously subject to the vagaries of memory and may not be accurate.

A smaller number of studies have followed a panel of patients prospectively over periods of one year or more to directly examine the relative onset and offset of depression and substance abuse over time. For example, Hasin et al. (2002), using the PRISM interview, followed 250 patients for one year to eighteen months after discharge from a dual diagnosis inpatient unit. This study found that substance-induced depression had important prognostic implications, including a reduced rate of remission in substance use disorders (Hasin et al., 2002). This finding illustrates the importance of recognizing substance-induced depression as a substantial clinical syndrome that warrants careful evaluation and treatment planning. A study that examined the same patient sample studied by Hasin et al. (2002) found that substance-induced depression is, in some measures, associated with an increased risk of suicidal behavior (Aharonovich, Liu, Nunes, & Hasin, 2002). Additionally, depression that emerged or persisted during an abstinent period during follow-up (i.e., primary depression) was associated with an increased risk of subsequent relapse to substance use disorder. Similarly, Greenfield et al. (1998) found that a diagnosis of major depression at admission to a hospital for treatment of alcohol dependence increased the risk of relapse to drinking after discharge from the hospital. These studies strongly suggest the importance of identifying and treating depression, since, in so doing, one may be treating one of the risk factors for ongoing substance abuse.

At the same time, evidence suggests that depression during the course of active substance use frequently resolves once the patient becomes abstinent. However, this evidence is based primarily upon observation of depressive symptoms at admission for short-term hospitalization for alcoholism rather than upon carefully diagnosed depressive disorder observed over a long follow-up.

ISSUES IN DIAGNOSIS: CHALLENGE OF DISTINGUISHING PRIMARY DEPRESSION FROM SUBSTANCE-INDUCED DEPRESSION FROM EXPECTED EFFECTS OF SUBSTANCES

This challenge has engendered controversy in this field for many years. *DSM-IV* has provided more guidance on making these distinctions than any previous diagnostic system. The PRISM interview (Hasin et al., 2006), which will be described in more detail in the next section, was designed to elicit these distinctions, and more research along such lines is needed. In the meantime, considerable uncertainty and room for clinical judgment remains. Some cases will be fairly clear. In the case example (See "Case Example"), social anxiety and dysthymia appeared to have had a clear onset prior to the onset of substance dependence. On the other hand, in the case example, the status of the patient's current depressive symptoms is unclear; for many years the symptoms have occurred only in the setting of chronic substance abuse. As the case example suggests, the clinician may wish to look to other aspects of the history, such as a history of severe symptoms (e.g., suicide attempts) and a history of prior response to treatment for depression, and then employ clinical judgment to determine in which category the patient likely fits.

The time course of the depressive symptoms may provide insight into which category a patient's symptoms fit. Depressive symptoms that result from substances will have the shortest duration. For example, a patient may experience sadness, loss of appetite, low energy, poor concentration, and difficulty sleeping during and immediately following an episode of drinking. These symptoms, however, should resolve within hours to days after the patient has stopped drinking and should not return unless the patient begins to drink again. Substance-induced depression results in symptoms that last between episodes of substance use but then resolve completely after a period of abstinence (these depressive symptoms last longer than those that occur as a result of substance use). Symptoms of primary depression, on the other hand, do not resolve after a period of abstinence and continue until the patient receives some form of psychosocial or pharmacologic treatment.

INSTRUMENTS AND METHODS FOR SCREENING AND DIAGNOSIS

Screening Instruments

Table 1-3 lists and briefly describes features of several common screening instruments that may be particularly useful in substance-dependent populations. The Beck Depression Inventory (BDI) is a brief self-administered questionnaire that detects the presence of depressive symptoms and is oriented toward the cognitive symptoms of depression, as opposed to the vegetative or physical symptoms (Beck, Steer, & Brown, 1996). The Hamilton Depression Scale (HAM-D or HDS) is the most widely used brief clinician-administered scale, and it is more oriented towards vegetative symptoms of depression (Hamilton, 1960; Williams, 1988). The Patient Health Questionnaire (PHQ), a newer instrument, asks patients to respond to items corresponding to each of the diagnostic criteria in the *DSM-IV* (Spitzer, Kroenke, & Williams, 1999); the instrument yields possible diagnostic classifications, as opposed to the BDI and the HAM-D, which yield symptom severity scores. The purpose of a screening instrument is to quickly identify those patients who may be at risk for depression and who warrant more detailed clinical evaluation. Each of these instruments meets that purpose because they take only a few minutes to complete, and elevated scores are suggestive of depressive illness. Clinicians should be encouraged to examine the items on the scales and apply the scales to their patients in order to efficiently identify cases of depression and to increase clinicians' facility in identifying depression. In addition, these scales are an excellent way for clinicians and patients to measure the response of depression to treatment interventions.

Diagnostic Instruments

Several structured and semistructured diagnostic instruments have been applied to, or evaluated in, substance-dependent patients. Arguably, the most sophisticated instrument for application in dually diagnosed populations is the PRISM, which requires approximately 120 minutes to administer to subjects with psychiatric and substance use symptoms (Hasin et al., 2006). The PRISM allows clinicians to evaluate each symptom separately in terms of its relationship to substance abuse, thereby helping clinicians to distinguish between primary and substance-induced depression and depressive symptoms that are expected effects of substance use. Unlike most other instruments, for which there has been relatively little study of the prognostic implications, the PRISM was applied in a longitudinal study of posthospitalization substance-dependent patients, and the categories of both primary depression and substance-induced depression were found to have important prognostic implications. In brief, the PRISM asks the interviewer to evaluate separately each symptom of a depressive syndrome (e.g., sleep disturbance, low energy) and to evaluate whether that symptom represents merely expected effects of substance intoxication or withdrawal or exceeds such expected effects, in which case it may be counted towards a diagnosis of either primary depression or substance-induced depression (see Tables 1-1A, 1-1B, and 1-1C for examples of questions from the PRISM). If the symptom emerged during a period of stable substance use, this is taken as evidence that the symptom exceeds expected effects of substances. If, on the other hand, the symptom emerged during a period of either escalating substance use or diminishing substance use, then the symptom more likely represents either toxic effects or withdrawal effects.

The Structured Clinical Interview for DSM-IV-TR Axis I Disorders (SCID-I) operationalizes a method for asking about each of the symptoms of various depressive

Table 1-3
Instruments for Screening and Diagnosis of
Depression in Substance-Dependent Patients

Beck Depression Inventory (BDI) (Beck et al., 1996)	– 21 items – self-administered screening questionnaire – focuses more on the cognitive symptoms of depression – indicates the severity of depressive symptoms
Hamilton Depression Scale (HAM-D) (Hamilton, 1960; Williams, 1988)	– 25 items – clinician-administered screening questionnaire – focuses more on the vegetative symptoms of depression – indicates the severity of depressive symptoms
Patient Health Questionnaire (PHQ) (Spitzer et al., 1999)	– self-administered screening questionnaire – items correspond to each of the *DSM-IV* diagnostic criteria – yields possible diagnostic classifications
Structured Clinical Interview for DSM-IV-TR Axis I Disorders (SCID-I) (First et al., 2002)	– clinician-administered diagnostic instrument – based on *DSM-IV-TR* criteria – provides a method for asking questions about symptoms of depression and other psychiatric disorders – usually used in research studies
Mini International Neuropsychiatric Interview (MINI) (Sheehan et al., 1998)	– clinician-administered diagnostic instrument – layout similar to the SCID-I but simplified
Primary Care Evaluation of Mental Disorders (PRIME-MD) (Spitzer et al., 1994)	– clinician-administered diagnostic instrument – tested in primary care medical settings
Psychiatric Research Interview for Substance and Mental Disorders (PRISM) (Hasin et al., 2006)	– clinician-administered diagnostic instrument – based on *DSM-IV* criteria – helps make the distinction between primary depression, substance-induced depression, and depressive symptoms expected given the effects of substances – usually used in research studies

disorders and other psychiatric disorders, as well as for applying the *Diagnostic and Statistical Manual of Mental Disorders,* 4th edition, text revision (*DSM-IV-TR*; American Psychiatric Association, 2000) criteria (First, Spitzer, Gibbon, & Williams, 2002). Although the SCID-I and PRISM are typically used in research studies rather than in clinical practice, clinicians should be encouraged to try out these instruments. The SCID-I and PRISM provide suggested questions and lines of questioning for inquiring about each of the symptoms of depression and other disorders and list the diagnostic criteria next to each question. Thus, they represent excellent training tools; experience using the PRISM or SCID-I will rapidly improve clinicians' ability to elicit a depression history.

Simpler versions intended to elicit *DSM-IV* criteria for depression and other psychiatric disorders in a briefer format also exist, including a SCID checklist, the Mini International Neuropsychiatric Interview (MINI) (Sheehan et al., 1998), and the Primary Care Evaluation of Mental Disorders (PRIME-MD), which has been tested in primary care medical settings (Spitzer et al., 1994). These instruments are faster to administer and should increase clinicians' familiarity with diagnosis of depression.

DIFFERENTIAL DIAGNOSIS AND OTHER OVERLAPPING DISORDERS

For the purposes of diagnosis and treatment planning, it is useful to think of depression as a disorder, but it is important to remember that the disorders described in *DSM-IV* are actually syndromes or clusters of symptoms that may have one of many causes. This is in contrast to many medical disorders (e.g., bacterial pneumonia or hepatitis C), for which the causative agent and mechanism of disease is known. Thus, depression may be a reaction to the impairment produced by one of the other syndromes or disorders with which it is associated, or the symptoms of depression, particularly fatigue and anhedonia, could be caused by other disorders, including many medical conditions. Once a history of depression has been obtained, it is useful to enumerate other disorders that the patient also suffers from and to generate a differential diagnosis or list of other disorders or conditions that might contribute to depression. Table 1-4 lists associated disorders that are commonly encountered in patients with both depression and substance dependence and that should be considered in the process of differential diagnosis. In some cases, further lines of questioning or diagnostic tests help to better understand the patient's problems and to determine a plan for treatment. It is recommended that patients presenting for the treatment of depression have a medical evaluation, including blood work, to rule out medical causes of major depression.

All substance use disorders should be to documented, and patients may be particularly sensitive to the depression producing effects of substances. Further, the substances themselves have differing depression-like effects when they are used chronically. For example, alcohol- or cocaine-dependent patients may appear quite severely depressed when presenting for treatment. Patients with cannabis dependence and regular heavy cannabis use more typically present with symptoms of apathy and lost of interest.

Nicotine dependence deserves special emphasis in evaluating depressed substance-dependent patients because (1) nicotine dependence is very common in such patients (Sullivan & Covey, 2002), (2) it poses substantial long-term health risk, and (3) the relationship between nicotine and depression is unique. Both a history of depression and the emergence of depressive symptoms during an attempt to quit smoking have been associated with greater difficulty in quitting cigarettes (Covey, Glassman, & Stetner, 1998). Further, there is evidence that depression, sometimes quite severe, may emerge after quitting cigarettes (almost as if the nicotine was functioning as an antidepressant); for most other addictive substances (e.g., alcohol, cocaine) chronic use seems to worsen depression. Nicotine dependence is treatable with a nicotine patch plus counseling and with noradrenergic antidepressants such as bupropion or nortriptyline (Hall et al., 1998; Hurt et al., 1997; Prochazka et al., 1998; for more information, see Chapter 13 of this volume). Depressed substance-dependent patients should be encouraged to quit smoking for the sake of their long-term health, but clinicians need to remember that depression may emerge or worsen if the patient successfully quits and that noradrenergic antidepressants may be particularly indicated in such patients.

**Table 1-4 Disorders Associated
With Depression**

Anxiety Disorders
    Generalized Anxiety Disorder (GAD)
    Obsessive Compulsive Disorder (OCD)
    Panic Disorder
    Substance Anxiety Disorder (SAD)
    Posttraumatic Stress Disorder (PTSD)

Conduct Disorder

Other Substance Use Disorders
    Alcohol Abuse or Dependence
    Cannabis Abuse or Dependence
    Cocaine Abuse or Dependence
    Nicotine Dependence
    Opiate Abuse or Dependence
    Stimulant Abuse or Dependence

Bipolar Disorder
Pathological Gambling

Medical Disorders
    Hypothyroidism
    Coronary Vascular Disease
    Cerebral Vascular Disease
    Chronic Pain Syndromes
    Chronic Infection
        Human Immunodeficiency Virus (HIV)
        Hepatitis B and C
    Multiple Sclerosis (MS)
    Fibromyalgia
    Polycystic Ovary Syndrome (PCOS)

Sleep Disorders
    Sleep Apnea
    Insomnia

Identification of bipolar disorder in depressed substance abusers is particularly critical because of its specific treatment implications. As can be seen in Table 1-4, a number of other psychiatric disorders commonly co-occur with depression, as well as with substance use disorders. The interrelationships between these disorders may be complicated, but it is useful to query the patient in order to try to determine which disorder is primary in a causative sense. For example, a patient with pathological gambling may become depressed because of the stress of overwhelming debt and financial losses that often mount up with this disorder. The presence of another disorder, the complications of which may contribute heavily to depression, would suggest that the disorder should receive emphasis in the treatment plan.

There are a number of medical conditions that can cause or mimic depression, and Table 1-4 lists those conditions that we most commonly encounter in clinical work with dually diagnosed patients. Thyroid disease, particularly hypothyroidism (low output of thyroid hormone), is quite common, particularly in female patients with depression, in whom it may be found up to 10 to 20 percent. Typical symptoms of low thyroid include fatigue, low activity level, and sometimes depressed mood. Thyroid hormone is easily supplemented, and this treatment may improve the effectiveness of treatment for depression.

Coronary vascular disease and cerebral vascular disease increasingly become an issue as depressed substance-dependent patients age. Such patients often smoke cigarettes, have poor dietary habits, do not exercise, and have other risk factors for the development of vascular disease. Interestingly, in recent years, depression has been identified as a likely risk factor for vascular disease. Vascular disease within the brain, and particularly within the frontal lobes, may impair brain functioning and produce depressive symptoms.

Chronic pain or chronic infections may also engender depression or fatigue and lack of activity that may mimic depression. It is well known that the human immunodeficiency virus (HIV) produces fatigue and cognitive impairment as the disease advances. Other chronic infections, such as hepatitis B and hepatitis C, are frequently encountered in such patients and can produce fatigue and other nonspecific symptoms that may overlap with depression. Hepatitis C can be treated with interferon, but this treatment often causes a secondary depression, which can be quite severe, and patients being treated with interferon for hepatitis C need to be monitored closely for the emergence of depression.

Other medical disorders that are associated with the development of depressive symptoms include MS, fibromyalgia, and PCOS. The depressive symptoms of MS, a central nervous system disorder characterized by waxing and waning of neurological symptoms as a result of the immune cells' attack on the coatings of neurons, occur as either a primary symptom or a psychological response to living with this debilitating disorder. Complaints of significant fatigue associated with diffuse tenderness and pain in muscles and joints are the hallmark signs of fibromyalgia. This disorder has been associated with a high co-occurrence of depression and anxiety disorders. PCOS, a hormonal abnormality in women, results in obesity, male-pattern baldness, acne, irregular periods, excessive hair growth, and depression.

Finally, sleep disorders are often overlooked and can result in sleep deprivation, which produces fatigue and depressed mood. Sleep apnea represents an intermittent physical obstruction of the upper airways during sleep and is signaled by the presence of excessive snoring. It results in multiple awakenings over the course of the night, which the patient may not be aware of but which produce sleep deprivation. Sleep may also be impaired by other medical disorders, by pain, or by medications. For example, antidepressant medications occasionally produce a stimulant-like effect, which impairs sleep. Patients on methadone maintenance who metabolize their medication rapidly may begin to develop mild withdrawal symptoms late in the day and into the night, resulting in disturbed sleep. Both depression and substance dependence can result in sleep disturbance, which compounds the depression. In our experience, sleep difficulties are among the most distressing symptoms to patients, and improvement resulting from direct focus on sleep problems can often be quite gratifying to patients. Steps in treatment can include recommending sleep studies for diagnosis of a sleep disorder, educating patients about sleep hygiene and methods for improving sleep, and encouraging patients to cut down on intake of caffeine and other drugs that may disturb sleep. Insomnia can also be treated with sedative-hypnotic medications, although many of these medications, including the commonly used benzodiazepines, have addictive potential and, thus, must be used with caution in patients with substance dependence. However, several other medications, including the antidepressant medication trazodone and the antihistamine diphenhydramine, are sedating with relatively little addictive potential and, in our experience, can be used safely in patients with addictions.

TREATMENT OPTIONS

Treatments for Depression

Extensive research in depressed patients without co-occurring substance use disorders has led to the development of a number of effective treatments, including antidepressant medications and psychotherapy. Brief descriptions of these approaches are given below.

Cognitive Behavioral Therapy. CBT focuses on the typical cognitive symptoms of depression, including pessimism, self-criticism, and low self-esteem. The effort in therapy is to help patients to understand the contribution of these cognitive distortions to their depressed mood and to develop new ways of thinking that permit a more positive outlook. A number of exercises and skills for this cognitive restructuring are taught. Particular emphasis is placed on challenging the automatic negative thinking that is characteristic of many depressed people. Patients are given homework assignments to practice the skills in between sessions. The behavioral component includes teaching relaxation skills and helping patients to increase their activity level, particularly to increase the number of pleasant and rewarding activities in which they take part. Behavioral Activation Therapy is a type of CBT that focuses largely on the latter. CBT is a short-term, goal-oriented treatment. Many clinicians who are working with substance-dependent patients and who are familiar with Cognitive Behavioral Relapse Prevention Therapy will recognize common elements; in fact, Relapse Prevention Therapy includes cognitive strategies for coping with bad feelings and low moods by means other than the use of substances.

Interpersonal Psychotherapy. Interpersonal Psychotherapy (IPT) is based on the theory that depression often stems from disruptions in valued relationships (e.g., death of a loved one or the loss of a marriage or life partner from separation or divorce). Treatment should help the patient to see the connection between depression and disruptions in relationships and then to replace what has been lost with new activities and relationships. Like CBT, IPT is a focused, short-term treatment that typically requires about twelve sessions.

Antidepressant Medications. A number of antidepressant medications are now available, and these can be thought of as falling into three broad classes: (1) tricyclic antidepressants (including imipramine, nortriptyline, and amitriptyline); (2) SSRIs (including fluoxetine, sertraline, paroxetine, fluvoxamine, and citalopram); and (3) other new generation medications (including bupropion, venlafaxine, trazodone, mirtazapine, and duloxetine). Tricyclics were among the first antidepressants to be introduced in the 1960s. In general, they produce more side effects than the newer medications, but one of the side effects, sedation, can be used to advantage by giving the medication at bedtime. Tricyclics frequently improve sleep in patients who complain of insomnia. Tricyclics must be used cautiously in patients with heart disease because they cause the delay of electrical impulses through the heart. SSRIs and other newer medications are generally well tolerated, and, as a result, their use has been more widespread than the use of tricyclics. However, these medications can produce some unpleasant side effects after long-term use, including weight gain, subtle memory deficits, and sexual dysfunction. When these medications are prescribed to patients who may be actively using alcohol or drugs, careful consideration must be given to the potential for interactions between alcohol or drugs and the medication, as well as to the possibility that increased intoxication or disorganizing effects of alcohol or drugs might result from the combination. Fortunately, clinical trials that have been conducted with substance-dependent patients to date suggest that these medications are, for the most part, safe in such patients. A significant benefit of the newer medications is their relative safety when taken in an overdose.

Choice of Treatment for Depression. The psychotherapies and medication treatments for depression share several features in common, including that they all generally take time to work (usually three to six weeks and sometimes longer), and that, as a gross generalization, any given patient has approximately a 50 percent chance of responding to any single course of treatment. Studies that have compared the effectiveness of one antidepressant to another antidepressant generally find about equal rates of effectiveness across groups of patients. However, it has been shown that patients who fail to respond to one medication will often respond to another medication. The choice of which particular treatment to try first is something of a guess, as the data on predictors of differential effectiveness are limited. The NIMH Treatment of Depression Collaborative Research Program, a multisite clinical trial (Elkin, Parloff, Hadley, & Autry, 1985), randomly assigned depressed outpatients to one of four treatment conditions: placebo, imipramine (a tricyclic antidepressant), CBT, or IPT. The therapies were found to be equally effective in treating depression overall (Elkin et al., 1989). However, secondary analyses suggested that more severe depressions responded better to imipramine than to placebo or psychotherapies (Elkin et al., 1995; Klein & Ross, 1993). On the other hand, associated symptoms of depression classified as atypical (i.e., overeating and oversleeping, as opposed to the typical symptoms of insomnia and weight loss) predicted poor response to imipramine (Stewart, Garfinkel, Nunes, Donovan, & Klein, 1998). A recommended treatment strategy is to try one of the specific psychotherapies for a milder depression and switch to or add an antidepressant medication if there has not been improvement after one or two months; if one medication fails, another may be tried. The most important strategy for treating depression is to continue to try alternative treatments until something works and not to give up if the first few attempts at treatment do not work. Most cases of depression will improve with one treatment or another, although up to 20 percent may be treatment-resistant (i.e., do not improve after multiple treatments have been tried).

Treatment of Substance Use Disorder

In evaluating a patient with substance dependence who also appears to have a depressive disorder, clinicians should remember that the first priority is to choose an effective treatment for the substance use disorder and to help the patient become abstinent or to significantly reduce substance use. Reduction in substance abuse or abstinence may result in considerable improvement or even resolution of depressive symptoms. This has been shown repeatedly in groups of alcohol-dependent, cocaine-dependent, and opiate-dependent patients who have detoxified in a hospital or entered outpatient treatment and reflects the extent to which depressive symptoms may reflect toxic or withdrawal effects of substances. Entry into treatment for substance dependence may also reduce the level of psychosocial stress that a patient is experiencing, and this, too, may contribute to improvement of depression. Further, it is unlikely that treatment of depression alone will result in the resolution of a substance use disorder, except in relatively rare cases. For this reason, substance use and depression should be considered as if they are separate but related disorders that require simultaneous treatment.

Treatment of Depression in Substance-Dependent Patients: What Is the Evidence?

More so than for most other co-occurring psychiatric disorders, a number of studies have been conducted to examine the treatment of depression among patients with alcoholism or other drug use disorders. A recent meta-analysis summarized the outcome of fourteen well-designed placebo-controlled trials of antidepressant medications in patients with current substance use disorders (Nunes & Levin, 2004). Medications examined across the studies included tricyclic antidepressants and SSRIs, as well as several other new generation agents. In the studies, depression was diagnosed with *Diagnostic and Statistical Manual of Mental Disorders,* 3rd edition (*DSM-III*; American Psychiatric Association, 1980) or *Diagnostic and Statistical Manual of Mental Disorders,* 3rd edition revised (*DSM-III-R*; American Psychiatric Association, 1987) criteria, which are very similar to the *DSM-IV* criteria presented earlier in this chapter. Many trials (although not all trials) included patients who were actively using substances at the time that they were diagnosed and entered into the trial. Overall, the results suggested that medication was effective and about equally as effective as would be expected in outpatients with depression. There were also wide differences between studies: some studies showed strong effects of medication, while six out of the fourteen studies showed no beneficial medication effects. Interestingly, studies that showed the strongest effects tended to be those that required abstinence for at least a brief period prior to diagnosis and treatment. Studies showing the least effect tended to be those that offered a systematic psychotherapy (such as CBT) to all patients included in the trial, including those in the placebo group, thereby suggesting the usefulness of certain psychotherapeutic techniques in such populations.

There are fewer controlled trials of specific psychotherapies for the treatment of substance-dependent patients with depression. One small preliminary study has shown the effectiveness of CBT for treatment of alcohol-dependent individuals with comorbid depression (Brown, Evans, Miller, Burgess, & Mueller, 1997). Another study showed the effectiveness of a combination regimen that included cognitive psychotherapy and medication for intravenous drug users (Stein et al., 2004). Further, psychotherapies designed for treating substance use disorders may improve mood outcome (Woody et al., 1983). In summary, more research in this area is needed, but the studies that exist are encouraging in suggesting that treatments effective for depression in the general population, including medication and psychotherapy techniques, are effective in patients with substance dependence. The psychotherapies tested in clinical trials require intensive training and monitoring in order for clinicians to develop proficiency.

What if the Patient Cannot Become Abstinent?

Few clinicians would disagree that if a substance-dependent patient achieves abstinence and continues to manifest a depressive disorder then the depressive disorder should be treated with either psychotherapy or medication. Clinicians may be faced with difficult decisions about treatment if a patient continues to be significantly depressed and to use alcohol or drugs (a situation that is frequently encountered in clinical work with comorbid patients). This situation has generated the greatest degree of controversy in the field, and there is no easy way to address it. The meta-analysis cited above (Nunes & Levin, 2004) included several studies that showed beneficial effects of antidepressant medication in comparison to placebo in alcohol- or drug-dependent

Table 1-5
Clinical Features to Consider in Judging Whether to
Start Antidepressant Treatment in Substance-Dependent Patients

Clinical Feature	Rationale
Severity of depression	As depression becomes more severe it exceeds expected effects of substances. Data from NIMH collaborative study in non-substance-abusing samples suggest severity of depression predicts response to antidepressant medication (Elkin et al., 1995).
Chronicity of depression	Persistence of depression for years may exceed expected effects of substances; chronic depression in non-substance-abusing patients has lower rate of response to treatment but greater superiority of response to medication over placebo (i.e., low likelihood that chronic depression will improve without active treatment).
DSM-IV primary versus substance-Induced	Both primary depression and substance-induced depression are distinguished from expected effects of substances; primary depression has occurred independently of substance use over the lifetime and ideally should be observed during a period of abstinence.
Associated disorders (e.g., anxiety disorders)	Many core features of anxiety disorders ([e.g., agoraphobia (fear of public places), social anxiety disorder (fear of social encounters)]) are not associated with drug toxicity or withdrawal. Depressive and anxiety disorders co-occur frequently, may have common mechanisms of illness, and respond to the same antidepressant medications.
History of suicide attempts and current suicide risk level	Common symptom of depression but not usually associated with drug toxicity or withdrawal; a marker of more severe depression; requires prompt evaluation to address suicide risk.
Treatment history	History of a favorable response to a past treatment for depression suggests the same treatment may help in a current episode.
Family history of mood disorder	History of depression in biological relatives, particularly parents or siblings, suggests possible genetic basis for vulnerability to depression.

patients who were actively using drugs at the time of diagnosis and when treatment was initiated. However, many of the studies that included patients who were actively using drugs showed no effect of medication, and it is not clear what exactly distinguished these studies. Thus, the choice to initiate antidepressant medication in an actively using outpatient depends upon clinical judgment.

Table 1-5 lists a number of features of the clinical presentation, and history of a patient should be considered in judging whether to start antidepressant treatment in a substance-dependent patient, along with a rationale for each feature. For the most part, these features are based on clinical experience and face validity, since little rigorous empirical data exists on factors that predict beneficial response to medication in such patients. Features, such as the overall severity of depressive symptoms and a history of suicide attempts or current suicidal ideation, highlight the potentially destructive and dangerous consequences of depression, and serious suicidal ideation should be addressed immediately. Patients with serious suicidal ideation should be hospitalized, or clinicians should significantly increase the intensity of the treatment. A history that establishes a depression that meets criteria for *DSM-IV* primary depression (i.e., it has clearly occurred in the past during times of abstinence) would suggest an independent mood disorder needing specific treatment. A history of an excellent symptomatic improvement during a prior course of antidepressant treatment would indicate that antidepressant treatment should be initiated for the current episode. Family history of depression or of suicides may indicate that a patient carries a biological vulnerability to depression, suggesting the possibility of an independent disorder warranting treatment. When determining which medication to prescribe to patients who cannot become abstinent, clinicians should consider the clinical features listed in Table 1-5.

Organization of Services

Since depression is common, it can be argued that all treatment programs and organizations should formulate a plan on how to approach depression at a system's level. Psychiatrists and other mental health clinicians with expertise in the evaluation of depression are in short supply, and many substance abuse treatment programs have either no access or very limited access to a psychiatric consultant. As a sensible first step, organizations should institute regular periodic screening for depression across all patients in treatment (like the regular screening for tuberculosis, HIV, or hepatitis B or C, which are medical problems that occur frequently in this population). Self-report instruments, such as the BDI (Beck et al., 1996) or the PHQ (Spitzer et al., 1999), take only a few minutes for a patient to complete, and an elevated score can suggest that further evaluation and action are required. Ideally, all counselors and clinicians in a program could be trained to recognize the basic symptoms of depression and to interpret the findings of a BDI or PHQ scale. Indeed, it is the overall goal of this book to increase such familiarity and clinical competence among substance abuse treatment clinicians. If a patient screens positive for depression, any clinician can take a history using guidelines like those provided in this chapter and can develop a preliminary diagnostic formulation regarding the depressive illness. Ultimately, a psychiatrist or a clinician who is an expert in the diagnosis and treatment of depression should evaluate such a patient, but a preliminary evaluation from the referring clinician can increase the efficiency with which the consultant's time is used. Programs that cannot arrange for a consultant to spend regular hours at their clinic should develop a referral arrangement with a local mental health clinic or professional. Alternatively, organizations might consider designating a clinician as the resource person for the clinic with respect to depression and related psychiatric disorders (just as many treatment programs designate HIV specialists, who help coordinate HIV risk reduction interventions and services for HIV-positive patients). Such an individual can serve as the local expert on depression and as a liaison with the psychiatric consultant.

Finally, mechanisms should be put in place for following the progress of a patient's depressive illness. Depression is a chronic and relapsing illness, much like addiction, and it can be treatment-resistant. Even if a patient has been referred outside the clinic for treatment, it is important to follow his/her progress, perhaps by periodically administering a screening instrument, such as the BDI, and to help the patient to secure the necessary help if the patient's symptoms are not improving.

It is also important for all treatment programs to have emergency procedures in place in case a patient presents with significant suicidal ideation or risks for other dangerous behavior. The emergency plan could include having a psychiatrist or other qualified mental health professional available on call or a procedure for transporting patients to a local psychiatric emergency room for evaluation. Suicide and other destructive behavior is always disturbing, particularly for clinicians who do not routinely evaluate it.

Treatment Planning for the Case Example

The case presented at the beginning of this chapter (see "Case Presentation") illustrates several features that, in our opinion, suggest that antidepressant medication should be considered for this patient. The patient has a long history of ongoing substance abuse, with only brief abstinent periods, and the patient had been abstinent for only a few days when the psychiatric evaluation was conducted. One would feel most confident in a diagnosis of depression if the patient could maintain abstinence for two to four weeks and remain persistently depressed during that time. However, the presence of early onset depression, which appears to precede the onset of substance abuse, and the presence of an associated social anxiety disorder, which began in childhood, increases the likelihood that the patient suffers from an independent depressive disorder (not substance-induced depression). Further, the patient has made a suicide attempt during a past depressive episode. Finally, the patient has a history of an excellent response to a prior trial of bupropion, an antidepressant medication. The value of diagnostic clarity that would be gained by observing the patient during a period of three to four weeks or more of abstinence must be weighed against evidence that the patient may have an independent depressive disorder that is adversely affecting the prognosis for the substance use disorder and perhaps preventing abstinence. After the patient has been enrolled in a good substance abuse treatment program, the clinician should focus on treatment of the depressive symptoms if they have not resolved.

SUMMARY

It is hoped that this chapter has provided a succinct introduction to the diagnosis and treatment of depressive disorders in patients with substance use disorders. A reader's learning objectives will differ depending on the background and experience of the reader, but the following main points should emerge:

1. Depression is common in the general population and even more common among patients with alcohol and drug use disorders, in whom the presence of depression predicts a worse outcome in comparison to those patients without depression.

2. The *DSM-IV* includes criteria for a diagnosis of major depression or dysthymia and for the distinction between primary depression and substance-induced depression.

3. With practice any clinician can become competent at eliciting a history and making the diagnosis.

4. In addition to the diagnosis of depression, there are several other psychiatric and medical disorders that may be associated with depression, and these disorders should be asked about in the course of eliciting the history.

5. Depression responds to treatment, either to psychotherapy or to antidepressant medication, and a growing body of evidence suggests that such treatments are effective in patients with alcohol or drug dependence.

Good treatment for substance use disorders and an effort to encourage abstinence in patients remains the cornerstone for the treatment of substance-dependent patients with depression. If depression persists after the achievement of abstinence, then it should be treated with either psychotherapy or medication. The decision to initiate antidepressant medication in a patient who is unable to achieve abstinence and who is still actively using substances is a difficult decision and has been a significant source of controversy for the field. However, we would argue that in the presence of significant ongoing depression one should not delay for too long before treating the patient with an antidepressant. Finally, treatment programs should consider initiating screening programs for depression, educating all staff about diagnosis and treatment of depression, and developing procedures and resources for referral and follow-up treatment.

Suggestions for Further Reading

For readers who wish to study further in this area, we recommend:

☐ **Prevalence and Prognostic Effects of Depression in Substance-Dependent Patients**

- Hasin, D., Nunes, E., & Meydan, J. (2004). Comorbidity of alcohol, drug and psychiatric disorders: Epidemiology. In H. R. Kranzler & J. A. Tinsley (Eds.), *Dual diagnosis and treatment: Substance abuse and comorbid disorders* (2nd ed., pp. 1-34). New York: Marcel Dekker.

☐ *DSM-IV* **Criteria for Depression and Case Examples**

- American Psychiatric Association. (1994). *Diagnostic and statistical manual of mental disorders* (4th ed.). Washington, DC: Author.

- Spitzer, R. L., Gibbon, M., Skodol, A. E., Williams, J. B. W., & First, M.B. (1994). *DSM-IV casebook: A learning companion to the diagnostic and statistical manual of mental disorders* (4th ed.). Washington, DC: American Psychiatric Association.

☐ **More on Depression**

- Stein, D., Kupfer, D., & Schatzberg, A. (Eds.) (2005). *American Psychiatric Association textbook of mood disorders*. Washington, DC: American Psychiatric Publishing.

☐ **Diagnostic Methods and Approach to Treatment Planning**

- Brady, K. T., & Malcolm, R. J. (2004). Substance use disorders and co-occurring axis I psychiatric disorders. In M. Galanter & H. D. Kleber (Eds.), *Textbook of substance abuse treatment* (3rd ed., pp. 529-537). Arlington, VA: American Psychiatric Publishing.

- Nunes, E. V., & Levin, F. R. (2004). Treatment of depression in patients with alcohol or other drug dependence: A meta-analysis. *Journal of the American Medical Association, 291*, 1887-1896.

- Nunes, E., Hasin, D., & Blanco, C. (2004). Substance abuse and psychiatric co-morbidity: Overview of diagnostic methods, diagnostic criteria, structured and semi-structured interviews, and diagnostic markers. In H. R. Kranzler &

J. A. Tinsley (Eds.), *Dual diagnosis and treatment: Substance abuse and comorbid disorders* (2nd ed., pp. 61-101). New York: Marcel Dekker.

- Spitzer, R. L., First, M. B., Gibbon, M., Williams, J. B. W. (2004). *Treatment companion to the DSM-IV-TR casebook*. Washington, DC: American Psychiatric Publishing.

☐ **Popular Press Books**

- Burns, D. D. (1999). *The feeling good handbook*. New York: Plume.

- Burns, D. D. (1999). *Feeling good: The new mood therapy*. New York: Avon Books.

- Casey, N. (2001). *Unholy ghost: Writers on depression*. New York: HarperCollins Publishers, Inc.

- Charney, D. S., & Nemeroff, C. B. (2004). *The piece of mind prescription: An authoritative guide to finding the most effective treatment for anxiety and depression*. New York: Houghton Mufflin Company.

- Dowling, C. (1993). *You mean I don't have to feel this way? New help for depression, anxiety, and addiction*. New York: Bantam Books.

- Klein, D. F., & Wender P. H. (1993). *Understanding depression: A complete guide to its diagnosis and treatment*. New York: Oxford University Press, Inc.

- Morrison, A. L. (1999). *The antidepressant sourcebook: A user's guide for patients and families*. New York: Main Street Books.

- Thase, M. E., & Lang, S. S. (2004). *Beating the blues: New approaches to overcoming dysthymia and chronic mild depression*. New York: Oxford University Press, Inc.

Authors' Note

The research in this chapter was supported in part by NIH grants K02 DA00288 (Dr. Nunes), K24 DA022412 (Dr. Nunes), and U10 DA13035 (Dr. Nunes) and the New York State Psychiatric Institute.

References

Aharonovich, E., Liu, X., Nunes, E., & Hasin, D. S. (2002). Suicide attempts in substance abusers: Effects of major depression in relation to substance use disorders. *American Journal of Psychiatry*, *159*, 1600-1602.

American Psychiatric Association. (1980). *Diagnostic and statistical manual of mental disorders* (3rd ed.). Washington, DC: Author.

American Psychiatric Association. (1987). *Diagnostic and statistical manual of mental disorders* (3rd ed. rev.). Washington, DC: Author.

American Psychiatric Association. (1994). *Diagnostic and statistical manual of mental disorders* (4th ed.). Washington, DC: Author.

American Psychiatric Association (2000). *Diagnostic and statistical manual of mental disorders* (4th ed., text rev.). Washington, DC: Author.

Beck, A. T., Steer, R. A., & Brown, G. K. (1996). *Beck depression inventory* (2nd ed. manual). San Antonio, TX: The Psychological Corporation.

Brown, R. A., Evans, D.M., Miller I. W., Burgess E. S., & Mueller T. I. (1997). Cognitive-behavioral treatment for depression in alcoholism. *Journal of Consulting and Clinical Psychology, 65*, 715-726.

Covey, L. S., Glassman, A. H., & Stetner, F. (1998). Cigarette smoking and major depression. *Journal of Addictive Diseases, 17*, 35-46.

Elkin, I., Shea, M. T., Watkins, J. T., Imber, S. D., Sotsky, S. M., Collins, J. F., et al. (1989). National Institute of Mental Health Treatment of Depression Collaborative Research Program: General effectiveness of treatments. *Archives of General Psychiatry, 46*, 971-982.

Elkin, I., Gibbons, R. D., Shea, M. T., Sotsky, S. M., Watkins, J. T., Pilkonis, P. A., et al. (1995). Initial severity and differential treatment outcome in the National Institute of Mental Health Treatment of Depression Collaborative Research Program. *Journal of Consulting and Clinical Psychology, 63*, 841-847.

Elkin, I., Parloff, M., Hadley, S., & Autry, J. (1985). NIMH Treatment of Depression Collaborative Research Program: Background and research plan. *Archives of General Psychiatry, 42,* 305-316.

First, M. B., Spitzer, R. L., Gibbon, M., & Williams, J. B. W. (2002, November). Structured Clinical Interview for DSM-IV-TR Axis I Disorders, Patient Edition (SCID-I/P). New York: Biometrics Research Department, New York State Psychiatric Institute.

Greenfield, S. F., Weiss, R. D., Muenz, L. R., Vagge L. M., Kelly, J. F., Bello, L. R., et al. (1998). The effect of depression on return to drinking: A prospective study. *Archives of General Psychiatry, 55*, 259-265.

Hall, S. M., Reus, V. I., Munoz, R. F., Sees, K. L., Humfleet, G., Hartz, D. T., et al. (1998). Nortriptyline and cognitive-behavioral therapy in the treatment of cigarette smoking. *Archives of General Psychiatry, 55*, 683-690.

Hamilton, M. (1960). A rating scale for depression. *Journal of Neurology, Neurosurgery, and Psychiatry, 23*, 56-62.

Hasin, D., Liu, X., Nunes, E., McCloud., S., Samet, S., & Endicott J. (2002). Effects of major depression on remission and relapse of substance dependence. *Archives of General Psychiatry, 59*, 375-380.

Hasin, D., Nunes, E., & Meydan, J. (2004). Comorbidity of alcohol, drug and psychiatric disorders: Epidemiology. In H. R. Kranzler & J. A. Tinsley (Eds.), *Dual diagnosis and treatment: Substance abuse and comorbid disorders* (2nd ed., pp. 1-34). New York: Marcel Dekker.

Hasin, D. S., Samet, S., Nunes, E., Meydan, J., Matseoane, K., & Waxman, R. (2006). Diagnosis of comorbid disorders in substance users: Psychiatric Research Interview for Substance and Mental Disorders (PRISM-IV). *American Journal of Psychiatry, 163,* 689-696.

Hurt, R. D., Sachs, D. P., Glover, E. D., Offord, K. P., Johnston, J. A., Khayrallah, M. A., et al. (1997). A comparison of sustained-release bupropion and placebo for smoking cessation. *New England Journal of Medicine, 337*, 1195-1202.

Joe, G. W., Simpson, D. D., & Broome, K. M. (1999). Retention and patient engagement models for different treatment modalities in DATOS. *Drug and Alcohol Dependence, 57*, 113-125.

Klein, D. F., & Ross, D. C. (1993). Reanalysis of the National Institute of Mental Health Treatment of Depression Collaborative Research Program General Effectiveness Report. *Neuropsychopharmacology, 8*, 241-251.

Nunes, E. V., & Levin, F. R. (2004). Treatment of depression in patients with alcohol or other drug dependence: A meta-analysis. *Journal of the American Medical Association, 291*, 1887-1896.

Nunes, E. V., & Raby, W. N. (2005). Comorbidity of depression and substance abuse. In J. Licinio & M. Wong (Eds.), *Biology of depression* (vol. 1) (pp. 341-364). Weinheim, Germany: Wiley-VCH Verlag GmbH & Co. KGaA.

Prochazka, A. V., Weaver, M. J., Keller, R. T. Fryer, G. E., Licari, P. A., & Lofaso, D. (1998). A randomized trial of nortriptyline for smoking cessation. *Archives of Internal Medicine, 158*, 2035-2039.

Rounsaville, B. J., & Kleber, H. D. (1985). Untreated opiate addicts. How do they differ from those seeking treatment? *Archives of General Psychiatry, 42*, 1072-1077.

Sheehan, D. V., Lecrubier, Y, Sheehan, K. H., Amorim, P., Janavs, J., Weiller, E., et al. (1998). The Mini-International Neuropsychiatric Interview (M.I.N.I): The development and validation of a structured diagnostic psychiatric interview for *DSM-IV* and ICD-10. *Journal of Clinical Psychiatry, 59*(Suppl. 20), 22-33.

Spitzer, R. L., Gibbon, M., Skodol, A. E., Williams, J. B. W., & First, M. B. (1994). *DSM-IV casebook: A learning companion to the diagnostic and statistical manual of mental disorders* (4th ed.). Washington, DC: American Psychiatric Association.

Spitzer, R. L., Kroenke, K., & Williams, J. B. (1999). Validation and utility of a self-report version of PRIME-MD: The PHQ primary care study. Primary Care Evaluation of Mental Disorders. Patient Health Questionnaire. *Journal of the American Medical Association, 282*, 1737-1744.

Spitzer, R. L., Williams, J. B., Kroenke, K., Linzer, M., deGruy, F.V., III, Hahn, S. R., et al. (1994). Utility of a new procedure for diagnosing mental disorders in primary care: The PRIME-MD 1000 study. *Journal of the American Medical Association, 272*, 1749-1756.

Stein, M. D., Solomon, D. A., Herman, D. S. Anthony, J. L., Ramsey, S. E., Anderson, B. J., et al. (2004). Pharmacotherapy plus psychotherapy for treatment of depression in active injection drug users. *Archives of General Psychiatry, 61*, 152-159.

Stewart, J. W., Garfinkel, R., Nunes, E. V., Donovan, S., & Klein, D. F. (1998). Atypical features and treatment response in the National Institute of Mental Health Treatment of Depression Collaborative Research Program. *Journal of Clinical Psychopharmacology, 18*, 429-434.

Sullivan, M. A., & Covey, L. S. (2002). Current perspectives on smoking cessation among substance abusers. *Current Psychiatry Reports, 4*, 388-396.

Weissman, M. M., Wickramaratne, P., Merikangas, K. R., Leckman, J. F., Prusoff, B. A., Caruso, K. A., et al. (1984). Onset of major depression in early adulthood: Increased familial loading and specificity. *Archives of General Psychiatry, 41*, 1136-1143.

Weissman, M. M., Gammon, G. D., John, K., Merikangas, K. R., Warner, V., Prusoff, B. A., et al. (1987) Children of depressed parents: Increased psychopathology and early onset major depression. *Archives of General Psychiatry, 44*, 847-853.

Wickramaratne, P. J., Greenwald, S., & Weissman, M. M. (2000). Psychiatric disorders in the relatives of probands with prepubertal-onset or adolescent-onset major depression. *Journal of the American Academy of Child and Adolescent Psychiatry, 39*, 1396-1405.

Williams, J. B. (1988). A structured interview guide for the Hamilton Depression Rating Scale. *Archives of General Psychiatry, 45*, 742-747.

Woody, G. E., Luborsky, L., McLellan, A. T., O'Brien, C. P., Beck, A. T., Blaine, J., et al. (1983). Psychotherapy for opiate addicts. Does it help? *Archives of General Psychiatry, 40*, 639-645.

Chapter 2

Bipolar Disorder in Patients With Substance Use Disorders

Timothy G. Benson, M.D., Rachel E. Bender, M.A., Patrice M. Muchowski, Sc.D., and Roger D. Weiss, M.D.

INTRODUCTION

Bipolar disorder and substance use disorders frequently occur together. Bipolar disorder is estimated to occur in approximately 0.8 percent of the general population, with similar rates in men and women (Hendrick, Altshuler, Gitlin, Delrahim, & Hammen, 2000). Rates of substance use disorders are significantly higher in individuals with bipolar disorder than in the general population (Regier et al., 1990). Indeed, bipolar disorder often co-occurs with substance use disorders: data from the National Comorbidity Study estimated a twelve-month prevalence of substance use disorder in 33 percent of those with bipolar disorder (Kessler et al., 1996).

Patients with a combination of bipolar disorder and substance use disorders typically have poor outcomes. However, until recently, very little research focused on this patient population. Rather, studies of bipolar disorder treatment focused almost exclusively on medication trials that excluded patients with substance use disorders.

In recent years, two encouraging trends have helped to change this situation. First, the past decade has seen a renaissance of interest in the use of psychosocial treatment in conjunction with pharmacotherapy for patients with bipolar disorder. Second, researchers have recognized the high prevalence rate of comorbidity and the importance of testing effective treatments for patients with bipolar disorder and substance use disorders.

This chapter will review the key features of bipolar disorder, methods to differentiate bipolar disorder from other disorders with similar clinical features (including substance intoxication or withdrawal), common pharmacological and psychological treatment strategies for patients with bipolar disorder, and integrated treatment approaches for patients with co-occurring bipolar disorder and substance use disorders.

CASE PRESENTATION

Chief Complaint

JM is an 18-year-old single Caucasian female requesting detoxification from alcohol. The patient states, "I can no longer drink controllably," and "I need help with my moods; I'm always either up or down."

Patient History

Substance Use History. The patient began using alcohol and marijuana at age 15. She states that she always socialized with an older crowd, so it was "normal" for her to use substances. She began to use marijuana daily at the age of 15; alcohol use progressed to weekend binges at age 16 and then to daily use at age 17. JM uses cocaine periodically and has used oxycodone, though she identifies neither drug as her drug of choice. She has not had previous substance use disorder treatment, but she reports that several months ago she was able to achieve a week-long period of abstinence from alcohol. JM has never stopped using marijuana and reports that she cannot stand to be "hyper." Currently, she thinks that it is time to stop drinking because she has recently begun to experience blackouts. The patient was referred for substance use disorder treatment from Emergency Mental Health Services following an episode of intoxication in which she was voicing suicidal threats, as well as exhibiting destructive behavior (e.g., smashing her car windshield). The patient says that she wants to stop drinking but requests a "medical prescription for marijuana," stating that it makes her feel calm.

Psychiatric History. The patient has been in counseling intermittently for four years. She reports that she usually feels "hyper" and often has difficulty sleeping; she has spent up to three days at a time without any sleep. JM was diagnosed with "something" a couple of years ago and was given medication, although she cannot recall what type of medication. She took the medication for a week, during which time she continued to use alcohol and cannabis; she reports that the medication did not work because she still felt hyper. JM also describes periods of depression and isolation. She lives in a basement apartment in her father's house and, at times, will not leave for several days. The patient denies any current suicidal ideation but reports two previous suicide attempts. She attempted suicide by carbon monoxide poisoning in a car, but the patient's boyfriend intervened. The second attempt was an overdose of antidepressants, but she eventually woke up. She made both of these attempts while intoxicated. She says that she does not really wish to die but acknowledges that she becomes suicidal and violent when intoxicated.

Developmental History. JM is the youngest of three girls. As a child, she was difficult to control and frequently fought with her parents. The patient did not enjoy school, indicating that she did not find it interesting and got bored easily. She had difficulty concentrating and finishing assignments. She therefore put little effort into studying, although she adds that "I could have if I'd wanted to." She dropped out of school in the twelfth grade, which corresponds to the time of her parents' divorce. The patient refuses to abide by her mother's rules and has been living with her father. The patient does not report any physical or sexual abuse as a child.

Family History. The patient was raised by both parents until the age of 17, at which time her parents divorced. The family history is positive for paternal alcohol dependence and maternal depression and "mood swings."

Medical History. The patient has no medical problems. Although JM has a prescription for birth control pills, she takes them inconsistently.

Social History. Although the patient is an assistant manager of a sporting goods store, she has missed work frequently and is unsure of the status of her job. She describes herself as "fantastic" at her job and states that she has great ideas for improving store productivity. JM reports no current social interests or hobbies other than listening to music. She has had hobbies in the past, but she gets bored easily.

Mental Status Examination

The patient looks younger than her stated age. She is dressed in jeans and a t-shirt. She sits cross-legged in her chair, quickly engages with the interviewer, and self-discloses immediately. JM is extremely talkative and anticipates questions before they are asked. Her speech is pressured and she exhibits difficulty maintaining focus. She complains of feeling "anxious"; in response to further questioning, she states that she feels "hyper." Her mood is elevated, and she says that her thoughts are racing. Although JM reports that she has barely slept for two days, she also indicates that she is not tired. She denies current suicidal or homicidal ideation, hallucinations, or delusions. She is alert and oriented to person, place, and time. The patient quickly becomes tearful when the issue of her parents' divorce is raised. Her judgment is somewhat impaired, as she has difficulty understanding the long-term consequences of her decisions. Immediate, recent, and remote memory are intact, but details of her history are often contradictory.

DIAGNOSTIC CRITERIA

DSM-IV Criteria for Bipolar Disorders

The four diagnostic subtypes of bipolar disorder, often referred to together as the bipolar spectrum, are bipolar I disorder, bipolar II disorder, cyclothymic disorder, and bipolar disorder not otherwise specified (see Tables 2-1C and 2-1D; American Psychiatric Association, 1994). A common misconception about bipolar disorder is that mania is always characterized by euphoria. In actuality, the core symptoms of mania are defined by the *Diagnostic and Statistical Manual of Mental Disorders, 4th edition (DSM-IV;* American Psychiatric Association, 1994) as either euphoria or irritability. An individual may experience one or both of these two core symptoms (plus the designated number of additional symptoms, which varies by core symptom type) in order to meet criteria for a manic episode (see Table 2-1A for *DSM-IV* criteria for a manic episode and suggested questions to aid diagnosis). Therefore, some people with bipolar disorder never experience euphoria at all. Mania is distinguished from hypomania primarily by its severity (see Table 2-1B for *DSM-IV* criteria for a hypomanic episode and suggested questions to aid diagnosis); a hypomanic episode cannot be accompanied by delusions or hallucinations (which may be present, though

Table 2-1A
DSM-IV Criteria for Bipolar Disorder, Manic Episode

Symptoms[a]	DSM-IV Criteria[a, b, c]	Issues in Substance-Dependent Patients	PRISM Questions to Aid Diagnosis[e, f]
Core Symptom	A. Distinct period of abnormality and persistently elevated, expansive, or irritable mood, lasting at least 1 week (or any duration if hospitalization is necessary).	Alcohol and other addictive substances can all produce elevated mood and, in some cases, irritability (e.g., cocaine, stimulants, alcohol). However, intoxication usually lasts only hours, bears a clear relationship to drug-taking, and may be supplanted by a crash (e.g., cocaine, stimulants) or withdrawal symptoms.	Was there ever a period of time when you felt so excited, elated, or energetic that other people thought you were not your normal self? ... Was there ever a period of time when you were "revved up," had a lot of extra energy, and at the same time, acted really angry, aggressive or argumentative?
Associated Symptoms	B. Three (or more) of the following symptoms have persisted (four if the mood is only irritable) and have been present to a significant degree	Associated symptoms of mania are quite similar to acute cocaine intoxication or other stimulant intoxication and, to a lesser extent, to alcohol or other substance intoxication. Substances with effects that are most likely associated with specific symptoms are listed below.	During that time you felt (the most) [elated/irritable] ...
	(1) inflated self-esteem or grandiosity	Cocaine, other stimulants, alcohol, other drugs	... did you feel especially good about yourself?
	(2) decreased need for sleep (e.g., feels rested after only 3 hours of sleep)	Cocaine, other stimulants	... did you need less sleep than usual?
	(3) more talkative than usual or pressure to keep talking	Cocaine, other stimulants, alcohol, other drugs	... were you more talkative than usual?
	(4) flight of ideas or subjective experience that thoughts are racing	Cocaine, other stimulants	... were your thoughts racing or rushing through your head? Did one thought spark another so fast that it was hard to follow your own thoughts?
	(5) distractibility (i.e., attention too easily drawn to unimportant or irrelevant external stimuli)	Any addictive substance	... did you have trouble concentrating because any little thing going on around you could get you off the track?
	(6) increase in goal-directed activity (either socially, at work or school, or sexually) or psychomotor agitation	Cocaine, other stimulants, opioids (some opioid-dependent patients describe increased energy and productivity during intoxication)	... were you a lot more active at work, with friends, around the house or pursuing other interests? Were you much more sexually active than usual?...Were you so physically restless that you had a lot of trouble sitting still?

(Continued)

Symptoms[a]	DSM-IV Criteria[a, b, c]	Issues in Substance-Dependent Patients	PRISM Questions to Aid Diagnosis[e, f]
	(7) excessive involvement in pleasurable activities that have a high potential for painful consequences (e.g., engaging in unrestrained buying sprees, sexual indiscretions, or foolish business investments).	Risky behavior that is associated with intoxication is more impulsive and disorganized (e.g., sexual indiscretions, fighting, driving under the influence)	... did you do anything that could have caused trouble for you or your family?
Other Criteria			
Rule out bipolar mixed	C. The symptoms do not meet criteria for a mixed episode [manic and depressive][d].		Have you ever had times when you went back and forth between feeling very [elated/irritable] and feeling very [depressed] in the same day?
Severity	D. The mood disturbance is sufficiently severe to cause marked impairment in occupational functioning or in usual social activities or relationships with others, or to necessitate hospitalization to prevent harm to self or others, or there are psychotic features.	Mania can manifest as acute psychosis and can be difficult to distinguish from schizophrenia and other psychotic disorders. Substance-induced psychosis is usually short-lived (hours to days).	During that time you felt (the most) [elated/irritable] ... ... were you in a hospital overnight or longer? ... did you lose a job or have serious problems with [major occupation] due to [manic symptoms]? ... did you have serious problems with other people? ... were you arrested or imprisoned?
Rule out substance effects, medical illness	E. The symptoms are not due to the direct physiological effects of a substance (e.g., a drug of abuse, a medication, or other treatment) or a general medical condition (e.g., hyperthyroidism).	See above	Were you using cocaine, stimulants, or PCP when you started feeling [elated/irritable]? ... Were you having medical problems around that time? What was wrong? ... Before that time began, had you been taking any medication? ... Were you taking any medication for depression when you started feeling [elated/irritable]?

(a) Mania may be diagnosed in patients who have experienced a manic episode with no past major depressive episodes (bipolar I), in patients who have recently experienced a manic episode with at least one past major depressive episode, manic episode or mixed episode (bipolar II), or in patients who have substance-induced mood disorder.
(b) American Psychiatric Association (1994).
(c) Reprinted with permission from the *Diagnostic and Statistical Manual of Mental Disorders*, Fourth Edition (Copyright 1994). American Psychiatric Association.
(d) Consult *DSM-IV* criteria (American Psychiatric Association, 1994) for mixed episode.
(e) Hasin et al. (2006).
(f) Reprinted with permission.

Table 2-1B
DSM-IV Criteria for Bipolar Disorder, Hypomanic Episode

Symptoms[a]	DSM-IV Criteria[a, b, c]	Issues in Substance-Dependent Patients	PRISM Questions to Aid Diagnosis[d, e]
Core Symptom	A. Distinct period of persistently elevated, expansive, or irritable mood, lasting throughout at least 4 days, that is clearly different from the usual non-depressed mood.	In diagnosing mania and hypomania clinicians are confronted with the same diagnostic issue in regard to duration of symptoms (see Table 2-1A). Alcohol and other addictive substances can produce elevated mood and, in some cases, irritability (e.g., cocaine, stimulants, alcohol). However, intoxication usually lasts only hours, bears a clear relationship to drug-taking, and may be supplanted by a crash (e.g., cocaine, stimulants) or withdrawal symptoms.	Was there ever a period of time when you felt so excited, elated, or energetic that other people thought you were not your normal self? ... Was there ever a period of time when you were "revved up," had a lot of extra energy, and at the same time, acted really angry, aggressive or argumentative?
Associated Symptoms	B. Three (or more) of the following symptoms have persisted (four if the mood is only irritable) and have been present to a significant degree	Associated symptoms of mania are quite similar to acute cocaine intoxication or other stimulant intoxication and, to a lesser extent, to alcohol or other substance intoxication. Substances with effects that are most likely associated with specific symptoms are listed below.	During that time you felt (the most) [elated/irritable] ...
	(1) inflated self-esteem or grandiosity	Cocaine, other stimulants, alcohol, other drugs	... did you feel especially good about yourself?
	(2) decreased need for sleep (e.g., feels rested after only 3 hours of sleep)	Cocaine, other stimulants	... did you need less sleep than usual?
	(3) more talkative than usual or pressure to keep talking	Cocaine, other stimulants, alcohol, other drugs	... were you more talkative than usual?

(Continued)

Symptoms[a]	DSM-IV Criteria[a, b, c]	Issues in Substance-Dependent Patients	PRISM Questions to Aid Diagnosis[d, e]
	(4) flight of ideas or subjective experience that thoughts are racing	Cocaine, other stimulants	… were your thoughts racing or rushing through your head? Did one thought spark another so fast that it was hard to follow your own thoughts?
	(5) distractibility (i.e., attention too easily drawn to unimportant or irrelevant external stimuli)	Any addictive substance	… did you have trouble concentrating because any little thing going on around you could get you off the track?
	(6) increase in goal-directed activity (either socially, at work or school, or sexually) or psychomotor agitation	Cocaine, other stimulants, opioids (some opioid-dependent patients describe increased energy and productivity during intoxication)	… were you a lot more active at work, with friends, around the house or pursuing other interests? Were you much more sexually active than usual? … Were you so physically restless that you had a lot of trouble sitting still?
	(7) excessive involvement in pleasurable activities that have a high potential for painful consequences (e.g., the person engages in unrestrained buying sprees, sexual indiscretions, or foolish business investments).	Risky behavior that is associated with intoxication is more impulsive and disorganized (e.g., sexual indiscretions, fighting, driving under the influence)	… did you do anything that could have caused trouble for you or your family?
Other Criteria			
Change in functioning	C. The episode is associated with an unequivocal change in functioning that is uncharacteristic of the person when not symptomatic.	Hypomania can enhance productivity and functioning (rather than cause impairment), but patients eventually cycle into depression or mania with impairment.	Did you have difficulties on your job (or as a homemaker) during this time? Did you have any trouble getting things done? … Was there any change in how you got along with people during that time?

(Continued)

Symptoms[a]	DSM-IV Criteria[a, b, c]	Issues in Substance-Dependent Patients	PRISM Questions to Aid Diagnosis[d, e]
Symptom visibility	D. The disturbance in mood and the change in functioning are observable by others.		Did anyone comment about this change?
Severity	E. The episode is not severe enough to cause marked impairment in social or occupational functioning, or to necessitate hospitalization, and there are no psychotic features.	Severity of symptoms distinguishes mania from hypomania. Hypomania can enhance productivity (rather than cause impairment).	During that time you felt (the most) [elated/irritable]… … were you in a hospital overnight or longer? … did you lose a job or have serious problems with [major occupation] due to [manic symptoms]? … did you have serious problems with other people? … were you arrested or imprisoned?
Rule out substance effects, medical illness	F. The symptoms are not due to the direct physiological effects of a substance (e.g., a drug of abuse, a medication, or other treatment) or a general medical condition (e.g., hyperthyroidism).	See above	Were you using cocaine, stimulants, or PCP when you started feeling [elated/irritable]? … Were you having medical problems around that time? What was wrong? … Before that time began, had you been taking any medication? … Were you taking any medication for depression when you started feeling [elated/irritable]?

(a) Hypomania may be diagnosed in patients who have experienced a hypomanic episode with at least one manic episode or mixed episode (bipolar I), in patients who have at least one hypomanic episode and one or more major depressive episodes without a history of a manic episode or mixed episode (bipolar II), and in patients who have cyclothymic disorder.
(b) American Psychiatric Association (1994).
(c) Reprinted with permission from the *Diagnostic and Statistical Manual of Mental Disorders*, Fourth Edition (Copyright 1994). American Psychiatric Association.
(d) Hasin et al. (2006).
(e) Reprinted with permission.

Table 2-1C
Types of *DSM-IV* Bipolar Disorder and Course Specifiers

Disorder	*DSM-IV* Criteria[a, b]	Issues in Substance-Dependent Patients
Bipolar I Disorder	Presence of [one or more manic episodes (see Table 2-1A) either currently or at other point(s) during the lifetime. May also include (and usually does include) other mood episodes over the course of the lifetime, especially major depression (see Chapter 1 of this volume), as well as mixed episodes (episodes meeting criteria for both mania and major depression), dysthymia, or hypomania.]	Chronic depression or frequent episodes of depression with less frequent mania is the most common pattern. It is important that clinicians obtain a thorough history from patients who present with depression, look for symptoms of mania, reevaluate the patient periodically, and consult significant others; patients often lack insight into manic episodes, and significant others may provide descriptions of mania. In patients with chronic depression and chronic substance use disorder (cases in which it is difficult to establish independence of depression from substance abuse), a history of episodes of mania or hypomania suggests an independent (primary) mood disorder (bipolar disorder).
Bipolar II Disorder	Presence (or history) of one or more [episodes of major depression (see Chapter 1 of this volume) and one or more episodes of hypomania (see Table 2-1B) but never any history of either episodes of mania or mixed episodes (episodes meeting criteria for both mania and major depression).]	Chronic or frequent depression with less frequent hypomanic episodes is the most common pattern, and identification of episodes of hypomania in a patient's history can help to establish a diagnosis of independent (primary) mood disorder in the setting of chronic substance use disorder. However, because symptoms of hypomania are milder than mania, the diagnosis is more difficult to make; symptoms of hypomania are easily confused with normal happiness or with substance-related symptoms.
Rule out psychotic disorder (applies to bipolar I and II)	The [core symptom is] ... not better accounted for by schizoaffective disorder and ... not superimposed on schizophrenia, schizophreniform disorder, delusional disorder, or psychotic disorder not otherwise specified.	See Chapter 7 of this volume
Rapid Cycling Course Specifier	At least 4 episodes ... in the previous 12 months that meet criteria for a major depressive, manic, mixed, or hypomanic episode. Episodes are [separated] either by partial or full remission for at least 2 months or a switch to an episode of opposite polarity (e.g., major depressive episode to manic episode).	More rapid cycling between manic and depressive symptoms (e.g., over days) would be diagnosed as bipolar disorder not otherwise specified and, like cyclothymic disorder (see Table 2-1D), can be difficult to distinguish from cycles of euphoria and depression that are associated with regular cocaine or other stimulant use. Clinicians should examine the relationship of symptoms to drug taking.

(a) American Psychiatric Association (1994).
(b) Reprinted with permission from the *Diagnostic and Statistical Manual of Mental Disorders*, Fourth Edition (Copyright 1994), American Psychiatric Association.

Table 2-1D
Criteria for Cyclothymic Disorder

Symptoms	DSM-IV Criteria[a, b]	Issues in Substance-Dependent Patients	PRISM Questions to Aid Diagnosis[d, e]
Core Symptom	A. For at least 2 years, the presence of numerous periods with hypomanic symptoms … and numerous periods of depressive symptoms that do not meet criteria for a major depressive episode … In children and adolescents, the duration must be at least 1 year.	May be difficult to distinguish from the cycles of euphoria and depression associated with cocaine or other stimulant intoxication. Clinicians should examine the relationship of symptoms to drug taking. Because symptoms can be relatively mild, cyclothymia can be difficult to distinguish from normal ups and downs of mood that occur in response to good and bad life events or from substance effects.	Was there a time lasting at least 2 years when you always felt either energetic and excited or low and down in the dumps? During [that long period/those long periods] of highs and lows, when your mood was up, did you need less sleep than usual, have trouble sitting still, talk a lot more or faster than usual, get involved in a lot more activities than usual? During [that long period/those long periods] of highs and lows, when your mood was down, did you sleep more or less than usual, lose or gain weight, feel very tired, have trouble concentrating, think a lot about death?
Other Criteria			
Chronicity and persistence (no long symptom-free periods)	B. During the above 2-year period (1 year in children and adolescents), the person has not been without the symptoms in Criterion A for more than 2 months at a time.		During [that time/those times] when your mood was going up and down a lot, did you ever feel just okay, without any highs or lows, for as long as 2 months?
Rule out major depression and bipolar disorder	C. No major depressive episode … manic episode … or mixed episode … has been present during the first 2 years of the disturbance.		Did you ever have a 2-year period of highs and lows that didn't include a period when you felt very depressed? … Did you ever have a 2-year period of highs and lows that didn't include a period when you felt very high?

(Continued)

Symptoms	DSM-IV Criteria[a, b]	Issues in Substance-Dependent Patients	PRISM Questions to Aid Diagnosis[d, e]
Rule out psychotic disorder	D. The symptoms in Criterion A are not better accounted for by schizoaffective disorder and are not superimposed on schizophrenia, schizophreniform disorder, delusional disorder, or psychotic disorder not otherwise specified[c].	See Chapter 7 of this volume	
Rule out substance effects, medical illness	E. The symptoms are not due to the direct physiological effect of a substance (e.g., a drug of abuse, a medication) or a general medication condition (e.g., hyperthyroidism).	See above	Were you drinking or using drugs a lot during the <u>whole time</u> your moods went up and down frequently? ... Were you physically ill during the <u>whole time</u> your moods went up and down frequently?
Functional impairment	F. The symptoms cause clinically significant distress or impairment in social, occupational, or other important areas of functioning.		Did [hypomanic/depressive symptoms] cause any difficulties for you at work, with your family or friends, or in your daily activities? ... Were you very troubled by [hypomanic/depressive symptoms]? Did you think of getting help or often wish that you could feel better?

[a] American Psychiatric Association (1994).
[b] Reprinted with permission from the *Diagnostic and Statistical Manual of Mental Disorders*, Fourth Edition (Copyright 1994). American Psychiatric Association.
[c] Consult *DSM-IV* criteria (American Psychiatric Association, 1994) for schizoaffective disorder, schizophrenia, schizophreniform disorder, delusional disorder, and psychotic disorder not otherwise specified.
[d] Hasin et al. (2006).
[e] Reprinted with permission.

not invariably so, in mania). Moreover, in contrast to hypomania, mania is characterized by severe disturbance in occupational or social functioning and may require hospitalization.

The key distinction between bipolar I and bipolar II is that the former disorder is characterized by at least one manic or mixed episode, whereas bipolar II is characterized by hypomania (see Table 2-1C). Cyclothymic disorder is characterized by chronic mood fluctuation between periods of hypomania and depression (see Table 2-1D for *DSM-IV* criteria for cyclothymic disorder and suggested questions to aid diagnosis); the periods of mood disturbance are shorter, less severe, and less regular than those of bipolar I disorder or bipolar II disorder. Nevertheless, these mood swings can interfere with optimal social and occupational functioning. Some people with cyclothymic disorder eventually develop a more severe form of bipolar illness. For patients who experience four or more mood episodes in a twelve-month period, the term rapid cycling is applied.

In some people, symptoms of mania and depression may occur together in what is called a mixed episode. Symptoms of a mixed episode may include agitation, difficulty sleeping, appetite change, psychosis, or suicidal ideation. A person may report feeling very sad or hopeless, while at the same time feeling extremely energized. A mixed episode can sometimes be difficult to recognize in light of its unusual constellation of symptoms.

How to Take a History

Review Substance Use History. A substance use history should be obtained carefully. It is crucial to view mood symptoms in the context of substance use in order to avoid misdiagnosis.

Inquire About History of Depressive Symptoms. The diagnosis of bipolar disorder requires the identification of at least one hypomanic or manic episode. Often patients experience premonitory depressive symptoms prior to mania. In addition, throughout their lifetime, patients with bipolar disorder are more likely to experience depressive episodes than mania. Consequently, it is important to inquire about periods of persistently low mood, anhedonia, difficulty concentrating, and fluctuating appetite (see Chapter 1 of this volume for information on diagnosing depression). Bipolar depression can be extremely challenging to treat and represents the phase of the illness that is most likely to result in suicidal behavior.

Identify Mania and Hypomania. Mania represents a distinctive set of symptoms that can be easily recognized; hypomania may be more subtle. A manic patient may exhibit physical signs of hyperactivity, fidgeting, or restlessness; heart rate may be elevated. The patient may be easily distracted and unable to focus during the interview. The speech pattern may be rapid, illogical, and disconnected. The term "pressured speech" is often used in referring to manic individuals; this type of speech refers to speech that is relatively uninterruptible, as patients experience an internal sense of pressure to talk. Inquiring about sleep is important, since manic patients may stay up for several days without need for sleep. Even if a patient reports sleeping at night, the interviewer should probe further by inquiring about how the patient's current sleep pattern compares to baseline. Patients often feel that they require less sleep when manic. Additional symptoms of mania include grandiosity, an increase in goal-directed activity, and impulsiveness. Impulsiveness may be characterized by hypersexuality, spending sprees, or substance abuse, which can lead to negative health, financial, and interpersonal consequences.

Because substance intoxication can mimic some manic symptoms, it is important to obtain a thorough substance use history in order to rule out a substance-induced condition; heavy use of stimulants can cause symptoms suggestive of mania. The presence of intoxication does not necessarily rule out concurrent mania. Sometimes, longitudinal observation may be required to clarify the role (or lack thereof) of substance use in precipitating a manic state.

Identifying hypomania can present a greater challenge in patients with substance use disorders. The symptoms of hypomania may be subtle, are less likely to be reported, and are more difficult to detect. Mood elevation, although not extreme, is distinctly different from baseline. By asking questions about periods of time in which the patient was highly productive and required less sleep, clinicians may gain clues about the presence of hypomania.

Ask About Prior Pharmacological Treatments. Some patients with bipolar disorder are misdiagnosed with unipolar depression because the clinician does not inquire about past manic or hypomanic episodes or because the patient does not recall these episodes. As a consequence, such patients may be treated with antidepressants, which can sometimes precipitate mania. Information about prior response to medications may provide a clue to the potential presence of bipolar disorder. Patients who report significant mood fluctuations, including euphoria or irritability, soon after the initiation of treatment with antidepressant medications should be carefully evaluated for bipolar disorder. Since patients without bipolar disorder can become agitated or anxious while taking antidepressants, such a response does not make a diagnosis of bipolar disorder. However, repeated adverse responses to antidepressants should raise suspicion and lead to a detailed inquiry about a history of manic or hypomanic symptoms.

Examine Family History. First-degree relatives of affected individuals can have up to a ten-fold increased risk for developing bipolar disorder (Smoller & Finn, 2003). A family history of bipolar disorder has also been correlated with an earlier onset of the disorder (Strober et al., 1988). Include family members in the diagnostic process to enhance the chance of obtaining a more accurate history (they may report symptoms of irritability that the patient does not recognize, for example).

NATURAL HISTORY AND ETIOLOGY

Onset and Diagnosis of Bipolar Disorder

A first episode of bipolar disorder can occur at any age, although the average age of onset is typically between the ages of 15 and 30. In recent years, bipolar disorder has been recognized as occurring in children as young as age 5. The initial episode may be mania, hypomania, depression, or a mixed episode, often with prodromal symptoms of depression. Although there does not appear to be a significant difference in age of onset between men and women, females are more likely to be diagnosed with bipolar II disorder, make more suicide attempts, and have a higher rate of comorbid anxiety disorders (Baldessano et al., 2005).

There is often a significant gap between the age of onset of bipolar disorder and the age at first treatment; the lag is typically five to ten years, although this varies (Lish, Dime-Meenan, Whybrow, Price, & Hirschfeld, 1994). Factors contributing to a delay in receiving treatment may include an extended time interval between episodes, a patient's reluctance to seek treatment, diagnostic confusion due to effects of patient's substance intoxication, and a misdiagnosis of unipolar depression.

Finally, in diagnosing bipolar disorder, clinicians should conduct a thorough review of the patient's current medication regimen. Some commonly prescribed medications (e.g., L-DOPA, corticosteroids) can produce behavior suggestive of mania. In addition, medical conditions, such as hyperthyroidism, multiple sclerosis, pheochromocytoma, adrenal tumors, and brain tumors, can also produce symptoms similar to mania. Therefore, obtaining a comprehensive medical history is required before making a diagnosis of bipolar disorder.

Course of Bipolar Disorder

The course of bipolar disorder is lifelong and highly variable. Several years may pass following the initial mood episode before a second episode is experienced; the amount of time prior to a second episode can vary greatly. When left untreated, bipolar disorder can result in numerous manic and depressive episodes, particularly when the disorder is rapid cycling (Shulman & Herrmann, 1999). Over time, bipolar disorder is likely to be dominated more by depression than by mania, and depressive episodes typically last longer than periods of mania (Joffe, MacQueen, Marriott, & Trevor Young, 2004).

The presence of a co-occurring substance use disorder has been associated with a worse course of bipolar disorder, including earlier onset of bipolar disorder, increased rates of anxiety and panic attacks, poor treatment response, more frequent relapse of mood symptoms, increased rates of psychiatric hospitalization, and a higher rate of suicide attempts (Brady, Casto, Lydiard, Malcolm, & Arana, 1991; Cassidy, Ahearn, & Carroll, 2001; Dalton, Cate-Carter, Mundo, Parikh, & Kennedy, 2003; Feinman & Dunner, 1996; Salloum & Thase, 2000). The presence of a substance use disorder can delay the diagnosis and treatment of bipolar disorder. For example, mood symptoms can be confused with substance use effects. Alternatively, mood symptoms may go unnoticed entirely when clinical attention is focused on addiction treatment.

ISSUES IN DIAGNOSIS: MAKING THE DIAGNOSIS OF BIPOLAR DISORDER IN SUBSTANCE-DEPENDENT PATIENTS

Diagnosing a co-occurring mood disorder can be difficult in a patient with an active substance use disorder. Bipolar disorder can be particularly difficult to identify because hypomanic symptoms can be misinterpreted as manifestations of drug intoxication or withdrawal. However, drug intoxication usually has a particular constellation of physiological symptoms that may help to differentiate it from mania. For instance, cocaine intoxication is often accompanied by dilated pupils, sweating, and elevated vital signs. On the other hand, mania is less likely to be accompanied by the characteristic physical manifestations of intoxication syndromes. Since patients in an acute agitated state may be unreliable informants, it may be critical to obtain additional information from a friend or relative, as well as a urine or blood toxicology screen, in order to understand the clinical picture.

To differentiate between manifestations of bipolar disorder and those of intoxication, clinicians should determine the temporal relationship between mood symptoms and drug use. Cocaine intoxication, for instance, is typically short-lived; most symptoms resolve within hours of the patient's last use. Thus, a patient displaying new-onset manic symptoms two days after his/her last cocaine use is unlikely to be experiencing drug intoxication symptoms alone.

To differentiate bipolar disorder symptoms from those of substance use, clinicians should ask several questions. Did the psychiatric symptoms begin before the onset of substance use? Did they persist for a significant period of time after the expected period of intoxication or withdrawal from the substance? Finally, are the quality and severity of psychiatric symptoms congruent with the expected nature and duration of the drug effects? Since there may often be subtle, protracted withdrawal symptoms following drug cessation, the *DSM-IV* recommends a four-week period of abstinence before the clinician attempts to differentiate a substance-induced mood disorder from an independent mood disorder. However, the latter diagnosis can be made before four weeks of abstinence have been achieved if the nature or severity of the symptoms is in excess of what would be expected as a result of substance use. Thus, acute mania in the context of a moderately heavy and unchanging drinking pattern would unlikely have resulted from alcohol use.

Unfortunately, ideal diagnostic circumstances may not always be present in acute situations; many patients seek treatment for bipolar disorder in the context of recent substance use. Thus, becoming familiar with common intoxication and withdrawal symptoms and differentiating these symptoms from mania and hypomania can help in the diagnostic process.

INSTRUMENTS AND METHODS FOR SCREENING AND DIAGNOSIS

Several standardized instruments have been utilized in research and clinical settings in order to improve proficiency in detecting bipolar disorder and charting progress (see Table 2-2). These tools are designed to elicit a history of symptoms that meet the criteria for bipolar disorder as outlined in the *DSM-IV*. Tools like the Psychiatric Research Interview for Substance and Mental Disorders (PRISM; Hasin et al., 2006) are often used in the research setting. The PRISM, which was designed for use among substance-dependent patients, permits clinicians to evaluate each psychiatric symptom separately in terms of its relationship to substance abuse. The PRISM quotes each *DSM-IV* criterion and offers questions for use by clinicians in eliciting information from patients about their symptoms (see Tables 2-1A, 2-1B, and 2-1D for examples of questions from the PRISM). The PRISM requires a trained interviewer and between 60 and 120 minutes to administer to subjects with psychiatric and substance use symptoms.

The Structured Clinical Interview for DSM-IV-TR Axis I Disorders (SCID-I; First, Spitzer, Gibbon, & Williams, 2002) is a comprehensive structured interview that yields *Diagnostic and Statistical Manual of Mental Disorders*, 4th edition, text revision (*DSM-IV-TR*; American Psychiatric Association, 2000) diagnoses. Like the PRISM, the SCID-I can be time consuming to use, requires a trained interviewer, and often is administered in a research setting.

An ideal screening tool is one that is highly sensitive, specific, brief, and easy to complete. In a review of bipolar disorder screening and assessment tools, Baldassano (2005) recommended three instruments: the Mood Disorder Questionnaire (MDQ), the Bipolar Spectrum Diagnostic Scale, and the Hypomanic Personality Scale.

Table 2-2
Instruments for Screening and Diagnosis of
Bipolar Disorder in Substance-Dependent Patients

Structured Clinical Interview for DSM-IV-TR Axis I Disorders (SCID-I) (First et al., 2002)	– clinician-administered diagnostic instrument – based on *DSM-IV* criteria – provides a method for asking questions about symptoms of depression and other psychiatric disorders – usually used in research studies
Mood Disorder Questionnaire (MDQ) (Hirschfield et al., 2000)	– 13 items – self-report questionnaire – offers estimate on probability of having bipolar disorder
Bipolar Spectrum Diagnostic Scale (Ghaemi et al., 2005)	– patients respond to 19 statements that describe various mood states – better than MDQ at detecting bipolar II disorder and bipolar disorder NOS
Hypomanic Personality Scale (Eckblad & Chapman, 1996)	– 48 items – self-report – more appropriate for psychiatric inpatient settings
Psychiatric Research Interview for Substance and Mental Disorders (PRISM) (Hasin et al., 2006)	– clinician-administered diagnostic instrument – based on *DSM-IV* criteria – often used in research studies but also suitable for clinical use

The MDQ is a brief, thirteen-item, self-report questionnaire that can be readily implemented in the acute clinical setting (Hirschfeld et al., 2000). It is designed to give a quick estimate of the probability of having bipolar disorder. If a patient positively endorses seven of the thirteen items, the sensitivity of this test (the likelihood of identifying a disorder that is present) is 73 percent; specificity (the likelihood of not diagnosing a disorder that is not present) is 90 percent.

The Bipolar Spectrum Diagnostic Scale (Ghaemi et al., 2005) is a narrative scale that consists of nineteen statements, describing various mood states, to which the patient responds. Scores are calculated and determined by high probability (11-18), moderate probability (6-10), and low probability (<6). This scale appears to be better than the MDQ at detecting bipolar II disorder and bipolar disorder not otherwise specified (NOS; Baldassano, 2005).

The Hypomanic Personality Scale (Eckblad & Chapman, 1986) is a self-report tool that is more time consuming to use than the MDQ; it contains forty-eight items. Because of its time intensiveness, it may be more appropriate for psychiatric inpatient settings than for outpatient settings, where time for clinical encounters is more limited.

DIFFERENTIAL DIAGNOSIS AND OTHER OVERLAPPING DISORDERS

Attention deficit hyperactivity disorder (ADHD) is an Axis I disorder that can be confused with bipolar disorder. ADHD is typically diagnosed in children and adolescents, while bipolar disorder typically has been diagnosed only in patients in late adolescence and in adults. However, there has been increasing recognition of childhood bipolar disorder, indicating that age alone may not be a definitive basis upon which to make a diagnosis.

ADHD can be difficult to distinguish from bipolar disorder in children because of shared core features, including excessive verbalization, motor hyperactivity, and high levels of distractibility. Children who fail to respond to ADHD medication may have a diagnosis of bipolar disorder. In children with bipolar disorder, manic symptoms are more likely to be dominated by irritability (Wozniak et al., 2005). For this reason, many children with bipolar disorder are likely to be misdiagnosed initially with ADHD or conduct disorder. It is also possible for children to suffer from both bipolar disorder and ADHD simultaneously, a phenomenon that has been associated with worse outcomes (Adler et al., 2005).

Distinguishing ADHD from bipolar disorder (especially bipolar II) in adults can be difficult, particularly in the context of a co-occurring substance use disorder. Adult ADHD is characterized more by disorganization and an inability to focus than by hyperactivity (Clarke, Heussler, & Kohn, 2005), and ADHD is a chronic state not characterized by distinct episodes of symptoms punctuated by episodes of different (e.g., depressive) symptoms or no symptoms.

TREATMENT OPTIONS

Pharmacological Treatment for Bipolar Disorder

Adequate pharmacological treatment of bipolar disorder significantly affects the rates of recurrence, morbidity, and mortality for individuals with the disorder. Pharmacological treatment is largely based on the phase of illness and the symptom picture. Thus, the goal may be either acute symptom reduction or relapse prevention. Medication treatment for acute mania (which may include psychosis) consists of a mood stabilizer, typically in combination with an antipsychotic medication. Because mood stabilizers take some time to attain full effectiveness, they alone are generally not sufficient to reduce racing or psychotic thoughts or mood lability during an acute manic episode. Therefore, rapid-acting antipsychotic agents are often used to contain acute agitated behaviors. To date, lithium, valproate, olanzapine, risperidone, and quetiapine have been approved by the Food and Drug Administration for the treatment of mania. In recent years valproate has been prescribed more frequently than lithium, perhaps because lithium requires careful monitoring and has side effects that many patients find noxious (e.g., tremors, excessive urination, and gastrointestinal upset). Side effects of valproate include sedation, weight gain, and hair loss. Despite these problematic side effects, the benefits of mood stabilizers in treating episodes of illness and in preventing recurrence of illness are clear. A significant clinical challenge is to help patients accept the need for maintenance medication once they are feeling well.

In patients with bipolar disorder, treatment of the depressive phase poses a particular challenge. Lifetime prevalence of depressive episodes in bipolar patients outweighs that of mania. Antidepressants are often avoided or used with caution because of an increased likelihood of precipitating mania. Research has indicated that the mood stabilizer lamotrigine can significantly improve depressive symptoms in bipolar patients (Calabrese et al., 1999). Because lamotrigine is associated with a small risk of causing a potentially lethal side effect called Stevens-Johnson syndrome (an allergic systemic reaction with a characteristic progressive rash), patients taking this medication should be continually monitored for suspicious rashes.

There is very little research focused specifically on bipolar patients with co-occurring substance use disorders. The best study of this population was conducted by Salloum et al. (2005), who found that bipolar patients with alcohol dependence who took valproate plus lithium experienced significantly less heavy drinking than did patients taking lithium alone. Another study found lithium superior to placebo for both mood and substance use outcome among adolescents with bipolar disorder and a substance use disorder (Geller et al., 1998). Despite the paucity of comparative trials, it is clear that medication adherence is critical in this population. Therefore, when treating patients with these two disorders, clinicians should discuss regularly the importance of taking medication as prescribed.

Psychosocial Treatment for Bipolar Disorder

Rationale for Psychosocial Treatments for Bipolar Disorder. Due to its general responsiveness to mood stabilizers and other forms of pharmacotherapy, bipolar disorder has typically been conceptualized as a biologically based illness. Consequently, less emphasis has been placed on psychosocial treatments for bipolar disorder than for many other psychiatric disorders (e.g., unipolar depression, anxiety). However, several characteristics of bipolar disorder and the patient population indicate that psychosocial treatment is an important adjunct to psychopharmacological approaches. First, despite the responsiveness of the disorder to pharmacotherapy, medication nonadherence is common and presents a well-recognized obstacle to the effective treatment of bipolar disorder. Thus, a critical goal of psychosocial treatments currently in development and in use for bipolar disorder is to enhance medication adherence. Second, even when patients are fully adherent to their medication regimens, mood relapses occur. Finally, evidence increasingly suggests that cognitive, behavioral, and external stressors can significantly affect the biological dysregulation underlying bipolar mood episodes, thereby influencing the course of the disorder (Craighead & Miklowitz, 2000). Stressful life events, family conflict, and instability of daily routines are among the most commonly cited factors; psychosocial interventions are capable of addressing each of these potentially destabilizing factors (Scott & Gutierrez, 2004).

In light of these issues and promising preliminary results from relevant studies, psychosocial treatments are becoming increasingly recognized as vital adjuncts to pharmacotherapy for patients with bipolar disorder. The following sections outline some of the issues in psychosocial treatment for bipolar disorder, as well as the major psychosocial approaches that have thus far garnered empirical support.

Timing of Treatment. The timing of the administration of psychosocial treatments for bipolar disorder may influence their efficacy. Thus far, there has been no evidence to suggest that such interventions can successfully help treat patients in the midst of a manic, hypomanic, or mixed episode, although some evidence suggests a degree of efficacy during depressive episodes (Colom & Vieta, 2004). Psychosocial treatments have exhibited their greatest utility in prophylactic or relapse prevention phases of treatment rather than during acute stabilization phases (Colom & Vieta, 2004).

Types of Treatment. The types of treatment recommended for patients with bipolar disorder are adaptations of treatments utilized in other psychiatric populations; the content and focus is altered to address the issues most relevant to bipolar disorder. Considerable overlap exists among empirically supported therapeutic approaches for bipolar disorder because there is a set of principles that must be included in any good psychosocial treatment for this disorder. These principles include psychoeducation, which provides patients with an understanding of the etiology, course, and treatment of the disorder; increased awareness of the importance of medication adherence; emphasis on stability of social rhythms and daily routines; and development of an ability to recognize prodromal symptoms (early signs of relapse). To varying degrees of emphasis, these themes are all present in the four main types of empirically validated psychosocial treatments for bipolar disorder (Colom & Vieta, 2004). The goal of these treatments is to improve both the course of the illness and the patient's quality of life.

Cognitive Behavioral Therapy. Cognitive Behavioral Therapy (CBT) has been studied less extensively in bipolar patients than in patients with unipolar depression. CBT for bipolar disorder employs the same theories and techniques as CBT for depression (see Chapter 1 of this volume) but with additional points of emphasis. The treatment is based on the theory that the mood swings experienced by bipolar patients are a result of negative or maladaptive thought patterns that can be corrected by cognitive and behavioral restructuring (Craighead, Miklowitz, Frank, & Vajk, 2002). Topics of focus that are above and beyond those employed in CBT for depression include adherence to both pharmacotherapy and psychosocial treatment; emphasis on monitoring mood, particularly with respect to prodromal symptoms; regularization of routines; and emphasis on resisting the temptation to engage in extreme behaviors (Lam et al., 2003).

Psychoeducation. The goal of psychoeducation is to provide patients with a fact-based, practical approach to understanding and coping with bipolar disorder and its consequences. The illness is conceptualized in a medical model; medication adherence is emphasized, illness management skills (e.g., early recognition of symptoms) are promoted, and methods to improve social and occupational functioning are discussed (Colom & Vieta, 2004; Colom et al., 2003). Psychoeducation can be delivered in individual or group settings and can also be an important part of family and marital therapy for patients with bipolar disorder. Some evidence indicates that even a brief psychoeducation session (e.g., a twelve-minute educational videotape and a handout containing factual information about lithium) can increase medication adherence (Peet & Harvey, 1991).

Interpersonal Social Rhythm Therapy. Interpersonal Social Rhythm Therapy (IPSRT) is a bipolar disorder-specific adaptation of Interpersonal Psychotherapy (IPT), which was originally developed for the treatment of depression (Frank et al., 1994). Like IPT, IPSRT focuses on the impact of social relationships and life events on the patient's mood. In contrast to IPT, IPSRT incorporates the hypothesis that disruption of normal daily routines (social rhythms) and sleep/wake cycles (circadian rhythms) plays an important role in precipitating symptoms of mania and depression (Frank et al., 1994; Frank, Swartz, & Kupfer, 2000; Frank et al., 2005). IPSRT instructs patients to keep track of daily activities such as sleep/wake times, levels of social stimulation, timing of routines, and mood. The goals of these activities are to (1) encourage understanding of the social context of mood symptoms and (2) help patients to recognize the impact of stress and interpersonal events on social and circadian rhythms. IPSRT tries to make these rhythms more regular in order to decrease vulnerability to mood cycling (Frank et al., 1994; Frank et al., 2000; Frank et al., 2005).

Family-Focused Therapy. Family-Focused Therapy (FFT) is based on the theory that the patient's family environment can strongly influence the likelihood of relapse (Miklowitz et al., 2000; Miklowitz, 2002). Research has shown that patients who return to a high-stress or high-conflict family environment after treatment fare significantly worse than those returning to a supportive environment (Miklowitz, Goldstein, Nuechterlein, Snyder, & Mintz, 1988). FFT aims to reduce tension and improve family functioning through psychoeducation, communication training, instruction in problem-solving and coping strategies, and relapse rehearsal (Miklowitz et al., 2000; Miklowitz, 2002).

Summary of Psychosocial Treatments for Bipolar Disorder. In summary, an increasing body of evidence has demonstrated that psychosocial treatment in conjunction with pharmacotherapy can assist with illness management and relapse prevention for bipolar disorder. These adjunctive treatments have been shown to impart some or all of the following benefits: increased medication adherence; enhanced patient ability to recognize warning signs of relapse; decreased relapse and rehospitalization rates; decreased denial of the impact of bipolar disorder on the patient's life; enhanced coping skills; improved occupational functioning; and increased overall quality of life (Craighead & Miklowitz, 2000; Scott & Gutierrez, 2004).

Psychosocial Treatments for Co-Occurring Bipolar Disorder and Substance Use Disorders

Despite the relatively high percentage of bipolar disorder patients with a co-occurring substance use disorder and the poor prognosis of these patients, very little research has been conducted on specific treatment approaches for this population. In response to the lack of evidence-based treatment guidelines, a manualized group treatment approach for patients with co-occurring bipolar disorder and substance use disorder (called Integrated Group Therapy (IGT)) has been developed.

Need for Specific Treatment for Bipolar Disorder and Substance Use Disorder. Bipolar disorder has several unique characteristics that make it amenable to a specialized treatment approach rather than to a more generalized dual diagnosis treatment strategy. For example, management of manic episodes offers a challenge that is unique to treatment of bipolar disorder. Research suggests that patients with bipolar disorder are more likely to use substances while manic or hypomanic than while depressed (Weiss, Mirin, Griffin, & Michael, 1988). Substance use and medication nonadherence can be influenced by positive attitudes toward manic and hypomanic symptoms; patients' ambivalence about recovery must be addressed. Furthermore, during periods of remission from bipolar episodes, patients often appear relatively asymptomatic (in comparison to patients with more severe psychiatric disorders such as schizophrenia). Thus, the pacing of treatment sessions and the treatment approaches that clinicians use may differ for patients with bipolar disorder and patients with schizophrenia.

Periods of remission can provide a window during which psychosocial treatments may have the greatest potential to effect change. At the same time, during periods of remission, bipolar disorder patients may believe that their disorder is under adequate control and may be at greater risk for medication nonadherence. During patients' periods of remission, clinicians should carefully monitor patients' medication adherence and capitalize on the opportunity to effect maximum therapeutic change.

Description of Integrated Group Therapy. IGT, which is a relapse prevention treatment for patients with bipolar disorder and a substance use disorder, simultaneously addresses both disorders using cognitive behavioral strategies. The core principle of IGT is that the same thought and behavioral patterns that promote recovery from one disorder will also facilitate recovery from the other disorder. IGT is designed to be administered weekly in hour-long sessions, with a different topic presented and discussed each week. Each group session begins with a "check-in," in which each patient is allotted several minutes to report on substance use, overall mood, medication adherence, high-risk situations, and coping strategies during the previous week. The previous week's discussion topic is reviewed briefly before a new topic is introduced and discussed. Whenever possible, clinicians should choose topics that are relevant to both disorders. Sample topics include "managing bipolar disorder without abusing substances;" "denial, ambivalence, admitting, and acceptance;" and "recovery versus relapse thinking." At the start of each session, group members are given a handout about the topic to be covered during that session; group members receive a take-home "skill practice" worksheet before leaving each session.

Features That Make Integrated Group Therapy "Integrated." Several key features make IGT "integrated." First, session topics are chosen to highlight both the similarities between bipolar disorder and substance use disorders and the interaction between the disorders. Second, during the check-in process patients are asked to focus on each of the check-in topics (particularly on substance use, mood, and medication adherence) and are encouraged to consider the importance of relapse and recovery behaviors for both bipolar disorder and substance use disorders.

Common Themes in Treatment of Patients With Bipolar Disorder and Substance Use Disorders. Common themes exist in the treatment of patients with bipolar disorder and substance use disorders (Weiss, 2004). First, patients with co-occurring bipolar disorder and a substance use disorder often consider one disorder as a "primary" illness and view the other disorder as of secondary importance in treatment. It is useful to suggest to patients that they view their illnesses as one disorder called "bipolar substance abuse" and that they view clinicians' recommendations as helpful in the treatment of "bipolar substance abuse" rather than in the treatment of either bipolar disorder or a substance use disorder. Thus, patients should be encouraged to view abstinence from drugs or alcohol as helpful in treatment of bipolar disorder and view medication adherence as helpful in treatment of substance use disorders. By training patients to conceptualize their illnesses and treatment in this manner, clinicians help patients to engage in recovery-oriented behaviors and promote recovery from both disorders (regardless of which disorder the patient initially considered as the primary problem).

The temptation to give up on recovery efforts after experiencing a setback is common in patients with substance abuse and in patients with depression. By helping patients to recognize similarities in symptoms of bipolar disorder and substance abuse disorders, and by aiding patients in challenging their pessimistic thoughts, clinicians can increase motivation in their patients to avoid relapse-oriented thought patterns and behavior patterns. Clinicians should also help patients to recognize the influence of one disorder on the other disorder. For example, by stressing the negative impact of drug and alcohol use on the course of bipolar disorder, a clinician might motivate a patient who is ambivalent about addressing his/her substance abuse problem to consider drug addiction treatment.

Finally, it is important for clinicians to encourage patients with bipolar disorder and substance use disorders to maintain structure in their day-to-day routines (a focus of IPSRT). Large amounts of unstructured time can lead to disruptions in sleep patterns (hypersomnia or insomnia), increased ruminative thinking, boredom, and behaviors that might place patients at risk for relapse. Clinicians should work with patients to facilitate the adoption of structured activities, including attendance at self-help meetings, regularly scheduled exercise, and a regular sleep schedule.

Organization of Services

The high prevalence of psychiatric illness in populations with substance use disorders ensures that all treatment programs for substance use disorders will encounter dually diagnosed patients. Some patients will have a previously established diagnosis at the time that they seek addiction treatment while other patients will not. The lack of a known diagnosis does not ensure the absence of a co-occurring illness, particularly if a psychiatric assessment has never been performed adequately.

The federal government has established a policy of "No Wrong Door" to ensure that dually diagnosed patients are assisted in obtaining appropriate services (Huber et al., 2000). This policy requires that all programs assist dually diagnosed patients by either providing services or referring patients to services. Treatment programs should be able to identify patients requiring further assessment. In addition, treatment programs should analyze their capacity to address the needs of patients who they serve and should address any gaps between the program's capabilities and the needs of the patients.

The American Society of Addiction Medicine has developed a model to define a program's capability to treat dually diagnosed patients (American Society of Addiction Medicine, 2001; Polcin, 2000). This model describes three levels of intensity of care: "addiction only," "dual diagnosis capable," and "dual diagnosis enhanced" (see also Chapter 19 of this volume). The presence or absence of psychiatric illness is insufficient to determine whether a program can adequately respond to a patient's needs. Rather, to determine if a particular program can provide adequate treatment for a patient, one must consider the level of care required by the patient. A bipolar patient who has been stabilized on medication can be easily treated by an addiction-only program; a patient with bipolar disorder who is experiencing depression with mild suicidal ideation may be appropriate for a dual diagnosis-capable program. Even though a patient with acute mania probably requires a dual diagnosis-enhanced program, an addiction-only service must be able to identify behaviors and symptoms that indicate that the patient requires a more comprehensive psychiatric assessment and be able to offer referral to appropriate treatment.

A thorough assessment of a treatment program may indicate that a large gap exists between what patients need and what the program can provide. Addiction treatment clinics with high rates of administrative or premature discharges have a responsibility to examine whether these administrative/premature discharges may have resulted from staff members who are unqualified to treat dually diagnosed patients or inadequate programs that enforce overly rigid rules and that fail to tailor programs to the needs of dually diagnosed patients (e.g., hypomanic patients who have difficulty following program rules or depressed patients who have difficulty getting out of bed for therapy sessions). A program can enhance its ability to handle dual diagnosis cases by identifying a dual diagnosis specialist within the organization who is able to identify dual diagnosis cases and treat these cases or refer the cases to appropriate treatment programs. Program directors can enhance an organization's services by promoting recruitment of staff with dual diagnosis or mental health experience, who not only treat dually diagnosed patients but also teach staff members the techniques required for treating these patients.

Treatment programs can also develop systems to efficiently identify dually diagnosed patients. Intake assessments that screen for co-occurring illnesses should include questions about past psychiatric treatment, including medications. Patients who report at the beginning of an evaluation session that they are not currently taking medications may reveal upon further questioning that they have taken medications (e.g., lithium) in the past. Through questions about a patient's response to antidepressants, staff members can further probe for the presence of bipolar disorder.

Collateral informant reports (obtained regularly with the patient's consent) offer a critical source of information. Information provided by a patient's family members about the patient's substance use and mental health issues can assist staff members in making a diagnosis. Family members of patients with bipolar disorder often provide more accurate data and complete histories about the patient's hypomanic and manic symptoms (particularly when patients have irritability as a core bipolar symptom) than the patient; patients with bipolar disorder may focus on periods of depression.

Staff members should be trained to be flexible in their approach to dually diagnosed patients. Rules in an addiction program may be too rigid for some bipolar patients who are experiencing a mood episode. Staff members may need to modify the treatment program for a bipolar patient (e.g., decrease the number and duration of group sessions). Just as addiction treatment professionals refuse to accept addiction-based behaviors as "willful misconduct," they should view behaviors and shifting moods of patients with bipolar disorder as symptoms of the patient's illness instead of acts of disobedience. A patient with bipolar disorder who will not stop talking and who interrupts others during group sessions is not necessarily doing so intentionally; this patient needs assistance in managing such behaviors, both with medication and with behavioral interventions that are appropriate to treat bipolar disorder.

Focus on treatment of addictions should not be minimized during treatment planning for dually diagnosed patients unless the psychiatric symptomatology is so severe that it makes discussion of substance use impossible. Indeed, concepts and techniques used in addiction treatment can inform treatment planning for dually diagnosed patients. The concepts of recovery, relapse prevention, and self-help (cornerstones of addiction treatment) should be applied to treatment of dually diagnosed patients. For example, addiction counselors can teach dually diagnosed patients that recovery (a concept in addiction treatment that implies that patients must assume responsibility for their improvement) from one disorder may assist with recovery from another disorder.

Since both bipolar disorder and substance use disorders are chronic illnesses, long-term treatment planning is necessary for this population. Acute care settings need to focus on facilitation of continuing care. For example, the aftercare plan for a dually diagnosed patient usually includes an appointment for medication monitoring and follow-up. Prior to discharge, a staff member from an acute care setting should review obstacles of implementation of the aftercare plan (e.g., since some patients do not fill their prescriptions because of the financial burden of purchasing medication, clinicians should discuss how, where, and when the patient will fill the prescription).

In summary, treatment of patients with addictions and bipolar illness presents unique challenges to addiction treatment programs. Symptoms of mania or hypomania may disrupt progress in an addiction program, and depressive symptoms may impede a patient's ability to actively participate in treatment. Psychiatric stabilization of a patient can make treatment of addictions and bipolar disorder easier. Since patients often attempt to simplify their illness (patients often feel more comfortable identifying themselves as having "only an addiction problem" or "just bipolar disorder"), clinicians should assist patients in recognizing the existence of two illnesses with symptoms that interact with each other, as well as the importance of participating in treatment that addresses the symptoms of both disorders (e.g., IGT). When providing treatment for dually diagnosed patients, clinicians should integrate the most effective aspects of addiction treatment while recognizing the unique challenges of treating patients with bipolar disorder and substance use disorders.

Treatment Planning for the Case Example

The case presented in this chapter (see "Case Presentation") illustrates the complexities that may be involved in diagnosing and treating bipolar disorder in patients with substance dependence. Although the patient possesses several symptoms suggestive of bipolar disorder, it is difficult to determine if these symptoms have manifested outside the context of alcohol or marijuana use. The most helpful clues in confirming a diagnosis of bipolar disorder include the patient's reports of hyperactivity, impulsive behavior, and periods of severe depression (characterized by her tendency to stay in her basement apartment for days), as well as her grandiose description of herself as being "fantastic" at her job and her many "great ideas." Since the patient has consistently abused drugs since age 15, it is difficult to determine whether these symptoms have ever occurred in the absence of substance use.

The patient reported significant difficulty concentrating prior to substance use. Although those symptoms could potentially reflect ADHD, conduct disorder, or anxiety, they may be signs of hypomanic irritability associated with childhood-onset bipolar disorder. The family history of "mood swings" and depression should be considered.

Although the patient's history and her presentation at examination are suggestive of bipolar disorder, a clinician should determine if she is currently under the influence of substances or in a withdrawal state before making a diagnosis. Stabilization and safety are always the first priority in treatment. If a diagnosis of bipolar disorder is established, a mood stabilizer, such as valproate or lithium, should be started. Since studies have shown valproate to be effective in reducing drinking in patients with bipolar disorder, valproate seems to be a reasonable medication choice for this patient (Salloum et al., 2005). Before a clinician prescribes valproate, however, liver enzymes and pregnancy tests should be performed. If psychotic symptoms are present, an antipsychotic agent could be added.

The patient should receive, in addition to pharmacologic treatment, psychoeducation about the nature and symptoms of bipolar disorder. The importance of good sleep hygiene and medication adherence should be emphasized. Discussions of substance use should focus on the adverse effects of drugs and alcohol on the course of bipolar disorder. In addition, family members can be helpful in early identification of manic or depressive symptoms and can encourage medication adherence.

SUMMARY

Recent research on the treatment of patients with bipolar disorder, both with and without substance use disorder, has been encouraging. A number of different adjunctive psychotherapeutic strategies have been shown to improve pharmacotherapy outcome, and recent developments in pharmacotherapy (e.g., the promise of lamotrigine for bipolar depression) have improved the prognosis for bipolar patients. Finally, promising results from studies using pharmacological treatments (valproate) and psychotherapeutic strategies (IGT) for treatment of bipolar disorder and substance use disorders may encourage more research and the development of new treatment options for this difficult-to-treat patient population.

Suggestions for Further Reading

For readers who wish to study further in this area, we recommend:

☐ *DSM-IV* **Criteria for Bipolar Disorder and Case Examples**

- American Psychiatric Association. (1994). *Diagnostic and statistical manual of mental disorders* (4th ed.). Washington, DC: Author.

- Spitzer, R. L., Gibbon, M., Skodol, A. E., Williams, J. B. W., & First, M. B. (1994). *DSM-IV casebook: A learning companion to the diagnostic and statistical manual of mental disorders* (4th ed.). Washington, DC: American Psychiatric Association.

☐ **More on Bipolar Disorder**

- Goodwin, F. K., & Jamison, K. R. (1990). *Manic-depressive illness*. New York: Oxford University Press.

- Stein, D. J., Kupfer, D. J., & Schatzberg, A. F. (Eds.) (2005). *Textbook of mood disorders*. Washington, DC: American Psychiatric Publishing.

☐ **Diagnostic Methods and Approach to Treatment Planning**

- Craighead, W. E., Miklowitz, D. J., Frank, E., & Vajk, F. C. (2002). Psychosocial treatments for bipolar disorder. In P. E. Nathan & J. M. Gorman (Eds.), *A guide to treatments that work* (2nd ed., pp. 263-275). New York: Oxford University Press.

- Craighead, W. E., & Miklowitz, D. J. (2000). Psychosocial interventions for bipolar disorder. *Journal of Clinical Psychiatry*, *61*(Suppl. 13), 58-64.

- Scott, J., & Gutierrez, M. J. (2004). The current status of psychological treatments in bipolar disorders: A systematic review of relapse prevention. *Bipolar Disorders*, *6*, 498-503.

- Weiss, R. D. (2004). Treating patients with bipolar disorder and substance dependence: Lessons learned. *Journal of Substance Abuse Treatment*, *27*, 307-312.

- Weiss, R. D., Greenfield, S. F., Najavits, L. M., Soto, J. A., Wyner, D., Tohen, M., et al. (1998). Medication compliance among patients with bipolar disorder and substance use disorder. *Journal of Clinical Psychiatry*, *59*, 172-174.

- Weiss, R. D., Ostacher, M. J., Otto, M. W., Calabrese, J. R., Fossey, M., Wisniewski, S. R., et al. (2005). Does recovery from substance use disorder matter in patients with bipolar disorder? *Journal of Clinical Psychiatry, 66*, 730-735.

☐ Specific Treatment Approaches and Supporting Evidence

- Colom, F., Vieta, E., Martinez-Aran, A., Reinares, M., Goikolea, J. M., Benabarre, A., et al. (2003). A randomized trial on the efficacy of group psychoeducation in the prophylaxis of recurrences in bipolar patients whose disease is in remission. *Archives of General Psychiatry, 60*, 402-407.

- Colom, F., & Vieta, E. (2004). A perspective on the use of psychoeducation, cognitive-behavioral therapy and interpersonal therapy for bipolar patients. *Bipolar Disorders, 6*, 480-486.

- Frank, E., Kupfer, D. J., Thase, M. E., Mallinger, A. G., Swartz, H. A., Fagiolini, A. M., et al. (2005). Two-year outcomes for interpersonal and social rhythm therapy in individuals with bipolar I disorder. *Archives of General Psychiatry, 62*, 996-1004.

- Lam, D. H., Hayward, P., Watkins, E. R., Wright, K., & Sham, P. (2005). Relapse prevention in patients with bipolar disorder: Cognitive therapy outcome after 2 years. *American Journal of Psychiatry, 162*, 324-329.

- Miklowitz, D. J., George, E. L., Richards, J. A., Simoneau, T. L., & Suddath, R. L. (2003). A randomized study of family-focused psychoeducation and pharmacotherapy in the outpatient management of bipolar disorder. *Archives of General Psychiatry, 60*, 904-912.

- Salloum, I. M., Cornelius, J. R., Daley, D. C., Kirisci, L., Himmelhoch, J. M., & Thase, M. E. (2005). Efficacy of valproate maintenance in patients with bipolar disorder and alcoholism: A double-blind placebo-controlled study. *Archives of General Psychiatry, 62*, 37-45.

- Weiss, R. D., Griffin, M. L., Kolodziej, M. E., Greenfield, S. F., Najavits, L. M., Daley, D. C., et al. (2007) A randomized trial of integrated group therapy versus group drug counseling for patients with bipolar disorder and substance dependence. *American Journal of Psychiatry, 164*, 100-107.

- Weiss, R. D., Najavits, L. M., & Greenfield, S. F. (1999). A relapse prevention group for patients with bipolar and substance use disorders. *Journal of Substance Abuse Treatment, 16*, 47-54.

☐ Popular Press Books

- Jamison, K. R. (1995). *An unquiet mind: A memoir of moods and madness.* New York: Knopf Publishing Group.

Authors' Note

The research in this chapter was supported in part by grants R01 DA15968, U10 DA15831, K24 DA0022288 from the National Institute on Drug Abuse.

References

Adler, C. M., Delbello, M. P., Mills, N. P., Schmithorst, V., Holland, S., & Strakowski, S. M. (2005). Comorbid ADHD is associated with altered patterns of neuronal activation in adolescents with bipolar disorder performing a simple attention task. *Bipolar Disorders, 7*, 577-588.

American Psychiatric Association. (1994). *Diagnostic and statistical manual of mental disorders* (4th ed.). Washington, DC: Author.

American Psychiatric Association (2000). *Diagnostic and statistical manual of mental disorders* (4th ed., text rev.). Washington, DC: Author.

American Society of Addiction Medicine. (2001). *Patient placement criteria for the treatment of substance-related disorders* (2nd ed., revised). Chevy Chase, MD: Author.

Baldassano, C. F. (2005). Assessment tools for screening and monitoring bipolar disorder. *Bipolar Disorders, 7*(Suppl. 1), 8-15.

Baldassano, C. F., Marangell, L. B., Gyulai, L., Ghaemi, S. N., Joffe, H., Kim D. R., et al. (2005). Gender differences in bipolar disorder: Retrospective data from the first 500 STEP-BD participants. *Bipolar Disorders, 7,* 465-470.

Brady, K., Casto, S., Lydiard, R. B., Malcolm, R., & Arana, G. (1991). Substance abuse in an inpatient psychiatric sample. *American Journal of Drug and Alcohol Abuse, 17,* 389-397.

Calabrese, J. R., Bowden, C. L., Sachs, G. S., Ascher, J. A., Monaghan, E., & Rudd, G. D. (1999). A double-blind placebo-controlled study of lamotrigine monotherapy in outpatients with bipolar I depression. Lamictal 602 Study Group. *Journal of Clinical Psychiatry, 60,* 79-88.

Cassidy, F., Ahearn, E. P. & Carroll, B. J. (2001). Substance abuse in bipolar disorder. *Bipolar Disorders, 3,* 181-188.

Clarke, S., Heussler, H., & Kohn, M. R. (2005). Attention deficit disorder: Not just for children. *Internal Medicine Journal, 35,* 721-725.

Colom, F., & Vieta, E. (2004). A perspective on the use of psychoeducation, cognitive-behavioral therapy and interpersonal therapy for bipolar patients. *Bipolar Disorders, 6,* 480-486.

Colom, F., Vieta, E., Martinez-Aran, A., Reinares, M., Goikolea, J. M., Benabarre, A., et al. (2003). A randomized trial on the efficacy of group psychoeducation in the prophylaxis of recurrences in bipolar patients whose disease is in remission. *Archives of General Psychiatry, 60,* 402-407.

Craighead, W. E., & Miklowitz, D. J. (2000). Psychosocial interventions for bipolar disorder. *Journal of Clinical Psychiatry, 61*(Suppl. 13), 58-64.

Craighead, W. E., Miklowitz, D .J., Frank, E., & Vajk, F. C. (2002). Psychosocial treatments for bipolar disorder. In P. E. Nathan & J. M. Gorman (Eds.), *A guide to treatments that work* (2nd ed., pp. 263-275). New York: Oxford University Press.

Dalton, E. J., Cate-Carter, T. D., Mundo, E., Parikh, S. V., & Kennedy, J. L. (2003). Suicide risk in bipolar patients: The role of co-morbid substance use disorders. *Bipolar Disorder, 5,* 58-61.

Eckblad M., & Chapman, L. J. (1986). Development and validation of a scale for hypomanic personality. *Journal of Abnormal Psychology, 95,* 214-222.

Feinman, J. A., & Dunner, D. L. (1996). The effect of alcohol and substance abuse on the course of bipolar affective disorder. *Journal of Affective Disorders, 37,* 43-49.

First, M. B., Spitzer, R. L., Gibbon, M., & Williams, J. B. W. (2002, November). Structured Clinical Interview for DSM-IV-TR Axis I Disorders, Patient Edition (SCID-I/P). New York: Biometrics Research Department, New York State Psychiatric Institute.

Frank, E., Kupfer, D. J., Ehlers, L. C., Monk, T. H., Cornes, C., Carter, S., et al. (1994). Interpersonal and social rhythm therapy for bipolar disorder: Integrating interpersonal and behavioral approaches. *Behavior Therapist, 17,* 143-149.

Frank, E., Kupfer, D. J., Thase, M. E., Mallinger, A. G., Swartz, H. A., Fagiolini, A. M., et al. (2005). Two-year outcomes for interpersonal and social rhythm therapy in individuals with bipolar I disorder. *Archives of General Psychiatry, 62,* 996-1004.

Frank, E., Swartz, H. A., & Kupfer, D. J. (2000). Interpersonal and social rhythm therapy: Managing the chaos of bipolar disorder. *Biological Psychiatry*, *48*, 593-604.

Geller, B., Cooper, T. B., Sun, K., Zimerman, B., Frazier, J., Williams, M., et al. (1998). Double-blind and placebo-controlled study of lithium for adolescent bipolar disorders with secondary substance dependency. *Journal of the American Academy of Child and Adolescent Psychiatry*, *37*, 171-178.

Ghaemi, S. N., Miller, C. J., Berv, D. A., Klugman, J., Rosenquist, K. J., & Pies, R.W. (2005). Sensitivity and specificity of a new bipolar spectrum diagnostic scale. *Journal of Affective Disorders*, *84*, 273-277.

Hasin, D. S., Samet, S., Nunes, E., Meydan, J., Matseoane, K., & Waxman, R. (2006). Diagnosis of comorbid disorders in substance users: Psychiatric Research Interview for Substance and Mental Disorders (PRISM-IV). *American Journal of Psychiatry, 163,* 689-696.

Hendrick, V., Altshuler, L. L., Gitlin, M. J., Delrahim, S., & Hammen, C. (2000). Gender and bipolar illness. *Journal of Clinical Psychiatry*, *61*, 393-396.

Hirschfeld, R. M., Williams, J. B., Spitzer, R .L., Calabrese, J. R., Flynn, L., Keck, P. E., Jr., et al. (2000). Development and validation of a screening instrument for bipolar spectrum disorder: The Mood Disorder Questionnaire. *American Journal of Psychiatry*, *157*, 1873-1875.

Huber, A., Lord, R. H., Gulati, V., Marinelli-Casey, P., Rawson, R., & Ling, W. (2000). The CSAT methamphetamine treatment program: Research design accommodations for "real world" application. *Journal of Psychoactive Drugs*, *32*, 149-156.

Joffe, R. T., MacQueen, G. M., Marriott, M., & Trevor Young, L. (2004). A prospective, longitudinal study of percentage of time spent ill in patients with bipolar I or bipolar II disorders. *Bipolar Disorders*, *6*, 62-66.

Kessler, R. C., Nelson, C. B., McGonagle, K. A., Edlund, M. J., Frank, R. G., & Leaf, P. J. (1996). The epidemiology of co-occurring addictive and mental disorders: Implications for prevention and service utilization. *American Journal of Orthopsychiatry*, *66*, 17-31.

Lam, D. H., Watkins, E. R., Hayward, P., Bright, J., Wright, K., Kerr, N., et al. (2003). A randomized controlled study of cognitive therapy for relapse prevention for bipolar affective disorder: Outcome of the first year. *Archives of General Psychiatry*, *60*, 145-152.

Lish, J. D., Dime-Meenan, S., Whybrow, P. C., Price, R. A., & Hirschfeld, R. M. (1994). The National Depressive and Manic-Depressive Association (DMDA) survey of bipolar members. *Journal of Affective Disorders*, *31*, 281-294.

Miklowitz, D. J. (2002). Family-focused treatment for bipolar disorder. In S. G. Hofmann & M. C. Tompson (Eds.), *Treating chronic and severe mental disorders: A handbook of empirically supported interventions* (pp. 159-174). New York: The Guilford Press.

Miklowitz, D. J., Goldstein, M. J., Nuechterlein, K. H., Snyder, K. S., & Mintz, J. (1988). Family factors and the course of bipolar affective disorder. *Archives of General Psychiatry*, *45*, 225-231.

Miklowitz, D. J., Simoneau, T. L., George, E. L., Richards, J. A., Kalbag, A., Sachs-Ericsson, N., et al. (2000). Family-focused treatment of bipolar disorder: 1-year effects of a psychoeducational program in conjunction with pharmacotherapy. *Biological Psychiatry*, *48*, 582-592.

Peet, M., & Harvey, N. S. (1991). Lithium maintenance: 1. A standard education programme for patients. *British Journal of Psychiatry*, *158*, 197-200.

Polcin, D. L. (2000). Professional counseling versus specialized programs for alcohol and drug abuse treatment. *Journal of Addictions and Offender Counseling*, *21*, 2-11.

Regier, D. A., Farmer, M. E., Rae, D. S., Locke, B. Z., Keith, S. J., Judd, L. L., et al. (1990). Comorbidity of mental disorders with alcohol and other drug abuse: Results from the Epidemiologic Catchment Area (ECA) Study. *Journal of the American Medical Association*, *264*, 2511-2518.

Salloum, I. M., Cornelius, J. R., Daley, D. C., Kirisci, L., Himmelhoch, J. M., & Thase, M. E. (2005). Efficacy of valproate maintenance in patients with bipolar disorder and alcoholism: A double-blind placebo-controlled study. *Archives of General Psychiatry, 62*, 37-45.

Salloum, I. M., & Thase, M. E. (2000). Impact of substance abuse on the course and treatment of bipolar disorder. *Bipolar Disorders, 2*(3 pt. 2), 269-280.

Scott, J., & Gutierrez, M. J. (2004). The current status of psychological treatments in bipolar disorders: A systematic review of relapse prevention. *Bipolar Disorders, 6*, 498-503.

Shulman, K. I., & Herrmann, N. (1999). The nature and management of mania in old age. *Psychiatric Clinics of North America, 22*, 649-665.

Smoller, J. W., & Finn, C. T. (2003). Family, twin, and adoption studies of bipolar disorder. *American Journal of Medical Genetics Part C: Seminars in Medical Genetics, 123*, 48-58.

Strober, M., Morrell, W., Burroughs, J., Lampert, C., Danforth, H., & Freeman, R. (1988). A family study of bipolar I disorder in adolescence: Early onset of symptoms linked to increased familial loading and lithium resistance. *Journal of Affective Disorders, 15*, 255-268.

Weiss, R. D., Mirin, S. M., Griffin, M. L., & Michael, J. L. (1988). Psychopathology in cocaine abusers: Changing trends. *Journal of Nervous and Mental Disease, 176*, 719-725.

Weiss, R. D. (2004). Treating patients with bipolar disorder and substance dependence: Lessons learned. *Journal of Substance Abuse Treatment, 27*, 307-312.

Wozniak, J., Biederman, J., Kwon, A., Mick, E., Faraone, S., Orlovsky, K., et al. (2005). How cardinal are cardinal symptoms in pediatric bipolar disorder? An examination of clinical correlates. *Biological Psychiatry, 58*, 583-588.

Part 2
Anxiety Disorders

Like depression, anxiety is a common disorder in substance-dependent patients and is often caused by substance intoxication or withdrawal. Specific anxiety syndromes—posttraumatic stress disorder (PTSD), panic disorder, agoraphobia (fear of public places), social anxiety disorder (formerly called social phobia, a fear of interpersonal situations), and generalized anxiety disorder—are relatively common and are often associated with substance abuse and dependence. In order to distinguish these syndromes from substance-related anxiety, clinicians must be familiar with the diagnostic criteria for these disorders. Symptoms of agoraphobia and social anxiety disorder and the reexperiencing symptoms of PTSD (e.g., surges of anxiety and flashbacks triggered by events that remind an individual of a trauma) are easily distinguished from symptoms of substance-related anxiety. However, symptoms of panic attacks and generalized anxiety disorder and the symptoms of psychic numbness of PTSD can be easily confused with symptoms of intoxication and withdrawal. Clinicians should determine carefully the relationship of anxiety symptoms to substance use over the course of a patient's history.

Substance-dependent patients who experience anxiety symptoms often seem to use substances in an effort to self-medicate anxiety disorders or may ask for prescriptions for benzodiazepines, which have potential for addiction. An accurate diagnosis allows clinicians to help patients to understand the source of their anxiety and to find ways to cope with their symptoms. Patients may be more motivated to achieve abstinence after a clinician informs them that their substance use may be causing or worsening their anxiety symptoms. Each of the anxiety syndromes covered in the chapters in Part 2 responds well to treatment with either cognitive behavioral psychotherapy methods or antidepressant medications that do not have potential for addiction. Clinicians who can recognize symptoms of anxiety disorders and distinguish them from substance-related anxiety should be able to improve treatment outcome for their substance-dependent patients.

Anxiety disorders also highlight the important role that stress plays in the development of both substance use disorders and psychiatric disorders. Substance-dependent patients tend to lead stressful lives (as a result, in part, of the disruptive effects of substance abuse on work, family, and physical health and the anxiety-inducing effects of substances). Stress seems to increase the drive to use addictive substances (a phenomenon that has been demonstrated in animal models of drug self-administration and observed in epidemiological studies that show an increase in substance use after disasters, such as the 9/11 terrorist attacks in New York City). Patients who are vulnerable to anxiety disorders (and mood disorders) may be vulnerable to the effects of stress. Indeed, an understanding of the complex relationships between substance abuse and other psychiatric disorders promotes an understanding of all psychiatric disorders.

Chapter 3

Posttraumatic Stress Disorder in Patients With Substance Use Disorders

by Kathleen Brady, M.D., Ph.D., Denise Hien, Ph.D.,
Louise Haynes, M.S.W., and Therese Killeen, Ph.D., A.P.R.N., B.C.

INTRODUCTION

Trauma and abuse are extremely common in the histories of substance-dependent patients. Obtaining a history of traumatic experiences during evaluation of substance-dependent patients can be difficult and can be a lengthy process, since patients often experience more than one trauma. It can be hard to listen to reports of trauma and abuse that patients have experienced—violence at the hands of loved ones, accidents and injuries, fights, beatings, or deaths of friends or loved ones. It is often painful for patients to discuss these experiences. However, in order to treat these patients, clinicians must understand trauma and its psychological consequences.

The high frequency of occurrence of trauma in the lives of substance-dependent patients is not a coincidence. Trauma and stress are risk factors for many forms of psychopathology, including depression and anxiety disorders (see Chapters 1 and 4 of this volume), as well as for substance dependence. Experiencing a trauma increases the likelihood that an individual will develop a substance use problem. For example, problem drinking increased in the weeks and months following the 9/11 attacks in direct relation to individuals' physical proximity to the site of the attacks (Vlahov et al., 2004). Further, stress seems to be fundamental to the biological mechanisms of addiction; for example, laboratory animals that are stressed are more likely to self-administer addictive drugs.

Posttraumatic stress disorder (PTSD), a serious psychological reaction to experiencing a trauma, consists of intrusive memories of the traumatic event that are accompanied by symptoms of anxiety and depression. PTSD is often chronic and disabling to varying degrees, and it is common among substance-dependent patients, in whom it is associated with poor treatment outcome. In a number of studies, lifetime prevalence of PTSD was found to be between 36 percent and 50 percent in individuals with substance use disorders, and current prevalence was found to be between 25 percent and 42 percent (Jacobsen, Southwick, & Kosten, 2001); the wide variability in prevalence rates reflects differing populations and diagnostic techniques used. Effective treatments for PTSD exist, including psychosocial or behavioral techniques and medications. It is important to recognize PTSD in order to initiate specific treatment.

CASE PRESENTATIONS

Two cases illustrating co-occurring PTSD and substance use disorders are presented below. While reading the case reports, readers might wish to note differences between the presentations of symptoms, formulate diagnoses, and devise a treatment plan. The outcome of these cases and a summary of the treatment plans for these two patients are offered at the end of the chapter.

Case 1

SR is a 33-year-old Caucasian female who is a high school graduate and who was referred by social services to the local community substance abuse treatment center for assessment and treatment of cocaine dependence. She has three children: two children (ages 15 and 12) from a previous marriage and one child (age 4) from her current boyfriend, with whom she is living. Social services became involved after a call from a neighbor, who suspected domestic violence and child abuse/neglect. When the complaint was investigated, SR's behavior was observed to be bizarre and guarded with some indications of paranoia. Discovery of drug paraphernalia in the house led to the substance abuse treatment referral. SR was ordered to complete a treatment program in order to maintain custody of her children.

SR married at age 18 when she became pregnant with her first child. Her husband was "an alcoholic and drug addict" and would become physically and emotionally abusive when he was intoxicated. SR left the relationship when she was 26; shortly thereafter she met her current boyfriend. She reports being physically and sexually abused by her stepfather from age 9 to 12. Her stepfather threatened her with harm if she ever told anyone about the abuse. Her mother was single, worked evening hours, and left the patient's stepfather as caretaker. SR reports that she has always felt depressed, has no close friends, and has no interest in activities. She has had several short-term unskilled jobs throughout her life and has had trouble maintaining employment for any substantial length of time. SR feels guilty; she feels that she does not care for her children as she should. She also reports chronic insomnia; when she does sleep, she often has vivid nightmares about her abuse. SR began using cocaine, marijuana, and alcohol in high school; her use slowly escalated and became problematic after the birth of her second child. She states that cocaine gives her more energy and helps her to "not think about the bad things that have happened to [her]." She uses alcohol and marijuana to help her sleep and to improve her mood. This is her first treatment experience.

Case 2

GB is a 45-year-old African American male college graduate who works as an engineer in a chemical plant. About eight months prior to his presentation for treatment there was an explosion at the plant while he was on duty. While trying to rescue one of his employees, GB sustained second- and third-degree burns to over 50 percent of his body. After a six-month hospitalization and recovery period, GB returned to work. However, GB has been very withdrawn, irritable, and anxious since the accident. He has had several angry outbursts and has been hypervigilant in regard to safety concerns, so much so that his productivity and relationships with colleagues have been affected. GB was referred for an assessment by his employee assistance program.

At intake, GB has a blunted affect and reports feeling nervous all the time since the accident. He startles easily and reports a sustained reaction to anything that startles him. He reports that he cannot stop thinking about ways he could have saved his employee. He has had several occasions when he has felt as if the accident is happening again. He states that he has not had a good night's sleep since the accident and has felt that his life is falling apart. Before the accident, GB was a "weekend beer drinker" who occasionally used marijuana. He states that he has never had problems as a result of alcohol or cannabis use. However, over the last several months, his wife has complained that his drinking and marijuana use have become excessive and that his use has caused problems in their relationship. He reports that he has called in sick to work more often. Even though he was reassigned to another department following the accident, he states that everything at work reminds him of the accident and that he cannot concentrate to get his job done.

DIAGNOSTIC CRITERIA

DSM-IV-TR Criteria for Posttraumatic Stress Disorder

PTSD is defined in the *Diagnostic and Statistical Manual of Mental Disorders*, 4th edition, text revision (*DSM-IV-TR*; American Psychiatric Association, 2000) as a set of signs and symptoms that persist for at least one month following the experience of a traumatic event. Symptoms of this disorder (see Table 3-1A) are characterized by three hallmark clusters:

1. *Reexperience cluster* (i.e., reexperience of the trauma in the form of flashbacks, nightmares, or intrusive thoughts);

2. *Avoidant cluster* (i.e., avoidance of reminders of the trauma; e.g., social withdrawal, feeling of detachment from others);

3. *Hyperarousal cluster* (i.e., a physiologic state of hyperarousal).

There are a number of issues that may make diagnosis of PTSD challenging. Often questions arise regarding the definition of trauma. Many hardships that a patient may consider traumatic may not qualify as a *DSM-IV-TR* Criterion A traumatic event (see Table 3-1A), including severe illnesses, homelessness, or loss of custody of children. Further, an individual exposed to a Criterion A traumatic event may not meet the necessary criteria for all three PTSD symptom clusters but may still exhibit a clinically significant syndrome that is, in many ways, indistinguishable from PTSD (e.g., partial or subthreshold PTSD (Marshall et al., 2001; Schutzwohl & Maercker, 1999)). Dissociation, the failure to integrate emotions, thoughts, and perceptions about specific events, is another hallmark symptom of PTSD. Dissociative symptoms, which are characterized by disruptions in functions of consciousness, memory, identity, or perception of the trauma, can make identification and self-report of PTSD symptoms challenging.

Mood Disorders, Acute Stress Disorder, and Disorders of Extreme Stress Not Otherwise Specified

The psychological consequences of trauma in individuals can present in the form of PTSD (the most well known and commonly occurring psychological consequence of trauma), as well as in the form of mood disorders, including other anxiety

Table 3-1A
DSM-IV-TR Posttraumatic Stress Disorder Criteria

Symptoms	DSM-IV-TR Criteria[a, b]	Issues in Substance-Dependent Patients	PRISM Questions to Aid Diagnosis[c, d]
Core Symptoms	A. The person has been exposed to a traumatic event in which both of the following were present:		
	1. the person experienced, witnessed, or was confronted with an event or events that involved actual or threatened death or serious injury, or a threat to the physical integrity of self or others	Substance-abusing patients may engage in more unsafe behavior in dangerous, high-risk situations; impaired cognition and decision making related to effects of substances of abuse	Were you ever … … in active military combat? … in a <u>very</u> serious accident? … in a serious fire, flood, earthquake, hurricane, or other disaster? … physically attacked, mugged, kidnapped, taken hostage, involved in a terrorist attack, or anything else like that? … sexually attacked or raped, or did you ever experience any unwanted sexual activity when you were a child or a teenager? … told you had a fatal illness? … very upset by hearing that any of these things had happened to someone you were close to? Did you ever see the serious injury or unnatural death of another person due to violent assault, accident, war, or disaster?
	2. the person's response involved intense fear, helplessness, or horror …. In children, this may be expressed instead by disorganized or agitated behavior.		At the time this happened, did you feel <u>extremely</u> frightened? Did you feel helpless to protect yourself or others? Did you feel horrified about what was happening?
Associated Symptoms	B. The traumatic event is persistently reexperienced in one (or more) of the following ways:	In general, symptoms in the reexperience cluster are not caused by substance intoxication or withdrawal	After [trauma] happened …

(Continued)

Symptoms	DSM-IV-TR Criteria[a, b]	Issues in Substance-Dependent Patients	PRISM Questions to Aid Diagnosis[c, d]
	1. recurrent and intrusive distressing recollections of the event, including images, thoughts, or perceptions … In young children, repetitive play may occur in which themes or aspects of the trauma are expressed		… did you remember it a lot, even though you didn't want to?
	2. recurrent distressing dreams of the event … In children, there may be frightening dreams without recognizable content		… did you have bad dreams about it?
	3. acting or feeling as if the traumatic event were recurring (includes a sense of reliving the experience, illusions, hallucinations, and dissociative flashback episodes, including those that occur on awakening or when intoxicated) … In young children, trauma-specific reenactment may occur	Certain drugs may cause psychotic symptoms (e.g., hallucinations, paranoia)	… did it ever seem like [trauma] was happening all over again?
	4. intense psychological distress at exposure to internal or external cues that symbolize or resemble an aspect of the traumatic event		… did you ever get <u>very</u> upset whenever anything reminded you of [trauma]? This could happen when you were in a situation that reminded you of it, or it could happen around the same time of year that it happened.
	5. physiological reactivity on exposure to internal or external cues that symbolize or resemble an aspect of the traumatic event.		… did you ever have any physical reactions when something reminded you of [trauma], like breaking out in a sweat, breathing fast, or feeling your heart pounding? Again, this could happen when you were in a situation that reminded you of it, or it could happen around the same time of year that it happened.
Other Criteria	C. Persistent avoidance of stimuli associated with the trauma and numbing of general responsiveness (not present before the trauma), as indicated by three (or more) of the following:		After [trauma] happened …

(Continued)

Symptoms	DSM-IV-TR Criteria[a, b]	Issues in Substance-Dependent Patients	PRISM Questions to Aid Diagnosis[c, d]
	1. efforts to avoid thoughts, feelings, or conversations associated with the trauma	Certain drugs may cause thought disturbances	… did you try to stop yourself from thinking or feeling anything about [trauma]?
	2. efforts to avoid activities, places, or people that arouse recollections of the trauma		… did you stay away from going places, doing things, or seeing people that might bring back memories of [trauma]?
	3. inability to recall an important aspect of the trauma		… did you [that] find that you couldn't remember some important part of what happened?
	4. markedly diminished interest or participation in significant activities	Certain drugs may cause lack of interest	… did you find [that] you were much less interested in activities you ordinarily enjoyed, or that you participated in such activities much less than usual?
	5. feeling of detachment or estrangement from others	Certain drugs may cause social withdrawal and isolation	… did you feel emotionally distant from other people or cut off from others?
	6. restricted range of affect (e.g., unable to have loving feelings)	Certain drugs may cause mood instability and depression	… did you feel as though you couldn't feel positive or loving feelings towards other people like you used to?
	7. sense of a foreshortened future (e.g., does not expect to have a career, marriage, children, or a normal life span).		… did you feel as if you couldn't really expect the future to turn out the way you had expected it to, in terms of your job, family, or the length of your own life?
	D. Persistent symptoms of increased arousal (not present before the trauma), as indicated by two (or more) of the following:	Certain drugs may cause hyperactivity and anxiety	After [trauma] happened …
	1. difficulty falling or staying asleep	Certain drugs may cause sleep disruption and insomnia	… did you have an unusual amount of trouble falling asleep or staying asleep?
	2. irritability or outbursts of anger	Certain drugs may cause irritability, apathy, and anger	… were you unusually angry or irritable a lot of the time?

(Continued)

Symptoms	DSM-IV-TR Criteria[a, b]	Issues in Substance-Dependent Patients	PRISM Questions to Aid Diagnosis[c, d]
	3. difficulty concentrating	Certain drugs may lead to impaired cognition	... did you find you were having unusual trouble concentrating on things?
	4. hypervigilance		... were you watchful or on guard, even when it probably wasn't necessary?
	5. exaggerated startle response.		... were you unusually jumpy or easily startled by sudden noises?
	E. Duration of the disturbance (symptoms in Criteria B, C, and D) is more than 1 month.		Did some of the after-effects of the trauma we've been talking about ever happen around the same time for at least 1 month?
	F. The disturbance causes clinically significant distress or impairment in social, occupational, or other important areas of functioning.		Did [symptoms]: ... interfere with your normal daily activities? ... make it harder for you to take care of your everyday responsibilities? ... cause any problems for you at [work/school]? ... cause any problems in your relationships or social life? Did anyone ever comment or complain about your [symptoms]? ... Did you often feel very upset about the [symptoms]?

(a) American Psychiatric Association (2000).
(b) Reprinted with permission from the *Diagnostic and Statistical Manual of Mental Disorders*, Fourth Edition, Text Revision (Copyright 2000). American Psychiatric Association.
(c) Hasin et al. (2006).
(d) Reprinted with permission.

disorders (see Chapter 4 of this volume), acute stress disorder (ASD; see Table 3-1B), and disorders of extreme stress not otherwise specified (DESNOS; see Table 3-1C); although the latter diagnosis currently is not listed as a distinct diagnosis in the *DSM-IV-TR*, the components of DESNOS have been explored in several research studies and are under consideration for inclusion in the *DSM-V* (Ford & Kidd, 1998; Pelcovitz et al., 1997; Zlotnick & Pearlstein, 1997).

Acute Stress Disorder. A diagnosis of acute stress disorder is associated with development of symptoms that are present while a patient is experiencing a traumatic stressor or after he/she has experienced a traumatic stressor. Symptoms of acute stress disorder last from two days to one month (a diagnosis of PTSD is made when symptoms persist beyond one month); cause clinically significant distress or impairment in social, occupational, or other important areas of functioning; and are classified into four criteria: (1) dissociative, (2) reexperiencing, (3) avoidance, and (4) increased anxiety and arousal (see Table 3-1B).

Disorders of Extreme Stress Not Otherwise Specified. In recent years, there has been increasing recognition that many individuals—men and women alike—have histories of longstanding abuse, including early childhood physical and sexual abuse; in many of these cases, experiences of revictimization occur throughout a lifetime. These individuals may present for substance abuse treatment with symptoms of DESNOS (also referred to as complex trauma). Although DESNOS has not yet been codified into a formal diagnosis, the symptom constellation of DESNOS (see Table 3-1C) offers a helpful framework through which to understand the disruptions in developmental processes caused by childhood maltreatment. An individual with DESNOS will often exhibit affect and impulse dysregulation, dissociation, somatization, and altered beliefs about identity and relationships to others. Adults who experience severe and chronic trauma early in life may exhibit impulse control deficits, unstable emotions or relationships, and dissociation (van der Kolk, McFarlane, & Weisaeth, 1996). Ninety-two percent of those who meet criteria for DESNOS also meet criteria for PTSD; however DESNOS may occur independently of PTSD (van der Kolk et al., 1996).

Using History of Trauma to Distinguish Mood Symptoms From Effects of Substances

When a patient has experienced traumatic events or other highly stressful events that clearly precede the onset of mood and anxiety symptoms, and especially when the full PTSD syndrome is present, it is likely that the patient's mood symptoms are more than just toxic effects of substances, and they should be addressed in treatment. Substance toxicity and withdrawal do not produce flashbacks or mood and anxiety symptoms triggered by reminders of a traumatic event. Thus, when a patient is having mood or anxiety symptoms that occur together with active substance use and when these symptoms are difficult to sort out from the toxic effects of substances, it is important to ask about trauma and to look for relationships between traumas and the symptoms that the patient is experiencing at the time of evaluation.

NATURAL HISTORY AND ETIOLOGY

Individuals with co-occurring PTSD and substance use disorders can present particular challenges in the treatment of their substance use disorders. Studies have shown

Table 3-1B
DSM-IV-TR Acute Stress Disorder Criteria

Symptoms	DSM-IV-TR Criteria[a, b]	Issues in Substance-Dependent Patients	PRISM Questions to Aid Diagnosis[d, e, f]
Core Symptoms	A. The person has been exposed to a traumatic event in which both of the following are present:		
	1. the person experienced, witnessed, or was confronted with an event or events that involved actual or threatened death or serious injury, or a threat to the physical integrity of self or others	Substance-abusing patients may engage in more unsafe behavior in dangerous, high-risk situations; impaired cognition and decision making related to effects of substances of abuse	Were you ever … … in active military combat? … in a very serious accident? … in a serious fire, flood, earthquake, hurricane, or other disaster? … physically attacked, mugged, kidnapped, taken hostage, involved in a terrorist attack, or anything else like that? … sexually attacked or raped, or did you ever experience any unwanted sexual activity when you were a child or a teenager? … told you had a fatal illness? … very upset by hearing that any of these things had happened to someone you were close to? Did you ever see the serious injury or unnatural death of another person due to violent assault, accident, war, or disaster?
	2. the person's response involved intense fear, helplessness, or horror.		At the time this happened, did you feel extremely frightened? Did you feel helpless to protect yourself or others? Did you feel horrified about what was happening?
Associated Symptoms	B. Either while experiencing or after experiencing the distressing event, the individual has three (or more) of the following dissociative symptoms:	Symptoms in Group B (e.g., numbing, detachment) may result from substance intoxication or withdrawal	After [trauma] happened …

(Continued)

Symptoms	DSM-IV-TR Criteria[a, b]	Issues in Substance-Dependent Patients	PRISM Questions to Aid Diagnosis[d, e, f]
	1. a subjective sense of numbing, detachment, or absence of emotional responsiveness		… did you feel emotionally distant from other people or cut off from others? … did you feel as though you couldn't feel positive or loving feelings towards other people like you used to?
	2. a reduction in awareness of his/her surroundings (e.g., "being in a daze")		
	3. derealization		
	4. depersonalization		
	5. dissociative amnesia (i.e., inability to recall an important aspect of the trauma).		… did you find that you couldn't remember some important part of what happened?
	C. The traumatic event is persistently reexperienced in at least one of the following ways: recurrent images, thoughts, dreams, illusions, flashback episodes, or a sense of reliving the experience; or distress on exposure to reminders of the traumatic event.	Symptoms in the *reexperience cluster* are not likely to be caused by substance intoxication or withdrawal	After [trauma] happened… … did you remember it a lot, even though you didn't want to? … did you have bad dreams about it? … did it ever seem like [trauma] was happening all over again? … did you ever get very upset whenever anything reminded you of [trauma]? … did you ever have any physical reactions when something reminded you of [trauma], like breaking out in a sweat, breathing fast, or feeling your heart pounding?
	D. Marked avoidance of stimuli that arouse recollections of the trauma (e.g., thoughts, feelings, conversations, activities, places, people).	Avoidance of specific trauma-related stimuli likely is not caused by substance intoxication or withdrawal	After [trauma] happened… … did you try to stop yourself from thinking or feeling anything about [trauma]? … did you stay away from going places, doing things, or seeing people that might bring back memories of [trauma]?

(Continued)

Symptoms	DSM-IV-TR Criteria[a, b]	Issues in Substance-Dependent Patients	PRISM Questions to Aid Diagnosis[d, e, f]
	E. Marked symptoms of anxiety or increased arousal (e.g., difficulty sleeping, irritability, poor concentration, hypervigilance, exaggerated startle response, motor restlessness).	Arousal or anxiety symptoms may relate to substance intoxication or withdrawal	After [trauma] happened … … did you have an unusual amount of trouble falling asleep or staying asleep? … were you unusually angry or irritable a lot of the time? … did you find you were having unusual trouble concentrating on things? … were you watchful or on guard, even when it probably wasn't necessary? … were you unusually jumpy or easily startled by sudden noises?
Other Criteria	F. The disturbance causes clinically significant distress or impairment in social, occupational, or other important areas of functioning or impairs the individual's ability to pursue some necessary task such as obtaining necessary assistance or mobilizing personal resources by telling family members about the traumatic experience.		Did [symptoms]: … interfere with your normal daily activities? … make it harder for you to take care of your everyday responsibilities? …cause any problems for you at [work/school]? … cause any problems in your relationships or social life? Did anyone ever comment or complain about your [symptoms]? … Did you often feel very upset about the [symptoms]?
	G. The disturbance lasts for a minimum of 2 days and a maximum of 4 weeks and occurs within 4 weeks of the traumatic event.		When did the [trauma] we've been talking about happen? … How long after [trauma] did you begin to have these reactions? … Have these reactions gone away completely? … When did that happen?
	H. The disturbance is not due to the direct physiological effects of a substance (e.g., a drug of abuse, a medication) or a general medical condition, is not better accounted for by brief psychotic disorder[c], and is not merely an exacerbation of a preexisting Axis I or Axis II disorder.		

(a) American Psychiatric Association (2000).
(b) Reprinted with permission from the *Diagnostic and Statistical Manual of Mental Disorders*, Fourth Edition, Text Revision (Copyright 2000). American Psychiatric Association.
(c) Consult *DSM-IV-TR* criteria (American Psychiatric Association, 2000) for brief psychotic disorder.
(d) PRISM does not provide questions for diagnosis of acute stress disorder; Table 3-1B includes questions from the PRISM's PTSD module that can be used for diagnosis of acute stress disorder.
(e) Hasin et al. (2006).
(f) Reprinted with permission.

Table 3-1C
Criteria for Disorders of Extreme Stress Not Otherwise Specified

Symptoms	Diagnostic Criteria[a, b, c]	Issues in Substance-Dependent Patients
Core Symptoms	The person must demonstrate alterations in six areas of functioning for diagnosis of DESNOS:	
Affect and impulses	I. Alteration in regulation of affect and impulses (A and one of B-F required): A. affect regulation B. modulation of anger C. self-destructive D. suicidal preoccupation E. difficulty modulating sexual involvement F. excessive risk taking.	Affective symptoms in this group of symptoms may be caused or worsened by substance intoxication or withdrawal.
Attention/consciousness	II. Alterations in attention or consciousness (A or B required): A. amnesia B. transient dissociative episodes and depersonalization.	May be caused or worsened by substance intoxication or withdrawal.
Self-perception	III. Alteration in self-perception (Two of A-F required): A. ineffectiveness B. permanent damage C. guilt and responsibility D. shame E. nobody can understand F. minimizing.	Substance dependence and associated impairment may contribute to poor self-image.
Relationships	IV. Alterations in relations with others (One of A-C required): A. inability to trust B. revictimization C. victimizing others.	Impairment resulting from substance dependence may contribute to poor relationships.
Somatization	V. Somatization (Two of A-E required): A. digestive system B. chronic pain C. cardiopulmonary symptoms D. conversion symptoms E. sexual symptoms.	May be worsened by substance use.
Systems of meaning	VI. Alterations in systems of meaning (A or B required): A. despair and hopelessness B. loss of previously sustaining beliefs.	May be caused or worsened by substance use or substance-induced depression.
Other Criteria		
Perception of Perpetrator	VII. Alterations in perception of the perpetrator (not required): A. adopting distorted beliefs B. idealization of the perpetrator C. preoccupation with hurting perpetrator.	Not likely caused by substances.

[a] Pelcovitz, D., van der Kolk, B. A., Roth, S., Mandel, F., Kaplan, S., & Resick, P. Development of a criteria set and a structured interview for disorders of extreme stress (SIDES). Journal of Traumatic Stress, Vol. 10, No. 1, pp. 3-16. Copyright, 1997, John Wiley & Sons, Inc.
[b] Disorders of Extreme Stress Not Otherwise Specified (DESNOS) is not a distinct diagnosis identified in *DSM-IV-TR*.
[c] Reprinted with permission of John Wiley & Sons, Inc.

that individuals with PTSD have poorer long-term substance-use-related outcomes, poorer psychosocial functioning, and higher treatment drop-out in comparison to substance abusers without PTSD (Brady, Killeen, Saladin, Dansky, & Becker, 1994; Ouimette, Finney, & Moos, 1999). On the other hand, improvement in PTSD symptoms during the course of treatment is associated with better substance-use-related outcomes (Read, Brown, & Kahler, 2004).

While PTSD and substance use disorders appear to be strongly linked, little is known about the nature of this relationship. The most widely held explanation is the self-medication hypothesis. This hypothesis is based primarily on the clinical observation that traumatized individuals sometimes use substances as a means of dampening traumatic memories and treating sleep disturbance and other painful symptoms of PTSD. A second hypothesis is that individuals with substance use disorders, because of high-risk lifestyles, are likely to experience a trauma and, therefore, are more likely to develop PTSD. It is not likely that there is a unidirectional, simple cause and effect relationship between PTSD and substance use disorders.

There are likely common genetic, neurobiologic, and environmental susceptibility factors for PTSD and substance use disorders. A full description of the commonalties in neurobiology between PTSD and substance use disorders is beyond the scope of this chapter. Indeed, there is growing evidence that shared neurobiological mechanisms may play a significant role in the co-occurrence of PTSD and substance use disorders (Brady & Sinha, 2005). Interestingly, both alcohol and a number of abused drugs exert their anxiolytic effects by inhibiting neuronal activity in brain areas associated with the symptoms of PTSD. Other investigations have focused on the hypothalamic-pituitary-adrenal (HPA) axis, the primary neuroendocrine system involved in stress response (Stewart, 2003). Abnormalities in the function of the HPA axis have been implicated in both PTSD and substance use disorders. Animal studies have demonstrated that exposure to stress facilitates both the initiation and reinstatement of substance use after a period of abstinence in previously substance-dependent animals (Kreek & Koob, 1998). This reinstatement is blocked by drugs that act on the HPA axis (Kreek & Koob, 1998; Stewart, 2003). The noradrenergic system is also intimately involved in stress response. This system is activated during withdrawal from many substances of abuse, thereby indicating another potential neurobiologic link between PTSD and substance use disorders. Other investigators have explored the role of endogenous opioids in both addictive disorders and PTSD.

ISSUES IN DIAGNOSIS: MAKING A POSTTRAUMATIC STRESS DISORDER DIAGNOSIS IN SUBSTANCE-DEPENDENT PATIENTS

There is considerable symptom overlap between PTSD and drug/alcohol intoxication and withdrawal, particularly in the PTSD symptoms in the *hyperarousal cluster*, such as sleep disturbance, irritability, and difficulty concentrating, which can all be caused by drug intoxication or withdrawal. Symptoms in the *avoidant cluster*, such as lack of interest, social withdrawal, and feeling of detachment from others, can also be caused by substance abuse. The symptoms in the *reexperience cluster*, which include recollections and reactions to reminders of the traumatic event, are relatively specific to the diagnosis of PTSD. For those symptoms that are common to PTSD and substance use disorders, it is important to ask the patient questions about relationships among the traumatic event, the patient's mood and anxiety symptoms, and the patient's substance use. If sleep disturbance, poor concentration, and other symptoms began shortly after a traumatic experience and/or are tied closely to distressing recollections of the traumatic event, the symptoms are likely a result of PTSD.

The common neurobiologic mechanisms that may link substance use disorders and PTSD make it likely that substance use and withdrawal will exacerbate PTSD symptoms. Thus, successful treatment of a substance use disorder is likely to mitigate PTSD symptoms.

INSTRUMENTS AND METHODS FOR SCREENING AND DIAGNOSIS

There are several assessment instruments that are used to make *Diagnostic and Statistical Manual of Mental Disorders,* 4th edition (*DSM-IV*; American Psychiatric Association, 1994) or *DSM-IV-TR* diagnoses of Axis I disorders, including PTSD and substance use disorders (see Table 3-2). Two diagnostic instruments that require trained clinicians to perform a structured interview are the Psychiatric Research Interview for Substance and Mental Disorders (PRISM; Hasin et al., 2006) and the Structured Clinical Interview for DSM-IV-TR Axis I Disorders (SCID-I; First, Spitzer, Gibbon, & Williams, 2002). Studies have shown that the PRISM, which requires approximately 120 minutes to administer, is reliable in making a *DSM-IV* diagnosis in research participants who have substance use disorders (Hasin et al., 1996; Hasin et al., 2006). Table 3-1A contains questions from the PRISM for aiding diagnosis of PTSD. The questions from the PRISM that are included in Table 3-1B for aiding diagnosis of acute stress disorder were extracted from the PTSD module of the PRISM; to date, the PRISM does not contain a separate module with questions for aiding diagnosis of acute stress disorder. Other common *DSM-IV* diagnostic instruments include the Mini International Neuropsychiatric Interview (MINI; Sheehan et al., 1998), Composite International Diagnostic Interview (CIDI; Robins et al., 1988), and Diagnostic Interview Schedule (DIS; Robins, Helzer, Croughan, Williams, & Spitzer, 1981) (see Table 3-2).

To screen for PTSD, an evaluator first must determine whether the individual was exposed to a Criterion A traumatic event. Trauma history may be gathered via a self-report measure or through clinical assessment. Typically, assessments of trauma that are based on a self-report are accurate. An inaccurate report may be a result of impairment caused by substance withdrawal or intoxication; inaccurate reporting may occur if the patient has legal or financial issues at stake, and inaccurate reporting may relate to coexisting psychopathology such as dissociative or psychotic disorders (Henderson & Jorm, 1990; Keane, Wolfe, & Taylor, 1987). Examples of screening tools that are used to assess lifetime traumatic events include the Hurt-Insult-Threaten-Scream (HITS; Sherin, Sinacore, Li, Zitter, & Shakil, 1998), which identifies partner abuse; the Primary Care PTSD Screen (Prins et al., 2004), which screens for key PTSD symptoms in general medical (and other) settings; and the Stressful Life Experiences questionnaire (Gray, Litz, Hsu, & Lombardo, 2004), which provides a checklist of a variety of types of traumas.

Several recently developed screening tools show promise in screening for PTSD. The Startle-Physiologic Arousal-Anger-Numb (SPAN) is a four-item, self-rated questionnaire that has demonstrated good correlation with structured clinical interviews for PTSD (Meltzer-Brody, Churchill, & Davidson, 1999). Breslau and colleagues (Breslau, Peterson, Kessler, & Schultz, 1999) developed a seven-item screening scale that compared well with diagnostic interviews for PTSD. However, neither this scale nor the SPAN has been systematically tested in individuals with substance use disorders.

There are a number of widely used assessment tools for ascertaining symptoms of PTSD for *DSM-IV-TR* diagnosis. A variety of self-report instruments, as well as those that are clinician-assisted, are presented in Table 3-2. These instruments can be used to make an initial diagnosis and/or to follow PTSD symptoms over time. Table 3-2 categorizes assessment tools according to constructs measured, methods of measurement, and psychometrics.

DIFFERENTIAL DIAGNOSIS AND OTHER OVERLAPPING DISORDERS

More often than not, PTSD co-occurs with other psychiatric disorders (Brady, 1997; Kessler, Sonnega, Bromet, Hughes, & Nelson, 1995). Approximately 80 percent of individuals with PTSD meet criteria for at least one other psychiatric diagnosis, and nearly 50 percent of individuals with PTSD have three or more additional diagnoses. Depressive disorders and substance use disorders are the most common conditions co-occurring with PTSD (see Table 3-3). The presence of a comorbid psychiatric disorder can exacerbate PTSD symptoms, make the presentation variable, and complicate clinical assessment and diagnosis.

Depression and Suicide Risk

The relationship between PTSD and major depression is complex because there is a substantial overlap of symptoms, such as sleep disturbance, difficulty concentrating, social avoidance and withdrawal, and anhedonia (see Chapter 1 of this volume). Those who meet criteria for both disorders are typically more distressed and have more chronic symptoms and a higher degree of impairment than those who have only one of the disorders. Further, PTSD, with or without major depression, is a significant risk factor for suicidal behavior (see Chapter 17 of this volume). Studies have shown that suicidality in patients who have been exposed to trauma is most frequent in individuals with a primary diagnosis of PTSD in comparison to other diagnoses (Ferrada-Noli, Asberg, Ormstad, Lundin, & Sundbom, 1998).

Other Anxiety Disorders

It is common for individuals with PTSD to have at least one other anxiety disorder diagnosis (see Chapter 4 of this volume); prevalence rates are estimated at 50 percent. Simple phobia and social anxiety disorder appear to be the most common comorbid anxiety conditions. Panic disorder also frequently occurs in patients with PTSD. PTSD also has many symptoms in common with other anxiety disorders, which can make the diagnostic process challenging. For example, symptoms of avoidance are characteristic of social anxiety disorder, specific phobia, agoraphobia, and PTSD. Hyperarousal, derealization, depersonalization, and fear of losing control are physiological features of both panic disorder and PTSD. Symptoms of disturbed sleep, difficulty concentrating, and restlessness are associated with all anxiety disorders.

Personality Disorders and Eating Disorders

Personality disorders with self-destructive behaviors, such as borderline personality disorder (see Chapter 9 of this volume), and eating disorders (see Chapter 12 of

Table 3-2

Commonly Used Measures for Diagnostic Assessment of Posttraumatic Stress Disorder

Instrument	Construct	Method	Psychometrics
Clinician-Administered PTSD Scale (CAPS) (Blake et al., 1990; Blake et al., 1995; Weathers, 1993)	Assesses frequency and intensity of PTSD symptoms	– clinician-administered – 20-40 minutes	Excellent reliability, validity, and consistency
Structured Clinical Interview for DSM-IV-TR Axis I Disorders (SCID-I) (First et al., 2002)	Assesses major Axis I psychiatric disorders, including substance abuse and PTSD	– clinician-administered – 1-3 hours	Most widely used, validated, and reliable assessment available
Psychiatric Research Interview for Substance and Mental Disorders (PRISM) (Hasin et al., 2006)	Assesses major Axis I psychiatric disorders, including substance abuse and PTSD	– clinician-administered – 2 hours	Good to excellent reliability demonstrated among substance-dependent patients
Mini International Neuropsychiatric Interview (MINI) (Sheehan et al., 1998)	Assesses most major psychiatric disorders, including substance use and PTSD	– clinician-administered – 30-60 minutes	Validity well established
Composite International Diagnostic Interview (CIDI) (Robins et al., 1988)	Assesses PTSD symptoms and course features, as in duration of PTSD symptoms, periods of remission, as well as severity	– interviewer-administered – 1-2 hours	Good reliability
Diagnostic Interview Schedule (DIS) (Robins, Helzer, Croughan, & Ratcliff, 1981; Robins, Helzer, Croughan, Williams, & Spitzer, 1981)	Assesses PTSD symptoms and course features, as in duration of PTSD symptoms, periods of remission, as well as severity	– interviewer-administered – 1-2 hours	Popular but reliability unsubstantiated
Posttraumatic Stress Diagnostic Scale (PSDS) (Foa, 1995; Foa, Riggs, Dancu, & Rothbaum, 1993)	Assesses frequency and intensity of PTSD symptoms	– self-report – 5-15 minutes	Good reliability and validity

Table 3-3
Percentage of Comorbid Diagnoses in Men and Women With Lifetime Posttraumatic Stress Disorder From the National Comorbidity Survey

Other Psychiatric Diagnoses Co-Occurring With PTSD	Men (%)	Women (%)
Affective Disorders		
Major depression	47.9	48.5
Dysthymia	21.4	23.3
Mania	11.7	5.7
Substance Use Disorders		
Alcohol abuse/dependence	51.9	27.9
Drug abuse/dependence	34.5	26.9
Anxiety Disorders		
Generalized anxiety disorder	16.8	15.0
Panic disorder	7.3	12.6
Simple phobia	31.4	29.0
Social anxiety disorder	27.6	28.4
Agoraphobia	16.1	22.4
Other Disorders		
Conduct disorder	43.3	15.4
Any Disorder		
No other diagnosis	11.7	21.0
1 diagnosis	14.9	17.2
2 diagnoses	14.4	18.2
> 3 diagnoses	59.0	43.6

Note: Kessler, Sonnega, Bromet, Hughes, & Nelson, Archives of General Psychiatry, December 1995, Vol. 52, p. 1056. Copyright © 1995, American Medical Association. All rights reserved. Reprinted with permission of American Medical Association.

this volume) commonly occur in persons with PTSD and substance use disorders. By regarding childhood abuse as an important factor in the development of borderline personality disorder, one might gain greater insight into the higher prevalence of this disorder among women. Specifically, because girls are two to three times more likely to be sexually victimized during childhood than boys, they are more frequently exposed to conditions that may put them at risk for developing borderline personality disorder.

TREATMENT OPTIONS

Psychosocial Treatments

This section briefly summarizes a number of psychosocial treatment options that have been specifically developed and tested for the treatment of patients with co-occurring PTSD and substance use disorders. While the treatments reviewed may differ with respect to how and when they are applied, they share features of psychoeducational and cognitive behavioral approaches and have an interdisciplinary theoretical framework. Typically, standard approaches to treatment of co-occurring PTSD and substance use disorders address both disorders simultaneously. Many of these approaches were originally developed for use with female populations but have been applied to therapy with both genders.

Psychoeducational and Cognitive Behavioral Techniques. Psychoeducational approaches teach patients about their illnesses and how to cope with them. Cognitive behavioral approaches teach patients techniques to cope with distorted thinking, symptoms, such as drug cravings, situations that may trigger substance use, and mood and anxiety symptoms associated with PTSD. Examples of techniques that aid patients in coping with mood and anxiety symptoms include thought stopping (recognizing and stopping negative thoughts associated with symptoms or substituting positive thoughts) and relaxation training. Homework is generally assigned to allow patients to practice techniques between sessions.

Exposure-Based Methods. Exposure-based methods represent a behavioral approach that has been found to be particularly effective for PTSD in patients without substance abuse. These methods involve some form of exposure to the traumatic experience, usually through guided remembering and reexperiencing of the traumatic event in the clinician's office. This approach provides patients with an opportunity to practice coping skills in the safety of a clinician's office and to gradually extinguish the emotional arousal associated with the memories. However, in substance-dependent patients, the painful emotions aroused by remembering the trauma in a therapy session may trigger cravings and relapse to substance use. More research is needed to determine guidelines for when and how to best use exposure-based methods with substance-dependent patients. In the meantime, exposure-based approaches should be used in conjunction with careful monitoring for excessive arousal or worsening of substance use symptoms.

Timing, Intensity, and Type of Psychosocial Treatment. Clinical decisions regarding the timing, intensity, and type of trauma-focused treatment must be made with course of illness in mind. When planning a treatment approach, clinicians should consider the order in which different interventions are applied. For example, for patients in the early stages of addictions recovery (a time when risk of lapses and relapses may be high), trauma-processing models that target trauma symptoms and experiences in an intensive way (such as exposure-based approaches) may be inappropriate until patients have gained some basic skills to manage their substance use disorder. Psychosocial approaches for managing active PTSD symptoms in the context of severe substance use typically involve a psychoeducational/coping skills format and typically leave trauma-processing work for later stages of recovery. Since patients with PTSD and substance use disorders often experience severe consequences as a result of their substance use, they have a more severe clinical profile (Najavits, Weiss, Shaw, & Muenz, 1998) and experience multiple other life problems, including medical problems (Brady et al., 1994). Considerations regarding how and when to treat both disorders require caution and sensitivity.

Summary of Empirically Supported Findings. Empirical studies have begun to yield findings that suggest that integrating treatment of PTSD and substance use disorders is possible and can lead to reductions in both PTSD and substance use symptoms. To date, five separate research teams have conducted and published trials of treatments for patients with co-occurring PTSD and substance use disorders; these trials are reviewed below and are summarized in Table 3-4. Although the findings are encouraging, to date, only one therapy is held by the American Psychological Association task force's rigorous standards (Chambless & Hollon, 1998) as "probably efficacious" ("Seeking Safety;" Najavits, 2002)—perhaps the result of a delay in reporting of findings from empirical studies that may still be under way or that have not been published yet.

Seeking Safety is a manualized cognitive behavioral intervention that was designed for the treatment of patients who have experienced trauma and have a substance use disorder. Seeking Safety sessions can be delivered in both individual and group format and focus on five areas of treatment: (1) safety; (2) simultaneous treatment of PTSD and substance use disorders; (3) ideals; (4) cognitive, behavioral, interpersonal, and case management content; and (5) attention to the therapist process.

While all studies related to Seeking Safety that are reported in this chapter found that treatment improved symptoms among patients with PTSD and a substance use disorder, there are limitations to these studies. First, most of the studies had relatively small sample sizes (sample sizes ranged from 19 to 107 subjects), thereby making generalization of findings difficult. One exception was the Hien et al. (in press) Clinical Trials Network study, which randomized 353 participants, who all received substance abuse treatment as usual, to twelve sessions of rolling admission Seeking Safety groups compared to twelve sessions of a women's health education curriculum. Only three of the studies (Hien, Cohen, Miele, Litt, & Capstick, 2004; Hien et al., in press; Triffleman, 2000) were controlled trials; however, the Hien et al. (in press) Clinical Trials Network study had a high proportion of participants who were abstinent upon study entry (about 50 percent), thereby rendering the lack of overall findings on substance use outcomes difficult to interpret. Uncontrolled trials limit ability to attribute outcomes to the specified treatment as opposed to nonspecific factors (e.g., exposure to the treatment milieu, treatment alliance, natural improvement with time). Other limitations include high drop-out rates (Back, Dansky, Carroll, Foa, & Brady, 2001; Brady, Dansky, Back, Foa, & Carroll, 2001; Coffey, Dansky, & Brady, 2003), lack of follow-up of participants who dropped out of the treatment (Najavits et al.,1998), short follow-up periods (Triffleman, 2000), and a requirement that patients be abstinent for thirty days before they could enter treatment for PTSD (Donovan, Padin-Rivera, & Kowaliw, 2001).

Other Widely Used Psychosocial Treatments. A number of manualized treatment approaches for trauma and addiction comorbidity have not been subjected to empirical testing but are widely used in the substance use treatment community. Many of these approaches were used in Substance Abuse and Mental Health Services Administration's (SAMHSA's) Women, Co-Occurring Disorders, and Violence Study (WCDVS; McHugo et al., 2005). All of these approaches incorporate elements of cognitive behavioral treatment, psychoeducation, and skill building:

- *The Addictions and Trauma Recovery Integration Model* (ATRIUM; Miller & Guidry, 2001) is a twelve-week model for use in individual treatment sessions and group sessions. It uses standard Cognitive Behavioral Therapy (CBT) techniques and focuses on relationships in mental, physical, and spiritual domains. This treatment also addresses somatic symptoms through expressive therapy approaches.

Table 3-4
Empirically Supported Treatments for Posttraumatic Stress Disorder and Substance Use Disorders

	Seeking Safety (Najavits et al., 1998)	Substance-Dependence PTSD Therapy (Triffleman, 2000)	Concurrent Treatment of PTSD and Cocaine Dependence (Brady et al., 2001)	Transcend (Donovan et al., 2001)	Seeking Safety (Hien et al., 2004)	Seeking Safety (Hien et al., in press)
N	27 women 17 (6 or + sessions)	19 (10 women)	39 (82% women) 15 (10 or + sessions)	46 men	107 women	353 women
Design	No control	Randomized trial	No control	No control	Randomized trial	Randomized trial
Length of treatment	3 months, 2x/week, 90-min/group	5 months, 2x/week, 45-min/individual	2 months, 2x/week, 90-min/individual	3 months, partial hospitalization, 10 hours/week	3 months, 2x/week, 45-min/individual	6 months, 2x/week, 90-min/group
Content	Psychoeducation & CBT	CBT, then stress inoculation, & exposure therapy vs. twelve-step facilitation (2-phase)	CBT and exposure therapies (2-phase)	CBT & peer social support (2-phase)	Seeking Safety vs. CBT vs. treatment-as-usual	Seeking Safety vs. women's health education
Follow-Up	3 months posttreatment	1 month posttreatment	6 months posttreatment	6 and 12 months posttreatment	3 and 6 months posttreatment	1 week and 3, 6, and 12 months posttreatment
Results	Improvement in SUD, PTSD, depression; increase in somatization	Improvement in SUD, PTSD, psych; no gender differences	Improvement in SUD, PTSD, & depression	Improvement in SUD, PTSD	Improvement at 3 months, diminished at 6 months	Improvement in PTSD sustained over 12 months in both Seeking Safety and women's health education
Limits	Small N, no control, did not follow up drop-outs	Small N, short follow-up period	Small N, no control, large drop-out rate	Small N, no control, 30-day abstinence required, one site	One site, non-randomized treatment-as-usual group	No comparison treatment-as-usual group; 50 percent were abstinent at baseline
Dependent variable	SUD, PTSD, psych cognitive	SUD, PTSD, psych	SUD, PTSD, depression	SUD, PTSD	SUD, PTSD, psych	SUD, PTSD

PTSD=posttraumatic stress disorder; SUD=substance use disorder; psych=other psychiatric symptoms.

- *Trauma Adaptive Recovery Group Education and Therapy* (TARGET; Ford, Kasimer, MacDonald, & Savill, 2000) is a trauma-focused intervention; it combines skills training with a psychoeducational approach that addresses the neurobiological impact of trauma. A seven-step "alarm" approach is geared toward helping participants in this group therapy to identify early signs of responses to trauma and to develop adaptive strategies for handling their responses to trauma without the use of substances.

- *Trauma Recovery and Empowerment Model* (TREM; Fallot & Harris, 2002) is a manualized group psychotherapy that was originally designed for women with severe mental disorders and trauma histories and that has been used in SAMHSA's WCDVS (McHugo et al., 2005). With a structured approach, TREM uses a skills-based model that addresses long-term effects of trauma and histories of childhood physical and sexual abuse; thirty-three topics are reviewed in patient workbooks that include exercises for completion between sessions.

- *Helping Women Recover* (Covington, 1999) is a manualized group treatment that offers a women's perspective on addiction and trauma treatment; seventeen sessions span four general areas of treatment: self, relationships, sexuality, and spirituality. This treatment may be used in residential, outpatient, and inpatient settings, as well as in criminal justice settings. Patient workbooks are also available.

Medication Treatment

While the treatment of PTSD is generally multimodal, pharmacotherapy is playing an increasingly important role. Pharmacotherapy aims to reduce key symptoms of PTSD so that individuals can "put greater distance" between themselves and the traumatic event(s) without the use of alcohol or nonprescribed drugs.

In early studies, tricyclic and monoamine oxidase inhibitor antidepressant agents were shown in double-blind, placebo-controlled trials to improve intrusive and depressive symptoms of PTSD. There are also uncontrolled reports of positive effects on PTSD symptoms of a number of medications, including carbamazepine (Tegretol), beta-blockers (e.g., propranolol (Inderal)), clonidine, benzodiazepines, and lithium. More recently, a number of placebo-controlled trials with relatively large sample sizes have demonstrated efficacy of selective serotonin reuptake inhibitors (SSRIs), specifically sertraline, fluoxetine, and paroxetine, in the treatment of PTSD (Friedman, Davidson, Mellman, & Southwick, 2000). In a recently published twelve-week placebo-controlled study of sertraline for treatment of PTSD in patients with comorbid alcohol dependence, a subgroup of individuals with early onset PTSD and less severe alcohol dependence showed improvement in PTSD symptoms and decreased alcohol consumption (Brady et al., 2005). There have also been advances made in the pharmacotherapeutic treatment of substance use disorders, particularly alcohol, opiate, and nicotine dependence. There are no controlled trials exploring the use of agents targeting alcohol use, such as naltrexone or acamprosate, in the treatment of alcohol dependence in individuals with comorbid PTSD. This is clearly an area that warrants investigation.

Organization of Services: Treating Posttraumatic Stress Disorder in Community Substance Abuse Treatment Settings

This section provides a community-based treatment perspective on using science-based assessments, screening tools, and models of care for PTSD to improve patient outcomes and to promote recovery. PTSD and trauma-related disorders are among the most common co-occurring disorders found in individuals with substance use problems. State-of-the-art assessment and treatment of trauma-related symptoms can substantially impact the overall quality of services offered by a community treatment program. Twenty years ago, counselors were taught not to address trauma in the first year of a patient's recovery. Today, the field is challenged to train counselors to integrate services for trauma-related psychopathology and substance use disorders into community treatment programs. Substance abuse treatment providers should learn to integrate the services that they provide for substance abuse with services that offer treatment for trauma-related psychopathology while maintaining the integrity of each intervention.

Slow Adoption of New Treatment Practices. It has been demonstrated that an evidence-based practice takes an average of seventeen years to make its way from the laboratory to the field (Balas & Boren, 2000); treatment practices for trauma in community substance abuse treatment programs are no exception. The use of evidence-based, manualized therapies is a relatively new approach for community treatment programs. In fact, most of the existing models for the integration of trauma and substance abuse services into community treatment programs are unknown within the treatment community. Although several models for integrated care have produced improved retention and outcome, community treatment programs have been slow to adopt them.

Selection and Adoption of Treatment Models. There are many challenges in moving a model from academia to the community. Successful adoption of an innovative practice by a community treatment program requires purchase of treatment manuals and training and practice in utilizing the intervention as described by the manual. SAMHSA's Addiction Technology Transfer Centers have developed a useful resource to facilitate the adoption of evidence-based models by community treatment programs: *The Change Book: A Blueprint for Technology Transfer* (*Blueprint*; originally published in 2000 and now in its second edition; Addiction Technology Transfer Center National Network, 2004). The *Blueprint* describes a process for successful organizational change and addresses such issues as the development of an agency planning team, assessment of organizational readiness, determination of the resources available versus resources necessary, assessment of staff needs, and measurement of results. These steps are conceptualized as part of a feedback loop for continuous evaluation and modification of the model.

Program administrators and supervisors must evaluate a new approach and be convinced that changing their current approach will make a difference in their patients' recovery and will be worth the necessary time and effort. Resources must be available to support the change. In his classic work on diffusion of innovations, Everett Rogers (1983) identifies key factors influencing a decision to adopt a new practice, including the relative advantage of the "new" versus the "existing" practice, the compatibility of a new practice with the organization's values, culture and current practices, and the degree of complexity involved in implementing the new practice. Each of these factors will influence an organization's selection of a model for their group.

There are no one-size-fits-all models to be adopted. Most manualized trauma treatment models were developed and evaluated for female trauma victims. Models used within the Veterans' Administration were developed for combat-related trauma. Although several models have been used in substance use disorder treatment programs, the amount of empirical evidence that supports their use varies. Many community treatment programs rely on SAMHSA to provide information concerning evidence-based interventions, yet SAMHSA's recommendations do not necessarily meet the most stringent scientific criteria. The efficacy of the promising practices described in SAMHSA's Treatment Improvement Protocols (TIPs) is not firmly established. Thus, community-based treatment programs need to carefully evaluate new models of treatment and decide which one to implement in order to improve treatment outcomes.

The Center for Substance Abuse Treatment and the National Trauma Consortium have written a report to assist community treatment programs in the evaluation of trauma models for use in their settings (Finkelstein et al., 2004). The report describes the four models that were studied in the SAMHSA-funded WCDVS (McHugo et al., 2005) and that are described above (TREM; Seeking Safety; ATRIUM; Helping Women Recover treatment). The report gives an overview of each model and compares them on theoretical approach, duration and intensity of services, open versus closed groups, adaptations for special populations, training and qualifications of group facilitator, and cost. However, the report does not explicitly address the strength of scientific evidence supporting each model. SAMHSA is also developing a TIP, Substance Abuse Treatment and Trauma, that includes screening and assessment instruments.

Role of Supervisors. Since training can be ineffective without broader organizational change that includes ongoing clinician feedback and coaching, effective clinical supervision is key to successful adoption of a new trauma treatment model. Manuals and/or training workshops without sufficient follow-up are likely to have negligible impact on practice (Miller, Yahne, Moyers, Martinez, & Pirritano, 2004). The typical staff response to the introduction of a manualized therapy is, "We already do that." Successful implementation requires a supervisor to become the resident expert in the intervention and to function as a "county extension agent" who provides on-site consultation for counselors with clinical questions. This staff member is also the "trauma champion," who advocates for changes that allow the organization and its staff to respond more sensitively to trauma issues. Clinical supervisors must help counselors maintain the integrity of the model, while, at the same time, recognizing that a model may need to be modified to fit the culture of the treatment organization and the community. Everett Rogers's work (1983) has demonstrated that a degree of "re-invention" is inevitable and, in fact, helps to promote adoption of new practices. The clinical supervisor must negotiate a balance between the degree of adaptation of a manualized treatment model and fidelity to the model. Supervisors should also be available to support counselors who are caring for trauma victims. Since strong clinical supervisors are essential for the successful adoption of new intervention strategies by treatment programs, it is fortunate that there has been an emphasis recently on training of clinical supervisors; training has focused on content and mechanics of effective clinical supervision.

Barriers to Using Medications. There are several barriers that community treatment programs encounter in using medications for the treatment of PTSD. First, many programs do not have easy access to a physician or other prescribing practitioners who can assess, treat, and follow all of the patients who might benefit from medication therapy. Second, even when help from a physician is available, many patients do not have the necessary resources to pay for medications. Many pharmaceutical companies have indigent care programs that make medications available to individuals with little or no insurance coverage. Treatment providers can help patients to access these programs. It is also important for clinicians to know which medications their patients are taking and to encourage medication compliance. When treating patients who are receiving treatment by several health care providers, counselors should maintain regular contact with all of the health care providers, especially with those who prescribe medication to their patients.

Conclusions. In the last ten years several efficacious models for simultaneous treatment of trauma and substance use disorders have been developed, but the models are seldom used. Community treatment programs face many challenges in implementing new evidence-based practices. In evaluating models, program administrators need to decide which model will have the best chance of improving patient outcomes and which model is the best fit for their organization. SAMHSA has published a blueprint for implementing new treatment approaches that agencies may find helpful. Effective clinical supervision is important for successful integration of innovative practices into existing programs. The supervisor should act as mentor, consultant, "trauma champion," and monitor. With strong program leaders, careful planning, thoughtful evaluation of treatment models, and good strategies for implementation and evaluation of new treatment models, community programs can offer the best treatment available to patients with co-occurring PTSD and substance use disorders.

Treatment Planning for the Case Examples

Case 1. After initial intake assessment, SR (whose case was presented at the beginning of this chapter (see "Case Presentations")) was referred to the Women's Intensive Outpatient Program, a four-hour-a-day, five-day-a-week program that lasts approximately six weeks and that is followed by a less intensive three-day-a-week program for another six weeks. Treatment consisted of group therapy, case management, parenting classes, self-help meetings, and weekly meetings with a counselor to work on treatment goals and to evaluate progress. Barriers to treatment, such as transportation and child care, were addressed. SR was referred to a trauma treatment specifically designed for women with substance use disorders and history of trauma (i.e., Seeking Safety model). Since SR continued to have depressed mood and sleep problems after her first six weeks in treatment, she was referred to a psychiatrist who visited the clinic weekly and who prescribed Paxil 20 mg daily.

SR completed the treatment program and remains in a weekly aftercare group. She has a network of supportive peers who are also attending aftercare. She has acquired skills to gain employment as a file clerk on a part-time basis. With the assistance of the program staff, she has been able to get subsidized housing so that she is no longer living with an abusive partner. SR reports feeling more optimistic about the future and has more confidence in her ability to care for her children.

Case 2. GB (whose case was presented at the beginning of this chapter (see "Case Presentations")) was diagnosed with PTSD and alcohol and marijuana abuse. A treatment plan was developed that included both pharmacotherapy and individual psychotherapy to address both the PTSD and substance use disorders. GB was started on sertraline (Zoloft) 50 mg daily, which was titrated to 200 mg daily. Individual psychotherapy initially involved psychoeducation and CBT. After GB's condition stabilized and he had acquired adequate coping skills, a referral was made for stress inoculation therapy and exposure therapy in order to desensitize GB to trauma-related stimuli. Individual sessions occurred twice weekly for six weeks and then weekly.

After twelve weeks of treatment, GB is responding well to the combined therapy. His mood has improved, and he experiences less intrusive thoughts about the trauma; he has been able to concentrate better. GB has stopped using alcohol and marijuana; he realized that this behavior only intensifies his distress and that these substances might adversely interact with his medication. He is sleeping better at night, and his work performance has improved.

Lessons Learned From Case Examples. As illustrated by these case descriptions, PTSD and substance use disorders commonly co-occur, but the presentation of these disorders and the relationship of one disorder to the other can vary widely. Patients in treatment for substance use disorders frequently report histories of childhood emotional and physical neglect or abuse, sexual or physical assault, robbery, or death of a loved one due to homicide. Individuals who experience traumatic events frequently report escalation of substance use after the trauma.

SUMMARY

In conclusion, individuals with substance use disorders have a high rate of trauma exposure and a higher rate of trauma-related psychiatric illnesses in comparison to the general population. Developing a treatment plan for patients with co-occurring substance use disorders and PTSD can be challenging for substance use treatment providers, since these patients have a poorer prognosis and more difficult course of treatment. There are several pharmacotherapeutic and psychotherapeutic treatments under investigation that show promise in the treatment of co-occurring PTSD and substance use disorders. Implementation and evaluation of these treatments in community treatment settings is important for optimizing treatment outcomes.

It is hoped that this chapter will help clinicians and treatment programs to recognize PTSD, to be aware of the potential impact of PTSD on the outcome of substance abuse treatment, to be aware of treatment options for this patient population, and to take important steps toward implementing well-informed treatment plans for patients with PTSD and other trauma-related disorders.

Suggestions for Further Reading

For readers who wish to study further in this area, we recommend:

- Brady, K. T., Sonne, S., Anton, R. F., Randall, C. L., Back, S. E., & Simpson, K. (2005). Sertraline in the treatment of co-occurring alcohol dependence and posttraumatic stress disorder. *Alcoholism: Clinical and Experimental Research, 29*, 395-401.

- Hien, D. A., Cohen, L. R., Miele, G. M., Litt, L. C., & Capstick, C. (2004). Promising treatments for women with comorbid PTSD and substance use disorders. *American Journal of Psychiatry, 161*, 1426-1432.

- Kessler, R. C., Sonnega, A., Bromet, E., Hughes, M., & Nelson, C. B. (1995). Posttraumatic stress disorder in the National Comorbidity Survey. *Archives of General Psychiatry, 52*, 1048-1060.

- Marshall, R. D., Olfson, M., Hellman, F., Blanco, C., Guardino, M., & Struening, E. L. (2001). Comorbidity, impairment, and suicidality in subthreshold PTSD. *American Journal of Psychiatry, 158*, 1467-1473.

References

Addiction Technology Transfer Center National Network (2004). *The change book: A blueprint for technology transfer* (2nd ed.). Kansas City, MO: Addiction Technology Transfer Center National Office.

American Psychiatric Association. (1994). *Diagnostic and statistical manual of mental disorders* (4th ed.). Washington, DC: Author.

American Psychiatric Association (2000). *Diagnostic and statistical manual of mental disorders* (4th ed., text rev.). Washington, DC: Author.

Back, S. E., Dansky, B. S., Carroll, K. M., Foa, E. B., & Brady, K. T. (2001). Exposure therapy in the treatment of PTSD among cocaine-dependent individuals: Description of procedures. *Journal of Substance Abuse Treatment, 21*, 35-45.

Balas, E. A., & Boren, S. A. (2000). Managing clinical knowledge for health care improvement. In J. Bemmel & A. T. McCray (Eds.), *Yearbook of medical informatics* (pp. 65-70). Stuttgart, Germany: Schattauer Verlagsgesellschaft mbH.

Blake, D. D., Weathers, F. W., Nagy, L. N., Kaloupek, D. G., Gusman, F. D., Charney, D. S., et al. (1995). The development of a Clinician-Administered PTSD Scale. *Journal of Traumatic Stress, 8*, 75-90.

Blake, D. D., Weathers, F. W., Nagy, L. M., Kaloupek, D. G., Klauminser, G., Charney, D. S., et al. (1990). A clinician rating scale for assessing current and lifetime PTSD: The CAPS-1. *Behavior Therapist, 18*, 187-188.

Brady, K. T. (1997). Posttraumatic stress disorder and comorbidity: Recognizing the many faces of PTSD. *Journal of Clinical Psychiatry, 58*, 12-15.

Brady, K. T., Dansky, B. S., Back S. E., Foa, E. B., & Carroll, K. M. (2001). Exposure therapy in the treatment of PTSD among cocaine-dependent individuals: Preliminary findings. *Journal of Substance Abuse Treatment, 21*, 47-54.

Brady, K. T., Killeen, T., Saladin, M. E., Dansky, B., & Becker, S. (1994). Comorbid substance abuse and posttraumatic stress disorder: Characteristics of women in treatment. *American Journal on Addictions, 3*, 160-163.

Brady, K. T., & Sinha, R. (2005). Co-occurring mental and substance use disorders: The neurobiological effects of chronic stress. *American Journal of Psychiatry, 162*, 1483-1493.

Brady, K. T., Sonne, S., Anton, R. F., Randall, C. L., Back, S.E., & Simpson, K. (2005). Sertraline in the treatment of co-occurring alcohol dependence and posttraumatic stress disorder. *Alcoholism: Clinical and Experimental Research, 29*, 395-401.

Breslau, N., Peterson, E. L., Kessler, R. C., & Schultz, L. R. (1999). Short screening scale for DSM-IV posttraumatic stress disorder. *American Journal of Psychiatry, 156*, 908-911.

Chambless, D. L., & Hollon, S. D. (1998). Defining empirically supported therapies. *Journal of Consulting and Clinical Psychology. 66*, 7-18.

Coffey, S. F., Dansky, B. S., & Brady, K. T. (2003). Exposure-based, trauma-focused therapy for comorbid posttraumatic stress disorder-substance use disorder. In P. Ouimette & P. J. Brown (Eds.), *Trauma and substance abuse: Causes, consequences, and treatment of comorbid disorders* (pp. 127-146). Washington, DC: American Psychological Association.

Covington, S. S. (1999). *Helping women recover: A program for treating addiction.* San Francisco: Jossey-Bass.

Donovan, B., Padin-Rivera, E., & Kowaliw, S. (2001). "Transcend": Initial outcomes from a posttraumatic stress disorder/substance abuse treatment program. *Journal of Traumatic Stress, 14*, 757-772.

Fallot, R. D., & Harris, M. (2002). The Trauma Recovery and Empowerment Model (TREM): Conceptual and practical issues in a group intervention for women. *Community Mental Health Journal, 38*, 475-485.

Ferrada-Noli, M., Asberg, M., Ormstad, K., Lundin, T., Sundbom, E. (1998). Suicidal behavior after severe trauma, part I: PTSD diagnoses, psychiatric comorbidity, and assessments of suicidal behavior. *Journal of Traumatic Stress, 11*, 103-112.

Finkelstein, N., VandeMark, N., Fallot, R., Brown, V., Cadiz, S., & Heckman, J. (2004). *Enhancing substance abuse recovery through integrated trauma treatment*. Sarasota, FL: National Trauma Consortium. Report prepared for the Center for Substance Abuse Treatment, Substance Abuse and Mental Health Services Administration.

First, M. B., Spitzer, R. L., Gibbon, M., & Williams, J. B. W. (2002, November). Structured Clinical Interview for DSM-IV-TR Axis I Disorders, Patient Edition (SCID-I/P). New York: Biometrics Research Department, New York State Psychiatric Institute.

Foa, E. B. (1995). *Posttraumatic stress diagnostic scale*. Minneapolis, MN: National Computer Systems.

Foa, E. B., Riggs, D. S., Dancu, C. V., & Rothbaum, B. O. (1993). Reliability and validity of a brief instrument for assessing post-traumatic stress disorder. *Journal of Traumatic Stress, 6*, 459-473.

Ford, J., Kasimer, N., MacDonald, M., & Savill, G. (2000). *Trauma Adaptive Recovery Group Education and Therapy (TARGET): Participant guidebook and leader manual*. Farmington, CT: University of Connecticut Health Center.

Ford, J. D., & Kidd, P. (1998). Early childhood trauma and disorders of extreme stress as predictors of treatment outcome with chronic posttraumatic stress disorder. *Journal of Traumatic Stress, 11, 743-761.*

Friedman, M., Davidson, J. R. T., Mellman, T. A., & Southwick, S. M. (2000). Pharmacotherapy. In E. B. Foa, T. M. Keane, & M. J. Friedman (Eds.), *Effective treatments for PTSD: Practice guidelines from the International Society for Traumatic Stress Studies* (pp. 84-105). New York: Guildford Press.

Gray, M. J., Litz, B. T., Hsu, J L., & Lombardo, T. W. (2004). Psychometric properties of the life events checklist. *Assessment, 11*, 330-341,

Hasin, D. S., Samet, S., Nunes, E., Meydan, J., Matseoane, K., & Waxman, R. (2006). Diagnosis of comorbid disorders in substance users: Psychiatric Research Interview for Substance and Mental Disorders (PRISM-IV). *American Journal of Psychiatry, 163,* 689-696.

Hasin, D. S., Trautman, K. D., Miele, G. M., Samet, S., Smith, M., & Endicott, J. (1996). Psychiatric Research Interview for Substance and Mental Disorders (PRISM): Reliability for substance abusers. *American Journal of Psychiatry, 153*, 1195-1201.

Henderson, A. S., & Jorm, A. F. (1990). Do mental health surveys disturb? *Psychological Medicine, 20*, 721-724.

Hien, D. A., Cohen, L. R., Miele, G. M., Litt, L. C., & Capstick, C. (2004). Promising treatments for women with comorbid PTSD and substance use disorders. *American Journal of Psychiatry, 161*, 1426-1432.

Hien, D. A., Wells, E., Jiang, H., Killeen, T., Suarez, L., Hansen, C., et al. (in press). Effectiveness of two behavior therapy groups for women with PTSD and comorbid substance use disorders: Findings from the National Institute of Drug Abuse Clinical Trials Network "Women and Trauma" multi-site study. *Journal of Consulting and Clinical Psychology.*

Jacobsen, L. K., Southwick, S. M., & Kosten, T. R. (2001). Substance use disorders in patients with posttraumatic stress disorder: A review of the literature. *American Journal of Psychiatry, 158*, 1184-1190.

Kessler, R. C., Sonnega, A., Bromet, E., Hughes, M., & Nelson, C. B. (1995). Posttraumatic stress disorder in the National Comorbidity Survey. *Archives of General Psychiatry, 52*, 1048-1060.

Keane, T. M., Wolfe, J., & Taylor, K. L. (1987). Post-traumatic stress disorder: Evidence for diagnostic validity and methods of psychological assessment. *Journal of Clinical Psychology, 43*, 32-43.

Kreek, M. J., & Koob, G. F. (1998). Drug dependence: Stress and dysregulation of brain reward pathways. *Drug and Alcohol Dependence, 51,* 23-47.

Marshall, R. D., Olfson, M., Hellman, F., Blanco, C., Guardino, M., & Struening, E. L. (2001). Comorbidity, impairment, and suicidality in subthreshold PTSD. *American Journal of Psychiatry, 158,* 1467-1473.

McHugo, G. J., Kammerer, N., Jackson, E. W., Markoff, L. S., Gatz, M., Larson, M.J., et al. (2005). Women, Co-occurring Disorders, and Violence Study: Evaluation design and study population. *Journal of Substance Abuse Treatment, 28,* 91-107.

Meltzer-Brody, S., Churchill, E., & Davidson, J. R. (1999). Derivation of the SPAN, a brief diagnostic screening test for post-traumatic stress disorder. *Psychiatry Research, 88,* 63-70.

Miller, D., & Guidry, L. (2001). *Addictions and trauma recovery: Healing the body, mind and spirit.* New York: W.W. Norton & Company.

Miller, W. R., Yahne, C. E., Moyers, T. B., Martinez, J., & Pirritano, M. (2004). A randomized trial of methods to help clinicians learn motivational interviewing. *Journal of Consulting and Clinical Psychology, 72,* 1050-1062.

Najavits, L. M. (2002). Seeking Safety: A new psychotherapy for posttraumatic stress disorder and substance use disorder. In P. Ouimette & P. Brown (Eds.), *Trauma and substance abuse: Causes, consequences, and treatment of comorbid disorders* (pp. 147-170). Washington, DC: American Psychological Association.

Najavits, L. M., Weiss, R. D., Shaw, S. R., & Muenz, L. (1998). "Seeking safety": Outcome of a new cognitive-behavioral psychotherapy for women with posttraumatic stress disorder and substance dependence. *Journal of Traumatic Stress, 11,* 437-456.

Ouimette, P. C., Finney, J. W., & Moos, R. H. (1999). Two-year posttreatment functioning and coping of substance abuse patients with posttraumatic stress disorder. *Psychology of Addictive Behaviors, 13,* 105-114.

Pelcovitz, D., van der Kolk, B. A., Roth, S., Mandel, F., Kaplan, S., & Resick, P. (1997). Development of a criteria set and a structured interview for disorders of extreme stress (SIDES). *Journal of Traumatic Stress, 10,* 3-16.

Prins, A., Ouimette, P., Kimerling, R., Cameron, R. P., Hugelshofer, D. S., Shaw-Hegwer, J., Thrailkill, A., Gusman, F. D., & Sheikh, J. I. (2004). The primary care PTSD screen (PC-PTSD): Development and operating characteristics. *Primary Care Psychiatry, 9,* 9-14.

Read, J. P., Brown, P. J., & Kahler, C. W. (2004). Substance use and posttraumatic stress disorders: Symptom interplay and effects on outcome. *Addictive Behaviors, 29,* 1665-1672.

Robins, L. N., Helzer, J. E., Croughan, J. L., & Ratcliff, K. S. (1981). National Institute of Mental Health diagnostic interview schedule: Its history, characteristics, and validity. *Archives of General Psychiatry, 38,* 381-389.

Robins, L. N., Helzer, J. E., Croughan, J., Williams, J. B. W., & Spitzer, R. L. (1981). *NIMH diagnostic interview schedule, version III* (DHHS Publication No. ADM-T-42-3). Washington, DC: U.S. Government Printing Office.

Robins, L. N., Wing, J., Wittchen, H. U., Helzer, J. E., Babor, T. F., Burke, J., et al. (1988). The Composite International Diagnostic Interview: An epidemiologic instrument suitable for use in conjunction with different diagnostic systems and in different cultures. *Archives of General Psychiatry, 45,* 1069-1077.

Rogers, E. (1983). *Diffusion of innovations* (3rd ed.). New York: Collier Macmillan.

Schutzwohl, M., & Maercker, A. (1999). Effects of varying diagnostic criteria for posttraumatic stress disorder are endorsing the concept of partial PTSD. *Journal of Traumatic Stress, 12,* 155-165.

Sheehan, D. V., Lecrubier, Y., Sheehan, K. H., Amorim, P., Janavs, J., Weiller, E., et al. (1998). The development and validation of a structured diagnostic psychiatric interview for DSM-IV and ICD-10. *Journal of Clinical Psychiatry, 59*(Suppl. 20), 22-23.

Sherin, K. M., Sinacore, J. M., Li, X. Q., Zitter, R. E., & Shakil, A. (1998). HITS: A short domestic violence screening tool for use in a family practice setting. *Family Medicine, 30*, 508-512.

Stewart, J. (2003). Stress and relapse to drug seeking: Studies in laboratory animals shed light on mechanisms and sources of long-term vulnerability. *American Journal on Addictions, 12*, 1-17.

Triffleman, E. (2000). Gender differences in a controlled pilot study of psychosocial treatments in substance dependent patients with post-traumatic stress disorder: Design considerations and outcomes. *Alcoholism Treatment Quarterly, 18*, 113-126.

van der Kolk, B. A., McFarlane, A. C., & Weisaeth, L. (Eds.) (1996). *Traumatic stress: The effects of overwhelming experience on mind, body and society.* New York: Guilford Press.

Vlahov, D., Galea, S., Ahern, J., Resnick, H., Boscarino, J. A., Gold, J., et al. (2004). Consumption of cigarettes, alcohol, and marijuana among New York City residents six months after the September 11 terrorist attacks. *American Journal of Drug & Alcohol Abuse, 30*, 385-407.

Weathers, F. W. (1993). *Empirically derived scoring rules for the clinician administered PTSD scale.* Unpublished manuscript.

Zlotnick, C., & Pearlstein, T. (1997). Validation of the Structured Interview for Disorders of Extreme Stress. *Comprehensive Psychiatry, 38*, 243-247.

Chapter 4

Other Anxiety Disorders in Patients With Substance Use Disorders: Panic Disorder, Agoraphobia, Social Anxiety Disorder, and Generalized Anxiety Disorder

by Carlos Blanco, M.D., Ph.D., Carrie A. Davies, B.S., and Edward V. Nunes, M.D.

INTRODUCTION

While major depression and posttraumatic stress disorder (PTSD), covered in Chapters 1 and 3 of this volume, are the most commonly encountered mood and anxiety disorders among substance-dependent patients seeking treatment, three other anxiety disorders are also prevalent in this population: panic disorder (with or without agoraphobia), social anxiety disorder (SAD; formerly called social phobia), and generalized anxiety disorder (GAD). The last three of these disorders have been less studied among substance-dependent patients, and many clinicians working with substance-dependent patients may be less familiar with them. However, these disorders cause significant suffering and functional impairment; they may promote substance abuse; and they respond to treatment with specific Cognitive Behavioral Therapies (CBTs), antidepressant medications, or combinations of the two. Thus, clinicians who are able to recognize these disorders will be better able to help their patients. This chapter aims to teach clinicians who are working with substance-dependent patients how to recognize and oversee the management of panic disorder, agoraphobia, SAD, and GAD.

Panic Disorder and Agoraphobia

Patients may speak of having "anxiety attacks," a term that patients may use to refer to anything from a feeling of sudden fear that normally occurs when someone feels physically threatened to states of heightened anxiety that are often part of stimulant intoxication or withdrawal from opioids, sedatives, or alcohol. These symptoms are not panic attacks. A panic attack (see Table 4-1A) has a more specific constellation of symptoms: it is an episode of an intense feeling of fear with sudden onset, rapid increase in intensity over less than ten minutes, accompanied by physical symptoms, often including chest pain and shortness of breath or a feeling of suffocating. Patients often vividly remember their first panic attack and frequently will have rushed to the hospital, believing that they are either dying of a heart attack or "going crazy." Panic attacks may occur in situations that patients fear (e.g., social situations in patients with SAD, heights, crowds, closed-in spaces, or public transportation in patients with agoraphobia). Panic attacks often occur "out of the blue" in routine situations with no apparent threat.

Agoraphobia (see Table 4-1B), literally the fear of open spaces, often develops after panic attacks. This phobia sometimes seems like a conditioned fear response (i.e., individuals begin to fear situations where they have experienced panic attacks or where they feel it would be particularly unpleasant to have a panic attack). Subways, buses, airplanes, bridges, crowded stores, traffic jams, elevators, or other closed-in spaces are among commonly feared situations. A common theme here is that these are situations for which it might be difficult to escape quickly, and during a panic attack people often feel a strong urge to escape or "get out and get air." Such individuals often begin to restrict their movements to avoid feared situations, causing them to have trouble getting to work, attending treatment sessions, and meeting other responsibilities. In its most severe form, agoraphobia causes patients to become house-bound, fearful of leaving their home. Thus, functional impairment can be significant.

Panic disorder (see Table 4-1C) consists of either frequent, repeated panic attacks or panic attacks with agoraphobia. In the general population, many individuals (around 23 percent) have had one or more isolated panic attacks, while large-scale surveys have shown that around 5 percent have had panic disorder at some point during their lifetime, and around 3 percent suffer from current panic disorder (Grant et al., 2006; Kessler et al., 1994; Kessler et al., 2006). These same surveys have shown that panic disorder increases the risk of having a substance use disorder (and vice versa) by a factor of at least 2 to 3 (Grant et al., 2006).

Social Anxiety Disorder

SAD (see Table 4-1D) is an extreme form of shyness in which individuals fear social situations, such as meeting new people, appearing at social events, or speaking at meetings, and feel physically sick, similar to a panic attack, if forced to engage in such situations. This disorder can be quite disabling; affected individuals may restrict their social lives (including dating) or pass up new opportunities or promotions at work that would require more interpersonal interaction (such as speaking at meetings) or that would "put them on the spot."

Patients who say that they do not like group therapy or self-help meetings, such as Alcoholics Anonymous (AA) or Narcotics Anonymous (NA), may not be resisting treatment. Some will have social anxiety disorder and fear such groups because they fear being asked to speak at meetings. Due to the nature of their disorder, individuals with social anxiety may also be afraid to make requests at the clinic to ensure that their needs are met (e.g., requesting a change of schedule or counselor, reporting any new symptoms, or talking about potential lapses).

Table 4-1A
DSM-IV Criteria for Panic Attack

Symptoms	DSM-IV Criteria[a, b, c]	Issues in Substance-Dependent Patients	PRISM Questions to Aid Diagnosis[d, e]
Core Criteria	A discrete period of intense fear or discomfort, in which four (or more) of the following symptoms developed abruptly and reached a peak within 10 minutes.	Symptoms of panic attacks may occur as part of intoxication or withdrawal from a variety of substances; common examples noted below.	During … [the] worst attack …
	(1) palpitations, pounding heart, or accelerated heart rate	Stimulant or cannabis intoxication. Alcohol, sedative, or opioid withdrawal	… did your heart race, pound, or skip a beat?
	(2) sweating	Stimulant, hallucinogen intoxication. Alcohol, sedative, or opioid withdrawal	… did you perspire or sweat?
	(3) trembling or shaking	Stimulant intoxication. Alcohol, sedative, or opioid withdrawal	… did you actually shake or tremble?
	(4) sensations of shortness of breath or smothering	Less common symptoms of intoxication or withdrawal	… were you short of breath? Did you feel that you were having trouble catching your breath? Did you feel as if you were smothering?
	(5) feeling of choking	Less common symptoms of intoxication or withdrawal	… did you feel as if you were choking?
	(6) chest pain or discomfort	Stimulant intoxication	… did you have chest pain or pressure?
	(7) nausea or abdominal distress	Alcohol, sedative, or opioid withdrawal	… did you feel nauseated, or have an upset stomach, or have the feeling that you were going to have diarrhea?
	(8) feeling dizzy, unsteady, lightheaded, or faint	Intoxication from most substances	… did you feel dizzy or unsteady? Did you feel lightheaded or as if you might faint?

(Continued)

Symptoms	DSM-IV Criteria[a,b,c]	Issues in Substance-Dependent Patients	PRISM Questions to Aid Diagnosis[d,e]
	(9) derealization (feelings of unreality) or depersonalization (being detached from oneself)	Cannabis, hallucinogen, or club drug intoxication	… did things around you seem unreal? Did you feel detached from things around you or detached from part of your body?
	(10) fear of losing control or going crazy	Cannabis, hallucinogen intoxication	… were you afraid you were going crazy or that you might lose control?
	(11) fear of dying	Severe stimulant, cannabis, or hallucinogen intoxication ("bad trip")	… were you afraid that you might die?
	(12) paresthesias (numbness or tingling sensations)	Stimulant intoxication	… did you have tingling or numbness in parts of your body?
	(13) chills or hot flashes	Various intoxication or withdrawal syndromes	… did you have flushes, hot flashes, or chills?

(a) A panic attack occurs as a symptom within the context of multiple anxiety disorders, including panic disorder with agoraphobia, panic disorder without agoraphobia, specific phobia, social anxiety disorder (formerly called social phobia), generalized anxiety disorder, and substance-induced anxiety disorder; a panic attack is not diagnosed as a separate entity.
(b) American Psychiatric Association (1994).
(c) Reprinted with permission from the *Diagnostic and Statistical Manual of Mental Disorders*, Fourth Edition (Copyright 1994). American Psychiatric Association.
(d) Hasin et al. (2006).
(e) Reprinted with permission.

Table 4-1B
DSM-IV Criteria for Agoraphobia

Symptoms	DSM-IV Criteria[a, b, c]	Issues in Substance-Dependent Patients	PRISM Questions to Aid Diagnosis[e, f]
Core Criteria	A. Anxiety about being in places or situations from which escape might be difficult (or embarrassing) or in which help may not be available in the event of having an unexpected or situationally predisposed panic attack or panic-like symptoms. Agoraphobic fears typically involve characteristic clusters of situations that include being outside the home alone; being in a crowd or standing in a line; being on a bridge; and traveling in a bus, train, or automobile.	Not typical of any substance intoxication or withdrawal syndrome. Hence presence of clear-cut agoraphobia is strong evidence of an anxiety disorder that is independent of substance use disorder.	Were you ever very afraid of panicking or losing control of yourself in any of the following situations: ... shopping in a big store or supermarket? ... being away from home by yourself? ... crossing busy or wide streets? ... being in a crowded place, such as a movie theater or restaurant? ... traveling in a car, bus or train? ... crossing a bridge or going through a tunnel? ... being in a crowd or standing in line? ... being in any other place or situation because you might suddenly feel panicky? Were you afraid that if you panicked you might not be able to get away or you might attract a lot of attention?
	B. The situations are avoided (e.g., travel is restricted) or else are endured with marked distress or with anxiety about having a panic attack or panic-like symptoms, or require the presence of a companion.	Not typical of any substance intoxication or withdrawal syndrome. Convincing evidence of an independent anxiety disorder.	Was there ever a time when you avoided [situation] because you were so afraid of panicking or losing control of yourself there?...Did you ever find that you needed to take someone with you if you were going to be [situation]?...When you were in [situation] were you very nervous the whole time?
Other Criteria	C. The anxiety or phobic avoidance is not better accounted for by another mental disorder such as [social anxiety disorder] [e.g., avoidance limited to social situations because of fear of embarrassment], specific phobia (e.g., avoidance limited to a single situation like elevators), obsessive compulsive disorder (e.g., avoidance of dirt in someone with an obsession about contamination), posttraumatic stress disorder (e.g., avoidance of stimuli associated with a severe stressor), or separation anxiety disorder (e.g., avoidance of leaving home or relatives)[d].		Were you afraid of [situation] because: ... you might be reminded of a traumatic event in your life? ... you would be in contact with germs or dirt? ... you would be embarrassed by a behavior you couldn't control? ... you were depressed and weren't interested in doing things? ... you thought you were being followed?

(a) Agoraphobia occurs as a symptom within the context of panic disorder with agoraphobia and agoraphobia without history of panic disorder; agoraphobia is not diagnosed as a separate entity.
(b) American Psychiatric Association (1994).
(c) Reprinted with permission from the *Diagnostic and Statistical Manual of Mental Disorders*, Fourth Edition (Copyright 1994). American Psychiatric Association.
(d) Consult *DSM-IV* criteria (American Psychiatric Association, 1994) for social anxiety disorder, specific phobia, obsessive compulsive disorder, posttraumatic stress disorder, separation anxiety disorder.
(e) Hasin et al. (2006).
(f) Reprinted with permission.

Table 4-1C
***DSM-IV* Criteria for Panic Disorder (With or Without Agoraphobia)**

Symptoms	*DSM-IV* Criteria[a, b, c]	Issues in Substance-Dependent Patients	PRISM Questions to Aid Diagnosis[f, g]
Core Symptoms	A. Both (1) and (2):		
	(1) recurrent unexpected panic attacks	Useful to ask whether panic attacks occur during intoxication or withdrawal or at times when there is no acute intoxication or withdrawal.	Have you ever had a panic attack, when you suddenly felt extremely frightened, overwhelmed, or uncomfortable and you didn't know why it was happening? ... Did you have at least 2 panic attacks that happened totally out-of-the-blue, for no real reason?
	(2) at least one of the attacks has been followed by 1 month (or more) of one (or more) of the following:	Preoccupation with panic attacks is not typical of substance intoxication or withdrawal. Patients sometimes describe avoiding cocaine or cannabis after having a panic attack while intoxicated.	
	(a) persistent concern about having additional attacks		After any [panic attack], did you ever worry for as long as a month about having another one?
	(b) worry about the implications of the attack or its consequences (e.g., losing control, having a heart attack, "going crazy")		Did you ever worry for as long as a month about what might happen as a result of the attack?
	(c) a significant change in behavior related to the attacks.		Did you make any changes in your everyday behavior or your plans for the future after you had one of these attacks?
Associated Symptoms	B. [Absence of agoraphobia for a diagnosis of panic disorder without agoraphobia; presence of agoraphobia for a diagnosis of panic disorder with agoraphobia].		

(Continued)

Symptoms	DSM-IV Criteria[a, b, c]	Issues in Substance-Dependent Patients	PRISM Questions to Aid Diagnosis[f, g]
Other Criteria	C. The panic attacks are not due to the direct physiological effects of a substance (e.g., a drug of abuse, a medication)[d] or a general medical condition (e.g., hyperthyroidism).	See Table 4-1A	Did this attack occur after you drank a lot of coffee or other caffeinated drink, used over-the-counter diet pills or sleep aid, or got high on drugs? … Did this attack occur while you were physically ill or had a medical condition?
	D. The panic attacks are not better accounted for by another mental disorder such as [social anxiety disorder] [e.g., occurring on exposure to feared social situations), specific phobia (e.g., on exposure to specific phobic situation), obsessive compulsive disorder (e.g., on exposure to dirt in someone with an obsession about contamination), posttraumatic stress disorder (e.g., in response to stimuli associated with a severe stressor), or separation anxiety disorder (e.g., in response to being away from home or close relatives)[e].	Remain alert to the common co-occurrence of multiple mood and anxiety syndromes.	

[a] Panic disorder is diagnosed in the presence or absence of agoraphobia.
[b] American Psychiatric Association (1994).
[c] Reprinted with permission from the *Diagnostic and Statistical Manual of Mental Disorders*, Fourth Edition (Copyright 1994). American Psychiatric Association.
[d] Consult *DSM-IV* criteria (American Psychiatric Association, 1994) for substance intoxication and withdrawal syndromes.
[e] Consult *DSM-IV* criteria (American Psychiatric Association, 1994) for social anxiety disorder, specific phobia, obsessive compulsive disorder, posttraumatic stress disorder, separation anxiety disorder.
[f] Hasin et al. (2006).
[g] Reprinted with permission.

SAD typically has onset in childhood, with a chronic lifelong course. Thus, it is important to get a good history of childhood experiences, including elementary school. When asked how they found elementary school, patients with SAD will often recall that they were nervous, that they never raised their hand in class, and that they feared being called upon by the teacher because it made them feel frightened and sick. Such individuals often report that they became involved with alcohol or drugs during adolescence because these substances helped them to relax temporarily and to engage socially with their peers. This disorder is surprisingly common, affecting 6-10 percent or more of the general population, according to large-scale surveys (Grant et al., 2005a; Kessler, Stein, & Berglund, 1998; Schneier, Johnson, Horning, Liebowitz, & Weissman, 1992). The same surveys show social anxiety disorder at least doubles the likelihood of having a substance use disorder and vice versa (Grant et al., 2005a; Schneier et al., 1992). Social anxiety disorder is a particularly common disorder among substance-dependent patients in treatment.

Generalized Anxiety Disorder

Patients with GAD (see Table 4-1E) experience excessive worry, accompanied by several associated symptoms including irritability, difficulty concentrating, or physical manifestations of anxiety such as restlessness, fatigue, muscle tension, and difficulty sleeping. GAD usually has a gradual onset in the late teens to early 20s, tends to run a chronic course, is associated with significant impairment, such as unemployment and divorce, and is often accompanied by other depressive or anxiety disorders. Population surveys show that GAD occurs in approximately 4 percent of the general population on a lifetime basis, and it increases the likelihood of alcoholism or another substance use disorder (or vice versa) by a factor of 3 or more (Grant et al., 2005b; Kessler, Chiu, Demler, Merikangas, & Walters, 2005; Kessler, Keller, & Wittchen, 2001). However, GAD can be particularly difficult to assess among substance-dependent patients, because its symptoms are relatively nonspecific. Substance-dependent patients often live under stressful circumstances and have many real problems to worry about. Virtually all of the symptoms of GAD also occur as part of either intoxication or withdrawal from alcohol and other drugs. Substance-dependent patients often are irritable and often complain of anxiety and insomnia among other GAD symptoms. Some of these patients may have experienced relief from benzodiazepines in the past and may ask for a prescription for benzodiazepines. A careful history and knowledge of the diagnostic criteria will enable the clinician to better understand such symptoms and to distinguish effects of substances and symptoms of other psychiatric disorders from symptoms of GAD.

Substance-Induced Anxiety Disorder

When evaluating anxiety disorders among substance-dependent patients, clinicians are faced with the challenge of determining if symptoms of anxiety disorders, particularly panic attacks and symptoms associated with GAD, represent an independent anxiety disorder or the usual or expected effects of substances (including effects from substance intoxication, withdrawal, and chronic exposure to substances). Table 4-2 describes common symptoms that are shared by *Diagnostic and Statistical Manual of Mental Disorders,* 4th edition (*DSM-IV;* American Psychiatric Association, 1994) anxiety disorders and *DSM-IV* syndromes of substance intoxication and withdrawal. Further, *DSM-IV* defines a diagnosis called substance-induced anxiety disorder.

Similar to substance-induced mood disorder (see Chapter 1 of this volume), substance-induced anxiety disorder is defined by the *DSM-IV* as an anxiety disorder that has occurred only during ongoing substance use intoxication and withdrawal in which symptoms of anxiety exceed expected symptoms of intoxication or withdrawal and warrant clinical attention in the form of follow-up and treatment (see Table 4-1F).

To date, very little research on *DSM-IV* substance-induced anxiety disorder has been conducted, and this chapter will not focus on it. Instead, we encourage readers to learn to diagnose anxiety disorders and to look for evidence that these disorders are independent of substance use, including a history of onset prior to substance abuse or occurrence of symptoms during periods of abstinence or symptoms that likely are not caused by substances (e.g., fear of public places (agoraphobia) or fear of social situations (SAD)). Substance-induced anxiety disorder exists as a fall-back diagnosis. If a patient presents with significant anxiety symptoms, but a clinician cannot establish that they are independent of substance use, then substance-induced anxiety disorder is the appropriate diagnosis. As the clinician follows the anxiety symptoms over time, he/she should continue to collect evidence to determine if the anxiety disorder is independent of substance use and if it interferes with functioning enough to warrant specific treatment despite uncertainty in the diagnosis.

Identifying Specific Mood or Anxiety Disorders in the Presence of Depression, Anxiety, Irritability, or Impaired Function

When patients present with emotional symptoms or difficulty functioning, clinicians are encouraged to heed the warning of the old saying "Where there's smoke, there's fire." Look for, and try to identify, a specific mood or anxiety disorder. Clinicians should not simply rely on a consulting psychologist or psychiatrist to evaluate these "difficult" or frustrating patients; further, a clinician who requests the aid of a consultant should not simply say, "Patient is anxious and not doing well in treatment; please evaluate." Since the time of consultants is limited, it is better to submit a more detailed and sophisticated consultation request, one in which the primary clinician relays a carefully gathered clinical history and evidence that supports the diagnosis of one or several psychiatric disorders. Detailed requests will help consultants to focus and use their time more efficiently. A detailed request might read:

> Patient is anxious and not doing well in treatment; patient has a history of childhood physical abuse and significant traumatic experiences as an adult. Patient may have social anxiety disorder: he feels anxious in many social situations such as in groups or when he meets strangers; see attached narrative for details. Please evaluate.

However, not all patients with mood or anxiety disorders are "difficult" (i.e., they complain a lot and demand attention). Like some fires that do not produce a lot of smoke, some patients (particularly those with chronic depression, agoraphobia, or SAD) suffer quietly, having accepted symptoms and functional limitations. In fact, paradoxically, these patients may appear as model patients, rarely complaining and hesitating to voice their needs or concerns. An example would be a talented patient with SAD who has always worked in entry-level positions and who has turned down promotions to avoid

Table 4-1D
DSM-IV Criteria for Social Anxiety Disorder

Symptoms	DSM-IV Criteria[a, b]	Issues in Substance-Dependent Patients	PRISM Questions to Aid Diagnosis[f, g]
Core Symptom	A. A marked and persistent fear of one or more social or performance situations in which the person is exposed to unfamiliar people or to possible scrutiny by others. The individual fears that he/she will act in a way (or show anxiety symptoms) that will be humiliating or embarrassing. . . . In children, there must be evidence of the capacity for age-appropriate social relationships with familiar people and the anxiety must occur in peer settings, not just in interactions with adults.	Not typical of any substance intoxication or withdrawal syndrome. Hence presence of clear-cut social anxiety is strong evidence of an anxiety disorder that is independent of substance use disorder.	Were you ever very afraid of being humiliated or embarrassed by: . . . speaking or performing in front of other people? . . . meeting new people or talking at social gatherings? . . . eating in front of others? . . . writing in front of others? . . . using public bathrooms? . . . any other social activity?
Associated Symptoms	B. Exposure to the feared social situation almost invariably provokes anxiety, which may take the form of a situationally bound or situationally predisposed panic attack. . . . In children, the anxiety may be expressed by crying, tantrums, freezing, or shrinking from social situations with unfamiliar people.	Not typical of any substance intoxication or withdrawal syndrome. Convincing evidence of an independent anxiety disorder.	Was there ever a time when you were always very nervous as soon as you knew you had to [activity]?. . . When you used to [activity], were you always very nervous as soon as you were in the situation?
	C. The person recognizes that the fear is excessive or unreasonable. . . . In children, this feature may be absent.		During the time that you were afraid of [activity], did you think: . . . that your [fear] was unreasonable? . . . that you were more afraid than you should have been?
	D. The feared social or performance situations are avoided or else are endured with intense anxiety or distress.	Not typical of any substance intoxication or withdrawal syndrome.	Was there ever a time when you avoided [activity] because you were so afraid of embarrassing yourself? . . . When you had to [activity], were you very nervous the whole time?

(Continued)

	DSM-IV Criteria[a, b]	Issues in Substance-Dependent Patients	PRISM Questions to Aid Diagnosis[f, g]
Symptoms	E. The avoidance, anxious anticipation, or distress in the feared social or performance situation(s) interferes significantly with the person's normal routine, occupational (academic) functioning, or social activities or relationships, or there is marked distress about having the [disorder].		Did your fear or avoidance ever: … interfere with your normal daily activities? … make it harder for you to take care of your everyday responsibilities? … cause any problems for you at work or school? … cause any problems in your relationships or social life? Did anyone ever comment or complain about your fear or the problems associated with it? … Did you often feel very upset about this fear even when you weren't in the situation?
	F. In individuals under age 18 years, the duration is at least 6 months.		How old were you when a fear of embarrassing or humiliating yourself in a specific situation first began to cause problems for you? … Did this go on for at least 6 months?
Other Criteria	G. The fear or avoidance is not due to the direct physiological effects of a substance (e.g., a drug of abuse, a medication)[c] or a general medical condition and is not better accounted for by another mental disorder (e.g., panic disorder with or without agoraphobia, separation anxiety disorder, body dysmorphic disorder, a pervasive developmental disorder, or schizoid personality disorder)[d].	A patient may have become frightened in a social situation because of being severely intoxicated, but this experience does not usually result in persistent fear and avoidance of such social situations in the absence of intoxication.	
	H. If a general medical condition or another mental disorder is present, the fear in Criterion A is unrelated to it (e.g., the fear is not of stuttering, trembling in Parkinson's disease, or exhibiting abnormal eating behavior in anorexia nervosa or bulimia nervosa)[e]		

(a) American Psychiatric Association (1994).
(b) Reprinted with permission from the *Diagnostic and Statistical Manual of Mental Disorders*, Fourth Edition (Copyright 1994). American Psychiatric Association.
(c) Consult *DSM-IV* criteria (American Psychiatric Association, 1994) for substance intoxication and withdrawal syndromes.
(d) Consult *DSM-IV* criteria (American Psychiatric Association, 1994) for panic disorder with agoraphobia, panic disorder without agoraphobia, separation anxiety disorder, body dysmorphic disorder, pervasive developmental disorders, schizoid personality disorder.
(e) Consult *DSM-IV* criteria (American Psychiatric Association, 1994) for anorexia nervosa and bulimia nervosa.
(f) Hasin et al. (2006).
(g) Reprinted with permission.

Table 4-1E
DSM-IV Criteria for Generalized Anxiety Disorder

Symptoms	DSM-IV Criteria[a, b]	Issues in Substance-Dependent Patients	PRISM Questions to Aid Diagnosis[e, f]
Core Symptom	A. Excessive anxiety and worry (apprehensive expectation), occurring more days than not for at least 6 months, about a number of events or activities (such as work or school performance).	Substance-dependent patients often live in stressful circumstances with many real worries.	In your entire life, was there ever a time lasting at least 6 months when you were very worried, nervous, or anxious about many different things?
	B. The person finds it difficult to control worry.		During that period when you were [worrying] the most, did you try to stop yourself from worrying?
Associated Symptoms	C. The anxiety and worry are associated with three (or more) of the following six symptoms (with at least some symptoms present for more days than not for the past 6 months). . . . Only one item required in children	These physical, emotional, and cognitive symptoms may result from a variety of intoxication or withdrawal syndromes.	During those months, when you felt most [worried] . . .
	(1) restlessness or feeling keyed up or on edge		. . . did you often feel restless, keyed up or on edge?
	(2) being easily fatigued		. . . did you often get tired easily?
	(3) difficulty concentrating or mind going blank		. . . did you often have trouble concentrating? Did your mind often go blank?
	(4) irritability		. . . were you often irritable or annoyed?
	(5) muscle tension		. . . did your muscles often feel tense?
	(6) sleep disturbance (difficulty falling or staying asleep, or restless unsatisfying sleep).		. . . did you often have trouble falling asleep or staying asleep? Did you wake up feeling as if you hardly slept at all?
Other Criteria	D. The focus of the anxiety and worry is not confined to features of an Axis I disorder (e.g., the anxiety or worry is not about having a panic attack (as in panic disorder), being embarrassed in public (as in [social disorder], being embarrassed in public (as in [social	General anxiety may be a sign of another anxiety or mood disorder.	Did this period of [anxiety/worry] begin after you were physically attacked or exposed to some horrible event, like a murder or fire? . . . Were there any times when you worried a lot (for at least six months) that didn't follow [trauma]?

(Continued)

Symptoms	DSM-IV Criteria[a, b]	Issues in Substance-Dependent Patients	PRISM Questions to Aid Diagnosis[e, f]
	anxiety disorder]), being contaminated (as in obsessive compulsive disorder), being away from home or close relatives (as in separation anxiety disorder), gaining weight (as in anorexia nervosa), having multiple physical complaints (as in somatization disorder), or having a serious illness (as in hypochondriasis), and the anxiety and worry do not occur exclusively during posttraumatic stress disorder)[c].		
	E. The anxiety, worry, or physical symptoms cause clinically significant distress or impairment in social, occupational, or other important areas of functioning.		During this time (when you felt the most [worried]) ... did you avoid seeing or talking to people because you didn't want to be around them as much as usual? ... did you depend on others to take care of your everyday responsibilities or to give you a lot of attention or comfort? ... did you have more arguments with others than usual? ... did you have more trouble with [work/school/ household task]? Did you feel that [worry/symptoms] were really a problem? Did you ever think about getting help for your [worry/symptoms]?
	F. The disturbance is not due to the direct physiological effects of a substance (e.g., a drug of abuse, a medication)[d] or a general medical condition (e.g., hyperthyroidism) and does not occur exclusively during a mood disorder, a psychotic disorder, or a pervasive developmental disorder.	See above.	Were you [psychotic symptoms] during that time? ... Were you [depressed/manic] during that time? ... Were you drinking or using drugs at all? ... During the whole time you were feeling [anxious/worried], were you taking any medicines prescribed by your doctor? ... Were you physically ill during the whole time you felt [anxious/worried]?

(a) American Psychiatric Association (1994).
(b) Reprinted with permission from the *Diagnostic and Statistical Manual of Mental Disorders*, Fourth Edition (Copyright 1994), American Psychiatric Association.
(c) Consult *DSM-IV* criteria (American Psychiatric Association, 1994) for panic disorder, social anxiety disorder, obsessive compulsive disorder, separation anxiety disorder, anorexia nervosa, somatization disorder, hypochondriasis, posttraumatic stress disorder.
(d) Consult *DSM-IV* criteria (American Psychiatric Association, 1994) for substance intoxication and withdrawal syndromes.
(e) Hasin et al. (2006).
(f) Reprinted with permission.

Table 4-1F
***DSM-IV* Criteria for Substance-Induced Anxiety Disorder**

Symptoms	*DSM-IV* Criteria[a, b, c]	PRISM Questions to Aid Diagnosis[d, e, f]
Core Symptoms	A. Prominent anxiety, panic attacks, or obsessions or compulsions predominate in the clinical picture.	
	B. There is evidence from the history, physical examination, or laboratory findings of either (1) or (2):	
	(1) the symptoms in Criterion A developed during, or within 1 month of, substance intoxication or withdrawal	Did [anxiety symptoms/panic attack] … occur after you drank a lot of coffee or other caffeinated drink, used over-the-counter diet pills or sleep aid, or got high on drugs? … Did the attack occur when you were coming down from alcohol, sedatives, or cocaine? What month did you start feeling [worried/symptoms]? Think about the month before that. Were you drinking or using drugs at all during that month? … During the month before you started feeling [worried/symptoms], were you [drinking/using drug] at least 4 times a week or 3 days straight? … During that entire time, did you keep [drinking/using drug] as much and as often as you just said?
	(2) medication use is etiologically related to the disturbance.	During the whole time you were feeling [anxious/worried/symptoms] were you taking any medicines prescribed by a doctor?
Other Criteria	C. The disturbance is not better accounted for by an anxiety disorder that is not substance induced. Evidence that the symptoms are better accounted for by an anxiety disorder that is not substance induced might include the following: the symptoms precede the onset of the substance use (or medication use); the symptoms persist for a substantial period of time (e.g., about a month) after the cessation of acute withdrawal or severe intoxication or are substantially in excess of what would be expected given the type or amount of the substance used or the duration of use; or there is other evidence suggesting the existence of an independent non-substance-induced anxiety disorder (e.g., a history of recurrent non-substance-related episodes).	Were you [worried/symptoms] … before you started [drinking/using drug]? During that entire time, did you keep [drinking/using drug] as much and as often as you just said? When did you [cut down/stop]? Were you still [worried/symptoms] … after that? Was there any other period … when you were [worried/symptoms] … and you were not drinking or using drugs?

(Continued)

Symptoms	DSM-IV Criteria[a, b, c]	PRISM Questions to Aid Diagnosis[d, e, f]
	D. The disturbance does not occur exclusively during the course of a delirium.	
	E. The disturbance causes clinically significant distress or impairment in social, occupational, or other important areas of functioning.	During this time … … did you avoid seeing or talking to people because you didn't want to be around them as much as usual? … did you depend on others to take care of your everyday responsibilities or to give you a lot of attention or comfort? … did you have more arguments with others than usual? … did you have more trouble with [work/school/household task]? Did you feel that [worry/symptoms] were really a problem? Did you ever think about getting help for your [worry/symptoms]?

(a) This diagnosis should be made instead of a diagnosis of substance intoxication or substance withdrawal only when the anxiety symptoms are in excess of those usually associated with the intoxication or withdrawal syndrome and when the anxiety symptoms are sufficiently severe to warrant independent clinical attention.
(b) American Psychiatric Association (1994).
(c) Reprinted with permission from the *Diagnostic and Statistical Manual of Mental Disorders*, Fourth Edition (Copyright 1994). American Psychiatric Association.
(d) PRISM does not provide questions for diagnosis of substance-induced anxiety disorder; questions from the PRISM's panic disorder module for diagnosis of substance-induced panic disorder and questions from the PRISM's GAD module for diagnosis of substance-induced GAD were adapted for inclusion in Table 4-1F.
(e) Hasin et al. (2006).
(f) Reprinted with permission.

Table 4-2
Common Symptoms Shared by *DSM-IV* Anxiety Disorders and
***DSM-IV* Syndromes of Substance Intoxication and Withdrawal**

Associated Anxiety Disorders	Symptoms	Associated Substance-Related Syndromes
generalized anxiety disorder; panic attack; panic disorder	nausea or vomiting, abdominal distress	alcohol withdrawal; amphetamine intoxication; caffeine intoxication; cocaine intoxication; opioid withdrawal; sedative, hypnotic, or anxiolytic withdrawal
acute stress disorder; agoraphobia; generalized anxiety disorder; panic attack; panic disorder; PTSD; social anxiety disorder, substance-induced anxiety disorder	anxiety	alcohol withdrawal; amphetamine intoxication; caffeine intoxication; cannabis intoxication; cocaine intoxication; hallucinogen intoxication; nicotine withdrawal; sedative, hypnotic, or anxiolytic withdrawal
generalized anxiety disorder; panic attack; panic disorder; social anxiety disorder	sweating	alcohol withdrawal; amphetamine intoxication; cocaine intoxication; hallucinogen intoxication; opioid withdrawal; sedative, hypnotic, or anxiolytic withdrawal
generalized anxiety disorder; panic attack; panic disorder	chills	amphetamine intoxication; cocaine intoxication; opioid withdrawal; sedative, hypnotic, or anxiolytic withdrawal
panic attack; panic disorder	cardiac arrhythmias, tachycardia	alcohol withdrawal; amphetamine intoxication; caffeine intoxication; cannabis intoxication; cocaine intoxication; hallucinogen intoxication; phencyclidine intoxication; sedative, hypnotic, or anxiolytic withdrawal
panic attack; panic disorder	respiratory depression, chest pain	amphetamine intoxication; cocaine intoxication
generalized anxiety disorder; panic attack; panic disorder; social anxiety disorder	dry mouth	cannabis intoxication
generalized anxiety disorder; panic attack; panic disorder	diuresis	caffeine intoxication
acute stress disorder; agoraphobia; generalized anxiety disorder; panic disorder; PTSD; social anxiety disorder; substance-induced anxiety disorder	impaired social or occupational functioning	alcohol intoxication; alcohol withdrawal; amphetamine intoxication; amphetamine withdrawal; caffeine intoxication; cannabis intoxication; cocaine intoxication; cocaine withdrawal; hallucinogen intoxication; inhalant intoxication; nicotine withdrawal; opioid intoxication; opioid withdrawal; phencyclidine intoxication; sedative, hypnotic, or anxiolytic intoxication; sedative, hypnotic, or anxiolytic withdrawal
social anxiety disorder	interpersonal sensitivity	amphetamine intoxication; cocaine intoxication
acute stress disorder; agoraphobia; PTSD; social anxiety disorder	social withdrawal	cannabis intoxication

(Continued)

Associated Anxiety Disorders	Symptoms	Associated Substance-Related Syndromes
acute stress disorder; generalized anxiety disorder; PTSD; social anxiety disorder	impaired attention or memory, difficulty concentrating	alcohol intoxication, nicotine withdrawal; opioid intoxication; sedative, hypnotic, or anxiolytic intoxication
generalized anxiety disorder; PTSD	irritability	nicotine withdrawal
acute stress disorder; PTSD	outbursts of anger	amphetamine intoxication; cocaine intoxication; inhalant intoxication; nicotine withdrawal; phencyclidine intoxication
acute stress disorder; generalized anxiety disorder; PTSD	insomnia	alcohol withdrawal; amphetamine withdrawal; caffeine intoxication; cocaine withdrawal; nicotine withdrawal; opioid withdrawal; sedative, hypnotic, or anxiolytic withdrawal
panic attack; panic disorder	fear of losing one's mind	cannabis intoxication; hallucinogen intoxication
acute stress disorder; panic attack; panic disorder; PTSD	depersonalization, derealization	cannabis intoxication; hallucinogen intoxication
acute stress disorder; PTSD	affective blunting	amphetamine intoxication; cocaine intoxication
acute stress disorder; PTSD	illusions, hallucinations	alcohol withdrawal; hallucinogen intoxication; sedative, hypnotic, anxiolytic withdrawal
acute stress disorder; PTSD	vivid, unpleasant dreams	amphetamine withdrawal; cocaine withdrawal
panic attack; panic disorder, social anxiety disorder	tremors	alcohol withdrawal; hallucinogen intoxication; inhalant intoxication; sedative, hypnotic, anxiolytic withdrawal
acute stress disorder; generalized anxiety disorder; PTSD	restlessness	alcohol withdrawal; amphetamine intoxication; amphetamine withdrawal; caffeine intoxication; cocaine intoxication; cocaine withdrawal; nicotine withdrawal; opioid intoxication; phencyclidine intoxication; sedative, hypnotic, or anxiolytic withdrawal
acute stress disorder; panic attack; panic disorder	numbness	phencyclidine intoxication
panic attack; panic disorder	dizziness, unsteadiness	alcohol intoxication; cannabis intoxication; hallucinogen intoxication; inhalant intoxication; opioid intoxication; sedative, hypnotic, anxiolytic intoxication
acute stress disorder; PTSD	hypervigilence	amphetamine intoxication; cocaine intoxication
generalized anxiety disorder	muscle aches	opioid withdrawal
generalized anxiety disorder	tension	amphetamine intoxication; cocaine intoxication
generalized anxiety disorder	fatigue	amphetamine withdrawal; cocaine withdrawal; opioid withdrawal

meetings at which he/she might have to speak. Often only a detailed history will capture symptoms of SAD, which may otherwise be overlooked. Since primary clinicians see their patients repeatedly over time, and since a detailed psychiatric history takes time to gather, primary clinicians ought to spend the time to gather a history. Further, by devoting time to take a detailed history, primary clinicians can help their patients to feel better understood, can better plan treatment, and can strengthen the treatment alliance between the patient and the clinician and the treatment program.

CASE PRESENTATIONS

Case 1

FS is a 55-year-old single man with opioid dependence in methadone maintenance treatment (dose: 120 mg per day) who complains of anxiety and insomnia. Other than having occasional temporary jobs, he is unemployed; he lives with his elderly parents. He frequently asks his counselor and the clinic physician for benzodiazepines, and when these requests are denied, he sometimes becomes irritable, argumentative, and even threatening. He also occasionally misses his clinic visits. The clinic has nearly discharged him several times for rule violations as a result of missed visits and hostile and irritable acts. At the same time, the staff members who know him describe him as a generally likeable and sympathetic fellow, with a good sense of humor. His urine tests are often positive for opioids and benzodiazepines, a pattern that has not changed despite increases in the methadone dosage.

History of Drug Problems. FS did well in elementary school but began having behavior problems during junior high school, when he began to hang out with peers who were using cigarettes, alcohol, and other drugs, and when he began using substances by age 14. After dropping out of high school, he worked in a family business for several years. He was drafted into the army and served with a combat unit in Vietnam, where he became addicted to heroin. He resumed regular heroin use following his discharge from the army and his return to the United States. He has been opioid-dependent since his return home, with no abstinent periods. He has been on methadone maintenance for twenty-five years, which has helped him markedly reduce his heroin use, although he still uses heroin intermittently. For many years, he has also used benzodiazepines (when he can get them) to relax and sleep better.

History of Mood and Anxiety Problems. When asked why he misses a clinic visit at least once a week, the patient explains that he cannot always find transportation to the clinic. Although reliable subway and bus service is available from his home to the clinic, FS admits that he stopped taking public transportation ten years ago following a series of "anxiety attacks" on the subway and that he fears having another anxiety attack on the subway or bus; he relies on friends with cars or, when he has enough money, a car service to drive him to the clinic. Further, FS is bothered by closed-in spaces and crowds; if there are long lines and a large crowd at the medication window, FS becomes anxious and irritable and bolts from the clinic.

When asked to describe his "anxiety attacks," FS describes episodes in which feelings of anxiety emerge from a relaxed state and escalate in intensity within a few minutes; he shakes, sweats, feels tightness in his chest and chest pain, feels short of breath, and feels the need to get outside to "get air." The episodes, which last approximately half an hour and occur about twice a week, sometimes occur in places that typically make him nervous (e.g., on the subway, in a crowded store, while waiting in line at the clinic) and occasionally occur "out of the blue" (e.g., times when he is relaxed while sitting at home or taking a walk). He vividly remembers his first panic attack (in his early 20s); he thought that he was dying of a heart attack and was rushed to the hospital, but the medical workup was normal and the symptoms cleared up.

The patient also presently meets criteria for major depressive disorder; he experiences insomnia, which is relieved by benzodiazepines that he buys on the street or gets by prescription from doctors outside of the clinic. He had a number of traumatic experiences during combat in Vietnam; he has met criteria for PTSD in the past, but the PTSD seems to be in remission at present. He denies any history of suicidal behavior but acknowledges frequent thoughts of suicide. He has occasionally lost control of his temper and has gotten into fights, but none, he asserts, have resulted in serious injury; he is frequently irritable. While experiencing panic attacks or while feeling the need "to get some air," he feels irritable and combative toward people around him.

Developmental History. FS was successful and well liked by his teachers during elementary school, but he began "hanging out with the wrong crowd" during junior high school. Around age 14, he began to skip school, to smoke cigarettes, and to experiment with alcohol and other drugs. He did not meet full criteria for substance dependence or conduct disorder as an adolescent. He did not appear to have mood or anxiety problems during childhood or adolescence.

Medical History. FS has smoked one pack of cigarettes per day since his tour of duty in Vietnam. His diet seems high in fatty foods and salt; he has borderline high blood pressure, and his cholesterol is elevated. Over the last five years, he has developed a chronic cough; in recent years he has experienced shortness of breath when climbing stairs or trying to run. Upon further questioning he describes tightness in his chest and chest pain during exertion at times when he is not having a panic attack. These symptoms may indicate that he is developing chronic lung disease from smoking, as well as coronary vascular disease. FS admits that he is afraid of doctors; he has refused to follow up on clinic staff members' recommendations for regular medical care.

Diagnostic Formulation. FS has a fairly typical case of panic disorder with agoraphobia. He has frequent attacks of anxiety that meet criteria for panic attacks (see Table 4-1A). He also has agoraphobia (see Table 4-1B), indicated by his fear and avoidance of public transportation and crowded places. Although clinic staff members have known for many years that he has anxiety, the specific anxiety disorder has never been diagnosed. Agoraphobia may be responsible for some of his functional impairment, including missed clinic visits and occasional irritable or unpredictable behavior while at the clinic, and may have contributed to his poor employment history. Not surprisingly (since mood and anxiety disorders tend to occur together), FS also meets criteria for major depression and has a past history of PTSD. Although benzodiazepines have relieved his anxiety symptoms and insomnia, his benzodiazepine use has been viewed by clinic staff as part of his drug problem. He clearly has serious substance dependence, with early onset and chronic course. Because of benzodiazepines' addictive potential, they do not usually represent an appropriate treatment for patients with substance dependence. However, it is important to remember that benzodiazepine-seeking behavior may be evidence of an untreated mood or anxiety disorder, for which better treatments (e.g., CBT or antidepressant medications) are available. Symptoms of a panic attack sometimes resemble symptoms of heart attacks (e.g., shortness of breath, chest discomfort). However, aging patients, particularly patients with risk factors, such as cigarette smoking and high cholesterol, may begin to develop heart disease and lung disease, which need medical attention. Finally, cigarette smoking has also been shown to increase the risk of panic attacks (Goodwin & Hamilton, 2002; Johnson et al., 2000).

Case 2

BN, a 37-year-old unmarried man who lives alone and is currently receiving disability benefits, presents for treatment for opioid dependence. He was first exposed to opioid analgesics after a painful back injury at age 24; he subsequently became dependent, alternating between prescription opioids and intranasal heroin. He has had several inpatient detoxifications, after which he has remained free of opioids for up to two years, always relapsing, apparently in response to stressful circumstances. He recently was started on buprenorphine maintenance at 16 mg per day, to which he has demonstrated a good response, despite continued cravings and occasional slips, when he uses small amounts of intranasal heroin. He was referred to a local treatment program for ongoing counseling, but he dropped out, complaining that he did not feel comfortable during group sessions; similarly, he has refused to attend AA or NA meetings.

History of Mood and Anxiety Problems. BN complains of anxiety and sensitivity to stress, to which he attributes his relapses. Further questioning reveals no evidence of panic attacks or agoraphobia. He describes chronic low mood and unhappiness and meets criteria for dysthymic disorder. When asked about childhood and elementary school, he recalls that he was a very shy child and was especially nervous about school. He reports that he did not feel nervous about leaving home or being away from his parents (as in separation anxiety disorder). Although he was an excellent student, and always earned good grades, he reports that he rarely spoke in class or raised his hand and was afraid that the teacher might call on him to answer a question or go to the blackboard. He reports that if the teacher called on him, he experienced a surge of anxiety, began sweating, and felt sick to his stomach. He had a few close friends but was nervous about attending birthday parties and other social gatherings. During junior high school and high school he found that alcohol reduced his anxiety temporarily, and he began drinking as a way of coping with the anxiety symptoms that he experienced during social gatherings and dating.

BN attended college, where he studied education; he gravitated toward special education because it allowed him to work one-on-one with students rather than stand before a classroom of students, which provoked anxiety. At the age of 24, he had an automobile accident that resulted in a painful back injury; he was introduced to opioid analgesics for treatment of his back pain and developed opioid dependence. He reports that the opioids temporarily improved his mood, energy, and anxiety. He achieved long periods of abstinence after several inpatient detoxifications. During these abstinent periods, his social anxiety persisted. Following inpatient detoxification, he was referred to several outpatient aftercare programs that emphasized group treatment, but he quickly dropped out of treatment because the group sessions made him anxious. Similarly, the intolerable anxiety that he experiences in anticipation of being asked to speak during meetings has discouraged him from attending AA or NA meetings.

Developmental History. Despite the anxiety that he experienced at school and at social gatherings, BN was a well-behaved, talented student with no history of conduct disorder or learning problems. He recalls feeling unhappy most of the time as a teenager, accompanied by low self-esteem, low energy, and intermittent sleep problems, a pattern that has persisted throughout his adult life. As a teenager he drank alcohol regularly during social engagements. Although he met criteria for alcohol abuse as an adolescent, due to occasional episodes of excessive intoxication and impaired judgment, he did not seem to meet criteria for alcohol dependence.

Diagnostic Formulation. BN displays a typical history of SAD (see Table 4-1D), with childhood onset and a chronic course throughout adult life. He also meets criteria for dysthymic disorder, with early onset; dysthymic disorder frequently co-occurs with SAD. Interestingly, BN does not have a typical history of early-onset substance dependence problems. He can be diagnosed with opioid dependence as early as his mid-20s (following his painful back injury). The onset of social anxiety in early childhood and the persistence of symptoms during periods of abstinence indicate that SAD is independent of opioid dependence. It is unclear if SAD or dysthymic disorder contributes to his risk of opioid dependence; it is possible that relief of his dysphoric symptoms with opioids provides a drive to take them. This case example illustrates the importance of taking a careful psychiatric history, including a history of early childhood and school experiences, in order to arrive at a precise diagnosis. This patient's social isolation and avoidance of groups are evidence of SAD.

Case 3

TN is a 31-year-old female, who drinks one to two six-packs of beer every day, along with several shots of vodka. She describes herself as a "nervous wreck." She has been admitted to an inpatient detoxification unit.

History of Drug and Alcohol Problems. Around the age of 15, TN began drinking alcohol and experimenting with other drugs, which, she says, she used during social situations. She denies any pattern of regular use or of impairment during her teenage years, other than a few episodes during which she got very drunk and sick and her friends had to help her home. She completed high school and two years of community college. Since she worried that she might go into debt to finance her college education and that she might have trouble paying her bills, she decided to complete training to become a real estate broker rather than continue with college. In her early 20s, her drinking became problematic: she would begin to drink beer or wine at lunchtime, followed by cocktails after work; she arrived home in the evening to continue drinking until she fell asleep. Over time, her total daily quantity of alcohol escalated, and she became more socially isolated, neglecting her friends and hobbies to stay at home and drink. Her work performance suffered. She felt nauseous, hot, sweaty, shaky, and anxious in the mornings and found herself craving alcohol by lunchtime. She clearly recalls that alcohol relieved these symptoms. Although her lunchtime drinks promptly relieved her physical symptoms, the alcohol only partly relieved the anxiety. She wanted to cut down on the number of drinks that she consumed, and often tried, but she always ended up drinking heavily in the evening, feeling sick with cravings for more alcohol when she awoke in the morning.

History of Mood and Anxiety Problems. TN remembers her childhood and teenage years as being relatively happy and uneventful, although she recalls that her father was often out of work and that money was tight. She recalls that her level of anxiety increased when she became responsible for her financial affairs, prompting her to cut short her college education in order to pursue stable work in real estate sales. However, she found work anxiety-provoking; she was always concerned that she would not make enough sales or generate enough income to make ends meet. In her early 20s she began to worry about her health and the health of her aging parents and her pet cats. Although her neighborhood was considered to be safe and she had never had any frightening experiences there, she felt nervous about being out alone at night. At this time, she developed a sense of worry, pessimism, and "doom and gloom" about the future, which was with her most of the time. She also recalls that she began to have trouble sleeping, particularly falling asleep. Although she felt tired when she climbed into bed, she felt tense and achy and was consumed with worries that often kept her awake for many hours before she could fall asleep; she often felt tired and short-tempered during the day, with frequent headaches and backaches.

However, while taking a history from TN, it seemed impossible to separate the increased anxiety and associated symptoms that TN experienced in her early 20s from the effects of her daily heavy drinking that occurred during the same period. She had never experienced any abstinent periods until the present admission for detoxification.

Course During Inpatient Detoxification. When TN was admitted to inpatient detoxification, she was started on a standard chlordiazepoxide (Librium) taper. Because of her longstanding history of anxiety, she was administered the Hamilton Anxiety Scale (Hamilton, 1959), a brief clinician-administered questionnaire that measures severity of anxiety symptoms, in addition to the Clinical Institute Withdrawal Assessment for Alcohol-Revised (CIWA-Ar; Sullivan, Sykora, Schneiderman, Naranjo, & Sellers, 1989), a standard brief measure of alcohol withdrawal severity. Her obvious physical symptoms of alcohol withdrawal (shakes, sweats, mild elevations in pulse and blood pressure) were eliminated, and her CIWA-Ar score fell to zero by the second hospital day. However, she continued to worry about money, family, pets, and the safety of her home; these worries, in addition to muscle tension and aches and pains, continued to keep her awake at night. After her first day in the hospital, her Hamilton Anxiety Scale score improved by about 25 percent, but she demonstrated no further improvement during the five days that followed, and the score remained in the range of moderate to severe anxiety. Although TN continued to ask for medication to lessen her anxiety, the clinicians on the unit wanted to taper her off of the benzodiazepine chlordiazepoxide because they were concerned that she might develop dependence on the drug.

Diagnostic Formulation. This case example illustrates a pattern of anxiety symptoms that matches that of GAD (Table 4-1E). However, it is difficult to distinguish the symptoms of an independent anxiety disorder from the effects of alcohol. According to the history, the anxiety symptoms emerged during the patient's early 20s; at the same time, she began to meet criteria for alcohol dependence. Since that time, she has experienced no periods of abstinence. The extent of her worry seems to exceed that which is expected from effects of chronic alcohol use. Yet many of the symptoms associated with the anxiety, including poor sleep, irritability, and muscle tension, can occur as a result of alcohol withdrawal. Although a clinician could make a diagnosis of substance-induced anxiety disorder at the time of evaluation, the clinician could clarify the diagnosis by observing the patient's symptoms during a period of abstinence, which should be achieved through hospitalization. Anxiety or depressive symptoms will often improve rapidly over days to several weeks upon abstinence from alcohol (Brown, Irwin, & Schuckit, 1991; Brown & Schuckit, 1988; see Nunes & Raby, 2005).

Following detoxification, the patient's symptoms of anxiety persisted. Although, ideally, one would like to observe persistence of mood or anxiety symptoms for several weeks following detoxification, it is decided to treat TN with buspirone, an antianxiety medication with no tranquilizing or sedating effects and no abuse potential. There is evidence that treatment with buspirone improves drinking outcome after discharge from the hospital among patients in whom generalized anxiety symptoms persist following detoxification (Kranzler et al., 1994).

DIAGNOSTIC CRITERIA

DSM-IV Criteria for Panic Attack, Agoraphobia, and Panic Disorder

The *DSM-IV* diagnostic criteria for panic attack, agoraphobia, and panic disorder (with or without agoraphobia) are presented in Tables 4-1A, 4-1B, and 4-1C, respectively. The tables also present questions from the Psychiatric Research Interview for Substance and Mental Disorders (PRISM; Hasin et al., 2006) that can be used to elicit information from patients about their symptoms, as well as issues to consider in distinguishing symptoms of panic attack from symptoms of drug intoxication or withdrawal. Panic attacks are characterized by sudden onset and rapid escalation of anxiety symptoms over a period of a few minutes in combination with a variety of associated physical symptoms that are typically associated with intense fear. Panic attacks may occur in isolation, may occur as part of a variety of anxiety disorders, or may seem to occur in response to substance intoxication or withdrawal. Agoraphobia is characterized by fear and avoidance of places or situations from which escape would be difficult (e.g., subways, buses, bridges, airplanes, crowded stores, elevators, traffic jams) or in which the individual fears having a panic attack. Agoraphobia often seems to develop as a consequence of panic attacks: a patient begins to fear and avoid places where panic attacks have occurred (behavior that appears to have been reinforced through classical (Pavlovian) conditioning). Panic disorder describes a syndrome in which panic attacks occur repeatedly and in which patients become preoccupied with the attacks, fearing recurrent attacks or changing their behavior as a result of the attacks. Panic disorder may occur with or without agoraphobia. Use of the PRISM (or a similar semistructured diagnostic interview) provides clinicians with practice in asking about these disorders and conducting an efficient diagnostic interview.

DSM-IV Criteria for Social Anxiety Disorder

The criteria for SAD and suggested questions from the PRISM for use in eliciting information from patients about their symptoms are presented in Table 4-1D. SAD is characterized by a marked or persistent fear of social situations that expose the person to unfamiliar people or possible scrutiny by others (e.g., speaking at a meeting); the person fears that his/her behavior (or display of anxiety symptoms) may result in embarrassment or humiliation. Since exposure to such social situations provokes marked anxiety or panic attacks, the feared situations are avoided or endured with significant distress. To distinguish anxiety that is generated by social situations from agoraphobia, one must consider that anxiety caused by social interactions becomes worse in the presence of other people while anxiety resulting from agoraphobia improves in the presence of other people.

Two subtypes of SAD are recognized: generalized and nongeneralized. A diagnosis of generalized SAD indicates that the individual fears most social situations; the generalized subtype is more severe and disabling than the nongeneralized subtype. A diagnosis of nongeneralized SAD (sometimes referred to as performance anxiety) indicates that the patient exhibits fear of performing in just one or a few particular situations; public speaking represents the most common example.

DSM-IV Criteria for Generalized Anxiety Disorder

The criteria for GAD, suggested questions from the PRISM for use in eliciting information from patients to address each criterion, and issues encountered in diagnosis of substance-dependent patients are listed in Table 4-1E. GAD is characterized by a state of chronic worry that is focused on more than one situation; the anxiety is accompanied by physical symptoms (e.g., sweating, heart pounding, muscle aches, insomnia) and emotional/cognitive symptoms (e.g., difficulty concentrating). Like symptoms of panic attacks, many symptoms of GAD resemble symptoms of substance intoxication and withdrawal.

NATURAL HISTORY AND ETIOLOGY

Genetics and Stress

The causes of panic disorder, SAD, and GAD are not precisely understood, but studies in twins suggest that these disorders are partly determined by inherited genetic vulnerabilities and partly attributable to environmental factors (Kendler, Neale, Kessler, Heath, & Eaves, 1992a; Kendler, Neale, Kessler, Heath, & Eaves, 1992b). Some evidence suggests that GAD and major depressive disorder may be alternative expressions of the same genetic vulnerability (Kendler, Neale, Kessler, Heath, & Eaves, 1992c). Among environmental factors, stress, loss, and psychological trauma appear to play a role in increasing risk for these disorders (Kendler, Kessler, Heath, Neale, & Eaves, 1991; Kendler et al., 1992c; Kendler, Prescott, Myers, & Neale, 2003). SAD often has an early onset, typically characterized by excessive shyness during childhood. Panic disorder, agoraphobia, and generalized anxiety disorder typically begin during adolescence or early adulthood, but some patients may have manifestations of anxiety during childhood (e.g., separation anxiety disorder). Each of these anxiety disorders tends to run a chronic relapsing course.

Relationship of Anxiety Disorders to Substance Use Disorders

Large scale community surveys have shown that substance use disorders and anxiety disorders occur together at rates greater than rates expected by chance, with the presence of one disorder increasing the risk of the other disorder by a factor of 2 or more (depending upon the combinations of disorders examined) (Conway, Compton,

Stinson, & Grant, 2006). Although the nature of the relationship between anxiety disorders and substance use disorders is not clearly understood, studies have yielded interesting clues. Substance abuse may activate the body's stress response system and stress hormones, predisposing patients to the development of mood or anxiety disorders (Brady & Sinha, 2005). Studies have shown that nicotine use (Breslau, Kilbey, & Andreski, 1993) or marijuana use (Brook, Brook, Zhang, Cohen, & Whiteman, 2002; Fergusson, Horwood, & Swain-Campbell, 2002; Patton et al., 2002) increases the risk for subsequent development of depressive or anxiety disorders. A shy yet aggressive temperament during childhood has been shown to increase the risk for development of substance problems during adolescence and adulthood; a shy temperament (i.e., shyness without aggressive tendencies) may be protective against the development of substance use problems (Crum et al., 2006; Ensminger, Juon, & Fothergill, 2002; Juon, Ensminger, & Sydnor, 2002). Deficiency in brain dopamine systems, in particular lower levels of D2 dopamine receptors measured through brain imaging techniques, has been associated with addictive disorders and is thought to represent reduced sensitivity of the brain reward system. Interestingly, deficits in the dopamine system also have been implicated in SAD in animal models (in studies that compared timid and aggressive monkeys; Grant et al., 1998) and in patients studied with brain imaging methods (Schneier et al., 2000). Anxiety disorders have been associated with greater severity or poorer outcome in substance-dependent patients in comparison to patients without substance dependence (Burns, Teesson, & O'Neill, 2005; Kushner et al., 2005; Schneider et al., 2001).

Thus, substance abuse may increase the risk for subsequent development of anxiety disorders, perhaps by sensitizing the body's stress response system. Anxiety disorders may increase the risk for subsequent development of substance use disorders, perhaps because patients may use substances to "self-medicate" or because anxiety is associated with alterations in the brain reward system that predispose patients to drugs. The two disorders, when they occur together, may worsen a patient's overall clinical outcome. Finally, symptoms of substance intoxication and withdrawal can mimic symptoms of anxiety disorders, particularly symptoms of panic attacks and GAD.

ISSUES IN DIAGNOSIS: DIAGNOSING ANXIETY DISORDERS IN SUBSTANCE-DEPENDENT PATIENTS

The third column in Tables 4-1A, 4-1B, 4-1C, and 4-1E lists issues that clinicians encounter during diagnosis of anxiety disorders among substance-dependent patients. Symptoms of substance intoxication and withdrawal often resemble symptoms of anxiety disorders, including nearly all of the physical symptoms of anxiety disorders, particularly the symptoms of panic attacks (Table 4-1A) and GAD (Table 4-1E).

The center column in Table 4-2 lists each of the emotional, cognitive, or physical symptoms shared by one or more of the anxiety disorders (listed in the left column) and one or more of the substance intoxication or withdrawal syndromes (listed in the right column). PTSD and acute stress disorder (ASD) (see Chapter 3 of this volume) are included in the table. When clinicians conduct diagnostic interviews, they should ask a patient about the substances that he/she has been using in order to determine if these substances might account for some of the anxiety symptoms that the patient reports.

As Table 4-2 illustrates, substance intoxication and withdrawal may mimic symptoms of panic attacks, GAD, and some associated symptoms of PTSD. However, the symptoms of agoraphobia and SAD and many symptoms of PTSD are distinct from the symptoms of substance use disorders; substance intoxication and withdrawal do not cause patients to fear buses and subways, avoid meetings, or experience flashbacks to past traumatic experiences. Case 3 (described above in "Case Presentations") demonstrates that when anxiety symptoms are difficult to distinguish from effects of chronic alcohol use and intoxication or withdrawal, it is helpful to observe the patient's symptoms during a period of abstinence. If the anxiety symptoms are due to the effects of alcohol, they should quickly resolve following abstinence. Persistence of anxiety symptoms following several weeks of abstinence suggests the presence of an independent anxiety disorder.

INSTRUMENTS AND METHODS FOR SCREENING AND DIAGNOSIS

Scales that measure levels of anxiety include the clinician-administered Hamilton Anxiety Scale (Hamilton, 1959) and the self-administered Symptom-Checklist-90 (SCL-90; Derogatis, 1983). Although these scales help to evaluate a patient's level of anxiety, they do not clearly point to specific diagnoses. Self-administered severity scales for specific disorders, such as SAD, also exist. Such scales require little time from clinicians and are useful for screening. Administration of these scales should be followed by a clinical interview to confirm whether a patient meets *DSM-IV* criteria for a given disorder. After a diagnosis has been made, these scales can be used to measure severity of anxiety symptoms in response to treatment (treatment of Case 3, described above in "Case Presentations," involved use of the Hamilton Anxiety Scale).

The PRISM (Hasin et al., 2006) was designed for use among substance-dependent patients; it covers the diagnoses discussed in this chapter. The PRISM quotes each *DSM-IV* criterion and offers questions for use by clinicians in eliciting information from patients about their symptoms. In addition, for each psychiatric disorder, the PRISM provides a list of substances with intoxication or withdrawal symptoms that mimic symptoms of the disorder. This information helps clinicians during diagnostic interviews to assess whether an anxiety disorder should be considered independent of ongoing alcohol or substance use. Training in use of the PRISM offers an opportunity to learn the *DSM-IV* diagnostic criteria and the procedure for conducting an effective psychiatric interview. Questions from the PRISM for eliciting information from patients about their anxiety symptoms are listed in Tables 4-1A, 4-1B, 4-1C, 4-1D, 4-1E, and 4-1F (note that since the PRISM does not provide questions for diagnosis of substance-induced anxiety disorder, questions from the PRISM's panic disorder module for diagnosis of substance-induced panic disorder and questions from the PRISM's GAD module for diagnosis of substance-induced GAD were adapted for inclusion in Table 4-1F).

Like the PRISM, the Structured Clinical Interview for DSM-IV-TR Axis I Disorders (SCID-I; First, Spitzer, Gibbon, & Williams, 2002) is a semistructured interview that offers guidance in asking about panic attacks, panic disorder, agoraphobia, SAD, and GAD, and in determining if criteria for the disorders have been met. The SCID-I also states exclusionary criteria and the number of symptoms that must be present for patients to meet criteria for a disorder.

Administration of the PRISM and the SCID-I requires training and clinical judgment. Other diagnostic instruments, including the Mini International Neuropsychiatric Interview (MINI; Sheehan et al., 1998), the Primary Care Evaluation of Mental Disorders (PRIME-MD; Spitzer et al., 1994), the Diagnostic Interview Schedule (DIS; Robins, Helzer, Croughan, Williams, & Spitzer, 1981), and the Composite International Diagnostic Interview (CIDI; Robins et al., 1988), require little or no training to administer. The Patient Health Questionnaire (PHQ; Spitzer, Kroenke, & Williams, 1999) is a self-report instrument that requires patients to respond on a Likert scale to questions addressing each criterion of a disorder.

DIFFERENTIAL DIAGNOSIS AND COMORBID PSYCHIATRIC DISORDERS

Co-Occurring Psychiatric Disorders

Anxiety disorders tend to co-occur. Up to 80 percent of patients with GAD will have at least one other anxiety disorder, and 30 percent or more of patients will have major depression (Grant et al., 2005b; Yonkers, Warshaw, Massion, & Keller, 1996). SAD tends to be accompanied by dysthymia (Schneier et al., 1992). Panic disorder often co-occurs with major depression and bipolar disorder (Grant et al., 2006). Thus, the identification of an anxiety disorder should prompt careful review for the presence of other mood or anxiety disorders. Each of the disorders is associated with somewhat different and specific treatment approaches; the optimal a treatment plan needs to address symptoms of all disorders. When evaluating a patient who presents with symptoms of panic attacks and GAD, clinicians should try to detect if the patient's anxiety symptoms represent symptoms of intoxication or withdrawal from substances subject to abuse.

Medical Conditions

Patients who have panic attacks or other forms of anxiety often experience a constellation of associated physical symptoms (e.g., palpitations, pounding heart, or accelerated heart rate, difficulty breathing, muscle tension, headaches, other aches and pains, insomnia). Often individuals with a history of an anxiety disorder are physically healthy. However, the physical symptoms of anxiety disorders are also characteristic of a number of serious medical problems, such as heart disease (coronary artery disease, cardiac arrhythmias), lung disease (asthma, bronchitis, especially in smokers), neurological problems, sleep disorders, endocrinological problems, among others. Many of these problems become more common with age, and some patients may have both an anxiety disorder and an independent general medical problem.

Management of treatment for both an anxiety disorder and a medical problem can be challenging: one illness may mask the presence of the other illness or interfere with treatment; further, the combination of a general medical problem and an anxiety disorder may result in exacerbation of the symptoms of both illnesses. Thus, a patient who presents with anxiety symptoms should be evaluated by a physician in general medicine, who should take a history, listen to the symptoms, and conduct a physical examination, including blood tests, electrocardiograms, or other appropriate tests. A clean bill of health can be reassuring for an anxious patient; discovery and treatment of a medical condition may ease anxiety symptoms.

TREATMENT OPTIONS

The first priority in treatment of this patient population is treatment of a patient's substance use disorders. Reduction or cessation of substance use may result in resolution of, or improvement in, anxiety symptoms.

Independent anxiety disorders respond to treatment with nearly all types of antidepressant medications that have been studied (with the exception of bupropion, which may worsen symptoms of panic attacks or GAD) and with CBTs. Some syndrome-specific medication approaches exist (e.g., beta-blockers for performance anxiety or "stage fright" in patients with or without nongeneralized SAD; pregabalin for GAD). In addition, specific versions of CBT have been tailored to the specific behavioral patterns and cognitive distortions associated with each of the anxiety disorders.

Numerous clinical trials have been conducted to evaluate the effectiveness of medications and behavioral therapies in the treatment of anxiety disorders. However, there are very few studies of these treatments among patients with substance use disorders. Hence, most of the information conveyed in this section is based on evidence from studies of psychiatric outpatients without comorbid disorders. Furthermore, in many, if not most, of these studies, patients with active substance use were excluded. More research is needed to evaluate the effectiveness of these treatments among substance-dependent patients. While most of these trials include comparisons to behavioral treatments or to placebo, some trials have also examined the efficacy of approaches that combine medication and cognitive behavioral approaches. These trials have shown that cognitive behavioral treatments and antidepressant medications are effective treatments for anxiety disorders, and these treatments may complement one another (Barlow, Gorman, Shear, & Woods, 2000). Thus, a combination of medication and CBT should be considered for cases that do not respond to one approach alone.

Caution in Prescribing Benzodiazepines

Benzodiazepines provide immediate relief from anxiety and insomnia and are widely used to assist in the treatment of patients with anxiety disorders. These medications can be especially useful when taken as needed to control panic attacks and anxiety in social situations or other feared situations or nightly to help patients to fall or stay asleep. Benzodiazepines can also be helpful when taken regularly as a daily medication. However, these medications are associated with abuse and dependence among patients with substance use disorders. Further, often substance-dependent patients with insomnia or anxiety take benzodiazepines for relief from anxiety and may pressure a clinician to prescribe them. In general, clinicians should avoid prescribing benzodiazepines to substance-dependent patients and, instead, should utilize behavioral approaches and medications without abuse potential such as antidepressants and anticonvulsants (e.g., neurontin, pregabalin).

However, not all substance-dependent patients are vulnerable to abuse of or dependence on benzodiazepines; some patients can take these medications safely and derive much-needed symptom relief. The choice to prescribe a benzodiazepine to a substance-dependent patient should be made by an experienced physician who has carefully considered the patient's history and the relative risks and benefits of prescribing a benzodiazepine. Once a benzodiazepine has been prescribed, the primary clinician should carefully monitor the patient's benzodiazepine use, particularly for periodic increases in the dose beyond the lowest dose necessary for symptom relief. Patients should be educated about the risks of taking benzodiazepines. Clinicians might encourage a family member or ask the treatment program to hold and distribute the medication.

Panic Disorder With or Without Agoraphobia

Receiving an accurate diagnosis of panic disorder and an explanation of the symptoms and treatment options can be very reassuring to patients and can result in significant improvement in symptoms. Panic attacks are frightening to patients, who often are scared that they are having a life-threatening medical event (e.g., a heart attack) or that they are "going crazy." The suddenness of a panic attack and a patient's inability to determine its apparent cause can amplify the patient's fear and discomfort. It is important to educate a patient about panic attacks and to assure patients that panic attacks are common, short-lived, and treatable, not dangerous and self-limited, and that they represent an overreaction of the nervous system. A good medical evaluation can confirm the absence of serious medical problems. Once a diagnosis of panic disorder has been confirmed and the patient has been issued a clean bill of health by his/her primary care physician, the primary clinician or counselor in a substance abuse treatment program can continue to educate the patient about panic attacks and panic disorder and reassure the patient that panic attacks are unpleasant but not life-threatening.

CBT for panic disorder begins with education about the disorder and focuses on the modification of cognitive distortions that are typical of panic disorder. A cognitive distortion, in the framework of CBT, is defined as a way of thinking that is inaccurate, exaggerated, or biased, and that makes a patient feel more anxious. For example, patients with panic disorder may overreact to internal sensations of discomfort, believing that these sensations are dangerous, and thereby cause their anxiety to escalate into a panic attack (Barlow et al., 2000). A cognitive therapist will try to help the patient to recognize these sensations and to think differently about them (e.g., "it's a little discomfort; it's not serious"). The therapist also will teach deep breathing and deep muscle relaxation techniques for use in countering escalating anxiety. Like treatment for other phobias, treatment for agoraphobia includes education about the disorder and a focus on addressing the cognitive distortions associated with feared situations, in addition to progressive desensitization. Clinicians encourage patients to gradually expose themselves to feared situations and to use tools (e.g., relaxation techniques, identification of cognitive distortions) to tolerate them. Although most clinicians can learn CBT techniques by studying a CBT treatment manual and practicing the techniques under supervision during sessions with patients, relatively few clinicians are trained in CBT methods. A primary counselor may need to search to find a referral for CBT, particularly if treatment costs are an issue.

Panic disorder was the first anxiety disorder in which a response to an antidepressant medication (imipramine) was discovered. The classic work by Klein and Fink (1962) reported that treatment with imipramine resulted in a gradual reduction in intensity and frequency of panic attacks over a period of weeks (a delayed response to antidepressants is typically observed when they are used to treat depression). Panic disorder has been found to respond to most other classes of antidepressants, including other tricyclic antidepressants (TCAs: desipramine, amitriptyline, nortriptyline), selective serotonin reuptake inhibitors (SSRIs: fluoxetine, sertraline, paroxetine, citalopram, among others), serotonin-norepinephrine reuptake inhibitors (SNRIs: venlafaxine), and monoamine oxidase inhibitors (MAOIs; bupropion may be an exception) (Bakker, van Balkom, & Stein, 2005). SSRIs and SNRIs are usually the first choice because they are well tolerated and have little sedative effect (and less potential for interactions with drugs of abuse). If a patient is having difficulty sleeping, the sedating antidepressant trazodone (Desyrel) can be given in low doses at bedtime (50 mg to 100 mg) in combination with another antidepressant. Before starting a patient on a course of antidepressant treatment, it is important to assess for bipolar illness, suicide history, and current suicide risk. There are no medications approved for use in the treatment of agoraphobia in the absence of panic attacks, although the medications used in the treatment of panic disorder can sometimes be useful for such patients.

Social Anxiety Disorder

Patients with SAD often suffer with the disorder for many years before it is detected; patients often have adapted their lifestyle to avoid social or employment situations and opportunities that trigger anxiety. Patients with SAD often have chronic depression (dysthymia or major depression). Thus, these patients may present as demoralized and may struggle to motivate themselves to try to overcome their anxiety. A primary clinician in a substance abuse treatment program can help patients with SAD by educating them about their illness and by using skills of motivational interviewing (MI) to help them to pursue treatment and follow through with referrals (for an introduction to MI, see Miller & Rollnick, 2002). Since group sessions make patients with SAD nervous, these patients may seem uncooperative if a clinician recommends group treatment or attendance at self-help groups (e.g., AA, NA). Support from the clinician may help the patient to tolerate group treatment. Clinicians should recognize that a patient may never feel comfortable in group treatment until the social anxiety is treated.

CBT approaches to social anxiety address cognitive distortions and try to help patients to feel more comfortable in social situations. Patients with SAD often fear that they will embarrass or humiliate themselves in social situations and believe that people perceive their faults and judge them negatively. Cognitive therapists aim to help patients to recognize these thoughts, to view these thoughts as exaggerated, and to understand the role of these thoughts in triggering anxiety. After cognitive therapists teach patients how to manage these thoughts and how to utilize relaxation techniques, therapists try to encourage patients to gradually expose themselves to social situations where they can practice using the strategies that they have been taught in order to manage and minimize anxiety.

When choosing medications for treatment of SAD, clinicians should determine if the SAD is of the generalized type (the patient is anxious in multiple social situations) or the nongeneralized type (fear is limited to a few performance situations, such as public speaking, and is commonly referred to as "stage fright"). Nongeneralized SAD often responds well to the class of medications known as beta-blockers (e.g., propranol (Inderal)), which are used to treat high blood pressure and other heart conditions. These medications block the response of the autonomic nervous system to anxiety, controlling symptoms that usually accompany SAD (e.g., heart palpitations or accelerated heart rate, a feeling of "butterflies in the stomach," sweating), thereby reducing the intensity of the overall anxiety experience. Beta-blockers, which are usually prescribed for patients who participate in few or intermittent performances, are usually taken as needed and immediately before a performance situation; when performances are frequent or daily, antidepressant medications are usually recommended. Although beta-blockers are usually well tolerated, they can be sedating and can lower blood pressure, leading to light-headedness upon standing or fainting. Patients should be warned about these risks and should be encouraged to remain well hydrated. Beta-blockers do not have abuse potential.

Antidepressant medications of the SSRI and MAOI classes are effective in treating the generalized form of SAD. TCAs have not been shown to be useful for treatment of this disorder. Antidepressants usually take effect slowly (i.e., over a period of weeks); successful treatment with antidepressants usually results in improved self-esteem, less self-critical thinking, less distorted thinking about what others are thinking, reduced intensity of anxiety, and improvement in associated depressed mood. Medication may be most effective when combined with cognitive and behavioral techniques. For example, as a patient becomes more comfortable with the treatment regime and more confident, the clinician should encourage the patient to gradually enter feared social situations. Clinicians should remember that any one antidepressant can only be expected to work only about half of the time and that other medications may need to be tried before an effective medication is found.

Generalized Anxiety Disorder

It is important to encourage patients with symptoms of GAD to become abstinent or to substantially reduce substance use, since abstinence or reduction in use can improve or even eliminate anxiety symptoms. Patients with GAD often experience cognitive distortions that are characterized by a view of the world as dangerous and full of pitfalls and the view that the worst is likely to happen in any situation (e.g., "I'll screw up the job"; "I'll get fired"; "my children are not safe"; "something bad is going to happen"). These cognitive distortions are similar to thought patterns of depressed patients. Cognitive therapists try to help patients to replace these cognitive distortions with a more balanced view and to teach them techniques, including relaxation techniques, for resisting anxiety-provoking thoughts.

Buspirone (Buspar), an antianxiety medication that is effective for the treatment of GAD, has no sedating or tranquilizing properties and no abuse potential; like antidepressant medications, it takes time to work. A placebo-controlled trial of buspirone in alcohol-dependent patients with generalized anxiety that persisted following acute detoxification in an inpatient unit found that buspirone was effective in improving not only anxiety symptoms but also treatment retention and drinking outcome (Tollefson, Lancaster, & Montague-Clouse, 1991). More studies are needed to examine treatments for anxiety disorders among substance-dependent patients. The anticonvulsant medication pregabalin has been found to be useful in treatment of GAD (Pande et al., 2003; Rickels et al., 2005).

GAD also responds to antidepressant medications of various classes; SSRIs and SNRIs are usually the first choice since they generally have fewer side effects and usually do not result in interactions with substances subject to abuse. Since patients with GAD often experience insomnia, sedating antidepressants, including tricyclics, trazodone, and mirtazepine (Remeron), may be considered; trazodone is often used in low doses to promote sleep at bedtime in conjunction with a nonsedating antidepressant such as an SSRI, SNRI, or buspirone.

SUMMARY

Panic disorder with or without agoraphobia, SAD, and GAD commonly co-occur with substance use disorders. A clinician who works in a substance abuse treatment program can anticipate that 10 percent or more of their patients might suffer from one or more anxiety disorders. By recognizing anxiety disorders and recommending appropriate treatment approaches, clinicians can improve a patient's overall clinical outcome.

Effective CBT approaches are available for each anxiety disorder discussed in this chapter and are appropriate for substance-dependent patients (since, unlike medications, these approaches do not have abuse potential or adverse interactions with substances subject to abuse). However, relatively few clinicians are trained in CBT methods. Treatment programs should consider training their clinicians to use some of these methods. Use of CBT techniques does not require prior clinical training, and motivated drug counselors should be able to learn and adequately apply the techniques. Since CBT techniques are manual-guided, most clinicians can learn the techniques by studying the manual and, under supervision, practicing these techniques during sessions with patients. Medications without abuse potential (antidepressants, buspirone, beta-blockers) are also effective for treatment of anxiety disorders in patients with substance use disorders. More research is needed to examine both behavioral and medication treatments for co-occurring anxiety and substance use disorders.

Suggestions for Further Reading

For readers who wish to study further in this area, we recommend:

- Hoehn-Saric, R., Borkovec, T. D., & Belzer, K. D. (2007). Generalized anxiety disorder. In G. O. Gabbard (Ed.), *Treatment of psychiatric disorders* (4th ed., pp. 1587-1622). Washington, DC: American Psychiatric Publishing.

- Katon, W. J. (2006). Clinical practice: Panic disorder. *New England Journal of Medicine, 354*, 2360-2367.

- Schneier, F. R., & Welkowitz, L. (1996). *The hidden face of shyness: Understanding & overcoming social anxiety*. New York: Avon Books.

- Schneier, F. R. (2006). Clinical practice: Social anxiety disorder. *New England Journal of Medicine, 355*, 1029-1036.

Authors' Note

The research in this chapter was supported in part by NIH grants K02 DA00288 (Dr. Nunes), K24 DA022412 (Dr. Nunes), U10 DA13035 (Dr. Nunes), K23 DA00482 (Dr. Blanco), R03 DA015559 (Dr. Blanco), and R01 DA019606 (Dr. Blanco) and the New York State Psychiatric Institute (Dr. Blanco and Dr. Nunes).

References

American Psychiatric Association. (1994). *Diagnostic and statistical manual of mental disorders* (4th ed). Washington, DC: Author.

Bakker, A., van Balkom, A. J., & Stein, D. J. (2005). Evidence-based pharmacotherapy of panic disorder. *International Journal of Neuropsychopharmacology, 8*, 473-482.

Barlow, D. H., Gorman, J. M., Shear, M. K., & Woods, S. W. (2000). Cognitive-behavioral therapy, imipramine, or their combination for panic disorder: A randomized controlled trial. *Journal of the American Medical Association, 283*, 2529-2536.

Brady, K. T., & Sinha, R. (2005). Co-occurring mental and substance use disorders: The neuro-biological effects of chronic stress. *American Journal of Psychiatry, 162,* 1483-1493.

Breslau, N., Kilbey, M. M., & Andreski, P. (1993). Nicotine dependence and major depression: New evidence from a prospective investigation. *Archives of General Psychiatry, 50,* 31-35.

Brook, D. W., Brook, J. S., Zhang, C., Cohen, P., & Whiteman, M. (2002). Drug use and the risk of major depressive disorder, alcohol dependence, and substance use disorders. *Archives of General Psychiatry, 59,* 1039-1044.

Brown, S. A., Irwin, M., & Schuckit, M. A. (1991). Changes in anxiety among abstinent male alcoholics. *Journal of Studies on Alcohol, 52,* 55-61.

Brown, S. A., & Schuckit, M. A. (1988). Changes in depression among abstinent alcoholics. *Journal of Studies on Alcohol, 49,* 412-417.

Burns, L., Teesson, M., & O'Neill, K. (2005). The impact of comorbid anxiety and depression on alcohol treatment outcomes. *Addiction, 100,* 787-796.

Conway, K. P., Compton, W., Stinson, F. S., & Grant, B. F. (2006). Lifetime comorbidity of *DSM-IV* mood and anxiety disorders and specific drug use disorders: Results from the National Epidemiologic Survey on Alcohol and Related Conditions. *Journal of Clinical Psychiatry, 67,* 247-257.

Crum, R. M., Juon, H. S., Green, K. M., Robertson, J., Fothergill, K., & Ensminger, M. (2006). Educational achievement and early school behavior as predictors of alcohol-use disorders: 35-year followup of the Woodlawn Study. *Journal of Studies on Alcohol, 67,* 75-85.

Derogatis, L. R. (1983). *The SCL-90 manual II.* Towson, MD: Clinical Psychometric Research.

Ensminger, M. E., Juon, H. S., & Fothergill, K. E. (2002). Childhood and adolescent antecedents of substance use in adulthood. *Addiction, 97,* 833-844.

Fergusson, D. M., Horwood, L. J., & Swain-Campbell, N. (2002). Cannabis use and psychosocial adjustment in adolescence and young adulthood. *Addiction, 97,* 1123-1135.

First, M. B., Spitzer, R. L., Gibbon, M., & Williams, J. B. W. (2002, November). Structured Clinical Interview for DSM-IV-TR Axis I Disorders, Patient Edition (SCID-I/P). New York: Biometrics Research Department, New York State Psychiatric Institute.

Goodwin, R., & Hamilton, S. P. (2002). Cigarette smoking and panic: The role of neuroticism. *American Journal of Psychiatry, 159,* 1208-1213.

Grant, B. F., Hasin, D. S., Blanco, C., Stinson, F. S., Chou, S. P., Goldstein, R. B., et al. (2005a). The epidemiology of social anxiety disorder in the United States: Results from the National Epidemiologic Survey on Alcohol and Related Conditions. *Journal of Clinical Psychiatry, 66,* 1351-1361.

Grant, B. F., Hasin, D. S., Stinson, F. S., Dawson, D. A., Goldstein, R. B., Smith, S., et al. (2006). The epidemiology of DSM-IV panic disorder and agoraphobia in the United States: Results from the National Epidemiologic Survey on Alcohol and Related Conditions. *Journal of Clinical Psychiatry, 67,* 363-374.

Grant, B. F., Hasin, D. S., Stinson, F. S., Dawson, D. A., June Ruan, W., Goldstein, R. B., et al. (2005b). Prevalence, correlates, co-morbidity, and comparative disability of DSM-IV generalized anxiety disorder in the USA: Results from the National Epidemiologic Survey on Alcohol and Related Conditions. *Psychological Medicine, 35,* 1747-1759.

Grant, K. A., Shively, C. A., Nader, M. A., Ehrenkaufer, R .L., Line, S. W., Morton, T. E., et al. (1998). Effect of social status on striatal dopamine D2 receptor binding characteristics in cynomolgus monkeys assessed with positron emission tomography. *Synapse, 29,* 80-83.

Hamilton, M. (1959). The assessment of anxiety states by rating. *British Journal of Medical Psychology, 32,* 50-55.

Hasin, D. S., Samet, S., Nunes, E., Meydan, J., Matseoane, K., & Waxman, R. (2006). Diagnosis of comorbid disorders in substance users: Psychiatric Research Interview for Substance and Mental Disorders (PRISM-IV). *American Journal of Psychiatry, 163,* 689-696.

Johnson, J. G., Cohen, P., Pine, D. S., Klein, D. F., Kasen, S., & Brook, J. S. (2000). Association between cigarette smoking and anxiety disorders during adolescence and early adulthood. *Journal of the American Medical Association, 284*, 2348-2351.

Juon, H. S., Ensminger, M. E., & Sydnor, K. D. (2002). A longitudinal study of developmental trajectories to young adult cigarette smoking. *Drug and Alcohol Dependence, 66*, 303-314.

Kendler, K. S., Kessler, R. C., Heath, A. C., Neale, M. C., & Eaves, L.J. (1991). Coping: A generic epidemiological investigation. *Psychological Medicine, 21*, 337-346.

Kendler, K. S., Neale, M. C., Kessler, R. C., Heath, A. C., & Eaves, L. J. (1992a). The genetic epidemiology of phobias in women: The interrelationship of agoraphobia, social phobia, situational phobia, and simple phobia. *Archives of General Psychiatry, 49*, 273-281.

Kendler, K. S., Neale, M. C., Kessler, R. C., Heath, A. C., & Eaves, L. J. (1992b). Generalized anxiety disorder in women: A population-based twin study. *Archives of General Psychiatry, 49*, 267-272.

Kendler, K. S., Neale, M. C., Kessler, R. C., Heath, A. C., & Eaves, L. J. (1992c). Major depression and generalized anxiety disorder: Same genes, (partly) different environments? *Archives of General Psychiatry, 49*, 716-722.

Kendler, K. S., Prescott, C. A., Myers, J., & Neale, M. C. (2003). The structure of genetic and environmental risk factors for common psychiatric and substance use disorders in men and women. *Archives of General Psychiatry, 60*, 929-937.

Kessler, R. C., Chiu, W. T., Demler, O., Merikangas, K. R., & Walters, E. E. (2005). Prevalence, severity, and comorbidity of 12-month DSM-IV disorders in the National Comorbidity Survey Replication. *Archives of General Psychiatry, 62*, 617-627.

Kessler, R. C., Chiu, W. T., Jin, R., Ruscio, A. M., Shear, K., & Walters, E. E. (2006). The epidemiology of panic attacks, panic disorder, and agoraphobia in the National Comorbidity Survey Replication. *Archives of General Psychiatry, 63*, 415-424.

Kessler, R. C., Keller, M. B., & Wittchen, H. U. (2001). The epidemiology of generalized anxiety disorder. *Psychiatric Clinics of North America, 24*, 19-39.

Kessler, R. C., McGonagle, K. A., Zhao, S., Nelson, C. B., Hughes, M., Eshleman, S., et al. (1994). Lifetime and 12-month prevalence of DSM-III-R psychiatric disorders in the United States: Results from the National Comorbidity Survey. *Archives of General Psychiatry, 51*, 8-19.

Kessler, R. C., Stein, M. B., & Berglund, P. (1998). Social phobia subtypes in the National Comorbidity Survey. *American Journal of Psychiatry, 155*, 613-619.

Klein, D. F., & Fink, M. (1962). Psychiatric reaction patterns to imipramine. *American Journal of Psychiatry, 119*, 432-438.

Kranzler, H. R., Burleson, J .A., Del Boca, F .K., Babor, T. F., Korner, P., Brown, J., et al. (1994). Buspirone treatment of anxious alcoholics: A placebo-controlled trial. *Archives of General Psychiatry, 51*, 720-731.

Kushner, M. G., Abrams, K., Thuras, P., Hanson, K. L., Brekke, M., & Sletten, S. (2005). Follow-up study of anxiety disorder and alcohol dependence in comorbid alcoholism treatment patients. *Alcoholism: Clinical and Experimental Research, 29*, 1432-1443.

Miller, W. R., & Rollnick, S. (2002). *Motivational interviewing: Preparing people for change* (2nd ed.). New York: Guilford Press.

Nunes, E. V., & Raby, W. N. (2005). Comorbidity of depression and substance abuse. In J. Licinio and M. Wong (Eds.), *Biology of Depression* (Vol. 2, pp. 341-364). Weinheim, Germany: Wiley-VCH-Verlag GmbH KGaA.

Pande, A. C., Crockatt, J. G., Feltner, D. E., Janney, C. A., Smith, W. T., Weisler, R., et al. (2003). Pregabalin in generalized anxiety disorder: A placebo-controlled trial. *American Journal of Psychiatry, 160*, 533-540.

Patton, G. C., Coffey, C., Carlin, J. B., Degenhardt, L., Lynskey, M., & Hall, W. (2002). Cannabis use and mental health in young people: Cohort study. *British Medical Journal, 325*, 1195-1198.

Rickels, K., Pollack, M. H., Feltner, D. E., Lydiard, R. B., Zimbroff, D. L., Bielski, R. J., et al. (2005). Pregabalin for treatment of generalized anxiety disorder: A 4-week, multicenter, double-blind, placebo-controlled trial of pregabalin and alprazolam. *Archives of General Psychiatry, 62,* 1022-1030.

Robins, L. N., Helzer, J. E., Croughan, J., Williams, J. B. W., & Spitzer, R. L. (1981). *NIMH diagnostic interview schedule, version III* (DHHS Publication No. ADM-T-42-3). Washington, DC: U.S. Government Printing Office.

Robins, L. N., Wing, J., Wittchen, H. U., Helzer, J. E., Babor, T. F., Burke, J., et al. (1988). The Composite International Diagnostic Interview: An epidemiologic instrument suitable for use in conjunction with different diagnostic systems and in different cultures. *Archives of General Psychiatry, 45,* 1069-1077.

Schneier, F. R., Johnson, J., Hornig, C. D., Liebowitz, M. R., & Weissman, M. M. (1992). Social phobia: Comorbidity and morbidity in an epidemiologic sample. *Archives of General Psychiatry, 49,* 282-288.

Schneier, F. R., Liebowitz, M. R., Abi-Dargham, A., Zea-Ponce, Y., Lin, S. H., & Laruelle, M. (2000). Low dopamine D(2) receptor binding potential in social phobia. *American Journal of Psychiatry, 157,* 457-459.

Schneider, U., Altmann, A., Baumann, M., Bernzen, J., Bertz, B., Bimber, U., et al. (2001). Comorbid anxiety and affective disorder in alcohol-dependent patients seeking treatment: The first multicentre study in Germany. *Alcohol and Alcoholism, 36,* 219-223.

Sheehan, D. V., Lecrubier, Y., Sheehan, K. H., Amorim, P., Janavs, J., Weiller, E., et al. (1998). The Mini-International Neuropsychiatric Interview (M.I.N.I.): The development and validation of a structured diagnostic psychiatric interview for DSM-IV and ICD-10. *Journal of Clinical Psychiatry, 59*(Suppl. 20), 22-33.

Spitzer, R. L., Kroenke, K., & Williams, J. B. (1999). Validation and utility of a self-report version of PRIME-MD: The PHQ primary care study. Primary Care Evaluation of Mental Disorders. Patient Health Questionnaire. *Journal of the American Medical Association, 282,* 1737-1744.

Spitzer, R. L., Williams, J. B., Kroenke, K., Linzer, M., deGruy, F. V., III, Hahn, S. R., et al. (1994). Utility of a new procedure for diagnosing mental disorders in primary care: The PRIME-MD 1000 study. *Journal of the American Medical Association, 272,* 1749-1756.

Sullivan, J. T., Sykora, K., Schneiderman, J., Narango, C. A., & Sellers, E. M. (1989). Assessment of alcohol withdrawal: The revised clinical institute withdrawal assessment for alcohold scale (CIWA-Ar). *British Journal of Addiction, 84,* 1353-1357.

Tollefson, G. D., Lancaster, S. P., & Montague-Clouse, J. (1991). The association of buspirone and its metabolite 1-pyrimidinylpiperazine in the remission of comorbid anxiety with depressive features and alcohol dependency. *Psychopharmacology Bulletin, 27,* 163-170.

Yonkers, K. A., Warshaw, M. G., Massion, A. O., & Keller, M. B. (1996). Phenomenology and course of generalized anxiety disorder. *British Journal of Psychiatry, 168,* 308-313.

Part 3

Disorders of Attention and Cognitive Functioning and Chronic Mental Illness

Disorders of cognition lie at the interface of medicine and neurology. While all psychiatric disorders have physiological causes, they are only dimly understood for most psychiatric disorders (e.g., depression and anxiety). However, the symptoms of delirium and dementia, which have clear physiological causes, are often treatable. Delirium is an acute state of mental confusion. In substance abusers, delirium most commonly is caused by substance intoxication or alcohol or sedative withdrawal, as well as a range of medical conditions (e.g., head injury or infections). Delirium represents a medical emergency and can lead to death if it is not promptly diagnosed and treated. Dementia is a chronic deterioration in mental functioning that is usually caused by a chronic medical condition that damages the brain. A neurological workup is essential in the identification and treatment of the underlying condition. While most substance abuse treatment programs do not expect their treatment providers to have expertise in medicine and neurology, any clinician can learn to recognize the symptoms of delirium and dementia and refer patients to appropriate medical care.

Subtle problems of attention and cognitive functioning are common in substance-dependent patients and, until recently, have been almost entirely overlooked by researchers and clinicians. Attention deficit hyperactivity disorder (ADHD) is characterized by symptoms of disordered attention, hyperactivity, and impulsivity that date to childhood, seem to be heritable, appear to be related to functioning of the neurotransmitter dopamine in the brain, and respond to stimulant-like medications that boost the functioning of the dopamine system. Interestingly, dopamine is an important neurotransmitter in the brain reward system, which mediates the reinforcing effects of addictive drugs. Although clinicians once believed that children "grew out" of ADHD during adolescence and early adulthood, it is now well documented that ADHD symptoms can persist into adulthood.

Many substance-dependent patients have other deficits in attention, memory, and executive cognitive functioning (e.g., difficulty in integrating and organizing information, formulating appropriate responses, making decisions, and controlling impulses). The frontal lobes of the brain and associated subcortical structures are thought to mediate many of these cognitive functions. Deficits are subtle (i.e., deficits may not be noticed during routine conversation or during clinical interview), but they can have a substantial adverse impact on patients' occupational and social functioning and on the outcome of treatment for substance use disorders (these deficits are associated with dropout and treatment failure). Some of these deficits often manifest as learning difficulties during early school years. In some cases, these deficits may result from the toxic effects of chronic substance use, and functioning may improve following abstinence. Neuropsychological testing can help diagnose these deficits. Treatment providers can adapt counseling methods in order to help patients with cognitive difficulties to understand the lessons that are taught.

Schizophrenia is a chronic mental illness that usually begins in adolescence. It consists of a combination of symptoms: hallucinations (usually hearing voices) and delusional beliefs ("positive symptoms") and a syndrome that includes symptoms of apathy, social isolation, and deterioration in social functioning ("negative symptoms"). Patients with schizoaffective illness, which is characterized by a constellation of symptoms that resemble symptoms of schizophrenia and symptoms of a severe mood disorder, experience chronic psychosis and episodes of depression and/or mania and exhibit poor social functioning. Most patients with schizophrenia smoke cigarettes and are nicotine-dependent. Dependence on alcohol, cannabis, cocaine, and other stimulants is common in these patients.

Interestingly, the symptoms of schizophrenia, like the symptoms of ADHD, are thought to relate to abnormal functioning of dopamine, which is an important neurotransmitter in the brain reward system and is implicated in the neurophysiology of addictive disorders. Positive symptoms (hallucinations and delusions) respond to neuroleptic medications that block dopamine functioning. Some evidence suggests that patients with schizophrenia seek the stimulant properties of nicotine (and perhaps other drugs) in an effort to counteract negative symptoms (e.g., apathy and social withdrawal).

Patients with schizophrenia usually enter treatment through the mental health treatment system (e.g., psychiatric inpatient units, community-based psychiatric services) rather than through the substance abuse treatment system. However, clinicians who work for programs that specialize in treatment of dual diagnosis patients or MICA (mentally ill, chemically addicted) routinely encounter patients with schizophrenia. Evidence suggests that patients with schizophrenia and substance dependence problems who receive treatment for both disorders from one program (rather than from separate programs) have a better treatment outcome. This finding has helped to encourage treatment programs to integrate substance abuse treatment and mental health services for patients with co-occurring disorders. Successful implementation of integrated care requires clinicians with expertise in the treatment of substance dependence and chronic mental illness.

Chapter 5

Adult Attention Deficit Hyperactivity Disorder in Patients With Substance Use Disorders

by John J. Mariani, M.D., and Frances R. Levin, M.D.

INTRODUCTION

Attention deficit hyperactivity disorder (ADHD) is the most common psychiatric disorder in children (Olfson, 1992), with an estimated prevalence in the United States of 5-10 percent (Adler & Cohen, 2004; Barbaresi et al., 2002). It is estimated that up to 60 percent of patients with ADHD during childhood will continue to have clinically significant symptoms of ADHD into adulthood (Barkley, Fischer, Smallish, & Fletcher, 2002; Biederman, Mick, & Faraone, 2000; Kessler, Adler, Barkley et al., 2005; Rasmussen & Gillberg, 2000). The prevalence of adult ADHD is estimated to be 2-4 percent (Kessler, Chiu, Demler, Merikangas, & Walters, 2005; Murphy & Barkley, 1996; Weiss & Murray, 2003). ADHD is characterized by persistent patterns of inattention and/or impulsivity and hyperactivity that are more extreme than would be expected for an individual at the same developmental stage or age. ADHD is burdensome to affected individuals and society at large. In adults, these burdens include workplace and automobile accidents, as well as impaired occupational and academic performance.

Adult ADHD is a common co-occurring mental disorder among patients with substance use disorders. While community-based epidemiologic studies historically have not surveyed the rates of ADHD in adults, the recently published National Comorbidity Survey Replication (Kessler, Adler, Barkley, et al., 2005) found that among the 8.1 percent of respondents classified as having had childhood ADHD, 36.3 percent demonstrated symptoms of ADHD as adults (prevalence of adult ADHD was 4.6 percent (Kessler, Adler, Barkley, et al., 2005)). In this sample of adults with ADHD, 2.8 percent met *Diagnostic and Statistical Manual of Mental Disorders,* 4th edition (*DSM-IV;* American Psychiatric Association, 1994) criteria for an alcohol use disorder and 2.4 percent met criteria for a substance use disorder, suggesting that the overall risk of substance use disorders in adults with ADHD is similar to that of the general population (Kessler, Adler, Barkley, et al., 2005). However, in clinical samples of treatment-seeking adult patients with substance use disorders rates of co-occurring ADHD are much higher, with the reported prevalence of adult ADHD ranging from 10 percent to 24 percent (Clure et al., 1999; Levin, Evans, & Kleber, 1998a; Schubiner et al., 2000). This disparity in rates of co-occurring ADHD and substance use disorders between community-based and clinical studies is likely due to Berkson's bias (Berkson, 1946), which is the phenomenon that patients in clinical treatment settings are more likely to exhibit a higher degree of association between two disorders. Further, ADHD and substance use disorders may be causally related. Neurobehavioral disinhibition in childhood and adolescence, typically manifested by impulsivity, aggressivity, and sensation-seeking, has been associated with the later development of substance use disorders (Hawkins, Catalano, & Miller, 1992; Kirisci, Tarter, Vanyukov, Reynolds, & Haybech, 2004; Tarter et al., 2003), and imbalances in the brain dopamine system have been implicated in the pathophysiology of both ADHD and substance use disorders (Volkow, Fowler, & Wang, 2004; Volkow, Wang, Fowler, & Ding, 2005). Further, the presence of ADHD might tend to cause substance use disorders to run a more severe, chronic, or treatment-resistant course, which could also explain the greater prevalence of ADHD among treatment-seeking substance-dependent patients.

This chapter will focus on the clinical issues of diagnosis and treatment of adult ADHD in patients with substance use disorders. The goal of the chapter is to offer clinicians providing substance use disorder treatment with a framework for evaluating possible co-occurring ADHD and developing a treatment plan. Given the profound impact that untreated adult ADHD can have on an individual's functioning, including ability to participate in and benefit from treatment for the substance use disorder, awareness of this disorder by clinicians of all disciplines is critical.

CASE PRESENTATION

The case presented below demonstrates the common diagnostic and therapeutic challenges that clinicians providing substance abuse treatment face when encountering a patient with co-occurring ADHD. The presentation is organized in the manner that we recommend for evaluating substance use disorder patients for psychiatric comorbidity. The case presentation will be used throughout the chapter to highlight important diagnostic and therapeutic issues.

Identifying Data

AJ is a 36-year-old, who is divorced, has one son who is 9 years old and lives with his ex-wife, is employed as a used car salesman, and lives alone.

Chief Complaint

The patient presents for treatment at an outpatient substance abuse treatment clinic for worsening cocaine use and related consequences.

Patient History

History of Present Illness. AJ reports using $100-$200 of cocaine intranasally three to four times per week. He reports starting to use cocaine intermittently about five years ago, but over the past two years, his use has become more frequent and he has been using increasing amounts. His cocaine use is causing financial difficulties, and he is behind in his child support payments. Approximately once a month, he uses more than he intends to, stays up until the next morning, and misses work. His supervisor has noticed this change in behavior and has told AJ that if it continues, he will lose his job. For the past year, the patient has recognized that his cocaine use is a problem and that he needs to do something about it, but his attempts to cut down or quit have been unsuccessful. He will make a promise to himself not to use that day, but when he runs into someone at his job who sells cocaine, he impulsively buys it. The patient reports that his cocaine use progressed from an activity that he would do with friends on a weekend night to a solitary activity that he does at home. Over the past year he has stopped playing basketball with his friends on the weekends and rarely makes social plans. He has never had treatment for a substance use problem before and has never attended any twelve-step meetings. He drinks alcohol when trying to get to sleep after a night of using cocaine but does not believe the alcohol abuse is the primary problem. He denies any other substance use.

Substance Use History. The patient began using marijuana at age 15 and continued to use regularly until the age of 25. The patient reports that he stopped smoking marijuana when he got married because of his wife's unhappiness with his daily use. He has drunk alcohol in social settings since the age of 15 but denies a pattern of problematic use. He denies any history of problematic use of opiates or sedatives. He denies ever being treated in an inpatient or outpatient facility for a substance use problem. He denies any history of legal problems related to substance use.

Psychiatric History. The patient denies any history of psychiatric treatment. He has never been hospitalized in a psychiatric hospital and has never been prescribed any psychiatric medications. He was in marital counseling briefly prior to his divorce but otherwise has not received any other psychotherapy.

Developmental History. The patient reports being a "below average" student and a "bad test taker." He described his academic performance as "mediocre" from grade school through his second year of community college. He reports that he has never read a book from "cover-to-cover" because he "gets bored and distracted." In grade school, his classroom behavior was frequently a source of conflict with his teachers and parents, and he had a great deal of difficulty sitting still in class. His mother used to complain that he had a "motor that wouldn't quit" in him. His older sister was always an excellent student and is now a lawyer, and the patient reports that he has been unfavorably compared to her by his parents for his entire life.

Family History. There is no history of psychiatric or substance use disorders in either parent. His son, who is now 9 years old, was diagnosed with ADHD at age 7 and has had a good response to methylphenidate treatment.

Medical History. The patient denies any significant medical problems.

Social History. The patient was born and raised in a suburban town outside New York City. He is the younger of two children; his sister is three years older than him. Both of his parents are still living. He was a below-average student, and after high school he attended a local community college for eighteen months before dropping out. His academic performance in college was poor. Since college, the patient has worked in a variety of sales positions, usually for a period of one to two years. Most recently, for the past four years, he has worked at a used car dealership. He married a coworker at an electronics store at age 25 and had a son at age 27. He describes his marriage as "tense" and reports that his wife was chronically dissatisfied with the impact his poor work performance had on the family finances. She often complained that he was "scattered and disorganized" and "couldn't finish anything he started." They divorced when the patient was age 30, and he sees his son on alternate weekends.

Mental Status Examination

The patient is adequately groomed and dressed in a somewhat disheveled manner (e.g., tie is askew and one shoelace is untied). During the interview, he continually shifts in his seat, fidgets with his cell phone, and frequently stares out the window. He is friendly and cooperative, although he frequently interrupts the interviewer. His speech is rapid and loud at times. He describes his mood as "frustrated," and his affect is somewhat irritable. He denies any suicidal or homicidal ideation. No delusions are elicited. He denies any perceptual disturbances. His thought process is generally linear and logical, although at times his answers to questions are circular. He is alert and oriented to person, place, and time. Brief cognitive testing reveals no gross cognitive or memory impairments. His insight and judgment are good.

DIAGNOSTIC CRITERIA

Clinical Diagnosis

The diagnosis of ADHD in children and adults remains a clinical diagnosis—that is, to date, there are no neuropsychiatric or laboratory tests that have been shown to have clinical utility in diagnosing ADHD. In adults, the clinical diagnosis of ADHD remains challenging, particularly in patients with co-occurring substance use disorders, since there is a lack of consensus on diagnostic criteria (McGough & Barkley, 2004), symptoms overlap with other psychiatric disorders, and there is a need for a retrospective diagnosis of childhood ADHD. The diagnostic criteria for ADHD in the *Diagnostic and Statistical Manual of Mental Disorders,* 4th edition, text revision *(DSM-IV-TR;* American Psychiatric Association, 2000) (see Table 5-1) were developed for diagnosing ADHD in children and are currently used for diagnosing adult ADHD.

The first step in working through the *DSM-IV* criteria for ADHD is to determine if six or more symptoms of inattention or hyperactivity-impulsivity are present to satisfy Criterion A. The symptoms have to have persisted for six months to a degree that is maladaptive and inconsistent with developmental level. For a patient's symptoms to meet Criterion B, some of the symptoms need to have caused impairment prior to the age of 7. When clinicians must diagnose an adult patient without the help of the patient's family members to corroborate the patient's report of symptoms prior to age 7, clinicians may be unable to determine if the patient's symptoms meet Criterion B. Under Criterion C impairment from the symptoms needs to have occurred in more than two settings (e.g., work and home for adults.) Criterion D requires clear evidence of clinically significant impairment in social, academic, and occupational functioning. Under Criterion E symptoms cannot be accounted for by another mental disorder. An obvious problem with this criteria set is that some symptoms are specific to children (e.g., "often runs about or climbs excessively") and are not exhibited by adults.

The *DSM-IV* recognizes three subtypes of ADHD: predominantly inattentive, predominantly hyperactive-impulsive, and combined. The clinical heterogeneity of ADHD necessitated the creation of these subtypes to aid diagnosis. Hyperactive symptoms present in childhood forms of the disorder tend to remit at a higher rate than inattention symptoms (Biederman et al., 2000). The predominately inattentive type is diagnosed if Criterion 1 (see Table 5-1), but not Criterion 2, is met for the past six months. The predominately hyperactive-impulsive type is diagnosed if Criterion 2, but not Criterion 1, is met for the past six months. The combined type is diagnosed if both Criteria 1 and 2 are met for the past six months.

There are several factors that can lead to underdiagnosis of ADHD in adults. The first factor is patients' inability to recall symptoms prior to the age of 7. Such recall is frequently unreliable (Mannuzza, Klein, Klein, Bessler, & Shrout, 2002). Further, this criterion is not based upon any empirical evidence, and some authorities have advocated abandoning this criterion or raising the age to 12 (Barkley & Biederman, 1997).

Table 5-1
DSM-IV-TR Criteria for Attention Deficit Hyperactivity Disorder

Symptoms	DSM-IV-TR Criteria[a, b]	Issues in Substance-Dependent Patients
	A. Either (1) or (2):	
Inattention	1. Six (or more) of the following symptoms of inattention have persisted for at least six months to a degree that is maladaptive and inconsistent with developmental level:	Substance intoxication or withdrawal effects that lead to inattention tend to fluctuate and do not persist for long during periods of abstinence.
	a. often fails to give close attention to details or makes careless mistakes in schoolwork, work, or other activities	
	b. often has difficulty sustaining attention in tasks or play activities	
	c. often does not seem to listen when spoken to directly	
	d. often does not follow through on instructions and fails to finish schoolwork, chores, or duties in the workplace (not due to oppositional behavior or failure to understand instructions)	
	e. often has difficulty organizing tasks and activities	
	f. often avoids, dislikes, or is reluctant to engage in tasks that require sustained mental effort (such as schoolwork or homework)	
	g. often loses things necessary for tasks or activities (e.g., toys, school assignments, pencils, books, or tools)	
	h. is often easily distracted by extraneous stimuli	
	i. is often forgetful in daily activities.	
	2. Six (or more) of the following symptoms of hyperactivity-impulsivity have persisted for at least six months to a degree that is maladaptive and inconsistent with developmental level:	Substance intoxication or withdrawal effects that lead to hyperactivity and/or impulsivity tend to fluctuate and do not persist for long during periods of abstinence.

(Continued)

Symptoms	DSM-IV-TR Criteria[a, b]	Issues in Substance-Dependent Patients
Hyperactivity	a. often fidgets with hands or feet or squirms in seat	
	b. often leaves seat in classroom or in other situations in which remaining seated is expected	
	c. often runs about or climbs excessively in situations in which it is inappropriate (in adolescents or adults, may be limited to subjective feelings of restlessness)	
	d. often has difficulty playing or engaging in leisure activities quietly	
	e. is often "on the go" or often acts as if "driven by a motor"	
	f. often talks excessively	
Impulsivity	g. often blurts out answers before questions have been completed	
	h. often has difficulty awaiting turn	
	i. often interrupts or intrudes on others (e.g., butts into conversations or games).	
	B. Some hyperactive-impulsive or inattentive symptoms that caused impairment were present before age 7 years.	May be difficult for patients to recall accurately; ask about symptoms during elementary school.
	C. Some impairment from the symptoms is present in two or more settings (e.g., at school [or work] and at home).	
	D. There must be clear evidence of clinically significant impairment in social, academic, or occupational functioning.	Substance use frequently leads to impairment in social, academic, or occupational functioning.
	E. The symptoms do not occur exclusively during the course of a pervasive developmental disorder, schizophrenia, or other psychotic disorder and are not better accounted for by another mental disorder (e.g. mood disorder, anxiety disorder, dissociative disorder, or a personality disorder).[c]	If the symptoms occur only during periods of substance intoxication or withdrawal or during the immediate recovery period, a diagnosis of ADHD cannot be made.

(a) American Psychiatric Association (2000).
(b) Reprinted with permission from the *Diagnostic and Statistical Manual of Mental Disorders*, Fourth Edition, Text Revision (Copyright 2000). American Psychiatric Association.
(c) Consult *DSM-IV-TR* criteria (American Psychiatric Association, 2000) for pervasive developmental disorders, schizophrenia, other psychotic disorders, mood disorders, anxiety disorders, dissociative disorder, and personality disorders.

The second factor is the assumption that other psychiatric disorders (e.g., hypomania, depression) preclude the diagnosis of ADHD. Individuals with substance use disorders comorbid with adult ADHD often have other psychiatric conditions. The third factor is clinicians' failure to discuss symptoms of ADHD during psychiatric evaluations of adult patients who were not diagnosed with ADHD in childhood. Finally, manifestation of ADHD symptoms in adults may differ from children and from the symptoms described in the *DSM-IV* (i.e., adult patients may display fewer symptoms, symptoms may be less severe, or patients may compensate and symptoms are not noticeable). In general, adults tend to present with more attentional symptoms and fewer hyperactivity symptoms than children, which may be due to the different social milieu of adulthood. Individuals with ADHD may also "self-select" occupations, and thereby environments, that favor their attentional capacity and activity level. The presentation of ADHD symptoms in patients in late adolescence tends to resemble the presentation of ADHD symptoms in adults. Similarly, the presentation of ADHD symptoms in patients in early adolescence tends to resemble the presentation of ADHD symptoms in children.

Potential for Under- or Overdiagnosis

A number of factors can lead to overdiagnosis of adult ADHD. These factors include not obtaining an adequate longitudinal history, relying on screening instruments or rating scales alone, not insuring that the symptoms occur in more than one setting, and not insuring that symptoms cause impairment. Most individuals experience some ADHD symptomology as part of their daily living. In the case of ADHD, the difference is the degree of impairment that the symptoms cause and their pervasive presence in different settings.

Application to Case Example

In the case presented above (see "Case Presentation"), the patient gave a clear history of ADHD symptoms beginning in early childhood and persisting into adulthood. Although ADHD was not diagnosed or treated during this patient's childhood, there is no better explanation for his symptoms. Ideally, the clinician would include the patient's family members in the diagnostic process to enhance the chance of obtaining an accurate history (family members might provide school report cards and any available educational or psychological testing). When an adult meets criteria for ADHD, but lacks a clear history of childhood ADHD, according to the *DSM-IV*, ADHD is not diagnosed. However, it is often unclear how to categorize such cases since it is possible that, in some cases, ADHD is present and the childhood symptoms were not evident or recalled, or in other cases, subthreshold ADHD symptoms may represent another disorder such as impairment secondary to chronic substance use.

NATURAL HISTORY AND ETIOLOGY

ADHD is a disorder that, by definition, is present before the age of 7 (although recall for such early symptoms may be poor). It is estimated that ADHD symptoms will persist into adulthood in approximately 50-60 percent of cases (Barkley et al., 2002; Biederman et al., 2000; Kessler, Adler, Barkley, et al., 2005; Rasmussen & Gillberg, 2000). As an individual with ADHD develops into an adult, the individual is at risk of developing co-occurring psychiatric disorders, including substance use disorders. It is estimated that up to 80 percent of adults with ADHD have at least one co-occurring psychiatric disorder (Kessler, Chiu, Demler, et al., 2005). ADHD symptoms result in a large individual and public burden; it is estimated that ADHD costs employers 120 million days of lost work time annually among U.S. employees or $19.5 billion in lost human capital (Kessler, Adler, Ames, et al., 2005).

There is overlap in the development of ADHD and substance use disorders. It is estimated that more than 25 percent of substance-abusing adolescents meet diagnostic criteria for ADHD (DeMilio, 1989; Halikas, Meller, Morse, & Lyttle, 1990; Thompson, Riggs, Mikulich, & Crowley, 1996). Studies of adults with ADHD have reported rates of substance use disorders that range from 9 percent to 45 percent (Wilens, Spencer, & Biederman, 1995c). Adults in substance abuse treatment have rates of ADHD ranging from 10 percent to 24 percent (Clure et al., 1999; Levin et al., 1998a; Schubiner et al., 2000). A recent large-scale epidemiologic survey, the National Comorbidity Survey Replication, found a significant correlation in rates of comorbidity between substance use disorders and ADHD (Kessler, Chiu, Demler, et al., 2005).

The etiology of ADHD is unknown. However, there is evidence of a strong genetic component to the development of ADHD. Twin studies report a greater concordance of ADHD symptoms between monozygotic twins in comparison to dizygotic twins, and adoptive relatives are less likely to have ADHD than biological relatives of ADHD children (Hechtman, 1996). First-degree relatives of children with ADHD have higher rates of ADHD than controls (Biederman et al., 1992; Biederman, Faraone, Keenan, Knee, & Tsuang, 1990).

Genes and familial factors may play a smaller role in the etiology of ADHD in individuals who have a remitting course (i.e., individuals who seem to grow out of ADHD rather than individuals who have persistent ADHD). Parents of adolescents with ADHD are twenty times more likely to have ADHD than parents of adolescents without ADHD. However, parents of adolescents whose ADHD symptoms have remitted are only five times more likely to have ADHD than parents of controls (Biederman et al., 1996). Siblings of adolescents with ADHD are seventeen times more likely to have ADHD than siblings of controls; however, siblings of adolescents whose ADHD symptoms have remitted are only four times more likely to have ADHD (Faraone, Biederman, Mennin, Gershon, & Tsuang, 1996).

While the exact cause of ADHD is unknown, available evidence supports the theory that dopamine neurotransmission dysfunction is at least partly responsible for the characteristic symptoms of ADHD. Evidence supporting dopamine involvement in ADHD symptomatology includes pharmacotherapy studies that have shown that stimulant medications, which increase dopamine levels, effectively treat ADHD symptoms (Greenhill, Halperin, & Abikoff, 1999; Greenhill et al., 2003; Schubiner et al., 2002; Shenker, 1992), genetic studies that have linked dopamine genes to ADHD (Cook et al., 1995; Ebstein, Nemanov, Klotz, Gritsenko, & Belmaker, 1997; LaHoste et al., 1996), and imaging studies of patients with ADHD that have shown abnormalities of dopamine function and structural abnormalities in regions of the brain with concentrations of dopamine-producing neurons (Bush et al., 1999; Giedd, Blumenthal, Molloy, & Castellanos, 2001; Volkow et al., 2005). Since the development of substance use disorders is also linked to dopamine (Kalivas & Volkow, 2005), there may be common factors that lead to the development of ADHD and co-occurring substance use disorders.

ISSUES INVOLVED IN MAKING THE DIAGNOSIS IN SUBSTANCE-DEPENDENT PATIENTS

Diagnosing ADHD in patients who are actively using substances or who recently initiated abstinence is challenging. Substances of abuse have many acute and chronic effects that mimic the symptoms of psychiatric disorders including ADHD. For example, the use of stimulants can lead to changes in attentional capacity and activity level both during intoxication and recovery from intoxication and chronic marijuana use may lead to deficits in attention. In addition, many patients are unable to describe recent periods of time when they were not actively using substances, making the distinction between primary and substance-induced symptoms difficult. When patients initially present for substance abuse treatment, other co-occurring psychiatric conditions, such as mood or anxiety disorders, may also require clinical attention.

While evaluating patients after a period of prolonged abstinence, as some authorities recommend (Milin, Loh, Chow, & Wilson, 1997), is ideal, in many cases this will not be possible. Often a careful clinical history of symptoms during past periods of abstinence or prior to the onset of substance use problems is the best available method to assess whether inattention and hyperactivity symptoms represent a primary disorder or are substance-induced. However, since retrospective diagnoses of childhood ADHD in adults, made on the basis of self-report, tend to overdiagnosis ADHD (Mannuzza et al., 2002), a conservative approach should be maintained. Symptoms that occur during periods of active substance use are difficult to interpret, since if they occur exclusively in the context of active substance use, a diagnosis of ADHD is inappropriate.

Assessment for malingering is an important component of evaluating a patient with a substance use disorder for ADHD since the mainstay of treatment for ADHD is stimulants that are potentially abusable. Since symptom assessment is based almost entirely on self-report, clinicians must be vigilant in spotting patients with substance use disorders who intend to mislead clinicians in order to obtain stimulants.

METHODS FOR SCREENING AND DIAGNOSIS

All patients with substance use disorders should be screened for the presence of ADHD since failure to treat ADHD symptoms can negatively impact on substance use disorder treatment outcome as well as overall social-occupational functioning. In order to complete a comprehensive assessment of a patient with a substance use disorder, the clinician must determine if the patient has symptoms of inattention or hyperactivity. If symptoms have been present during periods of prolonged abstinence or prior to the onset of the substance use disorder, further assessment is indicated.

The gold standard for diagnosing ADHD, as well as other psychiatric disorders, is a comprehensive psychiatric evaluation. Clinicians may use structured instruments, such as the Conners' Adult ADHD Diagnostic Interview for *DSM-IV* (CAADID; Epstein & Kollins, 2006), which systematically assesses adults for both childhood and adult symptoms. However, in many clinical settings, performing a CAADID is not practical or feasible. A more practical approach is to use a semistructured clinical interview that is based on *DSM-IV* criteria for ADHD as a guide. The ADHD Rating Scale-IV (DuPaul, Power, Anastopoulos, & Reid, 1998) and the Swanson, Nolan, and Pelham (SNAP) Checklist from the *Diagnostic and Statistical Manual of Mental Disorders*, 4th edition (SNAP-IV; Swanson, 1995) can be useful in screening for

ADHD symptoms. Rating scales, such as the Conners' Adult ADHD Rating Scales (CAARS; Conners et al., 1999), can be useful for monitoring symptom severity over time in response to prolonged abstinence or ADHD pharmacotherapy. One important caveat is that ADHD rating scales, when administered to patients who have not yet achieved a prolonged period of abstinence, will tend to capture substance-induced symptoms of inattention and hyperactivity in addition to possible symptoms due to ADHD. In such cases, repeated administration of the rating scale over time can help confirm the diagnosis; substance-induced symptoms should improve with abstinence, whereas symptoms due to ADHD will be stable in the absence of treatment. Obtaining school report cards and reports of the patient's symptoms from parents or other family members can be very helpful in determining whether ADHD symptoms caused significant impairment during childhood. If such reports are unavailable, it is often useful to ask patients to describe their experience in school, their relationship with teachers and classmates, the comments that they received about their school performance (e.g., report cards and comments from teachers), and the usual range of their grades.

DIFFERENTIAL DIAGNOSIS AND OVERLAPPING DISORDERS

ADHD frequently co-occurs with other psychiatric disorders in both children and adults (Faraone et al., 2000; McGough et al., 2005). This presents a diagnostic challenge since other psychiatric disorders (e.g., depression, bipolar illness, or substance use disorders) can mimic core ADHD symptoms. In patients receiving substance use disorder treatment, the most challenging aspect of an assessment for ADHD is determining whether inattention and hyperactivity symptoms are related to substance use or represent ADHD. Patients receiving treatment for addictive disorders frequently have comorbid mood, anxiety, and other psychiatric disorders (Grant et al., 2004; Kessler et al., 1997; Kessler, Chiu, Demler, et al., 2005; Regier et al., 1990), the presence of which further complicates the diagnostic evaluation. Psychiatric symptoms must be evaluated using a systematic and comprehensive approach.

For example, patients with major depressive disorder may present with poor concentration and memory, disorganization, and inability to accomplish tasks, but a careful history will reveal that in patients with depression, these symptoms should accompany and fluctuate with mood symptoms and should have cleared up at times during a patient's history when there was no depression. In contrast, in patients with ADHD, the symptoms and resulting impairment should be relatively stable (despite periods of remission from mood disorders or substance use disorders). Patients with hypomania will often have hyperactivity and distractibility, but a careful history will distinguish the fluctuating and episodic nature of mood disorders from the relatively stable and persistent symptoms of ADHD. It is also important to remember that a patient may have multiple disorders (e.g., both ADHD and bipolar illness).

TREATMENT OPTIONS

Importance of Treating ADHD

An important question for clinicians to answer is "how important is it to treat ADHD in patients with substance use disorders?" An initial approach to this question is to consider the impact of ADHD on individuals who do not have substance use disorders. Adults with ADHD have less educational attainment, greater likelihood of being fired from their jobs, greater sociopathy, more traffic accidents and car license suspensions, more psychosocial problems with social deficits, and a greater frequency of divorce (Mannuzza & Klein, 2000). There is evidence that ADHD affects the development and course of substance use disorders: individuals with substance use disorders and ADHD have (1) an earlier onset of substance abuse than those without ADHD, (2) a greater likelihood of having a continuous problem if they develop substance dependence and a reduced likelihood of going into remission, and (3) a tendency to take longer to reach remission (Wilens, Biederman, & Mick, 1998). Although individuals with ADHD have more treatment exposure, they seem to do less well with substance abuse treatment. Therefore, the diagnosis and treatment of ADHD in patients with substance use disorders is essential to achieve the best possible clinical outcome.

Treatment of ADHD With Stimulant Medications

The treatment of adult ADHD in patients with substance use disorders has been controversial, since the primary pharmacotherapy for ADHD is psychostimulants and, historically, there has been reluctance on the part of clinicians to use these medications in patients with addictive disorders. However, while nonstimulant treatments are available, none have been shown to have an equivalent efficacy to traditional stimulant medications. Some authorities (Castaneda, Levy, Hardy, & Trujillo, 2000; Riggs, 1998) have proposed approaches that emphasize use of medications with a lower risk of abuse, such as antidepressants, pemoline, or bupropion, before use of traditional stimulant medications, such as methylphenidate or amphetamine analogs. However, clinical trials of methylphenidate (Grabowski et al., 1997; Levin et al., 2006; Levin, Evans, McDowell, & Kleber, 1998b; Schubiner et al., 2002) and dextroamphetamine (Grabowski et al., 2001; Grabowski et al., 2004; Shearer et al., 2001; Shearer, Wodak, van Beek, Mattick, & Lewis, 2003) for the treatment of either cocaine dependence or ADHD in patients with co-occurring substance use disorders have shown that stimulant medications can be used safely in patients with substance use disorders and have a relatively low risk of abuse under monitored conditions.

Psychostimulant medications have been shown to have a clinically and statistically significant effect on reducing ADHD symptoms in adults (Wilens, Biederman, Spencer, & Prince, 1995b). Methylphenidate has been one of the first-line treatments for ADHD in children for decades and has been shown to be effective for the treatment of ADHD in adults (Faraone, Spencer, Aleardi, Pagano, & Biederman, 2004). Amphetamine analogs, also a first-line treatment for childhood ADHD, have also been shown to be effective for the treatment of ADHD in adults (Spencer et al., 2001).

Treatment of ADHD With Nonstimulant Medications

Nonstimulant medications, such as antidepressants, have a moderate effect on ADHD symptoms in adults (Wilens, Biederman, Mick, & Spencer, 1995a). Atomoxetine, a nonstimulant agent that was recently FDA approved for the treatment of ADHD in children and adolescents, also has evidence of efficacy in adults (Adler, Spencer, Milton, Moore, & Michelson, 2005; Michelson et al., 2003). Atomoxetine has no abuse potential, so it is an attractive candidate medication for study in the treatment of ADHD in patients with substance use disorders.

Studies of Medications for ADHD

The use of stimulants and nonstimulant medications has been studied in patients with co-occurring substance use disorders and adult ADHD. Methylphenidate has been shown to be effective in uncontrolled trials in reducing ADHD symptoms and cocaine use (Levin et al., 1998b; Somoza et al., 2004). A three-arm double-blind placebo-controlled trial of bupropion and methylphenidate for the treatment of ADHD in cocaine-dependent patients receiving methadone maintenance treatment for opioid dependence found no benefit of bupropion or methylphenidate on ADHD symptoms or cocaine use outcomes (Levin et al., 2006). A double-blind placebo-controlled trial of methylphenidate in the treatment of adult ADHD patients with comorbid cocaine dependence found that methylphenidate improved ADHD symptoms on some measures, but not others, and did not show a reduction in cocaine use (Schubiner et al., 2002). An uncontrolled trial of bupropion for the treatment of cocaine dependence and adult ADHD in eleven patients reported that ADHD and cocaine use symptoms decreased significantly (Levin, Evans, McDowell, Brooks, & Nunes, 2002). While the treatment literature for ADHD in patients with substance use disorders is not well developed, the trend that is emerging is that medications that are effective for adult ADHD are likely to be effective for adults with ADHD and co-occurring substance use disorders, but the therapeutic benefit may be less. The available evidence supports the use of stimulant medications over nonstimulant medications for adult ADHD and children with ADHD. While stimulant medications, such as methylphenidate and amphetamine analogs, have the potential for abuse, which is a heightened concern of clinicians who treat patients with comorbid substance use disorders, the available evidence suggests that this risk is relatively low when patients are under careful clinical monitoring. Results from clinical trials do not validate the concern that treatment with stimulant medication may worsen a patient's substance use disorder. Most clinicians experienced in the treatment of ADHD in patients with substance use disorders would likely recommend the use of sustained-release preparations of stimulants to reduce the potential for misuse, although clinical data are lacking to support this approach.

Psychosocial Treatments

The mainstay of treatment of adult ADHD and ADHD in children is pharmacotherapy. Psychosocial treatments for ADHD, which encompass a broad set of interventions, including behavior therapy, academic interventions, family therapy, and care coordination, have been extensively studied in children but not adults (Murphy, 2005). The optimal role of psychosocial treatment in adults with ADHD has not been determined. However, in the absence of data, it is reasonable to assume that multimodal treatment including medication and psychosocial treatments is likely to be the most effective and comprehensive approach.

Limitations of Treatments for ADHD

Pharmacotherapy can result in dramatic improvements in attentional deficits and hyperactivity-impulsivity. However, since ADHD is a chronic disorder with a childhood onset, the sequelae of a lifelong history of living with ADHD can persist even after the core ADHD symptoms have improved. Often important social and occupational skills have not been acquired. Adults with ADHD often have deficits in organization and planning that are not addressed with stimulant treatment. While the results from pharmacotherapy can be dramatic, it is important to manage a patient's expectations of medication treatment and reinforce the concept that cognitive and behavioral approaches will be needed to comprehensively address the deficits associated with ADHD.

SUMMARY

ADHD is a commonly co-occurring psychiatric disorder among patients with substance use disorders and results in substantial morbidity. While evaluation of ADHD in patients with substance use disorders is challenging, diagnostic criteria and rating scales exist to help guide the assessment. A variety of stimulant and nonstimulant medications have been shown to be effective in the treatment of ADHD in adults. While stimulant medications have the potential for abuse and must be used cautiously in patients with substance use disorders, the available evidence suggests that stimulant medications administered under monitored conditions can be safe and effective in patients with substance use disorders. The appropriate role of psychosocial treatment approaches in patients with ADHD and substance use disorders has not been determined, but it is reasonable to suggest that clinicians use a comprehensive treatment approach that includes psychosocial methods. Clinicians may wish to adapt their counseling methods to accommodate the difficulties with sustained attention, memory, and organization that are frequently manifested by such patients.

Suggestions for Further Reading

For readers who wish to study further in this area, we recommend:

- Hallowell, E. M. & Ratey, J. J. (1995). *Driven to distraction: Recognizing and coping with attention deficit disorder from childhood through adulthood.* New York: Touchstone.

- Levin, F. R., Sullivan, M. A., & Donovan, S. J. (2003). Co-occurring addictive and attention deficit/hyperactivity disorder and eating disorders. In A. W. Graham, T. K. Schultz, M. F. Mayo-Smith, R. K. Ries, & B. B. Wilford (Eds.), *Principles of addiction medicine* (3rd ed., pp. 1321-1346). Chevy Chase, MD: American Society of Addiction Medicine.

- Weiss, M. (2001). *ADHD in adulthood: A guide to current theory, diagnosis, and treatment.* Baltimore: Johns Hopkins University Press.

References

Adler, L., & Cohen, J. (2004). Diagnosis and evaluation of adults with attention-deficit/ hyperactivity disorder. *Psychiatric Clinics of North America, 27,* 187-201.

Adler, L. A., Spencer, T. J., Milton, D. R., Moore, R. J., & Michelson, D. (2005). Long-term, open-label study of the safety and efficacy of atomoxetine in adults with attention-deficit/ hyperactivity disorder: An interim analysis. *Journal of Clinical Psychiatry, 66,* 294-299.

American Psychiatric Association. (1994). *Diagnostic and statistical manual of mental disorders* (4th ed.). Washington, DC: Author.

American Psychiatric Association. (2000). *Diagnostic and statistical manual of mental disorders* (4th ed., text rev.). Washington, DC: Author.

Barbaresi, W. J., Katusic, S. K., Colligan, R. C., Pankratz, V. S., Weaver, A. L., Weber, K. J., et al. (2002). How common is attention-deficit/hyperactivity disorder? Incidence in a population-based birth cohort in Rochester, Minn. *Archives of Pediatrics and Adolescent Medicine, 156,* 217-224.

Barkley, R. A., & Biederman, J. (1997). Toward a broader definition of the age-of-onset criterion for attention-deficit hyperactivity disorder. *Journal of the American Academy of Child and Adolescent Psychiatry, 36,* 1204-1210.

Barkley, R. A., Fischer, M., Smallish, L., & Fletcher, K. (2002). The persistence of attention-deficit/hyperactivity disorder into young adulthood as a function of reporting source and definition of disorder. *Journal of Abnormal Psychology, 111,* 279-289.

Berkson, J. (1946). Limitations of the application of fourfold table analyses to hospital data. *Biometrics Bulletin, 2,* 47–53.

Biederman, J., Faraone, S. V., Keenan, K., Knee, D., & Tsuang, M. T. (1990). Family-genetic and psychosocial risk factors in DSM-III attention deficit disorder. *Journal of the American Academy of Child and Adolescent Psychiatry, 29,* 526-533.

Biederman, J., Faraone, S. V., Keenan, K., Benjamin, J., Krifcher, B., Moore, C., et al. (1992). Further evidence for family-genetic risk factors in attention deficit hyperactivity disorder: Patterns of comorbidity in probands and relatives psychiatrically and pediatrically referred samples. *Archives of General Psychiatry, 49,* 728-738.

Biederman, J., Faraone, S., Milberger, S., Guite, J., Mick, E., Chen, L., et al. (1996). A prospective 4-year follow-up study of attention-deficit hyperactivity and related disorders. *Archives of General Psychiatry, 53,* 437-446.

Biederman, J., Mick, E., & Faraone, S. V. (2000). Age-dependent decline of symptoms of attention deficit hyperactivity disorder: Impact of remission definition and symptom type. *American Journal of Psychiatry, 157,* 816-818.

Bush, G., Frazier, J. A., Rauch, S. L., Seidman, L. J., Whalen, P. J., Jenike, M. A., et al. (1999). Anterior cingulate cortex dysfunction in attention-deficit/hyperactivity disorder revealed by fMRI and the Counting Stroop. *Biological Psychiatry, 45,* 1542-1552.

Castaneda, R., Levy, R., Hardy, M., & Trujillo, M. (2000). Long-acting stimulants for the treatment of attention-deficit disorder in cocaine-dependent adults. *Psychiatric Services, 51,* 169-171.

Clure, C., Brady, K. T., Saladin, M. E., Johnson, D., Waid, R., & Rittenbury, M. (1999). Attention-deficit/hyperactivity disorder and substance use: Symptom pattern and drug choice. *American Journal of Drug and Alcohol Abuse, 25,* 441-448.

Conners, C. K., Erhardt, D., Epstein, J. N., Parker, J. D. A., Sitarenios, G., & Sparrow, E. (1999). Self-ratings of ADHD symptoms in adults I: Factor structure and normative data. *Journal of Attention Disorders 3,* 141-151.

Cook, E. H., Jr., Stein, M. A., Krasowski, M. D., Cox, N. J., Olkon, D. M., Kieffer, J. E., et al. (1995). Association of attention-deficit disorder and the dopamine transporter gene. *American Journal of Human Genetics, 56,* 993-998.

DeMilio, L. (1989). Psychiatric syndromes in adolescent substance abusers. *American Journal of Psychiatry, 146,* 1212-1214.

DuPaul, G. J., Power, T. J., Anastopoulos, A. D., & Reid, R. (1998) *ADHD Rating Scale-IV: Checklists, norms, and clinical interpretation.* New York: Guilford Press.

Ebstein, R. P., Nemanov, L., Klotz, I., Gritsenko, I., & Belmaker, R. H. (1997). Additional evidence for an association between the dopamine D4 receptor (D4DR) exon III repeat polymorphism and the human personality trait of novelty seeking. *Molecular Psychiatry, 2,* 472-477.

Epstein, J. N., & Kollins, S. H. (2006). Psychometric properties of an adult ADHD diagnostic interview. *Journal of Attention Disorders, 9,* 504-514.

Faraone, S. V., Biederman, J., Mennin, D., Gershon, J., & Tsuang, M. T. (1996). A prospective four-year follow-up study of children at risk for ADHD: Psychiatric, neuropsychological, and psychosocial outcome. *Journal of the American Academy of Child and Adolescent Psychiatry, 35,* 1449-1459.

Faraone, S. V., Biederman, J., Spencer, T., Wilens, T., Seidman, L. J., Mick, E., et al. (2000). Attention-deficit/hyperactivity disorder in adults: An overview. *Biological Psychiatry, 48,* 9-20.

Faraone, S. V., Spencer, T., Aleardi, M., Pagano, C., & Biederman, J. (2004). Meta-analysis of the efficacy of methylphenidate for treating adult attention-deficit/hyperactivity disorder. *Journal of Clinical Psychopharmacology, 24,* 24-29.

Giedd, J. N., Blumenthal, J., Molloy, E., & Castellanos, F. X. (2001). Brain imaging of attention deficit/hyperactivity disorder. *Annals of the New York Academy of Sciences, 931,* 33-49.

Grabowski, J., Roache, J. D., Schmitz, J. M., Rhoades, H., Creson, D., & Korszun, A. (1997). Replacement medication for cocaine dependence: Methylphenidate. *Journal of Clinical Psychopharmacology, 17,* 485-488.

Grabowski, J., Rhoades, H., Schmitz, J., Stotts, A., Daruzska, L. A., Creson, D., et al. (2001). Dextroamphetamine for cocaine-dependence treatment: A double-blind randomized clinical trial. *Journal of Clinical Psychopharmacology, 21,* 522-526.

Grabowski, J., Rhoades, H., Stotts, A., Cowan, K., Kopecky, C., Dougherty, A., et al. (2004). Agonist-like or antagonist-like treatment for cocaine dependence with methadone for heroin dependence: Two double-blind randomized clinical trials. *Neuropsychopharmacology, 29,* 969-981.

Grant, B. F., Stinson, F. S., Dawson, D. A., Chou, S. P., Dufour, M. C., Compton, W., et al. (2004). Prevalence and co-occurrence of substance use disorders and independent mood and anxiety disorders: Results from the National Epidemiologic Survey on Alcohol and Related Conditions. *Archives of General Psychiatry, 61,* 807-816.

Greenhill, L. L., Halperin, J. M., & Abikoff, H. (1999). Stimulant medications. *Journal of the American Academy of Child and Adolescent Psychiatry, 38,* 503-512.

Greenhill, L. L., Swanson, J. M., Steinhoff, K., Fried, J., Posner, K., Lerner, M., et al. (2003). A pharmacokinetic/pharmacodynamic study comparing a single morning dose of Adderall to twice-daily dosing in children with ADHD. *Journal of the American Academy of Child and Adolescent Psychiatry, 42,* 1234-1241.

Halikas, J. A., Meller, J., Morse, C., & Lyttle, M. D. (1990). Predicting substance abuse in juvenile offenders: Attention deficit disorder versus aggressivity. *Child Psychiatry and Human Development, 21,* 49-55.

Hawkins, J. D., Catalano, R. F., & Miller, J. Y. (1992). Risk and protective factors for alcohol and other drug problems in adolescence and early adulthood: Implications for substance abuse prevention. *Psychological Bulletin, 112,* 64-105.

Hechtman, L. (1996). Families of children with attention deficit hyperactivity disorder: A review. *Canadian Journal of Psychiatry, 41,* 350-360.

Kalivas, P. W., & Volkow, N. D. (2005). The neural basis of addiction: A pathology of motivation and choice. *American Journal of Psychiatry, 162,* 1403-1413.

Kessler, R. C., Crum, R. M., Warner, L. A., Nelson, C. B., Schulenberg, J., & Anthony, J. C. (1997). Lifetime co-occurrence of DSM-III-R alcohol abuse and dependence with other psychiatric disorders in the National Comorbidity Survey. *Archives of General Psychiatry, 54,* 313-321.

Kessler, R. C., Adler, L., Ames, M., Barkley, R. A., Birnbaum, H., Greenberg, P., et al. (2005). The prevalence and effects of adult attention deficit/hyperactivity disorder on work performance in a nationally representative sample of workers. *Journal of Occupational and Environmental Medicine, 47,* 565-572.

Kessler, R. C., Adler, L. A., Barkley, R., Biederman, J., Conners, C. K., Faraone, S. V., et al. (2005). Patterns and predictors of attention-deficit/hyperactivity disorder persistence into adulthood: Results from the National Comorbidity Survey Replication. *Biological Psychiatry, 57,* 1442-1451.

Kessler, R. C., Chiu, W. T., Demler, O., Merikangas, K. R., & Walters, E. E. (2005). Prevalence, severity, and comorbidity of 12-month DSM-IV disorders in the National Comorbidity Survey Replication. *Archives of General Psychiatry, 62,* 617-627.

Kirisci, L., Tarter, R. E., Vanyukov, M., Reynolds, M., & Habeych, M. (2004). Relation between cognitive distortions and neurobehavior disinhibition on the development of substance use during adolescence and substance use disorder by young adulthood: A prospective study. *Drug and Alcohol Dependence, 76,* 125-133.

LaHoste, G. J., Swanson, J. M., Wigal, S. B., Glabe, C., Wigal, T., King, N., et al. (1996). Dopamine D4 receptor gene polymorphism is associated with attention deficit hyperactivity disorder. *Molecular Psychiatry, 1,* 121-124.

Levin, F. R., Evans, S. M., & Kleber, H. D. (1998a). Prevalence of adult attention-deficit hyperactivity disorder among cocaine abusers seeking treatment. *Drug and Alcohol Dependence, 52,* 15-25.

Levin, F. R., Evans, S. M., McDowell, D. M., & Kleber, H. D. (1998b). Methylphenidate treatment for cocaine abusers with adult attention-deficit/hyperactivity disorder: A pilot study. *Journal of Clinical Psychiatry, 59,* 300-305.

Levin, F. R., Evans, S. M., McDowell, D. M., Brooks, D. J., & Nunes, E. (2002). Bupropion treatment for cocaine abuse and adult attention-deficit/hyperactivity disorder. *Journal of Addictive Diseases, 21,* 1-16.

Levin, F. R., Evans, S. M., Brooks, D. J., Kalbag, A. S., Garawi, F., & Nunes, E. V. (2006). Treatment of methadone-maintained patients with adult ADHD: Double-blind comparison of methylphenidate, bupropion and placebo. *Drug and Alcohol Dependence, 81,* 137-148.

Mannuzza, S., & Klein, R. G. (2000). Long-term prognosis in attention-deficit/hyperactivity disorder. *Child and Adolescent Psychiatric Clinics of North America, 9,* 711-726.

Mannuzza, S., Klein, R. G., Klein, D. F., Bessler, A., & Shrout, P. (2002). Accuracy of adult recall of childhood attention deficit hyperactivity disorder. *American Journal of Psychiatry, 159,* 1882-1888.

McGough, J. J., & Barkley, R. A. (2004). Diagnostic controversies in adult attention deficit hyperactivity disorder. *American Journal of Psychiatry, 161,* 1948-1956.

McGough, J. J., Smalley, S. L., McCracken, J. T., Yang, M., Del'Homme, M., Lynn, D. E., et al. (2005). Psychiatric comorbidity in adult attention deficit hyperactivity disorder: Findings from multiplex families. *American Journal of Psychiatry, 162,* 1621-1627.

Michelson, D., Adler, L., Spencer, T., Reimherr, F. W., West, S. A., Allen, A. J., et al. (2003). Atomoxetine in adults with ADHD: Two randomized, placebo-controlled studies. *Biological Psychiatry, 53,* 112-120.

Milin, R., Loh, E., Chow, J., & Wilson, A. (1997). Assessment of symptoms of attention-deficit hyperactivity disorder in adults with substance use disorders. *Psychiatric Services, 48,* 1378-1380, 1395.

Murphy, K., & Barkley, R. A. (1996). Attention deficit hyperactivity disorder adults: Comorbidities and adaptive impairments. *Comprehensive Psychiatry, 37,* 393-401.

Murphy, K. (2005). Psychosocial treatments for ADHD in teens and adults: A practice-friendly review. *Journal of Clinical Psychology, 61,* 607-619.

Olfson, M. (1992). Diagnosing mental disorders in office-based pediatric practice. *Journal of Developmental and Behavioral Pediatrics, 13,* 363-365.

Rasmussen, P., & Gillberg, C. (2000). Natural outcome of ADHD with developmental coordination disorder at age 22 years: A controlled, longitudinal, community-based study. *Journal of the American Academy of Child and Adolescent Psychiatry, 39,* 1424-1431.

Regier, D.A., Farmer, M. E., Rae, D. S., Locke, B. Z., Keith, S. J., Judd, L. L., et al. (1990). Comorbidity of mental disorders with alcohol and other drug abuse: Results from the Epidemiologic Catchment Area (ECA) Study. *Journal of the American Medical Association, 264,* 2511-2518.

Riggs, P.D. (1998) Clinical approach to treatment of ADHD in adolescents with substance use disorders and conduct disorder. *Journal of the American Academy of Child and Adolescent Psychiatry, 37,* 331-332.

Schubiner, H., Tzelepis, A., Milberger, S., Lockhart, N., Kruger, M., Kelley, B.J., et al. (2000). Prevalence of attention-deficit/hyperactivity disorder and conduct disorder among substance abusers. *Journal of Clinical Psychiatry 61,* 244-251.

Schubiner, H., Saules, K. K., Arfken, C. L., Johanson, C. E., Schuster, C. R., Lockhart, N., et al. (2002). Double-blind placebo-controlled trial of methylphenidate in the treatment of adult ADHD patients with comorbid cocaine dependence. *Experimental and Clinical Psychopharmacology, 10,* 286-294.

Shearer, J., Wodak, A., Mattick, R. P., Van Beek, I., Lewis, J., Hall, W., et al. (2001). Pilot randomized controlled study of dexamphetamine substitution for amphetamine dependence. *Addiction, 96,* 1289-1296.

Shearer, J., Wodak, A., van Beek, I., Mattick, R. P., & Lewis, J. (2003). Pilot randomized double blind placebo-controlled study of dexamphetamine for cocaine dependence. *Addiction, 98,* 1137-1141.

Shenker, A. (1992). The mechanism of action of drugs used to treat attention-deficit hyperactivity disorder: Focus on catecholamine receptor pharmacology. *Advances in Pediatrics, 39,* 337-382.

Somoza, E. C., Winhusen, T. M., Bridge, T. P., Rotrosen, J. P., Vanderburg, D. G., Harrer, J. M., et al. (2004). An open-label pilot study of methylphenidate in the treatment of cocaine dependent patients with adult attention deficit/hyperactivity disorder. *Journal of Addictive Diseases, 23,* 77-92.

Spencer, T., Biederman, J., Wilens, T., Faraone, S., Prince, J., Gerard, K., et al. (2001). Efficacy of a mixed amphetamine salts compound in adults with attention-deficit/hyperactivity disorder. *Archives of General Psychiatry, 58,* 775-782.

Swanson, J. M. (1995). *SNAP-IV Scale.* Irvine, CA: University of California Child Development Center.

Tarter, R. E., Kirisci, L., Mezzich, A., Cornelius, J. R., Pajer, K., Vanyukov, M., et al. (2003). Neurobehavioral disinhibition in childhood predicts early age at onset of substance use disorder. *American Journal of Psychiatry, 160,* 1078-1085.

Thompson, L. L., Riggs, P. D., Mikulich, S. K., & Crowley, T. J. (1996). Contribution of ADHD symptoms to substance problems and delinquency in conduct-disordered adolescents. *Journal of Abnormal Child Psychology, 24,* 325-347.

Volkow, N. D., Fowler, J. S., & Wang, G. J. (2004). The addicted human brain viewed in the light of imaging studies: Brain circuits and treatment strategies. *Neuropharmacology, 47*(Suppl. 1), 3-13.

Volkow, N. D., Wang, G. J., Fowler, J. S., & Ding, Y. S. (2005). Imaging the effects of methylphenidate on brain dopamine: New model on its therapeutic actions for attention-deficit/hyperactivity disorder. *Biological Psychiatry, 57,* 1410-1415.

Weiss, M., & Murray, C. (2003). Assessment and management of attention-deficit hyperactivity disorder in adults. *Canadian Medical Association Journal, 168,* 715-722.

Wilens, T. E., Biederman, J., Mick, E., & Spencer, T. J. (1995a). A systematic assessment of tricyclic antidepressants in the treatment of adult attention-deficit hyperactivity disorder. *Journal of Nervous and Mental Disease, 183,* 48-50.

Wilens, T. E., Biederman, J., Spencer, T. J., & Prince, J. (1995b). Pharmacotherapy of adult attention deficit/hyperactivity disorder: A review. *Journal of Clinical Psychopharmacology, 15,* 270-279.

Wilens, T. E., Spencer, T. J., & Biederman, J. (1995c). Are attention-deficit hyperactivity disorder and the psychoactive substance use disorders really related? *Harvard Review of Psychiatry, 3,* 160-162.

Wilens, T. E., Biederman, J., & Mick, E. (1998). Does ADHD affect the course of substance abuse? Findings from a sample of adults with and without ADHD. *American Journal on Addictions, 7,* 156-163.

Chapter 6

Delirium, Dementia, and Other Cognitive Disorders in Patients With Substance Use Disorders

by Petros Levounis, M.D., M.A., and Efrat Aharonovich, Ph.D.

INTRODUCTION

People who use alcohol and drugs may suffer from a variety of cognitive problems or impairments. Cognition refers to higher mental processes such as attention, concentration, memory, planning, problem solving, and abstract reasoning. Cognitive problems fall under a wide variety of psychiatric disorders but can be organized in three broad categories:

- Delirium;
- Dementia; and
- Nonspecific cognitive disorders associated with drug and alcohol dependence.

Delirium is a disturbance of consciousness during which a person experiences confusion and disorientation and may display grossly impaired judgment and behavior. Delirium may be caused by substance intoxication, withdrawal, acute medical conditions, or a combination of the above. It typically develops within a short period of time (i.e., minutes or hours) from the onset of its physiological cause. Delirium is considered a medical emergency for two reasons:

1. It may represent a rapidly evolving medical condition that could be life threatening if not treated rapidly and appropriately (e.g., delirium tremens due to severe alcohol withdrawal or subdural hematoma (bleeding inside the brain) after head trauma); and

2. The potential for injury is high due to impaired judgment and disorganized behavior (e.g., severe alcohol intoxication).

Thus, it is important for every health care worker to be able to recognize delirium and to ensure that a patient with symptoms of delirium is monitored and treated.

Dementia refers to a cognitive decline that evolves over a long period of time (i.e., months to years). People who suffer from dementia typically lose their memory and frequently have problems following conversation, remembering names and/ or places, or performing simple daily tasks (e.g., eating or bathing). Dementia is caused by permanent damage to the brain. The most common causes of dementia are Alzheimer's disease and cerebral vascular disease. Dementia may also result from chronic poisoning (e.g., lead poisoning) or from chronic effects of substances (e.g., brain damage from abuse of inhaled solvents). Another cause of dementia is alcohol-induced dementia syndrome, which results from chronic alcohol intoxication and related vitamin deficiencies.

Nonspecific Cognitive Disorders: Alcohol and drug dependence are often associated with problems in attention, memory, and ability to organize, plan, learn, and process information. These are relatively subtle deficits that may not be evident during a routine conversation or a clinical interview and require use of objective measures such as formal neuropsychological evaluation. They can, nonetheless, underlie significant impairment in occupational and social functioning and predict failure to benefit from substance abuse treatment (Aharonovich et al., 2006; Fals-Stewart & Schafer, 1992). Such impairments may result from chronic substance use or may represent a preexisting condition (sometimes dating to childhood) that increases the risk for developing substance use disorders. Subtle cognitive dysfunction is a common condition in substance-dependent patients that is underrecognized by most health care professionals. Neuropsychological studies indicate that one-third to one-half of patients entering treatment for alcohol or other substance dependence are cognitively impaired (Vik, Cellucci, Jarchow, & Hedt, 2004); some studies find even higher rates of cognitive impairment (Bates et al., 2004). It is important to be able to recognize the signs of such problems in the history or clinical presentation, since accurate assessment may help to shape an appropriate treatment plan or to determine why a patient may be having difficulty in treatment.

Specific and nonspecific disorders of cognition are common among substance-dependent patients and are generally underrecognized. The ability to recognize the various disorders of cognition will improve a clinician's effectiveness. Thus, the purpose of this chapter is to introduce readers to the diagnosis and treatment of delirium, dementia, and other types of cognitive impairments in substance-dependent patients.

CASE PRESENTATIONS

Case 1: Delirium and Dementia

The case presented below reflects the challenge of evaluating and treating patients with co-occurring substance use disorders and cognitive impairments.

Chief Complaint and History of Present Illness. CR is a 27-year-old Puerto Rican man with a history of alcohol and drug use and ill-defined psychiatric diagnosis who presented to an urban hospital. On admission, he reports that he was thrown out of his aunt's house because he was drinking, approached a policeman, knelt on the ground, and said to him "Shoot me in the head; I am … crazy." The officer found CR to be intoxicated by alcohol, tearful, agitated, and suspicious, and the officer brought him to the hospital for admission into the detoxification unit. When CR is reevaluated three hours after his arrival, he cannot recall the circumstances that brought him to the hospital but continued to express suicidal ideation and begins to sing. Hospital staff members contact the patient's aunt, who reported that although CR has been "a drunken menace" for a long time, he has become "impossible within the last several days" (i.e., two to three days prior to admission to the hospital), following a brawl at the local bar.

Patient History.
Alcohol and Other Drug History. CR started drinking alcohol at the age of 12 and began smoking marijuana shortly thereafter. He describes his teenage years as "a fog" due to his use of many illicit substances, including cannabis, hallucinogens, and, occasionally, opioids. He reports, "I would use whatever I could get my hands on." He currently abuses alcohol, cocaine, marijuana, heroin, and benzodiazepines almost every day, except when hospitalized. He smokes about a pack of cigarettes a day. During withdrawal from drugs, he typically becomes aggressive, verbally abusive, and hostile, and sometimes he expresses suicidal and homicidal ideation.

Psychiatric and Treatment History. In the past several years, the patient has had several hospital admissions for psychiatric problems, primarily for suicidal ideation and disinhibited behavior. He has been treated in the past with several medications, including haloperidol, chlorpromazine, risperidone, lithium, valproate, sertraline, amitriptyline, trazodone, propranolol, buspirone, and lorazepam. He has a long history of poor adherence to medications.

CR has a history of suicide gestures, including superficially slashing his wrists two months prior to the current admission. The patient has a history of violent behavior, including a recent assault on the property manager of his apartment building and an employee of the company that manages his apartment building, where he destroyed a door.

Developmental History. CR dropped out of high school in the eleventh grade; he has been supporting himself by "hustling on the streets." He has been arrested twice for larceny and three times for possession of illicit substances. He has spent seven months in jail. He has never had a romantic relationship and reports "not being sure if [he]'d like a girlfriend."

Family History. CR reports that both his mother and his father used excessive amounts of alcohol. However, he does not recall any history of suicide or psychiatric problems in his family. One of his sisters "drinks a lot, even when she is pregnant."

Medical History. The patient denies any history of medical problems other than occasional "bruises and scratches" following fights. He has no surgical history.

Mental Status Examination. The patient is well dressed and well groomed. His speech is normal in volume, rate, and prosody. No psychomotor agitation or retardation is noted. He reports that his mood is "fine" and adds "I just want to go home." Since his admission to the hospital, his affect seems improved and euthymic, but he remains irritable and occasionally demanding and, at times, displays labile affect. The patient denies any suicidal or homicidal ideation (active or passive). He denies any perceptual disturbances. His orientation is intact, but his concentration, memory, and higher cognitive functions (as tested by a series of questions, including a question that asks the patient to name the president of the United States) are impaired. He scores 23 (out of 30) on the Mini Mental State Examination (MMSE; Folstein, Folstein, & McHugh, 1975); he misses 2 points for orientation, 3 points for concentration, and 2 points for recall. His insight and judgment are compromised but adequate for basic activities of daily living.

Physical Examination. Physical examination of the patient reveals superficial scrapes and bruises on the patient's arms and legs and tenderness of his scalp on the left side.

Medical Workup. The patient's instability and cognitive impairment (as indicated by the MMSE) indicate delirium and possibly an underlying medical/neurological condition that may account for part of the clinical presentation. Medical/neurological work-up results include:

- *Laboratory Examinations.* Results from laboratory examinations of all major medical functions (including hematologic, metabolic, thyroid, and hepatic functioning) are all within normal limits, except for mildly elevated liver function tests (LFTs) with AST = 86, ALT = 96, and Alkaline Phosphatase = 110. The patient tests human immunodeficiency virus (HIV) negative. The test for syphilis is also negative. Urinalysis and urine toxicology examination for drugs of abuse administered on admission) are negative. The patient's tuberculosis test and chest X-ray are negative. Electrocardiogram (EKG) is normal.

- *Prior Neuropsychological Testing.* Records from a previous hospitalization at a state hospital reveal that neuropsychological testing that was completed two years prior to the current admission showed deficits in sustained concentration, executive function, language expression, visual-motor abilities, ability to learn, and immediate, recent, and delayed memory. The treatment team gave the patient the Axis I diagnoses of dementia NOS (not otherwise specified) and polysubstance dependence with physiological dependency.

- *Neuropsychological Testing.* Neuropsychological testing, completed two weeks after the current admission, confirms the state hospital's results and reveals "very real and significant impairment in memory, attention, and concentration."

- *Head Scans.* Since the patient reports tenderness of the scalp from a brawl three days prior to his admission to the hospital, head Computed Tomography (CT) scans with and without contrast and Magnetic Resonance Imaging (MRI) scans are ordered. These scans reveal an evolving subdural hematoma (bleeding inside the brain) that probably resulted from head trauma sustained during the recent brawl.

Follow-Up. A hospital neurosurgeon, who is consulted about the patient's brain pathology, recommends draining the hematoma and repairing the injury to stop the bleeding. The procedure is uneventful, and CR has a speedy recovery. Two weeks following the procedure, CR was fully conscious and showed significant improvement in his cognitive functioning (although not complete recovery). He can concentrate better on different tasks, and his mood lability improves dramatically. However, both his short-term memory and long-term memory remain impaired.

Diagnosis. On admission, CR suffers from delirium; he has (1) clear disturbance of consciousness with reduced ability to attend to any one task; (2) change in cognition, poor memory, and some orientation difficulties; (3) acute deterioration of his condition over a period of a few days; and (4) a medical condition that caused the disturbance: subdural hematoma. His case is formulated as delirium due to a medical condition, in addition to alcohol and drug dependence. CR may also suffer from a substance-induced persisting dementia, perhaps as a result of toxic effects of alcohol. The *Diagnostic and Statistical Manual of Mental Disorders,* 4th edition, text revision (*DSM-IV-TR;* American Psychiatric Association, 2000) diagnosis is:

Axis I:	Delirium due to subdural hematoma
	Rule out substance-induced persisting dementia
	Alcohol dependence
	Polysubstance dependence
Axis II:	Rule out mental retardation
Axis III:	Subdural hematoma, followed up with draining and repair
Axis IV:	Poor social support, homelessness, unemployment, poor finances
Axis V:	On admission to the hospital: 22
	Highest during the year prior to admission: 40

Clinical Summary. This case illustrates how an acute and life-threatening medical condition can develop in a substance-dependent patient and manifest as delirium (an acute and fluctuating impairment in cognitive functioning). These types of cases can be mismanaged and misdiagnosed; delirium in patients with alcohol dependence or drug dependence can be mistaken for effects of intoxication. CR became delirious after sustaining a head injury in a fight, but his aunt attributed his condition to drunkenness (she referred to him as a "drunken menace"), as did the police officer (fortunately, the police officer took him to a hospital). Sometimes medical personnel do not recognize the symptoms of delirium. Thus, clinicians working at detoxification units and other programs for treatment of substance dependence should be able to recognize the signs and symptoms of delirium.

Case 2: Cognitive Impairments

The case study below illustrates the subtleties of the cognitive impairments experienced by a large proportion of substance-dependent patients. Relevant treatment recommendations are discussed in "Treatment Options."

Chief Complaint and History of Present Illness. DL is a 32-year-old Caucasian woman with a long history of snorting cocaine and smoking crack. On admission to an outpatient drug treatment program, she reports that she is tired of being arrested for drug possession and states "I want my life back; I can't continue living like this."

Patient History.
Alcohol and Other Drug History. DL started snorting cocaine at the age of 19; her boyfriend at the time introduced her to the drug. From the age of 19 to 24 she "had as much cocaine as [she] wanted because [her] boyfriend was a dealer." She started to freebase and to smoke crack at age 24. She reports "I immediately knew this was it: the high was so strong; I loved it and could not stop." At this time, DL used alcohol (mostly beer) and, occasionally, used valium that she bought off the street to "calm [her] down from the high." At age 27, when her boyfriend was sentenced to jail, she paid for her drug use by dealing: "I would cop for others and get a cut." She reports regular cocaine and crack use (spending $60 to $100 per day four to five days per week). She denies any regular use of other substances. During withdrawal from cocaine she becomes agitated, irritable, and slightly depressed.

Psychiatric and Treatment History. The patient denies any past hospital admissions for psychiatric problems but reports that she has two failed attempts to become abstinent in drug treatment programs. Her first attempt in a drug treatment program was three years ago, when she was 29 years old: she enrolled in a short-term residential treatment program, but she was unable to follow all of the program guidelines or attend all of the meetings, and she left the program three weeks after she had entered it. Her second attempt in a drug treatment program was one year ago: she participated in group therapy sessions and individual therapy sessions in an outpatient treatment program. She completed the program and was abstinent for one month but "then [she] went to a party, did a line, and, within a week, was using regularly again."

Developmental History. Born into a middle-class family from New York, DL is the youngest of three siblings. She reports that she had "a normal childhood." All developmental milestones (e.g., beginning to crawl, walk, talk) were reached without difficulty. DL reports that she was an average student. After graduating from high school, she attended a school for visual arts, but she dropped out after the second semester when she "met the wrong guy." She worked odd jobs and could not hold a job for longer than four months. She reports that she "got bored with the work very easily," "missed work when [she] went on cocaine binges," and "was laid off many times."

Family History. DL reports that no one in her family has a history of drug use or excessive drinking.

Medical History. The patient denies any history of medical problems.

Mental Status Examination. The patient arrives at the examination neatly dressed and appears slightly younger than her stated age. Her speech is within normal limits of volume and rate. She displays minor psychomotor agitation when she moves uneasily in her chair. She reports her mood to be "good" and adds "I am glad to be here today to start treatment." Her affect is generally euthymic (occasionally labile). Her thought process seems goal-oriented and concrete. She denies any suicidal or homicidal ideation (active or passive). She displays no gross cognitive impairments (e.g., problems with attention, short- and long-term memory, and reality judgment) during the examination.

Treatment Attendance/Participation. DL has problems arriving at weekly sessions on time (she was frequently one to two hours late and twice forgets that she had a session) and has difficulty paying attention during the sixty-minute sessions. She easily converses with her therapist during her sessions, but after the first twenty minutes of the session she begins to move around in her chair. DL has difficulty with assignments that require her to plan activities that she might do instead of using drugs. She frequently says, "I never plan ahead; I can't do it."

Clinical Summary. To appropriately refer a patient for neuropsychological services and treatment planning, clinicians must carefully observe the patient during intake and during interviews. Certain symptoms or behaviors can indicate the need for further assessment, including a neuropsychological evaluation. Many substance-dependent patients with mild cognitive impairments may not display or report these symptoms. Failure to identify these symptoms may lead to failure to diagnosis or diagnosis properly.

DIAGNOSTIC CRITERIA

The *DSM-IV-TR* criteria for substance-induced delirium (i.e., substance intoxication delirium or substance withdrawal delirium) and substance-induced persisting dementia are summarized in Table 6-1A and Table 6-1B. Other cognitive disorders described in the *DSM-IV-TR* (e.g., delirium due to a medical condition and dementia of the Alzheimer's type, dementia due to head trauma, and dementia due to HIV disease) are seen in people who use drugs and alcohol. Distinguishing among these types of cognitive disorders can be challenging since they share several core symptoms and associated symptoms. Table 6-2 describes some differences between delirium and dementia.

Delirium

The hallmark of delirium is disorientation and shifting levels of consciousness (sometimes called waxing and waning consciousness) that develops over a period of a few hours or a few days. Disorientation refers to an inability to correctly identify oneself (i.e., a patient cannot remember his/her name), location (i.e., a patient cannot identify where he/she is), and date (i.e., a patient cannot identify the day of the week or the date). A patient who cannot correctly state the date, day of the week, or time of day (e.g., the patient is interviewed in the middle of winter, but the patient says that it is July) is "disoriented to time." A patient who cannot correctly identify where he/she is located (e.g., a patient in the emergency room insists that he/she is at home) is "disoriented to place." A patient who cannot correctly identify himself/herself is "disoriented to person" (the most severe disturbance of consciousness). A patient who correctly identifies person, place, and time is said to be "awake, alert, and oriented times three" (sometimes abbreviated in medical charts as AAO × 3). The waxing and waning level of consciousness that is typical of delirium can be tricky to evaluate because it requires repeated assessments over time; at times, a patient is fully conscious, oriented

Table 6-1A
***DSM-IV-TR* Criteria for Substance-Induced Delirium
(Substance Intoxication Delirium and Substance Withdrawal Delirium)**

Criteria Common to Both Substance Intoxication Delirium and Substance Withdrawal Delirium		
Symptoms	***DSM-IV-TR* Criteria**[a, b]	**Issues in Substance-Dependent Patients**
Changes in consciousness	A. Disturbance of consciousness (i.e., reduced clarity of awareness of the environment) with reduced ability to focus, sustain, or shift attention.	Elderly patients who use alcohol and over-the-counter medications are particularly vulnerable.
Changes in cognition	B. A change in cognition (such as memory deficit, disorientation, language disturbance) or the development of a perceptual disturbance that is not better accounted for by a preexisting, established, or evolving dementia.	Substance-abusing patients are subject to common medical conditions, such as head trauma or stroke, which can present with similar symptoms.
Changes are abrupt	C. The disturbance develops over a short period of time (usually hours to days) and tends to fluctuate during the course of the day.	
Criterion Specific to Substance Intoxication Delirium		
Symptoms	***DSM-IV-TR* Criteria**[a, b]	**Issues in Substance-Dependent Patients**
Changes are due to intoxication	D. There is evidence from the history, physical examination, or laboratory findings of either (1) or (2):	Commonly seen with alcohol, other sedatives (benzodiazepines and barbiturates), cocaine, amphetamines, cannabis, inhalants, hallucinogens, phencyclidine, over-the-counter medications.
	(1) the symptoms in Criteria A and B developed during substance intoxication	
	(2) medication use is etiologically related to the disturbance	
Criterion Specific to Substance Withdrawal Delirium		
Symptoms	***DSM-IV-TR* Criteria**[a, b]	**Issues in Substance-Dependent Patients**
Changes are due to withdrawal	E. There is evidence from the history, physical examination, or laboratory findings that the symptoms in Criteria A and B developed during, or shortly after, a withdrawal syndrome.	Commonly seen with alcohol, other sedatives (benzodiazepines and barbiturates).

[a] American Psychiatric Association (2000).
[b] Reprinted with permission from the *Diagnostic and Statistical Manual of Mental Disorders*, Fourth Edition, Text Revision (Copyright 2000). American Psychiatric Association.

Table 6-1B
***DSM-IV-TR* Criteria for Substance-Induced Persisting Dementia**

Symptoms	*DSM-IV-TR* Criteria[a, b]	Issues in Substance-Dependent Patients
	A. The development of multiple cognitive deficits manifested by both (1) and (2):	
Memory loss	(1) Memory impairment (impaired ability to learn new information or to recall previously learned information)	If the patient remains abstinent from alcohol, memory loss is halted and possibly partially reversed.
Problems including:	(2) one (or more) of the following cognitive disturbances:	Alcohol-induced cognitive disturbances are complicated by a variety of nutritional deficiencies, brain infections, traumatic injuries, and liver failure (all commonly seen in alcoholic patients).
a. speaking or understanding	a. aphasia (language disturbance)	
b. doing things	b. apraxia (impaired ability to carry out motor activities despite intact motor function)	
c. recognizing things	c. agnosia (failure to recognize or identify objects despite intact sensory function)	
d. planning and organizing	d. disturbance in executive functioning (i.e., planning, organizing, sequencing, abstracting).	
Functional impairment	B. The cognitive deficits in Criteria A1 and A2 each cause significant impairment in social or occupational functioning and represent a significant decline from a previous level of functioning.	
Changes are not due to intoxication or withdrawal	C. The deficits do not occur exclusively during the course of a delirium and persist beyond the usual duration of substance intoxication or withdrawal.	See Table 6-1A for symptoms of substance intoxication delirium and substance withdrawal delirium (symptoms can mimic dementia).
Changes are due to chronic substance use	D. There is evidence from the history, physical examination, or laboratory findings that the deficits are etiologically related to the persisting effects of substance use (e.g., a drug of abuse, a medication).	Commonly seen with alcohol, inhalants, polysubstance use.

[a] American Psychiatric Association (2000).
[b] Reprinted with permission from the *Diagnostic and Statistical Manual of Mental Disorders,* Fourth Edition, Text Revision (Copyright 2000). American Psychiatric Association.

(to person, place, and time), and conversational, while moments later the patient may be disoriented and easily distracted and may have lost touch with reality. Delirious patients also have memory deficits and can experience hallucinations and delusions. Hallucinations experienced during delirium are often visual and quite vivid.

Table 6-2
Differences Between Delirium and Dementia

Question	Delirium	Dementia
Is the person fully conscious?	Always no	Almost always yes
Is the person oriented? Does the person know who he/she is, what the date is, and where the interview takes place?	Often no	Often yes
How does the person feel?	Often anxious, fearful, confused, labile, irritable, or silly	Typically stable, sometimes detached
How is the person's thinking?	Fragmented	Coherent
How is the person's sleep?	Fragmented	Normal
What's the course of the illness?	It comes on fast and lasts hours to a few days, depending on course of the underlying acute medical problem	It comes on slowly and lasts years; in many cases the impairment is irreversible

Note: Adapted from Manley (2003); reprinted with permission.

Delirium exists on a continuum of physiological disturbances of brain functioning. A patient with less severe delirium may have mild disturbances in cognition (as indicated by a score lower than 29 or 30 (out of 30) on the MMSE) with loss of performance in areas like memory or calculation. Such mild disturbances can progress to delirium if the underlying physiological cause worsens. In a patient with more severe delirium, delirium can progress to stupor, coma, and, ultimately, to death as the physiological disturbance becomes more severe. *Stupor* refers to a state in which a patient is extremely lethargic and somnolent and cannot be aroused to a higher level of alertness. *Coma* refers to a state of complete unconsciousness from which a patient cannot be aroused. As the underlying physiological disturbance goes untreated and becomes more severe (e.g., blood accumulates inside the skull during a subdural hematoma), a patient's mental state will progress from delirium to stupor to coma and, possibly, to death if the underlying cause is not recognized and treated. Unlike patients with stupor or coma, patients who are simply tired, sleepy, or asleep can be quickly awakened to a fully alert state and oriented level of consciousness (oriented to person, place, and time, and otherwise in their usual state of mental functioning). Stupor and coma are medical emergencies. A patient with symptoms of stupor or coma should be rushed to a hospital so that the underlying cause can be identified and treated.

Common Causes of Delirium in Substance-Dependent Patients. Common causes of delirium in substance-dependent patients are summarized in Table 6-3 and discussed below.

Substance Intoxication. All substances, including alcohol, street drugs, and prescription medications, can cause delirium when taken in high doses. Intoxication is the most common cause of delirium among substance users. The most likely substances to cause delirium during intoxication are alcohol and other sedatives such as benzodiazepines, as well as cocaine, amphetamines, cannabis, inhalants, phencyclidine (PCP), and over-the-counter medications (Schuckit, 2000). Special attention should be paid to the elderly and people who use combinations of drugs, because of increased risk of delirium with lower doses of substances. Aging slows down liver function, so a relatively small dose of a substance taken by an elderly person does not get neutralized as quickly as in an average adult, lingers in the body longer than in an average adult, and can cause intoxication and delirium. People who take combinations of drugs are at increased risk of delirium due to a possible synergistic effect (the overall effect of a combination of two drugs can be larger than the sum of their individual effects). Therefore, delirium ensues at lower doses than what we would normally expect. For example, the combination of alcohol and sleeping pills can cause delirium and significant respiratory depression (and possibly death) at doses that are lower than what would be considered dangerous if each substance had been taken not in combination.

Head Trauma. People who are addicted to alcohol and drugs are at high risk for head trauma, secondary to falls, fights, or accidents. Head trauma can cause internal bleeding in the brain (subdural hematoma), whether there is evidence of external injury or not, which leads to delirium because the accumulating pocket of blood gradually compresses the brain tissue. Thus, emergency room clinicians routinely order a CT examination of the heads of all patients who have history of trauma in order to rule out internal bleeding. If a patient says, "I am having the worst headache of my life" following a blow to the head or a fall, a CT scan must be ordered. Symptoms of internal bleeding (subdural hematoma) can be more subtle, in part because the bleeding can progress slowly over several days and in part because intoxication can mask symptoms or confuse the symptom picture. Clinicians should carefully observe for several days patients who have had a head injury and should look for changes in level of consciousness, emerging somnolence, delirium, or changes in functioning (e.g., sudden difficulty speaking, walking, coordinating) that could indicate an evolving intracranial bleed.

Wernicke's Encephalopathy and Korsakoff's Dementia. Patients who abuse alcohol often suffer from malnutrition and poor absorption of vitamins like B12 and thiamine. Thiamine deficiency can lead to a specific form of delirium called Wernicke's encephalopathy, which is characterized by confusion, unsteady gait (i.e., ataxia), and abnormal eye movements (i.e., ophthalmoplegia). Intravenous administration of thiamine is essential in order to reverse the delirium and prevent Wernicke's encephalopathy from progressing to Korsakoff's dementia, which is often irreversible. Emergency rooms routinely add thiamine to intravenous fluids for patients suspected of having an alcohol use disorder, in an effort to treat this potentially serious medical consequence of alcoholism.

Substance Withdrawal. If a patient has developed physical dependence on alcohol or other sedatives (e.g., benzodiazepines and barbiturates), then he/she may experience withdrawal symptoms of high blood pressure and pulse, tremors, anxiety, and insomnia. Sometimes alcohol or sedative withdrawal can include seizures and, rarely, can progress to delirium called "delirium tremens" (in the case of alcohol withdrawal delirium). Delirium tremens is characterized by severe tremors, confusion, extreme fear, and vivid hallucinations. These symptoms may wax and wane: at one moment a patient may seem rational, while, a few minutes later, the patient may insist that there are people hiding under the bed or snakes crawling around the floor. Delirium tremens is a serious medical emergency with a significant risk of death, even among patients who receive treatment; early recognition and hospitalization for intensive care are essential.

Table 6-3
Common Causes of Delirium in Patients
With Substance Abuse or Dependence

Substance Use
• Alcohol or sedative intoxication • Cocaine or amphetamine intoxication
Neurological Emergencies
• Head trauma • Stroke • Seizures
Other Medical Emergencies
• Severe infection • High fever • Low blood sugar level • Hormonal or electrolyte imbalance

Acute Infections. Substance-dependent patients are susceptible to a variety of infections. This vulnerability is promoted by poor nutrition, intravenous drug use (which can promote serious bacterial infections of the skin and heart valves, as well as viral hepatitis and HIV), poor hygiene, cramped quarters in shelters or jails, and injuries. HIV infection impairs the immune system, thereby promoting vulnerability to a range of infections. Acute infections can present with delirium, due to high fever, high levels of circulating bacteria (sepsis), or direct infections of the brain such as encephalitis (infection of the brain tissue itself), meningitis (infection of the fibrous tissue that covers the brain), or brain abscess (a mass consisting of organisms, immune cells, and dead material, that displaces or destroys brain tissue as it expands). Patients with acute infections will generally present with fever and/or pain or other symptoms related to the infected body part (e.g., cough and chest pain in patients with pneumonia), but confusion and agitation may be the most prominent symptom.

Distinguishing Delirium From Psychosis. Delirium can be difficult to distinguish from an acute exacerbation of a psychotic disorder (e.g., schizophrenia) or a mood disorder (e.g., bipolar disorder with mania). Hallucinations resulting from delirium tend to be visual or tactile and are often quite vivid (the patient sees or feels snakes or bugs, which may be described in detail). In contrast, hallucinations of patients with schizophrenia or psychotic mood disorder are typically auditory (i.e., the patient hears voices). Patients with psychosis resulting from schizophrenia or a mood disorder generally will remain oriented to person, place, and time. For example, a patient with schizophrenia may hear voices that he/she believes come from a device implanted in his/her brain by the CIA, but the patient will score well on the MMSE (he/she knows who and where he/she is, knows the day, date, and time of day, remembers facts presented by the interviewer, and completes simple calculations easily).

Dementia

The hallmark of dementia is loss of memory and inability to learn new information or recall previously learned information while fully conscious. The memory loss of dementia (amnesia) is accompanied by decline in social and occupational functioning decline, as well as one or more of the following cognitive impairments:

- Difficulty speaking or understanding language (aphasia);

- Inability to do things despite intact muscular function (apraxia);

- Failure to recognize people or objects despite intact sensory function (agnosia); or

- Disturbances in planning, organizing, or abstracting (executive function disturbance).

Dementia starts in adulthood, develops slowly over a period of several months and years (with the exception of vascular dementia that can develop abruptly following a stroke), and is, for the most part, irreversible. It shares many symptoms with mental retardation, but mental retardation is typically a genetic, congenital, or early developmental illness. The most common causes of dementia are dementia of the Alzheimer's type and vascular dementia (see Table 6-4). The initial manifestations of dementia of the Alzheimer's type are mild cognitive deficits—memory loss, apathy, and loss of intellectual acuity. During more advanced stages of Alzheimer's disease, patients show profound cognitive deficits, emotional lability, loss of social skills, and sometimes hallucinations and delusions. Eventually, patients are not able to attend to the basic activities of daily living, including eating and personal hygiene. Patients may become completely unresponsive before succumbing to the illness. Vascular dementia is often the result of several small brain infarcts (strokes), which manifest clinically in step-wise deteriorations of cognitive function.

Chronic use of a number of substances can result in cognitive impairments. However, the full syndrome of substance-induced persisting dementia is primarily due to chronic, excessive use of alcohol. The symptoms of alcohol dementia are similar to dementia of the Alzheimer's type (forgetfulness and motor ability), but alcohol dementia progresses slowly, unlike Alzheimer's disease. Furthermore, there is evidence that the cognitive and functional deterioration due to alcoholism can be partially reversed in early stages of the illness if the patient stops drinking (Nunes, Hwang, & Lazaridis, 2001). Alcohol-abusing patients who suffer from thiamine deficiency can develop Wernicke's encephalopathy, a form of delirium, which, if left untreated, can progress to Korsakoff's dementia, which is characterized by severe short-term and long-term memory impairments (although immediate registration of information can remain intact). Patients who suffer from Korsakoff's syndrome routinely invent stories to hide their memory deficits.

HIV infection can cause dementia, particularly in the advanced stages of the disease. It is important to counsel substance-dependent patients about HIV risk and to encourage testing for HIV and follow-up and treatment for patients found to be HIV positive. HIV has become increasingly treatable. Careful medical follow-up and timely treatment with antiviral medications can virtually stop the progression of the disease and prevent the development of its late-stage manifestations such as dementia and opportunistic infections. Proper care for HIV generally requires chronic treatment and careful adherence to the regimen of treatment and follow-up, and it is important for substance abuse treatment counselors to be aware of their patients' medication regimens and help them to adhere to their regimens.

Early signs of dementia are often difficult to distinguish from normal aging. While symptoms of dementia and normal aging both include a decline of mental processes and motor agility, the memory problems of normal aging typically are due to difficulty with recall of information rather than registration of information, which is often seen in patients with dementia.

Another condition that may mimic dementia is pseudodementia, which refers to deterioration in mental functioning accompanying depression. Depressed patients often

**Table 6-4
Common Causes of Dementia in Patients
With Substance Abuse or Dependence**

Substance Use
• Alcohol dementia
Neurological Disorders
• Alzheimer's disease • Vascular dementia (stroke, multiple brain infarcts) • Hydrocephalus (excessive cerebrospinal fluid in the brain) • Parkinson's disease
Other Medical Disorders
• Infections (e.g., HIV) • Cancer (e.g., lymphoma) • Hormonal disorders (e.g., thyroid) • Vitamin deficiency (e.g., thiamine) • Heavy metal poisoning (e.g., lead)

will complain of difficulty concentrating or remembering things, which may result from being uninterested or preoccupied with self-critical, guilty, or other morbid thought's. Until recently, it has been believed that depression in the elderly can manifest itself as apparent cognitive loss, including forgetfulness, difficulty with attention and calculation, apathy, and frustration with cognitive loss, and that, unlike true dementia, when the depression symptoms of pseudodementia are adequately treated, the cognitive symptoms disappear. However, recent evidence suggests that loss of cognitive functioning in an elderly patient that has been measured objectively (e.g., low score on the MMSE), combined with depression, likely represents the early stages of a real dementia (Modrego & Ferrandez, 2004).

Cognitive Impairments Not Otherwise Specified

Diagnosis of nonspecific cognitive disorders associated with chronic drug use is a difficult task (even for the seasoned clinician) due to the subtle clinical presentation of these impairments. In order to accurately diagnose general and more specific cognitive impairments, clinicians must complete a formal neurocognitive assessment.

Principal Domains of Cognitive Function: Attention, Memory, and Executive Functions. The occurrence of certain signs or symptoms in a patient's history (e.g., previously diagnosed with learning difficulties or attention deficits disorder), irregularities in a patient's general appearance (e.g., failure to dress appropriately), motor difficulties (e.g., unstable gait, poor eye-hand coordination), language incompetence (e.g., laconic speech, derailment), and memory problems (e.g., cannot recall parts of the interview) may indicate compromised neurological status. However, the majority of substance abusers presenting to treatment do not exhibit easily recognizable diagnostic signs of impairments in cognitive function. Clinicians should learn to assess three principal domains of cognitive function: attention, memory, and executive function (abstraction). During clinical interviews and treatment sessions, clinicians should monitor patients' attention span, concentration, ability to learn new material, and memory of the interview and session content. In Case 2 (see "Case Presentations"), DL consistently demonstrated an inability to sit still during treatment sessions, difficulty in attending sessions on time, and an inability to maintain concentration during the sixty-minute sessions; these difficulties indicate mild impairments in attention, memory, and overall level of functioning.

Attention. Impaired attention and concentration are among the most common cognitive problems associated with brain damage (Lezak, 2004). In substance-abusing patients, even mild attention deficits have predicted negative treatment outcome (Aharonovich et al., 2006; Aharonovich, Nunes, & Hasin, 2003; Teichner, Horner, & Harvey, 2001). When impaired attention occurs, overall cognitive abilities suffer. For example, an inattentive or drowsy patient may have difficulty following and comprehending conversation and may fail to make right decisions. Thus, problems in attention and concentration should be the first to be assessed. In substance-abusing patients, two major types of attentional disturbance may be identified: (1) impaired alertness or drowsiness and (2) impairments in concentration with distractibility and fluctuating attention. Impaired alertness, if present, is evident during the intake or clinical interview and in the subsequent treatment sessions.

The neurophysiological and neuroanatomic aspects of attention are normally integrated into a functional unit mediating arousal, concentration, and sensory awareness. Deficits in alertness, if present, are evident during the interview and manifested by drowsiness and the need for repeated stimulation to keep the patient engaged with the examiner. Several degrees of reduced arousal are recognized, including clouding (mildly reduced wakefulness or awareness), obtundation (mildly to moderately reduced alertness with lessened interest in the environment, drowsiness, and increased sleep), and stupor (deep sleep or similar unresponsive state from which the patient can be aroused only with vigorous and repeated stimuli).

Useful tests for attention include:

- *Digit span:* this simple, useful test assesses alertness and arousal.

- *Continuous performance test (CPT):* patients are asked to respond by lifting their hands whenever the letter A is heard in a list of letters read aloud by the examiner.

Memory. Memory is often divided into three functions: immediate, recent, and remote. Immediate memory represents the very short-term memory tested with digit span. Recent memory represents the ability to learn new information. Remote memory represents the recall of material learned in the past. Immediate memory or short-term memory is best considered an attentional capacity, since the information is not memorized or committed to memory for later recall. Working memory and mental control tasks utilize this aspect of memory. Attention is a necessary prerequisite for all aspects of memory, and the presence of intact attention must be demonstrated before conclusions about memory can be drawn.

Recent memory refers to the ability to learn and recall new information. Two types of tests are commonly used to assess recent memory: orientation and recall of recently presented verbal and nonverbal information. Orientation in time and space must be learned on a daily basis, and inquiring whether one knows the correct day, month, and year as well as one's current location ("Can you tell me where you are now?") will reveal learning and memory abilities (recommended testing—MMSE).

Executive Functions (Abstraction). Executive functions are higher-order cognitive abilities mediated primarily by the prefrontal cortex and subcortical regions connected to this area (e.g., amygdala, putamen). A good index of the patient's executive functioning, as well as general intellectual function, is ability of abstraction. It depends on intact language functions and on the patient's level of educational achievement and cultural experience. One of the ways to assess abstract ability is administration of proverbs. Proverbs can be understood by most individuals with a high school education. An inability to interpret proverbs despite advanced educational achievement is evidence of compromised executive function. Testing with proverbs should include both simple proverbs ("don't cry over spilled milk") and complex proverbs ("people who live in glass houses shouldn't throw stones"). Note, however, that proverbs may be culture- or language-specific; patients for whom English is a second language may have difficulty interpreting such proverbs.

Clinicians working with special populations, such as substance-abusing patients, should understand the complex way in which various neurological and other medical conditions mimic or masquerade as psychological in origin. The ability to identify and differentiate between a psychological disorder and neurological condition is critical in determining when neuropsychological referral is warranted and in tailoring the treatment for the patient.

Neuropsychological Assessment. Formal neuropsychological assessment is useful in refining the clinical observations made during the clinical intake and in discriminating between psychiatric and neurological symptoms. The clinical picture regarding the cognitive abilities of the patient emerges through systematic testing of individual neuropsychological functions. In most cases, clinical experience guides the decision of the seasoned clinician as to which aspects of the cognitive functions (e.g., attention, memory, decision making, and planning) should be explored and which tests should be chosen in any particular case. Nevertheless, the major areas of neuropsychological functions can be assessed at least briefly in most patients. Clinicians can ask substance-abusing patients who appear to be cognitively intact to perform a difficult task derived from each of the principal domains of cognitive function (e.g., attention, memory, executive function). If the patient is able to perform these tasks, no further evaluation is required. If a failure occurs, the patient's case should be discussed with a neuropsychologist or a clinician specializing in neuropsychological assessment.

Interpretation of a patient's cognitive performance scores on tests needs to take into account the patient's age, education level, sociocultural background, and overall engagement during the testing. For example, an elderly patient with limited education may have difficulties with psychomotor tasks and will likely have restricted expressive language ability. A patient from a minority culture may not do as well on information and vocabulary tests because of unfamiliarity with the leading culture historical or social cues. Anxiety during testing may hamper a patient's ability to do well on parts of the assessment that he/she would be able to perform under less strenuous circumstances. Thus, interpretation of a patient's level of cognitive functioning should be done with great caution. Clinicians should avoid overinterpretation of the results. Deficits in a patient's specific and general level of cognitive functioning should be attributed to a cognitive disorder only when there is a consistent pattern of behavior and supporting evidence of a neurocognitive impairment.

NATURAL HISTORY AND ETIOLOGY OF NEUROPSYCHOLOGICAL IMPAIRMENT IN SUBSTANCE-DEPENDENT PATIENTS

The causes and clinical course of delirium and dementia are related to their underlying physiological or medical conditions (see "Diagnostic Criteria" and Tables 6-3 and 6-4). Readers seeking detail on these topics should consult standard textbooks of medicine or neurology and textbooks on addiction medicine and addiction psychiatry that devote entire chapters to the discussion of delirium and dementia caused by intoxicating substances (see "Suggestions for Further Reading"). The present section will focus on the subtle cognitive deficits common in substance-dependent patients, their potential causes, and clinical course.

Controversy exists over whether cognitive deficits are the cause or consequence of drug abuse. Some researchers argue that use of cocaine causes abnormalities in brain functioning (e.g., Volkow & Fowler, 2000), whereas others posit that preexisting neurobiological and cognitive deficits (e.g., childhood brain dysfunction, learning disabilities, or electro-cerebral brain abnormalities) predispose certain individuals to use cocaine (Campbell, 2003). Impairment revealed by tests of neuropsychological functioning has been shown in longitudinal studies to be part of a constellation of "neurobehavioral disinhibition" in childhood associated with increased risk for development of substance use disorders (Kirisci, Vanyukov, & Tarter, 2005; Tarter, Kirisci, Reynolds, & Mezzich, 2004). Learning disabilities and trouble functioning in school are common in children who later develop addictions, and school failure is an important risk factor predicting development of substance use disorders. Both mechanisms are probably valid and operate to different extents in different patients. Further research is needed to help determine which mechanism operates in specific types of patients. However, at this stage, it is sufficient to know that cognitive impairments exist in this population, suggesting the need to address their effects on treatment planning and outcome.

Alcohol

Extensive literature on alcohol abusers indicates that heavy drinking contributes to structural and functional damage to the prefrontal and temporal cortices, areas essential for memory, strategic planning, use of environmental feedback, goal selection, and response inhibition. Chronic alcohol abuse can eventually lead to permanent disorders such as alcohol-induced dementia (Cummings, 1995; Fals-Stewart, Schafer, Lucente, Rustine, & Brown, 1994; Goldman-Rakic, 1987). Research on other classes of drugs is less extensive, but studies suggest that drugs impact cognitive functioning differently than alcohol.

Cocaine

Over the past two decades, many investigations of brain and cognitive functioning (e.g., neuropsychological and neurobiological measures) in chronic cocaine abusers have shown that they suffer from significant deficits in brain metabolism and cognitive abilities. These deficits were most commonly found in memory and learning, attention, and executive functioning, but also in psychomotor functioning and abstract reasoning (e.g., Berry et al., 1993; Browndyke et al., 2004; Gottschalk, Beauvais, Hart, & Kosten, 2001; Hopper et al., 2004; Lee, Telang, Springer, & Volkow, 2003; O'Malley, Adamse, Heaton, & Gavin, 1992; Verdejo-Garcia, Lopez-Torrecillas, Gimenez, & Perez-Garcia, 2004).

Studies examining short-term effects of cocaine use extending after initiation of abstinence consistently have found that these deficits persist into the abstinent period (Verdejo-Garcia et al., 2004). In one study, patients demonstrated impairment in visuomotor tracking, cognitive flexibility, and speed of information processing after ten days of abstinence (Melamed, 1987). After fourteen days of abstinence, cocaine users still showed impairment in psychomotor speed, concentration, and memory, relative to controls (Berry et al., 1993), and impaired attention, memory, learning, and verbal fluency (Cunha, Nicastri, Gomes, Moino, & Peluso, 2004). In a carefully designed study, Bolla, Rothman, and Cadet (1999) found that, compared to non-drug-using control subjects closely matched for age, education, and intelligence, chronic cocaine users who were abstinent for four weeks had persistent deficits in neurobehavioral performance on complex tasks of higher cortical functioning. The results are consistent with other studies that have reported deficits on similar tests of neuropsychological functioning in cocaine abusers (Hoff et al., 1996; Mittenberg & Motta, 1993; Strickland et al., 1993). Moreover, Bolla et al. (1999) found a dose-effect relationship, in which changes in neurobehavioral performance correlated more strongly with intensity of cocaine use (grams per week) than with frequency (times per week) or years of cocaine use.

Some researchers suggest that there are no long-term neuropsychological consequences from cocaine use (Verdejo-Garcia et al., 2004); others have found only incomplete recovery of short-term verbal memory deficits (Manschreck et al., 1990). In one study, patients, after six months of abstinence, demonstrated impairments in attention, concentration, new learning, visual and verbal memory, word production, and visuomotor integration (Strickland et al., 1993). In a more recently completed study, cocaine-dependent patients demonstrated deficits in attention, executive functioning, and spatial processing after six months of abstinence (Di Sclafani, Tolou-Shams, Price, & Fein, 2002).

Taken together, these findings suggest that even abstinent patients may continue to have cognitive impairments (to some degree) throughout twelve weeks of treatment. Therefore, careful treatment planning and aftercare should be provided beyond the twelve weeks.

Amphetamines

Research on methylenedioxymethamphetamine (MDMA, Ecstasy) use indicates long-term damage to serotonergic nerve terminals (Vik et al., 2004). Amphetamine use has been associated with impairment in visual and verbal memory (McKetin & Mattick, 1998; Ornstein et al., 2000).

Cannabis

Prolonged cannabis use is associated with deficits in attention, memory, perceptual-motor abilities, and reaction time (Snyder & Nussbaum, 1998).

Other Drugs and Polysubstance Dependence

Brain damage from prolonged sedative-hypnotic use may resemble damage from alcohol and may lead to deterioration in reasoning, visuospatial ability, and executive functioning (Bergman, Borg, Hindmarsh, Idestrom, & Mutzell, 1980), although, in general, sedative-hypnotics are not thought to be directly toxic in the same way as alcohol. Results from studies on hallucinogens and heroin are inconsistent, but studies generally fail to find significant long-term cognitive impairments (e.g., Halpern & Pope, 1999; Rounsaville, Novelly, Kleber, & Jones, 1981). Some of the most severe long-term cognitive damage occurs in polysubstance-abusing patients, perhaps due to additive effects of different drugs (Fals-Stewart & Schafer, 1992; Miller et al., 1995; Snyder & Nussbaum, 1998). In a large sample of polysubstance users, 45 percent were still impaired three weeks after admission to outpatient treatment (Grant & Judd, 1976). Among 246 polysubstance-abusing patients, 22.4 percent were cognitively impaired one month after inpatient admission (Fals-Stewart & Lucente, 1994).

ISSUES INVOLVED IN MAKING A DIAGNOSIS IN SUBSTANCE-DEPENDENT PATIENTS

Despite the accumulated empirical evidence of the high prevalence of cognitive impairments in substance abusers, clinicians tend to neglect this issue in the delivery of substance abuse treatments. Several reasons may account for the difficulties in identi-fying cognitive impairments and treating cognitively impaired substance abusers. One of the reasons is that the verbal articulation of cognitively impaired patients is rarely impaired. With either intact or mildly impaired verbal articulation, patients appear cog-nitively intact. Furthermore, patients' ability to "talk the talk" masks their mild deficits in other cognitive domains, which is consistent with results showing that even seasoned therapists cannot informally detect cognitive impairment in areas such as attention, memory, planning, and decision making (Fals-Stewart, 1997; Weinstein & Shaffer, 1993). Therapists who are working with such patients may attribute the effects of the cognitive impairments on the treatment to other causes. For example, a patient with mild memory problems may not readily recall the content of a previous session with his/her therapist or may be late to appointments or miss appointments altogether. The patient will likely be labeled as "not ready for treatment/change." Lastly, substance-abusing patients presenting for treatment are often unaware of their own cognitive deficits (Horner, Harvey, & Denier, 1999). The patient may be unable to report the problem and the dif-ficulties in processing the session. Mildly impaired cognitive abilities of the patient may continue to go unnoticed (an exception is cannabis users, who are more likely to report that memory impairment is among their top reasons for seeking treatment).

INSTRUMENTS AND METHODS FOR SCREENING AND DIAGNOSIS

A useful tool in assessing cognitive abnormalities is the MMSE (Folstein, Folstein, & McHugh, 1975). This test is simple to conduct, can be given in almost any setting, and typically takes less than ten minutes to complete. The MMSE is comprised of thirty items and tests the following:

1. *Orientation* (10 points)—the clinician asks the patient to give information about the time and place of the interview.

2. *Language* (9 points)—the clinician asks the patient to name objects, repeat a phrase, follow verbal and written commands, write a sentence, and copy a design.

3. *Memory* (6 points)—the clinician asks the patient to repeat the names of three unrelated objects that the clinician recites and then asks the patient to recall these names after one to two minutes.

4. *Attention* (5 points)—the clinician asks the patient to count backwards by inter-vals of seven (starting at 100).

Most people without cognitive problems score either 29 or 30 (out of 30). The patient in Case 1 (CR; see "Case Presentations") scored 23, which suggests significant cognitive impairment. A score lower than 20 indicates definite cognitive impairment. Although the MMSE is not specific for any one cognitive disorder, it gives a summary "cognitive status snapshot" of a patient. The MMSE is the most widely accepted and most widely used quantitative tool for reporting cognitive functioning.

TREATMENT OPTIONS

Delirium and Dementia

Delirium and dementia need to be recognized, and the underlying medical disorder needs to be diagnosed and treated if possible. As noted in the "Introduction" to this chapter, delirium is a medical emergency both because it may represent a rapidly evolving, serious medical condition (such as intracranial bleeding after head trauma) and because patients may be injured as a result of their disorganized and confused behavior. The most common cause of delirium in substance-dependent patients is substance intoxication. However, if the intoxication is severe enough to cause delirium, medical attention should be sought, and the patient should be evaluated and observed in a safe medical setting, such as an emergency room, where other medical conditions can be ruled out, sedative and/or antipsychotic medications can be given (if appropriate) to manage agitation, and the patient can be monitored for worsening symptoms or complications such as lapse into stupor or coma, fluid and electrolyte imbalances, or vomiting and aspiration. A full toxicology screen will determine which substances the patient has taken or whether an overdose of medications might be involved. Fortunately, in most cases, severe intoxication can be treated supportively and will resolve without permanent consequences.

Dementia represents a chronic and relatively severe deficit in cognitive functioning, most prominently memory. Referral for medical and neurological evaluation is an important first step. Occasionally, underlying medical conditions that are reversible, such as endocrine abnormalities (e.g., hypothyroidism), vitamin deficiencies, such as vitamin B_{12} and thiamine (as may occur in alcohol- or drug-dependent patients with poor diets), or chronic heavy metal poisoning (e.g., lead), are discovered. However, the most common causes of dementia, such as cerebral vascular disease and Alzheimer's disease, are chronic diseases that follow a slowly deteriorating course. Some medications may be mildly helpful. Most importantly, clinicians should ensure that patients live in an appropriate environment where they can be cared for, including skilled nursing facilities or nursing homes if the patient can no longer live safely at home.

Cognitive Impairments Not Otherwise Specified

There are many important occupational, social, and treatment consequences following even subtle impairments in attention, memory, and executive functioning. These can be observed either during treatment sessions or outside of sessions and include (1) impaired self-monitoring and inability to use feedback to change behaviors and (2) difficulty identifying relevant goals or organizing and monitoring behavior regarding goals. In particular, impairments of attention (e.g., short attention span) lead to high distractibility, which, in turn, makes learning of any behavioral change difficult for the patient. Patients with deficits in attention often have delayed processing and responses and may not be able to grasp complex tasks in the confined time period of a treatment session. Memory deficits affect multitasking ability, processing speed, use of acquired skills and knowledge, and recognition of mistakes. Furthermore, patients may have difficulty remembering the strategies and assignments discussed in therapy during sessions and from one session to the next. Executive functioning deficits can affect willingness and ability to cooperate with the therapist and self-regulation (crucial components in the relapse-prevention type of the therapy). Executive functioning deficits may also compromise self-awareness, thereby causing difficulty in recognizing substance use as a problem, proximal antecedents of use, or behavior patterns leading to use.

Alcohol researchers hypothesized that cognitive impairments interfere with treatment processes and negatively impact outcome (Fals-Stewart, Lucente, Shanahan, & Brown, 1995; McCrady & Smith, 1986; Morgenstern & Bates, 1999). Empirical results confirm these hypotheses and show that, among alcohol abusers, cognitive impairments impede: acquisition of new coping behaviors, learning and retention of new material, therapeutic interventions, and treatment retention. Cognitively impaired substance users also have significantly higher attrition rates and lower rates of successful treatment completion, including abstinence (Aharonovich et al., 2006; Aharonovich et al., 2003; Horner, 1999; Teichner et al., 2001) and difficulty receiving and using treatment-relevant information to change behavior (Fals-Stewart et al., 1995). In other studies, cognitively impaired substance abusers, in comparison to their cognitively intact peers, have greater dropout rates from residential programs, faster relapse rates, and poorer long-term outcomes (Abbott & Gregson, 1981; Berglund, Leijonquist, & Horlen, 1977; Fabian & Parsons, 1983; Fals-Stewart, 1993; Guthrie & Elliott, 1980; Yohman, Parsons, & Leber, 1985).

This body of research indicates that in order to be successful, the clinician must identify cognitive impairments, incorporate this information into cognitive and behavioral treatments, and adjust the treatment as necessary so that the patient can fully participate in treatment.

Counseling Techniques

Since many substance abuse treatment settings do not formally evaluate patients with a neuropsychological battery and assess their cognitive functioning, we encourage clinicians to conduct treatment as if the patient has mild impairments in the areas of attention, memory, and decision making. We believe that this approach can assist both impaired and nonimpaired patients. A number of strategies for dealing with the cognitive difficulties seen in this population are discussed below.

Compensation for Deficits in Attention During Counseling. For a successful psychological intervention, the patient must be able to attend to and understand verbally communicated information and therapeutic dialogue as it unfolds during a session. We propose several strategies that a clinician can easily implement, regardless of the intervention type (e.g., interpersonal, cognitive behavioral). At the outset of treatment, and as part of the therapeutic contract, the therapist should establish rules for refocusing the session dialogue if it derails because of a patient's inattention. The patient and therapist agree on a verbal or nonverbal prompt, such as raising the hand and saying "Let's get back on track." At the beginning of each session, the therapist should avoid overwhelming the patient with numerous topics for discussion and should restrict themes or topics to a few (no more than three topics are recommended for the first few weeks). Therapists should refrain from long and complex sentences and monologues. For most patients with short attention spans, noncomplex and brief sentences are easier to understand and remember. Presenting new material several times in the session, reducing session length, and increasing session frequency are all recommended strategies to accommodate patients with attention problems. Therapists should consider shorter therapy sessions of thirty to forty minutes, when appropriate, instead of sixty-minute sessions.

Compensation for Deficits in Memory During Counseling. Three types of memory are integral to the success of psychological interventions:

1. *Working Memory:* Working memory is the limited, temporary store where new information is held while it is manipulated in a meaningful way to solve a current problem (Baddeley, Logie, Bressi, Della Sala, & Spinnler, 1986). Strategies that minimize the harmful effect of working memory deficits on treatment often utilize encoding of the content to be remembered by frequent rehearsals, visual aids, and slower rate of presentation of the therapeutic material. Therapy sessions may include frequent rehearsals of verbal/visual-didactic information and regulation of the rate (slower pace) at which therapeutic content is presented. Therapists should consider conducting frequent but shorter sessions. For example, patients with memory problems do better attending shorter (thirty minutes) sessions twice a week than the standard sixty-minute weekly sessions.

2. *Long-Term Memory:* Long-term memory involves memories lasting several minutes or longer, deficits that often thwart therapeutic gains (Tulving, 2002). Long-term memory deficits hamper patients' use of the therapeutic suggestions and recommendations, as they cannot build cumulatively on previous therapeutic work or retrieve strategies (e.g., coping skills for dealing with drug-related situations that arise). Mnemonic strategies are helpful in assisting with encoding of new learning material, and treatment should be adjusted to include many of these devices (e.g., use acronyms to help patients remember skills and goals).

3. *Metamemory:* Metamemory is the aspect of cognition that monitors memory capacity. It is often described as the component that "reminds us to remember" (Metcalfe & Shimamura, 1994). To aid patients with deficits in metamemory, clinicians should help patients recognize and monitor their limitations. This awareness motivates the patient to learn and use compensatory strategies. Treatment can incorporate a "memory notebook," a journal in which the patient can record therapeutic highlights, changes in treatment goals, homework assignments, and date and time of appointments (Avants, 2001). This notebook may help a patient to be more organized and may encourage the patient to rehearse treatment information.

Compensation for Deficits in Executive Functioning During Counseling. The term executive functioning refers to a group of organizational and integrative cognitive abilities associated with various neural pathways involving the prefrontal cortex

(Verdejo-Garcia et al., 2004). Executive functioning deficits compromise patients' motivation, self-awareness (Ben-Yishay & Diller, 1993), abstract reasoning, decision making, initiation of behaviors, and self-regulatory competencies (Lezak, 2004). Structure, goal, and action-based therapeutic strategies are recommended. Methods that address patients' lack of self-regulation include practicing verbal self-monitoring during therapy sessions (Cicerone et al., 2000). Therapy can incorporate a patient workbook in which a patient can record his/her daily and weekly activities and complete a record of daily drug craving. The patient workbook also includes handouts, quizzes, daily and weekly planners, and activity lists. Practice in using these strategies should occur both during and outside the session (e.g., patient workbook exercises). Use of this patient workbook approach can facilitate organization and planning, encourage patients to rehearse treatment content, and foster coping skill building.

SUMMARY

People who suffer from substance use disorders often present with cognitive symptoms such as disorientation, confusion, loss of memory, and difficulties with attention and concentration. A clinician should first decide if the problem is acute (e.g., delirium) or chronic (e.g., dementia, other neurocognitive impairments). Delirium requires immediate medical attention and is often reversible, while dementia and chronic neurocognitive impairments require long-term management and are typically irreversible. Then a clinician should investigate the cause of the cognitive symptoms (e.g., alcohol or drugs or a medical or neurological condition). A careful evaluation of the acuity and the etiology of the disturbance can help a clinician to determine the most appropriate treatment management strategy.

Finally, clinicians should remember that substance-dependent patients may have subtle deficits in attention, memory, and executive functioning that may not be easily recognizable during the first interview with the patient but that may have a significant impact on the patient's level of psychosocial functioning and the patient's ability to benefit from counseling. Clinicians should consider adapting their counseling methods to compensate for these common deficits in attention, memory, executive functioning, and self-organization. Strategies may include shorter but more frequent sessions, repetition of key points and concepts, an agreed-upon way for the patient or therapist to signal if the patient has lost track of the focus of the session, presentation of material both visually and verbally, mnemonic strategies, and use of a notebook or journal to build scheduling and planning skills.

Suggestions for Further Reading

For readers who wish to study further in this area, we recommend:

- Allen, J. B. (Ed.). (2002). *Treating patients with neuropsychological disorders: A clinician's guide to assessment and referral.* Washington, DC: American Psychological Association.

- Andreasen, N. C., & Black, D. W. (Eds.). (2006). *Introductory textbook of psychiatry* (4th ed.). Washington, DC: American Psychiatric Publishing.

- Braunwald, E., Fauci, A., Hauser, S., & Kasper, D. L. (Eds.). (2001). *Harrison's principles of internal medicine* (15th ed.). New York: McGraw Hill Medical Publishing Division.

- Galanter, M., & Kleber, H. D. (Eds.). (2004). *Textbook of substance abuse treatment* (3rd ed.). Washington, DC: American Psychiatric Publishing.

- Graham, S., Mayo-Smith, R., Ries, R. K., Shultz, T. K., & Wilford, B. B. (Eds.). (2003). *Principles of addiction medicine* (3rd ed.). Chevy Chase, MD: American Society of Addiction Medicine.

- Manley, M. R. S. (2003). Delirium and dementia. In *Psychiatry clerkship guide* (pp. 236-247). St. Louis, MO: Mosby.

- Rowland, L. P. (Ed.). (1995). *Merritt's textbook of neurology* (9th ed.). Baltimore: Williams & Wilkins.

- Spreen, O., & Strauss, E. (Eds.). (1998). *A compendium of neuropsychological tests: Administration, norms, and commentary* (2nd ed.). Oxford, UK: Oxford Press.

- Vanderploeg, R. D. (Ed.). (2000). *Clinician's guide to neuropsychological assessment* (2nd ed.). Mahwah, NJ: Laurence Erlbaum Associates.

References

Abbott, M. W., & Gregson, R. A. (1981). Cognitive dysfunction in the prediction of relapse in alcoholics. *Journal of Studies on Alcohol, 42*, 230-243.

Aharonovich, E., Hasin, D. S., Brooks, A. C., Liu, X., Bisaga, A., & Nunes, E. V. (2006). Cognitive deficits predict low treatment retention in cocaine dependent patients. *Drug and Alcohol Dependence, 81*, 313-322.

Aharonovich, E., Nunes, E., & Hasin, D. (2003). Cognitive impairment, retention and abstinence among cocaine abusers in cognitive-behavioral treatment. *Drug and Alcohol Dependence, 71*, 207-211.

American Psychiatric Association (2000). *Diagnostic and statistical manual of mental disorders* (4th ed., text rev.) Washington, DC: Author.

Avants, K. S. (2001). *The HIV+ Harm Reduction Program for HIV-positive infection drug users (HHRP+)*. New Haven, CT: Yale University School of Medicine.

Baddeley, A., Logie, R., Bressi, S., Della Sala, S., & Spinnler, H. (1986). Dementia and working memory. *Quarterly Journal of Experimental Psychology. A, Human Experimental Psychology, 38*, 603-618.

Bates, M. E., Barry, D., Labouvie, E. W., Fals-Stewart, W., Voelbel, G., & Buckman, J. F. (2004). Risk factors and neuropsychological recovery in clients with alcohol use disorders who were exposed to different treatments. *Journal of Consulting and Clinical Psychology, 72*, 1073-1080.

Ben-Yishay, Y., & Diller, L. (1993). Cognitive remediation in traumatic brain injury: Update and issues. *Archives of Physical Medicine and Rehabilitation, 74*, 204-213.

Berglund, M., Leijonquist, H., & Horlen, M. (1977). Prognostic significance and reversibility of cerebral dysfunction in alcoholics. *Journal of Studies on Alcohol, 38*, 1761-1770.

Bergman, H., Borg, S., Hindmarsh, T., Idestrom, C. M., & Mutzell, S. (1980). Computed tomography of the brain and neuropsychological assessment of male alcoholic patients and a random sample from the general male population. *Acta Psychiatrica Scandinavica. Supplementum, 286*, 77-88.

Berry, J., van Gorp, W. G., Herzberg, D. S., Hinkin, C., Boone, K., Steinman, L., et al. (1993). Neuropsychological deficits in abstinent cocaine abusers: Preliminary findings after two weeks of abstinence. *Drug and Alcohol Dependence, 32*, 231-237.

Bolla, K., Rothman, R., & Cadet, J. L. (1999). Dose-related neurobehavioral effects of chronic cocaine use. *Journal of Neuropsychiatry and Clinical Neurosciences, 11*, 361-369.

Browndyke, J. N., Tucker, K. A., Woods, S. P., Beauvals, J., Cohen, R. A., Gottschalk, P. C., et al. (2004). Examining the effect of cerebral perfusion abnormality magnitude on cognitive performance in recently abstinent chronic cocaine abusers. *Journal of Neuroimaging, 14*, 162-169.

Campbell, W. G. (2003). Addiction: A disease of volition caused by a cognitive impairment. *Canadian Journal of Psychiatry. Revue Canadienne de Psychiatrie, 48*, 669-674.

Cicerone, K. D., Dahlberg, C., Kalmar, K., Langenbahn, D. M., Malec, J. F., Bergquist, T. F., et al. (2000). Evidence-based cognitive rehabilitation: Recommendations for clinical practice. *Archives of Physical Medicine and Rehabilitation, 81*, 1596-1615.

Cummings, P. (1995). Association of alcohol with fatal snowmobile accidents. *Annals of Emergency Medicine, 25*, 717-718.

Cunha, P. J., Nicastri, S., Gomes, L. P., Moino, R. M., & Peluso, M. A. (2004). Alterações neuropsicológicas em dependentes de cocaína/crack internados: Dados preliminares [Neuropsychological impairments in crack/cocaine-dependent inpatients: Preliminary findings]. *Revista Brasileira de Psiquiatria, 26*, 103-106.

Di Sclafani, V., Tolou-Shams, M., Price, L. J., & Fein, G. (2002). Neuropsychological performance of individuals dependent on crack-cocaine, or crack-cocaine and alcohol, at 6 weeks and 6 months of abstinence. *Drug and Alcohol Dependence, 66*, 161-171.

Fabian, M. S., & Parsons, O. A. (1983). Differential improvement of cognitive functions in recovering alcoholic women. *Journal of Abnormal Psychology, 92*, 87-95.

Fals-Stewart, W. (1993). Neurocognitive defects and their impact on substance abuse treatment. *Journal of Addiction and Offender Counseling, 13*, 46-57.

Fals-Stewart, W. (1997). Ability of counselors to detect cognitive impairment among substance-abusing patients: An examination of diagnostic efficiency. *Experimental and Clinical Psychopharmacology, 5*, 39-50.

Fals-Stewart, W., & Lucente, S. (1994). The effect of cognitive rehabilitation on the neuropsychological status of patients in drug abuse treatment who display neurocognitive impairment. *Rehabilitation Psychology, 39*, 75-94.

Fals-Stewart, W., Lucente, S., Shanahan, T., & Brown, L. (1995). The relationship of patients' cognitive status and therapists' ratings of psychological distress among psychoactive substance users in long-term residential treatment. *Journal of Substance Abuse, 7*, 205-222.

Fals-Stewart, W., & Schafer, J. (1992). The relationship between length of stay in drug-free therapeutic communities and neurocognitive functioning. *Journal of Clinical Psychology, 48*, 539-543.

Fals-Stewart, W., Schafer, J., Lucente, S., Rustine, T., & Brown, L. (1994). Neurobehavioral consequences of prolonged alcohol and substance abuse: A review of findings and treatment implications. *Clinical Psychology Review, 14*, 775-788.

Folstein, M. F., Folstein, S. E., & McHugh, P. R. (1975). "Mini-mental state." A practical method for grading the cognitive state of patients for the clinician. *Journal of Psychiatric Research, 12*, 189-198.

Goldman-Rakic, P. S. (1987). Circuitry of the frontal association cortex and its relevance to dementia. *Archives of Gerontology and Geriatrics, 6*, 299-309.

Gottschalk, C., Beauvais, J., Hart, R., & Kosten, T. (2001). Cognitive function and cerebral perfusion during cocaine abstinence. *American Journal of Psychiatry, 158*, 540-545.

Grant, I., & Judd, L. L. (1976). Neuropsychological and EEG disturbances in polydrug users. *American Journal of Psychiatry, 133*, 1039-1042.

Guthrie, A., & Elliott, W. A. (1980). The nature and reversibility of cerebral impairment in alcoholism; treatment implications. *Journal of Studies on Alcohol, 41*, 147-155.

Halpern, J. H., & Pope, H. G., Jr. (1999). Do hallucinogens cause residual neuropsychological toxicity? *Drug and Alcohol Dependence, 53*, 247-256.

Hoff, A. L., Riordan, H., Morris, L., Cestaro, V., Wieneke, M., Alpert, R., et al. (1996). Effects of crack cocaine on neurocognitive function. *Psychiatry Research, 60*, 167-176.

Hopper, J. W., Karlsgodt, K. H., Adler, C. M., Macklin, E. A., Lukas, S. E., & Elman, I. (2004). Effects of acute cortisol and cocaine administration on attention, recall and recognition task performance in individuals with cocaine dependence. *Human Psychopharmacology, 19*, 511-516.

Horner, M. D. (1999). Attentional functioning in abstinent cocaine abusers. *Drug and Alcohol Dependence, 54*, 19-33.

Horner, M. D., Harvey, R. T., & Denier, C.A. (1999). Self-report and objective measures of cognitive deficit in patients entering substance abuse treatment. *Psychiatry Research, 86*, 155-161.

Kirisci, L., Vanyukov, M., & Tarter, R. (2005). Detection of youth at high risk for substance use disorders: A longitudinal study. *Psychology of Addictive Behaviors, 19*, 243-252.

Lee, J. H., Telang, F. W., Springer, C. S., Jr., & Volkow, N. D. (2003). Abnormal brain activation to visual stimulation in cocaine abusers. *Life Sciences, 73*, 1953-1961.

Lezak, M. D. (2004). *Neuropsychological assessment* (4th ed.). New York: Oxford University Press.

Manley, M. R. S. (2003). Delirium and dementia. In *Psychiatry clerkship guide* (pp. 236-247). St. Louis, MO: Mosby.

Manschreck, T. C., Schneyer, M. L., Weisstein, C. C., Laughery, J., Rosenthal, J., Celada, T., et al. (1990). Freebase cocaine and memory. *Comprehensive Psychiatry, 31*, 369-375.

McCrady, B. S., & Smith, D. E. (1986). Implications of cognitive impairment for the treatment of alcohol. *Alcoholism Clinical and Experimental Research, 10*, 145-149.

McKetin, R., & Mattick, R. P. (1998). Attention and memory in illicit amphetamine users: Comparison with non-drug-using controls. *Drug and Alcohol Dependence, 50*, 181-184.

Melamed, J. I. (1987). Neuropsychological deficits after cessation of freebase cocaine abuse. Ph.D. dissertation, Northwestern University, United States—Illinois. *Dissertation Abstracts International*. Retrieved May 29, 2008, from ProQuest Digital Dissertations database (Publication No. AAT 8710365).

Metcalfe, J., & Shimamura, A. P. (1994). *Metacognition: Knowing about knowing*. Cambridge, MA: MIT Press.

Miller, W. R., Brown, J., Simpson, T. L., Handmaker, N. S., Bien, T. H., Luckie, L. F., et al. (1995). What works? A methodological analysis of the alcohol treatment outcome literature. In R. K. Hester & W. R. Miller (Eds.), *Handbook of alcoholism treatment approaches: Effective alternatives* (2nd ed., pp. 12-44). Boston: Allyn and Bacon.

Mittenberg, W., & Motta, S. (1993). Effects of chronic cocaine abuse on memory and learning. *Archives of Clinical Neuropsychology, 8*, 477-483.

Modrego, P. J., & Ferrández, J. (2004). Depression in patients with mild cognitive impairment increases the risk of developing dementia of Alzheimer type: A prospective cohort study. *Archives of Neurology, 61*, 1290-1293.

Morgenstern, J., & Bates, M. E. (1999). Effects of executive function impairment on change processes and substance use outcomes in 12-step treatment. *Journal of Studies on Alcohol, 60*, 846-855.

Nunes, E. V., Hwang, M. Y., & Lazaridis, P. G. (2001). Substance induced persisting dementia and substance induced persisting amnestic disorders. In G. O. Gabbard (Ed.). *Treatments of psychiatric disorders* (3rd ed., pp. 575-607). Washington, DC: American Psychiatric Publishing.

O'Malley, S., Adamse, M., Heaton, R. K., & Gawin, F. H. (1992). Neuropsychological impairment in chronic cocaine abusers. *American Journal of Drug and Alcohol Abuse, 18*, 131-144.

Ornstein, T. J., Iddon, J. L., Baldacchino, A. M., Sahakian, B. J., London, M., Everitt, B. J., et al. (2000). Profiles of cognitive dysfunction in chronic amphetamine and heroin abusers. *Neuropsychopharmacology, 23*, 113-126.

Rounsaville, B. J., Novelly, R. A., Kleber, H. D., & Jones, C. (1981). Neuropsychological impairment in opiate addicts: Risk factors. *Annals of the New York Academy of Sciences, 362*, 79-80.

Schuckit, M. A. (2000). *Drug and alcohol abuse: A clinical guide to diagnosis and treatment* (5th ed.). New York: Kluwer Academic/Plenum Publishers.

Snyder, P. J., & Nussbaum, P. D. (1998). *Clinical neuropsychology: A pocket handbook for assessment*. Washington, DC: American Psychological Association.

Strickland, T. L., Mena, I., Villanueva-Meyer, J., Miller, B. L., Cummings, J., Mehringer, C. M., et al. (1993). Cerebral perfusion and neuropsychological consequences of chronic cocaine use. *Journal of Neuropsychiatry and Clinical Neurosciences, 5*, 419-427.

Tarter, R. E., Kirisci, L., Reynolds, M., & Mezzich, A. (2004). Neurobehavior disinhibition in childhood predicts suicide potential and substance use disorder by young adulthood. *Drug and Alcohol Dependence, 76*(Suppl. 1), S45-52.

Teichner, G., Horner, M. D., & Harvey, R. T. (2001). Neuropsychological predictors of the attainment of treatment objectives in substance abuse patients. *International Journal of Neuroscience, 106*, 253-263.

Tulving, E. (2002). Episodic memory: From mind to brain. *Annual Review of Psychology, 53*, 1-25.

Verdejo-Garcia, A., Lopez-Torrecillas, F., Gimenez, C. O., & Perez-Garcia, M. (2004). Clinical implications and methodological challenges in the study of the neuropsychological correlates of cannabis, stimulant, and opioid abuse. *Neuropsychology Review, 14*, 1-41.

Vik, P. W., Cellucci, T., Jarchow, A., & Hedt, J. (2004). Cognitive impairment in substance abuse. *Psychiatric Clinics of North America, 27*, 97-109.

Volkow, N. D., & Fowler, J. S. (2000). Addiction, a disease of compulsion and drive: Involvement of the orbitofrontal cortex. *Cerebral Cortex, 10*, 318-325.

Weinstein, C. S., & Shaffer, H. J. (1993). Neurocognitive aspects of substance abuse treatment: A psychotherapist's primer. *Psychotherapy and Psychosomatics, 30*, 317–333.

Yohman, J. R., Parsons, O. A., & Leber, W. R. (1985). Lack of recovery in male alcoholics' neuropsychological performance one year after treatment. *Alcoholism, Clinical and Experimental Research, 9*, 114-117.

Chapter 7

Schizophrenia and Schizoaffective Illness in Patients With Substance Use Disorders

by Serge Sevy, M.D., M.B.A., Rachel Miller, Ph.D., and Joanne McCormack, L.C.S.W.

INTRODUCTION

Schizophrenia is a disorder of the brain that affects people's thinking, feeling, and behavior. People with schizophrenia experience symptoms such as delusions, hallucinations, and disorganized thinking and behavior. It is a chronic illness affecting about 1 percent of the population. Although the prevalence rate of schizophrenia is lower than the rate of other psychiatric disorders (e.g., depression), it is one of the most disabling psychiatric disorders, and it places an enormous burden on patients, caregivers, and society (Knapp, Mangalore, & Simon, 2004). The course of the illness is often complicated by co-occurring substance use disorders. It is estimated that more than half of patients with schizophrenia are also addicted to at least one substance.

There are three main theories for explaining the high co-occurrence of substance use disorders and schizophrenia:

1. *The Vulnerability Hypothesis* states that substances cause or precipitate the onset of schizophrenia. This hypothesis is supported by the fact that the onset of schizophrenia (a) follows the onset of substance use in more than half of patients and (b) is earlier in patients using substances compared to patients not using substances.

2. *The Self-Medication Hypothesis* states that patients use substances to (a) decrease symptoms, (b) improve cognition, and (c) decrease side effects of medication. This hypothesis is supported by findings that patients with schizophrenia who experience depressed mood are especially susceptible to development of substance use disorders (Siris et al., 1988).

3. *The Common-Disease Hypothesis* states that there is a common biological factor (e.g., a dysfunction in some areas of the brain) that may lead to schizophrenia and substance use disorders.

Co-occurring substance use disorders in patients schizophrenia have been associated with an earlier age at onset of psychosis, less compliance with treatment (Drake & Wallach, 1989; Owen, Fischer, Booth, & Cuffel, 1996; Swofford, Kasckow, Scheller-Gilkey, & Inderbitzin, 1996), higher rates of relapse (Gupta, Hendricks, Kenkel, Bhatia, & Haffke, 1996; Linszen, Dingemans, & Lenior, 1994; Swofford et al., 1996), more positive symptoms and disorganization (Drake & Wallach, 1989; Hambrecht & Häfner, 1996), more depression and cognitive impairment (Mueser, Bellack, & Blanchard, 1992; Sevy, Kay, Opler, & van Praag, 1990), poorer treatment response (Bowers, Mazure, Nelson, & Jatlow, 1990), poorer outcome (Hambrecht & Häfner, 1996), more violent behavior (Räsänen et al., 1998), and higher suicide rates (Siris, 2001). Given the poorer prognosis of patients with schizophrenia and co-occurring substance use disorders compared to nonsubstance users with schizophrenia, it is essential to identify and treat co-occurring substance use disorders early in the course of this illness.

Making the diagnosis of schizophrenia with co-occurring substance use disorders is challenging for clinicians, in part because substances, as well as mental disorders, can induce psychotic symptoms. Despite this difficulty, determining the diagnosis is essential for developing a treatment plan that will fit the various needs of the patient. The purpose of this chapter is to provide practical guidelines for clinicians working with substance abuse patients who have a history of psychotic symptoms in order to help clinicians learn to identify and diagnose schizophrenia, differentiate schizophrenia from other psychotic disorders, diagnose substance use disorders in patients with schizophrenia, identify treatments available for psychosis and co-occurring substance use disorders in schizophrenia, and formulate a treatment plan.

CASE PRESENTATION

The following vignette describes a young man who is being seen for the first time for outpatient treatment following a six-week inpatient hospitalization. He presents with a complex combination of symptoms, which include cannabis and alcohol misuse, psychosis, depression, and possible character disorder. The presentation is organized in the manner that we recommend for evaluating patients with psychotic disorder and substance use. Although it is presented in the order in which the information is generally elicited from the patient during a diagnostic interview, patients with psychosis may be extremely anxious or confused. At such times, it is useful to begin the interview with the developmental history in order to help patients organize their thinking. The interview takes approximately one hour to conduct and provides the information necessary for a preliminary diagnostic evaluation according to the *Diagnostic and Statistical Manual of Mental Disorders,* 4th edition (*DSM-IV;* American Psychiatric Association, 1994). The case will be referred to as an illustrative example throughout this chapter. After reading the case report, readers may wish to formulate the case and develop a treatment plan.

Chief Complaint

BC is a 21-year-old young man who lives at home and worked several odd jobs until two months ago. Seven weeks ago, following a suicide attempt, BC was brought into a psychiatric hospital by EMS. According to the records, he was fearful people were going to hurt him, believed people were watching and looking at him, and thought the radio and television were talking about him specifically and were affecting his movements. He thought people could put thoughts into his mind and take them out. He believed there was something seriously wrong with his stomach and that he had brain cancer. BC heard several unknown people talking about him, saw shadows of people following him, and smelled burning odors that no one else smelled. Two months prior to the time of hospitalization, he made several suicide attempts, including overdosing on Tylenol, cutting his wrists, and attempting to hang himself. According to BC, at the time of hospitalization, he felt life had nothing to offer him, and he wanted to die. The patient was treated on an inpatient unit for six weeks and is now seeking help to prevent a return of his symptoms.

Patient History

Alcohol and Other Drug History. BC reports that he began using alcohol (about 40 ounces of beer mostly on weekends) at the age of 18. He changed his group of friends, cut classes, and became an active participant in a gang of "hoodlums." He dropped out of high school and worked at several jobs. Cannabis use started at age 19 and quickly became a daily habit of three to four "blunts," which he describes as about three to four "joints" rolled up like a cigar. Most of his pay was used to purchase cannabis. He attempted to stop cannabis use on his own but was unsuccessful. He has not experimented with other drugs. He smokes ten cigarettes a day, which he has been unable to stop, despite several attempts, including the use of a nicotine patch. He reports his last use of alcohol (two 12-ounce cans of beer) was the weekend following discharge from the hospital; he denies use of cannabis since his hospitalization.

Psychiatric History. At age 16, BC was seen in family therapy because he was experiencing problems in school, and his family thought something was wrong with him. He reports he was sad because of family problems but was social and enjoyed activities. He was not referred for a psychiatric evaluation at that time. BC states that at age 17 he felt that someone put a curse on him and took his soul. He reports three brief episodes of depression from age 19 to the present. Beginning at age 20, BC felt that his thoughts were being broadcasted to everyone, that people could place thoughts into his mind or take them out, and that people could read his mind. He also believed he heard people talking about him and thought he saw them standing on a corner near his home on several occasions. Prior to hospitalization, he attempted suicide four times, including two overdoses with intention to die and one attempt to hang himself with a belt. He stopped all alcohol and cannabis for eight weeks but restarted two weeks before hospitalization. Psychotic symptoms persisted throughout his two months of abstinence. His symptoms were treated with risperidone (Risperdal) 6 mg a day, sertraline (Zoloft) 50 mg a day, and lorazepam (Ativan) 1 mg three times daily, with fair remission of symptoms. He was discharged from the psychiatric hospital one week ago.

Developmental History. BC reports he was born in Haiti. His parents left him in the care of a grandmother from age 1 to 3 while they established life in the United States.

He reports that he was a good student until age 8, when his parents divorced. Since age 14, he has had little contact with his father, despite many attempts to engage his father in a relationship. The patient reports that abandonment by his father led to feelings of anger and depression that continue to trouble him. He did poorly in high school and dropped out after failing many classes.

Family History. There is no known family history of schizophrenia or substance abuse.

Medical History. The patient has no medical problems.

Social History. BC believes that he functioned well in school until age 14. He then became uninterested, did little work, and failed. BC reports that he was a good student and had many friends throughout his early school years but had only one close friend in high school. He had two girlfriends during his teenage years. In high school, he became involved with a group of friends who robbed people and used drugs and alcohol.

Mental Status Examination

This is an adult male who appears his stated age. He slouches in his seat and makes little eye contact throughout the interview. During the interview his leg moves up and down as much as eighteen inches, a movement that the patient cannot explain but says happens sometimes. The patient denies paranoid delusions, denies thought insertion and thought withdrawal, and denies auditory, visual, and olfactory hallucinations (see "Diagnostic Criteria" for a definition of these terms). He is convinced that there is "something wrong" inside his body and requests tests of his brain and stomach (although he had such tests while hospitalized). Since discharge, he is socially isolated and does not leave his home except occasionally with family or friends (outings are short because he becomes anxious and irritable). BC states he feels depressed, anxious, and hopeless; he has thoughts of wanting to die but has no plan or intent. He states that at times he wants to hurt someone but is sure he will not act on these feelings. He denies feelings of restlessness. He continues to enjoy playing his video games in his room. He states his appetite is "too good" and that he sleeps ten to twelve hours. He is alert and oriented to person, place, and time. Brief cognitive testing reveals no abnormalities. He has partial insight and fair judgment.

DIAGNOSTIC CRITERIA

Symptoms of Schizophrenia

In order to make a diagnosis of schizophrenia, clinicians must be able to recognize the symptoms of schizophrenia. These symptoms fall into two broad categories, often referred to as positive symptoms and negative symptoms. After studying this section, the reader is encouraged to review the case of BC (see "Case Presentation") and identify each of the positive and negative symptoms that he has experienced.

Positive Symptoms. Positive symptoms, also called psychotic symptoms, are the presence of sensations, beliefs, and behaviors that would not normally occur or are an excess or distortion of normal functions. Positive symptoms include delusions, hallucinations, disorganized speech, and disorganized or catatonic behavior.

Hallucinations. Hallucinations are sensations about something that is not really there, such as hearing voices (auditory hallucinations), seeing visions (visual hallucinations), feeling as if one is being touched (tactile hallucinations), smelling foul odors (olfactory hallucinations), or tasting something that is not there (gustatory hallucinations).

Delusions. Delusions are beliefs that are not true. There are many kinds of delusions. The most frequent ones are paranoid delusions (the belief that others are trying to harm the patient), delusions of reference (the belief that things in the environment are related to the patient (e.g., being convinced that the radio is talking about him/her), somatic delusions (the belief that the body is changed because of an illness or because of something foreign inside the body), and delusions of grandeur (the belief that the patient has special powers or abilities). Other delusions that are particularly characteristic of schizophrenia are delusions of thought insertion (the belief that thoughts are being placed in the patient's mind by someone else), thought withdrawal (the belief that thoughts are taken out of the mind), and thought broadcasting (the belief that thoughts are being broadcast out loud so that others can hear them).

Disorganized Thinking. Disorganized thinking should be suspected when speech is hard to follow or understand. Ideas may slip off track from one topic to another that is completely unrelated or only indirectly related (called loosening of associations or derailment). At times, there may be no logical connection between words and phrases, thereby making speech incomprehensible (called incoherence).

Disorganized Behavior. Disorganized behavior is when the person has difficulty with goal-directed behavior. The patient may appear disheveled, dress or behave in an unusual way, or have unpredictable agitation.

Catatonic Behavior. Catatonic behavior is an inhibited or excited behavioral disturbance in which motor activity is affected. The person may be mute and unresponsive, repeat in a parrot-like way words (echolalia) or movements (echopraxia), or have aimless agitation that does not appear to be influenced by anything in the environment.

Negative Symptoms. Negative symptoms are the lack of important abilities and include: (1) lack of or reduced emotional or facial expression (called blunted or flat affect); (2) reduced amount of speech (poverty of speech) or vague, overabstract speech (poverty of thought), which indicates that thought processes are slow or empty (called alogia); (3) low energy; (4) low motivation (amotivation); (5) difficulty initiating or following through with activities (avolition); (6) inability to make or keep friends or not caring to have friends; and (7) poor awareness of hygiene and clothing.

Cognitive Symptoms. Schizophrenia also affects thinking or cognition in other ways. Many people experience poor concentration, poor memory, or have difficulty integrating their thoughts, feelings, and behavior. These symptoms are not considered when making the diagnosis but are important to take into account in treatment planning.

DSM-IV Criteria for Schizophrenia and Related Disorders

The *DSM-IV* criteria for schizophrenia, schizoaffective disorder, and substance-induced psychotic disorder are summarized in Tables 7-1A, 7-1B, 7-2, and 7-3. For a more detailed discussion of the associated features for each disorder, readers should refer to the *DSM-IV*; for further examples and case discussions, readers should refer to the *DSM-IV Casebook* (Spitzer, Gibbon, Skodol, Williams, & First, 1994). Schizophrenia is basically a syndrome of chronic (at least six months in duration) psychosis (delusions, hallucinations) with a chronic deterioration in social functioning, which is not explained by other disorders (effects of substances, mood disorders, medical disorders). Schizoaffective disorder includes both symptoms that resemble schizophrenia and clear episodes of a mood disorder, that is, major depression, mania, or mixed mood episodes (see Chapter 1 and Chapter 2 of this volume). Substance-induced psychotic disorder describes a syndrome of psychosis, mainly delusions and/or hallucinations, which occurs only during active substance use and resolves during abstinence, but where the psychotic symptoms exceed what would be expected from the usual effects of the substances that the patient is using. Each syndrome will be described in detail. After studying this section, the reader is encouraged to the case of BC (see "Case Presentation") and make a diagnosis: Which syndrome review (schizophrenia, schizoaffective disorder, or substance-induced psychotic disorder) best describes BC's history?

***DSM-IV* Criteria for Schizophrenia.** As can be seen in Table 7-1A, the core feature of schizophrenia is the presence of prominent psychotic symptoms. Two or more types of symptoms are required for Criterion A. However, only one symptom is required if it is one of the more characteristic symptoms of schizophrenia: delusions are bizarre (thought insertion, thought withdrawal, or thought broadcasting) or hallucinations consist of a voice keeping a running commentary on the person's behavior or thoughts or two or more voices conversing with each other. The symptoms must be present for a significant portion of the time during a one-month period and must not be substance induced. To be diagnosed with schizophrenia, patients must meet criteria for the core symptoms, must show deterioration in social and occupational functioning, and must exhibit symptoms for at least six months. Patients who have symptoms and social/occupational dysfunction for less than six months are diagnosed with schizophreniform disorder.

Once a diagnosis of schizophrenia is made, subtypes are determined in order to describe the type of schizophrenia (see Table 7-1B). Since the core symptoms of schizophrenia (see Table 7-1A, Criteria A(1) through A(5)) are quite varied, the subtypes provide useful descriptions of patterns or clinical presentations that occur frequently.

***DSM-IV* Criteria for Schizoaffective Disorder.** The criteria for schizoaffective disorder are outlined in Table 7-2 on page 7-13. In schizoaffective disorder, major depressive, manic, or mixed mood episodes occur at the same time as Criterion A symptoms of schizophrenia. However, there are also periods when the core symptoms of schizophrenia occur without mood symptoms. For the diagnosis of schizoaffective disorder to be made, the mood episodes need to be present for a substantial portion of the total duration of the illness (i.e., 30 percent or more). For information regarding mood disorders and diagnostic criteria for major depression, mania, and mixed mood episodes, see Chapter 1 and Chapter 2 of this volume. The distinction between schizophrenia and schizoaffective disorder is useful in guiding treatment. Both disorders generally require antipsychotic medications (see Table 7-6 on page 7-29). Patients with schizoaffective disorder are likely to be helped by a combination of antipsychotic medication and antidepressant medications or mood stabilizer medications used to treat mood disorders (see Chapter 1 and Chapter 2 of this volume).

Table 7-1A
DSM-IV Criteria for Schizophrenia

Symptoms	DSM-IV Criteria[a, b]	Issues in Substance-Dependent Patients	PRISM Questions to Aid Diagnosis[d, e]
Core Symptoms			
Characteristic symptoms	A. Two (or more) of the following, each present for a significant portion of time during a one-month period (or less if successfully treated)[c]:	Substance intoxication (cocaine, methamphetamine, or other stimulants; PCP, LSD, or other hallucinogens; cannabis) can cause delusions; hallucinations, or disorganization; these effects should clear up within days to a week or two of abstinence. Substance withdrawal (mainly alcohol or sedatives) can cause delusions and hallucinations, usually as part of a delirium (see Chapter 6 of this volume); these effects should clear up within days to a week or two of abstinence.	
	(1) delusions [which may include persecutory, referential, somatic, religious, grandiose themes, or thought broadcasting, thought insertion, or thought withdrawal]	Rule out substance intoxication, withdrawal, or substance-induced psychotic disorder (see Table 7-3).	Was there ever a time when you often noticed people talking about you or paying particular attention to you? ... Did you ever think that anyone was going out of their way to give you a hard time or harm you? ... Did you ever think that you were exceptionally important in some way? ... Did you ever think that parts of your body had changed or stopped working? ... Did you ever think that you did something terrible that you should be punished for? ... Did you ever think that someone was unfaithful to you, even though no one else would believe it? ... Did you ever think that your thoughts, feelings, or actions were being completely controlled by a force or power outside yourself?
	(2) hallucinations [auditory, visual, olfactory, gustatory, or tactile hallucinations]	Rule out substance intoxication, withdrawal, or substance-induced psychotic disorder (see Table 7-3).	Did you ever hear things that other people couldn't hear, such as noises or the voices of people whispering or talking? ... Did you ever have visions or see things that other people couldn't see? ... Did you ever have strange or unusual sensations on your body or under your skin? ... Did you ever smell specific or peculiar odors that no one else could smell? [Did you ever] have a definite or strange taste in your mouth for no ordinary reason? ... Did you ever hear a voice talking about what you were doing or thinking?
	(3) disorganized speech (e.g., frequent derailment or incoherence)	Rule out substance intoxication.	Did people ever have a very hard time making out what you were saying or what you meant?

(Continued)

Symptoms	DSM-IV Criteria[a, b]	Issues in Substance-Dependent Patients	PRISM Questions to Aid Diagnosis[d, e]
	(4) grossly disorganized or catatonic behavior	Rule out substance intoxication.	Have you ever done anything that other people considered very strange or even crazy or that got you in trouble with the neighbors, your family, or the police? Was there ever a time when … … you didn't react to things going on around you? … you didn't move for a long time? … you didn't talk for a long time?
	(5) negative symptoms (i.e., affective flattening, alogia, or avolition).	Long-term substance use can cause anhedonia and flat affect.	Was there ever a time when… … you didn't show interest in doing anything? … you didn't have conversations with people? … you didn't have feelings or had very little feelings?
Other Criteria			
Social/ occupational dysfunction	B. For a significant portion of time since the onset of the disturbance, one or more major areas of functioning, such as work [or school], interpersonal relations, or self-care, are markedly below the level achieved prior to the onset [of psychotic symptoms] (or when the onset is in childhood or adolescence, failure to achieve expected level of interpersonal, academic, or occupational achievement).	Long-term substance use can cause deterioration in functioning.	At the time when you [active phase symptoms], were you having problems … … with people? … at work or school? … getting a job? … taking care of your everyday responsibilities? … taking care of yourself? … keeping your clothes clean and neat?
Duration	C. Continuous signs of the disturbance persist for at least 6 months. This 6-month period must include at least 1 month of symptoms (or less if successfully treated) that meet Criterion A (i.e., active-phase symptoms) and may include periods of prodromal or residual symptoms. During these prodromal or residual periods, the signs of the disturbance may be manifested by only negative symptoms or 2 or more symptoms listed in Criterion A present in an attenuated form (e.g., odd beliefs, unusual perceptual experiences).	Chronic substance use can cause chronic symptoms resembling schizophrenia (positive, negative, prodromal, residual); symptoms caused by substances should clear up during periods of abstinence.	Did you ever take any medication(s) for [psychotic symptoms]? IF YES: Which medication(s) did you take? IF DID NOT TAKE MEDICATION(S): Did you ever have some of these experiences around the same time for more than one month? Which ones? When did [prodromal symptoms] start? … Did [residual symptoms] go away? … When?

(Continued)

Symptoms	DSM-IV Criteria[a, b]	Issues in Substance-Dependent Patients	PRISM Questions to Aid Diagnosis[d, e]
Rule out schizoaffective disorder and mood disorders	D. Schizoaffective disorder and mood disorder with psychotic features have been ruled out because either (1) no major depressive, manic, or mixed episodes have occurred concurrently with the active-phase symptoms; or (2) if mood episodes have occurred during the active-phase symptoms, their total duration has been brief relative to the duration of the active and residual periods.	See Table 7-2 for DSM-IV criteria for schizoaffective disorder; both major depression (see Chapter 1 of this volume) and mania (see Chapter 2 of this volume) can present as psychosis with delusions and hallucinations, but this psychosis resolves when the mood episode resolves.	Were you [depressed/manic] for at least 2 weeks during the time you [active phase symptoms]? ... Were you [depressed/manic] for most of the time you [active phase symptoms] and had some of the other problems we talked about?
Rule out effects of substances and medical illness	E. The disturbance is not due to the direct physiological effects of a substance (e.g., a drug of abuse, a medication) or a general medical condition.	Rule out effects of substance intoxication, substance withdrawal; see Table 7-3 for DSM-IV criteria for substance-induced psychotic disorder. Substance-dependent patients may be in poor health (see Chapter 14 of this volume). Medical evaluation and follow-up are advisable. Ask about head trauma.	Were you drug- and alcohol-free [or drink/use drugs only occasionally] ... ... when you began [active phase symptoms]? ... for the first month after you began [active phase symptoms]? ... for at least a month while you [active phase symptoms]? Did you have any medical problems during that time? ... Did you have any of the following medical problems at [onset]: a brain tumor, a stroke, epilepsy, thyroid problems, liver disease, kidney disease?
Relationship to a pervasive developmental disorder	F. If there is a history of autistic disorder or another pervasive developmental disorder, the additional diagnosis of schizophrenia is made only if prominent delusions or hallucinations are also present for at least one month (or less if successfully treated).	Obtain a developmental history of childhood and school performance.	

(a) American Psychiatric Association (1994).
(b) Reprinted with permission from the *Diagnostic and Statistical Manual of Mental Disorders*, Fourth Edition (Copyright 1994). American Psychiatric Association.
(c) Only one Criterion A symptom is required if delusions are bizarre or hallucinations consist of a voice keeping ... a running commentary on the person's behavior or thoughts or two or more voices conversing with each other.
(d) Hasin et al. (2006).
(e) Reprinted with permission.

Table 7-1B
Subtypes Schizophrenia

Subtype	Symptoms
Paranoid type	Delusions or frequent hallucinations, but speech and behavior are organized, and affect is not flat or inappropriate
Disorganized type	Disorganized speech and behavior and flat or inappropriate affect
Catatonic type	Patient may be motionless, may have inappropriate postures, may have excessive, purposeless, repetitive movements, and may repeat words
Undifferentiated type	Diagnostic criteria for schizophrenia are met, but criteria are not met for any of the above subtypes (paranoid, disorganized, or catatonic)
Residual type	One or more episodes in the past, but the current illness is characterized by mostly negative symptoms (i.e., poverty of speech and affect, social withdrawal) and by some mild positive symptoms (i.e., hallucinations, delusions)

Note: Reprinted with permission from *the Diagnostic and Statistical Manual of Mental Disorders,* Fourth Edition (Copyright 1994). American Psychiatric Association.

***DSM-IV* Criteria for Substance-Induced Psychotic Disorder.** As can be seen in Table 7-3, the core symptoms of substance-induced psychotic disorder are prominent hallucinations or delusions. The presence of only one of the core symptoms is required for the diagnosis. In contrast, a diagnosis of schizophrenia and schizoaffective disorder requires the presence of at least two core symptoms. The psychotic symptoms in substance-induced psychotic disorder are present during or within a month of substance use, and, most of the time, they remit within a month of stopping use. In addition, the psychotic symptoms appear to be more severe than the expected effects of the substances that the patient is using. For example, paranoid delusions are common during cocaine or methamphetamine intoxication, but they usually occur at the height of intoxication and clear up quickly (within hours) after the drug's effect wears off. Substance-induced psychotic disorder is an appropriate diagnosis for a patient who exhibits psychotic symptoms that persist at a steady level and take several weeks to resolve after the patient becomes abstinent.

How to Take a History

A critical aspect in making a diagnosis when a patient has psychotic symptoms and substance use problems is identifying the specific symptoms and the timing of those symptoms. Because this can often be a complex and confusing task, we recommend the use of a timeline. When obtaining diagnostic information for a timeline, clinicians should prompt patients by asking about memorable times in their lives, such as birthdays and holidays. For example, BC (see "Case Presentation") was able to provide

Table 7-2
DSM-IV Criteria for Schizoaffective Disorder

Symptoms	DSM-IV Criteria[a, b]	Issues in Substance-Dependent Patients	PRISM Questions to Aid Diagnosis[c, d]
Combined mood episode and psychotic symptoms	A. An uninterrupted period of illness during which, at some time, there is either a major depressive episode, a manic episode, or a mixed episode concurrent with symptoms that meet Criterion A for schizophrenia.	See Chapter 1 of this volume (depression), Chapter 2 of this volume (bipolar disorder), and Table 7-1A (DSM-IV criteria for schizophrenia; substance intoxication or withdrawal or chronic substance use can cause mood and psychotic symptoms, which should clear up within days to a few weeks of abstinence.	Were you [depressed/manic] for at least 2 weeks during the time you [active phase symptoms]?
Psychotic symptoms with no mood symptoms	B. During the same period of illness there have been delusions or hallucinations for at least 2 weeks in the absence of prominent mood symptoms.	If hallucinations and delusions occur only during mood episodes (major depression or mania), then a diagnosis of mood disorder is more appropriate. Rule out substance intoxication, withdrawal, or substance-induced psychotic disorder.	Did you [active phase symptoms] for at least 2 weeks when you were not [depressed/manic]?
Duration	C. Symptoms that meet criteria for a mood episode are present for a substantial portion of the total duration of the active and residual periods of the illness.		Were you [depressed/manic] for most of the time you [active phase symptoms] and had some of the other problems we talked about?
Rule out effects of substances and medical illness	D. The disturbance is not due to the direct physiological effects of a substance (e.g., a drug of abuse, a medication) or a general medical condition.	Rule out substance intoxication or withdrawal; see Table 7-3 for DSM-IV criteria for substance-induced psychotic disorder.	Were you drug- and alcohol-free [or drink/use drugs only occasionally] … … when you began [active phase symptoms]? … for the first month after you began [active phase symptoms]? … for at least a month while you [active phase symptoms]? Did you have any medical problems during that time? … Did you have any of the following medical problems at [onset]; a brain tumor, a stroke, epilepsy, thyroid problems, liver disease, kidney disease?

(a) American Psychiatric Association (1994).
(b) Reprinted with permission from the Diagnostic and Statistical Manual of Mental Disorders, Fourth Edition (Copyright 1994). American Psychiatric Association.
(c) Hasin et al. (2006).
(d) Reprinted with permission.

Table 7-3
DSM-IV Criteria for Substance-Induced Psychotic Disorder

Symptoms	*DSM-IV* Criteria[a, b]	Suggested Operationalization for Clinical Application	PRISM Questions to Aid Diagnosis[c, d]
Core Symptoms	A. Prominent hallucinations or delusions … do not include hallucinations if the person has insight that they are substance induced.	Do not consider hallucinations or delusions experienced only during intoxication or withdrawal.	
Other Criteria	B. There is evidence from the history, physical examination, or laboratory findings of either (1) or (2):		
	(1) the symptoms in Criterion A developed during, or within a month of, substance intoxication or withdrawal	Establish by careful history taking; identify the presence of psychotic symptoms and then relate the time of their occurrence to that of substance use.	How long after … [active phase symptoms] began did you start drinking or using drugs heavily? By heavily, I mean 4 or more days a week or 3 days straight … What were you using? How often did you [drink/use drug]?
	(2) medication use is etiologically related to the disturbance.		Did you start taking [medication(s)] before you began [active phase symptoms]? How long did you take [it/them]?
Rule out primary psychotic disorder	C. The disturbance is not better accounted for by a psychotic disorder that is not substance induced. Evidence that the symptoms are better accounted for by a psychotic disorder that is not substance induced might include the following:		
	(1) the [psychotic] symptoms precede the onset of the substance use (or medication use)	Compare the age of onset of psychotic symptoms and substance use.	At any time, were you drug- and alcohol-free when you began [psychotic symptoms]?

(Continued)

Symptoms	DSM-IV Criteria[a, b]	Suggested Operationalization for Clinical Application	PRISM Questions to Aid Diagnosis[c, d]
	(2) the [psychotic] symptoms persist for a substantial period of time (e.g., about a month) after the cessation of acute withdrawal or severe intoxication	Identify if the psychotic symptoms continued for more than a month after last substance use.	At any time, were you drug- and alcohol-free during the month before you began [psychotic symptoms]?
	(3) [the psychotic symptoms] are substantially in excess of what would be expected given the type or amount of the substance used or the duration of use	Identify the type and amount of substances used and duration of substance use and relate to the extent of psychotic symptoms.	What were you using? How often did you [drink/use drug]?
	(4) there is … evidence that suggests the existence of an independent non-substance-induced psychotic disorder (e.g., a history of recurrent non-substance-related [psychotic] episodes).	Establish by careful history taking; if there have been previous episodes of psychosis, identify substance use during those periods.	Did you have more than one time like that, when you [psychotic symptoms] and you were (drug- and alcohol-free or drinking or using drug occasionally)?
Rule out delirium	D. The disturbance does not occur exclusively during the course of delirium.	See Chapter 6 of this volume.	

(a) American Psychiatric Association (1994).
(b) Reprinted with permission from the *Diagnostic and Statistical Manual of Mental Disorders*, Fourth Edition (Copyright 1994). American Psychiatric Association.
(c) Hasin et al. (2006).
(d) Reprinted with permission.

the timing of the beginning of paranoid delusions by determining what grade he was in at that time, whether those symptoms began before or after his birthday that year, and whether he was experiencing these feelings during Christmas of that year.

Identify the Chief Complaint. Clinicians should find out why the patient is coming to treatment, who referred the patient, and why the patient feels that he/she needs treatment, what type of treatment is desired by the patient, and what treatments have been given to the patient in the past. This basic overview will help clinicians to evaluate substance use and psychotic symptoms.

Identify the Psychotic Symptoms. Information about psychotic symptoms is often more difficult to elicit than information about other symptoms such as depression or anxiety. The patient may volunteer some symptoms, and some information obtained from referral sources, family, or medical records may identify symptoms that can be explored in the assessment. However, it is also important to ask the patient about specific psychotic symptoms often seen in schizophrenia. The unusual experiences symptom section of the Psychiatric Research Interview for Substance and Mental Disorders (PRISM; Hasin et al., 2006) and the psychotic symptom section of the Structured Clinical Interview for DSM-IV-TR Axis I Disorders (SCID-I; First, Spitzer, Gibbon, & Williams, 2002) provide suggested questions for inquiring about specific psychotic symptoms.

Since psychotic symptoms often progress gradually, we recommend that clinicians identify the age of onset for each symptom, the course of the symptom (e.g., continuous, episodic, brief), and the current status. As can be seen in Figure 7-1 (based on our case example), the patient first experienced paranoid delusions at age 17, and those delusions continued until the time of his hospitalization. At age 20, he began to hear voices of people talking about him and felt that people were reading his mind, putting thoughts in his mind, taking thoughts out, and hearing his thoughts like they were broadcast out loud. The symptoms continued until his hospitalization. At age 21, he began to see people who were not there and to experience strong foul tastes for no apparent reason (gustatory hallucinations). These hallucinations occurred only episodically.

As noted on the timeline (see Figure 7-1), the core symptoms of schizophrenia are present. They are hallucinations and delusions, which have been present for over three years (more than the one month required for diagnosis).

Determine Whether Psychotic Symptoms Should Be Classified as Primary (Independent) or Substance Induced. Clinicians can determine whether psychotic symptoms should be classified as primary (independent) or substance induced by identifying the history of substance use. Clinicians first should determine specific substances used at any time by the patient and then should determine (1) the age and amount when first used, (2) the age that substances were regularly used several times per week or more, (3) the age of onset and length of any periods of abstinence, and (4) the current usage. Figure 7-2, which is based on the case example (see "Case Presentation") shows onset of alcohol use at age 18 and onset of other abuse at age 19. Cannabis use began at age 19 and quickly increased to dependence. There was a two-month period when he stopped using both alcohol and cannabis, but he then resumed use just prior to his hospitalization.

As noted on the timeline in Figure 7-2, the paranoid delusions began before the use of alcohol or cannabis. Also, the hallucinations and delusions continued during the

Figure 7-1
Onset and Course of Psychosis in the Case Example

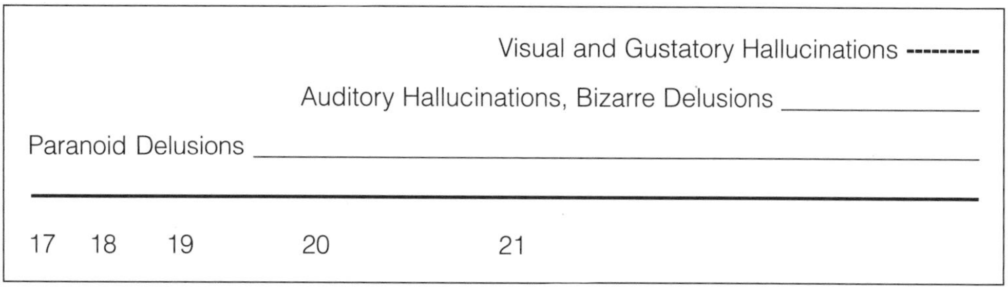

Visual and Gustatory Hallucinations --------

Auditory Hallucinations, Bizarre Delusions _____

Paranoid Delusions _____

17   18   19   20   21

Figure 7-2
Onset and Course of Psychosis and Substance Use in the Case Example

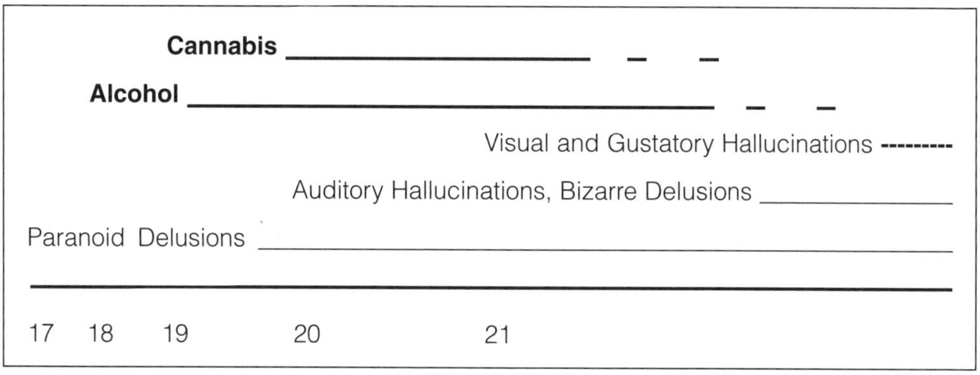

Cannabis _____   _   _

Alcohol _____   _   _

Visual and Gustatory Hallucinations --------

Auditory Hallucinations, Bizarre Delusions _____

Paranoid Delusions _____

17   18   19   20   21

two-month period of abstinence from all substances. These periods of continued psychotic symptoms in the absence of substance use indicate that the psychotic symptoms are primary and not substance induced.

Determine Whether Disorder Should Be Classified as Schizophrenia or Schizoaffective Disorder. Clinicians can determine if a disorder should be classified as schizophrenia or schizoaffective disorder by evaluating if there have been any major depressive episodes or manic episodes (see Chapter 1 and Chapter 2 of this volume) and then relating any mood episodes to the periods of psychosis. In our case example (see "Case Presentation") the patient reported three brief major depressive episodes, which can be seen in Figure 7-3.

As noted on the timeline in Figure 7-3, the patient had periods when a major depressive episode was present along with the hallucinations and delusions. There were also periods of over two weeks when the patient did not experience mood symptoms, but the hallucinations and delusions remained. However, the depressive episodes were not considered to be present for a substantial portion of the total duration of the psychotic symptoms. For this reason schizoaffective disorder is ruled out.

Ask About Past Treatments. We recommend asking about all prior treatment, including treatment for schizophrenia. In the early stages of the illness, called the prodrome,

Figure 7-3
Onset and Course of Psychosis, Substance
Use, and Depression in the Case Example

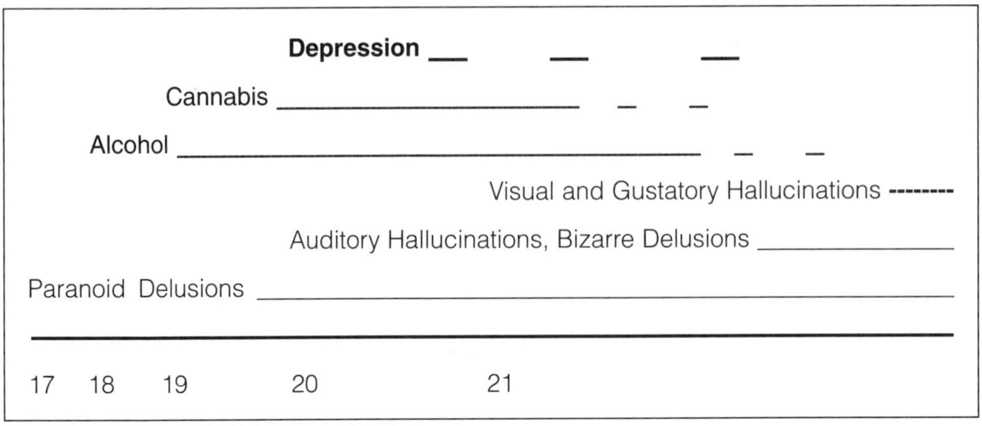

```
                    Depression ___        __            __

          Cannabis _____    _    _

      Alcohol _____    _    _

                                   Visual and Gustatory Hallucinations --------

                    Auditory Hallucinations, Bizarre Delusions _____

   Paranoid  Delusions _____


   ─────────────────────────────────────────────────────────────────

   17   18   19        20              21
```

many people become withdrawn, isolate themselves more from social situations, and have difficulty in school or at work. This sometimes looks like depression, and patients are often treated for depression prior to the onset of the psychotic symptoms. It is also important to ask about specific treatments for schizophrenia and the patient's response to the treatments. Information should be obtained about the specific medications taken in the past as well as maximum dosage, length of treatment, adherence to treatment, and response to treatment, including any side effects or adverse reactions. This information helps to guide treatment decisions. If a patient has taken medication in the past that has caused serious side effects or has not helped with the symptoms, other medications should be considered. In the case example (see "Case Presentation"), BC did not have any previous treatment for schizophrenia but was seen at age 16 by a family therapist as a result of problems in school. These problems could have been related to prodromal symptoms, to the changes occurring in the family, or to both.

Examine Family History. Schizophrenia, to some degree, is genetically determined. Having a family member with schizophrenia increases the risk for both psychotic disorders and mood disorders. Clinicians should take a family history of substance use disorders, psychotic disorders, and mood disorders.

Ask About Suicide and Potential for Violence. Patients with schizophrenia are at a higher risk for suicide, and the presence of substance abuse increases that risk. It is crucial to ask about previous suicidal thoughts, plans, and attempts, as well as the context. It is also necessary to ask about the patient's access to guns or other dangerous items that the patient may be thinking of using to harm himself/herself. Some suicidal behavior may be related to depression, but some may be in response to delusions or voices telling patients to hurt themselves (termed command hallucinations). The same is true for those patients who have a history of violent thoughts or behaviors. Violent acting out may be related to poor impulse control, antisocial behavior, or a response to psychotic symptoms. An understanding of the history of suicide attempts or violence will help in the ongoing assessment of risk for suicide and violence.

Ask About Other Psychiatric Disorders. It is important to understand other disorders that may be present along with schizophrenia and substance abuse. Some patients have preexisting anxiety disorders, such as social anxiety disorder or obsessive compulsive disorder, which also need to be addressed in treatment. We have found that, as psychotic symptoms decrease, some patients experience a reduction in the symptoms related to anxiety disorders, but other patients require additional treatment aimed at the anxiety disorder. Some patients with schizophrenia and substance abuse problems may also have personality disorders such as antisocial personality disorder.

Take Brief Developmental Childhood History. Patients with schizophrenia sometimes have a history of school or social problems early on or show a decline in functioning during adolescence. A developmental childhood history helps to identify the course of illness, rule out other possible disorders, such as pervasive developmental disorders (autism, Asperger's syndrome), and identify issues that need to be addressed in treatment. In our case example (see "Case Presentation"), the patient began to have difficulty in adolescence. It is unclear whether this change was in response to his parents' divorce or related to prodromal symptoms of schizophrenia. However, his feelings of anger and depression related to his father continue to trouble him and need to be addressed.

Ask About Trauma and Abuse. Unfortunately, past trauma is common in patients with schizophrenia and substance abuse problems and, in some patients, this leads to posttraumatic stress disorder. Current trauma or abuse needs to be addressed immediately as part of the treatment plan, but we recommend addressing past trauma after the psychotic symptoms stabilize.

Ask About Family or Home Environment. Schizophrenia tends to be worsened by home or family environments that are full of emotion, anger, and open confrontation (termed "high expressed emotion"). This type of stress appears to be an important risk factor for episodes of psychotic relapse in patients with schizophrenia. Conversely, schizophrenia tends to be less severe in family environments that are calm and relaxed ("low expressed emotion"). Further, interventions that teach families to foster an atmosphere of low expressed emotion have been shown, when used in combination with appropriate antipsychotic medication, to help reduce symptoms of schizophrenia and the frequency of hospitalizations for episodes of worsening psychosis. Analysis of family structure and family interventions are also important tools in the treatment of substance dependence. Thus, evaluating how family members or other coinhabitants relate to each other and to the patient can be important in developing the treatment plan.

NATURAL HISTORY AND ETIOLOGY

Risk Factors and Possible Causative Mechanisms

The cause of schizophrenia is still unclear, but it may be related to both genetic and environmental factors. Parents, brothers, and sisters of patients with schizophrenia have higher rates of schizophrenia than the general population. Rates of schizophrenia are higher in children born during periods of famine or in the winter and early spring compared to other seasons, thereby suggesting that nutrition and viral infection may play a role in this illness (Torrey, Miller, Rawlings, & Yolken, 1997).

Course of Schizophrenia in Relation to Course of Substance Use Over Lifetime

The onset of schizophrenia is usually in late adolescence and early adulthood (Häfner, Maurer, Löffler, & Reicher-Rossler, 1993), which is the same high-risk period for the onset of substance use disorders. Schizophrenia is characterized by high rates of relapse (Breier, Schreiber, Dyer, & Pickar, 1991), severe impairment in social and occupational functioning, and higher rates of death by suicide than the general population (Siris, 2001). Several factors can complicate the treatment of schizophrenia. A number of people have a poor response to medication. Others frequently do not take medication as prescribed, which results in higher rates of relapse and possible decreased response to treatment over time. Another complicating factor is the high rate of substance use disorders in patients with schizophrenia. More than half of the patients abuse drugs. According to the Epidemiologic Catchment Area Study (Regier et al., 1990), a large epidemiological study of rates of mental disorders in the general population in five communities in the United States, the odds of having a substance use disorder is 4.6 times higher in patients with schizophrenia than in the general population. Table 7-4 summarizes the prevalence rates of substance use disorders in patients with schizophrenia from different studies.

Type of substances used and lifetime prevalence rates vary between studies due to demographics (e.g., gender, urban/rural, inpatients/outpatients), diagnostic criteria, and sources of information. Young males are at higher risk for substance use disorders than females and older patients. About half of patients with schizophrenia and substance use disorders use more than one substance (excluding nicotine), usually cannabis and alcohol or cannabis and cocaine.

Although there have been many studies of the incidence of substance use disorders for people with schizophrenia, there are fewer on outcomes of treatment. However, recent research holds promise that integrated treatments may be effective in reducing substance use (Mueser, Drake, & Bond, 1997; RachBeisel, Scott, & Dixon, 1999). It has also been shown that, when assertive community treatment (ACT) programs adhere to the ACT model, outcomes are more favorable with decreases in substance use (McHugo, Drake, Teague, & Xie, 1999). ACT involves assigning a patient an advocate or care manager who oversees and coordinates both psychiatric treatment (monitoring medication compliance and attendance at appointments and ensuring that a patient's treatment needs are being met) and help with other needs (housing, public assistance, vocational training).

ISSUES INVOLVED IN DIAGNOSING SCHIZOPHRENIA IN SUBSTANCE-DEPENDENT PATIENTS

Distinguishing Primary Schizophrenia From Substance-Induced Psychosis or Mood Disorder

To differentiate substance-induced psychotic disorder from schizophrenia, clinicians should determine the onset of psychotic symptoms in relation to the onset of substance use:

1. The psychotic symptoms began before the substance use began; or

2. The psychotic symptoms began after substance use but stopped when there was no further substance use for a period of one month or more; or

3. The psychotic symptoms continued despite the fact that the person was no longer using substances for at least a month.

Table 7-4
Lifetime Prevalence Rates of Substance
Use Disorders in Patients With
Schizophrenia

Substance	Lifetime Prevalence
nicotine	70-90%
alcohol	20-60%
cannabis	12-42%
cocaine	15-50%
amphetamines	2-25%

If psychotic symptoms occurred before the substance use started or continued after stopping substance use for a month, a primary psychotic disorder is most likely. On the other hand, if the psychotic symptoms occurred after substance use started and then stopped within a month of discontinuing substance use, a substance-induced psychotic disorder is most likely.

Similarly, to differentiate a mood disorder from schizophrenia, clinicians should determine the timing of mood symptoms in relation to the timing of psychotic symptoms:

1. Was there major episode of depression or mania (see Chapter 1 and Chapter 2 of this volume) at the same time as the hallucinations and delusions began?

2. Within the same period of illness, was there an episode of major depression or mania prior to hallucinations and delusions?

3. Was there a period of at least two weeks when there were hallucinations and delusions *without* any significant mood symptoms?

Clinicians should consider the following guidelines for conducting diagnostic evaluations.

Conduct Thorough Psychiatric Evaluation. It is not possible to determine whether someone has schizophrenia by forming an impression based only on how the patient presents. A patient presenting with delusions and hallucinations may have a mood disorder, schizophrenia, schizoaffective disorder, substance-induced psychosis, substance intoxication or withdrawal, or a medical problem. Thus, a complete history, with attention to the lifetime course of illness, is necessary to make an accurate diagnosis. Multiple sources of information, including reports from family members and prior medical records, are also useful.

Assess Substance Use. In some cases, patients may prefer to say they were using substances around the time of illness, even when this is not the case. This occurs because many patients prefer to blame substance use for their psychosis rather than accept a diagnosis of schizophrenia.

Recognizing Diagnosis as an Ongoing Process. Some patients appear at first to have a substance-induced psychosis. When their psychotic symptoms do not remit after several months of abstinence or when it becomes clear that the psychotic symptoms exceed expected effects of the substances that they are using, the clinician may change the diagnosis to schizophrenia.

Maintain Nonjudgmental Stance. There are patients who report psychotic symptoms that they do not actually experience (although this is uncommon). In general, this is done to obtain additional government benefits or to avoid legal problems. This is sometimes referred to as "malingering" ("faking it," in essence), although we believe that this term should be used with caution because it has derogatory and judgmental implications. In general, during the evaluation of psychopathology, clinicians should maintain a nonjudgmental stance and attempt to empathize with the patient's situation and point of view. This approach will yield the best information and helps to build therapeutic alliance, thereby increasing the chances that the patient will follow treatment recommendations.

Avoid Making Diagnosis of Schizophrenia Based Only on Negative Symptoms. In patients with co-occurring disorders, the cause of negative symptoms is often impossible to determine. Negative symptoms may be related either to schizophrenia or to chronic substance use (e.g., psychostimulant withdrawal). For this reason, the diagnosis of schizophrenia should not be made if there are no other Criterion A symptoms.

Consider All Symptoms of Substance Intoxication and Withdrawal. Some symptoms are more characteristic of intoxication or withdrawal associated with a particular substance (e.g., visual hallucinations associated with hallucinogen or alcohol withdrawal and tactile hallucinations associated with psychostimulant intoxication). The *DSM-IV* lists specific criteria for intoxication and withdrawal for each of the major substances of abuse and is a useful reference. A caveat is that the lists of symptoms found in *DSM-IV* may not be complete; patients may experience symptoms that are clearly related to substance use but that are not listed in the *DSM-IV* as intoxication or withdrawal symptoms for a particular substance.

Be Aware of Attempts to Hide Substance Use. Despite careful assessment and use of urine and blood testing, clinicians may fail to diagnose substance-induced psychosis in patients who are skilled at hiding their substance use. Clinicians should reassess their patients when patients' symptoms lessen, when patients exhibit clearer thinking, and after a strong therapeutic alliance has been established. A reassessment may simply require members of a treatment team to share updates on a patient's progress and may not require a comprehensive psychiatric evaluation (like the initial psychiatric evaluation when a patient enters treatment). The following example illustrates the case of a patient who was initially diagnosed with psychotic disorder but who, in fact, had substance-induced psychosis.

> *Example:* JS, a 22-year-old female, has two children and lives with her mother, who reports that, for the last five months, JS has been acting strangely, has feared leaving the house, and has been argumentative and anxious. JS reports that people "are after [her]," that she was raped by a "ghost-like person," and that she has been "held down in [her] bed for the last several months." She has been unable to work and requires help from her mother to care for her children. Although JS admits that she has used ecstasy, she states that she has not used the drug in four months. Her symptoms meet criteria for schizophrenia, and she continues to experience symptoms throughout the first months of treatment. After two months of treatment, JS admits that she has continued to use ecstasy on a regular basis. Once she stops its use, she recovers rapidly.

Substances Often Used by Patients With Schizophrenia

The following is a review of the substances often used by patients with schizophrenia.

Alcohol. Twenty to sixty percent of people with schizophrenia have a lifetime diagnosis of alcohol use disorder. Most of these patients also have a nicotine addiction, and more than half of them also have a lifetime diagnosis of cannabis use disorder and other substance use disorders. Long-term use of alcohol in patients with schizophrenia has been associated with more frequent and longer hospitalizations, poorer functioning, and higher suicide rates (Allebeck, Varla, Kristjansson, & Wistedt, 1987; Gerding, Labbate, Measom, Santos, & Arana, 1999; Heilä et al., 1997). Long-term use of alcohol increases the chances of cardiovascular and liver diseases.

Acute alcohol intoxication does not induce psychosis. However, long-term use has been associated with a psychotic state often referred to as alcoholic hallucinosis. In contrast to schizophrenia, alcoholic hallucinosis does not have prominent negative symptoms or thought disorder, and patients sometimes have insight into the fact that the hallucinations are not real. In severe withdrawal, alcohol withdrawal delirium (delirium tremens) is associated with hallucinations and marked confusion as well as seizures. Severe alcohol withdrawal is a medical emergency requiring hospitalization and can end in death if not properly treated. Patients with this type of delirium with confusion (see Chapter 6 of this volume), called impaired sensorium, do not know what time of day it is, where they are, or who the people around them are. The level of confusion waxes and wanes (e.g., hospitalized patients may seem fully aware of their surroundings and what is happening to them at one moment, and then one hour later they may believe that they are at home, and snakes are crawling around the floor). Hallucinations are often visual and vivid (e.g., snakes, bugs). Hallucinations and confusion associated with alcohol withdrawal cease within a few days to a week of sobriety.

Cannabis. Cannabis, the most common illicit drug used by patients with schizophrenia, is often used in conjunction with nicotine and alcohol. Cannabis intoxication can induce brief episodes of psychosis or exacerbate preexisting psychotic symptoms (Negrete, Knapp, Douglas, & Smith, 1986; Thornicroft, 1990). Cannabis may precipitate psychosis in some individuals (Andréasson, Allebeck, Engström, & Rydberg, 1987), and several studies (Andréasson, Allebeck, & Rydberg, 1989; Hambrecht & Häfner, 1996) have found that patients with schizophrenia and a history of cannabis use experience onset of psychosis at an earlier age than patients who did not use cannabis. Long-lasting psychotic effects of cannabis seem to be related to preexisting schizophrenia or bipolar illness (Bowers, 1987). Some individuals develop psychotic symptoms after smoking a combination of cannabis and phencyclidine (PCP), although psychosis can result from use of either alone. To determine whether psychotic symptoms are a result of cannabis, clinicians must evaluate patients after they have been abstinent from this substance for a minimum of one month.

Hallucinogens. Hallucinations, particularly visual hallucinations, as well as a feeling of altered reality, are typical symptoms of hallucinogen intoxication on hallucinogens (lysergic acid diethylamide (LSD), phencyclidine (PCP), mescaline or psilocybin from mushrooms). A state of heightened anxiety and feelings of dread ("bad trip") can also occur. Hallucinogen use has been associated with brief psychotic episodes and schizophreniform psychoses—that is, psychotic episodes that resemble schizophrenia but resolve weeks to a few months after last drug use (Mueser et al., 1990). Bowers and Swigar (1983) found that patients with positive family histories of major mental illness become psychotic with smaller amounts of hallucinogens compared to patients without family histories of major mental illness. This finding suggests that such patients may have a vulnerability to psychosis that is brought out by drug use. The use of hallucinogens must be thoroughly investigated in patients with a history of psychotic episodes. Sometimes PCP can induce a psychosis similar to schizophrenia that can last for several weeks (Javitt & Zuckin, 2005).

Psychostimulants. Compared to the general population, patients with schizophrenia have higher rates of psychostimulant use (Mueser et al., 1990). Psychostimulants (amphetamines and related substances (e.g., methylphenidate), metamphetamine, and cocaine) can induce brief psychotic episodes or exacerbate preexisting psychosis. The effect of psychostimulants on dopamine neurotransmission in the brain can result in repetitive and stereotyped movements. One particular psychostimulant-induced psychosis is formication (often referred to as "coke bugs" or "snow bugs"): a sensation that resembles the feeling of insects or snakes crawling on or under the skin. Some people have used a knife or tweezers in an effort to cut out the imagined bugs, sometimes leading to death by bleeding (Gahlinger, 2001). Transient cocaine-induced paranoia may increase the risk of developing psychosis (Satel & Edell, 1991). Psychotic symptoms caused by stimulants generally subside within hours after cessation of drug use and can be diagnosed as part of stimulant intoxication. Delusions or hallucinations that continue for days or weeks after cessation of stimulant use suggest another diagnosis (substance-induced psychosis, schizophrenia, schizoaffective disorder, mood disorder with psychosis, delirium).

Psychostimulant withdrawal may result in depression, lethargy, and anhedonia (inability to feel pleasure) that may last for up to four months, although usually there is substantial improvement in such withdrawal symptoms within days to a week of stopping drug use. These symptoms are similar to the negative symptoms of schizophrenia and further complicate diagnosis of schizophrenia in a long-term psychostimulant user. Chronic use of amphetamines can cause mood swings, anxiety, sleep problems, violent behavior, paranoia, and auditory and visual hallucinations (Jaffe, Ling, & Rawson, 2005). To determine if a patient's psychotic symptoms are a result of psychostimulant use, clinicians should evaluate patients after they have been abstinent from all substances for at least one week.

Nicotine. Up to 90 percent of patients with schizophrenia have a lifetime diagnosis of nicotine dependence. According to the Epidemiologic Catchment Area (ECA) study, nicotine addiction is three times higher in patients with schizophrenia than the general population (Regier et al., 1990). The stimulating effects of nicotine may help counteract the negative symptoms of schizophrenia, may help patients to be more vigilant and focused, and may improve their working memory (George et al., 2002; Lee, Frangou, Russel, & Gray, 1997). Nicotine intoxication and withdrawal do not cause psychosis, although withdrawal may increase anxiety. Cigarette smoking has devastating effects on the health of patients with schizophrenia by increasing the risk of cardiovascular diseases and lung and pharyngeal cancers (Lichtermann, Ekelund, Pukkala, Transkanen, & Lonnqvist, 2001).

Club Drugs. Club drugs (MDMA (Ecstasy), GHB (gamma hydroxybutyrate), and others) are a group of drugs with diverse pharmacology that have in common that they are relatively new on the drug scene and often available at nightclubs or other party venues (e.g., parties on college campuses). MDMA (Ecstasy) resembles stimulants and hallucinogens and has been associated with psychosis (see the example of JS in "Be Aware of Attempts to Hide Substance Use"). GHB is more like a sedative and can produce confusion, delirium, stupor, or coma in excessive doses.

INSTRUMENTS AND METHODS FOR SCREENING AND DIAGNOSIS

Screening and Assessment Instruments

Screening tools (e.g., CAGE Questionnaire (Ewing, 1984; Mayfield, McLeod, & Hall, 1974), which is named for its four questions; Michigan Alcoholism Screening Test (MAST; Selzer, 1971)) and tools that assess symptom severity and degrees of impairment from drug use (e.g., Addiction Severity Index) are useful in evaluating this patient population (Appleby, Dyson, Altman, & Luchins, 1997). The Dartmouth Assessment of Lifestyle Instrument (DALI) was specifically designed to screen for substance use in patients with severe mental illness (Rosenberg et al., 1998). Table 7-5 briefly describes features of several common screening and assessment instruments for identifying substance abuse and psychotic symptoms.

Since patients with schizophrenia often are reluctant to disclose information about substance use, clinicians should collect information about patients from sources in addition to the diagnostic interview (e.g., significant others, medical records, urine toxicology, and alcohol breathalyzers). Finally, risk factors for a substance use disorder include heavy smoking (more than twenty-five cigarettes per day), homelessness, legal problems, a history of verbal threats and violence, need for higher doses of antipsychotics, multiple medical problems, frequent visits to the emergency room, frequent hospitalizations, and a history of suicidal ideation or attempts (Ziedonis, 2004).

Diagnostic Instruments

The best method for confirming a diagnosis of schizophrenia and assessing the co-occurrence of substance use disorders is the use of a structured interview based on the *DSM-IV* criteria. The PRISM (Hasin et al., 2006), which was designed for use among substance-dependent patients, permits clinicians to evaluate each psychiatric symptom separately in terms of its relationship to substance abuse. The PRISM quotes each *DSM-IV* criterion and offers questions for use by clinicians in eliciting information from patients about their symptoms (see Tables 7-1A, 7-2, and 7-3 for examples of questions from the PRISM). The PRISM requires approximately 120 minutes to administer to subjects with psychiatric and substance use symptoms. Training in use of the PRISM offers an opportunity to learn the *DSM-IV* diagnostic criteria and the procedure for conducting on effective psychiatric interview.

The SCID-I (First et al., 2002) has been widely used in studies of schizophrenia. Although it is lengthy (an interview can take up to two hours) and requires some training, the SCID-I interview consists of detailed questions regarding the onset and the course of schizophrenia and other *DSM-IV* diagnoses, including mood, anxiety, and substance use disorders.

PSYCHOTIC DISORDERS DUE TO GENERAL MEDICAL CONDITION

Many medical disorders can present with schizophrenia-like symptoms and can be confused with schizophrenia: (1) endocrine disorders (i.e., disorders associated with body

Table 7-5
Instruments for Screening and Diagnosis of
Schizophrenia in Patients With Substance Use Disorders

Instrument	Features
CAGE Questionnaire (Ewing, 1984; Mayfield, McLeod, & Hall, 1974)	– 4 items (yes/no) – Self-report or clinician-administered – Screens for alcohol problems
Michigan Alcoholism Screening Test (MAST) (Selzer, 1971)	– 25 items (yes/no) – Self-report or clinician-administered – Identifies lifetime problems related to alcohol use
Addiction Severity Index (ASI) (Appleby, Dyson, Altman, & Luchins, 1997)	– 142 items – Clinician-administered, semi-structured interview – Identifies problems in several areas of functioning that are often affected by substance abuse
Dartmouth Assessment of Lifestyle Instrument (DALI) (Rosenberg et al., 1998)	– 18 items – Clinician-administered scale – Screens for substance use disorders in psychiatric population
Brief Psychiatric Rating Scale (BPRS) (Overall & Gorham, 1962)	– 18 items – Clinician-administered assessment instrument – Assesses the severity of symptoms in individuals with moderate to severe psychotic disorders – Usually used in research studies
Positive and Negative Syndrome Scale (PANSS) (Kay, Fiszbein, & Opler, 1987)	– 30 items – Clinician-administered assessment instrument – Assesses the severity of symptoms and general psychopathology in individuals with schizophrenia and other psychotic disorders – Provides a method for asking questions about symptoms – Usually used in research studies
Structured Clinical Interview for DSM-IV-TR Axis I Disorders (SCID-I) (First et al., 2002)	– Clinician-administered diagnostic instrument – Based on *DSM-IV-TR* criteria – Provides a method for asking questions about symptoms of schizophrenia and other psychiatric disorders – Usually used in research studies
Psychiatric Research Interview for Substance and Mental Disorders (PRISM) (Hasin et al., 2006)	– Clinician-administered diagnostic instrument – Based on *DSM-IV* criteria – Often used in research studies but also suitable for clinical use

glands such as the thyroid, adrenal glands, and pituitary); (2) heavy metal (e.g., mercury) and carbon monoxide poisoning; (3) epilepsy including complex partial seizures (a type of epilepsy with psychosensory phenomena); (4) Wernicke-Korsakov syndrome (a continuum of delirium, dementia, and neurological symptoms associated with chronic alcohol use, thought to represent a combination of nutritional (e.g., vitamin B_{12}) deficiency and alcohol-related brain damage); (5) infectious diseases (Creutzfeldt-Jakob disease, herpes encephalitis, neurosyphilis); (6) metabolic disorders (acute intermittent porphyria, B_{12} deficiency, pellagra, cerebral lipidoses, homocystinuria, metachromatic leukodystrophy, Wilson's disease, Fabry's disease, Fahr's disease, Hallervorden-Spatz syndrome); (7) immune disorders (acquired immune deficiency syndrome, systemic lupus erythematosus); and (8) other neurological disorders (brain tumors, cerebrovascular diseases, normal pressure hydrocephalus, Huntington's disease).

Because psychiatric symptoms can emerge early in the course of medical disorders before other symptoms become apparent, a patient who presents with a first episode of psychosis requires a thorough evaluation to rule out a medical diagnosis. The initial evaluation should include collection of a complete family history for medical, neurological, and psychiatric disorders, a physical examination, comprehensive blood and urine tests, and brain imaging when indicated (Kirkpatrick & Tek, 2005).

TREATMENT OPTIONS

Treatments for Schizophrenia

Importance of Integrated Treatment. Treatment of schizophrenia and co-occurring substance use disorders requires an integrated treatment approach that is provided by a team of clinicians who can address each disorder and their interactions (Mueser, Noordsy, Drake, & Fox, 2003). The evidence is clear that integrated treatment approaches are superior to approaches in which schizophrenia and substance use disorders are each treated at separate programs by separate teams of clinicians. Each patient is a unique individual who is likely to be affected in a variety of ways by schizophrenia, substance use, and life events. Many patients do not follow up on medical problems that may affect their health, and they often require assistance getting the medical care they need. Antipsychotic medications are usually effective in decreasing or eliminating the positive symptoms of schizophrenia such as delusions and hallucinations. However, negative symptoms, such as social withdrawal, low motivation, flat affect, and apathy, do not respond as well to medications and can be treated with psychosocial interventions. Similarly, cognitive impairments in areas like memory, attention, problem solving, and abstract thinking require different treatment approaches. Patients often are nonadherent to medication regimes. All of these problems make it difficult to provide appropriate treatment for patients with both schizophrenia and substance use problems.

Selecting the appropriate treatment setting will require matching available facilities to the severity of the patient's symptoms. Such settings range from specialized outpatient programs, to psychiatric day programs, to residential programs and inpatient psychiatric treatment. The ideal integrated treatment program includes behavioral and pharmacological treatments and emphasizes communication (1) among members of the treatment team in charge of psychiatric, substance use disorder, and medical care and (2) between treatment providers and significant others (e.g., relatives, spouses or partners, friends). Patients require regular monitoring (weekly if possible) for medication management (compliance and side effects) and use of substances (weekly urine toxicology with immediate results if possible).

Antipsychotic Medication Therapy for Treatment of Schizophrenia. In the 1950s, antipsychotic medications were discovered and found to help with symptoms of psychosis. This first group of medications is referred to as "typical" or "conventional" medications. A new class of medications, called "atypical" (not typical), was recently introduced; these medications are supposed to have fewer side effects and be better at addressing negative symptoms. Clinical experience suggests that patients who fail to improve on a typical antipsychotic may improve when switched to an atypical. There is also some evidence that the atypical antipsychotic medication clozapine may be more beneficial in reducing substance use. Table 7-6 presents a list of typical and atypical antipsychotic medications.

Antipsychotic medications are believed to work by adjusting the actions of dopamine, serotonin, and other chemicals, called neurotransmitters, that are involved in brain functioning. These medications help many people to varying degrees by alleviating symptoms such as delusions and hallucinations. They are less effective in improving cognitive abilities (such as attention and memory) and negative symptoms (such as lack of initiative and flat affect). Antipsychotic medications do not provide a cure but, like medications for diabetes and high blood pressure, help decrease symptoms and reduce relapse rates.

As with all medications, some of the benefits are accompanied by unwanted side effects. Common side effects of the typical antipsychotic medications include muscle stiffness, muscle cramping, tremors, dry mouth, weight gain, and tardive dyskinesia (persistent involuntary muscle movements). Common side effects of atypical antipsychotic medications are sedation, fatigue, and weight gain, which sometimes results in diabetes and high levels of cholesterol. All of the medications except for clozapine may cause persistent involuntary muscle movements (tardive dyskinesia). Clozapine has the potential side effect of lowering the white blood count (agranulocytosis) to dangerous levels where the body cannot fight infections, and therefore patients require regular blood tests. All antipsychotic medications can cause a rare but dangerous condition called neuroleptic malignant syndrome, which causes muscle rigidity, high fevers, and seizures. Some side effects can be treated with adjunctive medication or require a switch to a different medication. For more specific information regarding side effects, refer to Marder and van Kammen (2005) for typical antipsychotics and van Kammen and Marder (2005) for atypical antipsychotics.

Medication Treatment of Co-Occurring Substance Use Disorders. Standard pharmacotherapies for intoxication and withdrawal states are used in patients with schizophrenia. The long-term treatment goal should be psychiatric stability, since the likelihood of success in reducing substance use is low when patients are psychiatrically unstable (George, Vessicchio, & Termine, 2003).

Antipsychotic Medications. For people with schizophrenia, antipsychotics are beneficial and reduce the likelihood of psychotic relapse even in people who are actively using drugs (Hunt, Bergen, & Bashir, 2002). Antipsychotics may also be used to treat agitation in acute intoxication. Compared to typical antipsychotics, atypical antipsychotics may help reduce substance use (Drake, Xie, McHugo, & Green, 2000; Littrell, Petty, Hilligoss, Peabody, & Johnson, 2001; Smelson et al., 2002). Clozapine decreases self-reported cigarette smoking, particularly in heavy smokers (George et al., 2003; McEvoy, Freudenreich, & Wilson, 1999). In contrast, typical antipsychotics such as haloperidol seem to increase smoking (McEvoy, Freudenreich, Levin, & Rose, 1995).

Benzodiazepines, Barbiturates, and Opiates. These medications have the potential for abuse or dependence, and therefore it is better to avoid prescribing these medications if possible. In addition, these medications are sedating and may augment the sedative effects of alcohol, opioids, or tranquilizers. At times, benzodiazepines such as lorazepam are used for agitation related to acute intoxication. Benzodiazepines also are used to treat symptoms of agitation, severe anxiety, and restlessness in patients with schizophrenia.

Medications for Alcohol Abuse. Disulfiram (Antabuse) is usually not recommended because of side effects and a paucity of data regarding its efficacy in people with schizophrenia. Psychotic episodes have been described as a rare side effect of disulfiram particularly with doses in the higher range of what historically has been prescribed.

Table 7-6
Antipsychotic Medications

Typical Antipsychotic Medication[a]	Atypical Antipsychotic Medications
haloperidol (Haldol)	clozapine (Clorzaril)
fluphenazine (Prolixin)	risperidone (Risperdal)
chlorphromazine (Thorazine)	olanzapine (Zyprexa)
molidone (Moban)	quetiapine (Seroquel)
thioridazine (Mellaril)	ziprasidone (Geodon)
perphenazine (Trilafon)	aripiprazole (Abilify)

[a] For a complete list of typical antipsychotic medications, see Marder & van Kammen (2005).

Lower doses of 125 to 250 mg per day of disulfiram are usually well tolerated, but the patient should be monitored for worsening of psychosis. Disulfiram exerts a powerful effect: most patients who take it regularly will be physically unable to tolerate drinking any alcohol. Naltrexone (Revia) seems to be helpful in treating patients with schizophrenia who are abusing alcohol (Petrakis et al., 2004) and does not interact with most psychotropic medications. Its effect is more subtle than the effect of disulfiram. A long-acting depot naltrexone injection is now available for patients. Like long-acting depot injections of antipsychotic medications (prolixin, haloperidol, risperidone), long-acting depot naltrexone injections should be helpful in treating patients who have difficulty adhering to a medication regime. Acamprosate (Campral) is a medication that has been available in Europe for several years for treatment of alcoholism, and, like naltrexone, it exerts modest but significant beneficial effects. There is less experience using acamprosate in patients with schizophrenia.

Medications for Nicotine Dependence. Nicotine dependence is very common among patients with schizophrenia, and clinicians may view its treatment as a low priority when they are faced with the task of managing a patient's psychosis, disorganized or dangerous behavior, and use of more intoxicating substances that produce acute behavioral impairment (e.g., alcohol, stimulants, or cannabis). However, cigarettes cause serious long-term damage. Heart and lung disease related to smoking are among the most common causes of death in patients with schizophrenia. Thus, once a patient has been stabilized, clinicians should encourage patients to quit smoking.

There are three FDA-approved treatments for nicotine dependence: nicotine replacement, bupropion sustained-release, and varenicline. Nicotine replacement therapies (patch, gum, lozenge, nasal spray, inhaler) facilitate reduction in nicotine use and cessation. Patients must be instructed not to smoke when using the patch in order to avoid nicotine toxicity (tremors, nausea, vomiting, dizziness). Bupropion is a stimulant-like antidepressant that can be used safely in patients with schizophrenia, as long as patients are monitored regularly. However, because of increased risk of seizures, clinicians should avoid prescribing bupropion to patients who are taking clozapine. Varenicline is a medication that has complex effects at nicotinic receptors and was more effective than bupropion in a study of smoking cessation (Gonzales et al., 2006). Nicotine dependence is difficult to treat in patients with schizophrenia, and clinicians and patients should not become discouraged if the first attempts to quit fail. If a patient continues to attempt to quit, the likelihood of success is increased (see Chapter 13 of this volume for detailed coverage of diagnosis and treatment of nicotine dependence).

Antidepressant and Mood-Stabilizing Medications. People with schizophrenia and co-occurring abuse disorders may also have mood disorders that require prescription of additional medications. In patients who abuse psychostimulants, depression is common and often requires treatment with antidepressant medications. Mood disorders are treated in the same way in patients with schizophrenia as in people without schizophrenia (see Chapter 1 and Chapter 2 of this volume).

Treatment of Co-Occurring Medical Disorders

Patients with schizophrenia and co-occurring substance use disorders are at increased risk for medical problems associated with substance use (e.g., human immunodeficiency virus (HIV), hepatitis B or hepatitis C, cardiovascular diseases, cancer) and for medical problems associated with use of medications to treat schizophrenia (e.g., use of atypical antipsychotics has been associated with diabetes, weight gain, and increased cholesterol). Chronic alcohol use is associated with multiple medical problems, including liver disease and cardiovascular diseases. Tobacco use is associated with an increase in bronchitis, emphysema, and other chronic lung diseases, and a higher incidence of lung cancer. Tobacco use is also a main risk factor for cardiovascular disease, which is the primary cause of death in both male and female patients with schizophrenia.

The prognosis of medical complications associated with substance use disorders is worse in patients with schizophrenia compared to the general population because patients with schizophrenia are less likely to practice health-promoting behaviors, are less adherent to treatment, and are likely to have more limited access to health care (Casey & Hansen, 2003). Medical treatment should be accompanied by strategies to enhance adherence to medical treatment, that is, psychoeducation, motivational therapies, psychosocial support, and monitoring of medication intake whenever possible.

Psychotherapies for Co-Occurring Schizophrenia and Substance Abuse

Several forms of psychotherapeutic interventions have been recommended for people with schizophrenia and co-occurring substance abuse. While these take a variety of formats, the following are frequently recommended interventions: supportive individual and group therapies, family therapy, Cognitive Behavioral Therapy (CBT), Motivational Enhancement Therapy, Compliance Therapy, peer support, modified self-help groups (sometimes referred to as "double trouble" groups), psychoeducation, substance abuse counseling, social skills training, and case management services.

Supportive Psychotherapy. Patients with schizophrenia require a supportive treatment setting where the therapist provides "emotional support, empathy, warmth, authenticity, transparency, and reliability" (Bachmann, Resch, & Mundt, 2003, p. 169). This therapeutic stance is necessary for patients with schizophrenia and co-occurring substance use problems. The following example illustrates how a counselor can provide support to a patient with schizophrenia in a group therapy session.

Example: AJ is in a substance abuse treatment group session and suddenly leaves the room. In some settings, group members are penalized for such behavior. However, the counselor, who is experienced in working with patients with schizophrenia, speaks to AJ and learns that he was unable to stay in the group because he felt paranoid. The counselor praises AJ for letting her know why he left the group session and teaches him skills that help him to cope with his feelings of paranoia.

Patients are not encouraged to explore their memories of losses, abuse, or other traumas. Feelings are validated, but it is most important to help patients move forward rather than risk setting off a cascade of emotions that may be destabilizing. Cognitive behavioral approaches can be utilized as part of supportive psychotherapy to help patients to understand how thoughts can trigger psychological changes and behaviors. Patients may also require help when they have close family members who use substances. It is safe and useful to help patients understand that they are not the same person as the substance-abusing family member and that, as adults, they can make their own choices.

Psychoeducation. The goal of psychoeducation is to provide patients with information regarding their psychiatric disorder and their substance use disorder as well as the interaction between both. This information helps patients develop the insight that is necessary to build motivation for abstinence and adherence to medications (Miller, McCormack, Sevy, & Robinson, 2005). Psychoeducation is enhanced by using illustrations of the brain to explain how medications work and how substances interfere with medication and affect the brain. Additional topics of psychoeducation include safer sex practices and complications such as HIV and hepatitis.

Cognitive Behavioral Therapy. CBT can help patients to recognize triggers for substance abuse. It is useful for work with impulsive behaviors and appears to be a promising treatment for some psychotic symptoms (Jones, Cormac, Silveira da Mota Neto, & Campbell, 2004).

Behavioral Therapy. Behavioral Therapy aims to change behavior without necessarily exploring the thinking processes that underlie feelings or behavior. It is useful for working with patients with schizophrenia whose cognitive deficits may make it difficult for them to remember triggers for their problems and identify thinking processes that contribute to their problems. Behavioral Therapy includes role-playing and rehearsals.

Skills Building Therapy. The goal of Skills Building Therapy is to help patients improve their social skills. These skills are vital for improving functioning in work and social settings (Bellack, Mueser, Gingerrich, & Agresta, 1997). Treatment is directed at improving interactions in social settings.

Cognitive Enhancement Therapy. There are two basic approaches to improving memory, language, and attention. The first is by restitution, or repair of impairments, through practicing skills and relearning them. The second approach focuses on compensating for deficits by finding alternative strategies.

Co-Occurring Substance Abuse Therapy. A widely used treatment strategy for co-occurring substance abuse and schizophrenia integrates treatment by taking into account the patients' therapeutic needs as well as deficits. Ziedonis & D'Avanzo (1998) identify five levels of psychosocial interventions that are at the core of treatment: (1) establishing a therapeutic alliance, (2) addressing low motivation, (3) addressing cognitive limitations, (4) addressing low self-efficacy, and (5) addressing maladaptive interpersonal skills.

Treatment recognizes that people do not change behaviors rapidly; instead people move from one stage of change to the next and often fall backwards so that they must begin the process again. The transtheoretical model describes change as gradually moving from one stage to the next (Prochaska & DiClemente, 1983) and delineates five stages of change: (1) precontemplation (denial and minimization of the problem), (2) contemplation (ambivalence about changing), (3) preparation (desire to change within the next month), (4) action (significant steps toward changes), and (5) maintenance (commitment to long-term abstinence).

According to Ziedonis (2004), six to nine months may be required for patients with schizophrenia and substance abuse to move from one motivational level to another, and about two years may be required for patients to move from precontemplation to maintenance.

Motivational Enhancement. This intervention has been demonstrated to be useful in helping patients build the motivation necessary to change behaviors (Miller, 1996). Motivational interviewing (MI) as described by Miller (1996; Miller & Rollnick 2002) recommends the following strategies for increasing motivation: (1) expressing empathy, (2) identifying the discrepancy between a goal and current behavior, (3) avoiding arguments with patient, (4) rolling with resistance rather than confronting it, and (5) supporting efficacy of the patient.

Case Management and Assertive Case Management

Case management is a general method according to which clinicians work in teams and carry individual caseloads with a focus on coordinating all aspects of the patients' care, from medication treatment for schizophrenia and counseling for substance abuse, to helping patients access community resources and other support systems related to housing, psychosocial issues, entitlements, rehabilitation, work, and community services needs. Assertive case management (Essock et al., 2006) is a more intensive model that was developed especially for chronically mentally ill patients with poor psychosocial functioning, poor adherence to usual community treatment, frequent relapses, and hospitalizations. The model has been carefully developed and extensively tested, with strong evidence of efficacy. In this model, teams of clinicians follow a caseload and share responsibility for each patient. The overall clinician-to-patient ratio is relatively high (one clinician per ten or fifteen patients), so that each patient has access to more time with the clinician. The model emphasizes delivery of services in the community and by the team rather than through referral to other agencies. Both assertive case management and standard case management were found to be effective in a recent controlled trial among patients with chronic mental illness and substance dependence, while assertive case management was more effective among patients with more prior hospitalizations and institutionalizations (Essock et al., 2006). This study provides good support for the case management approach and suggests that Assertive Case Management may be particularly effective among the most severely ill patients.

Treatment of Schizophrenia in Substance-Abusing Patients: What Is the Evidence?

Unlike for several other disorders, such as depression and anxiety disorders, for schizophrenia, once a diagnosis of schizophrenia is established, medication treatment is almost always started immediately. It is widely accepted that people with schizophrenia require antipsychotic medication. In the Schizophrenia Patient Outcomes Research Team (PORT) report on evidence-based practice, treatment with antipsychotic medication is clearly recommended based on a review of scientific studies (Lehman & Steinwachs, 1998). Davis et al. found that "all patients not treated with any form of antipsychotic drug will relapse within 3 years" (1993, p. 24). Much of the current research regarding antipsychotic medications focuses on the benefits of the atypical antipsychotic medications over the older, typical antipsychotic medications and the efficacy of the various new medications. In a meta-analysis of fifty-two research studies, Geddes, Freemantle, Harrison, & Bebbington (2000) concluded that there is no clear evidence favoring atypical antipsychotic medication. A recently published multisite clinical trial also supports this conclusion that response to atypical antipsychotics is, overall, not better than response to typical antipsychotics (Lieberman, Stroup, McEnvoy, Swattz, Rosenheck, Perkins et al., 2005). However, patients who fail to improve on a typical antipsychotic may improve when switched to an atypical.

While antipsychotic medications may be less effective for patients who are abusing substances, these medications remain essential to treatment of psychotic symptoms. The benefits of medication, even for those abusing substances, was demonstrated in a four-year study by Hunt et al. (2002), who found that (1) poor medication treatment adherence was the strongest predictor of hospital readmission and (2) medication treatment-adherent patients who abused substances required fewer hospital readmissions than those who were not adherent.

To date, studies of psychosocial treatments for people with schizophrenia and people with schizophrenia and co-occurring substance use disorders, have provided some encouraging results, but there is also a need for more research. Family therapy and assertive community treatment have been shown to have good results although there have been some resports of negative results more recently. Supported employment programs and CBT have positive results; and social skills training and cognitive remediation models show promising results (Bustillo, Lauriello, Horan, & Keith, 2001). The general principle of integrated treatment—that is, treatment of both schizophrenia and substance use disorders by one team or in one program—makes sense. Patients with schizophrenia are generally best treated by mental health clinicians or programs that specialize in severe mental illness. Referral of such patients to outside clinicians or programs for treatment of substance use is likely to result in a lower rate of adherence to, and engagement in, substance abuse treatment than if such treatment is available at the agency at which patients receive treatment for schizophrenia. Thus, integrated treatment is recommended. One way to achieve this would be to train mental health clinicians to use methods for treating substance abuse; another way would be for substance abuse treatment specialists to spend time at mental health clinics and join the teams that are treating patients with schizophrenia. Reviews of the evidence supporting integrated treatment have generally been supportive of its efficacy, although the results of the studies are somewhat mixed, and more research is needed (RachBeisel et al., 1999; Jeffery, Ley, McLaren, & Siegfried, 2000). In summary, treatment with antipsychotic medication has been shown to be effective; psychosocial treatments and integrated treatment are preferable, although more research is needed in this area.

How to Manage Patients Who Cannot Achieve Abstinence

Despite every effort to stop substance use, abstinence may be difficult for many patients to achieve. Abstinence may be more difficult to reach if psychotic symptoms, which impair impulse control and judgment, persist. People with schizophrenia who continue to use substances present significant problems. Their recovery from schizophrenia may be limited, which will compromise their ability to function in society. They may become alienated from family and friends who can provide support for recovery. Furthermore, they are at increased risk for dangerous behaviors (Cuffel, Shumway, Choulijian, & MacDonald, 1994). If patients repeatedly refuse or are unable to stop abusing substances, it is highly likely that they will relapse and require rehospitalization. If this occurs, residential treatment may be useful. In some states, it may be necessary to go to court to have residential or inpatient treatment mandated. Once patients return to the community, intensive case management and ACT can provide additional services that are helpful for people with schizophrenia and co-occurring substance abuse. ACT teams are available in some areas and offer comprehensive treatment that mobilizes community resources. Similarly, case managers reach out to patients, help mobilize resources, and encourage adherence to treatment recommendations.

Treatment Planning for the Case Example

In the case discussed at the beginning of this chapter (see "Case Presentation"), BC's treatment was provided within an integrated treatment program for patients with a first episode of schizophrenia. BC's psychotic symptoms partially responded to treatment after trials of several antipsychotic medications, a medication for keeping the mood more even (usually called a "mood stabilizer"), and an antidepressant. Following hospitalization, BC was transferred to a day program, where he began each day in a special group for patients who have their first episode of psychosis and histories of substance abuse. Treatment focused on building insight and motivation for adherence to medication and abstinence from substances (Miller et al., 2005). Psychoeducation regarding schizophrenia, medications, and substances was provided daily; urine testing to monitor drug use was conducted weekly. Coping skills, skills building, and anxiety management were regular topics of treatment. CBT was utilized to help BC and other group members to recognize triggers for substance use and to decrease impulsive and antisocial behaviors. BC's family attended family groups and maintained regular telephone contact. He was seen weekly by the psychiatrist for medication management and was seen individually for psychotherapy to target problems timely (Miller & Mason, 1999). Case management services were utilized to help BC to obtain Medicaid and Supplemental Security Income (SSI) benefits.

After one year of treatment, BC denied paranoid feelings except when attempting to travel independently. BC used some alcohol early in treatment but remained abstinent from marijuana following hospitalization through year one. His insight and motivation for abstinence and treatment adherence were good. Although he continued to have difficulty regulating his mood and anxiety, he no longer experienced suicidal ideation, and he did not make suicidal gestures or attempts. He developed the capacity to feel empathy for peers and did not engage in antisocial behaviors. He passed his general educational development (GED) exam, set appropriate new goals, and utilized desensitization treatment to help him travel independently. He gained a significant amount of weight (side effect of medication), which he was not able to lose, but he set a goal to reduce his weight next year.

SUMMARY

More than half of patients with schizophrenia have a lifetime diagnosis of a substance use disorder other than nicotine dependence. Substance use disorders worsen the prognosis of the illness. For this reason, early identification and treatment of substance use disorders are essential for people with schizophrenia. The diagnostic interview should include a thorough assessment of drug use, screening for co-occurring mood or anxiety disorders, and assessment of the timing of the onset and duration of substance use, psychotic symptoms, and periods of sobriety. Changes in symptoms related to substance use and sobriety may be critical in distinguishing between substance-induced psychosis and schizophrenia. The optimal treatment strategy is multidimensional and integrates the treatment of mental, medical, and substance use disorders. Poor compliance and limited insight should be addressed from the beginning of treatment. Antipsychotic medications are indicated in patients with schizophrenia and substance use disorders. In our experience, atypical antipsychotics are used as first-line antipsychotic treatment because they are often better tolerated (in terms of side effects) and may help decrease substance use. When available, pharmacological treatments for substance use disorder should be considered. Psychosocial interventions aim to establish a therapeutic alliance and improve motivation, self-efficacy, and social skills. A wide variety of interventions are available, but case management should be considered especially in patients who are doing poorly.

Integrating treatment for people with schizophrenia and co-occurring substance use disorders requires a specialized approach to treatment that may be set in either a mental health clinic or addiction treatment setting. However, it is essential that the program recognizes the unique needs of people with schizophrenia and is designed to provide the specialized services required.

Most patients with schizophrenia have nicotine dependence. Clinicians may view its treatment as a low priority in comparison to treatment of schizophrenia or treatment of other drug and alcohol use. However, cigarette smoking causes serious long-term health damage. Thus, after a patient has been stabilized, clinicians should encourage patients to quit smoking and offer treatment for nicotine dependence.

Suggestions for Further Reading

For readers who wish to study further in this area, we recommend:

☐ ***DSM-IV* Criteria for Schizophrenia and Case Examples**

- American Psychiatric Association. (1994). Diagnostic and statistical manual of mental disorders (4th ed.). Washington, DC: Author.

- Spitzer, R. L., Gibbon, M., Skodol, A. E., Williams, J. B. W., & First, M. B. (1994). *DSM-IV casebook: A learning companion to the diagnostic and statistical manual of mental disorders* (4th ed.). Washington DC: American Psychiatric Association.

☐ **Understanding Substances**

- Gahlinger, P. M. (2001). *Illegal drugs: A complete guide to their history, chemistry, use and abuse.* Las Vegas, NV: Sagebrush Press.

☐ **Treatment of Schizophrenia and Co-Occurring Substance Use Disorders**

- Barnes, K., Mueser, K., Noordsy, D., & Drake, R. (2003). *Integrated treatment of dual disorders: A guide to effective practice.* New York: Guilford Press.
- Bellack, A. S., & DiClemente, C. C. (1999). Treating substance abuse among patients with schizophrenia. *Psychiatric Services, 50,* 75-80.
- Drake, R. E., Essock, S. M., Shaner A., Carey, K. B., Minkoff, K., Kola, L., et al. (2001). Implementing dual diagnosis services for clients with severe mental illness. *Psychiatric Services, 52,* 469-476.
- Hinton, M., Elkins, K., Edwards, J., & Donovan, K. (2002). *Cannabis and psychosis: An early psychosis treatment manual.* Parkville VIC Australia: EPPIC.
- Miller, R., McCormack, J., Sevy, S., & Robinson, D. (2005). An integrated treatment program for first-episode schizophrenia. *Bulletin of the Menninger Clinic, 63,* 499-519.
- Miller, W., & Rollnick, S. (2002). *Motivational interviewing: Preparing people for change* (2nd ed.). New York: Guilford.
- Mueser, K. T., Noordsy, D. L., Drake, R. E., & Fox, L. (2003). *Integrated treatment for dual disorders: A guide to effective practice.* New York: Guilford Press.
- Velasquez, M. M., Maurer, G. G., Crouch, C., & DiClemente, C. C. (2001). *Group treatment for substance abuse.* New York: Guildford Press.
- Ziedonis, D. M., & D'Avanzo, K. (1998). Schizophrenia and substance abuse. In H. R. Kranzler & B. J. Rounsaville (Eds.), *Dual diagnosis and treatment* (pp. 427-465). New York: Marcel Dekker.

☐ **General Treatment of Schizophrenia**

- Bellack, A. S., Mueser, K., Gingerich, S., & Agresta, J. (1997). *Social skills training for schizophrenia.* New York: Guilford Press.
- Hogarty, G. E. (2002). *Personal therapy for schizophrenia & related disorders.* New York: Guilford Press.

☐ **Popular Press Books and Web sites**

- Miller, R., & Mason, S. E. (2002). *Diagnosis: Schizophrenia.* New York: Columbia University Press.
- National Institute of Mental Health: http://www.nimh.nih.gov.
- Schiller, L., & Bennett, A. (1994). *The quiet room: A journey out of the torment of madness.* New York: Warner Book.
- Substance Abuse and Mental Health Services Administration, Center for Substance Abuse Treatment: http://csat.samhsa.gov.
- Torrey, F. E. (2001). *Surviving schizophrenia: A manual for families, consumers, and providers* (4th ed.). New York: Harper Collins.

References

Allebeck, P., Varla, A., Kristjansson, E., & Wistedt, B. (1987). Risk factors for suicide among patients with schizophrenia. *Acta Psychiatrica Scandanavica, 76,* 414-419.

American Psychiatric Association. (1994). *Diagnostic and statistical manual of mental disorders,* (4th ed.). Washington, DC: Author.

Andréasson, S., Allebeck, P., Engström, A., & Rydberg, U. (1987). Cannabis and schizophrenia. A longitudinal study of Swedish conscripts. *Lancet, 26,* 1483-1486.

Andréasson, S., Allebeck, P., & Rydberg, U. (1989). Schizophrenia in users and nonusers of cannabis. *Acta Psychiatrica Scandanavica, 79,* 505-510.

Appleby, L., Dyson, V., Altman, E., & Luchins, D. J. (1997). Assessing substance use in multi-problem patients: Reliability and validity of the addiction severity index in a mental hospital population. *Journal of Nervous and Mental Disease, 185,* 159-165.

Bachmann, S., Resch, F., & Mundt, C. (2003). Psychological treatments for psychosis: History and overview. *Journal of the American Academy of Psychoanalysis and Dynamic Psychiatry, 31,* 155-176.

Bellack, A. S., Mueser, K., Gingerich, S., & Agresta, J. (1997). *Social skills training for schizophrenia.* New York: Guilford Press.

Bowers, M. B., Jr. (1987). The role of drugs in the production of schizophreniform psychoses and related disorders. In H.Y. Meltzer (Ed.), *Psychopharmacology. The third generation of progress* (pp. 819-823). New York: Raven Press.

Bowers, M. B., Jr., & Swigar, M. E. (1983). Vulnerability to psychosis associated with hallucinogen use. *Psychiatry Research, 9,* 91-97.

Bowers, M. B., Mazure, C. M., Nelson, J. C., & Jatlow, P. I. (1990). Psychotogenic drug use and neuroleptic response. *Schizophrenia Bulletin, 16,* 81-85.

Breier, A., Schreiber, J. L., Dyer, J., & Pickar, D. (1991). National Institute of Mental Health longitudinal study of chronic schizophrenia. *Archives of General Psychiatry, 48,* 239-246.

Bustillo, J. R., Lauriello, J., Horan, W. P., & Keith, S. J. (2001). The psychosocial treatment of schizophrenia: An update. *American Journal of Psychiatry, 158,* 163-175.

Casey, D. E., & Hansen, T. E. (2003). Excessive mortality and morbidity associated with schizophrenia. In J. M. Meyer & H. A. Nasrallah (Eds.), *Medical illness and schizophrenia* (pp. 13-34). Arlington, VA: American Psychiatric Publishing.

Cuffel, B. J., Shumway, M., Chouljian, T. L., & MacDonald, T. (1994). A longitudinal study of substance use and community violence in schizophrenia. *Journal of Nervous Mental Disease, 182,* 704-708.

Davis, J. M., Kane, J. M., Marder, S. R., Brauzer, B., Gierl, B. Schooler, N., et al. (1993). Dose response of prophylactic antipsychotics. *Journal of Clinical Psychiatry, 54*(Suppl.), 24-30.

Drake, R. E., & Wallach, M. A. (1989). Substance abuse among chronically mentally ill. *Hospital and Community Psychiatry, 40,* 1041-1046.

Drake, R. E., Xie, H., McHugo, G. J., & Green, A. I. (2000). The effects of clozapine on alcohol and drug use disorders among patients with schizophrenia. *Schizophrenia Bulletin, 26,* 441-449.

Essock, S. M., Mueser, K, T., Drake, R. E., Covell, N. H., McHugo, G.J., Frisman, L. K., et al. (2006). Comparison of ACT and standard case management for delivering integrated treatment for co-occurring disorders. *Psychiatric Services, 57*(2), 185-196.

Ewing, J. A. (1984). Detecting alcoholism: The CAGE questionnaire. *Journal of the American Medical Association, 252,* 1905-1907.

First, M. B., Spitzer, R. L., Gibbon, M., & Williams, J. B. W. (2002, November). Structured Clinical Interview for DSM-IV-TR Axis I Disorders, Patient Edition (SCID-I/P). New York: Biometrics Research Department, New York State Psychiatric Institute.

Gahlinger, P. M. (2001). *Illegal drugs: A complete guide to their history, chemistry, use and abuse.* Las Vegas, NV: Sagebrush Press.

Geddes, J., Freemantle, N., Harrison, P., & Bebbington, P. (2000). Atypical antipsychotics in the treatment of schizophrenia: Systematic overview and meta-regression analysis. *British Medical Journal, 321,* 1371-1376.

George, T. P., Vessicchio, J. C., Termine, A., Sahady, D. M., Head, C. A., Pepper, et al. (2002). Effects of smoking abstinence on visuospatial working memory function in schizophrenia. *Neuropsychopharmacology, 26,* 75-85.

George, T. P., Vessicchio, J. C., & Termine, A. (2003). Nicotine and tobacco use in schizophrenia. In J. M. Meyer & H. A. Nasrallah (Eds.), *Medical illness and schizophrenia* (pp. 85-98). Washington, DC: American Psychiatric Publishing.

Gerding, L. B., Labbate, L. A., Measom, M. O., Santos, A. B., & Arana, G. W. (1999). Alcohol dependence and hospitalization in schizophrenia. *Schizophrenia Research, 38,* 71-75.

Gonzales, D., Rennard, S. I., Nides, M., Oncken, C., Azoulay, S., Billing, C. B., et al. (2006). Varenicline, an alpha4beta2 nicotinic acetylcholine receptor partial agonist, vs sustained-release bupropion and placebo for smoking cessation: A randomized controlled trial. *Journal of the American Medical Association, 296,* 47-55.

Gupta, S., Hendricks, S., Kenkel, A. M., Bhatia, S. C., & Haffke, E. A. (1996). Relapse in schizophrenia: Is there a relationship to substance abuse? *Schizophrenia Research, 20,* 153-156.

Häfner, H., Maurer, K., Löffler, W., & Reicher-Rossler, A. (1993). The influence of age and sex on the onset and early course of schizophrenia. *British Journal of Psychiatry, 162,* 80-86.

Hambrecht, M., & Häfner, H. (1996). Substance abuse and the onset of schizophrenia. *Biological Psychiatry, 40,* 115-1163.

Hasin, D. S., Samet, S., Nunes, E., Meydan, J., Matseoane, K., & Waxman, R. (2006). Diagnosis of comorbid disorders in substance users: Psychiatric Research Interview for Substance and Mental Disorders (PRISM-IV). *American Journal of Psychiatry, 163,* 689-696.

Heilä, H., Isometsä, E. T., Henriksson, M. M., Heikkinen, M. E., Marttunen, M. J., & Lonnqvist, J. K. (1997). Suicide and schizophrenia: A nationwide psychological autopsy study on age- and sex-specific clinical characteristics of 92 suicide victims with schizophrenia. *American Journal of Psychiatry, 154,* 1235-1242.

Hunt, G. E., Bergen, J., & Bashir, M. (2002). Medication compliance and comorbid substance abuse in schizophrenia: Impact on community survival 4 years after a relapse. *Schizophrenia Research, 54,* 253-264.

Jaffe, J. H., Ling, W., & Rawson, R. A. (2005). Amphetamine (or amphetamine-like)-related disorders. In B. J. Sadock & V. A. Sadock (Eds.), *Kaplan & Sadock's comprehensive textbook of psychiatry* (8th ed., pp. 1188-1200). Philadelphia: Lippincott Williams & Wilkins.

Javitt, D., & Zukin, S. R. (2005). Phencycline (or phencyclidine-like)-related disorders. In B. J. Sadock & V. A. Sadock (Eds.), *Kaplan & Sadock's comprehensive textbook of psychiatry* (8th ed., pp. 1290-1300). Philadelphia: Lippincott Williams & Wilkins.

Jeffery, D. P., Ley, A., McLaren, S., & Siegfried, N. (2000). Psychosocial treatment programmes for people with both severe mental illness and substance misuse. *Cochrane Database of Systematic Reviews, 2,* CD001088.

Jones, C., Cormac, I., Silveira da Mota Neto, J. I., & Campbell, C. (2004). Cognitive behaviour therapy for schizophrenia. *Cochrane Database of Systematic Reviews, 4,* CD000524.

Kay, S. R., Fiszbein, A., & Opler, L. A. (1987). The positive and negative syndrome scale (PANSS) for schizophrenia. *Schizophrenia Bulletin, 13,* 261-276.

Kirkpatrick, B., & Tek, C. (2005). Schizophrenia: Clinical features and psychopathology concepts. In B. J. Sadock & V. A. Sadock (Eds.), *Kaplan & Sadock's comprehensive textbook of psychiatry* (8th ed., pp. 1416-1433). Philadelphia: Lippincott Williams & Wilkins.

Knapp, M., Mangalore, R., & Simon, J. (2004). The global costs of schizophrenia. *Schizophrenia Bulletin, 30,* 279-293.

Lee, C., Frangou, S., Russel, M. A., & Gray, J. A. (1997). Effect of haloperidol on nicotine-induced enhancement of vigilance in human subjects. *Journal of Psychopharmacology, 11,* 253-257.

Lehman, A. F., & Steinwachs, D. M. (1998). Translating research into practice: The Schizophrenia Patient Outcomes Research Team (PORT) treatment recommendations. *Schizophrenia Bulletin, 24,* 1-10.

Lichtermann, D., Ekelund, J., Pukkala, E., Transkanen, A., & Lonnqvist, J. (2001). Incidence of cancer among persons with schizophrenia and their relatives. *Archives of General Psychiatry, 58*, 573-578.

Lieberman, J. A., Stroup, T. S., McEnvoy, J. P., Swattz, M. S., Rosenheck, R. A., Perkins, D. O., et al. (2005). Effectiveness of antipsychotic drugs in patients with chronic schizophrenia. *New England Journal of Medicine, 353*, 1209-1223.

Linszen, D. H., Dingemans, P. M., & Lenior, M. E. (1994). Cannabis abuse and the course of recent-onset schizophrenic disorders. *Archives of General Psychiatry, 51*, 273-279.

Littrell, K. H., Petty, R. G., Hilligoss, N. M., Peabody, C. D., & Johnson, C. G. (2001). Olanzapine treatment for patients with schizophrenia and substance abuse. *Journal of Substance Abuse Treatment, 21*, 217-221.

Marder, S. R., & van Kammen, D. P. (2005). Dopamine receptor antagonists (typical antipsychotics). In B. J. Sadock & V. A. Sadock (Eds.), *Kaplan & Sadock's comprehensive textbook of psychiatry* (8th ed., pp. 2817-2838). Philadelphia: Lippincott Williams & Wilkins.

Mayfield, D., McLeod, G., & Hall, P. (1974). The CAGE questionnaire: Validation of a new alcoholism screening instrument. *American Journal of Psychiatry, 131*, 1121-1123.

McEvoy, J. P., Freudenreich, O., Levin, E. D., & Rose, J. E. (1995). Haloperidol increases smoking in patients with schizophrenia. *Psychopharmacology, 119*, 124-126.

McEvoy, J. P., Freudenreich, O., & Wilson, W. H. (1999). Smoking and therapeutic response to clozapine in patients with schizophrenia. *Biological Psychiatry, 46*, 125-129.

McHugo, G. J., Drake, R. E., Teague, G. B., & Xie, H. (1999). Fidelity to assertive community treatment and client outcomes in the New Hampshire dual disorders study. *Psychiatric Services, 50*, 818-824.

Miller, R., & Mason, S. E. (1999). Phase-specific psychosocial interventions for first episode schizophrenia. *Bulletin of the Menninger Clinic, 63*, 499-519.

Miller, R., McCormack, J., Sevy, S., & Robinson, D. (2005). The Insight-Adherence-Abstinence triad: An integrated treatment program for cannabis-using first-episode schizophrenia patients. *Bulletin of the Menninger Clinic, 69*, 220-236.

Miller, W. R. (1996). Motivational interviewing: Research, practice, and puzzles. *Addictive Behaviors, 21*, 835-842.

Miller, W. R., & Rollnick, S. (2002). *Motivational interviewing: Preparing people for change* (2nd ed.). New York: Guilford Press.

Mueser, K. T., Arnold, P. R., Levinson, D. F., Singh, H., Bellack, A. S., Kee, K., et al. (1990). Prevalence of substance abuse in schizophrenia: Demographic and clinical correlates. *Schizophrenia Bulletin, 16*, 31-56.

Mueser, K. T., Bellack, A. S., & Blanchard, J. J. (1992). Comorbidity of schizophrenia and substance abuse: Implications for treatment. *Journal of Clinical and Consultation Psychology, 60*, 845-856.

Mueser, K. T., Drake, R. E., & Bond, G. R. (1997). Recent advances in psychiatric rehabilitations for patients with severe mental illness. *Harvard Review of Psychiatry, 5*, 123-137.

Mueser, K. T., Noordsy, D. L., Drake, R. E., & Fox, L. (2003). *Integrated treatment for dual disorders: A guide to effective practice.* New York: Guilford Press.

Negrete, J. C., Knapp, W. P., Douglas, D. E., & Smith, W. B. (1986). Cannabis affects the severity of schizophrenic symptoms: Results of a clinical survey. *Psychological Medicine, 16*, 515-520.

Owen, R. R., Fischer, E. P., Booth, B. M., & Cuffel, B. J. (1996). Medication noncompliance and substance abuse among patients with schizophrenia. *Psychiatric Services, 47*, 853-858.

Overall, J. E., & Gorham, D. R. (1962). The Brief Psychiatric Rating Scale. *Psychological Reports, 10*, 799-812.

Petrakis, I. L., O'Malley, S., Rounsaville, B., Poling, J., McHugh-Strong, C., Krystal, J. H., et al. (2004). Naltrexone augmentation of neuroleptic treatment in alcohol abusing patients with schizophrenia. *Psychopharmacology, 172*, 291-297.

Prochaska, J. O., & DiClemente, C. C. (1983). Stages and processes of self-change of smoking: Toward an integrative model of change. *Journal of Consulting and Clinical Psychology, 51*, 390-395.

RachBeisel, J., Scott, J., & Dixon, L. (1999). Co-occurring severe mental illness and substance use disorders: A review of recent research. *Psychiatric Services, 50,* 1427-1434.

Räsänen, P., Tiihonen, J., Isohanni, M., Rantakallio, P., Lehtonen, J., & Moring, J. (1998). Schizophrenia, alcohol abuse, and violent behavior: A 26-year follow up study of an unselected birth cohort. *Schizophrenia Bulletin, 24,* 437-441.

Regier, D. A., Farmer, M. E., Rae, D. S., Locke, B. Z., Keith, S. J., Judd, L. L., et al. (1990). Comorbidity of mental disorders with alcohol and other drug abuse. Results from the Epidemiologic Catchment Area (ECA) study. *Journal of the American Medical Association, 264,* 2511-2518.

Rosenberg, S. D., Drake, R .E., Wolford, G. L., Mueser, K. T., Oxman, T. E., Vidaver, R. M., et al. (1998). Dartmouth Assessment of Lifestyle Instrument (DALI): A substance use disorder screen for people with severe mental illness. *American Journal of Psychiatry, 155,* 232-238.

Satel, S. L., & Edell, W. S. (1991). Cocaine-induced paranoia and psychosis proneness. *American Journal of Psychiatry, 148,* 1708-1711.

Selzer, M. (1971). The Michigan Alcoholism Screening Test: The quest for a new diagnostic instrument. *American Journal of Psychiatry, 127,* 1653-1658.

Sevy, S., Kay, S. R., Opler, L., & van Praag, H. M. (1990). Significance of cocaine history in schizophrenia. *Journal of Nervous and Mental Disease, 178,* 642-648.

Siris, S. G. (2001). Suicide and schizophrenia. *Journal of Psychopharmacology, 15,* 127-135.

Siris, S. G., Kane, J. M., Frechen, K., Sellew, A. P., Mandeli, J., & Fasano-Dube, B. (1988). Histories of substance abuse in patients with postpsychotic depressions. *Comprehensive Psychiatry, 29,* 550-557.

Smelson, D. A., Losonczy, M. F., Davis, C. W., Kaune, M., Williams, J., & Ziedonis, D. (2002). Risperidone decreases craving and relapses in individuals with schizophrenia and cocaine dependence. *Canadian Journal of Psychiatry, 4,* 671-675.

Spitzer, R. L., Gibbon, M., Skodol, A. E., Williams, J. B. W., & First, M. B. (1994). *DSM-IV casebook: A learning companion to the diagnostic and statistical manual of mental Disorders* (4th ed.). Washington DC: American Psychiatric Association.

Swofford, C. D., Kasckow, J. W., Scheller-Gilkey, G., & Inderbitzin, L. B. (1996). Substance use: A powerful predictor of relapse in schizophrenia. *Schizophrenia Research, 20,* 145-151.

Thornicroft, G. (1990). Cannabis and psychosis. Is there epidemiological evidence for an association? *British Journal of Psychiatry, 157,* 25-33.

Torrey, E. F., Miller, J., Rawlings, R., & Yolken, R. H. (1997). Seasonality of births in schizophrenia and bipolar disorder: A review of the literature. *Schizophrenia Research, 28,* 1-38.

van Kammen, D. P., & Marder, S. R. (2005). Serotonin-dopamine antagonists (atypical or second-generation antipsychotics). In B. J. Sadock & V. A. Sadock (Eds.), *Kaplan & Sadock's comprehensive textbook of psychiatry* (8th ed., pp. 1416-1433). Philadelphia: Lippincott Williams & Wilkins.

Ziedonis, D. M., & D'Avanzo, K. (1998). Schizophrenia and substance abuse. In H. R. Kranzler & J. B. Rounsaville (Eds.), *Dual diagnosis and treatment* (pp. 427-465). New York: Marcel Dekker.

Ziedonis, D. M. (2004). Integrated treatment of co-occurring mental illness and addiction: Clinical intervention, program, and system perspectives. *CNS Spectrums, 9,* 892-904, 925.

Part 4

Personality Disorders

The "addictive personality," a notion in popular discourse, is a vague concept with a derogatory, bleak overtone (a person with an addiction has an addictive personality, and personality is impossible to change). However, substantial scientific evidence suggests that specific personality characteristics are associated with addictions. Large-scale longitudinal studies have consistently shown that a constellation of character traits that are measured during early childhood (impulsivity, inattention, irritability, and aggressiveness) increases the risk for the development of substance use disorders during adolescence and adulthood. Conduct disorder, which manifests as an extreme expression of these character traits, often develops into antisocial personality disorder in adulthood. Conduct disorder and antisocial personality disorder, which are common in adolescents and adults with substance use disorders, are among the strongest risk factors for the development of substance use disorders. However, all patients with substance use disorders do not have antisocial traits. Research on the specific subgroup of patients who possess these traits has led to a better understanding of their problems and to the development of effective treatments.

Borderline personality disorder consists of a constellation of symptoms that includes severe moodiness, particularly intense mood swings between anger and depression, unstable interpersonal relationships, and impulsive and self-destructive behavior. The personality traits of borderline personality disorder overlap with traits of conduct disorder and antisocial personality disorder; substance use disorders are common in these patients. Patients with borderline personality disorder are particularly difficult to treat: they tend to be angry and aggressive, and treatment providers may label them as "bad" patients and terminate treatment. However, specific psychotherapeutic techniques have been developed for treatment of patients with borderline personality disorder, and medications may be helpful, particularly for treatment of mood problems. Clinicians may need to refer these patients to specialists for psychological and pharmacological treatment. The principles of psychological treatments for borderline personality disorder that are covered in the chapters in Part 4 may help clinicians to develop a strong treatment alliance and effective treatment plans. Treatment of co-occurring substance use disorders may improve patients' moodiness and interpersonal relationships.

Chapter 8

Antisocial Personality Disorder in Patients With Substance Use Disorders

by Robert K. Brooner, Ph.D., Elizabeth R. Disney, Ph.D., Karin J. Neufeld, M.D., M.P.H., Van L. King, M.D., Michael Kidorf, Ph.D., and Kenneth B. Stoller, M.D.

INTRODUCTION

Antisocial personality disorder (ASPD) is one of the most common co-occurring psychiatric diagnoses among individuals with a substance use disorder. At least a quarter of patients who seek treatment for a substance use disorder have ASPD; the disorder is more commonly diagnosed in men than in women (Brooner, King, Kidorf, Schmidt, & Bigelow, 1997; Moran, 1999). About 80 percent of patients with a diagnosis of ASPD have had at least one lifetime substance use disorder (Kessler et al., 1994). Clinicians who work with substance abusers often associate a diagnosis of ASPD with poor treatment prognosis (and for good reason). As early as during the intake process of a substance abuse treatment program, patients with ASPD quickly distinguish themselves from patients without ASPD: patients with ASPD are usually dependent on multiple substances and have a history of earlier onset of substance use, heavier substance use, and more family, social, and legal problems than patients without ASPD (Alterman & Cacciola, 1991; Compton, Conway, Stinson, Colliver, & Grant, 2005).

Despite the severity and chronicity of problems in this population of substance users, there is no compelling reason to despair when they arrive for treatment. Although little is known about treatment of ASPD, more is known about treatment of substance use problems in patients with ASPD. Indeed, these patients can respond well to substance abuse treatment. For example, multiple studies of methadone maintenance treatment for opioid-dependent patients have shown that patients with ASPD responded to treatment as well as patients without ASPD, based on a number of important treatment outcome measures, including retention in treatment (King, Kidorf, Stoller, Carter, & Brooner, 2001). There is also growing evidence that patients with ASPD respond favorably to specialized behavioral and educational interventions that are easily integrated into many substance abuse treatment programs (Brooner, Kidorf, King, & Stoller, 1998; Havens & Strathdee, 2005).

This chapter aims to dispel the pessimism that often accompanies the treatment of patients with ASPD. With the aid of a case presentation, we discuss how to accurately assess ASPD in patients with substance use disorders. Information obtained during an assessment and knowledge of the course of the disorder can be used to develop a treatment approach that is tailored to the specific issues faced by this population. Further, we discuss use of contingency management and other clinical interventions to reinforce engagement in treatment and reductions in drug use. Since day-to-day interactions with patients with ASPD present a unique clinical challenge, we offer recommendations for developing and enhancing the therapeutic relationship between clinician and patient in order to facilitate behavior change in the patient.

CASE PRESENTATION

The following case presentation may be familiar to clinicians who have worked with patients who have ASPD and substance use disorders. We will refer back to this case example during discussion of diagnosis and treatment of patients with ASPD.

Chief Complaint

TP is a 47-year-old divorced Caucasian male who requested admission to a substance disorder treatment program. His entrance complaint was "I don't want to go back to jail; somebody has to help me soon or they will be sorry."

Patient History

Alcohol and Drug History. TP began drinking alcohol at age 11 and began smoking cannabis at age 14. At age 14, he began drinking cough syrup with codeine on a daily basis, and he remembers experiencing withdrawal symptoms, including diarrhea and joint aches at age 15, when he tried to stop. TP started using heroin by intravenous injection at age 16 and progressed to daily use within weeks of first use. He continued to use heroin throughout his life until this admission. He reported that he frequently shared used syringes and denied any sustained periods of abstinence (except during methadone maintenance treatment and during periods of incarceration). He continues to use intravenous cocaine monthly. TP reported taking illegally obtained benzodiazepines each day in the past year and has noticed shakiness, confusion, and extreme anxiety when he tries to stop. He received treatment at a methadone maintenance clinic on two separate occasions: at age 27, he attended a treatment program for six months before dropping out of treatment as a result of incarceration; at age 44, he attended a treatment program for six months and was administratively discharged for chronic loitering on hospital property and suspicion of drug dealing.

Other Psychiatric History. TP has always had trouble getting along with other people. He regards himself as "too trusting" and believes that people "take advantage" of him. People tell him that he is untrustworthy, but he believes that he is misunderstood and that people often lie about him. He complains of becoming bored easily. He denies any history of anxiety or abnormal mental experiences, such as hallucinations, and he reports that he has never been prescribed psychiatric medications. One episode of low mood, which lasted at least two weeks, occurred during incarceration in his early 30s, and he was required to see a prison psychiatrist and attend group psychotherapy with other prisoners. TP did not report any history of trying to commit suicide, but he described several overdoses with heroin and other substances that resulted in need for resuscitation. He described these overdoses as simply "going too far in trying to see how high [he] could get."

Developmental History. TP is the younger of two boys. His father ran a family-owned bar and had a middle-class income. The patient's birth and development were normal without significant childhood illnesses. He described his home atmosphere as chaotic and unsafe. His father's "problem with alcohol" resulted in violent and unpredictable behavior and frequent physical abuse of his children and wife. On several occasions, the patient's father fractured the patient's limbs and the limbs of his brother. The abuse was never reported to authorities and stopped only when the boys were old enough to protect themselves from the abuse.

Educational History. TP started school at the age of 5 but had to repeat first grade due to disruptive behavior and problems following rules. He was slow to read and had some difficulties sitting still and paying attention. TP recalled being involved in many fights with other children and proudly stated that they described him as "the meanest and scariest kid" in elementary school. He described the enjoyment that he received from hearing cats screech as he swung them around by their tails. He was suspended from school at age 10 after intentionally breaking a window and threatening a teacher. Due to repeated truancy at age 12, he transferred to several schools. With increasing demands from his drug dependency, he dropped out of school in the ninth grade (at age 15); he earned a general equivalency diploma (GED) in prison.

Family History. TP reported that his father used alcohol heavily and died in his 60s of alchohol abuse, secondary to congestive heart failure and coronary artery disease. The patient's mother experienced significant anxiety (never diagnosed) but abstained from use of all substances. His older brother developed heavy alcohol dependence at a young age and died secondary to alcoholic liver cirrhosis at age 47.

Medical History. One year before admission, TP had a severe closed head injury after a brawl in a local bar. Loss of consciousness lasted several days, and for one to two months following the brawl, he had grand mal seizures weekly. Physicians prescribed phenytoin, an antiepileptic medication. He discontinued this medication on his own because of being "scared of taking pills from a doctor." He has not had any seizures for the last six months. He denied other medical problems, except for being seropositive for the hepatitis C virus.

Employment History. TP has never held a job for longer than two months; his employment has been terminated frequently as a result of his poor attitude or drug use on the job. He has held a variety of labor positions. He lost a position as a truck driver when he stole a truck to transport drugs across state lines. He currently is unemployed and receives a limited income from a state social services program.

Criminal History. The patient's long criminal history began at age 13 with a conviction for vandalism, followed by a drug distribution conviction at age 14. He has been charged with numerous drug possession crimes from age 16 until the present. As an adult, he has been charged with drug smuggling, breaking and entering, forgery, robbery, and assault and battery. He has served a total of seven years in prison.

Relationship History. TP reports a heterosexual orientation with first intercourse at age 12 and forty to fifty sexual partners over his lifetime. He currently hires prostitutes and does not use a condom during intercourse. TP married once; the couple lived together for less than one year before his incarceration. His wife divorced him while he was in prison. He has an 18-year-old son from this marriage; his ex-wife supports herself and their son without the patient's help. TP refuses all contact with his son. He has no close friends and is currently living with his mother at her home.

Mental Status Examination

During his interview, TP appears healthy and his stated age. Despite intermittent irritability and restlessness, he seems alert and forthcoming and makes appropriate eye contact. His speech is goal-directed, and there is no evidence of a thought disorder. He reports his mood as "okay," and he displays a normal range of affective expressions during the interview. He reports feeling that he is a good person but admits that he feels physically sick from withdrawal symptoms. He denies any current thoughts, intent, or plans to harm himself or other people. There is no evidence of abnormal mental phenomena (e.g., hallucinations, delusions, obsessions, compulsions, phobias, or panic attacks). He is oriented to person, place, and time. He has limited insight into the severity of his substance use disorder and his personality vulnerabilities.

DIAGNOSTIC CRITERIA

Making Diagnosis Using *DSM-IV*

Table 8-1A lists the *Diagnostic and Statistical Manual of Mental Disorders,* 4th edition (*DSM-IV;* American Psychiatric Association, 1994) diagnostic criteria for ASPD. A diagnosis of ASPD requires that the individual has reached the age of 18 and has engaged in a pervasive pattern of behavior as a child and adult that reflects disregard for, and violation of, the rights of other people. A patient's behavior during childhood must be consistent with a diagnosis of conduct disorder (CD), which requires that the patient meet at least three of fifteen criteria before age 15. These behaviors fall into four general areas: (1) a pattern of aggression toward people or animals, (2) destruction of property, (3) repeated deceitfulness or theft, or (4) serious repeated rule violations. The behavioral disturbance must result in significant impairment in social, academic, or occupational functioning. Table 8-1B presents the diagnostic criteria for CD.

Table 8-1A
DSM-IV Criteria for Antisocial Personality Disorder

Symptoms	DSM-IV Criteria[a, b]	PRISM Questions to Aid Diagnosis[e, f]
	A. There is a pervasive pattern of disregard for and violation of the rights of others occurring since age 15 years, as indicated by three (or more) of the following:	I'd like to ask you about experiences you might have had repeatedly since age 15 *and* in the last 12 months.
Core Symptoms	(1) failure to conform to social norms with respect to lawful behaviors as indicated by repeatedly performing acts that are grounds for arrest	Since age 15, have you often done things you could have been arrested for, such as drug dealing, using illegal drugs, shoplifting, or prostitution? ... Since age 15, have you often done any other things you could have been arrested for, such as robbery, rape, mugging?
	(2) deceitfulness, as indicated by repeated lying, use of aliases, or conning others for personal profit or pleasure	Since age 15, have you ever ... ... scammed or conned anyone for money or to get something else from them? ... committed fraud? ... used a false or made-up name? ... forged a signature or document? Since age 15, have you often lied? Did you often use a false ID for underage drinking?
	(3) impulsivity or failure to plan ahead	Since age 15, have you often made spur of the moment decisions, like moving or changing jobs?
	(4) irritability and aggressiveness, as indicated by repeated physical fights or assaults	Since age 15, have you often ... ... gotten into fights or used a weapon on someone in a fight? ... hit your [wife/husband/partner], your [child/children], or any other family member? ... gotten really angry and injured someone or left a mark on them?
	(5) reckless disregard for safety of self or others	Since age 15, have you often done things like driving at very high speeds, driving or operating heavy machinery while high or drunk, high diving? Since age 15, did you ever leave your child or a child in your care alone for several hours or send a young child out to run errands for you? Since age 15, have you often had unprotected sex with people who could have been exposed to HIV or with IV drug users or their partners?

(Continued)

Symptoms	DSM-IV Criteria[a, b]	PRISM Questions to Aid Diagnosis[e, f]
	(6) consistent irresponsibility, as indicated by repeated failure to sustain consistent work behavior or honor financial obligations	Since age 15, were there ever periods of time … … when you weren't working and other people thought that you should have been? … when you were often absent from work? … when you quit jobs without notice or without plans for another one? Were others dependent on you? Since age 15, have you often failed to pay financial obligations, such as child support, alimony, mortgages, loans, or credit card bills? Were there any other bills or debts you never paid?
	(7) lack of remorse, as indicated by being indifferent to or rationalizing having hurt, mistreated, or stolen from another.	Since age 15, have you felt any regrets about any of these things, for example [assaults/fights]?
Other Criteria	B. The individual is at least age 18 years.	
	C. There is evidence of conduct disorder[c] with onset before age 15 years.	How old were you when [conduct symptoms] before age 15 began?
	D. The occurrence of antisocial behavior is not exclusively during the course of schizophrenia or a manic episode.[d]	

(a) American Psychiatric Association (1994).
(b) Reprinted with permission from the *Diagnostic and Statistical Manual of Mental Disorders*, Fourth Edition (Copyright 1994). American Psychiatric Association.
(c) Consult *DSM-IV* criteria (American Psychiatric Association, 1994) for conduct disorder or see Table 8-1B.
(d) Consult *DSM-IV* criteria (American Psychiatric Association, 1994) for schizophrenia, manic episode.
(e) Hasin et al. (2006).
(f) Reprinted with permission.

Table 8-1B
DSM-IV Criteria for Conduct Disorder

Symptoms	DSM-IV Criteria[a, b]	PRISM Questions to Aid Diagnosis[e, f]
	A. A repetitive and persistent pattern of behavior in which the basic rights of others or major age-appropriate societal norms or rules are violated, as manifested by the presence of three (or more) of the following criteria in the past 12 months, with at least one criterion present in the past 6 months:	I'd like to ask you some questions about experiences you might have had *before age 15.*
Core Symptoms		
Aggression toward people and animals	(1) often bullies, threatens, or intimidates others	Before age 15, did you *often* threaten others or try to make them afraid of you?
	(2) often initiates physical fights	Before age 15, did you often get into a lot of fights?
	(3) has used a weapon that can cause serious physical harm to others (e.g., a bat, brick, broken bottle, knife, gun)	Before age 15, did you ever use a weapon or some other object to hurt someone?
	(4) has been physically cruel to people	Before age 15, did you ever … … hurt or injure another person on purpose? … get back at someone by hurting them physically?
	(5) has been physically cruel to animals	Before age 15, did you ever hurt an animal or pet on purpose or "just for fun?"
	(6) has stolen while confronting a victim (e.g., mugging, purse snatching, extortion, armed robbery)	Before age 15, did you ever … … steal something from someone directly, for example, by mugging them, threatening them with a weapon, or snatching their purse?
	(7) has forced someone into sexual activity	Before age 15, did you ever force anyone to have sex with you?
Destruction of property	(8) has deliberately engaged in fire setting with the intention of causing serious damage	Before age 15, did you ever purposely set something on fire?
	(9) has deliberately destroyed others' property (other than by fire setting)	Before age 15, did you ever damage or destroy anyone else's property, like a car, their home, or other personal belongings?

(Continued)

Symptoms	DSM-IV Criteria[a, b]	PRISM Questions to Aid Diagnosis[e, f]
Deceitfulness or theft	(10) has broken into someone else's house, building, or car	Before age 15, did you ever break into someone's house, apartment, building, or car?
	(11) often lies to obtain goods or favors or to avoid obligations (i.e., "cons" others)	Before age 15, did you often lie .... to get things you wanted or to get special favors from people? ... to get out of doing things you were supposed to do?
	(12) has stolen items of nontrivial value without confronting a victim (e.g., shoplifting, but without breaking and entering; forgery)	Before age 15, did you ever ... ... steal money from someone? ... shoplift? ... forge a check or any other document? ... use someone else's credit card without their permission? ... use a computer or telephone to steal?
Serious violations of rules	(13) often stays out at night despite parental prohibitions, beginning before age 13 years	Before age 15, did you often stay out at night when your [parent(s)/caregiver] had told you to stay home? ... Did you start staying out late like that before you were 13 years old?
	(14) has run away from home overnight at least twice while living in parental or parental surrogate home (or once without returning for a lengthy period)	Before age 15, did you ever run away from home for at least one night?
	(15) often truant from school, beginning before age 13 years.	Before age 15, did you often skip school or cut classes?...Did you start [cutting class] before you were 13 years old?
	B. The disturbance in behavior causes clinically significant impairment in social, academic, or occupational functioning.	Did any of these experiences, such as [conduct symptoms], cause any problems with your family or friends, at school, or with the law?
	C. If the individual is age 18 years or older, criteria are not met for antisocial personality disorder.[c]	

(a) American Psychiatric Association (1994).
(b) Reprinted with permission from the *Diagnostic and Statistical Manual of Mental Disorders*, Fourth Edition (Copyright 1994). American Psychiatric Association.
(c) Consult *DSM-IV* criteria (American Psychiatric Association, 1994) for antisocial personality disorder or see Table 8-1A.
(d) Hasin et al. (2006).
(e) Reprinted with permission.

Meeting at least three of seven diagnostic criteria at age 18 or older establishes the adult behavior pattern. These criteria cover a range of aggressive and irresponsible actions, including (1) repeated law breaking; (2) lying or conning other people; (3) impulsivity and failure to plan ahead; (4) irritability, aggressiveness, and instigation of physical fights; (5) repeated disregard for safety of self or other people; (6) a history of a lack of sustained work; and (7) lack of remorse for harm caused to other people. These behaviors should not be restricted to periods of time when the individual is suffering from another major mental illness (e.g., bipolar disorder or a worsening of schizophrenia); rather, these behaviors should be observed as part of the patient's usual pattern of interaction with other people. The diagnostic criteria for ASPD emphasize observable behaviors (e.g., repeatedly getting into fights) rather than emotional states or drives of the patient.

How to Take a History

A routine assessment that covers childhood development and adult behaviors provides the basis for making the diagnosis of ASPD. One of the most important components of the interview is a detailed assessment of substance use and abuse, including acts to acquire and regularly use alcohol and drugs (e.g., lying, stealing, drug dealing). This type of assessment depends largely on the accuracy of a patient's self-report, which, especially in cases of patients with ASPD, may be suspect. School and criminal records (obtained with the patient's consent) may provide additional information for the diagnosis. Speaking to family members may be useful (clinicians should consider that ASPD and substance abuse tends to run in families). Surprisingly, patients with ASPD are often open (and sometimes even boastful) about their criminal record and past interpersonal conflicts.

Assess for Conduct Disorder. Clinicians should ask about four areas to determine if a patient meets criteria for CD:

1. Relationships with parents and other authority figures;

2. Relationships with peers;

3. Educational history; and

4. Violence and criminal history.

Relationships With Parents and Other Authority Figures. Individuals with a history of CD often report stormy and difficult relationships with parents or other authority figures (e.g., teachers, police). The interviewer might ask the patient if he/she frequently lied to his/her parents about attending school or using alcohol or drugs or if the patient attempted to "con" them to grant favors. Patients who exhibit these behaviors before the age of 15 meet criteria for CD. In the above case example (see "Case Presentation"), TP meets the first criterion for CD (threatens others): he reports that he was suspended from elementary school for threatening a teacher. A patient who ran away from home (even once for several days) before the age of 15 meets a criterion for CD. However, clinicians should not count this behavior toward a diagnosis of CD if the patient reports that he/she ran away from home because of emotional or physical abuse and ran to a responsible adult.

Relationships With Peers. CD is also associated with peer relationships characterized by conflict. Clinicians should inquire if patients have bullied other children. If the patient reports that he/she only occasionally bullied other people, the clinician should ask the patient if other children considered him/her to be a bully or seemed intimidated by the patient. Carrying a weapon meets a CD criterion only if the patient has used the weapon to intimidate other people. In the above case example (see "Case Presentation"), TP boasted that he was the "meanest and scariest" child in elementary school and reported multiple fights with other children; he meets two criteria: (1) often bullies, threatens, or intimidates others (Criterion A(1) of CD) and (2) often initiates physical fights (Criterion A(2) of CD). Information about a patient's sexual behavior also aids diagnosis: a patient who has initiated sexual behavior through physical force or intimidation (even on one occasion) meets the threshold for a CD criterion.

Educational History. Clinicians should gather information not only on a patient's relationships with teachers and students but also on the patient's progress in school. Clinicians should determine why a patient left school before attaining a diploma and if the patient skipped school. To meet Criterion A(15) of CD, patients must have been often truant from school before age 13. In the above case example (see "Case Presentation"), TP transferred to several schools due to repeated truancy at age 12 (meeting Criterion A(15) of CD).

Violence and Criminal History. CD is associated with violence and criminal activity. Clinicians should note if a patient reports a pattern of initiating verbal or physical fights, if the patient ever fought with teachers, and if the patient reports any incidents of cruelty toward people or animals. Clinicians should inquire about a patient's criminal record and about behaviors that might lead to arrest or other penalties. Individuals with CD often steal or extort lunch money, steal personal property, including jackets or sneakers from other children, write graffiti on walls, shoplift significant items, and break into houses. In the above case example (see "Case Presentation"), TP spoke about torturing cats and fighting with other children. His criminal record began at age 13 with charges for vandalism, followed by a conviction for drug distribution at age 14. TP meets Criterion A(5) of CD (has been physically cruel to animals) and Criterion A(9) of CD (has deliberately destroyed others' property). Interestingly, drug dealing does not meet any of the CD criteria. Clinicians should inquire if patients have engaged in other wrongful behaviors, including stealing (Criterion A(6) and Criterion A(12) of CD) and conning others (Criterion A(11) of CD) to obtain drugs or to sell drugs.

Assess for Antisocial Personality Disorder. Adult behaviors meet criteria for ASPD only when they occur frequently across time and situations and with a variety of people. To rule in or rule out a diagnosis of ASPD, clinicians should evaluate a patient's functioning in four domains:

1. Employment history;

2. Relationship history;

3. Violence and criminal history; and

4. Patient's appraisal of past behavior.

Employment History. Patients with ASPD often have an employment history characterized by instability. Patients with ASPD act impulsively and irresponsibly (e.g., repeatedly argue with, and lie to, supervisors; are chronically late to, or absent from, work; use drugs on the job; leave a job without having another job in place). Homelessness or prolonged reliance on parents or other family members for financial support may also indicate irresponsibility and inadequate planning. In the above case example (see "Case Presentation"), TP reported that he has had long-standing difficulties in maintaining employment and that he continues to live with his mother since he cannot support himself financially; he meets Criterion A(3) of ASPD (impulsivity or failure to plan ahead) and Criterion A(6) of ASPD (consistent irresponsibility, as indicated by repeated failure to sustain consistent work behavior or honor financial obligations).

Relationship History. Assessment of a patient's past romantic relationships, current relationship with spouse, and current relationship with children helps the interviewer to understand the quality of important relationships. A clinician should ask the patient to describe his/her relationship with his/her spouse and children and determine if the patient pays child support. Individuals with ASPD may physically abuse or threaten their spouses and may abuse or neglect their children. In the above case example (see "Case Presentation"), TP failed to support, or maintain contact with, his only child and denied any sustained meaningful relationships; this information provides further support for meeting Criterion A(3) of ASPD and Criterion A(6) of ASPD. Clinicians should seek from patients' family members and acquaintances evidence that corroborates the diagnosis.

Violence and Criminal History. Patients with ASPD often act impulsively or engage in intentionally harmful or irresponsible behavior, such as driving while intoxicated or sharing needles for intravenous drug use. Clinicians should collect from patients a thorough history of unlawful acts for which patients were prosecuted and for which patients did not experience legal consequences. In the above case example (see "Case Presentation"), TP has a long-standing pattern of fighting and engaging in criminal acts, including drug-dealing, forgery, and breaking and entering. He reported frequent needle sharing and unprotected sex with prostitutes. This patient meets Criterion A(1) of ASPD (failure to conform to social norms with respect to lawful behaviors), Criterion A(2) of ASPD (deceitfulness), Criterion A(3) of ASPD (impulsivity or failure to plan ahead), Criterion A(4) of ASPD (irritability and aggressiveness), and criterion A(6) of ASPD (consistent irresponsibility).

Patient's Appraisal of Past Behaviors. It is helpful to ask patients how they feel about some of the behaviors that they report during the interview in order to determine if patients exhibit any feelings of remorse. Clinicians should ask patients how they might change their behavior if faced with a similar situation and how patients think that their behavior has affected other people. Clinicians should also determine if a patient seems to express more concern about penalties received than about the impact of his/her behavior on others and if he/she expresses any remorse. In general, patients with ASPD often minimize the consequences of their actions than about assign blame to other people. In the above case example (see "Case Presentation"), TP entered treatment with a statement that, interestingly, focused on the legal consequences of his behavior and with a threat to cause harm to other people if treatment was not provided to him. He expressed little concern about the impact of substance use on his family or other people in his life.

Identify Other Major Psychiatric Disorders. It is not uncommon for patients with ASPD to have coexisting mood disorders (see Chapter 1 and Chapter 2 of this volume) and anxiety disorders (see Chapter 3 and Chapter 4 of this volume); disorders that involve difficulty with impulse control (e.g., pathological gambling, see Chapter 10 of this volume) and explosive aggression (see Chapter 11 of this volume) are also prevalent in these patients. Techniques for assessing and treating many of these disorders are found in other chapters of this volume, and a complete list of psychiatric conditions that often co-occur with ASPD is presented below. Patients with ASPD who suffer from an Axis I psychiatric disorder may have more motivation to engage in treatment, and there is some evidence that suggests that patients with depression may have a more favorable prognosis (Woody, McLellan, Luborsky, & O'Brien, 1985). Psychiatric comorbidity may also be associated with drug preference. A recent study conducted with methadone maintenance patients showed that patients with ASPD alone (i.e., patients who did not have any co-occurring psychiatric disorders) favored cocaine to other drugs, while patients with co-occurring Axis I disorders preferred benzodiazepines and other sedatives (King et al., 2001).

In the above case example (see "Case Presentation"), TP described symptoms of two psychiatric disorders (depression and attention deficit hyperactivity disorder (ADHD)) in addition to symptoms of ASPD. He reported that he experienced two consecutive weeks of depressed mood while incarcerated (this episode may have met criteria for major depression). Although the patient denied a history of manic episodes, he reported pervasive impulsiveness and irritability; the interviewer should inquire further about these symptoms in order to rule in or rule out bipolar disorder. The patient also reported that he experienced difficulties paying attention as a child; the interviewer should inquire further about these difficulties in order to rule in or rule out ADHD, which can persist until adulthood. Mood disorders and ADHD commonly co-occur in patients with ASPD.

Assess Current Suicidal and Homicidal Thinking. The interviewer must carefully assess patients' intentions and plans to harm themselves or other people. The combination of impulsivity from ASPD and disinhibition from drug use can be lethal, and some patients with ASPD may have brief but intense suicidal or homicidal thoughts. Many patients with ASPD have a concurrent psychiatric disorder (e.g., major depression) that may be independently associated with higher rates of suicidal behavior. A clinician should clarify how close a patient has come to suicide or homicide in the past in order to determine a patient's risk for committing suicide or homicide.

In the above case example (see "Case Presentation"), TP denied current or past suicidal and homicidal ideation or behavior. Nevertheless, the patient's treatment provider should ask him regularly about suicidal and homicidal ideation and behavior. TP has a long-standing history of aggressiveness and impulsive behavior. Several factors increase suicide and homicide risk: age, medical and psychosocial problems and stressors, and little family or social support. Further, many drugs of abuse, including benzodiazepines (which TP takes regularly), are associated with acute periods of disinhibition that may increase risk of harming oneself and other people.

NATURAL HISTORY AND ETIOLOGY

Risk Factors and Possible Causative Mechanisms

ASPD runs in families, and patients with ASPD (in comparison to patients without ASPD) tend to have more relatives with both ASPD and substance use disorders. These associations are likely a result of a combination of genetic and environmental factors, and studies of children who have been adopted at birth have shed some light on the nature-versus-nurture puzzle. One important study demonstrated that genetically vulnerable children placed in adoptive households developed ASPD at higher rates than nonvulnerable children. Rates of aggression in youth and diagnoses of ASPD and substance use disorder in adulthood increased more dramatically when vulnerable children lived in homes that were characterized as stressful (stress resulting from legal, marital, or psychiatric problems faced by adoptive parents) (Cadoret, Yates, Troughton, Woodworth, & Stewart, 1995). Findings from this study dovetail with studies that show that adults with ASPD are more likely to have been raised in a chaotic and impoverished environment and to have had parents who used harsh discipline and who abused or neglected their children (Holmes, Slaughter, & Kashani, 2001; Luntz & Widom, 1994).

Investigation of specific genes associated with the development of ASPD is ongoing. The neurotransmitter serotonin may be involved in aggression and other impulsive behaviors, and genes related to its metabolism are being studied. A recent study in New Zealand followed a group of male subjects from childhood to adulthood; some of the children experienced maltreatment at home. The researchers found that a certain type of gene encoding the activity of an enzyme (MAO A) that regulates serotonin and other neurotransmitters seemed to protect against the development of ASPD in adulthood (independent of parenting received in childhood) (Caspi et al., 2002). This study suggests a genetic-environment interaction that may be quite complex.

In the above case example (see "Case Presentation"), TP reported that both his father and brother had serious substance-related problems that eventually took their lives. The patient's report of his father's physical and emotional abuse of his wife and children indicates that the patient's father may have had ASPD. Patients with ASPD often have had a troubled start to life, perhaps as a result of genetic predisposition and/ or chronic mistreatment and abuse by parents or caretakers. Childhood maltreatment can leave scars that rarely heal quickly or completely.

Course of Disorder

While all individuals with ASPD have a history of CD, not all children with CD will develop ASPD; in fact, only about one quarter of children with CD develop ASPD (Robins, 1966). Factors that predict increased risk for development of ASPD are unclear; biology and environment appear to play prominent roles. Other childhood conditions that are frequently associated with the development of ASPD include ADHD and educational problems, including difficulties in learning to read. These problems correlate with earlier onset of ASPD and more severe ASPD symptoms in adulthood (Moffitt, Caspi, Dickson, Silva, & Stanton, 1996; Moran, 1999). Children with CD appear to be more vulnerable to developing other psychiatric disorders in adulthood.

Individuals with ASPD have a troubled adulthood that is characterized by higher rates of divorce, unemployment, homelessness, criminality, suicidal and homicidal behavior, and incarceration than patients without ASPD (Moran, 1999; Thompson & Bland, 1995). A study that followed men with ASPD for an average of twenty years after inpatient psychiatric treatment showed that of those patients who remained alive, one quarter no longer reported ASPD symptoms, one quarter were improved but still met ASPD criteria, and one half continued to have significant psychiatric, medical, and social problems (Black, Baumgard, & Bell, 1995).

In the above case example (see "Case Presentation"), TP appears to be following a downward trajectory. He continues to exhibit symptoms of ASPD and has little insight into his behavior or its effect on other people. He is approaching age 50 and has multiple medical and psychosocial problems and has little social support or financial support. Older patients with ASPD who present to treatment are often very lonely and demoralized and demonstrate a loss in confidence that they are able to manage the many problems that seem to be inflicted on them.

ISSUES INVOLVED IN DIAGNOSING ANTISOCIAL PERSONALITY DISORDER IN SUBSTANCE-DEPENDENT PATIENTS

Since substance users often engage in a variety of antisocial behaviors (e.g., stealing, lying during periods of drug use), it is common for adult patients with substance use disorders to endorse ASPD criteria. The *DSM-IV* instructs clinicians to count these behaviors toward a diagnosis of ASPD, even if the behaviors occur only during periods of drug use. Nevertheless, most substance users will not meet the full criteria for ASPD because they do not fulfill CD criteria in childhood. In fact, adult patients without a history of CD are more likely to stop their antisocial behavior during periods of abstinence from substance use. Clinical prognosis appears to be less favorable if a patient continues to exhibit antisocial behavior while substantially reducing substance use (Brooner, Greenfield, Schmidt, & Bigelow, 1993).

Clinicians may count antisocial behaviors toward a diagnosis of ASPD as long as these behaviors do not occur exclusively during the course of another psychiatric syndrome (e.g., schizophrenia or a manic episode in a patient with bipolar disorder). Thus, it is important for clinicians to carefully evaluate a patient to determine if a patient meets criteria for other major psychiatric disorders and if the antisocial behaviors occur only during the course of other psychiatric disorders. For example, a patient with bipolar disorder who is involved in criminal activity and is violent only during manic episodes does not meet criteria for ASPD. However, if this patient exhibited this pattern of disregard for other people during childhood (when the patient met criteria for CD) and exhibits this pattern of behavior in adulthood outside episodes of other psychiatric disorders (e.g., manic episodes), then the patient may be diagnosed with ASPD.

Some patients diagnosed with ASPD (approximately 10 percent) exhibit psychopathy. Psychopathy is a psychological construct that measures antisocial characteristics along a continuum of severity that places more emphasis on psychological traits (e.g., glibness, lack of affect and emotional depth) than on discrete behaviors (Hare, 1980). Individuals with psychopathy are more manipulative, callous, and self-centered, and they demonstrate little guilt, remorse, or anxiety. Individuals who rate high on psychopathy may be even less amenable to psychosocial treatment than the average patient with ASPD. A discussion of psychopathy is beyond the scope of this chapter.

In the above case example (see "Case Presentation"), TP has engaged in antisocial behaviors since childhood and into adulthood; he meets criteria for both CD and ASPD. The patient's long history of antisocial behavior confers a poor treatment prognosis and suggests that the patient will continue to exhibit antisocial behaviors regardless of success in treatment for his substance use disorders. Further evaluation may help a treatment provider to determine if TP also has psychopathy and co-occurring Axis I disorders (e.g., a mood disorder, adult ADHD). While some symptoms of ASPD can mimic symptoms of other psychiatric disorders, it is unlikely that further evaluation of the patient's symptom profile will not yield a diagnosis of ASPD; further evaluation will likely confirm a diagnosis of ASPD plus the presence of one or more co-occurring psychiatric disorders.

INSTRUMENTS AND METHODS FOR SCREENING AND DIAGNOSIS

Screening Instruments

Although it is difficult to diagnose ASPD through a brief screening process, many self-report instruments can identify personality profiles that are consistent with patients with ASPD. The most popular and thoroughly tested instruments include the psychopathic deviate subscale of the Minnesota Multiphasic Personality Inventory (MMPI; Butcher, Dahlstrom, Graham, Tellegen, & Kaemmer, 1989) and the socialization subscale of the California Personality Inventory (CPI; Gough & Bradley, 1996). These instruments can identify a subset of individuals who have antisocial profiles but who would not meet criteria for ASPD because they report little or no criminal history or misbehavior. These scales correlate quite poorly with each other and with diagnoses of ASPD derived from structured diagnostic interviews and are not recommended for diagnostic purposes (Hare, 1985).

Diagnostic Instruments

There are a number of *DSM*-based diagnostic interviews that can be used in the evaluation of ASPD. The Psychiatric Research Interview for Substance and Mental Disorders (PRISM; Hasin et al., 2006) was designed for use among substance-dependent patients. The PRISM quotes *DSM-IV* criteria and consists of detailed questions that help clinicians to ask patients about symptoms, including symptoms of CD and ASPD. Administration of the PRISM requires training and clinical judgment. The PRISM requires approximately 120 minutes to administer to subjects with psychiatric and substance use symptoms. Table 8-1A includes questions from the PRISM for aiding diagnosis of ASPD, and Table 8-1B includes questions from the PRISM for aiding diagnosis of CD.

The Structured Clinical Interview for DSM-IV Axis II Personality Disorders (SCID-II) (First, Spitzer, Gibbon, & Williams, 1997) lists *DSM-IV* criteria for CD and ASPD, and it offers questions that may be used by the interviewer to gather information from the patient about his/her symptoms. To help the interviewer to determine if the patient's symptoms meet each criterion for CD and ASPD, the SCID-II provides a coding system that allows the interviewer to determine if the patient's symptoms are "threshold" (symptom meets the criterion) or "sub-threshold" (symptom is evident but does not meet the criterion).

Clinicians who wish to learn to administer the PRISM or the SCID-II should use a two-step training process: didactic instruction followed by experiential learning under the supervision of an expert. New interviewers should corate interviews with an expert in order to develop consistency; corating interviews can also reduce gradual changes over time in application of the interview technique (referred to as "interview drift"). Through the process of learning to administer the PRISM or the SCID-II, clinicians will acquaint themselves with the criteria for ASPD and CD. Increased familiarity with these criteria may enhance a clinician's ability to identify the presence of these disorders through standard psychosocial interviews.

DIFFERENTIAL DIAGNOSIS AND OVERLAPPING DISORDERS

Depressive Disorders

Individuals with ASPD have exceptionally high rates of alcohol dependence and other substance use disorders and are at higher risk for other psychiatric conditions. Dysthymia and major depressive episodes (see Chapter 1 of this volume) may be present in up to one third of patients with ASPD and substance use disorders (Brooner et al., 1998). Mood disorders can worsen symptoms of irritability, labile mood, and impulsivity that are prevalent in patients with ASPD and may result in changes in sleep pattern, sexual drive, appetite, interest, and energy, in addition to pervasively depressed mood. Adequate treatment of mood disorders can ameliorate symptoms of irritability and labile mood and may enhance engagement in treatment but may have less impact on substance use disorders. Treatment of substance use disorders should occur simultaneously with treatment of psychiatric disorders.

Bipolar Spectrum Disorders

In the small percentage of patients with ASPD who have bipolar disorder (see Chapter 2 of this volume), mania or hypomania can increase impulsivity and irritability and can prevent engagement in treatment. These patients are more likely to act on antisocial impulses and to break the law. Clinicians may fail to diagnosis bipolar disorder if a patient enters treatment when his/her mood is stable or euthymic. If a patient with ASPD develops symptoms of mania or hypomania after entering treatment for a substance use disorder, a treatment provider can mistake these symptoms for irritability and pugnacity (characteristics of patients with ASPD). Thus, it is important that clinicians perform a careful evaluation of a patient's psychiatric symptoms when the patient presents to treatment, in order to rule in or rule out a diagnosis of bipolar disorder and to determine if mood stabilizer medications might improve a patient's stability and ability to engage in treatment.

Anxiety Disorder

Patients with ASPD are about twice as likely as patients without ASPD to have an anxiety disorder (Goodwin & Hamilton, 2003), including panic disorder (with and without agoraphobia), generalized anxiety disorder, posttraumatic stress disorder, social anxiety disorder, and specific phobias (see Chapter 3 and Chapter 4 of this volume). By diagnosing and treating anxiety disorders in patients with ASPD and substance use disorders, clinicians may help to improve a patient's treatment engagement. Treatment providers should avoid prescribing benzodiazepines to this patient population. Patients with ASPD, a substance use disorder, and another psychiatric syndrome are particularly vulnerable to misuse of benzodiazepines, and when these patients become dependent on benzodiazepines, they tend to have worse outcomes in substance use treatment programs (Havens & Strathdee, 2005; King et al., 2001). There are several good alternatives to benzodiazepines for treatment of anxiety disorders in patients with ASPD and substance use disorders; these alternative treatments, which have little or no abuse potential and are effective in treatment of anxiety disorders, include serotonin reuptake inhibitors and other antidepressant medications and buspirone. Unlike benzodiazapines, antidepressants are not fast-acting and are not overly sedating in most patients. For anxious patients who require medications that have a fast-acting soporific effect and have little abuse potential, treatment providers might consider prescribing sedating antidepressants (e.g., trazodone), anticonvulsants (e.g., valproate (Depakote), gabapentin (Neurontin)), and neuroleptic medications (e.g., olanzapine (Zyprexa), quetiapine (Seroquel)).

Attention Deficit Hyperactivity Disorder

ADHD often co-occurs with ASPD and substance use disorders. Characterized by symptoms of hyperactivity, impulsivity, and poorly sustained attention to tasks, ADHD begins in childhood and often accompanies conduct-disordered behaviors (see Chapter 5 of this volume). As patients age, hyperactivity and impulsivity tend to recede more than attention problems. Given the abuse potential of stimulant medications, treatment providers should be cautious in prescribing them to patients with ADHD, ASPD, and substance use disorders. However, treatment providers should not rule out a trial of a stimulant, since the potential benefit may be significant. Treatment providers might reduce the risk of abuse of stimulant medications by prescribing slow-release forms of methylphenidate (e.g., Ritalin SR, Concerta) or amphetamine (e.g., Dexedrine Spansules, Adderall XR), which have less abuse potential and, likely, less street value. Other precautions can be taken to lower the likelihood of abuse of medication, including writing prescriptions at frequent intervals for small amounts of medication, dispensing medication at the clinic, asking a significant other to monitor the patient's medication, or instituting random call-backs that require patients to produce their medication bottle for pill counting. Although nonstimulant medications for ADHD, such as the antidepressant bupropion (Wellbutrin, others), atomoxetine (Strattera), modafinil (Provigil), or guanfacine, may be less efficacious, treatment providers should consider prescribing them as a first course of treatment.

Medical Problems

Medical problems (see Chapter 14 of this volume) often result from risky and impulsive behaviors that are characteristic of patients with ASPD, who experience high rates of human immunodeficiency virus (HIV), viral hepatitis, and sexually transmitted diseases (Brooner et al., 1993). Physical injuries from fighting, gunshots, and motor vehicle accidents are common in these patients. Age and the accumulating burden of physical and emotional problems often encourage these patients to seek treatment for substance abuse problems and psychiatric disorders. Since these patients often neglect medical and psychiatric problems, it is important that clinicians help these patients to access medical and psychiatric treatment during rehabilitation.

TREATMENT PLANNING

Development of Therapeutic Relationship

Treatment of patients with co-occurring ASPD and substance use disorders can be challenging, and more is known about treatment of substance use disorders than treatment of ASPD. Patients with ASPD have difficulty maintaining warm, lasting relationships, often demand immediate results, fail to view their behavior as problematic, blame other people for lack of progress, and resort to threats when they are dissatisfied. Close work with patients with ASPD can evoke from counselors feelings of frustration and hopelessness that can interfere with the development of good rapport with the patient and can impede a patient's progress. Indeed, the development and maintenance of a strong therapeutic relationship can facilitate success in treatment for substance use disorders regardless of treatment modality. Clinicians should try the following four strategies to avoid feelings of frustration and hopelessness and to create a strong therapeutic relationship that is necessary for encouraging behavior changes in patients.

Develop Empathy Toward Patients. Through a careful evaluation, clinicians can identify a patient's strengths and the challenges that he/she has faced. In the above case example (see "Case Presentation"), TP endured an extremely difficult childhood and has faced considerable challenges and hardships throughout his life. Clinicians can use information gathered from their evaluation of the patient to develop empathy toward the patient. A therapist might display empathy by saying to a patient, "you have remained persistent in the face of many difficulties; I admire your tenacity."

Praise Patients (Rather Than Criticize). Patients with ASPD prefer instant reward and gratification. Critical or harsh words tend to anger and mystify patients with ASPD, who often fail to take responsibility for their actions. For example, it is more helpful to praise patients for attending sessions on time rather than criticize them for tardiness.

Set Limits. Patients with ASPD tend to respond best to a consistent and predictable environment. Therapists should explain the policies and contingencies of the program at the start of treatment and should help patients throughout treatment to manage their feelings when they encounter undesirable consequences (a therapist might say, "I know that this situation is frustrating to you; I think that we can get through this together."). Therapists should have a repository of problem-solving strategies for helping patients to manage feelings of frustration and anger. Objective measures (e.g., urinalysis) and information from corroborating sources (e.g., probation officer) can help clinicians to measure patients' progress and can help clinicians to avoid manipulation by the patient.

Use Team Approach in Treatment. Treating patients with ASPD is challenging and often draining. Substance abuse treatment programs should utilize a team approach when managing patients with ASPD in order to provide these patients with individual therapy, group therapy, and support for psychiatric disorders and medical problems. To help therapists who are treating patients with ASPD to remain objective and focused on the treatment goals, therapists should meet regularly with their supervisors and with other clinicians who are treating these patients in order to discuss the patients' progress.

Contingency Management

Contingency management is a system of behavioral reinforcement designed to increase motivation. Positive or negative consequences are systematically arranged to compete with the short-term benefits of drug use (or other maladaptive behavior) and to encourage patients to engage in behaviors that are consistent with recovery. For example, patients enrolled in treatment at a methadone maintenance clinic may receive methadone take-home doses as a reward for giving a drug-negative urine sample or for attending a counseling session; this incentive may be withdrawn if the patient tests drug-positive or misses a counseling session. Studies have demonstrated the efficacy of contingency management in treating substance use disorders (Petry et al., 2001). Contingency management may be ideal for patients with ASPD, who often have difficulty motivating themselves to change their behavior and who often ignore potential long-term risks and consequences of maladaptive behavior (Strand, 2002).

A recent study showed that contingency management techniques could be used in a methadone maintenance program to help patients with ASPD to attend counseling sessions and to reduce drug use (Brooner et al., 1998; Neufeld et al., 2008). With each counseling session that patients attended and with each drug-negative urine sample that patients submitted, patients received progressively more clinic-based incentives (e.g., take-home methadone doses); these incentives were withdrawn when patients missed counseling sessions or gave a drug-positive urine sample. Contingency management produced good results: over a six-month period patients attended 83 percent of their counseling sessions and submitted almost 70 percent drug-free urine samples.

Behavioral strategies can also be combined with other models of treatment, such as a stepped-care approach (Sobell & Sobell, 2000), in which patients receive more intensive treatment if they have a poor or partial response to less intensive care. Brooner et al. (2004) showed that a combination of stepped-based care and behavioral reinforcement encouraged both patients with ASPD and patients without ASPD to attend more counseling sessions and to submit more drug-negative urine samples. These results are as good as most outcomes reported in studies of patients without ASPD.

Individual Therapy

Although patients with ASPD are not the best candidates for insight-oriented therapy, they may benefit from supportive or cognitive behavioral approaches (Beck, Freeman, & Davis, 2004). The effectiveness of any treatment approach depends upon the rapport that the therapist can establish with the patient; therapists should try to utilize the four strategies described above (see "Development of Therapeutic Relationship") in order to develop a strong therapeutic relationship. We have had some success in helping patients to anticipate the immediate and long-term consequences of certain behaviors. For example, a clinician might encourage a patient who wants to "tell off" his probation officer to place himself in the "shoes" of the probation officer, to try to anticipate the response of the probation officer, and to try to understand the consequences of the patient's actions. A clinician should review with the patient effective ways that the patient can communicate with his probation officer.

Motivational Interviewing

Therapists might improve outcomes with patients with ASPD by using motivational interviewing (MI) and motivational enhancement techniques (Miller & Rollnick, 2002), and clinicians should obtain training in these techniques. The primary objective of these techniques is to create "dissonance" by helping patients to consider both the advantages and drawbacks of engaging in certain behaviors and to resolve their ambivalence by acting in ways that are aligned with their best interests. In the example cited above (see "Individual Therapy"), the patient's therapist might encourage the patient to consider how he might feel if he returned to jail. MI emphasizes a collaborative, empathic style of working with patients; this style, which may be particularly useful when working with angry patients who are resistant to change, requires therapists to avoid confrontation with the patient and encourages therapists to listen to patients' points of view while helping them to determine reasons for making positive changes.

Group and Community-Oriented Therapies

Patients with ASPD are poor candidates for unstructured process-oriented groups, since they tend to exploit group members and to waste time with unproductive distractions (Yalom, 1995). Nevertheless, group treatment sessions that are offered by substance use treatment programs may be appropriate for patients with ASPD if the sessions are structured and skills oriented. We have had some success in using these group sessions to help patients with ASPD to manage problems that occur during their participation in treatment. Since patients with ASPD and substance use disorders engage in high-risk behaviors and are at increased risk for HIV infection (Brooner et al., 1993), these patients should receive HIV risk-reduction counseling, to which they often respond well (Compton, Cotler, Ben-Abdallah, Cunningham-Williams, & Spitznagel, 2000). Unfortunately, therapeutic communities that offer a combination of therapeutic interventions within a residential setting have generally been unsuccessful in helping patients with ASPD and substance use disorders (Salekin, 2002).

Medications

No single medication regimen is widely supported for the treatment of ASPD. There is ongoing research on medications that lessen impulsiveness, aggressiveness, and explosiveness (see Chapter 11 of this volume). In brief, evidence from controlled clinical trials supports the effectiveness of serotonin reuptake inhibitors (e.g., fluoxetine) in decreasing emotional lability in patients with excessive aggression and personality disorders, including ASPD (Coccaro & Kavoussi, 1997). Controlled trials also indicate that anticonvulsant medications (e.g., valproate (Depakote)) can be helpful in reducing irritability and aggressiveness in adolescents and adults (Donovan et al., 1997; Donovan et al., 2000; Kavoussi & Coccaro, 1998).

Further, as discussed above (see "Differential Diagnosis and Overlapping Disorders"), clinicians should conduct a thorough psychiatric evaluation in order to identify the presence of other co-occurring psychiatric disorders, many of which may respond to specific medication treatments. Since patients with substance use disorders are at high risk for dropout, a thorough psychiatric evaluation is warranted during the early stages of treatment. Initiation of an effective treatment strategy for a co-occurring disorder may help to reduce the risk of dropout and improve long-term outcome. Further, clinicians should regularly reevaluate patients for co-occurring disorders; during these evaluations, a clinician may discover the presence of another potentially treatable disorder. Although treatment of co-occurring disorders may not impact the core features of ASPD, such treatment may relieve suffering, improve the treatment alliance, or improve a patient's functioning, thereby facilitating a patient's rehabilitation.

Treatment Planning for the Case Example

In the above case example (see "Case Presentation"), TP reported abuse of two substances, which requires immediate attention. First, the patient has a long-standing problem with opioid dependence, which has responded only to methadone maintenance treatment. Second, he meets diagnostic criteria for concurrent benzodiazepine dependence; he will almost certainly require detoxification, possibly on an inpatient basis (given his seizure history and prominent withdrawal symptoms). The patient should be referred to a comprehensive methadone maintenance clinic that can help him to access inpatient treatment for sedative dependence. Ideally, the methadone maintenance clinic should offer a contingency management program in which TP must provide regular urine samples for drug screening and in which incentives (e.g., methadone take-home doses) are offered in order to encourage patients to attend counseling sessions regularly and to reduce drug use.

The patient's therapist should conduct a comprehensive psychosocial assessment, including identification of physical and emotional abuse that the patient experienced as a child. While the therapist should not encourage the patient to discuss childhood abuse in detail until he has been stabilized in treatment, the therapist should demonstrate empathy toward the patient and ensure that he feels understood by the therapist. The therapist should also identify the patient's strengths (e.g., the patient's attainment of a GED while he was incarcerated required determination) and the patient's motivations for seeking treatment.

TP probably will require treatment for other psychiatric disorders and medical problems. A thorough psychiatric evaluation may reveal the presence of one or more Axis I psychiatric conditions (e.g., a mood disorder). The patient experienced an episode of depressed mood while in prison, and he regularly takes benzodiazepines, perhaps to relieve symptoms of a mood disorder. The patient should receive HIV risk-reduction counseling.

Individual and group therapy sessions may help TP to remain in treatment. Treatment retention is almost always associated with good treatment response and is a prerequisite for sustained abstinence and improved psychosocial and medical functioning. Therapy sessions may help the patient to manage negative feelings that often arise in treatment programs that have many rules and require interaction with different staff members. Since substance abuse treatment takes time, and since patients with ASPD often become frustrated if they do not meet their treatment goals quickly, the patient should receive coping and social skills training that may help him to appropriately interact with program staff members and to handle frustrating situations during treatment.

Individual and group therapy sessions also might help TP to resolve ambivalence toward behavior change and to recognize the results of continued drug use, including more time in prison. Although patients with ASPD often have little insight into the consequences of their actions, TP may exhibit willingness to change (e.g., reduce his drug use) if he perceives this change as consistent with his own interests.

The patient's therapist should help him to identify short-term and long-term treatment goals (including employment and cessation of substance use), to identify activities that might replace substance use, and to devise a daily schedule that encourages the patient to avoid using substances and that provides structure. The therapist might use cognitive behavioral strategies to help the patient to manage difficulties encountered during the job search process or while on the job and MI techniques to encourage the patient to utilize vocational rehabilitation services and job search services.

Finally, all staff members who are involved in the patient's care should meet regularly to discuss this case in order to review the patient's progress and to ensure that staff members properly manage negative countertransference and remain focused on the primary treatment goals (i.e., reduction of drug use and improved psychosocial functioning).

SUMMARY

Since ASPD frequently co-occurs with substance use disorders, a large number of patients with ASPD present to substance abuse treatment. The accurate diagnosis of ASPD and other co-occurring psychiatric disorders during the early stages of treatment can facilitate the development of a treatment plan that is tailored toward the special needs of this population. The diagnosis of ASPD can be made using a routine psychiatric interview or with structured assessments, including the PRISM and the SCID-II; therapists should collect information from corroborating sources to confirm the accuracy of patients' self-reports. Familiarity with the diagnostic criteria for ASPD (including the criteria for CD) is required for accurate diagnosis.

Patients with ASPD are probably most easily treated within the context of a comprehensive treatment program that uses a team approach. Therapists should work with patients to establish a therapeutic relationship. Cognitive behavioral approaches, motivational approaches, and supportive approaches can be used to help the patient to remain in treatment, to manage negative feelings about recovery and specific aspects of the treatment program, and to remain focused on the goals of treatment. Contingency management strategies can support this work by providing a structured framework to facilitate behavior change. This behavioral approach can focus on drug use or on modification of other behaviors to improve treatment response (e.g., adherence to scheduled appointments, employment-seeking). Objective measures of treatment response, such as urinalysis, help therapists to assess patients' progress.

Patients with ASPD are likely to demand more attention than many other patients (e.g., therapists will spend more time with these patients and will spend more time discussing these patients with a supervisor or during team meetings). Although patients with ASPD present to treatment with more severe substance use problems (e.g., dependence on multiple substances, a history of earlier onset of substance use, heavier substance use), these patients can respond favorably to substance abuse treatment and can attain positive outcomes that are similar to patients without ASPD. Behavior change following sustained abstinence is possible when the patient perceives that these changes benefit his/her own interests.

Suggestions for Further Reading

For readers who wish to study further in this area, we recommend:

☐ **Prevalence and Prognostic Effects of ASPD in Substance-Dependent Patients**

- Compton, W. M., Conway, K. P., Stinson, F. S., Colliver, J. D., & Grant, B. F. (2005). Prevalence, correlates, and comorbidity of DSM-IV antisocial personality syndromes and alcohol and specific drug use disorders in the United States: Results from the National Epidemiologic Survey on Alcohol and Related Conditions. *Journal of Clinical Psychiatry, 66*, 677-685.

- Havens, J. R., & Strathdee, S. A. (2005). Antisocial personality disorder and opioid treatment outcomes: A review. *Addictive Disorders & Their Treatment, 4*, 85-97.

☐ **Diagnostic Methods and Treatment Planning**

- Beck, A., Freeman, A., & Davis, D. (2004). *Cognitive therapy of personality disorders*. New York: Guilford Press.

- Brooner, R. K., Kidorf, M., King, V. L., & Stoller, K. (1998). Preliminary evidence of good treatment response in antisocial drug abusers. *Drug and Alcohol Dependence, 49*, 249-260.

- Hare, R. D., Hart, S. D., & Harpur, T. J. (1991). Psychopathy and the DSM-IV criteria for antisocial personality disorder. *Journal of Abnormal Psychology, 100*, 391-398.

- Messina, N., Farabee, D., & Rawson, R. (2003). Treatment responsivity of cocaine-dependent patients with antisocial personality disorder to cognitive-behavioral and contingency management interventions. *Journal of Consulting and Clinical Psychology, 71*, 320-329.

- Sperry, L. (2003). *Handbook of diagnosis and treatment of DSM-IV-TR personality disorders*. New York: Brunner-Routledge.

☐ **Popular Press Books and Web Sites**

- Alcohol Medical Scholars Program: http://www.alcoholmedicalscholars.org.

- Black, D. (1999). *Bad boys, bad men: Confronting antisocial personality disorder*. New York: Oxford University Press.

References

Alterman, A. I., & Cacciola, J. S. (1991). The antisocial personality disorder diagnosis in substance abusers: Problems and issues. *The Journal of Nervous and Mental Disease, 179*, 401-409.

American Psychiatric Association. (1994). *Diagnostic and statistical manual of mental disorders* (4th ed). Washington, DC: Author.

Beck, A., Freeman, A., & Davis, D. (2004). *Cognitive therapy of personality disorders*. New York: Guilford Press.

Black, D. W., Baumgard, C. H., & Bell, S. E. (1995). A 16- to 45-year follow-up of 71 men with antisocial personality disorder. *Comprehensive Psychiatry, 36*, 130-140.

Brooner, R. K., Greenfield, L., Schmidt, C. W., & Bigelow, G. E. (1993). Antisocial personality disorder and HIV infection among intravenous drug abusers. *American Journal of Psychiatry, 150*, 53-58.

Brooner, R. K., Kidorf, M., King, V. L., & Stoller, K. (1998). Preliminary evidence of good treatment response in antisocial drug abusers. *Drug and Alcohol Dependence, 49*, 249-260.

Brooner, R. K., Kidorf, M. S., King, V L., Stoller, K B., Peirce, J. M., Bigelow, G. E., et al. (2004). Behavioral contingencies improve counseling attendance in an adaptive treatment model. *Journal of Substance Abuse Treatment, 27*, 223-232.

Brooner, R. K., King, V. L., Kidorf, M., Schmidt, C. W., & Bigelow, G. E. (1997). Psychiatric and substance use comorbidity among treatment-seeking opioid abusers. *Archives of General Psychiatry, 54*, 71-80.

Butcher, J. N., Dahlstrom, W. G., Graham, J. R., Tellegen, A., & Kaemmer, B. (1989). *Minnesota Multiphasic Personality Inventory-2 (MMPI-2): Manual for administration and scoring.* Minneapolis: University of Minnesota Press.

Cadoret, R. J., Yates, W. R., Troughton, E., Woodworth, G., & Stewart, M. A. (1995). Adoption study demonstrating two genetic pathways to drug abuse. *Archives of General Psychiatry, 52,* 42-52.

Caspi, A., McClay, J., Moffitt, T. E., Mill, J., Martin, J., Craig, I. W., et al. (2002). Role of genotype in the cycle of violence in maltreated children. *Science, 297,* 851-854.

Coccaro, E. F., & Kavoussi, R. J. (1997). Fluoxetine and impulsive aggressive behavior in personality-disordered subjects. *Archives of General Psychiatry, 54,* 1081-1088.

Compton, W. M., Conway, K. P., Stinson, F. S., Colliver, J. D., & Grant, B. F. (2005). Prevalence, correlates, and comorbidity of DSM-IV antisocial personality syndromes and alcohol and specific drug use disorders in the United States: Results from the National Epidemiologic Survey on Alcohol and Related Conditions. *Journal of Clinical Psychiatry, 66,* 677-685.

Compton, W. M., Cottler, L. B., Ben-Abdallah, A., Cunningham-Williams, R., & Spitznagel, E. L. (2000). The effects of psychiatric comorbidity on response to an HIV prevention intervention. *Drug and Alcohol Dependence, 58,* 247-257.

Donovan, S. J., Stewart, J. W., Nunes, E. V., Quitkin, F. M., Parides, M., Daniel, W., et al. (2000). Divalproex treatment for youth with explosive temper and mood lability: A double-blind, placebo-controlled crossover design. *American Journal of Psychiatry, 157,* 818-820.

Donovan, S. J., Susser, E. S., Nunes, E. V., Stewart, J. W., Quitkin, F. M., & Klein, D. F. (1997). Divalproex treatment of disruptive adolescents: A report of 10 cases. *Journal of Clinical Psychiatry, 58,* 12-15.

First, M. B., Spitzer, R. L., Gibbon, M., & Williams, J. B. W. (1997). Structured Clinical Interview for DSM-IV Axis II Personality Disorders (SCID-II). Washington, DC: American Psychiatric Publishing.

Goodwin, R. D., & Hamilton, S. P. (2003). Lifetime comorbidity of antisocial personality disorder and anxiety disorders among adults in the community. *Psychiatry Research, 117,* 159-166.

Gough, H. G., & Bradley, P. (1996). *The California Personality Inventory manual* (3rd ed.). Palo Alto, CA: Consulting Psychologists Press.

Hare, R. D. (1980). A research scale for the assessment of psychopathy in criminal populations. *Personality and Individual Differences, 1,* 111-119.

Hare, R. D. (1985). Comparison of procedures for the assessment of psychopathy. *Journal of Consulting and Clinical Psychology, 53,* 7-16.

Hasin, D. S., Samet, S., Nunes, E., Meydan, J., Matseoane, K., & Waxman, R. (2006). Diagnosis of comorbid disorders in substance users: Psychiatric Research Interview for Substance and Mental Disorders (PRISM-IV). *American Journal of Psychiatry, 163,* 689-696.

Havens, J. R., & Strathdee, S. A. (2005). Antisocial personality disorder and opioid treatment outcomes: A review. *Addictive Disorders & Their Treatment, 4,* 85-97.

Holmes, S. E., Slaughter, J. R., & Kashani, J. (2001). Risk factors in childhood that lead to the development of conduct disorder and antisocial personality disorder. *Child Psychiatry and Human Development, 31,* 183-193.

Kavoussi, R. J., & Coccaro, E. F. (1998). Divalproex sodium for impulsive aggressive behavior in patients with personality disorder. *Journal of Clinical Psychiatry, 59,* 676-680.

Kessler, R. C., McGonagle, K. A., Zhao, S., Nelson, C. B., Hughes, M., Eshleman, S., et al. (1994). Lifetime and 12-month prevalence of DSM-III-R psychiatric disorders in the United States: Results from the National Comorbidity Survey. *Archives of General Psychiatry, 51,* 8-19.

King, V. L., Kidorf, M. S., Stoller, K. B., Carter, J. A., & Brooner, R. K. (2001). Influence of antisocial personality subtypes on drug abuse treatment response. *The Journal of Nervous and Mental Disease, 189*, 593-601.

Luntz, B. K., & Widom, C. S. (1994). Antisocial personality disorder in abused and neglected children grown up. *American Journal of Psychiatry, 151*, 670-674.

Miller, W. R., & Rollnick, S. (2002). *Motivational interviewing: Preparing people for change* (2nd ed.). New York: Guilford Press.

Moffitt, T. E., Caspi, A., Dickson, N., Silva, P., & Stanton, W. (1996). Childhood-onset versus adolescent-onset antisocial conduct problems in males: Natural history from ages 3 to 18 years. *Development and Psychopathology, 8*, 399-424.

Moran, P. (1999). The epidemiology of antisocial personality disorder. *Social Psychiatry and Psychiatric Epidemiology, 34*, 231-242.

Neufeld, K. J., Kidorf, M. S., Kolodner, K., King, V. L., Clark, M., & Brooner, R.K. (2008). A behavioral treatment for opioid-dependent patients with antisocial personality. *Journal of Substance Abuse Treatment, 34,* 101-111.

Petry, N. M., Petrakis, I., Trevisan, L., Wiredu, G., Boutros, N. N., Martin, B., et al. (2001). Contingency management interventions: From research to practice. *American Journal of Psychiatry*, 158, 694-702.

Robins, L. N. (1966). *Deviant children grown up: A sociological and psychiatric study of sociopathic personality*. Baltimore: Williams and Wilkins.

Salekin, R. T. (2002). Psychopathy and therapeutic pessimism: Clinical lore or clinical reality? *Clinical Psychology Review, 22*, 79-112.

Sobell, M .B., & Sobell, L. C. (2000). Stepped care as a heuristic approach to the treatment of alcohol problems. *Journal of Consulting and Clinical Psychology, 68*, 573-579.

Strand, P. S. (2002). Treating antisocial behavior: A context for substance abuse prevention. *Clinical Psychology Review, 22*, 707-728.

Thompson, A. H., & Bland, R. C. (1995). Social dysfunction and mental illness in a community sample. *Canadian Journal of Psychiatry, 40*, 15-20.

Woody, G., McLellan, A. T., Luborsky, L., & O'Brien, C. P. (1985). Sociopathy and psychotherapy outcome. *Archives of General Psychiatry, 42*, 1081-1086.

Yalom, I. D. (1995). *The theory and practice of group psychotherapy* (4th ed.). New York: Basic Books.

Chapter 9

Borderline Personality Disorder in Patients With Substance Use Disorders

Andrew Ekblad, M.A., Alexander L. Chapman, Ph.D., and Thomas R. Lynch, Ph.D.

INTRODUCTION

Borderline personality disorder is a serious psychiatric disorder that often co-occurs with other disorders (e.g., substance use disorders) and must be given special clinical attention. Borderline personality disorder involves instability across a variety of important life domains—emotional, cognitive, interpersonal, and behavioral. Persons who meet criteria for borderline personality disorder tend to experience extremely intense and unstable emotions. This intense emotional arousal makes it difficult for them to plan ahead and to inhibit impulsive behaviors. In addition, persons with borderline personality disorder have difficulty maintaining a stable sense of identity and often feel a pervasive sense of emptiness. They frequently have unstable interpersonal relationships and engage in impulsive behavior such as reckless driving, binge eating, substance abuse, and self-damaging behaviors (e.g., suicidal behavior, self-injury).

Although borderline personality disorder is relatively rare in the general population, it is very common among patients seeking treatment for psychiatric disorders or substance use disorders. Approximately 15 percent of all psychiatric inpatients and 50 percent of all inpatients with a personality disorder meet diagnostic criteria for borderline personality disorder (Widiger & Weissman, 1991). Up to 58 percent of individuals with borderline personality disorder meet criteria for a substance use disorder (cf. Trull, Sher, Minks-Brown, Durbin, & Burr, 2000), and between 5 percent and 32 percent of individuals with substance use disorders meet diagnostic criteria for borderline personality disorder (Brooner, King, Kidorf, Schmidt, & Bigelow 1997; Weiss, Mirin, Griffin, Gunderson, & Hufford, 1993). Borderline personality disorder also commonly co-occurs with major depressive disorder (see Chapter 1 of this volume), bipolar disorder (see Chapter 2 of this volume), posttraumatic stress disorder (see Chapter 3 of this volume), and other anxiety disorders (see Chapter 4 of this volume). Borderline personality disorder is more frequently diagnosed among females than males, with estimates indicating that up to 75 percent of persons with borderline personality disorder are women (American Psychiatric Association, 1994).

Individuals with borderline personality disorder have a disproportionately high rate of health care utilization, primarily due to risky behaviors that often come to the attention of mental health treatment providers. Patients with borderline personality disorder are at high risk for suicide. Approximately 40 percent to 65 percent of individuals who commit suicide meet criteria for a personality disorder, and borderline personality disorder is the personality disorder most strongly associated with suicide:

8 to 10 percent of patients diagnosed with borderline personality disorder commit suicide (Frances, Fyer, & Clarkin, 1986); 75 percent attempt suicide (Frances et al., 1986); and 69 to 80 percent engage in nonsuicidal self-injury (Clarkin, Widiger, Frances, Hurt, & Gilmore, 1983; Cowdry, Pickar, & Davies, 1985; Gunderson, 1984; Grove & Tellegen, 1991; Stone, 1993).

One of the most challenging aspects of working with substance-dependent patients is their tendency to engage in impulsive, unpredictable, and dangerously self-destructive behavior. Patients with the combination of borderline personality disorder and substance use disorders are at greater risk of committing self-destructive behavior than patients without both of these disorders. The instability that characterizes relationships held by patients with borderline personality disorder (including relationships with clinicians) and the tendency of these patients to engage in self-destructive behavior often make clinicians feel frustrated, angry, and helpless. Fortunately, there are empirically tested methods for evaluation and treatment of patients with borderline personality disorder. Accurate diagnosis of borderline personality and implementation of an evidence-based treatment plan can lead to both improved treatment outcome and a more rewarding experience for treatment staff.

This chapter aims to provide an overview of the issues and strategies associated with the diagnosis and treatment of borderline personality disorder in patients with comorbid substance use disorders and to help clinicians who work with substance-dependent patients to learn how to recognize symptoms of borderline personality disorder, to be aware of treatment options, and to develop a treatment plan. This chapter provides a detailed description of one form of treatment for borderline personality disorder: Dialectical Behavior Therapy (DBT), which has been adapted and tested for patients with borderline personality disorder and co-occurring substance use disorders. An understanding of DBT will help clinicians to improve their ability to diagnose and treat patients with borderline personality disorder and substance use disorders.

CASE PRESENTATION

The following case example illustrates important issues in the assessment of individuals with borderline personality disorder and substance use disorders. Assessment of the patient in this case example follows the DBT model for assessing psychiatric symptoms and problems. The patient's difficulties are organized into five categories:

1. Behavior dysregulation;
2. Emotion dysregulation;
3. Cognitive dysregulation;
4. Interpersonal dysregulation; and
5. Self-dysregulation.

These five categories correspond to the criteria for borderline personality disorder that are listed in the *Diagnostic and Statistical Manual of Mental Disorders,* 4th edition (*DSM-IV*; American Psychiatric Association, 1994; see Tables 9-1 and 9-2). The case example presented in this section does not represent a specific case but is an amalgam of typical cases of co-occurring borderline personality disorder and substance use disorders. A discussion of treatment planning for the case example is included at the end of the chapter.

Chief Complaint

JN is a 36-year-old single, Caucasian male. He presents at the suggestion of his sister, who is worried about his addiction to heroin.

Assessment of Domains of Dysregulation

Behavior Dysregulation. JN presents with an extensive history of polysubstance abuse. He began smoking marijuana at age 12 and progressed to heroin by age 17. At intake, he reports that he injects heroin five to six days per week, is unemployed, and is financially destitute; his landlord has been threatening to evict him from his apartment.

He demonstrates many of the key features of heroin dependence. For example, JN reports tolerance to heroin (he requires greater amounts of heroin to get the same effect) and reports withdrawal symptoms (including severe flu-like symptoms, agitation, sweating, and intense general malaise) when he abstains from heroin for more than eight to sixteen hours. In addition, JN frequently uses more heroin than he intends and uses it more frequently than he intends; he chastises himself after overusing heroin. He often feels panicky that his "stash" might run out before he has enough money to buy more heroin.

JN also engages in a variety of reckless, impulsive, self-damaging behaviors that appear to be related to borderline personality disorder rather than substance abuse. For example, JN periodically burns himself, engages in high-risk sexual activity, and has made several serious suicide attempts both while intoxicated and while sober. He reports that he burns himself and engages in reckless behaviors when he experiences strong emotional distress; he feels that these self-injurious behaviors provide him with relief from the distress. JN also reports difficulties with gambling; he has gambled primarily to obtain money for purchase of heroin.

Emotion Dysregulation. JN reports that he experiences intense, rapidly shifting moods throughout the day and considerable difficulty in regulating his emotional reactions. He feels shame over his addiction to heroin and his drug-related behavior that has alienated him from his family and friends (e.g., stealing, verbal abuse). He also reports frequent sadness and anger, and he indicates that these emotions tend to occur suddenly, quickly become unmanageably intense, and take several hours to diminish, unless he engages in dysfunctional behavior to lessen these feelings (e.g., cutting, burning).

Cognitive Dysregulation. When JN is distressed, overwhelmed, or involved in conflict with friends, he often feels disconnected from his body and his surroundings. He reports that he sometimes believes that people are talking about him or trying to steal from him (although these worries do not seem unreasonable given his social circle (e.g., drug users)).

Interpersonal Dysfunction. JN experiences intense, chaotic relationships. He has frequent intense arguments with his girlfriend (after which he usually uses heroin). He engages in extreme efforts to prevent people from leaving him (e.g., pleading, begging) and undergoes extreme emotional distress when his relationships with significant others end.

Report From Relatives

During a brief phone interview, two of the patient's close relatives indicate that the patient's symptoms of borderline personality disorder are long-standing and are present even during periods when JN is not actively using drugs or experiencing episodes of Axis I disorders (e.g., major depression).

Diagnosis

JN meets seven of the nine criteria in the *DSM-IV* for borderline personality disorder (see Table 9-1):

1. Frantic efforts to avoid real or imagined abandonment (Criterion 1);

2. A pattern of unstable and intense interpersonal relationships characterized by alternation between extremes of idealization and devaluation (Criterion 2);

3. Impulsivity in at least two areas that are potentially self-damaging (e.g., sex, substance abuse) (Criterion 4);

4. Recurrent suicidal behavior, gestures, and self-mutilating behavior (Criterion 5);

5. Affective instability due to marked reactivity of mood (Criterion 6);

6. Inappropriate, intense anger or difficulty controlling anger (Criterion 8); and

7. Transient, stress-related paranoid ideation or severe dissociative symptoms (Criterion 9).

The patient's symptoms of borderline personality disorder seem to occur independently of the patient's drug use. JN also meets *DSM-IV* criteria for opioid dependence. JN does not meet criteria for cyclothymia or bipolar disorder, since his rapid mood shifts appear to be more consistent with affective instability characteristic of borderline personality disorder.

DIAGNOSTIC CRITERIA

Borderline personality disorder is a complex and serious disorder that is difficult to diagnose. The *DSM-IV* defines borderline personality disorder as "a pervasive pattern of instability of interpersonal relationships, self-image, and affects and marked impulsivity beginning by early adulthood and present in a variety of contexts" (American Psychiatric Association, 1994, p. 650). To be diagnosed with borderline personality disorder, patients must meet at least five of nine *DSM-IV* criteria. A defining feature of borderline personality disorder includes instability in a variety of life domains, including interpersonal functioning, mood, identity, and cognition (American Psychiatric Association, 1994).

To accurately assess borderline personality disorder in patients with substance use disorders, clinicians must determine if the patient experiences symptoms of borderline personality disorder in the absence of active drug use or if the symptoms occur only within the context of drug use. If symptoms of borderline personality disorder occur only within the context of drug use, the patient's borderline personality features may be secondary to the substance use disorder. Table 9-1 presents the *DSM-IV* criteria, issues involved in diagnosis of borderline personality disorder in substance-dependent patients, and questions from the Psychiatric Research Interview for Substance and Mental Disorders (PRISM; Hasin et al., 2006), which should aid clinicians in asking patients about each criterion.

There are several problems associated with the categorical diagnostic system used by the *DSM-IV* to diagnose borderline personality disorder. Most notably, there is a lack of general empirical support for the boundaries of the diagnostic criteria (Morey, 1988). Critics of the *DSM-IV* criteria have suggested that there is considerable overlap between and within personality disorder diagnostic categories (Clarkin et al., 1983; Oldham, Skodol, Kellman, & Hyler, 1992; Widiger, Sanderson, & Warner, 1986) and that there is too much heterogeneity among persons diagnosed with the same disorder. In fact, Skodol et al. (2002a) pointed out that there are 151 different combinations of symptoms that result in a diagnosis of borderline personality disorder. As a result, some researchers have conceptualized borderline personality disorder in terms of general personality features or dimensions (Hyman, 2002). For example, several authors have characterized borderline personality disorder as consisting of three core features: (1) disturbed interpersonal relatedness, (2) affective dysregulation, and (3) behavioral dyscontrol (Sanislow et al., 2002; Skodol et al., 2002a, 2002b; Siever, Torgersen, Gunderson, Livesley, & Kendler, 2002).

Similarly, Linehan (1993a) has characterized borderline personality disorder as a disorder of dysregulation in several domains and has reorganized the *DSM-IV* criteria into five different domains consistent with research on borderline personality disorder (see Table 9-2):

1. Emotion dysregulation includes the criteria that specify affective instability and problems with anger;

2. Interpersonal dysregulation includes frantic efforts to avoid abandonment and relationship instability;

3. Behavior dysregulation includes life-threatening behaviors, such as deliberate self-injury or suicide attempts, in addition to a variety of mood-driven impulsive behaviors, such as binge eating, recklessness, and alcohol and drug abuse;

4. Cognitive dysregulation includes difficulty with information processing, dissociative mental states, and paranoid cognition under conditions of stress; and

5. Self-dysregulation involves an unstable sense of self or identity and chronic feelings of emptiness.

The first three symptom categories described by Linehan (1993a) share many similarities with the three core features proposed by Skodol et al. (2002a, 2002b).

NATURAL HISTORY AND ETIOLOGY

Personality disorders (e.g., borderline personality disorder) are chronic, lifelong conditions. Thus, onset of symptoms of borderline personality disorder should be evident in childhood or by adolescence, and the course of the symptoms should be chronic. Researchers have noted a variety of possible contributors to the etiology of borderline personality disorder (Lieb, Zanarini, Schmahl, Linehan, & Bohus,

Table 9-1

DSM-IV **Criteria for Borderline Personality Disorder**

Symptoms	*DSM-IV* Criteria[a, b]	Issues in Substance-Dependent Patients	PRISM Questions to Aid Diagnosis[c, d]
Core Criteria	A pervasive pattern of instability of interpersonal relationships, self-image, and affects, and marked impulsivity beginning in early adulthood and present in a variety of contexts, as indicated by five (or more) of the following:		
	1. frantic efforts to avoid real or imagined abandonment (do not include suicidal or self-mutilating behavior covered in Criterion 5)		Since early adulthood … … when you've gotten close to someone, have you needed them to reassure you that they would never leave you? … would you put in a lot of time and effort doing things to keep someone from leaving you?
	2. a pattern of unstable and intense interpersonal relationships characterized by alternating between extremes of idealization and devaluation	Substance abuse and dependence may undermine relationships with family members and significant others; relapses and deceptiveness and antisocial behavior resulting from substance use often cause anger, disappointment, and loss of trust in family members and significant others.	Since early adulthood … … have you usually gotten very attached to people very quickly? … have your close relationships had lots of highs and lows? … have you often started out thinking that someone was a great person only to be disappointed when they did not live up to your expectations?
	3. identity disturbance: markedly and persistently unstable self-image or sense of self	Self-image is often low in substance-dependent patients but usually not unstable.	Since early adulthood … … have you often changed your mind about your goals, your friends, or your lovers? … have you often looked at what others were doing to know how to act in a situation? … have you sometimes wondered who you really are?
	4. impulsivity in at least two areas that are potentially self-damaging (e.g., spending, sex, substance abuse, reckless driving, binge eating) (do not include suicidal or self-mutilating behavior covered in Criterion 5)	Substance intoxication increases impulsivity and may cause or promote these symptoms.	Since early adulthood, have there been periods in your life when you often … … had sex with a lot of different people, people who meant very little to you, or had unsafe sex? … spent too much money while shopping or gambling? … binged on food? … drank a lot more or used a lot more drugs than you meant to? … took many risks while driving?

(Continued)

Symptoms	DSM-IV Criteria[a, b]	Issues in Substance-Dependent Patients	PRISM Questions to Aid Diagnosis[c, d]
	5. recurrent suicidal behavior, gestures, or threats, or self-mutilating behavior	Severe dysphoria during stimulant withdrawal or hallucinogen intoxication rarely results in suicidal or self-destructive behavior.	Since early adulthood, have you ever hurt yourself on purpose without wanting to die? Since early adulthood … … have you ever threatened to kill yourself? … have you ever tried to kill yourself?
	6. affective instability due to a marked reactivity of mood (e.g., intense episodic dysphoria, irritability, or anxiety usually lasting a few hours and only rarely more than a few days)	Intense, transient mood states are associated with substance intoxication and withdrawal across a variety of substances.	Since early adulthood … … have you often become very sad, anxious, or angry over "little" things? … have others often wondered why you get upset so easily?
	7. chronic feelings of emptiness		Since early adulthood, have you often felt like your life had no purpose or meaning?
	8. inappropriate, intense anger or difficulty controlling anger (e.g., frequent displays of temper, constant anger, recurrent physical fights)	Irritability and intense anger may occur with alcohol or stimulant intoxication or with opioid or cannabis withdrawal.	Since early adulthood, have you often lost control of yourself when you were very angry?
	9. transient, stress-related paranoid ideation or severe dissociative symptoms.	Paranoia may occur during cocaine or other stimulant intoxication or during alcohol or sedative withdrawal; dissociative symptoms may occur during hallucinogen intoxication.	Since early adulthood, during difficult and stressful times, have you often felt … … that you weren't real? … like you were outside of your body? Since early adulthood, during difficult and stressful times, have you often felt suspicious or distrustful in your relationships with others?

(a) American Psychiatric Association (1994).
(b) Reprinted with permission from the *Diagnostic and Statistical Manual of Mental Disorders*, Fourth Edition (Copyright 1994). American Psychiatric Association.
(c) Hasin et al. (2006).
(d) Reprinted with permission.

Table 9-2
Conceptualization of *DSM-IV* Criteria for Borderline Personality Disorder in the Framework of Dialectical Behavior Therapy

DSM-IV Diagnostic Criteria for Borderline Personality Disorder[a]	Domains of Dysregulation[a]
1. Affective instability	Emotion dysregulation
2. Problems with anger	
3. Chaotic relationships	Interpersonal dysregulation
4. Fears of abandonment	
5. Impulsive behavior	Behavior dysregulation
6. Self-injurious behavior	
7. Cognitive disturbances	Cognitive dysregulation
8. Unstable self-image	Self-dysregulation
9. Chronic feelings of emptiness	

[a] Adapted from Linehan (1993a, p. 13); reprinted with permission of the Guilford Press.

2004). Recent research suggests that genetic factors may influence the onset of borderline personality disorder. In a study of monozygotic and dizygotic twins, 35 percent of both monozygotic twins had borderline personality disorder while only 7 percent of both dizygotic twins had the disorder (Torgersen et al., 2000). Other studies have suggested both genetic and environmental components to personality features possibly associated with borderline personality disorder (Livesley, Jang, & Vernon, 1998).

Environmental factors have been implicated in the etiology of borderline personality disorder. One study revealed that 91 percent of inpatients with borderline personality disorder reported some type of childhood abuse; 92 percent reported some type of childhood neglect; 75 percent of these inpatients reported emotional or verbal abuse; and 60 percent reported physical or sexual abuse. In addition, 70 percent of these inpatients reported that they had a caretaker who denied their thoughts and feelings (Zanarini, Williams, Lewis, & Reich, 1997).

Other studies have suggested that childhood sexual abuse among patients with borderline personality disorder tends to be frequent and severe, and that both childhood abuse and neglect are associated with greater severity of symptoms of borderline personality disorder (Zanarini et al., 2002). However, not all individuals with borderline personality disorder experience childhood abuse or neglect. Additionally, many individuals who do experience childhood abuse or neglect do not develop borderline personality disorder. In other words, early childhood trauma is neither necessary nor sufficient for the development of borderline personality disorder (Zanarini et al., 1997).

INSTRUMENTS AND METHODS FOR SCREENING AND DIAGNOSIS

There are several ways to assess the presence of borderline personality disorder, including self-report questionnaires (e.g., Borderline Symptom List (BSL; Bohus et al., 2007), Personality Assessment Inventory (PAI; Morey, 1991)) and structured clinical interviews (e.g., PRISM (Hasin et al., 2006), Structured Clinical Interview for DSM-IV AXIS-II Personality Disorders (SCID-II; First, Spitzer, Gibbon, & Williams, 1997), International Personality Disorder Examination (IPDE; Loranger, 1995)). The PRISM, a diagnostic instrument that requires approximately 120 minutes to administer, was designed for use among substance-dependent patients; training in use of the PRISM offers clinicians an opportunity to learn the *DSM-IV* diagnostic criteria and the procedure for conducting an effective psychiatric interview. Table 9-1 includes questions from the PRISM for each of the diagnostic criterion for borderline personality disorder. In addition to employing self-report instruments and structured clinical interviews, clinicians should seek from patients' family members and acquaintances evidence that corroborates the diagnosis.

DIFFERENTIAL DIAGNOSIS AND COMORBID PSYCHIATRIC DISORDERS

Borderline Personality Disorder and Substance Use Disorders

Borderline personality disorder frequently co-occurs with other psychiatric disorders. Borderline personality disorder is highly comorbid with substance use disorders. In fact, substance abuse is included in the *DSM-IV* criteria for borderline personality disorder as one example of impulsivity (Criterion 4; see Table 9-1). Up to 57.4 percent of individuals with borderline personality disorder meet criteria for a substance use disorder (cf. Trull et al., 2000), and between 5 percent and 32 percent of individuals with a substance use disorder meet diagnostic criteria for borderline personality disorder (Brooner et al., 1997; Weiss et al., 1993).

The frequent co-occurrence of borderline personality disorder and substance use disorders poses unique clinical challenges (Skodol, Oldham, & Gallagher, 1999). For example, the presence of borderline personality disorder is associated with a more chronic and problematic course of substance use disorders, including more severe physical dependence and more adverse social, emotional, and legal consequences (Linehan et al., 1999; Links, Heslegrave, Mitton, & van Reekum, 1995; Ross, Dermatis, Levounis, & Galanter, 2003). In addition, the co-occurrence of borderline personality disorder and substance use disorders makes treatment of borderline personality disorder difficult (van den Bosch, Verheul, Schippers, & van den Brink, 2002), makes treatment of substance use disorders difficult (Martinez-Raga, Marshall, Keaney, Ball, & Strang, 2002), and makes simultaneous treatment of both disorders difficult (Dimeff, Rizvi, Brown, & Linehan, 2000; Ross et al., 2003). Patients with borderline personality disorder and substance use disorders are more likely to engage in suicidal and other life-threatening behaviors than patients with substance use disorders alone (Kosten, Kosten, & Rounsaville, 1989); therapists who treat patients with borderline personality disorder and substance use disorders must be familiar with strategies for managing high-risk or suicidal behaviors and have access to community resources that can ensure a patient's safety (e.g., inpatient psychiatric care).

Individuals with borderline personality disorder are prone to risky, self-damaging behaviors; the presence of substance use disorders amplifies the risk. For example, the use of substances can erode the inhibitions of patients with borderline personality disorder, thereby resulting in increased risk for self-harm, suicide, and other self-damaging behaviors (Welch, 2001). Interestingly, one of the most common features shared by individuals with borderline personality disorder and substance use disorders is impulsivity (Trull, 2001). Indeed, it is possible that patients with borderline personality disorder and patients with substance use disorders share personality or temperament features that are related to impulsive behavior. In addition, patients with borderline personality disorder often engage in impulsive behaviors in an attempt to quickly relieve overwhelming emotions, and substance use has been cited as an example of this type of coping style (Bornovalova, Lejuez, Daughters, Rosenthal, & Lynch, 2005).

Treatment of patients who engage in potentially lethal, high-risk behaviors and who have substance use disorders can be challenging for therapists. It is common for therapists to feel overwhelmed, frustrated, or unmotivated when treating patients with co-occurring borderline personality disorder and substance use disorders. Patients with borderline personality disorder periodically engage in behaviors that are demoralizing to therapists (e.g., expressions of extreme hostility or anger, suicidal behavior) (Linehan, 1993a) and that leave therapists feeling incompetent or lacking in skill to help their patients (Robins & Koons, 2004). The tendency of patients with borderline personality disorder to engage in these behaviors may account for avoidance of these patients in the past by mental health practitioners. However, over the past two decades, the emergence of effective treatments for borderline personality disorder and substance use disorders justifies a more optimistic outlook on treatment of patients with co-occurring borderline personality disorder and substance use disorders. DBT (Linehan, 1993a), which was initially designed to treat suicidal women and which has been applied to borderline personality disorder with considerable success (see Robins & Chapman, 2004), addresses therapist burnout and has been adapted with promising results for patients with co-occurring borderline personality disorder and substance use disorders ("Treatment Options" contains a detailed description of DBT).

Comorbidity With Personality Disorders

Borderline personality disorder is classified by the *DSM-IV* as a "Cluster B" personality disorder. Other personality disorders in the Cluster B category of the *DSM-IV* are antisocial personality disorder, narcissistic personality disorder, and histrionic personality disorder. The *DSM-IV* indicates that these personality disorders share several common symptoms. Specifically, these personality disorders are characterized by dramatic and erratic behavior, sometimes marked by impulsivity and aggression toward self or others (American Psychiatric Association, 1994). One study reported that 30 percent of people meeting strict diagnostic criteria for borderline personality disorder also met criteria for an additional Cluster B personality disorder (Zanarini et al., 1998).

Comorbidity With Other Psychiatric Disorders

Axis I disorders often co-occur with borderline personality disorder. A study by Zanarini et al. (1998) found that 83 percent of people with borderline personality disorder met criteria for major depressive disorder; 64 percent met criteria for substance use disorders; 1.3 percent met criteria for a psychotic disorder; 88 percent met criteria for at least one anxiety disorder; and 53 percent met criteria for at least one eating disorder.

Co-occurring disorders, particularly mood disorders, are sometimes difficult to distinguish from borderline personality disorder. For example, patients with depression or bipolar disorder may be impulsive, suicidal, irritable, or paranoid, and may have mood swings or feelings of emptiness. In patients with mood disorders, these symptoms tend to wax and wane with the severity of mood episodes (e.g., episodes of major depression); these symptoms are chronic in patients with borderline personality disorder (although symptoms may wax and wane depending on level of stress). Mood disorders also may be chronic.

A careful psychiatric evaluation is necessary in order to identify symptoms of Axis I disorders and to design an effective treatment plan (see Chapter 1, Chapter 2, Chapter 3, and Chapter 4 of this volume). When clinicians identify and treat Axis I disorders (e.g., major depression) in patients with borderline personality disorders, they should determine if symptoms of borderline personality disorder change during treatment.

TREATMENT OPTIONS

Importance of Careful Assessment of Symptoms for Effective Treatment Planning

For patients who have both borderline personality disorder and substance use disorders, a comprehensive treatment to address both problems is required. First, clinicians should conduct a thorough assessment of various problem areas. During the assessment, clinicians should record the substances that the patient is using, the symptoms of borderline personality disorder that are most prominent, and the aspects of interpersonal functioning that are most impaired. Clinicians should also determine if the patient has any co-occurring disorders (e.g., depression, anxiety disorders, posttraumatic stress disorder). A treatment plan should address each of these areas.

Challenges of Treatment

Patients with borderline personality disorder can be among the most difficult patients to manage. The unstable quality of their interpersonal relationships is often reflected in their relationships with treatment staff. The anger, feelings of emptiness, or impulsivity experienced by patients with borderline personality disorder and substance use disorders can often leave clinicians feeling helpless or frustrated, which may lead to difficulties in the therapeutic relationship and may drive away clinicians, thereby resulting in failure or termination of treatment. It is challenging for clinicians to establish and build a treatment alliance with these patients and to encourage patients to continue with treatment. A clear treatment plan and a team approach are effective strategies for treatment. A team approach prevents a single clinician from feeling solely responsible for an unstable patient; team members can share the inevitable challenges and strategize.

Given the plethora of life difficulties that patients with borderline personality disorder tend to experience, therapy can feel like an exercise in stabilizing one crisis after another. It can be challenging for the therapist to adhere to the treatment plan of reducing drug and alcohol use behavior. At the same time, patients with borderline personality disorder may experience life difficulties that must be addressed before substance use behavior may be addressed (e.g., suicide attempts and other life-threatening behaviors). In planning treatment for patients with multiple problems, clinicians may find it useful to prioritize treatment targets (problem areas) and to devote the most attention to treatment targets with the highest priority (e.g., suicidal behavior). Clinicians often must accept that they may not be able to alleviate all of the patient's symptoms simultaneously.

In recent years, controlled clinical trials have tested specific treatments for borderline personality disorder. This section will review evidence-based treatments. There has been less systematic research on treatment approaches for patients with co-occurring borderline personality disorder and substance use disorders; DBT is the psychosocial treatment with the most evidence of efficacy in these patients (Linehan, 1993a, 1993b). The final subsection of this section is devoted to a detailed discussion of the use of DBT in patients with borderline personality disorder and substance use disorders.

Psychotherapeutic Approaches

Psychosocial or psychotherapeutic treatment approaches that have been systematically tested in patients with borderline personality disorder include Cognitive Behavioral Therapy (CBT; Davidson et al., 2006), Schema-Focused Therapy (another cognitive approach; Beck, Freeman, & Davis, 2004; Young, 1994), Transference-Focused Therapy (a psychodynamic approach; Giesen-Bloo et al., 2006), Interpersonal Therapy (Bellino, Zizza, Rinaldi, & Bogetto, 2006), and DBT (Linehan, 1993a, 1993b). CBT, Schema-Focused Therapy, Transference-Focused Therapy, and Interpersonal Therapy have shown some evidence of efficacy from a limited number of clinical trials; DBT has received the most study and has the most evidence for efficacy. The last subsection of this section provides a detailed description of DBT and its approach to substance-dependent patients with borderline personality disorder.

Medications

Medications can be helpful as an adjunct to psychosocial treatment for patients with borderline personality disorder and substance use disorders. There have been few controlled clinical trials of medications for borderline personality disorder; most of these studies have been conducted only in recent years, and most have not focused specifically on patients with the combination of borderline personality disorder and substance use disorders.

Clearcut co-occurring psychiatric disorders should be identified and treated with medication, if appropriate. Depression (see Chapter 1 of this volume), bipolar disorder (see Chapter 2 of this volume), anxiety disorders (see Chapter 4 of this volume) and posttraumatic stress disorders (see Chapter 3 of this volume) are all known to co-occur with borderline personality disorder and often respond well to antidepressant medications and/or mood stabilizer medications. Successful treatment of a co-occurring disorder may help to reduce the severity of a patient's symptoms of borderline personality disorder.

Similarly, clinicians should consider medications that may be helpful in treating substance use disorders, including disulfiram, naltrexone, or acamprosate for alcohol dependence and buprenorphine (Suboxone) or methadone maintenance for opioid dependence. Medication that improves symptoms of substance dependence may help to stabilize a patient and reduce the overall severity of illness.

Several types of medications have been tested as treatments for borderline personality disorder, including antidepressant medications, anticonvulsant mood stablizers, and neuroleptics (see Mercer, 2007). A recent Cochrane Library Review of pharmacological interventions for borderline personality disorder (Binks et al., 2006a) concluded that there is evidence for a substantial positive effect of antidepressant medication (although the number of well-designed studies is small). A number of symptoms of borderline personality disorder (e.g., irritability, dysphoric mood, suicidal thoughts and behaviors) resemble symptoms of depression. In addition, antidepressant medications, particularly selective serotonin reuptake inhibitors (e.g., fluoxetine (Prozac)), have been associated with improvements in impulsivity and impulsive anger among patients with personality disorders (Coccaro & Kavoussi, 1997).

Anticonvulsant medications that have been used to treat epilepsy and bipolar disorder, such as carbamazepine (Tegretol), divalproex (Depakote) and lamotrigine (Lamictal), have shown some promise in treatment of borderline personality disorder (Cowdry & Gardner, 1988; Hollander et al., 2001; Tritt et al., 2005). The purpose of using these medications is to reduce mood swings, irritability, and impulsivity (symptoms that frequently characterize borderline personality disorder). In controlled trials, anticonvulsants, such as valproate (Depakote), have been found to be effective for patients with explosive anger (Donovan et al., 2000; Hollander, Swann, Coccaro, Jiang, & Smith, 2005).

Atypical neuroleptic medications, such as aripiprazole (Abilify), quetiapine (Seroquel), and olanzapine (Zyprexa), have shown some promise in controlled trials for treatment of borderline personality disorder (Nickel et al., 2006; Soler et al., 2005; Villeneuve & Lemelin, 2005). These medications are used to treat psychosis in patients with schizophrenia and mood disorders, and they are often helpful as adjuncts in the treatment of bipolar disorder and other mood disorders without psychosis. The rationale for using atypical neuroleptic medications for treatment of borderline personality disorder is similar to the rationale for using anticonvulsant medications: atypical neuroleptics may reduce mood swings, depression, impulsivity, and irritability. Atypical neuroleptics may target the transient stress-related paranoia that some patients with borderline personality disorder experience.

In treatment of borderline personality disorder, the management of medications must be carefully integrated into the psychosocial treatment plan. Dialectical behavior treatment for patients with substance use disorders (DBT-SUD) provides five useful guiding principles for managing medication treatment in patients with substance use disorders. First, medications with little or no lethal potential should be prescribed. Prescribers should take particular care with regard to dosage when prescribing medications to patients with a history of drug abuse and overdose (e.g., clinicians might give these patients only a small amount of medication at each visit instead of entrusting patients with several weeks' worth of medication). Second, it is important that prescribers ensure that the prescribed medication regimen is kept to the simplest possible combination. Third, prescribers should avoid overprescribing medication, should consider potential drug interactions, and should closely monitor side effects. Fourth, the choice of medications prescribed should always be guided by knowledge of the most current, rigorously controlled efficacy studies of medications. Fifth, since there is high value placed on speed of clinical improvement, medications (including appropriate drug replacement medications) should be prescribed at a maximally effective dosage.

Dialectical Behavior Therapy

DBT originally was designed to address the problems of suicidal women, but Linehan (1993a) tailored the treatment to the problems of patients with borderline personality disorder, in whom there is a high prevalence of suicidal behavior. Several well-controlled trials support the efficacy of DBT for borderline personality disorder. In fact, DBT is the only treatment currently considered to be "efficacious and specific" for borderline personality disorder (Robins & Chapman, 2004) or for any personality disorder (Linehan, Davidson, Lynch, & Sanderson, 2005).

Theoretical Foundations of Dialectical Behavior Therapy. DBT is based on Linehan's biosocial theory of borderline personality disorder (1993a) and also is rooted in dialectical philosophy, Zen practice, and behavioral science. Dialectical philosophy is at the core of DBT and is an adoption of thought posited by Marx (Marx & Engels, 1970). Dialectical thinking posits that reality consists of a continual interplay of opposing forces, (i.e., thesis and antithesis). Any statement (thesis) naturally leads to consideration of its opposite (antithesis). Thesis and antithesis exist in dialectical tension until they are synthesized. For example, the notion that therapists need to push patients with borderline personality disorder to change their destructive behavior (thesis) can be countered with the opposing statement that therapists need to accept their patients' destructive behavior (antithesis). Either position on its own is incomplete: by pushing a patient too hard to change, a therapist risks pushing the patient out of treatment; by accepting the patient's dysfunctional behavior, the therapist is unlikely to help the patient to change his/her behavior.

The primary dialectic in DBT centers around two poles: acceptance and change. Acceptance refers to the stance that all behaviors are acceptable and worthy of validation. For example, while patients may resist acknowledging that they were abused during childhood, they cannot change their childhood history and must accept and acknowledge it in order to improve their present situation. At the same time, as a patient works to accept his/her past, the therapist works with the patient toward making changes in the patient's life that will alleviate suffering. Instead of simply soothing a patient's distress or strictly adhering to a therapeutic regimen that constantly pushes for change, DBT requires both acceptance and change (as illustrated by a therapist's statement, "I understand why you want to use drugs—they reduce your shame and anger; we must work on finding ways to reduce shame and anger without the use of drugs.").

A focus on the synthesis of polarities and opposites helps to reduce standoffs between the patient and the therapist. For example, in the above case example (see "Case Presentation"), if, during a treatment session, the patient argues that the therapist's suggested alternate driving route to the office (which will ensure that the patient avoids the area where he has purchased heroin) will add too much time to his commute, the therapist should acknowledge the patient's concern about a longer commute and should suggest that the patient consider modifying his work hours (to avoid rush-hour traffic) or to car-pool with a colleague (who will prevent the patient from purchasing heroin). Adopting a dialectical philosophy allows the therapist in the above case example to accept the patient's position, while not giving up on the goal of helping the patient to avoid the area where he has purchased heroin. In dialectics, the key is to find a way to synthesize the thesis and antithesis. Therapists should not become wedded to a particular stance or solution.

Many of the mindfulness strategies and skills in DBT derive from Zen practice (Hanh, 1987). Use of mindfulness-related skills requires radical acceptance of reality and the stance that everything "is as it should be" (Linehan, 1993b). These strategies encourage patients to accept troubling thoughts and feelings (rather than fighting them or trying to "put them out of their mind"), thereby making the thoughts and feelings less distressing. In addition, the therapist uses validation strategies that are consistent with strategies of client-centered and emotion-focused approaches in order to convey acceptance of the patient and to help the patient to learn to validate himself/herself. These acceptance-based approaches are balanced with a strong emphasis on behavioral principles and change-based strategies, such as skills training, exposure, behavior modification, problem solving, and cognitive modification, among others.

DBT is a comprehensive treatment that addresses the numerous serious life difficulties that patients with borderline personality disorder experience. DBT aims to fulfill five important functions: (1) increasing patients' skills and capabilities, (2) increasing and maintaining patients' motivation for change, (3) generalizing or transferring treatment gains to patients' natural environment, (4) structuring the treatment in an effective way, and (5) helping therapists improve their skills and maintain their motivation in treating challenging patients. In order to serve these functions, DBT has several components: (1) outpatient individual psychotherapy that is focused on transferring skills to the natural environment, maintaining and enhancing motivation, and dealing with crises; (2) outpatient group skills training, which is focused on increasing behavioral skills in the areas of mindfulness, interpersonal effectiveness, emotion regulation, and distress tolerance; and (3) a therapist consultation team that provides therapists with support, encouragement, training, and supervision. Patients with borderline personality disorder may also require pharmacotherapy, case management, and/or inpatient psychiatric treatment during times of crisis. Patients must commit to treatment for a set period of time (often twelve months).

One of the hallmarks of DBT is therapists' use of a hierarchy of treatment targets; this hierarchy helps therapists to determine which behaviors should be addressed during a session. Patients with borderline personality disorder often present with a myriad of life difficulties, and it can be challenging to determine treatment priorities. Consequently, Linehan (1993a) developed a framework to guide therapists in their organization of treatment targets: at the top of the hierarchy are life-threatening behaviors (e.g., suicidal behavior, self-injurious behavior), followed by behaviors that interfere with success in therapy, and followed by behaviors that interfere with the patient's quality of life.

Dialectical Behavior Therapy's Conceptualization of Borderline Personality Disorder. Linehan's biosocial theory (Linehan, 1993a), on which the theoretical foundation of DBT partly rests, proposes that borderline personality disorder results from an interplay between biology/temperament and a particular type of environment in which a person is reared, which produces pervasive difficulties in regulating emotions. Patents with borderline personality disorder are born with a temperament that is characterized by emotional vulnerability or quick, strong, and long-lasting emotional reactions to events. Unfortunately, people often have difficulty understanding or responding effectively to children with temperaments that are characterized by intense emotional reactions. According to Linehan's biosocial theory, individuals with borderline personality disorder are often reared in environments in which caregivers punish, ignore, or trivialize the child's communication of thoughts and emotions. The environment fails to validate the child because the caregiver may not possess the skills required for raising the child, may become overwhelmed by the child's intense emotional reactions and fail to respond effectively, or may have problems with emotion dysregulation. The invalidating environment might involve sexual, physical, and emotional abuse (Wagner & Linehan, 1997).

In a self-perpetuating cycle, the child's intense emotional reactions prohibit validation by the child's environment, thereby exacerbating the child's tendency to display intense emotional reactions. Ultimately, the child is left bereft of skills needed to manage emotions. Persons with borderline personality disorder also have difficulty diverting their attention from the emotions elicited by an event. As a result, individuals with borderline personality disorder often have difficulty thinking, paying attention, problem solving, and inhibiting impulsive behaviors. Thus, many of the behaviors associated with borderline personality disorder either result directly from extreme emotional arousal or represent ways that patients cope with overwhelming emotions (e.g., self-injury, suicide attempts, binge eating, substance abuse).

Standard Dialectical Behavior Therapy for Treatment of Substance Use Disorders.
Standard DBT has been applied in mixed settings to patients with borderline personality disorder and patients with borderline personality disorder and a substance use disorder (van den Bosch et al., 2002; Verheul et al., 2003). A study conducted in the Netherlands compared DBT to treatment as usual in women who met criteria for borderline personality disorder (n = 58), many of whom had a comorbid substance use disorder (53 percent). Compared with patients receiving treatment as usual, patients receiving DBT had significantly greater decreases in total number of parasuicidal acts and in impulse control problem behaviors (e.g., binge eating, gambling, reckless driving). In addition, larger differences between DBT and treatment as usual were found among patients with a high frequency of parasuicidal behaviors (i.e., 14 to over 1,000 instances of parasuicidal behavior over lifetime) in comparison to patients with lower frequencies of parasuicidal behavior (i.e., 0 to 14 instances of parasuicidal behavior over lifetime). A significantly higher proportion of patients receiving DBT (63 percent) continued with the same therapist for the entire twelve months in comparison to patients receiving treatment as usual (23 percent). However, no differences were found between the two treatment conditions in terms of reduction of substance abuse. The investigators noted that standard DBT generally does not specifically target substance use unless treatment of substance use is an important goal for the patient (van den Bosch et al., 2002).

Researchers at the Centre for Addiction and Mental Health (CAMH) in Canada compared standard DBT to treatment as usual in women with borderline personality disorder and substance use disorders (n = 27, mean age = 36) (McMain, 2004). In comparison to patients who received treatment as usual, patients who received DBT showed greater reductions in suicidal and parasuicidal behaviors and greater decreases in alcohol use. However, the treatment groups did not differ in terms of reduction in use of substances other than alcohol. According to a twelve-month assessment, patients who received DBT maintained the reductions in self-harm and substance use behaviors that were demonstrated at four and eight months; however, between the eight-month assessment and the twelve-month assessment, patients who received treatment as usual experienced a "rebound" of self-harm behaviors. Finally, patients who received DBT and patients who received treatment as usual did not differ significantly in treatment retention. This study had many limitations, including a small sample size and an absence of follow-up assessments following treatment; in addition, the treatment as usual was not manualized (unlike DBT). Findings from this study suggest that treatment of substance use disorders may require a more targeted form of DBT.

Despite enthusiasm for DBT, further study is needed. Binks et al. expressed their skepticism of psychological therapies for borderline personality disorder in a recent Cochrane Library Review: "[although] some of the problems frequently encountered by people with borderline personality disorder may be amenable to talking/behavioral treatments, ... [available studies] are too few and small to [inspire] ... full confidence in their results" (2006b, p. 21). A recent study that compared DBT, Transference-Focused Psychotherapy, and supportive treatment (Clarkin et al., 2007) found that patients in all three groups showed improvement in several symptom domains. Although this study included adherence coding for DBT, the method for coding adherence was not developed or approved by the developer of the treatment. In addition, it is unclear whether training of therapists who provided DBT was sufficient or commensurate with the training of therapists in other studies of DBT (e.g., Linehan et al., 2006). Patients with active substance dependence were excluded from this study.

Modified Dialectical Behavior Therapy for Treatment of Substance Use Disorders.
When Linehan and Dimeff (1997) began to apply standard DBT to the treatment of individuals with borderline personality disorder and substance use disorders, they encountered several challenges: patients with borderline personality disorder and substance use disorders often have difficulty forming an attachment to their therapist, frequently miss therapy appointments or arrive late, frequently drop out of therapy, and often have difficulties with housing, finances, abusive relationships, unemployment, and the law. These problems often frustrate therapists and lead them to feel discouraged and apathetic.

Techniques used in standard DBT were adapted to address the challenges of treating patients with both borderline personality disorder and substance use disorders. To modify standard DBT techniques for use in patients with borderline personality disorder and substance use disorders, Linehan et al. (1999, 2002) followed guidelines for the development of psychosocial treatment that were formulated at workshops of the National Institute of Mental Health (NIMH) and the National Institute on Drug Abuse (NIDA; e.g., Rounsaville, Carroll, & Onken, 2001). DBT-SUD targets drug use and abuse, and therapy sessions focus on reduction of use of all substances (regardless of the amount that the patient is using, the frequency with which the patient is using, and the legality of the substance). DBT-SUD shares many elements with other treatments for substance use disorders: the goal of increasing patients' coping skills and emotion regulation skills, a focus on motivation to change (by modifying inhibitions and reinforcement contingencies), an emphasis on preventing relapse, and the inclusion of accommodating clinicians, who are available to speak to patients by telephone, permit patients to frequently reschedule their appointments, and are widely available for appointments. Treatments for substance dependence that overlap with DBT-SUD include Higgins's regimen of contingency management in conjunction with the Community Reinforcement Approach (Higgins et al., 1993) for cocaine dependence and Marlatt's relapse prevention approach for alcohol dependence (Witkiewicz & Marlatt, 2004).

DBT-SUD treatment techniques that apply specifically to substance use are referred to as "the path to clear mind" (Rosenthal, Lynch, & Linehan, 2005). To increase the likelihood that patients attend sessions and stay in treatment, strategies that emphasize outreach efforts to engage patients were developed. These strategies are called attachment strategies. A therapist who calls a patient or sends a patient a card after the patient has failed to attend a therapy session is utilizing attachment strategies.

Like standard DBT, DBT-SUD requires therapists to address life-threatening behaviors and any behaviors that may interfere with therapy before addressing other problems. However, the overall goal of DBT-SUD is abstinence from drugs (which will improve patients' quality of life). Therapists work with patients to (1) decrease use of substances, including use of illicit drugs and prescription drugs, (2) ensure an appropriate dose of a maintenance medication, (3) decrease the intensity and frequency of cravings to use drugs, (4) decrease physical discomfort associated with withdrawal, (5) decrease behaviors linked to drug use, and (6) limit the opportunities that patients have to use drugs. Strategies of acceptance that are practiced in standard DBT (Linehan, 1993b) may be used during treatment of patients with substance use disorders in order to help patients tolerate physical pain and psychological distress associated with drug withdrawal.

Although the goal of DBT-SUD is abstinence from drugs, some patients with borderline personality disorder and substance use disorders are unable to permanently discontinue their drug use. DBT-SUD permits therapists to use harm-reduction approaches in anticipation of the possibility of relapse to substance use (Marlatt & Gordon, 1985). Harm-reduction approaches aim to reduce harm from substance use (rather than to encourage lifelong abstinence from drug use). The use of harm-reduction approaches to reduce the frequency and intensity of drug relapse and the use of abstinence approaches to lengthen the intervals between periods of use is called dialectical abstinence. If a therapist utilized DBT-SUD techniques to treat the patient in the above case example (see "Case Presentation"), the therapist would encourage the patient to remain abstinent while he was abstinent and encourage the patient to commit again to abstinence when he relapsed (rather than criticizing the patient for relapsing).

DBT-SUD includes individual therapy sessions and group therapy sessions. DBT-SUD may also include use of pharmacotherapy (see "Medications") and case management. DBT-SUD also utilizes a therapist consultation team, which provides therapists with peer support for challenging patients (not discussed in this chapter; see Chapman & Linehan, 2005; Linehan, 1993a).

Individual Therapy. Individual therapy usually consists of fifty- to sixty-minute sessions once per week. Individual therapy sessions during the early stages of treatment (referred to as pretreatment sessions) include psychoeducation on borderline personality disorder and DBT-SUD, discussion of the differences between DBT-SUD and other types of treatment, and an emphasis on the patient's commitment to reducing substance use and self-harm and eliminating suicidal behavior. The following dialogue illustrates how a therapist who is treating the patient in the above case example (see "Case Presentation") might motivate the patient to commit to treatment.

Therapist: "Are you willing to agree that our goal is for you to work toward not using drugs?" (The therapist asks the patient to commit to treatment.)

Patient: "I think so."

Therapist: "It's up to you. This is going to be a lot of work. Wouldn't it be easier if you had a therapist who thought that heroin wasn't a serious problem?" (The therapist plays "devil's advocate" to strengthen the patient's commitment to treatment.)

Patient: "Yes, probably. What's the big deal anyway?"

Therapist: "I don't know. Perhaps you could have a reasonable life on heroin. You could continue to hide it from your boss and your sister, and things would go along okay." (The therapist plays "devil's advocate.")

Patient: "You might have a point."

Therapist: "It is up to you. You could continue to use heroin. If you do, you may get kicked out of the apartment, and your girlfriend already told you that she is going to leave you if that happens." (The therapist highlights the patient's freedom to choose to use drugs and lists the consequences.)

Patient: "I'm here to quit drugs. I can't lose my girlfriend; I'd kill myself. I have to stop."

Therapist: "It sounds like we agree that stopping heroin is one of our most important goals, right?"

Patient: "Right."

After patients complete the pretreatment sessions, individual therapy sessions focus on reduction of cravings, self-harm, suicidal behavior, and emotional distress through use of a diary card and other techniques (e.g., role playing), use of chain analyses to understand problematic behaviors and to determine the focus of therapy sessions, and reduction of "apparently irrelevant behaviors." Between sessions, therapists may provide telephone consultations, in which therapists help patients to apply skills that they have learned during individual sessions or group sessions and provide crisis intervention and coaching in order to discourage patients from engaging in drug use or life-threatening behaviors.

Diary cards are used by patients to record drug use, emotional distress, suicidal behavior, self-harm, and other behaviors, and aid therapists each week in determining which behaviors to target during sessions (e.g., heroin use). Therapists may conduct a chain analysis in which they analyze a problematic behavior, the events that led to the specific problematic behavior, and the events that followed the problematic behavior. Unlike a behavioral analysis (Bandura & Goldman 1995; Cone & Hawkins, 1997), which yields a broad conceptualization of the conditions that typically influence a patient's behavior, a chain analysis is a detailed analysis of one specific instance of a problematic behavior (Chapman & Linehan, 2005). To conduct a chain analysis, a therapist must ask numerous questions (e.g., When did you first feel an urge to use drugs? Where were you? What were you doing?) in order to dissect the patient's problematic behavior and to elicit information that will help the therapist and the patient find solutions to problems (sometimes called solution analysis). For example, if a therapist treating the patient in the above case example (see "Case Presentation") conducted a chain analysis to uncover the chain of events that led the patient to purchase heroin following one of his recent arguments with his girlfriend, the therapist might discover that the patient felt shame after the argument and then experienced strong urges to use heroin, which he purchased from a drug dealer (whose pager number was posted on the patient's refrigerator). Using the information collected from the chain analysis, the therapist might encourage the patient to remove from the refrigerator the note with the drug dealer's pager number, and might help the patient to identify healthy methods for coping with strong emotions like shame (i.e., alternatives to drug use), such as placing one's face in ice water, which reduces arousal of the sympathetic nervous system.

Patients learn a variety of techniques to reduce urges to use drugs, including removal of environmental cues to use drugs, acceptance of situations (instead of escape from a situation through drug use), and "urge surfing," a skill in which patients observe urges come and go like waves on an ocean (Marlatt & Gordon, 1985). In our experience, techniques that divert patients' attention from cravings for drugs are the easiest for patients with borderline personality disorder and substance use disorders to learn and are often the most useful. As patients master these techniques, they are encouraged to seek out environments that will reinforce abstinence, including Alcoholics Anonymous meetings or Narcotics Anonymous meetings, stable employment and housing, and groups of peers who do not use drugs.

Patients also learn skills to help them to identify and reduce "apparently irrelevant behaviors" (similar to "apparently irrelevant decisions," defined by Marlatt and Gordon, 1985). Apparently irrelevant behaviors are acts, thought patterns, or emotional responses that seem irrelevant but that often lead patients to use drugs (e.g., driving by the house of a drug dealer while traveling home from the office, socializing with drug dealers and peers who use drugs, renting an apartment in an area that is known for drug trafficking).

Group Therapy. Each group therapy session is usually two hours or two and one-half hours in length, consists of six to ten people, is led by two coleaders (one leader teaches skills and reviews homework, and the second leader attends to the group process and tries to balance the change-oriented approach of the other leader with acceptance, validation, and encouragement), and focuses on skill-building, which is designed to enhance patients' capabilities in four skill domains: mindfulness, distress tolerance, emotion regulation, and interpersonal effectiveness (see Linehan, 1993b). Skill-building approaches in DBT-SUD and standard DBT are similar, except DBT-SUD requires therapists to teach patients several additional skills that target problems common in patients with substance use disorders and borderline personality disorder (e.g., alternative rebellion).

Although mindfulness skills are primarily derived from Zen practice, they are consistent with Western contemplative practices. Mindfulness requires openness to the present moment (i.e., "keeping one's consciousness alive to the present reality," as Hanh stated (1987, p. 11). Linehan (1993a) distilled the practice of mindfulness into three discrete "what" skills (observe, describe, participate) and three distinct "how" skills (nonjudgmentally, one-mindfully, and effectively). DBT also describes three states of mind ("emotion mind," "reasonable mind," and "wise mind"). DBT-SUD includes states of mind that are specific to substance use problems: (1) "clear mind" (state of mind in which patients are likely to abstain from drugs), (2) "addict mind" (state of mind focused on obtaining and using drugs), and (3) "clean mind" (state of mind in which patients are naïve about the risks of drug use). DBT-SUD aims to encourage patients to spend more time in "clear mind." Since patients with borderline personality disorder and substance use disorders may use drug use as a way to rebel against societal norms, these patients may be taught the skill of alternate rebellion; patients are encouraged to engage in other forms of rebellion (e.g., engage in social action, protest, modify their clothing style) instead of drug use.

In both standard DBT and DBT-SUD, patients are taught distress tolerance skills to help them to tolerate distressing emotions, thoughts, and situations (e.g., distract themselves, self-sooth, improve the moment, and accept the current reality). Linehan and her colleagues have identified additional skills that may be taught to patients with substance use disorders, including adaptive denial and burning bridges (to drug use) (Linehan & Dimeff, 1997). Adaptive denial requires patients to block thoughts that are intolerable or overwhelming and that would likely lead to drug use (Dimeff et al., 2000). Burning bridges (to drug use) eliminates options to use drugs and access to drugs; after committing themselves to abstinence, patients avoid contact with drug-dealers and friends who use drugs and avoid situations in which patients used drugs. Distress tolerance skills allow patients to use adaptive ways to respond to difficult situations (instead of using drugs or engaging in self-harm behaviors).

Emotion regulation skills help patients to modify their emotional experiences and to reduce their vulnerability to unwanted emotions (Linehan, 1993b). All of the emotion regulation skills that are taught to patients undergoing standard DBT may be taught to patients undergoing DBT-SUD. To help patients reduce their sensitivity and reactivity to events that elicit emotions, clinicians teach patients the skill of "opposite action." Drawing upon the same principles as the principles of exposure therapy, the "opposite action" skill allows patients to break the link between an emotion and a stimulus (Foa & Kozak 1986; Wolpe, 1990). After a therapist helps a patient to identify the emotions that he/she is feeling, the therapist asks the patient how he/she intends to act (e.g., patients who experience anxiety may have an urge to escape the situation) and then encourages the patient to determine if the emotion is justified by the situation; if the emotion is not justified by the situation, then the patient is encouraged to act in the opposite way to the way that he/she intended to act. For example, since the fear of leaving the house that a patient with agoraphobia experiences is not justified, the therapist should encourage the patient to perform the opposite action (i.e., leave the house repeatedly). The following dialogue illustrates how a therapist who is treating the patient in the above case example (see "Case Presentation") might teach the patient emotion regulation skills.

Therapist:	"It sounds like you felt shame when your girlfriend left the apartment after your argument with her."
Patient:	"Yes. I wish that I hadn't yelled at her. I lose control and say horrible things."
Therapist:	"Did you feel shame mainly over what you said or about overusing drugs again?"
Patient:	"I guess that I felt shame over both."
Therapist:	"Interesting. "Let's discuss the shame that you felt when you yelled at your girlfriend. Do you think that this feeling was justified?"
Patient:	"It's justified."
Therapist:	"I'm not sure about that. Shame is justified when your behavior may result in the termination of a relationship. Do you really think that your girlfriend will leave you because you yelled at her?"

Patient: "No. Actually, she puts up with a lot. She won't leave me, but she will be really hurt and sad."

Therapist: "Yes: she will be sad. If you hurt your girlfriend, a feeling of guilt would be justified, right? Guilt is justified when your behaviors go against your values. Verbally abusing your girlfriend is against one of your core values. Let's agree that you felt guilt, not shame. How do you address justified guilt?"

Patient: "I learned in skills training class that I should solve the problem or try to repair my relationship with my girlfriend."

Therapist: "What could you do?"

Patient: "I could commit to not yelling at her. I could show her that I intend to take this commitment seriously: I could act sweetly to her and tell her what I am doing to ensure that I will not yell at her. I also could work toward a goal of not using drugs."

Therapist: "You read my mind. The shame that you felt about yelling at your girlfriend was not justified. You are justified to feel shame over your drug use. Your girlfriend probably will leave you if you continue to use heroin. In this situation, you cannot apply the skill of "opposite action" (i.e., continuing to use drugs); you could apply the skill of "opposite action" if your girlfriend would not leave you. You need to stop using drugs; then you will not feel shame when you see your girlfriend."

Since erratic relationships are common among patients with borderline personality disorder and substance use disorders and may trigger patients to use drugs, patients are taught interpersonal effectiveness skills to help them to refuse unwanted requests (e.g., to use drugs), to request that people change their behavior, to navigate interpersonal conflict, to end relationships with people who use drugs or sell drugs, and to build adaptive relationships that do not increase risk of drug use. Use of interpersonal effectiveness skills requires assertiveness.

Case Management. Case management, which is considered an optional component of DBT-SUD, provides support to therapists with patients who cannot secure regular housing, food, or basic health care services. The case manager does not provide or procure specific services that will address patients' problems of inadequate housing, food, and health care but will provide patients with skills coaching that augments the skills coaching that patients receive during individual therapy sessions. The case manager serves as a resource for therapists seeking referrals for particular services for their patients and as a consultant on patients' progress in treatment.

Studies on the Effectiveness of Dialectical Behavior Therapy for Substance Use Disorders. Several studies have evaluated the effectiveness of DBT-SUD in the treatment of borderline personality disorder and substance use disorders. The first study to evaluate DBT-SUD was a randomized controlled trial that compared DBT-SUD with treatment as usual for women (ages 18-45) who met criteria for borderline personality disorder and substance use disorders (Linehan et al., 1999). Subjects were matched for age, severity of drug dependence, readiness to change, and global adjustment, and were randomly assigned to DBT-SUD or treatment as usual (treatment as usual consisted of ongoing therapy with either a clinician with whom a patient had already started treatment or with a local treatment provider who offered substance abuse treatment or mental health treatment). Clinical outcomes were assessed after four months, eight months, and twelve months of treatment and at a sixteen-month follow-up visit. In comparison to patients who received treatment as usual, patients who received DBT-SUD showed greater reductions in drug use over the course of treatment and at follow-up and had a better retention rate. In addition, according to the sixteen-month follow-up assessment, patients who received DBT-SUD demonstrated greater improvements in social functioning and global functioning than patients who received treatment as usual.

Linehan et al. (2002) examined the efficacy of DBT-SUD to treat women with borderline personality disorder and heroin dependence. DBT-SUD was compared to a manualized treatment called Comprehensive Validation Therapy Plus 12-Step (CVT-12S), which is similar to DBT but which does not include strategies to modify patients' behavior and cognition. This study design controlled for time of access to treatment, academic treatment setting, and therapist experience and commitment. Patients were treated with DBT or CVT-12S for twelve months. Patients in both treatment conditions received opiate agonist replacement medication (levo-alpha-acetylmethadol (LAAM)). Both patients who received DBT and patients who received CVT-12S showed significant reduction in opiate use over the course of treatment and showed significantly increased global functioning and reduced psychopathology over twelve months of treatment and at follow-up. However, in comparison to patients who received CVT-12S, patients who received DBT showed more sustained abstinence from opiate use according to a sixteen-month follow-up assessment and were significantly more accurate in their self-report of opiate use (indexed against urinalysis results). Interestingly, the dropout rate for DBT was 36 percent, while the dropout rate for CVT-12S was 0 percent. Results from this study should be interpreted with caution; the sample size was small (n = 23), and three of the four patients who received DBT and who dropped out of treatment were patients of the same therapist.

In a small pilot study, DBT-SUD was evaluated for the treatment of three women (age 22-37) with borderline personality disorder and methamphetamine use (Dimeff et al., 2000). Two of the three patients completed twelve months of DBT-SUD treatment; these two patients were abstinent from methamphetamine after six months of treatment and remained abstinent through the sixteen-month follow-up assessment.

Findings from these studies suggest that DBT-SUD may be an effective treatment for patients with borderline personality disorder and substance use disorders. Additional randomized clinical trials of this treatment must be conducted before DBT-SUD may be considered a well-established treatment for borderline personality disorder and substance use disorders.

Treatment Planning for the Case Example

For twelve months, JN received DBT, including fifty-two weeks of individual therapy and group-based skills training, in addition to buprenorphine/naloxone (an opiate replacement medication). At the beginning of treatment, JN used heroin five to six days per week, burned himself once per week, and experienced intense, episodic suicidal ideation several times per month. By the end of treatment, he had gone for eight months without burning himself and had gone for three months without using heroin. He had a brief relapse four weeks prior to termination, but, following his relapse, he reestablished his regimen of buprenorphine/naloxone and committed himself to abstinence. By the end of treatment, JN experienced suicidal ideation approximately twice per month. He found a job and was able to maintain his relationship with his girlfriend; he moved into her apartment, which is located far from the area in which JN bought heroin. Although he continued to report emotional vulnerability, he made frequent and effective use of his emotion regulation skills. Following the advice of his therapist, he took a different route home from work in order to avoid the area where he bought heroin.

SUMMARY

It is hoped that this chapter has provided an introduction to the diagnosis and treatment of borderline personality disorder in patients with substance use disorders. The presence of both borderline personality disorder and substance use disorders poses serious and unique challenges in treatment. Work by Linehan et al. (2002) and others (Verheul et al., 2003) has produced a package of interventions that has considerable promise for the treatment of borderline personality disorder and substance use disorders. DBT-SUD may be the behavioral treatment of choice for reducing impulse control problems and parasuicidal behaviors (Verheul et al., 2003), and it has shown promise in the treatment of self-harm behaviors, emotion dysregulation, interpersonal chaos, and substance use. Studies that have examined other psychotherapeutic approaches have yielded some evidence of efficacy (Beck, Freeman, & Davis, 2004; Bellino, Zizza, Rinaldi, & Bogetto, 2006; Davidson et al., 2006; Giesen-Bloo et al., 2006; Young, 1994). Medications may be helpful in management of substance use disorders (e.g., buprenorphine or methadone) and Axis I disorders (including bipolar disorder, major depression, anxiety disorders, and posttraumatic stress disorder) in patients with borderline personality disorder. Studies support efficacy of antidepressant medications, anticonvulsant mood stabilizers, and atypical neuroleptics as treatments for borderline personality disorder. However, there is need for more research, and promising findings require replication by different investigators with larger and more diverse patient populations. In the interplay between science and practice, the challenges and successes of clinicians and treatment developers will advance treatments, thereby cultivating hope for patients with borderline personality disorder and substance use disorders.

Suggestions for Further Reading

For readers who wish to study further in this area, we recommend:

- American Psychiatric Association. (2001). Practice guideline for the treatment of patients with borderline personality disorder. *American Journal of Psychiatry, 158*(10 Suppl.), 1-52.

- Behavioral Tech, LLC: http://www.behavioraltech.com/.

- Chapman, A. L., & Glatz, K. L. (2007). *The borderline personality disorder survival guide: Everything you need to know about living with BPD*. Oakland, CA: New Harbinger Publications.

- Linehan, M. M. (1993). *Cognitive-behavioral treatment of borderline personality disorder*. New York: Guilford Press.

- Linehan, M. M. (1993) *Skills training manual for treating borderline personality disorder*. New York: Guilford Press.

- Linehan, M. M., Davidson, G. C., Lynch, T. R., & Sanderson, C. (2005). Technique factors in treating personality disorder. In L. G. Castonguay & L. E. Beutler (Eds.), *Principles of therapeutic change that work* (pp. 239-252). New York: Oxford University Press.

References

American Psychiatric Association. (1994). *Diagnostic and statistical manual of mental disorders (*4th ed.). Washington, DC: Author.

Bandura, M. M., & Goldman, C. (1995). Expanding the contextual analysis of clinical problems. *Cognitive and Behavioral Practice, 2*, 119-141.

Beck, A. T., Freeman, A., & Davis, D. D. (2004). *Cognitive therapy of personality disorders* (2nd ed.). New York, NY: Guilford Press.

Bellino, S., Zizza, M., Rinaldi, C., & Bogetto, F. (2006). Combined treatment of major depression in patients with borderline personality disorder: A comparison with pharmacotherapy. *Canadian Journal of Psychiatry, 51*, 453-460.

Binks, C. A., Fenton, M., McCarthy, L., Lee, T., Adams, C. E., & Duggan, C. (2006a). Pharmacological interventions for people with borderline personality disorder. *Cochrane Database of Systematic Reviews, 1*, CD005653.

Binks, C. A., Fenton, M., McCarthy, L., Lee, T., Adams, C. E., & Duggan, C. (2006b). Psychological therapies for people with borderline personality disorder. *Cochrane Database of Systematic Reviews, 1*, CD005652.

Bohus, M., Limberger, M. F., Frank, U., Chapman, A. L., Kühler, T., & Stieglitz, R. D. (2007). Psychometric properties of the Borderline Symptom List (BSL). *Psychopathology, 40*, 126-132.

Bornovalova, M. A., Lejuez, C. W., Daughters, S. B., Rosenthal, M. Z., & Lynch, T. R. (2005). Impulsivity as a common process across borderline personality and substance use disorders. *Clinical Psychology Review, 25*, 790-812.

Brooner, R. K., King, V. L., Kidorf, M., & Schmidt, C. W., Jr., & Bigelow, G. E. (1997). Psychiatric and substance use comorbidity among treatment-seeking opioid abusers. *Archives of General Psychiatry, 54,* 71-80.

Chapman, A. L., & Linehan, M. M. (2005). Dialectical behavior therapy for borderline personality disorder. In M. Zanarini (Ed.), *Borderline personality disorder* (pp. 211-242). New York: Taylor and Francis.

Clarkin, J. F., Widiger, T. A., Frances, A., Hurt, S. W., & Gilmore, M. (1983). Prototypic typology and the borderline personality disorder. *Journal of Abnormal Psychology, 92,* 263-275.

Clarkin, J. F, Levy, K. N., Lezenweger, W. F., & Kernberg, O. F. (2007). Evaluating three treatments for borderline personality disorder: A multiwave study. *American Journal of Psychiatry, 164*, 922-928.

Coccaro E. F., & Kavoussi R. J. (1997). Fluoxetine and impulsive aggressive behavior in personality-disordered subjects. *Archives of General Psychiatry, 54*, 1081-1088.

Cone J. D., & Hawkins R. P. (1997). *Behavioral assessment: New directions in clinical psychology.* New York: Brunner/Mazel.

Cowdry, R. W., & Gardner, D. L. (1988). Pharmacotherapy of borderline personality disorder: Alprazolam, carbamazepine, trifluoperazine, and tranylcypromine. *Archives of General Psychiatry, 45*, 111-119.

Cowdry, R. W., Pickar, D., & Davies, R. (1985). Symptoms and EEG findings in the borderline syndrome. *International Journal of Psychiatry Medicine, 15*, 201-211.

Davidson, K., Norrie, J., Tyrer, P., Gumley, A., Tata, P., Murray, H., et al. (2006). The effectiveness of cognitive behavior therapy for borderline personality disorder: Results from the borderline personality disorder study of cognitive therapy (BOSCOT) trial. *Journal of Personality Disorders, 20*, 450-465.

Dimeff, L., Rizvi, S. L., Brown, M., & Linehan, M. M. (2000). Dialectical behavior therapy for substance abuse: A pilot application to methamphetamine-dependent women with borderline personality disorder. *Cognitive and Behavioral Practice, 7*, 457-468.

Donovan, S. J., Stewart, J. W., Nunes, E. V., Quitkin, F. M., Parides, M., Daniel, W., et al. (2000). Divalproex treatment for youth with explosive temper and mood lability: A double-blind, placebo-controlled crossover design. *American Journal of Psychiatry, 157*, 818-820.

First, M. B., Spitzer, R. L., Gibbon, M., & Williams, J. B. W. (1997). Structured Clinical Interview for DSM-IV Axis II Personality Disorders (SCID-II). Washington, DC: American Psychiatric Publishing.

Foa, E. B., & Kozak, M. J. (1986). Emotional processing of fear: Exposure to corrective information. *Psychological Bulletin, 99,* 20-35.

Frances, A. J., Fyer, M., & Clarkin, J. F. (1986). Personality and suicide. *Annals of the New York Academy of Sciences, 487*, 281-293.

Giesen-Bloo, J., van Dyck, R., Spinhoven, P., van Tilburg, W., Dirksen, C., van Asselt, T., et al. (2006). Outpatient psychotherapy for borderline personality disorder: Randomized trial of schema-focused therapy versus transference-focused psychotherapy. *Archives of General Psychiatry, 63*, 649-658.

Gunderson, J. G. (1984). *Borderline personality disorder*. Washington DC: American Psychiatric Press.

Grove, W. M., & Tellegen, A. (1991). Problems in the classification of personality disorders. *Journal of Personality Disorders, 5*, 31-41.

Hanh, T. N. (1987). *The miracle of mindfulness: A manual on meditation* (rev. ed; M. Ho, Trans.). Boston: Beacon Press.

Hasin, D. S., Samet, S., Nunes, E., Meydan, J., Matseoane, K., & Waxman, R. (2006). Diagnosis of comorbid disorders in substance users: Psychiatric Research Interview for Substance and Mental Disorders (PRISM-IV). *American Journal of Psychiatry, 163,* 689-696.

Higgins, S. T., Budney, A. J., Bickel, W. K., Hughes, J. R., Foerg, F., & Badger, G. (1993). Achieving cocaine abstinence with a behavioral approach. *American Journal of Psychiatry, 150,* 763-769.

Hollander, E., Allen, A., Lopez, R. P., Bienstock, C. A., Grossman, R., Siever, L. J., et al. (2001). A preliminary double-blind, placebo-controlled trial of divalproex sodium in borderline personality disorder. *Journal of Clinical Psychiatry, 62*, 199-203.

Hollander, E., Swann, A. C., Coccaro, E. F., Jiang, P., & Smith, T. B. (2005). Impact of trait impulsivity and state aggression on divalproex versus placebo response in borderline personality disorder. *American Journal of Psychiatry, 162*, 621-624.

Hyman, S. E. (2002). A new beginning for research on borderline personality disorder. *Biological Psychiatry, 51,* 933-935.

Kosten, T. A., Kosten, T. R., & Rousaville, B. J. (1989). Personality-disorders in opiate addicts show prognostic specificity. *Journal of Substance Abuse Treatment, 6,* 163-168.

Lieb, K., Zanarini, M. C., Schmahl, C., Linehan, M. M., & Bohus, M. (2004). Borderline personality disorder. *The Lancet, 364*, 453-461.

Linehan, M. M. (1993a). *Cognitive-behavioral treatment of borderline personality disorder.* New York: Guilford Press.

Linehan, M. M. (1993b). *Skills training manual for treating borderline personality disorder.* New York: Guilford Press.

Linehan, M. M., Comtois, K. A., Murray, A. M., Brown, M. Z., Gallop, R. J., Heard, H. L., et al. (2006). Two-year randomized controlled trial and follow up of dialectical behavior therapy versus therapy by experts for suicidal behaviors and borderline personality disorder. *Archives of General Psychiatry, 63,* 757-766.

Linehan, M. M., Davidson, G. C., Lynch, T. R., & Sanderson, C. (2005). Technique factors in treating personality disorder. In L. G. Castonguay & L. E. Beutler (Eds.), *Principles of therapeutic change that work* (pp. 239-252). New York: Oxford University Press.

Linehan, M. M., & Dimeff, L. A. (1997). *Dialectical behavior therapy manual of treatment interventions for drug abusers with borderline personality disorder.* Seattle: University of Washington.

Linehan, M. M., Dimeff, L. A., Reynolds, S. K., Comtois, K. A., Welch, S. S., Heagerty, P., et al. (2002). Dialectal behavior therapy versus comprehensive validation therapy plus 12-step for the treatment of opioid dependent women meeting criteria for borderline personality disorder. *Drug and Alcohol Dependence, 67,* 13-26.

Linehan, M. M., Schmidt, H., III, Dimeff, L. A., Craft, J. C., Kanter, J., & Comtois, K. A. (1999). Dialectical behavior therapy for patients with borderline personality disorder and drug-dependence. *American Journal on Addictions, 8,* 279-292.

Links, P. S., Heslegrave, R. J., Mitton, J. E., & Van Reekum, R. (1995). Borderline personality disorder and substance abuse: Consequences of comorbidity. *Canadian Journal of Psychiatry, 40,* 9-14.

Livesley, W. J., Jang, K. L., & Vernon, P. A. (1998). Phenotypic and genetic structure of traits delineating personality disorder. *Archives of General Psychiatry, 55,* 941-948.

Loranger, A. W. (1995). *International Personality Disorder Examination (IPDE) manual.* White Plains, NY: Cornell Medical Center Press.

Marlatt, G. A., & Gordon, J. R. (1985). *Relapse prevention: Maintenance strategies in the treatment of addictive behaviors.* New York: Guilford Press.

Martinez-Raga, J., Marshall, E. J., Keaney, F., Ball, D., & Strang, J. (2002). Unplanned versus planned discharges from in-patient alcohol detoxification: Retrospective analysis of 470 first-episode admissions. *Alcohol & Alcoholism, 37,* 277-281.

Marx, K., & Engels, F. (1970). *Selected works* (Vol. 3). New York: International Publishers.

McMain, S. (2004, November). Dialectical behavior therapy for individuals with borderline personality disorder and substance abuse: A randomized, controlled pilot study. Paper presented at the meeting of the Association for the Advancement of Behavior Therapy, New Orleans, LA.

Mercer, D. (2007). Medications in the treatment of borderline personality disorder. *Current Psychiatry Reports, 9,* 53-62.

Morey, L. C. (1988). A psychometric analysis of the DSM-III-R personality disorder criteria. *Journal of Personality Disorders, 2,* 109-124.

Morey, L. C. (1991). *The Personality Assessment Inventory professional manual.* Odessa, FL: Psychological Assessment Resources.

Nickel, M. K., Muehlbacher, M., Nickel, C., Kettler, C., Pedrosa Gil, F., Bachler, E., Buschmann, W., et al. (2006). Aripiprazole in the treatment of patients with borderline personality disorder: A double-blind, placebo-controlled study. *American Journal of Psychiatry, 163,* 833-838.

Oldham, J. M., Skodol, A. E., Kellman, H. D., & Hyler, S. E. (1992). Diagnosis of DSM-III-R personality disorders by two structured interviews: Patterns of comorbidity. *American Journal of Psychiatry, 149,* 213-220.

Robins, C. J., & Chapman, A. L. (2004). Dialectical behavior therapy: Current status, recent developments, and future directions. *Journal of Personality Disorders, 18,* 73-79.

Robins, C. J., & Koons, C. R. (2004). Dialectical behavior therapy of severe personality disorders. In J. J. Magnavita (Ed.), *Handbook of personality disorders: Theory and practice.* (pp. 221-253). New York: John Wiley and Sons.

Rosenthal, M. Z., Lynch, T. R., & Linehan, M. M. (2005). Dialectical behavior therapy for individuals with borderline personality disorder and substance use disorders. In R. J. Frances, S. I. Miller, & A. H. Mack (Eds.), *Clinical textbook of addictive disorders* (pp. 615-636). New York: Guilford Press.

Ross, S., Dermatis, H., Levounis, P., & Galanter, M. (2003). A comparison between dually diagnosed inpatients with and without Axis II comorbidity and the relationship to treatment outcome. *American Journal of Drug & Alcohol Abuse. 29,* 263-279.

Rounsaville, B. J., Carroll, K. M., & Onken, L. S. (2001). A stage model of behavioral therapies research: Getting started and moving on from stage I. *Clinical Psychology-Science and Practice, 8,* 133-142.

Sanislow, C. A., Grilo, C. M., Morey, L. C., Bender, D. S., Skodol, A. E., Gunderson, J. G., et al. (2002). Confirmatory factor analysis of DSM-IV criteria for borderline personality disorder: Findings from the Collaborative Longitudinal Personality Disorders Study. *American Journal of Psychiatry, 159,* 284-290.

Siever, L. J., Torgersen, S., Gunderson, J. G., Livesley, W. J., & Kendler, K. S. (2002). The borderline diagnosis III: Identifying endophenotypes for genetic studies. *Biological Psychiatry, 51,* 964-968.

Skodol, A. E., Oldham, J. M., & Gallaher, P. E. (1999). Axis II comorbidity of substance use disorders among patients referred for treatment of personality disorders. *American Journal of Psychiatry. 156,* 733-738.

Skodol, A. E., Gunderson, J. G., Pfohl, B., Widiger, T. A., Livesley, W. J., & Siever, L. J. (2002a). The borderline diagnosis I: Psychopathology, comorbidity, and personality structure. *Biological Psychiatry, 51,* 936-950.

Skodol, A. E., Siever, L. J., Livesley, W. J., Gunderson, J. G., Pfohl, B., & Widiger, T. A. (2002b). The borderline diagnosis II: Biology, genetics, and clinical course. *Biological Psychiatry, 51,* 951-963.

Soler J., Pascual J. C., Campins J., Barrachina J., Puigdemont D., Alvarez E., et al. (2005). Double-blind, placebo-controlled study of dialectical behavior therapy plus olanzapine for borderline personality disorder. *American Journal of Psychiatry, 162,* 1221-1224.

Stone, M. H. (1993). Long-term outcome in personality disorders. *British Journal of Psychiatry, 162,* 299-313.

Torgersen, S., Lygren, S., Oien, A., Skre, I., Onstad, S., Edvardsen, J., et al. (2000). A twin study of personality disorders. *Comprehensive Psychiatry, 41,* 416-425.

Tritt, K., Nickel, C., Lahmann, C., Leiberich, P. K., Rother, W. K., Loew, T. H., et al. (2005). Lamotrigine treatment of aggression in female borderline-patients: A randomized, double-blind, placebo-controlled study. *Journal of Psychopharmacology, 19,* 287-291.

Trull, T. J. (2001). Structural relations between borderline personality disorder features and putative etiological correlates. *Journal of Abnormal Psychology, 110,* 471-481.

Trull, T. J., Sher, K. J. Minks-Brown, C., Durbin, J., & Burr, R. (2000). Borderline personality disorder and substance use disorders: A review and integration. *Clinical Psychology Review, 20,* 235-253.

van den Bosch, L. M. C., Verheul, R., Schippers, G. M., & van den Brink, W. (2002). Dialectical behavior therapy of borderline patients with and without substance use problems: Implementation and long-term effects. *Addictive Behaviors, 27,* 911-923.

Verheul, R., van den Bosch, L. M. C., Koeter, M. W. J., de Ridder, M. A. J., Stijnen, T., & van den Brink, W. (2003). Dialectical behavior therapy for women with borderline personality disorder: 12-month, randomized clinical trial in the Netherlands. *British Journal of Psychiatry, 182,* 135-140.

Villeneuve, E., & Lemelin, S. (2005). Open-label study of atypical neuroleptic quetiapine for treatment of borderline personality disorder: Impulsivity as main target. *Journal of Clinical Psychaitry, 66,* 1298-1303.

Wagner, A. W., & Linehan, M. M. (1997). Biosocial perspective on the relationship of childhood sexual abuse, suicidal behavior, and borderline personality disorder. In M. C. Zanarini (Ed.), *Role of sexual abuse in the etiology of borderline personality disorder* (pp. 203-223). Washington, DC: American Psychiatric Association.

Weiss, R. D., Mirin, S. M., Griffin, M. L., Gunderson, J. G., & Hufford, C. (1993). Personality-disorders in cocaine dependence. *Comprehensive Psychiatry, 34,* 145-149.

Welch, S. S. (2001). A review of the literature on the epidemiology of parasuicide in the general population. *Psychiatric Services, 52,* 368-375.

Widiger, T. A., & Weissman, M. M. (1991). Epidemiology of borderline personality disorder. *Hospital and Community Psychiatry, 42,* 1015-1021.

Widiger, T. A., Sanderson, C., & Warner, L. (1986). The MMPI, prototypal typology, and borderline personality disorder. *Journal of Personality Assessment, 50,* 540-553.

Witkiewicz, K., & Marlatt, G. A. (2004). Relapse prevention for alcohol and drug problems: That was zen, this is tao. *American Psychologist, 59,* 224-235.

Wolpe, J. (1990). *The practice of behavior therapy* (4th ed.). New York: Elmsford.

Young J. E. (1994). *Cognitive therapy for personality disorders: A schema-focused approach.* Sarasota, FL: Professional Resource Press.

Zanarini, M. C., Williams, A. A., Lewis, R. E., & Reich, R. B. (1997). Reported pathological childhood experiences associated with the development of borderline personality disorder. *American Journal of Psychiatry, 154,* 1101-1106.

Zanarini, M. C., Yong, L., Frankenburg, F. R., Frances R., Hennen, J., Reich, D. B., et al. (2002). Severity of reported childhood sexual abuse and its relationship to severity of borderline psychopathology and psychosocial impairment among borderline inpatients. *Journal of Nervous and Mental Disease, 190,* 381-387.

Zanarini, M. C., Frankenburg, F. R., Dubo, E. D., Sickel, A. E., Trikha, A., Levin, A., et al. (1998). Axis I comorbidity of borderline personality disorder. *American Journal of Psychiatry, 155,* 1733-1739.

Part 5

Impulse Control Disorders and Eating Disorders

Although pathological gambling, intermittent explosive disorder, and eating disorders are not uncommon among patients who seek treatment for substance dependence, clinicians often fail to diagnose these disorders. The criteria for each of these disorders assess the loss of control over a set of behaviors (i.e., gambling, aggression, eating). Similarly, patients with substance use disorders lose control over their use of addictive substances (perhaps as a result of the reinforcing effects of drugs and their action on the brain reward system).

The tendency of patients with intermittent explosive disorder to "fly into rages" with minimal provocation can occur independently of, or as a result of, mood disorders, personality disorders, or substance intoxication. Since patients' uncontrolled anger can be disruptive to treatment and dangerous, clinicians should tailor their treatment plan to target these behaviors; behavioral treatment approaches to anger management and mood-stabilizing medications can be effective.

Pathological gambling and eating disorders have been described as behavioral addictions. Problem gamblers experience cravings to gamble, euphoria while gambling, and difficulty in cutting down on gambling and continue to gamble despite mounting losses (criteria for pathological gambling are similar to criteria for substance dependence). Although results of clinical trials of antidepressants for treatment of pathological gambling have been disappointing, the opioid antagonist naltrexone (used to treat alcohol dependence and opioid dependence) has shown promise in treatment of pathological gambling. Patients with bulimia or overeating disorders experience urges to overeat that they struggle to control. Patients with these disorders may respond to cognitive and behavioral treatment approaches; antidepressant medications, particularly selective serotonin reuptake inhibitors (e.g., fluoxetine), are effective for treatment of bulimia.

Chapter 10

Pathological Gambling Among Patients With Substance Use Disorders

by Carlos Blanco, M.D., Ph.D., Oshra Cohen, Ph.D., Juan José Luján, M.D., and Edelgard Wulfert, Ph.D.

INTRODUCTION

Over the last two decades gambling and its related problems have been on the rise in many countries, and pathological gambling is now considered a major public health concern. Pathological gambling (PG), which is characterized by a maladaptive pattern of increased gambling behavior despite its adverse consequences, has a negative impact on gamblers' personal, professional, economic, and social lives. Despite the increasing prevalence of pathological gambling, our knowledge of the etiology, development, and treatment of pathological gambling remains limited. Although considerable progress has been made in the development of methods for diagnosis and treatment of pathological gambling, more research on the different aspects of pathological gambling is needed in order to identify strategies for effective prevention and treatment for this increasing problem.

Legalization of gambling and the rise within recent decades in the number of places to gamble and the types of games available to adults, adolescents, and children clearly have contributed to the increasing prevalence of pathological gambling. Pathological gambling often begins in adolescence or early adulthood in men; although onset tends to be later in women, women progress from "recreational" gambling to pathological gambling faster than men (although treatment rates are similar for men and women with pathological gambling). Just as easy access to substances and early onset of substance use increase risk for development of addiction problems, easy access to gambling venues and games and introduction to gambling at an early age increase risk for development of pathological gambling.

Epidemiological studies that have been conducted in several countries using random samples of adults living in the community reveal lifetime prevalence rates of pathological gambling (i.e., percentage of individuals with pathological gambling at any point in their lifetime) ranging from 0.4 percent to 2.5 percent of the population (Cunningham-Williams, Cottler, & Womack, 2004). Studies indicate that men, adolescents, ethnic minorities, and individuals in lower socioeconomic levels are at highest risk for developing pathological gambling. Pathological gambling is found more often in urban residents and in individuals with other psychiatric diagnoses.

The prevalence of pathological gambling may be 10 percent or more in samples of patients with substance use disorders. Clinicians who work with substance-dependent patients should be familiar with the symptoms of pathological gambling, methods for distinguishing pathological gambling from "recreational" gambling, and types of treatment for pathological gambling. This chapter provides an introduction to the diagnosis and treatment of pathological gambling for clinicians who work with substance-dependent patients.

CASE PRESENTATION

TM, a 40-year-old male, started to go with friends to off-track betting (OTB) parlors at age 17 to win extra pocket money. He enjoyed the "rush" that he felt when he placed bets. As TM became more involved with gambling, he started to go to OTB parlors two to three times a week without his friends, who, he thought, were "not serious about making money." Despite frequent trips to OTB parlors, his academic performance did not suffer, and he was accepted to college. In college TM joined a betting pool during the football season. His interest in sports gambling increased, and he devoted several hours per day to the study of football team statistics in an effort to figure out the probable outcome of the games.

Upon graduation from college, TM began work at a software company; he continued to go to OTB parlors and placed bets year-round on sports teams. Although TM was occasionally late in paying his bills and making loan payments, he was "able to make ends meet." However, after four years of working at the software company, TM no longer could pay his bills. Too ashamed to tell his family and friends about his gambling losses, he turned to credit card companies for loans; he planned to use the money from the loans for gambling and to recover the money that he lost.

At age 35, TM no longer found gambling exciting but was unable to quit. His credit card debt had reached $20,000. He felt constantly depressed and anxious. His preoccupation with obtaining money for gambling and his frequent tardiness at work caused his job performance to deteriorate. In an effort to relieve his anxiety, he tried heroin at the suggestion of friend, who told him that heroin "might help [him] to relax." He began to crave the relief from anxiety that heroin provided. He began to develop tolerance and required larger amounts of heroin in order to achieve the same level of relief. Since TM had depleted his savings and since his credit card debt had escalated further, he began to steal software from work to sell to rival companies in order to obtain money for gambling and for buying heroin. When his boss discovered the theft and fired TM, he acknowledged to both himself and to his family his addiction to heroin and his problem with gambling.

Supportive of TM, his family helped him to settle a payment schedule with his creditors. TM was admitted into a rehabilitation clinic; he began to attend Gamblers Anonymous (GA) meetings and Narcotics Anonymous (NA) meetings and began individual therapy sessions for treatment of his problems with gambling and heroin. His recovery was slow but steady. TM was able to quit his heroin use. He learned to identify triggers that lead to gambling and learned coping skills to deal with urges to gamble. His family was supportive throughout his recovery process. At the time of discharge, TM had been abstinent from heroin and gambling for three months. He is currently attending GA meetings and NA meetings regularly, as well as monthly follow-up sessions with his therapist.

DIAGNOSTIC CRITERIA

DSM-IV Criteria for Pathological Gambling

The criteria for pathological gambling that are listed in the *Diagnostic and Statistical Manual of Mental Disorders,* 4th edition (*DSM-IV*; American Psychiatric Association, 1994; see Table 10-1) describe a progression in gambling behavior from a preoccupation with gambling to a display of dysfunctional behaviors (e.g., illegal acts or behaviors that cause a patient to lose a significant relationship or job). Criteria for pathological gambling are similar to criteria for other addictions. Criteria for pathological gambling include loss of control ("chasing"), tolerance (an escalation in betting over time), withdrawal-like symptoms (restlessness and irritability), repeated unsuccessful attempts to quit, impaired role performance, and continuation despite negative consequences. Like substance abusers, pathological gamblers engage in high-risk behaviors that lead to short-term rewards but long-term negative consequences.

Table 10-1
DSM-IV Criteria for Pathological Gambling

Symptoms	DSM-IV Criteria[a, b]	A Sample of DIGS Questions[c, d]
Core Symptoms	A. Persistent and recurrent maladaptive gambling behavior as indicated by five (or more) of the following:	
	(1) is preoccupied with gambling (e.g., preoccupied with reliving past gambling experiences, handicapping or planning the next venture, or thinking of ways to get money with which to gamble)	Have there been periods in the past six months when you spent a lot of time thinking about past gambling experiences or thinking about future gambling venues?
	(2) needs to gamble with increasing amounts of money in order to achieve the desired excitement	Have you needed to gamble with larger amounts of money or with larger bets in order to obtain the same feeling of excitement?
	(3) has repeated unsuccessful efforts to control, cut back, or stop gambling	Have you tried to cut down or control your gambling several times in the past and found it difficult?
	(4) is restless or irritable when attempting to cut down or stop gambling	Did you feel quite restless or irritable after you tried to cut down or stop gambling?
	(5) gambles as a way of escaping from problems or of relieving a dysphoric mood (e.g., feelings of helplessness, guilt, anxiety, depression)	Do you feel that you gamble as a way to escape personal problems?
	(6) after losing money gambling, often returns another day to get even ("chasing" one's losses)	When you lose money on a given day, do you often return soon on another day to win back your losses?
	(7) lies to family members, therapist, or others to conceal the extent of involvement with gambling	Have you often lied to family members, friends, co-workers or teachers about the extent of your gambling or of your gambling debt?
	(8) has committed illegal acts such as forgery, fraud, theft, or embezzlement to finance gambling	Have you committed any illegal acts, such as embezzlement or fraud, to support your gambling habit?
	(9) has jeopardized or lost a significant relationship, job, or educational or career opportunity because of gambling	Have you had periods when your gambling caused problems in your relationships with family, friends, co-workers or teachers?
	(10) relies on others to provide money to relieve a desperate financial situation caused by gambling.	Have you frequently thought about ways of getting money with which to gamble?
Other Criteria	B. The gambling behavior is not better accounted for by a manic episode.[e]	

[a] American Psychiatric Association (1994).
[b] Reprinted with permission from the *Diagnostic and Statistical Manual of Mental Disorders*, Fourth Edition (Copyright 1994). American Psychiatric Association.
[c] Stinchfield & Winters (1996).
[d] Reprinted with permission.
[e] Consult *DSM-IV* criteria (American Psychiatric Association, 1994) for manic episode.

Conceptualization of Gambling on a Continuum

Some researchers propose that pathological gambling can be considered the extreme on a continuum that ranges from occasional "recreational" gambling without negative consequences to problem gambling to pathological gambling. Gamblers who suffer from a subthreshold form of pathological gambling (i.e., patients who have less than five symptoms that meet *DSM-IV* criteria) are referred to as *problem gamblers*. Although most research, to date, has focused on patients who meet *DSM-IV* criteria for pathological gambling, there is an increased interest in problem gambling. To some extent, the *DSM-IV* requirement for the presence of five or more symptoms for a diagnosis of pathological gambling is arbitrary; both problem gambling and pathological gambling warrant clinical attention.

Debate About the Classification of Pathological Gambling

There is debate about how to classify pathological gambling. The World Health Organization and the American Psychiatric Association currently consider pathological gambling as an impulse control disorder because of the difficulty that individuals have in resisting the impulse to gamble, the emotional distress that individuals experience before engaging in a gambling activity, the pleasure that individuals usually experience while gambling, and the potential for individuals to experience negative feelings of guilt or regret. However, some researchers believe that pathological gambling has characteristics that resemble characteristics of addictions (e.g., the intense desire to satisfy a need, loss of control over gambling behavior, continuous thoughts about gambling, abstinence and tolerance symptoms, and persistence of the behavior despite negative consequences). Some researchers place pathological gambling into the spectrum of obsessive compulsive disorders, and yet others have considered it as an affective disorder (Blanco, Moreyra, Nunez, Saiz-Ruiz, & Ibañez, 2001).

NATURAL HISTORY AND ETIOLOGY

Onset, Course, and Consequences of Pathological Gambling

Playing games of chance is a normal activity for most people. Pathological gamblers are individuals who develop a gambling pattern that is characterized by a lack of control over gambling behavior and a progressive focus on activities related to gambling. Pathological gambling is a disorder with a chronic course that can manifest itself either in continuous episodic patterns or with periods of abstinence of variable duration (sometimes years) followed by periodic lapses or full relapses. Although pathological gambling can develop shortly after initial exposure to gambling activities, in most cases, the development is gradual, taking several years for individuals to progress to pathological gambling. Occasionally, the development of pathological gambling may be accelerated by external factors, including increased exposure to gambling opportunities, changes in the type of gambling in which an individual engages, and stressors (Ibañez & Saiz, 2000; Lesieur, 1979). Most pathological gamblers are between the ages of 18 and 44; onset of pathological gambling tends to occur in patients' mid-20s or early 30s.

Although the natural history of pathological gambling has not been systematically studied, the clinical picture of a gambler may be conceptualized in four stages.

1. *Winnings phase*: With a variable length, this phase is stimulated by initial wins. The individual devotes increasing amounts of time and money to gambling.

2. *Loss phase*: This phase is characterized by significant money losses. The individual desperately tries to recover the money lost by increasing the frequency and size of bets (known as chasing losses); the greater the monetary loss, the more the individual attempts to recover the money through gambling. Often uncontrollable, individuals' gambling behaviors progress in a downward spiral, leading individuals to deceive and lie in order to justify the money lost and the need to borrow money to continue gambling and to pay debts. Gambling now controls the individual's life; consumed by thoughts of gambling and obtaining money for gambling, the individual often abandons his/her friends and hobbies, leading to deterioration of personal and family relationships and performance in school or on the job.

3. *Desperation phase*: It is not uncommon for gamblers at this stage to engage in criminal activities (e.g., stealing money from relatives, forging checks, committing embezzlement and fraud).

4. *Hopelessness phase*: Some gamblers progress to a fourth phase, in which they may seek help or develop depressive symptoms, often with suicidal ideation or behavior.

Pathological gambling is associated with numerous difficulties for gamblers and their families, including marital difficulties, family dysfunction, domestic violence, isolation from the community, problems with substance abuse, occupational and financial difficulties, criminal activity, suicidal ideation or attempts, and comorbidity with other psychiatric disorders. Ongoing studies seek to determine if pathological gambling is a cause or a consequence of these difficulties or if there is a common factor that causes both pathological gambling and the difficulties associated with this disorder.

Pathological gamblers are predisposed to suffer from psychosomatic disorders, such as high blood pressure, upper gastrointestinal pathology, and migraines. These symptoms are probably related to the stress brought on by gambling. Studies have found that pathological gamblers have high rates of personality disorders, anxiety disorders, substance abuse disorders (particularly alcoholism), and impulse control disorders. Finally, individuals suffering from both psychiatric disorders and pathological gambling tend to have more severe pathological gambling problems (Ibáñez et al., 2001).

Possible Causative Mechanisms

Psychological theories and biological theories offer explanations for the origins of pathological gambling. Studies of genetics and molecular biology have examined causes of pathological gambling, incidence, and risk factors.

Psychological Theories. Psychoanalysts provided the first systematic attempt to diagnose and treat pathological gambling and posited some initial theories about the development of pathological gambling. More recently developed psychological theories emphasize the role of cognitive and behavioral influences on the origin and maintenance of pathological gambling.

Cognitive theories propose that individuals with pathological gambling have irrational beliefs and distorted cognitions about gambling. For example, pathological gamblers may make a common cognitive error of having an illusion of control (the mistaken belief that one is able to influence the outcome of a random event). In addition, pathological gamblers tend to make false inferences about their chances of winning and often distort the significance of gambling results; pathological gamblers often attribute gains to personal skill and attribute losses to bad luck or view losses as a sign that a win "is due" soon. Pathological gamblers frequently exhibit superstitious behavior (e.g., believing that a specific slot machine will bring luck) and selective memory (e.g., gains are remembered and overestimated and losses are forgotten and underestimated).

Behavioral theories posit that gambling is a behavior learned through a process of intermittent reinforcement. As monetary consequences are delivered on an irregular schedule (with many losses interspersed with small and occasional large wins), the gambler concludes that persistence pays off. Over time, this unpredictable temporal pattern of occasional monetary gains acts as a powerful reinforcer and eventually results in the development of pathological gambling. Other theories state that the most powerful reinforcer in pathological gambling is the high excitement and physiological arousal that gambling provokes in the central nervous system. Pathological gamblers continuously attempt to experience this emotion (i.e., "thrill"), regardless of the consequences of gambling. Agreement has not been reached on the reinforcing properties of pathological gambling (Gaboury & Ladouceur, 1989).

Biological Theories. After pathological gambling was recognized as a disorder, three lines of neurobiological research on etiologic and pathophysiological mechanisms of pathological gambling emerged. The three leading theories are (1) pathological gambling as an impulse control disorder, which suggests the implication of serotoninergic mechanisms; (2) pathological gambling as a disorder of arousal, which supports the hypothesis of an alteration of the noradrenergic system; and (3) pathological gambling as a nonpharmacological addiction, which suggests the implication of dopaminergic pathways. A detailed summary of published biological studies on pathological gambling can be found in a paper by Ibañez, Blanco, and Saiz-Ruiz (2002).

Genetic Studies. Studies of genetics and molecular biology have investigated possible causes of pathological gambling. Studies of clinical samples have shown that, among first degree relatives (i.e., parents, siblings, children) of patients with pathological gambling, around 20 percent will have pathological gambling at some point during their lifetime. In order to tease apart the contribution of genetic factors and environmental factors to this disorder, studies of twins and adopted children have been undertaken. A meta-analysis of pathological gambling studies of families and twins confirms the existence of a genetic risk factor that seems to be higher among boys and is especially elevated in severe cases of pathological gambling (Walters, 2001).

To clarify the possible role of genetic factors in the development of pathological gambling, studies of molecular genetics have been conducted. Gene candidates (i.e., genes chosen for study) were selected according to neurobiological theories on pathological gambling and theories on neurotransmitters and brain systems involved in pathological gambling. The results of those studies suggest possible associations between pathological gambling and specific polymorphisms (i.e., variants) of the genes for monoamine oxidase (MAO) A, the serotonin transporter (SERT), and dopamine receptors D1, D2, and D4. Taken together, these preliminary results suggest a genetic role in the etiopathogenesis of pathological gambling; replication studies conducted in large samples are needed. Different psychological and biological explanatory models acquire more significance and utility when they are integrated with a biopsychosocial perspective that emphasizes the interaction of several factors in the development of a disorder, particularly the interaction of genetic and environmental factors.

INSTRUMENTS AND METHODS FOR SCREENING AND DIAGNOSIS

Several instruments are available for screening and diagnosis of pathological gambling. Screening instruments should be used to identify patients with symptoms that require a detailed evaluation. Table 10-2 briefly describes features of several screening and diagnostic instruments.

The Structured Clinical Interview for Pathological Gambling (SCI-PG) (Grant, Steinberg, Kim, Rounsaville, & Potenza, 2004) is a clinician-administered, structured clinical interview that consists of probe and follow-up questions about gambling symptoms and a rating scale that helps interviewers to determine if a patient's symptoms meet *DSM-IV* criteria for pathological gambling. Although the SCI-PG has demonstrated high reliability and validity, replication of findings in other populations is required. Practice in using this tool may help clinicians to learn how to ask patients about their gambling symptoms and to recognize symptoms of pathological gambling.

The oldest and most frequently used instrument in epidemiological studies of pathological gambling is the South Oaks Gambling Screen (SOGS; Lesieur & Blume, 1987), a twenty-item self-report questionnaire based on *Diagnostic and Statistical Manual of Mental Disorders*, 3rd edition, revised (*DSM-IIIR;* American Psychiatric Association, 1987) criteria for pathological gambling. Clinicians who familiarize themselves with the items on this questionnaire may improve their ability to interview patients about their gambling. The SOGS yields a numerical score that reflects severity of pathological gambling and provides a suggested cutoff (or threshold score) for making the diagnosis of pathological gambling (a score of five or more indicates probable pathological gambling). This questionnaire has demonstrated high diagnostic accuracy, high sensitivity, and modest specificity, with high positive and negative predictive power. The original version of the SOGS is based on lifetime gambling and does not differentiate pathological gamblers in remission from current problem gamblers (Lesieur & Blume, 1987).

Several instruments for diagnosis and evaluation of problem gambling have been developed recently: the Diagnostic Interview for Gambling Severity (DIGS; Stinchfield & Winters, 1996), a structured clinical interview that evaluates gambling symptoms, gambling treatment history, onset of gambling problems, and family and social functioning; the Gambling Assessment Module (GAM-IV); the Gambling Behavior Interview (GBI); the Gamblers Anonymous 20 Questions (Ursua & Uribelarrea, 1998), which differentiates between problem gamblers and social gamblers and which has a high sensitivity and specificity and overall diagnostic accuracy (a score of seven or more indicates problem gambling); and the Lie/Bet Questionnaire (Johnson et al., 1997), which has a high sensitivity and specificity and contains only two questions (its use in research studies has been scarce to date). Further investigation into psychometric properties of the DIGS, GAM-IV, and GBI is required.

Table 10-2
Instruments for Screening and Diagnosis of Pathological Gambling in Substance-Dependent Patients

Instrument	Features
Structured Clinical Interview for Pathological Gambling (SCI-PG) (Grant et al., 2004)	– 11 inclusionary questions – 1 exclusionary question – based on the DSM-IV criteria
South Oaks Gambling Screen (SOGS) (Lesieur & Blume, 1987)	– 20 items – self-administered screening questionnaire – does not differentiate subjects in remission from those actively gambling
Gamblers Anonymous 20 Questions (Ursua & Uribelarrea, 1998)	– 20 items – self-administered screening questionnaire – assesses only past year
Massachusetts Gambling Screen (MAGS) (Shaffer, LaBrie, Scanlan, & Cummings, 1994)	– 14 items – self-administered screening questionnaire
Lie/Bet Questionnaire (Johnson et al., 1997)	– 2 items
Patient Health Questionnaire, Pathological Gambling module (PHQ-PG) (unpublished)	– 11 items – self-administered screening questionnaire – based on *DSM-IV*
Diagnostic Interview for Gambling Severity (DIGS) (Stinchfield & Winters, 1996)	– 20 items – structured clinical interview – evaluates treatment history and social and family functioning

DIFFERENTIAL DIAGNOSIS AND OVERLAPPING DISORDERS

Differentiating Types of Gamblers

Clinicians should differentiate the following three types of gamblers from pathological gamblers: social (or recreational) gamblers, gamblers with bipolar disorder, and professional gamblers.

Social Gamblers. In contrast to pathological gamblers, social gamblers usually limit their gambling to social situations, engage in gambling activities during a short period of time, and can keep their gambling under control.

Gamblers With Bipolar Disorder. Excessive gambling that occurs exclusively in the context of manic episodes is not considered pathological gambling, since the excessive gambling behavior can be explained by a diagnosis of bipolar disorder.

Patients who have symptoms of mania and hypomania (e.g., euphoria, grandiose thinking, high energy, and tendency toward risk taking; see Chapter 2 of this volume) and symptoms of pathological gambling usually engage in other risky problem behaviors such as substance abuse, excessive spending, and impulsive sexual indiscretions. Symptoms of pathological gambling in these patients should subside spontaneously or when the symptoms of mania or hypomania are treated. If a patient exhibits problem gambling outside the context of a manic episode (e.g., during periods of depression), then the patient should be diagnosed with both bipolar disorder and pathological gambling.

Professional Gamblers. Some gamblers consider themselves to be professional gamblers; some individuals make a living at playing games that require both skill and chance (e.g., poker) and do not display symptoms of pathological gambling. However, the label of professional gambler seems irrelevant in making a diagnosis and can cloud the diagnosis by providing a rationalization for pathological gambling behavior. Clinicians must focus on the patient's gambling behavior (i.e., determine if the gambling behavior is progressive and maladaptive), not on the patient's motivation for gambling or the patient's justification for gambling. Patients who consider themselves to be professional gamblers are not precluded from a diagnosis of pathological gambling.

Pathological Gambling and Substance Use Disorders

Substance abuse and substance dependence have been consistently reported in persons with pathological gambling. An average of 40 percent of individuals seeking help for pathological gambling have a history of substance abuse (Lesieur, Blume, & Zoppa, 1986), and the rates of substance abuse are even higher in individuals who are not seeking help for pathological gambling. In 1998, Spunt, Dupont, Lesieur, Liberty, and Hunt (1998) reported that 21 percent of patients enrolled in a methadone maintenance program were probable pathological gamblers; in 65 percent of cases, the onset of problem gambling was found to occur within two years of the onset of a substance use disorder.

In the largest study of comorbidity conducted to date, Petry, Stinson, and Grant (2005) reported that 73 percent of pathological gamblers were found to have an alcohol use disorder, 60 percent had nicotine dependence, and 38 percent had another drug use problem. The strong association between pathological gambling and substance abuse disorders (especially alcoholism) may indicate the presence of shared genetic, environmental, or social factors that may contribute to both of these disorders.

Problem gambling may be one of many risky behaviors that individuals engage in during substance abuse or dependence, and it is possible for problem gambling to occur exclusively during episodes of substance use disorder. In patients who have symptoms that meet criteria for both pathological gambling and substance use disorders, clinicians should diagnose both disorders rather than attributing one syndrome to the other syndrome (as in cases of bipolar patients who display symptoms of pathological gambling only during periods of mania). Although one of several disorders may seem predominant in the clinical picture, each disorder should be addressed in treatment. For example, a patient who has severe alcohol dependence, who gambles, and who takes cocaine during some of her bouts of drinking, may receive treatment that initially focuses on her drinking, but her problems with gambling and cocaine should be addressed at some point during treatment.

Comorbidity With Other Psychiatric Disorders

Although comorbidity research is still in its infancy, studies, to date, have indicated that pathological gamblers tend to have higher rates of mood disorders, including depression (72 percent), bipolar disorder (24 percent), and hypomania (38 percent) (Linden, Pope, & Jonas, 1986). Increased rates of lifetime anxiety disorders (ranging from 9 percent (Grant & Kim, 2001) to 40 percent (Black & Moyer, 1998)) have been reported in pathological gamblers. Since mania is the most common mood disorder associated with pathological gambling, clinicians should avoid quickly dismissing gambling as a symptom of mania and should determine if pathological gambling instead should be diagnosed as a comorbid disorder.

Consistent with the notion of classifying pathological gambling as an impulse control disorder (ICD), pathological gambling has been linked to other ICDs such as compulsive shopping. Indeed, gambling and compulsive shopping have common elements—monetary exchange and reinforcement through monetary gains (Specker, Carlson, Edmonson, Johnson, & Marcotte, 1996).

Research indicates that close to 61 percent of pathological gamblers have a comorbid personality disorder. Rates of avoidant personality disorder (14 percent), dependant personality disorder (4 percent), paranoid personality disorder (24 percent), and schizoid personality disorder (15 percent) are consistently higher in pathological gamblers than in the general population. Rates of antisocial personality disorder (ASPD) in pathological gamblers range from 15 to 40 percent; these rates are significantly higher than rates found in the general population (Black & Moyer, 1998; Bland, Newman, Orn, & Steblsky, 1993). Other personality disorders that may co-occur with pathological gambling include borderline personality disorder (14 percent), histrionic personality disorder (13 percent), and obsessive compulsive personality disorder (28 percent) (Cunningham-Williams et al., 2004; Petry et al., 2005).

Some gender differences have been observed in the presentation of gambling and comorbid conditions. Alcohol dependence and drug use or drug abuse have a higher prevalence among young males with gambling problems (Kim, Grant, Adson, & Shin, 2001). Women are more likely than men to have a diagnosis of pathological gambling in addition to a diagnosis of major depression and/or anxiety. Gambling problems are present in all strata of the population and among all socioeconomic groups.

TREATMENT OPTIONS

In the past few years, important advances have been made in the treatment of pathological gambling. Although no one treatment method has been established as superior to other treatment methods, clinicians and general practitioners may choose from a variety of methods for treatment of pathological gambling.

Psychological Treatment

Behavioral interventions, including cognitive behavioral treatment and self-help programs, are currently available. Treatment models may be individual-based or group-based, may incorporate patients' relatives or acquaintances in the treatment process, and may consist of one session or require multiple sessions. Some treatment options are specific to patients with a diagnosis of pathological gambling. Some treatment options require the help of a specialist, while other options may simply require therapists to follow instructions in a manual.

Cognitive Behavioral Therapy (CBT) is the most commonly used treatment for pathological gambling. In the treatment of pathological gamblers, cognitive behavioral therapists utilize the principal strategy of functional analysis, which allows patients to recognize triggers and precipitants of their gambling behavior and to evaluate the positive and negative consequences of gambling. Cognitive behavioral therapists also use strategies that teach patients to control their responses to gambling-related stimuli, that help patients to increase the frequency of non-gambling-related behaviors, that help patients to cope with gambling urges, and that teach patients problem solving strategies, social skills, and assertiveness (Cunningham-Williams et al., 2004; Oakley-Browne, Adams, & Mobberley, 2000; Petry et al., 2005). According to a meta-analysis of interventions used in the treatment of pathological gambling, CBT has been found to be the most efficacious in treatment of pathological gambling in short-term follow-up studies.

Self-help groups, such as GA, are comprised of pathological gamblers who may be trying to quit or are already abstinent. GA provides financial, legal, and vocational advice and support to its participants. Although GA is probably the most common treatment for pathological gambling, its efficacy as a single treatment for pathological gambling has not been established. It is hypothesized that the use of cognitive and behavioral strategies in its model (which is based on the model used by Alcoholics Anonymous (AA)), may aid efficacy. Data from some studies indicate that participation in some formal psychotherapy, combined with assistance from a self-help group, promotes better results than GA attendance alone (Oakley-Browne et al., 2000).

Pharmacological Treatment

Several pharmacological approaches based on biological theories of the origins of pathological gambling have been developed. Theories implicating the serotonin system in the pathophysiology of pathological gambling call for the treatment of the disorder with serotonin reuptake inhibitors (SRIs); theories implicating the endogenous opioid system in the pathophysicology of pathological gambling call for treatment of the disorder with opioid antagonists. In a few cases, mood stabilizers (e.g., lithium and carbamazepine), which are used to treat impulsivity in patients with other psychiatric disorders, have been used to treat pathological gambling.

The efficacy of clomipramine (an SRI) has been described in one case. Selective serotonin reuptake inhibitors (SSRIs) have been studied in several clinical trials. Although results of open trials have been encouraging, results of controlled trials have been mixed, and further research is needed in order to determine which patients are more likely to benefit from SSRI treatment.

Use of opiate antagonists in pathological gambling is based on a conceptual model of pathological gambling as a nonpharmacological addiction. The exact mechanism of action of opioid antagonists remains controversial, but researchers hypothesize that opioid antagonists may decrease pleasure derived from gambling-related activities, may decrease urges to gamble, or may increase ability to stop gambling activities shortly after they have been started. The potential efficacy of naltrexone in treatment of pathological gambling is supported by a recent open trial and double-blind, placebo-controlled trial (Kim & Grant, 2001; Kim et al., 2001).

Although there is a growing literature on pharmacotherapy for pathological gambling, results of published studies should be interpreted with caution, since these studies have high placebo-response rates and high drop-out rates and include little data on long-term outcome. However, given the increasing interest in pathological gambling and the lack of established treatments for this disorder, it is expected that other medications for the treatment of pathological gambling will be systematically studied.

SUMMARY

Rates of pathological gambling and problem gambling are on the rise. The increase in the accessibility and availability of gambling and the potential devastating consequences of pathological gambling have prompted research into the development of diagnostic tools and treatments for this disorder. Use of CBT and psychopharmacological treatments is being explored and requires further study. The increase in gambling and its resulting problems highlights the need for better understanding of the clinical phenomenology, etiology, and treatment of pathological gambling.

Suggestions for Further Reading

For readers who wish to study further in this area, we recommend:

☐ **Diagnosis and Treatment of Pathological Gambling**

- Grant, J. E., & Potenza, M. N. (2004). *Pathological gambling: A clinical guide to treatment*. Washington DC: American Psychological Association.

- Ladouceur, R., Sylvain, C., Boutin, C., & Doucet, C. (2002). *Understanding and treating the pathological gambler*. New York: John Wiley & Sons.

- Petry, N. M. (2004). *Pathological gambling: Etiology, comorbidity, and treatment*. Washington DC: American Psychological Association.

☐ **Juvenile Gamblers**

- Derevensky, J. L., & Gupta, R. (Eds.). (2004).*Gambling problems in youth: Theoretical and applied perspectives*. New York: Kluwer.

☐ **Web Sites About Pathological Gambling**

- National Council on Problem Gambling: http://www.ncpgambling.org/.

- Gamblers Anonymous: http://www.gamblersanonymous.org/.

- New York Council on Problem Gambling: http://www.nyproblemgambling.org/.

Authors' Note

The research in this chapter was supported in part by grants K23 DA00482 (Dr. Blanco), R03 DA015559 (Dr. Blanco), R01 DA019606 (Dr. Blanco), and R01 DA020783

(Dr. Blanco), a Level I Research Award from the Ontario Problem Gambling Research Center (Dr. Cohen), and the New York State Psychiatric Institute (Dr. Blanco).

References

American Psychiatric Association. (1987). *Diagnostic and statistical manual of mental disorders* (3rd ed. rev.). Washington, DC: Author.

American Psychiatric Association. (1994). *Diagnostic and statistical manual of mental disorders* (4th ed.).Washington, DC: Author.

Blanco, C., Moreyra, P., Nunes, E., Saiz-Ruiz, J., & Ibañez, A. (2001). Pathological gambling: Addiction or compulsion. *Seminars in Clinical Neuropsychiatry, 6,* 167-176.

Black, D. W., & Moyer, T. (1998). Clinical features and psychiatric comorbidity of subjects with pathological gambling behavior. *Psychiatric Services 49,* 1434-1439.

Bland, R. C., Newman, S. C., Orn, H., & Steblsky, G. (1993). Epidemiology of pathological gambling in Edmonton. *Canadian Journal of Psychiatry, 38,* 108-112.

Cunningham-Williams, R., Cottler, L., & Womack, S. (2004). Epidemiology. In J. Grant & M. Potenza (Eds.), *Pathological gambling: A clinical guide to treatment* (pp. 25-36). Washington, DC: American Psychiatric Publishing.

Gaboury, A., & Ladouceur, R. (1989). Erroneous perceptions and gambling. *Journal of Social Behavior and Personality, 4,* 411-420.

Grant, J. E., & Kim, S. W. (2001). Demographic and clinical features of 131 adult pathological gamblers. *Journal of Clinical Psychiatry, 62,* 957-962.

Grant, J. E., Steinberg, M. A., Kim, S.W., Rounsaville, B. J., & Potenza, M. N. (2004). Preliminary validity and reliability testing of a structured clinical interview for pathological gambling. *Psychiatry Research, 128, 79-88.*

Ibáñez, A., & Saiz, J. (2000). *La ludopatía: Una nueva enfermedad.* Barcelona, Spain: Masson S.A.

Ibáñez, A., Blanco, C., Donahue, E., Lesieur, H. R., Perez de Castro, I., Fernandez-Piqueras, J. et al. (2001). Psychiatric comorbidity in pathological gamblers seeking treatment. *American Journal of Psychiatry, 158:*1733-1735.

Ibáñez, A., Blanco, C., & Saiz-Ruiz, J. (2002). Neurobiology and genetics of pathological gambling. *Psychiatry Annals, 32,* 181-185.

Johnson, E. E., Hamer, R., Nora, R. M., Tan, B., Eisenstein, N., & Engelhart, C. (1997). The Lie/Bet Questionnaire for screening pathological gamblers. *Psychological Reports, 80,* 83-88.

Kim, S. W., & Grant, J. E. (2001). An open naltrexone treatment study in pathological gambling disorder. *International Clinical Psychopharmacology, 16,* 285-289.

Kim, S. W., Grant, J. E., Adson, D. E., & Shin, Y. C. (2001). Double-blind naltrexone and placebo comparison study in the treatment of pathological gambling. *Biological Psychiatry, 49,* 914-921.

Lesieur, H. R. (1979). The compulsive gamblers spiral of options and involvement. *Psychiatry, 42,* 79-87.

Lesieur, H. R., Blume, S. B., & Zoppa, R. M. (1986). Alcoholism, drug abuse, and gambling. *Alcoholism Clinical and Experimental Research, 10,* 33-38.

Lesieur, H. R., & Blume, S. B. (1987). The South Oaks Gambling Screen (SOGS): A new instrument for the identification of pathological gamblers. *American Journal of Psychiatry, 144*, 1184-1188.

Linden, R. D., Pope, H. G., Jr., & Jonas, J. M. (1986). Pathological gambling and major affective disorder: Preliminary findings. *Journal of Clinical Psychiatry, 47*, 201-203.

Oakley-Browne, M. A., Adams, P., & Mobberley, P. M. (2000). Interventions for pathological gambling. *Cochrane Database of Systematic Reviews, 2*, CD001521.

Petry, N. M, Stinson, F. S, & Grant, B. F. (2005). Comorbidity of DSM-IV pathological gambling and other psychiatric disorders: Results from the national epidemiologic survey on alcohol and related conditions. *Journal of Clinical Psychiatry, 66*, 564-574.

Shaffer, H. J., LaBrie, R., Scanlan, K. M., & Cummings, T. N. (1994) Pathological gambling among adolescents: Massachusetts Gambling Screen (MAGS). *Journal of Gambling Studies, 10*, 339-362.

Specker, S. M., Carlson, G. A., Edmonson, K. M., Johnson, P. E., & Marcotte, M. (1996). Psychopathology in pathological gamblers seeking treatment. *Journal of Gambling Studies, 12*, 67-81.

Spunt, B., Dupont, I., Lesieur, H., Liberty, H. J., & Hunt, D. (1998). Pathological gambling and substance abuse: A review of the literature. *Substance Use and Misuse, 33*, 2535-2560.

Stinchfield, R. D., & Winters, K. C. (1996). *Treatment effectiveness of six state-supported compulsive gambling treatment programs in Minnesota*. St. Paul, MN: Compulsive Gambling Program, Mental Health Division, Minnesota Department of Human Services.

Ursua, M. P., & Uribelarrea, L. L. (1998). 20 questions of gamblers anonymous: A psychometric study with population of Spain. *Journal of Gambling Studies, 14*, 3-15.

Walters, G. D. (2001). Behavior genetic research on gambling and problem gambling: A preliminary meta-analysis of available data. *Journal of Gambling Studies, 17*, 255-271.

Chapter 11

Intermittent Explosive Disorder and Impulsive Aggression in Patients With Substance Use Disorders

by Stephen J. Donovan, M.D.

INTRODUCTION

A moment's reflection on clinical experience will convince one that substance abuse and aggression commonly coexist. Fights often occur during substance intoxication (alcohol, sedatives, cocaine, stimulants, and phencyclidine (PCP)) and/or withdrawal (alcohol, sedatives, opioids, cannabis, and nicotine). Functional impairment from arguments and abusive relationships is often observed in the histories of patients seeking treatment for substance dependence. Impulsivity, hyperactivity, inattention, and aggression are components of a childhood temperament that predicts the development and persistence of substance abuse in adolescence and young adulthood (Ialongo, Edelsohn, Werthamer-Larsson, Crockett & Kellam, 1996; Tarter et al., 2003).

Aggressive behavior is frightening, disturbing, and difficult for clinicians to manage. Recidivism is high in patients with histories of serious violence, thereby forcing clinicians to take seriously threats to significant others and to the general public. Sometimes clinicians have a legal obligation to warn others. The treatment team itself may feel physically threatened either immediately or as a consequence of a duty to warn others. The various causes of aggression and their corresponding treatment or management strategies are highly relevant to clinicians working with substance-dependent patients.

Just as a rational approach to suicidal behavior is part of standard clinical practice (see Chapter 17 of this volume), a rational approach to violent behavior is also possible. Given the disturbing, disruptive nature of aggression, the default response to violence in substance abuse treatment clinics is usually administrative: expel the offender. The physical safety of clinical staff is paramount, but, once established, the clinician may collect a thorough clinical history that may permit an understanding of the source of the violent tendencies and suggest possible treatments that may allow the patient to avoid expulsion and remain in treatment. This chapter aims to provide clinicians working with substance-dependent patients with a framework for distinguishing different types of aggression and for planning treatment based on available evidence.

The terminology of aggression is not standardized, even though aggression is a common problem in substance abuse treatment programs. Clinically, a cold hard stare from an individual with a violent history and a grudge against the clinic feels very different from the ranting of a hot head making all kinds of threats. We feel chilled in the first instance and emotionally upset in the second. This is how we are supposed to feel. We have been programmed to feel that way by evolution. In one case we are the object of predatory (cold) aggression, and in the other case we are the object of affective (hot) aggression.

Until recently, psychiatry has been reluctant to study aggression as a separate area of psychopathology. There are anxiety and mood disorders, but no aggressive disorders, in the various editions of the *Diagnostic and Statistical Manual of Mental Disorders*, 3rd edition (*DSM-III*; American Psychiatric Association, 1980); *Diagnostic and Statistical Manual of Mental Disorders*, 3rd edition, revised (*DSM-III-R*; American Psychiatric Association, 1987); *Diagnostic and Statistical Manual of Mental Disorders*, 4th edition (*DSM-IV*; American Psychiatric Association, 1994); *Diagnostic and Statistical Manual of Mental Disorders*, 4th edition, text revision (*DSM-IV-TR*; American Psychiatric Association, 2000). As late as 1994, the DSM-IV Taskforce questioned whether there should be any disorder that dealt just with aggression, let alone an attempt to subclassify the problem. The DSM-IV Taskforce planned to eliminate intermittent explosive disorder (IED) from the *DSM-IV* because there was little evidence that uncharacteristic eruptions of violence were a clinical problem.

However, the DSM-IV Taskforce noted a paradox. Clinicians were using IED to characterize eruptions of violence that could not be explained by another *DSM* diagnosis. The DSM-IV Taskforce members reasoned that clinicians may be identifying a neglected area of research and modified the IED criteria to include interepisode dispositions toward aggression (Bradford, Geller, Lesieur, Rosenthal, & Wise, 1996). It then became "legitimate" to study characteristic outbursts of aggression not explained by conduct disorder, psychosis, or affective disorders.

While this new definition of IED promoted some academic research and indicated that it was a common problem in patients seeking psychiatric care (Coccaro, Posternak, & Zimmerman, 2005), many questions remained (Coccaro, 2002; Coccaro & Siever, 2002). Child psychiatry has led the way in classifying aggression as predatory (cold) versus affective or "impulsive" (hot) types (Conner, 2002; Soller, Karnik, & Steiner, 2006). This is a useful starting point for understanding aggression, as the following clinical vignettes will illustrate. The environmental contributions to aggression (family discord, high crime neighborhoods, availability of substance abuse and weapons) are well known in the epidemiologic literature (Earls & Mezzacappa, 2002) and have been ignored in these case presentations for the sake of clinical simplicity.

CASE PRESENTATIONS

All these cases are males because overt aggression is far more common in males. Overt aggression in females is essentially the same, although the proportion of types of aggression may be different.

Case 1

JM was 10 years old when he was arrested for breaking a younger boy's leg and stealing his money. He was unafraid of the family court judge and stared at her, not so much in defiance, but as though he was memorizing her face. At reform school, he was often accused of violence but was rarely caught and always got even. After he was released, at age 18, he stole and dealt drugs, and he always got even. After he was arrested. he was given a choice of jail or drug treatment, and while staring at his probation officer, he chose treatment. After arriving at the center, he kept his criminal activities quiet, but he arrived at his sessions with his cold, hard stare. He had several positive urines and would have to go to prison if he did not turn in clean urines. His counselor was afraid of his reputation for always getting even.

This is a case of cold aggression. It leads directly to antisocial behavior. It is planned and premeditated, and the individual has the sense of "being quietly targeted." There is no known treatment for cold, predatory aggression. Medication does not help, and no psychotherapy claims success. This is a case in which a purely administrative approach is justified.

The cases that follow are all examples of different types of hot aggression. Here psychiatric understanding has a great deal to contribute.

Case 2

AP has been in special education since the second grade. Now 10 years old, he has recently been referred for a psychiatric evaluation because he threw a chair at a teacher that left a hole in the wall. AP was notorious for these eruptions of anger and had been suspended five times in the past six months, with the last three being "superintendent suspensions," indicating that someone could have been seriously hurt. He had few friends, although he received a lot of attention from his fellow classmates. They both feared him and goaded him to explode. The classroom was chaotic, with few children present every day.

AP felt fear and remorse after each explosive episode, but he had little apparent understanding of what had led up to it. He was not the only violent child in the classroom. Children who were not violent tended to be victimized. Within this deviant subculture, AP was not outside the norm until he threw the chair at the teacher and could have seriously hurt him.

This vignette illustrates the complex presentation of hot or affective aggression in school. AP always had a tendency to explode with aggression. It anteceded his placement in special education. Once he was in the special education class, his unpredictable rage became "adaptive" in that new environment. The other children were afraid of him. The worst aggression was directed to the more vulnerable members of the group. Throwing the chair at the teacher represents both a biological vulnerability toward explosive temper and, most likely, a maladaptive form of learning, encouraged by his peers.

The patient's mother recognized his tendency to throw tantrums, and she was afraid of him. His temper reminded her of his biological father, long gone from her life but still an intimidating memory. The patient's mother sought help with his temper and learned some techniques for managing his temper, but she could not withstand the explosive rage that often followed her attempt to place limits.

It is only a matter of time before the patient's family will lose control over him entirely, and his peer group will assume total control over reinforcers of his behavior. Lack of supervision, combined with intermittent rage, makes his membership in a deviant substance abusing subculture very likely. Unless his rage is brought under control, it will be difficult for any system, including reform school, to alter his trajectory.

Note that both JM ("Case 1") and AP are on an antisocial trajectory, but in the case of JM, his cold aggression led directly to antisocial behavior. In the case of AP, complex maladaptive coercive reciprocal social interactions led to antisocial behavior, and the outcome is still not settled; his rage is impulsive, out of his control, and disturbing to him; but he gradually learned that it is adaptive in certain social situations. His rage enables him to coerce others to act as he wishes, while others may respond by coercing him. There are opportunities to intervene, in order to reduce the intensity of the anger and to teach him more prosocial ways of interacting with others.

Case 3

ML was 14 years old and rarely went to school. When he did, he usually started a fight and, half the time, was beaten up himself. A recent sweep of the school had rid it of gang elements, and any use of gang logos in school was strictly forbidden. However, ML was largely rejected by gang members, and he could find no protection. He found, however, that if he smoked large amounts of marijuana, he could remain calm for at least part of the day and maintain something of a social life. Not having the backing of a gang, he turned to an inchoate group of youngsters who arrived at the school early and were stoned by first period, often cutting classes after the third period. Despite his regular use of marijuana, he continued to have explosive episodes. When interviewed, he vigorously defended his use of marijuana as necessary for staying out of fights to the extent that he could.

In contrast to AP ("Case 2"), ML has some insight into his temper, enough insight to seek to control it with marijuana. However, marijuana does at best a mediocre job of controlling his behavior and gets him more deeply involved in a deviant subculture, where exposure to other substances of abuse is inevitable, thereby raising the risk for cannabis dependence and long-term heavy use of cannabis. At this point, ML has learned that it is not so easy to coerce people with rage attacks, although he will do it with his mother and weaker adolescents. A host of related problems begins to emerge at this time: school failure, arrest for petty crime, family discord. These problem behaviors are so characteristic of adolescent substance abuse that some argue that adolescent substance abuse is simply one aspect of a larger concept of problem behaviors. In the case of ML, it seems clear that his aggression plays an important role in initiating and maintaining these problem behaviors, thereby raising the question of whether early intervention could reverse or prevent this psychosocial deterioration.

Case 4

MB has been called a hot head all his life. At age 24, he remains a follower and has followed his friends into heroin use and methadone maintenance. He smokes marijuana to help him calm down, but one would never know it from the way he blows in and blows out of the clinic each morning. His aggressive outbursts do not feel personal, but the slightest frustration leads to what can only be called a temper tantrum. Whereas the other patients engage in intense indignant interchanges with each other in the parking lot, MB does this in the middle of the line to pick up his methadone. MB still challenges authority directly. He knows if he is expelled from the methadone program, his parole officer will send him back to prison, but he cannot help himself. Shouting, threatening, abusive words, and stomping around were once so adaptive. Now he knows that if he throws a chair or damages property in front of the staff, he will be expelled and left to his own resources.

The patient's behavior is a product of three factors: his biological predisposition to explode in hostile rages, his drug use (self-medication with illegal substances), and negative feedback (including punishment) that he has received from society. It is very difficult for MB to abandon his use of coercive interaction patterns with others, including authority figures, because they were adaptive in the past and are resistant to change. Unless his explosive aggression is treated, it is only a matter of time before he is expelled from treatment.

Case 5

EW was 24 years old when he was released from the hospital following his second suicide attempt in three years. A skinny young man with tattoos covering both arms, he seemed unaware of the first impression his tank top and tattoos made in the clinic. He spoke in casual but educated speech, as though at some time in the past he had ambitions to go to college. He hated his family and he hated himself. He drew people to him but could not hold on to friendships. When he felt betrayed, he would hurt himself, other people, or both. His girlfriend had an order of protection against him, and when he showed up at her house screaming abuse, she called the police. By the time that the police had arrived, he had destroyed her television set, and as the police carried him away, he ranted and raved. After his release from jail, he took cocaine and cut his throat in front of his girlfriend's brother.

This case highlights the need to pay attention to symptoms of depression in individuals who present with aggressive features. The mixture of self-hatred and self-abuse suggests that a different type of mood disturbance is driving the aggression than that in the previous cases. It is important to explore whether aggression is accompanied by depressive symptoms (see Chapter 1 and Chapter 2 of this volume), as its presence may affect treatment decisions. In the first three cases, the aggression was driven by irritable mood, but the irritability was always directed outward, never at the self. A mood stabilizer, such as lithium or divalpreox (Depakote), is often helpful in reducing this kind of outward-directed irritability and aggression. For patients with inner-directed irritability and depression, a serotonin reuptake inhibitor (SRI) or other antidepressant often needs to be part of the treatment.

Thus far, hot aggression driven by mood disturbances has been discussed. There are two more types of aggression that can be considered hot or affective. These are aggression driven by pure impulsivity, such as that seen in attention deficit hyperactivity disorder (ADHD) (see Chapter 5 of this volume), and aggression driven by paranoid states (see Chapter 7 of this volume). The case of EW ("Case 5") has elements of paranoia in his preoccupation with betrayal and jealousy, but the mood component is dominant. The case of ML ("Case 3") has elements of attention deficit hyperactivity disorder (ADHD), evident in his long-standing tendency to act on his impulses even when he was not in a bad mood. However, pure states of impulsive aggression (ADHD-type) and paranoid aggression do exist.

Case 6

RT was diagnosed with ADHD as a child. Now 22, he never finished high school due to learning problems that were never addressed. He often started fights in school, but he did not think of himself as a troublemaker. He thought he was just playing. He repeatedly found himself in fights after being warned by an adversary "I'm not playing with you." He did not hold grudges or plan revenge. He could make friends but he could not keep them. He would always hit first and think later. When he thought about his aggression, he was often sorry, but the outbursts and fights kept happening. Now in treatment for cocaine abuse, he still blurts things out and is constantly on the verge of confrontation. His aggression is driven by impulsivity related to ADHD. Stimulant medication may both improve his ADHD symptoms and control his aggression, and one wonders whether his life course might have been quite different had his ADHD been identified and appropriately treated at an early age.

Case 7

In contrast to RT ("Case 6"), BG held grudges. If he was slighted or felt slighted, he would get even. From his perspective, he was not out looking for trouble. He just wanted to "even the score." When he saw his opponent, an intense feeling of humiliation came over him. It was unbearable. If someone laughed at his rage, that person entered the list of persons who he would attack. BG was paranoid. He misinterpreted the intentions of others, imagined that people saw his humiliation as the most important issue, and acted accordingly. BG could benefit from a low-dose antipsychotic medication.

DSM-IV CRITERIA

The above case presentations suggest a clinically useful theory of aggression must distinguish aggression that is cold ("predatory") and required planning from aggression that is hot ("affective"). Hot aggression can be impulsive, paranoid, inner-directed irritable, or outer-directed irritable in origin. Hot aggression can be called "affective aggression," following the convention in affective neuroscience. IED defines a clinical situation in which affective (hot) aggression appears with no reasonable purpose. There is no threat to ward off and no reason to explode with rage. The *DSM-IV* diagnostic criteria for IED are presented in Table 11-1.

The criteria operationalize the loss of "top-down" "executive" control over affective (hot) aggression. The hot character of the aggression is revealed in the use of the word "impulses"; the loss of top-down control is revealed in the words "failure to resist"; and the dysfunctional nature of the aggression is revealed in the words "out of proportion." Criterion C requires that the episodes not be the direct consequence of substance use or a medical condition.

NATURAL HISTORY AND ETIOLOGY

The etiology and natural history of hot or affective aggression are not well known, since the concepts are only starting to emerge. Among studies that have simply applied IED criteria, two are exemplary. One looked at how many people met criteria in one year in the United States and estimated about 2 percent of those surveyed did (Kessler, Chiu, Demler, Merikangas, & Walters, 2005). Another looked at a clinical sample and estimated the lifetime prevalence of IED in that group to be 6 percent (Coccaro et al., 2005). It would appear that nonpredatory, or affective or hot aggression is a mild to moderate public health problem in terms of prevalence and a moderate clinical problem in adults. In children, hot aggression is a much more serious problem, accounting for, along with ADHD and disruptive behavior disorders, about half of all clinic visits (Earls & Mezzacappa, 2002).

The natural history of IED (as pieced together from adults who report having the problem in a clinical setting) suggests it often begins in childhood, is well-established by young adulthood, and fades as the individual ages (Coccaro et al., 2005). Follow-up studies of children with antisocial behaviors are abundant and suggest a chronic course of problems into adulthood (Earls & Mezzacappa, 2002), but studies focusing on tantrums in childhood are almost nonexistent, with the one available study suggesting persistence of problems with authority and temper into adulthood for the group as a whole (Caspi, Elder, & Bem, 1987), but the amount of variability in outcome is greater (i.e., some individuals age out). If aggression is combined with antisocial spectrum problems, then the long-term connection with substance abuse (Boyle et al., 1992) is clear-cut (Robins, 1966), but for tantrums alone, the outcome is largely unknown.

The etiology of pathologic affective aggression is also unknown. Most speculation in this area acknowledges the role of social learning and attributes the biological role to a failure of "self-regulation." Self-regulation is a generic term that refers to the ways people filter and respond to the innumerable influences that impinge on them. There is evidence that specific neural pathways subserve self-regulation and that when these are disrupted, neurobehavioral disinhibition results. The latter refers to a failure of top-down control or executive functioning. This failure is connected not only to affective aggression but also to substance abuse (Tarter et al.,

Table 11-1
***DSM-IV* Criteria for Intermittent Explosive Disorder**

Symptoms	*DSM-IV* Criteria[a, b]	SCID-ICD Questions to Aid Diagnosis[c, d]
Core Symptoms	A. Several discrete episodes of failure to resist aggressive impulses that result in serious assaultive acts or destruction of property.	Have you ever lost control of your anger, resulting in your hitting or seriously threatening someone or damaging things? If yes, what did you do? When did you do it? How often did it happen?
Other Criteria	B. The degree of aggressiveness expressed during the episodes is grossly out of proportion to any precipitating psychosocial stressors.	What happened that set you off? Do you think your reaction was much stronger than it should have been given the circumstances? Has anyone told you that your reaction was way off-base given the situation?
	C. The aggressive episodes are not better accounted for by another mental disorder (e.g., antisocial personality disorder, borderline personality disorder, a psychotic disorder, a manic episode, conduct disorder, or ADHD) and are not due to direct physiological effects of a substance (e.g., a drug of abuse, a medication) or a general medical condition (e.g., head trauma, Alzheimer's disease).	Did this happen only when you were drinking or using drugs? Did this happen only when you were sick with a medical illness? IF HISTORY OF MANIA OR PSYCHOSIS: Did this happen only when you were feeling excited or irritable or only when you had [psychotic symptoms]? Did you do [assaultive acts] because you were hearing voices or because your thinking was confused? Did you do [assaultive acts] on purpose or was it really beyond your control?

[a] American Psychiatric Association (1994).
[b] Reprinted with permission from the *Diagnostic and Statistical Manual of Mental Disorders,* Fourth Edition (Copyright 1994). American Psychiatric Association.
[c] First (2004); to date SCID-ICD has not been field-tested.
[d] Reprinted with permission from the Structured Clinical Interview for DSM-IV-TR Impulse Control Disorders Not Elsewhere Classified (2004).

2003). In adults, drug/alcohol use is more prevalent among, patients diagnosed with *DSM-IV* IED than controls (Coccaro et al., 2005). More significantly, the presence of neurobehavioral disinhibition at age 11 predicts substance abuse at age 15 (Tarter et al., 2003) and beyond (Tarter et al., 2003).

As can be seen in the clinical vignettes (see "Case Presentations"), hot or affective aggression is almost certainly not one clinical entity. It is very likely that there are different types of hot aggression. The clearest evidence for this point is the fact that radically different pharmacological agents (stismulants, antipsychotics, antidepressants, and mood stabilizers) are sometimes useful and sometimes not. Since these agents are very different in character, (i.e., in what they do in the brain), it is likely that there are multiple clinical entities or disease processes underlying affective aggression. Different types of hot aggression seen in clinical practice are illustrated to in the vignettes (see "Case Presentations") and discussed below.

ISSUES INVOLVED IN MAKING A DIAGNOSIS IN SUBSTANCE-DEPENDENT PATIENTS

Since individuals who become substance dependent often have preexisting problems with self-regulation (Tarter et al., 2003), it is possible that some adolescent and young adults may attempt to self-medicate hot or affective aggression with substances of abuse. We have found that under double-blind placebo-controlled conditions, treatment with divalproex of irritable, aggressive patients who use marijuana to calm down both improves irritability and aggression (often dramatically) and reduces their marijuana use (Donovan, Stewart, & Nunes, 2004). A pattern of chronic marijuana use in a patient with aggressive episodes should raise the suspicion that some form of self-medication is taking place, and should prompt further investigation into the nature of the aggressive symptoms.

Individuals seek out substances of abuse for pleasure, or for positive reinforcement in behavioral terms. When a patient uses drugs for pleasure, secondary effects on control of aggression may ensue. Alcohol, cocaine (Chermack & Blow, 2002), and PCP (McCardle & Fishbein, 1989) promote expression of aggression during intoxication, especially in individuals who are predisposed to aggressive outbursts (Giancola, Godlaski, & Parrott, 2005). Irritability can occur during withdrawal from alcohol or other sedatives, opioids, cannabis, and nicotine and, if sufficiently severe, can result in aggression. Thus, a clinical picture can emerge in some substance abusers of chronic explosive episodes surrounded by periods of intoxication and/or withdrawal. Whether an aggressive disposition is permanently worsened by exposure to drugs of abuse is not known.

The key to distinguishing IED from the consequences of chronic intoxication and withdrawal is the presence of symptoms prior to the onset of substance use or during periods of extended abstinence. Thus, a developmental history, focusing on childhood and adolescent behavior problems, school suspensions, school yard fights, recommendations for medication, and other indications of neurobehavioral disinhibition in childhood or early adolescences should be gathered. When aggressiveness and substance use are difficult to separate in the history because both are chronic, attention should be paid to the pattern of irritability and aggression and whether its timing corresponds closely and consistently with periods of intoxication or withdrawal from substances that characteristically boost irritability.

INSTRUMENTS AND METHODS FOR SCREENING AND DIAGNOSIS

There are several ways to assess aggression, including structured clinical interview (e.g., Structured Clinical Interview for DSM-IV-TR Impulse Control Disorders Not Elsewhere Classified (SCID-ICD; First, 2004), and scales (e.g., Overt Aggression

Scale (OAS; Endicott, Tracy, Burt, Olson, & Coccaro, 2002)). The SCID-ICD, a recently developed module for the Structured Clinical Interview for DSM-IV-TR Axis I Disorders (SCID-I; First, Spitzer, Gibbon, & Williams, 2002), quotes *DSM-IV-TR* criteria for impulse control disorders and suggests questions to elicit information from patients about their symptoms. To date, the SCID-ICD has not been field tested. Table 11-1 includes questions from the SCID-ICD for each of the diagnostic criterion for IED. Scores on assessment instruments, like the OAS, should reflect both the frequency and the magnitude of aggression. For example, a single episode of physical aggression should contribute more to the final score than a single episode of verbal aggression, but multiple verbal rages should add up in clinical significance to a single fight. Various forms of the OAS are available (Endicott et al., 2002).

The idea behind the OAS is to use specific anchors with four types of aggression: against other people, against the self, against property, and purely verbal aggression. Each type of aggression is "weighted" differently in arriving at a total score from purely verbal aggression, considered least severe and given a weight of 1, to aggression against people, considered most severe and given a weight of 4. Aggression against property gets a weight of 2, and aggression against self gets a weight of 3. The usual frame of reference is the past week. To arrive at a total score, each incident in each of those domains that has occurred over the past week is multiplied by the weight, and then all the weighted episodes are summed. Thus, one physical fight in the past week would yield a score of 4; two fights would yield a score of 8, and so forth. Each severe outburst of verbal rage would add one point. Each episode of destruction of property would add two points. Each episode of harm to self (e.g., hitting one's head, pounding one's fist against a wall) would add three points. The points are then summed to arrive at a measure of how severe the person's aggression has been over the past week. For example, a patient with one fight over the past week (1 episode times the weight of 4 = 4) plus three verbal outbursts over the past week (3 episodes times the weight of 1 = 3) and no episodes of destruction of property or harm to self would get a total score of 4 + 3 = 7 for the past week. This scale is useful in establishing a baseline for the type and frequency of aggressive episodes and for following progress during treatment.

DIFFERENTIAL DIAGNOSIS AND OVERLAPPING DISORDERS

The first and most important differential to make is whether the aggression is cold (predatory) or hot (nonpredatory), as this will govern whether treatment is possible. Predatory aggression is characterized by pleasure—a thrill, often likened to the thrill of the hunt. There is little emotional excitement, even with probing by a clinician, on recounting the violence, as the emotion of anger or rage was not present during the act. If this is the pattern to the violence, and the violence is serious, then little can be done to alter the course of the disorder in an outpatient therapeutic setting.

Inappropriate outbursts of affective or hot aggression may be accounted for by a variety of states in which top-down control is compromised or the state of aggressive arousal is increased (see Table 11-2). Thus, intoxications with some substances, such as alcohol, promote aggression in those predisposed by compromising inhibition of aggressive impulses. Intoxication with PCP appears to promote aggression by increasing aggressive arousal. Other substances are less likely to promote hot aggression, for example, marijuana and heroin are more calming and sedating, although withdrawal from these substances can increase aggressive arousal. Thus, the second question in a substance abuse treatment setting when confronting aggression is whether the individual is under the influence.

Table 11-2
Common Psychiatric, Medical, and Substance-Related Conditions Associated
With Irritability and Aggression (Affective Aggression)

Diagnosis	Difference From Intermittent Explosive Disorder
schizophrenia (see Chapter 7 of this volume)	Presence of delusions, hallucinations, blunting of affect; aggression is usually a response to paranoid delusions (e.g., a patient feeling convinced he must defend himself because others intend to harm him) or to command hallucinations (the patient hears voices commanding him to harm others).
bipolar disorder (see Chapter 2 of this volume)	Presence of cycling into and out of depressive and manic states; the mood disturbance in either depression or mania can be irritability; in severe mania, patients often become psychotic and may have delusions or hallucinations that prompt aggression.
major depression, dysthymia (see Chapter 1 of this volume)	Presence of depressive episodes or chronic depression; depressed mood may be irritable; look for suicidal thoughts and plans (aggression toward self); severe major depression may evolve into psychosis.
ADHD (see Chapter 5 of this volume)	Constellation of symptoms including hyperactivity, difficulty with attention, memory, and organization dating to childhood; irritability and aggression typically occur impulsively when such patients are kept waiting (e.g., waiting in line or in traffic) or otherwise frustrated.
borderline personality disorder (see Chapter 9 of this volume)	Lifelong pattern of mood swings, stormy, unstable interpersonal relationships, sense of abandonment, and poor sense of self and identity; irritability is typically focused on significant others or treatment staff and is related to feelings that they have been abandoned or their needs have not been met.
head injury	Clear onset of symptoms after a discrete point in time, history of head injury; as with intoxications, aggression is impulsive in nature and reflects brain dysfunction as a result of the head injury.
metabolic conditions, including delirium, dementia, and intoxications (see Chapter 6 and Chapter 14 of this volume)	Presence of global impairment in cognitive functioning as evidenced in the mental status exam (e.g., disorientation, confusion, gross memory impairment), presence of a relevant medical condition, or history of recent substance ingestion.
	– Substances associated with irritability or aggression during intoxication: alcohol, sedatives, cocaine, other stimulants, PCP.
	– Substances associated with irritability or aggression during withdrawal: alcohol or sedatives, opioids, and cannabis.

Certain medical conditions can promote aggression through the same mechanism. Head injury, particularly to the frontal lobe, can compromise top-down control. Certain forms of epilepsy are implicated in aggressive outbursts. The original description of IED as uncharacteristic episodes of violence was founded on the idea that some individuals had an unusual form of epilepsy. This idea has fallen by the wayside, but it has never been refuted.

Aggression is may also be caused by a psychiatric disorder, such as schizophrenia, mania, and attention deficit spectrum disorders. By definition, such individuals do not have IED because the aggression is presumably better explained by another psychiatric diagnosis.

As mentioned earlier, part of the reluctance to view aggression as a distinct psychiatric problem stemmed from its co-occurrence with many psychiatric conditions. Thus, affective aggression can (but need not) occur in any condition that disturbs self-regulation. Schizophrenia disrupts normal cognitions, thereby allowing the person to think that affective aggression is appropriate when it is not. Bipolar disorder disrupts affect regulation, which can create a mood in which everything appears to annoy and frustrate the patient and to interfere with grandiose plans, thereby making it appear appropriate to use affective aggression to make people back off, when, in fact, people are needed to constrain the person. ADHD leads to loss of top-down control. Thus, a person with ADHD, by definition, may have already yelled at or hit someone because the aggressive impulse was, like all other impulses, not constrained. Some forms of depression bring forth irritable mood in which the person not only attacks himself/herself but also attacks others. The predominant mood disturbance of depression can be irritability.

The main difference between these disorders and problems with affective aggression alone is the presence of the associated symptoms of delusions and hallucinations (schizophrenia), decreased need for sleep, flight of ideas (bipolar disorder), and chronic depressed mood with loss of interest (major depression).

An important differential is whether there is truly loss of control. Children with explosive tantrums often learn that contingent rage is a powerful means of controlling their microenvironment, such as the home or the schoolyard. Thus, although explosive episodes are not inherently antisocial, they have the potential of offering a kind of deviant empowerment, such that the individual senses the power gained from coercing and intimidating others (reciprocal coercive social interactions). Working with children and adults with explosive episodes requires an ability to resist the temptation to give in to the demands associated with the tantrum (Dishion, French, & Patterson, 1995). However, it is often difficult to tolerate the interminable rages of a child and often impossible to ignore the explosive threats of an adult. The distinction between predatory and affective aggression is important, since to the extent that the aggression is affectively driven determines its likelihood of being responsive to medication treatments.

Table 11-3 outlines a classification system to summarize the different types of aggression and medications most useful in treating each type. The scheme is derived in part from the types of medications (e.g., antipsychotic, mood stabilizer, etc.) that different types of aggression seem to respond to in treatment. This scheme can be used to determine medications that might be helpful to a particular patient during treatment planning. It also presents a way of thinking about the causes and underlying mechanisms of aggression.

TREATMENT OPTIONS

Clinically relevant aggression generally starts with verbal aggression on the part of the patient, followed by verbally aggressive behavior on the part of the clinician, followed by physically aggressive behavior by the patient, and then counteraggression by the staff. It is obvious that the point at which to de-escalate this process is when staff must respond to verbal aggression. Once the patient shows physical agression, it is too

Table 11-3
Proposed Subtypes of Aggression and Treatment Implications

Major Division	Subdivision	Second Subdivision	Implications for First Medication Choice	Relation to Antisocial Behavior
predatory	none	none	none	direct
affective	cognitive	impulsive (e.g., ADHD)	stimulant	indirect
affective	cognitive	paranoid (e.g., schizophrenia; paranoid or schizoid personality)	low dose antipsychotic	indirect
affective	mood	mixed irritable (outer- and inner-directed) (e.g., major depression, dysthymia, borderline personality disorder)	SRI or other antidepressant medication	indirect
affective	mood	outer-directed irritable (e.g., mania, hypomania, explosive mood disorder)	mood stabilizer/ anticonvulsant	indirect

Note: Reprinted with permission from *Clinical Manual of Impulse-Control Disorders* (copyright 2005). American Psychiatric Publishing.

late. A firm, quiet response is therefore almost always the only sane one. Quiet means one does not raise one's voice. Firm means the clinician has adequate physical forces in evident reserve (a show of force in terms of presence of other staff) should the patient not listen. If the patient is sober, a firm quiet response will usually prevent escalation. However, if the patient is intoxicated or has a history of aggression, then a show of force must be present before anyone approaches the client. The clinician should speak in a calm, rational tone, and, unless an arrest or necessary detention is planned (e.g., the patient is judged to be sufficiently dangerous to self or others that involuntary confinement is necessary), the patient should be allowed an obvious escape route.

Any setting that treats potentially violent people must have a well-tested system for surreptitiously summoning help should an interview spin out of control. A button under the desk is one such option. As support staff congregates outside the interview, the clinical manager might comment, "I think you would feel more comfortable if you waited outside" in order to preserve something of a clinical continuity in a frightening situation. No clinician can help a patient he/she is afraid of, and if the clinician fears the patient, the interview must end.

For the treatment of aggression, there are two approaches: psychotherapy and pharmacotherapy.

Psychosocial and Behavioral Treatments

Two evidence-based behavioral treatments for children and adolescents with aggression and antisocial features illustrate the main concepts of treatment. Parent Management Training is the most common approach in treatment of children, and its lessons generalize to management of aggression by clinical staff. It emphasizes the need to change reciprocal social interactions typical of children with affective aggression (i.e., coercion—the child (or adult) has learned that aggressive behavior intimidates others and gets them to do what he/she wants; Kazdin, 2000). The important lesson for parents to learn is every time the child avoids a task by throwing a tantrum, the tantrum has been reinforced. If the tantrum does not result in the child avoiding a task, then lack of reinforcement will gradually extinguish the tantrum tactic. Patients must withstand the patient's intensity of rage without giving in. Medication can make a big difference. Medication can diminish the intensity of the aggression, then it is easier for the relevant authority (parents, clinicians, etc.) to maintain the supervisory role.

Another evidence-based psychotherapy is Problem Solving Skills Training (PSST). PSST builds on the inner resources of the adolescent or adult patients and teaches behavioral and cognitive skills for coping with aggressive urges through practice sessions in which graded provocations require patients to use cognitive problem solving skills (Kazdin, 2000; Kazdin & Weisz, 2003). For example, if an adolescent has an art project ruined by another student, the adolescent is taught (through practice and role playing) to think of nonaggressive alternatives to handling this serious provocation. Similarly, an adult version of this approach would use role playing and increasingly more provocative situations to encourage patients to come up with alternative ways of approaching the problem. The difficulty, of course, is that rage and fury can inhibit the implementation of newly learned behavior. Here too, medication can decrease the pressure to revert to maladaptive habits and allow the individual to practice and develop new habits. For both treatments, medications that address the underlying aggressive temperament have the potential to enhance psychotherapies for aggression.

Anger management based on cognitive behavioral principles has become a standard nonpharmacological treatment for explosive adults (Freeman, Felgoise, Nezu, Nezu, & Reinecke, 2005). There are many different forms of this intervention, but they all rely on the principle of problem solving in provocative situations. Clearly, the use of substances like alcohol and other drugs, which generally inhibit problem solving, is strongly discouraged in treatment programs.

Pharmacologic Treatments

Although pharmacologic agents are commonly used to treat aggressive children, adolescents, and, to some extent, adults, there is no theory-driven algorithm for their prescription. A theory-driven approach of first choice of medication has been developed (Donovan, 2005; see Table 11-3), and it proposes that clinical practice already indicates an approach to first choice of medications for affective aggression based on clinical presentation.

Briefly, the approach requires clinicians to make inferences based on the clinical presentation of what is driving the affective or hot aggression, as it will vary from case to case. In some instances, it will be clear that there is little rage in the individual and that pure impulsivity (hitting first and thinking later) drives the aggression. In this case, the first medication choice is a psychostimulant. Pure impulsive aggression overlaps with (but is not always the same as) ADHD (Klein et al., 1997).

Some hot aggression is not impulsive, but rather is driven by a failure to test reality (for example during psychosis). Such individuals are prone to paranoid thinking, and antipsychotic medications are the first line of treatment.

Irritability is often present in aggressive individuals. This is a state characterized by impatience, intolerance, and poor anger control (Snaith & Taylor, 1985). It appears to be a mood in that if one examines the clinical history, the explosive episodes occur in states that are global but temporary. Two classes of medications are useful, and there appears to be some difference in the kind of person who benefits from one class (as opposed to the other). Some patients benefit from SRI antidepressant medications, such as fluoxetine (Coccaro & Kavoussi, 1997). Others fail to benefit from fluoxetine but respond to divalproex (Kavoussi & Coccaro, 1998).

Work by our group, including a randomized placebo-controlled trial, suggests children, adolescents, and young adults with pure "outer-directed" irritability unquestionably respond to divalproex (Donovan et al., 1997, 2000, 2003). Outer-directed irritability means the angry feelings are directed only at the outside world, never at the self. Clinically, we have found that individuals with pure outer-directed irritability do not do well on serotonin uptake inhibitors (sometimes they even become more explosive).

The irritable, aggressive patients who have benefited from SRI antidepressants in placebo-controlled trials are described as having personality disorders, indicating a chronic or lifelong pattern of maladaptive interpersonal functioning. We suspect this latter group has both inner-directed as well as outer-directed irritability; the inner-directed irritability is characterized by self-criticism, self-loathing, self-harm (suicidal behavior or self-injury), and depressive symptoms. Indeed the mood disturbance in major depression, dysthymia (i.e., chronic depression), bipolar depression, or mixed affective episodes (simultaneous presentation of depression and mania) can present as irritability (see Chapter 1 and Chapter 2 of this volume).

Organization of Services

It is a major tragedy that due to lack of attention to the origins and potential treatment options for aggression, it largely remains an administrative problem from grade school to substance abuse treatment programs—that is, such individuals are expelled from the classroom or a treatment program and are transferred to special education classrooms, other treatment programs, or the criminal justice system. Dual diagnosis programs reflect increased interest in helping these explosive, unpredictable individuals, but a deeper understanding of aggression is needed.

Individuals with aggression problems are usually aggregated in special education classes as children. If they develop substance abuse problems, they often drop out of school and perhaps have a brief hospitalization, where they are prescribed medications, often with little follow-up. If problems with aggression and substance abuse persist, some contact with the criminal justice system is almost inevitable, often with consequences that tend to promote antisocial attitudes, just as an earlier exposure to special education might (Kellam, Ling, Merisca, Brown, & Ialongo, 1998). If the individual is fortunate and finds a dual diagnosis program that offers treatment for explosive aggressive outbursts, it may be possible to retain the person long enough to provide a program of rehabilitation. However, the reality is that explosive aggressive adolescents and young adults are difficult to retain and difficult to bring into a structured setting. For this reason, judicious use of pharmacologic agents should be considered. It is no more possible to help these individuals when they are throwing tantrums at age 25 than when they were throwing tantrums in special education classes at age 8. Ultimately, the frightening coercive aspects of explosive rage must be confronted, but first the rage must be dampened. Confrontation of coercion is possible only if the contingent rage is dampened to the point that those trying to help the individual can tolerate and forgive it.

SUMMARY

Aggression is a common problem in substance abuse treatment settings. Substances of abuse can promote aggression directly through intoxication and withdrawal, and they also foster lifestyles in which antisocial behaviors and aggressive activities, are common. Furthermore, aggression often predates and promotes substance abuse.

Aggression that is part of an antisocial lifestyle is difficult to treat. Agression that exists independent of it is quite possible to treat.

Individuals with a long history of thrill-seeking violence (cold, predatory aggression) are antisocial by definition, and there is no clear treatment for this type aggression aside from restraining them in some way. Individuals with affective (hot) aggression are amenable to treatment, although they can often have an antisocial lifestyle as a consequence of a long history of maladaptive forms of social learning. It is often possible with a combination of medication and psychotherapy to dampen the hot aggression and, with surveillance and supervision, decrease the antisocial behavior, at least to the point that the person can stay in treatment.

Medications that are useful for hot aggression suggest that there are different tributaries to ultimate expression of the behavior. In some individuals, one tributary is so dominant that a medication immediately suggests itself. In other cases, the clinical phenomena are more mixed. Dismissal of patients should not be a universal response to aggressive behavior.

Suggestions for Further Reading

For readers who wish to study further in this area, we recommend:

- Coccaro, E. F. (Ed.). (2003). *Aggression: Psychiatric assessment and treatment.* New York: Marcel Dekker.

- Hollander, E., & Stein, D. (Eds.). (2005). *Clinical manual of impulse control disorders.* Washington, DC: American Psychiatric Publishing.

- Kazdin, A., & Weisz, J. R. (2003). *Evidence-based psychotherapies for children and adolescents.* New York: Guilford Press.

Author's Note

The research in this chapter was supported in part by grants K20 DA00246 (Dr. Donovan) and K02 DA00451 (Dr. Donovan) from the National Institute on Drug Abuse and grant R01 DA12234 (Dr. Donovan).

References

American Psychiatric Association. (1980). *Diagnostic and statistical manual of mental disorders* (3rd ed.). Washington, DC: Author.

American Psychiatric Association. (1987). *Diagnostic and statistical manual of mental disorders* (3rd ed., rev.). Washington, DC: Author.

American Psychiatric Association. (1994). *Diagnostic and statistical manual of mental disorders* (4th ed.). Washington, DC: Author.

American Psychiatric Association. (2000). *Diagnostic and statistical manual of mental disorders* (4th ed., text rev.). Washington, DC: Author.

Boyle, M. H., Offord, D. R., Racine, Y. A., Szatmari, P., Fleming, J. E., & Links, P. S. (1992). Predicting substance use in late adolescence: Results from the Ontario Child Health Study follow-up. *American Journal of Psychiatry, 149*, 761-767.

Bradford, J., Geller, J., Lesieur, H., Rosenthal, R., & Wise, M. (1996). Impulse control disorders. In T. A. Widiger, A. J. Frances, H. A. Pincus, M. B. First, R. Ross, & W. Davis (Eds.), *DSM-IV sourcebook* (Vol. 2, pp. 1007-1031). Washington, DC: American Psychiatric Publishing.

Caspi, A., Elder, G. H., & Bem, D. J. (1987). Moving against the world: Life-course patterns of explosive children. *Developmental Psychology, 23*, 308-313.

Chermack, S. T., & Blow, F. C. (2002). Violence among individuals in substance abuse treatment. The role of alcohol and cocaine consumption. *Drug and Alcohol Dependence, 66*, 29-37.

Coccaro, E. (2002). Intermittent explosive disorder. In E. Coccaro (Ed.), *Aggression: Psychiatric assessment and treatment* (pp. 149-166). New York: Marcel Dekker.

Coccaro, E. F., & Kavoussi, R. J. (1997). Fluoxetine and impulsive aggressive behavior in personality disordered subjects. *Archives of General Psychiatry, 54*, 1081-1088.

Coccaro, E. F., Posternak, M. A., & Zimmerman, M. (2005). Prevalence and features of intermittent explosive disorder in a clinical setting. *Journal of Clinical Psychiatry, 66*, 1221-1227.

Coccaro, E. F., & Siever, L. J. (2002). Pathophysiology and treatment of aggression. In K. L. Davis, D. Charney, J. T. Coyle, & C. Nemeroff (Eds.), *Neuropsychopharmacology: The fifth generation of progress* (pp. 1709-1723). Philadelphia: Lippincott, Williams and Williams.

Connor, D. F. (2002). *Aggression and antisocial behavior in children and adolescents: Research and treatment*. New York: Guilford Press.

Dishion, T. J., French, D. C., & Patterson, G. R. (1995). The development and ecology of antisocial behavior. In D. Cicchetti & D. J. Cohen (Eds.), *Developmental psychopathology* (Vol. 2, pp. 421-471). New York: John Wiley & Sons.

Donovan, S. (2005). Childhood conduct disorder and the antisocial spectrum. In E. Hollander & D. Stein (Eds.), *Clinical manual of impulse-control disorders* (pp. 39-62). Washington, DC: American Psychiatric Publishing.

Donovan, S. J., Nunes, E. V., Stewart, J. W., Ross, D., Quitkin, F. M., Jensen, P. S., et al. (2003). "Outer Directed Irritability:" A distinct mood syndrome in explosive youth with a disruptive behavior disorder? *Journal of Clinical Psychiatry, 64*, 698-701.

Donovan, S., Stewart, J. W., & Nunes, E. V. (2004). *Temper, mood and marijuana—A link at the biological level?* New Research Presentation #129 at the Scientific Proceedings of the American Academy of Child and Adolescent Psychiatry.

Donovan, S. J., Stewart, J. W., Nunes, E. V., Quitkin, F. M., Parides, M., Daniel, W., et al. (2000). Divalproex treatment for youth with explosive temper and mood lability: A double-blind, placebo-controlled crossover design. *American Journal of Psychiatry, 157*, 818-820.

Donovan, S. J., Susser, E. S., Nunes, E. V., Stewart, J. W., Quitkin, F. M., & Klein, D. F. (1997). Divalproex treatment of disruptive adolescents: A report of 10 cases. *Journal of Clinical Psychiatry, 58*, 12-15.

Earls, F., & Mezzacappa, E. (2002). Conduct and oppositional disorders. In M. Rutter & E. Taylor (Eds.), *Child and adolescent psychiatry* (4th ed., pp. 419-436). Oxford, UK: Blackwell Science Ltd.

Endicott, J., Tracy, K., Burt, D., Olson, E., & Coccaro, E. F. (2002). A novel approach to assess inter-rater reliability in the use of the overt aggression scale-modified. *Psychiatry Research, 112*, 153-159.

First, M. B. (2004, September). Structured Clinical Interview for DSM-IV-TR Impulse Control Disorders Not Elsewhere Classified (SCID-ICD). New York: Biometrics Research Department, New York State Psychiatric Institute.

First, M. B., Spitzer, R. L., Gibbon, M., & Williams, J. B. W. (2002, November). Structured Clinical Interview for DSM-IV-TR Axis I Disorders, Patient Edition (SCID-I/P). New York: Biometrics Research Department, New York State Psychiatric Institute.

Freeman, A., Felgoise, S. H., Nezu, A. M., Nezu, C. M., & Reinecke, M. A. (Eds.). (2005). *Encyclopedia of cognitive behavior therapy.* New York: Springer Science + Business Media.

Giancola, P. R., Godlaski, A. J., & Parrott, D. J. (2005). So I can't blame the booze? Dispositional aggressivity negates the moderating effects of expectancies on alcohol-related aggression. *Journal on Studies of Alcohol, 66,* 815-824.

Ialongo, N., Edelsohn, G., Werthamer-Larsson, L., Crockett, L., & Kellam, S. (1996). The course of aggression in first-grade children with and without comorbid anxious symptoms. *Journal of Abnormal Child Psychology, 24,* 445-456.

Kavoussi, R. J., & Coccaro, E. F. (1998). Divalproex sodium for impulsive aggressive behavior in patients with personality disorder. *Journal of Clinical Psychiatry, 59*, 676-680.

Kazdin, A. E. (2000). Treatments for aggressive and antisocial children. *Child and Adolescent Psychiatric Clinics of North America, 9*, 841-858.

Kazdin, A. E., & Weisz, J. R. (2003). *Evidence-based psychotherapies for children and adolescents.* New York: Guilford Press.

Kellam, S. G., Ling, X., Merisca, R., Brown, C. H., & Ialongo, N. (1998). The effect of the level of aggression in the first grade classroom on the course and malleability of aggressive behavior into middle school. *Development and Psychopathology, 10,* 165–185.

Kessler, R. C., Chiu, W. T., Demler, O., Merikangas, K. R., & Walters, E. E. (2005). Prevalence, severity, and comorbidity of 12-Month DSM-IV disorders in the National Comorbidity Survey Replication. *Archives of General Psychiatry, 62*, 617-627.

Klein, R. G., Abikoff, H., Klass, E., Ganeles, D., Seese, L. M., & Pollack, S. (1997). Clinical efficacy of methylphenidate in conduct disorder with and without attention deficit hyperactivity disorder. *Archives of General Psychiatry, 54,*1073-1080.

McCardle, L., & Fishbein, D. H. (1989). The self-reported effects of PCP on human aggression. *Addictive Behaviors, 14*, 465-472.

Robins, L. N. (1966). Deviant children grown up: A sociological and psychiatric study of sociopathic personality. Baltimore: Williams & Wilkens.

Soller, M. V., Karnik, N. S., & Steiner, H. (2006). Psychopharmacologic treatment in juvenile offenders. *Child and Adolescent Psychiatric Clinics of North America, 15,* 477-499.

Snaith, R. P., & Taylor, C. M. (1985). Irritability: Definition, assessment and associated factors. *British Journal of Psychiatry, 147*, 127-136.

Tarter, R. E., Kirisci, L., Mezzich, A., Cornelius, J. R., Pajer, K., Vanyukov, M., et al. (2003). Neurobehavioral disinhibition in childhood predicts early age at onset of substance use disorder. *American Journal of Psychiatry, 160*, 1078-1085.

Chapter 12

Eating Disorders in Patients With Substance Use Disorders: Bulimia, Anorexia, Overeating Disorder, and Obesity

by Shelly F. Greenfield, M.D., M.P.H., Susan M. Gordon, Ph.D., Lisa Cohen, Ph.D., and Elisa Trucco, B.A.

INTRODUCTION

Eating disorders commonly co-occur in patients with substance use disorders. Individuals receiving treatment for eating disorders frequently report alcohol and other drug use and abuse. Similarly, individuals entering treatment for substance use disorders often report a preoccupation with food and body image. In both treatment settings, patients often have symptoms that meet diagnostic criteria for both substance use disorders and eating disorders.

Surveys of the general population report that eating disorders occur in 2.8 percent of individuals under the age of 18 and in 1.3 percent of those 19 to 23 years of age. Two of the most common eating disorders are anorexia nervosa and bulimia nervosa, and 90 to 95 percent of individuals with these disorders are female. In the general population, in the course of the lifetime, 0.3 to 0.7 percent of all females are estimated to have anorexia nervosa, and 1.7 to 2.5 percent of all females have bulimia nervosa. Surveys also report a 0.1 percent lifetime prevalence of bulimia nervosa for males ages 15 to 65.

Among patients with substance use disorders, co-occurring bulimia nervosa and binge-eating disorder are more prevalent than anorexia nervosa. Holderness, Brooks-Gunn, and Warren (1994) estimate that, among patients with substance use disorders, approximately 8 to 14 percent will have bulimia nervosa, and 2 to 10 percent will have anorexia nervosa.

In a population-based study, 22.9 percent of bulimic women had alcohol dependence and 48.6 percent had co-occurring alcohol abuse compared to control female subjects, who had prevalence rates of 8.6 percent for alcohol abuse and 0.0 percent for alcohol dependence (Bulik, 1987). Goldbloom, Naranjo, Bremner, and Hicks (1992) studied two different populations of women: those receiving treatment for alcohol abuse and those receiving treatment for an eating disorder. In women presenting for treatment of alcohol problems, 30.1 percent met criteria for an eating disorder, while

26.9 percent of women seeking outpatient treatment for an eating disorder met criteria for alcohol dependence. Other studies report that, by the age of 35, 50 percent of individuals with bulimia nervosa had met criteria for alcohol abuse or dependence at some point in their lives (Beary, Lacey, & Merry, 1986). Other studies have reported that the diagnosis of eating disorder not otherwise specified (NOS) was more likely to be made in individuals with substance use disorders than those without a substance use disorder (Grilo, Levy, Becker, Edell, & McGlashan, 1995; Grilo, Sinha, & O'Malley, 2002).

Research has examined possible factors that may account for the increased risk that eating disorders pose in the development (or worsening) of an alcohol use disorder (and vice versa). For example, patients who have been diagnosed with bulimia nervosa report alcohol consumption as a primary trigger for binge eating. Research also suggests that individuals with eating disorders develop problem drinking patterns at a more rapid rate than individuals with only alcohol dependence and without an eating disorder.

The relationship between eating disorders (particularly bulimia nervosa) and substance use disorders highlights the importance of screening patients with substance use disorders for symptoms of eating disorders. It is also important to determine if patients with substance use disorders have symptoms that meet standard diagnostic criteria for eating disorders such as those described in the *Diagnostic and Statistical Manual of Mental Disorders*, 4th edition, text revision (*DSM-IV-TR*; American Psychiatric Association, 2000). The assessment of symptoms of an eating disorder in patients who come to treatment for a substance use disorder can help guide effective treatment planning for patients with both disorders.

This chapter will outline the assessment and treatment of patients with co-occurring eating and substance use disorders. Since bulimia is more prevalent than anorexia in patients with substance use disorders, and since eating disorders occur predominantly in women, most of the available literature addresses the treatment of co-occurring bulimia and substance use disorders in women. Therefore, this chapter will focus primarily on substance use disorders and co-occurring bulimia nervosa or binge-eating disorder in females. More specifically, the chapter will outline the various classifications and subtypes of eating disorders, present evidence for the heightened risk that eating disorders pose in the development of substance use disorders (and vice versa), and describe psychometrically validated measures for screening and diagnosing eating disorders and substance use disorders. The chapter will present current options available to treat substance-dependent patients with eating disorders and will offer a method for effective treatment planning.

CASE PRESENTATION

The case presented below is a synopsis of a number of patients encountered by the authors in their clinical work. It represents a fairly typical pattern of substance abuse in patients with a co-occurring eating disorder.

Chief Complaint

TG is a 20-year-old female full-time second-year college student. She sought treatment when the manager of a local campus bar banned her from the bar because of disruptive behavior. TG also reported that she may have been date raped following an evening of drinking. Her friends frequently worried about her safety because she often was "overly friendly" and loud with male patrons at the bar. TG felt that her drinking habits did not appear to be more excessive than others; she did not believe that she had a problem with alcohol. However, she admitted that she was concerned that she had woken up in the bed of a stranger and could not remember how she got there. She also wondered if she might be smoking too much marijuana because she was gaining weight and had to rely on laxatives to lose weight.

Patient History

Alcohol and Other Drug History. TG reported that she began to smoke cigarettes at age 13 and began to smoke approximately one pack a day by age 16. TG began drinking alcohol (mainly beer and wine coolers) at the beginning of high school (around the age of 15). At that time, she also started smoking marijuana. She tended to use both substances once or twice weekly at parties and always smoked cigarettes while she was drinking or smoking marijuana.

When TG moved to an apartment in her second year of college, her marijuana use increased to three or four nights per week because she was able to smoke alone in her apartment. She also began to drink more heavily in college and reported that, on weekend evenings, when she went to a bar with friends, she consumed up to four or five beers, followed by three or four shots of scotch. After these evenings of binge drinking, TG often experienced hangovers. She occasionally could not remember events that occurred while drinking. TG continued to combine her marijuana and alcohol use with cigarettes.

TG also occasionally used lysergic acid diethylamide (LSD) and Ecstasy when they were available at parties or dance raves. She briefly experimented with cocaine in her first year of college, but she did not like the "jitteriness" that she experienced when snorting cocaine. TG had been offered heroin (snorting) but did not try it because its reputation scared her. However, she appeared interested in the weight-loss aspects of cocaine and heroin.

TG never tried to stop or reduce her drug or alcohol use. She tried to stop smoking cigarettes a few times but was unable to maintain abstinence for more than a day. TG reported that she was not interested in decreasing her cigarette smoking, which helped her to control her weight. She was interested in curbing her alcohol use and decreasing her marijuana use in order to lose weight. TG reported no prior treatment for substance use disorders.

Psychiatric History. TG reported that she received treatment for depression when she was 13 years old. At that time, her parents separated and divorced, and TG recollected that she had felt hopeless and blamed herself for her parents' marital difficulties. During an interview, TG's mother reported that at the time of her divorce TG became argumentative, irritable, and verbally abusive to her younger sister. TG's pediatrician had recommended psychiatric treatment following an episode in which TG had swallowed some of her mother's sleeping medication. TG and her mother did not view the episode as a suicide attempt and described it as "experimentation."

At the time of her parents' divorce, TG became much more self-conscious and concerned about her weight. At that time, TG was undergoing puberty-related changes. She had been an active gymnast, but she quit her team when she turned 15 years old because the shift in body fat and breast development made it difficult for her to perform advanced gymnastics. TG initially tried dieting and fasting to control her weight but could not control her eating behavior. She tended to fast or eat very little until dinnertime when she would begin to binge. Her mother agreed that TG was a "good" (i.e., light) eater until dinner (when she could consume over 1,000 calories). The situation worsened when TG's mother increased her work hours and could not supervise her children's dinners. TG reported that in middle school (around 14 to 15 years of age) a friend taught her how to self-induce vomiting to control her weight. She did not like the experience of vomiting and turned to laxative abuse in high school.

At the time of the initial evaluation, TG was consuming eight to ten over-the-counter laxatives three or four times a week. She realized that her use of laxatives had dramatically increased (from one laxative per day). She experienced gastrointestinal symptoms from laxative abuse. However, she was reluctant to stop the use of laxatives because of the "light and airy" feeling that she experienced following laxative abuse. In fact, TG thought that she could smoke marijuana and then overeat in order to have an excuse to take the laxatives, which would relax her. She also feared that cessation of laxative use would cause bloating, constipation, and weight gain.

Developmental History. TG reported an average suburban childhood marred only by the birth of her younger sister and her parents' marital conflicts. She felt that her father preferred her sister because she was thinner. In a session with TG's father, he denied favoring his younger daughter but focused on his desire for TG to "maintain her appearance" and to avoid looking like her obese mother. TG described herself as an average student who was popular with other students who liked to have fun. She tended to be inattentive in class and had difficulty concentrating. She felt that marijuana helped her to focus on schoolwork.

Treatment History. Following the episode with her mother's sleeping medication, TG was treated in outpatient individual child-centered psychotherapy for six months. Treatment was terminated when the symptoms subsided. She also participated in a few family therapy sessions in high school when her younger sister was admitted to an inpatient unit for anorexia.

Family History. TG's father has a history of alcohol abuse. He reported heavy drinking in college and during the difficult period leading up to his divorce. At the time of the interview, he reported that he was in control of his drinking, but he would not describe his alcohol use patterns. TG's mother has a history of depression and anxiety. TG described her mother as having symptoms of obsessive compulsive disorder (OCD), but her mother has not been diagnosed or treated for it. TG's sister has a history of anorexia nervosa; when TG presented for treatment, her sister was receiving inpatient treatment for anorexia nervosa for the third time. Her sister had been diagnosed also with OCD and had no history of substance abuse.

Medical History. TG has no serious medical problems other than laxative-related gastrointestinal problems and alcohol withdrawal symptoms.

Social History. TG reported considerable scholastic problems in college and complained that her college classes were more difficult and boring than her high school classes. She described herself as a mediocre student with a GPA of 2.5. TG also was experienced difficulties forming steady intimate relationships. She dated one boy in high school but admitted to "cheating" on him. The relationship ended when she moved to college. In college she has had a series of one-night sexual relationships and fears that she will never meet the "right person."

Mental Status Examination

TG is a young adult female who looks younger than her stated age. She is average height and weight. During the admission interview she initially is superficial and artificially cheerful. She becomes more serious and engaged as the interview progresses, and her mood shifts to thoughtful with sad affect. She reports low energy, sleep disturbance, appetite disturbance, and hopeless mood. She denies suicidal or homicidal ideation and auditory, visual, and olfactory hallucinations. She is oriented to person, place, and time. Brief cognitive testing reveals average intelligence with possible symptoms of attention deficit hyperactivity disorder. Her insight and judgment are poor. Stressors include poor scholastic performance, difficulties with forming intimate relationships, and body image distortion.

DIAGNOSTIC CRITERIA AND TECHNIQUE

DSM-IV Criteria for Eating Disorders

The current classification for eating disorders in the *DSM-IV* specifies two specific diagnoses (anorexia nervosa and bulimia nervosa) and also includes eating disorders NOS; the *Diagnostic and Statistical Manual of Mental Disorders*, 4th edition, text revision (*DSM-IV-TR;* American Psychiatric Association, 2000) includes a new eating disorder subtype, binge-eating disorder, as a research category. Because it is still considered a research diagnosis and requires further study, binge-eating disorder is diagnosed and coded as eating disorder NOS. The criteria for these four eating disorder classifications are summarized in Tables 12-1A, 12-1B, 12-1C, and 12-1D, respectively. The *DSM-IV* and the *DSM-IV* casebook (Spitzer, Gibbon, Skodol, Williams, & First, 1994) include detailed explanations of subtypes (purging type and nonpurging type).

As outlined in Tables 12-1A through 12-1D, eating disorders are characterized by severe disturbances in the way in which body weight or shape is perceived and an excessive influence of body weight or shape on self-evaluation. The core features for anorexia nervosa are refusal to maintain a minimally normal body weight and an intense fear of gaining weight. Therefore, it is essential to ask patients if they weigh much less than other people think they ought to weigh and to collect information on the patients' height, weight, and age. Although an individual in childhood and early adolescence may not exhibit significant weight loss, he/she may fail to meet expected weight gains. If a patient weighs less than 85 percent of the weight that is considered normal for the patient's age and height (standards are based on pediatric growth charts), the patient is considered underweight. However, when determining minimum normal weight for a patient, clinicians should consider the individual's body build and weight history. Individuals with anorexia nervosa may lack insight or have extreme denial of their weight loss; therefore, weight history and other information about the patient's illness should be obtained from the patient's parents or another source.

Weight loss in patients with anorexia nervosa is primarily achieved through a very restricted diet coupled at times with purging (i.e., self-induced vomiting or the misuse of laxatives or diuretics) or excessive exercise. Despite significant weight loss through dieting and exercise, patients become increasingly concerned about weight gain. Significant weight loss may result in an associated symptom of anorexia, amenorrhea (i.e., the absence of at least three consecutive menstrual cycles in postmenarcheal females, or a delay in menarche in prepubertal females), as outlined in Table 12-1A.

Table 12-1A
DSM-IV Criteria for Anorexia Nervosa

Symptoms	DSM-IV Criteria[a, b]	PRISM Questions to Aid Diagnosis[c, d]
Core Symptoms	A. Refusal to maintain body weight at or above a minimally normal weight for age and height (e.g., weight loss leading to maintenance of body weight less than 85% of that expected; or failure to make expected weight gain during period of growth, leading to body weight less than 85% of that expected).	When your weight was [lowest weight], did you refuse to gain any weight, even though other people thought you should?
	B. Intense fear of gaining weight or becoming fat, even though underweight.	During the time your weight was [lowest weight], were you very afraid of gaining weight or getting fat?
	C. Disturbance in the way in which one's body weight or shape is experienced, undue influence of body weight or shape on self-evaluation, or denial of the seriousness of the current low body weight.	When your weight was [lowest weight] … … did you think you looked fat? … did you think your weight was one of the most important things about you? … did you think that it might have been unhealthy or believe people who told you it was?
	D. In postmenarcheal females, amenorrhea (i.e., the absence of at least three consecutive menstrual cycles). (A woman is considered to have amenorrhea if her periods occur only following hormone (e.g., estrogen) administration.)	Before you reached [lowest weight], were you having your periods? Did they stop when you lost weight? … Did they stop for at least 3 months?
Types of Anorexia Nervosa		
Restricting Type	During the current episode of anorexia nervosa, the person has not regularly engaged in binge-eating or purging behavior (i.e., self-induced vomiting or the misuse of laxatives, diuretics, or enemas).	
Binge-Eating/Purging Type	During the current episode of anorexia nervosa, the person has regularly engaged in binge-eating or purging behavior (i.e., self-induced vomiting or the misuse of laxatives, diuretics, or enemas).	During the time your weight was [lowest weight], did you ever make yourself vomit or use laxatives, diuretics, or enemas as often as twice a week?

(a) American Psychiatric Association (1994).
(b) Reprinted with permission from the *Diagnostic and Statistical Manual of Mental Disorders*, Fourth Edition (Copyright 1994). American Psychiatric Association.
(c) Hasin et al. (2006).
(d) Reprinted with permission.

There are two major patterns of eating behavior in anorexia nervosa. In the restrictive subtype, food restriction is utilized as the primary means of weight loss. These patients do not exhibit binge/purge behavior and generally have less diffuse impulsivity. They are less likely than patients with the binge/purge subtype of anorexia nervosa to have substance use disorders. Patients with the binge/purge subtype of anorexia nervosa lack the more rigid discipline of those with the restrictive subtype. While they may restrict food intake for periods of time, they also have powerful urges to binge. Because of their fear of weight gain, they engage in counteractive measures, which can include self-induced vomiting, laxative abuse, diuretic abuse, fasting, and compulsive exercise. Those with the binge/purge subtype are more likely than those with the restrictive subtype to abuse substances.

Although both anorexia nervosa and bulimia nervosa have criteria that reflect an extreme preoccupation with weight and body shape, individuals with bulimia nervosa exhibit periods of binge eating followed by inappropriate compensatory behaviors to prevent weight gain. Unlike individuals with anorexia, individuals with bulimia nervosa are able to maintain body weight that is at or above a normal level. A binge is defined as eating a larger amount of food in a shorter amount of time than most people would eat under similar circumstances (see Table 12-1B). An episode is usually triggered by dysphoric mood states and associated with an acute feeling of loss of control (e.g., a feeling that one cannot stop eating). To evaluate an individual for an eating disorder, a clinician should begin by asking if the individual often feels like he/she is "eating out of control." The binge-eating episode ends when the individual is uncomfortably satiated and typically leads to feelings of guilt and depressed mood. Binge eating is normally secretive in order to conceal symptomatology. Holiday meals or continuous snacking throughout the day are not classified as binges.

Another core feature of bulimia nervosa is recurrent inappropriate and maladaptive compensatory behaviors to control weight gain after binge episodes. Common behaviors include self-induced vomiting; misuse of laxatives, diuretics, or enemas; fasting; or excessive exercise. To compensate for the binge episode, individuals with bulimia nervosa may fast for a day or two. Exercise is considered excessive when it interferes with daily activities, occurs at inappropriate times or in appropriate settings, or continues despite medical injury or complications.

For a patient's symptoms to meet a diagnosis of anorexia or bulimia nervosa, the patient must exhibit all associated symptoms, as outlined in Tables 12-1A and 12-1B. A diagnosis of bulimia nervosa requires both binge eating and the occurrence of inappropriate compensatory behaviors, on average, at least twice a week for three months. For other problems of weight and eating that do not meet all the necessary criteria for a specific eating disorder, eating disorder NOS may be the more appropriate diagnosis (see Table 12-1D). If an individual meets criteria for binge eating but does not exhibit inappropriate compensatory behaviors that are characteristic of bulimia nervosa, a diagnosis of binge-eating disorder may be more appropriate (see Table 12-1C).

How to Take a History

Outline Substance Abuse History. We recommend starting the assessment by asking about current and past drug and alcohol use and documenting the landmarks of use. For each specific substance that has been used, document the chronology of (1) age of first use, (2) age of first regular use (e.g., two or three times per week or more), (3) age of first problem caused by the substance, (4) age of first treatment for the substance,

Table 12-1B
DSM-IV Criteria for Bulimia Nervosa

Symptoms	*DSM-IV* Criteria[a, b]	PRISM Questions to Aid Diagnosis[c, d]
Core Symptoms	A. Recurrent episodes of binge eating. An episode of binge eating is characterized by both of the following:	
	(1) eating, in a discrete period of time (e.g., within any 2-hour period), an amount of food that is definitely larger than most people would eat during a similar period of time and under similar circumstances	Have you ever eaten an <u>unusually large amount</u> of food within any 2-hour period?
	(2) a sense of lack of control over eating during the episode (e.g., a feeling that one cannot stop eating or control what or how much one is eating.	While you were [binging], did you feel that you couldn't control what or how much you were eating?
	B. Recurrent inappropriate compensatory behavior in order to prevent weight gain, such as self-induced vomiting; misuse of laxatives, diuretics, enemas, or other medications; fasting; or excessive exercise.	
Other Criteria	C. The binge eating and inappropriate compensatory behaviors both occur, on average, at least twice a week for 3 months.	Did you ever [binge] at least twice a week? ... Did this last for three months? ... If you added up all the times you [compensatory behaviors], would you say you were ever doing those things at least twice a week on average?
	D. Self-evaluation is unduly influenced by body shape and weight.	During the time(s) when you were binging and [compensatory behaviors], did your weight seem like one of the most important things about you?
	E. The disturbance does not occur exclusively during episodes of anorexia nervosa (see Table 12-1A).	Were there any times when you were [binging] and [compensatory behaviors] at least twice a week when you weighed <u>more</u> than [15% below expected body weight]?
Types of Bulimia Nervosa		
Purging Type	During the current episode of bulimia nervosa, the person has regularly engaged in self-induced vomiting or misuse of laxatives, diuretics, or enemas.	During any period that you were binging at least twice a week ... ... did you make yourself vomit after [binging]? ... did you take laxatives after [binging]? ... did you take diuretics or other medicine after [binging]?
Nonpurging Type	During the current episode of bulimia nervosa, the person has used other inappropriate compensatory behaviors, such as fasting or excessive exercise, but has not regularly engaged in self-induced vomiting on the misuse of laxatives, diuretics, or enemas.	During any period that you were binging at least twice a week ... ... did you fast to keep from gaining weight? ... did you exercise a lot to keep from gaining weight?

[a] American Psychiatric Association (1994).
[b] Reprinted with permission from the *Diagnostic and Statistical Manual of Mental Disorders,* Fourth Edition (Copyright 1994). American Psychiatric Association.
[c] Hasin et al. (2006).
[d] Reprinted with permission.

Table 12-1C
DSM-IV **Research Criteria for Binge-Eating Disorder**

Symptoms	*DSM-IV* Criteria[a, b]	SCID-I Questions to Aid Diagnosis[c, d]
Core Symptoms	A. Recurrent episodes of binge eating. An episode of binge eating is characterized by both of the following:	
	(1) eating, in a discrete period of time (e.g., within any 2-hour period), an amount of food that is definitely larger than most people would eat in a similar period of time under similar circumstances	
	(2) a sense of lack of control over eating during the episode (e.g., a feeling that one cannot stop eating or control what or how much one is eating).	
	B. The binge-eating episodes are associated with three (or more) of the following:	During these binges …
	(1) eating much more rapidly than normal	… did you eat much more rapidly than normal?
	(2) eating until feeling uncomfortably full	… eat until you felt uncomfortably full?
	(3) eating large amounts of food when not feeling physically hungry	… eat large amounts of food when you didn't feel physically hungry?
	(4) eating alone because of being embarrassed by how much one is eating	… eat alone because you were embarrassed by how much you were eating?
	(5) feeling disgusted with oneself, depressed, or very guilty after overeating.	… feel disgusted with yourself, depressed, or feel very guilty after overeating?
Other Criteria	C. Marked distress regarding binge eating is present.	Was it very upsetting to you that you couldn't stop eating or control what or how much you were eating?
	D. The binge eating occurs, on average, at least 2 days a week for 6 months.	How often did you binge? For how long? At least two days a week for at least six months?
	E. The binge eating is not associated with the regular use of inappropriate compensatory behaviors (e.g., purging, fasting, excessive exercise) and does not occur exclusively during the course of anorexia nervosa (see Table 12-1A) or bulimia nervosa (see Table 12-1B).	

(a) American Psychiatric Association (1994).
(b) Reprinted with permission from the *Diagnostic and Statistical Manual of Mental Disorders*, Fourth Edition (Copyright 1994), American Psychiatric Association.
(c) First, Spitzer, Gibbon, & Williams (2002); note that since the PRISM does not provide specific questions for diagnosis of binge-eating disorder, questions from the SCID-I for diagnosing binge-eating disorder were included in Table 12-1C.
(d) Reprinted with permission.

Table 12-1D
DSM-IV Criteria for Eating Disorder Not Otherwise Specified

Symptoms	*DSM-IV* Criteria[a, b]
Core Symptoms	(1) For females, all of the criteria for anorexia nervosa (see Table 12-1A) are met except that the individual has regular menses.
	(2) All of the criteria for anorexia nervosa (see Table 12-1A) are met except that, despite significant weight loss, the individual's current weight is in the normal range.
	(3) All of the criteria for bulimia nervosa (see Table 12-1B) are met except that binge eating and inappropriate compensatory mechanisms occur at a frequency of less than twice a week or for a duration of less than three months.
	(4) The regular use of inappropriate compensatory behavior by an individual of normal body weight after eating small amounts of food (e.g., self-induced vomiting after the consumption of two cookies).
	(5) Repeatedly chewing and spitting out, but not swallowing, large amounts of food.
	(6) Binge-eating disorder (see Table 12-1C): recurrent episodes of binge eating in the absence of the regular use of inappropriate compensatory behaviors characteristic of bulimia nervosa (see Table 12-1B).

Note: The eating disorder not otherwise specified category is for disorders of eating that do not meet the criteria for any specific eating disorder.
[a] American Psychiatric Association (1994).
[b] Reprinted with permission from the *Diagnostic and Statistical Manual of Mental Disorders,* Fourth Edition (Copyright 1994). American Psychiatric Association.

(5) efforts to cut down or quit use, and (6) periods of abstinence and any treatments or support that were helpful in promoting abstinence. It is helpful to establish each of these landmarks for each substance used throughout the patient's lifetime. Then the clinician should document the pattern and quantity of all substances used most recently. One helpful way to elicit this history is to ask patients a series of questions such as: "Tell me about your pattern of use of alcohol/marijuana/cocaine over the (1) past week, (2) past four weeks, (3) month before that ... etc." The clinician then can ask the patient if this more-recent pattern characterizes use for the last six months, the last year, etc. After establishing substance use patterns, periods of abstinence, triggers for relapse, and past treatments, the clinician should ask questions in order to establish whether substance use has (1) resulted in failure to complete obligations at work, school, or home; (2) taken place in a physically hazardous situation; (3) resulted in legal problems; and/or (4) resulted in any physiological or psychological problems.

The clinician then can ask the patient about eating disorder symptoms. The clinician can begin by asking the patient if he/she has ever (1) had concerns about weight or body image, (2) restricted food intake because of these concerns, (3) engaged in patterns of overexercising, (4) used laxatives because of concerns about weight, (5) engaged in binge eating, and (6) engaged in purging. If a patient has exhibited these symptoms, it is helpful to establish a lifetime history of these symptoms (e.g., age of onset, age when these behaviors became regular, periods of time when the patient did not exhibit these symptoms or engage in these behaviors) and to ask about previous treatments.

Noting the temporal relationships between patterns of substance abuse or abstinence and the patterns of eating disorder symptoms is important since reemergence of eating disorders during periods of cessation of alcohol or drug abuse is common. The opposite pattern is also common, particularly in women with co-occurring substance use disorders and bulimia nervosa: individuals who cease eating disorder behaviors may find themselves relapsing into alcohol or drug use.

Examine Family History. It is important to examine family history that focuses on eating disorders, substance use disorders, and mood disorders. Studies suggest that a strong genetic predisposition exists among these disorders. Also, parental and sibling modeling may be a risk factor for both eating and substance use disorders. In the case of TG (see "Case Presentation"), her father reported having problems with alcohol in the past. TG's mother was diagnosed with both anxiety and depression. TG's sister was diagnosed with, and treated for, anorexia nervosa on several occasions. Several family members have had symptoms of OCD. Although research on familial tendency toward obesity and bulimia is lacking, TG's therapist might posit that the mother's obesity may have increased the patient's risk of developing an eating disorder.

Stressors from familial discord and the divorce of their parents may have also contributed to the emergence of eating disorders in both sisters (see "Case Presentation"). Individuals with eating disorders often attempt to cope with feelings and emotions associated with parental separation or divorce by binging or controlling food intake. Some patients may use dieting, binging, and purging to cope with life stressors, comfort themselves during times of stress, or punish themselves if they feel responsible for their parents' problems. As outlined in the case report (see "Case Presentation"), TG noted that she felt more self-conscious about her weight during her parents' divorce. TG reported feelings of helplessness and guilt about her parents' marital problems. Around the time of the divorce, TG began abusing laxatives to alleviate stress and to relax.

Take Brief Developmental or Childhood History. Developmental stages and major transitions may be associated with the onset of eating disorders. Eating disorders may stem from an inability to cope or adapt to developmental challenges, especially during adolescence (i.e., puberty, autonomy from parents, forming new friendships, solidifying an identity). Other stressors, such as an increase in academic demands when transitioning to high school or college, changes in the family makeup because of parental divorce or separation, or other major life changes, can contribute to the onset and persistence of eating disorders.

Ask About Trauma and Abuse. The incidence of emotional, physical, and sexual abuse appears higher in patients with eating disorders or substance use disorders than in the general population. Studies suggest that food becomes a source of comfort and numbs the feelings associated with unwanted sexual encounters, especially in patients with bulimia nervosa. Trauma and abuse are important aspects of the patient's history that ought to be taken into consideration when formulating a treatment plan. TG (see "Case Presentation") reported that she may have been date raped following a night of drinking. In the course of treatment, the clinician and patient should focus on her current pattern of one-night sexual encounters and her inability to develop a meaningful relationship.

Ask About Other Psychiatric Disorders. Eating disorders are strongly associated with other psychiatric disorders besides substance use disorders. The most common co-occurring psychiatric disorders include mood disorders (particularly dysthymic disorder and major depressive disorder in patients with bulimia), OCD, which may or may not be directly related to food (particularly in patients with anorexia), anxiety symptoms (e.g., fear of social situations) or anxiety disorders, and personality disorders (particularly borderline personality disorder in patients with bulimia). In the case presented, TG (see "Case Presentation") received treatment for depression at the age of 13.

CAUSE OF EATING DISORDERS AND COURSE OF ILLNESS

Risk Factors and Possible Causative Mechanisms

Several hypotheses have been posited for the etiology of eating disorders. Table 12-2 outlines a list of possible risk factors. Kendler et al. (1991) conducted twin studies and estimated the heritability of bulimia nervosa to be around 50 percent. Kaye (1999) gives a similar estimate of around 50 percent heritability for anorexia nervosa. Heritability is an estimate of the extent to which a disorder is caused by genetic factors, as opposed to environmental factors; 50 percent heritability means approximately 50 percent of risk for the disorder (e.g., bulimia nervosa) is attributable to genetic factors. Another biological risk factor associated with eating disorders (particularly bulimia nervosa and binge-eating disorder) is brain chemistry and neurotransmitter activity. Research has demonstrated that psychoactive drugs and overeating operate on neurotransmitters (i.e., serotonin, dopamine, and gamma-aminobutyric acid (GABA)) in similar ways. Other research suggests that eating disorders and alcohol use disorders may be related to atypical endogenous opioid peptide (EOP) activity (Grilo et al., 2002; Wolfe & Maisto, 2000). EOP activity has been found to have effects on both food and alcohol consumption. Research in this area has spurred an increasing focus on psychopharmacologic treatment, such as the opiate antagonist naltrexone, for individuals with both eating disorders and substance use disorders (Wolfe & Maisto, 2000).

Wade, Martin, and Tiggemann (1998), in contrast, suggest that shared environmental factors are more important than biological contributions. Many studies suggest that family conflict and parental modeling (especially from the mother or same sex siblings) are also major risk factors for both disorders. Children may learn to use substances as a coping mechanism to relieve stress from parents. Similarly, children, especially girls, of mothers who emphasize physical appearance and are overly concerned about their own weight and dieting may foster unhealthy ideals and behaviors. If parents view weight and physical appearance as significant indicators of self-worth, their children may be more prone to internalize these beliefs and engage in unhealthy eating behaviors. As outlined in the case history (see "Case Presentation") TG's father used substances on a regular basis and cautioned TG to watch her weight and to not become obese like her mother. TG also reported feelings of resentment toward her sister and her father's favoritism toward her sister because of her slimmer figure.

Eating disorders and substance use disorders are another major contributor to sociocultural factors. Social environment and peers play a significant role, not only in the initial use of substances or dieting but also in the persistence of substance abuse problems and unhealthy eating behaviors. Young females going through puberty are often concerned about changes in body weight and appearance and are more sensitive to the cultural ideal of a slender body; for them, the use of substances, especially cigarette smoking, often becomes a way to suppress appetite. Members of athletic groups, such as ballet dancing or gymnastics, may experience even more emphasis on weight and appearance and may feel greater pressure to adhere to an ideal body weight. TG (see "Case Presentation") reported increased body dissatisfaction after puberty, and she quit the gymnastics team because of her increase in weight and breast development. TG also reported learning from a friend how to self-induce vomiting during adolescence.

Individual factors, such as personality, are considered important in the development of both eating and substance use disorders. It has been suggested that individuals may have

Table 12-2
Risk Factors Thought to Contribute to Development of Eating Disorders

Biological factors
    Genetic
    Brain chemistry

Familial risk factors
    Family history
    Family conflict

Sociocultural factors   Trauma or abuse

Individual factors
    Personality
        Impulsivity
        Addictive personality

Other psychiatric disorders
    Posttraumatic stress disorder
    Obsessive-compulsive disorder
    Mood disorders
    Personality disorders
        Borderline
        Antisocial
        Histrionic
        Obsessive compulsive
        Avoidant

certain personality traits that put them at greater risk of becoming addicted to both food and alcohol and drugs. Impulsivity and an addictive personality type, for instance, are also suggested as risk factors for both substance use and eating disorders. Fairburn (1995), however, finds major flaws in this theory and argues against the claim that food is an addictive substance. Substance abuse treatment programs typically emphasize skills to increase control and restraint in high-risk situations, while treatment of eating disorders usually addresses perfectionism, overconcern with body image, and pathological overcontrol and obsession with calorie counting that are typical among individuals with eating disorders.

A number of other psychiatric disorders, such as OCD, are highly associated with eating disorders. Studies have consistently reported elevated levels of anxiety disorders, including specific phobias, separation anxiety, posttraumatic stress disorder (PTSD), and OCD, among individuals with eating disorders. Childhood trauma, especially sexual abuse, is reported to be highest in individuals with bulimia nervosa and a lifetime history of substance dependence disorders (Deep, Lilenfeld, Plotnicov, Pollice, & Kaye, 1999). Women who have been abused are at a greater risk of developing PTSD, which increases the risk of developing both eating disorders and substance use disorders (Brady, Killeen, Brewerton, & Lucerini, 2000; Dansky, Brewerton, & Kilpatrick, 2000).

Personality disorders, such as borderline, antisocial, histrionic, obsessive compulsive, and avoidant, frequently co-occur in individuals with both eating disorders and substance use disorders. Several studies have found that individuals with comorbid disorders tend to be diagnosed with borderline personality disorder and report affective instability and impulsivity (Sansone, Fine, & Nunn, 1994). There is strong evidence suggesting that borderline personality traits are common among individuals with co-occurring eating disorders and substance use disorders (not necessarily a result of predisposing personality traits).

Finally, the risk of having a co-occurring mood disorder is high among individuals with eating disorders. Major depression has an estimated lifetime prevalence of 50 to 65 percent in individuals with bulimia nervosa (Pearlstein, 2002) and an estimated prevalence of 50 percent in women with anorexia nervosa (Wade, Bulik, Sullivan, Neale, & Kendler, 2000). Mood disorders also commonly co-occur in individuals with substance use disorders. Twenty to 50 percent of patients who seek treatment for alcohol and drug problems report a history of major depression sometime in their lifetime. Depression has been noted as a strong component linking the co-occurrence of substance use disorders and eating disorders (Holderness et al., 1994). The "self-medication hypothesis" has been posited based on the high prevalence of depression among individuals with eating disorders (Kendler et al., 1991; Wolfe & Maisto, 2000). This hypothesis suggests that individuals with dysphoria, depression, or high dissatisfaction with body weight and shape use alcohol and other substances to alleviate these symptoms. However, there is a lack of evidence to support the theory that self-medication of depressive symptoms increases the risk for substance use among patients with eating disorders.

Course of Eating Disorders in Relation to Course of Substance Use Over Lifetime

In most cases, eating disorders emerge during adolescence, when individuals experience changes in weight due to puberty and greater social pressure to conform to ideals of thinness. However, onset of an eating disorder may occur in adulthood as well. Cross-sectional research suggests that alcohol and drug use disorders tend to occur after the onset of anorexia (Deep, Nagy, Weltzin, Rao, & Kaye, 1995). Limited availability of drugs and alcohol during adolescence and limited concern for adolescents who diet or engage in excessive exercise might account for the research finding. In fact, research on dieting behaviors of adolescents has demonstrated predictive value of later alcohol abuse. Several studies with rats have demonstrated an association between food deprivation and an increase in self-administration of alcohol and other drugs, such as cocaine and amphetamines, thereby suggesting that eating disorders may predispose or unmask a vulnerabililty to substance use disorders (Carroll et al., 1979). The food deprivation hypothesis posits that the removal of one reinforcer (i.e., food) will result in an increased reinforcement value of another reinforcer (alcohol and drugs). This theory would support the association between starvation or anorexia nervosa and substance use disorders; however, it does not account for the fact that bulimia nervosa and binge-eating disorders are also more prevalent in patients with substance use disorders.

Other studies report an older age of onset of eating disorders than of alcohol and cigarette use. In a prospective longitudinal study of adolescents with a substance use disorder and co-occurring eating disorders (either bulimia nervosa or binge-eating disorder), the mean age of onset of alcohol use was younger than the age of onset of eating problems (Zaider, Johnson, & Cockrell, 2002). This finding was seen in adolescents with a history of smoking; age of onset of cigarette smoking was significantly lower than the mean age of onset of eating problems (Zaider et al., 2002). In the case example (see "Case Presentation"), onset of eating disorder behavior is age 15 (a typical age of onset). The first report of TG using compensatory behaviors following a binge is at age 14 to 15, while she began smoking at age 13. Even though she started smoking before the onset of regular use of laxatives following binge episodes, her problems with alcohol and drugs did not develop until high school and early college years.

ISSUES INVOLVED IN MAKING THE DIAGNOSIS IN SUBSTANCE-DEPENDENT PATIENTS

Although research studies document a high co-occurrence of eating disorders and substance use disorders, especially in women, patients with these co-occurring disorders are most often treated in programs that address only one disorder. For example, eating disorder programs focus on treating bulimia and anorexia and usually do not evaluate or treat substance abuse; similarly, substance abuse treatment programs rarely evaluate or treat eating disorders. This "don't ask, don't tell" policy often leads to underdetection of eating disorders among patients being treated for substance abuse, as well as underdetection of substance use disorders in patients being treated for eating disorders. Patients with both disorders often experience feelings of shame and often minimize the severity of eating disorder symptoms and substance abuse symptoms.

A complete assessment of symptoms of both disorders is the key to accurate diagnosis of the disorders. Often treatment of one disorder can exacerbate symptoms of the other disorder. For example, a woman who has completed alcohol treatment may find that she is able to maintain abstinence from alcohol, but she may relapse into bulimic behaviors. A patient newly recovered from cocaine dependence or nicotine dependence may relapse into food restricting behavior or laxative abuse in order to lose the weight that she may have recently gained following abstinence from stimulants. Similarly, individuals who are recovering from eating disorders may be at risk for relapse to substance use, abuse, or dependence; external stressors or internal mood states serve as triggers for substance use.

Because of the high rates of co-occurrence of these disorders, because of the shame that many patients feel in reporting their symptoms, and because of the negative prognostic implications that each disorder poses for recovery from these disorders, it is very important that disorder-specific programs develop approaches for screening and assessment of symptoms and behaviors of both disorders. A treatment plan must address both disorders.

INSTRUMENTS AND METHODS FOR SCREENING AND DIAGNOSIS

Screening and Preliminary Assessment Instruments

Table 12-3 lists and briefly describes features of several common eating disorder screening instruments that may be used in substance-dependent populations.

The Eating Attitudes Test was originally developed by Garner and Garfinkel (Garner & Garfinkel, 1979) to examine symptoms of anorexia nervosa. This self-administered questionnaire has been shortened to twenty-six items (EAT-26; Garner, Olmstead, Bohr, & Garfinkel, 1982) and is most frequently used to identify individuals with disordered eating attitudes and behaviors. Its authors suggest a cut-off score of 20 and above to indicate "abnormal eating behavior." The Bulimia Test-Revised (BULIT-R; Thelen, Farmer, Wonderlich, & Smith, 1991) is a self-report questionnaire that assesses the frequency of bulimic behaviors, such as binging, inappropriate compensatory behaviors (e.g., vomiting, laxative use), and a sense of loss of control while eating. It is also a brief, well-validated measure and is useful in screening for bulimia. A cutoff score of 104 on the BULIT-R is used by researchers to identify probable cases of bulimia nervosa. The

Table 12-3

Instruments for Screening and Diagnosis of Eating Disorders in Substance-Dependent Patients

Instrument	Features
Eating Attitudes Test (EAT-26) (Garner et al., 1982)	– 26 items – self-administered screening questionnaire – measure of general eating disorder pathology – brief, simple to administer and score, widely used
Bulimia Test-Revised (BULIT-R) (Thelen et al., 1991)	– 28 items – self-administered screening questionnaire – measures symptoms of bulimia – brief, simple to administer and score, widely used
Questionnaire on Eating and Weight Patterns-Revised (QEWP-R) (Spitzer, Yanovski, & Marcus, 1993)	– 28 items – self-administered screening questionnaire – measures problem eating and dieting behaviors – provides diagnosis of binge-eating disorder with purging or nonpurging bulimia nervosa subtypes – brief, simple to administer and score, widely used
Eating Disorder Examination (EDE) (Fairburn & Cooper, 1993; Smith, Marcus, & Eldredge, 1994; Williamson, Anderson, Jackman, & Jackson, 1995)	– clinician-administered diagnostic instrument – provides measure of key behavioral and attitudinal items on four subscales (eating concern, shape concern, dietary restraint, weight concern); can also calculate global severity of eating disorder score and can generate *DSM-IV-TR* eating disorder diagnoses – strong psychometrics; often considered method of choice for assessing specific eating disorder pathology – commonly used in treatment outcome research studies – requires training and may take one hour to complete
Eating Disorder Examination Questionnaire (EDE-Q) (Black & Wilson, 1996; Fairburn & Beglin, 1994; Wilfley, Schwartz, Spurrell, & Fairburn, 1997)	– 36 items – self-administered version of Eating Disorder Examination interview – detailed information on behavioral and attitudinal features of eating disorder – has been used specifically with substance abusers – brief, simple to administer and score, widely used
Structured Clinical Interview for DSM-IV-TR Axis I Disorders (SCID-I) (First, Spitzer, Gibbon, & Williams, 2002)	– clinician-administered diagnostic instrument – based on *DSM-IV-TR* criteria – provides a method for asking questions about symptoms of eating disorders and other psychiatric disorders – usually used in research studies
Psychiatric Research Interview for Substance and Mental Disorders (PRISM) (Hasin et al., 2006)	– clinician-administered diagnostic instrument – based on *DSM-IV* criteria – provides a method for asking questions about symptoms of eating disorders and other psychiatric disorders – usually used in research studies

Questionnaire on Eating and Weight Patterns-Revised (QEWP-R; Spitzer et al., 1993) is based on *DSM-IV* diagnostic criteria for binge-eating disorder. It assesses the presence or absence of binge episodes as well as purging behaviors, distress about eating, dieting, and weight. Scoring is based on rules used to diagnose binge-eating disorder with purging or nonpurging subtypes. The QEWP-R has been widely used in research programs in order to differentiate between clinical and nonclinical binge eaters.

Diagnostic Instruments

The Eating Disorder Examination (EDE; Fairburn & Cooper, 1993) is a semistructured interviewer-rated diagnostic assessment of eating pathology. The EDE is often considered the method of choice for assessing the specific psychopathology associated with eating disorders (Smith et al., 1994). The twelfth edition of the EDE includes four subscales (Eating Concern, Shape Concern, Dietary Restraint, and Weight Concern) and frequency ratings of behaviors such as binge eating, vomiting, and laxative misuse. The EDE also assesses the frequency of three different types of overeating: objective bulimic episodes (large quantities of food coupled with subjective loss of control), subjective bulimic episodes (subjective loss of control while eating a quantity of food not judged to be large given the context), and objective overeating episodes (overeating without a loss of control). The EDE focuses primarily on the previous twenty-eight days, except for diagnostic items, which rate behaviors over longer periods. Items are rated on seven-point scales (0 to 6); higher scores reflect greater severity or frequency. The EDE provides a measure of behavior and attitudes and can be used to calculate a global severity score and to generate *DSM-IV-TR* eating disorder diagnoses.

Since the EDE generates comprehensive information and has high reliability and validity, it is recommended for use in research and treatment outcome evaluation (Williamson et al., 1995). However, since it requires extensive training to reliably administer and often takes about an hour to complete, the EDE may not be the most practical tool for use in clinical settings. A good alternative is the self-report questionnaire version of the EDE—the Eating Disorder Examination Questionnaire (EDE-Q; Fairburn & Beglin, 1994). Like the EDE, the EDE-Q has four subscales, focuses on a twenty-eight-day time frame, and uses a seven-point rating scale. The EDE-Q has shown generally good correspondence with the EDE in both community and clinical samples (Fairburn & Beglin, 1994; Wilfley et al., 1997), and it has been found to be an effective screening instrument for detecting the presence of eating disorder symptoms in a clinic sample of substance abusers (Black & Wilson, 1996).

The PRISM (Hasin et al., 2006), a diagnostic instrument that requires approximately 120 minutes to administer, was designed for use among substance-dependent patients. The PRISM quotes *DSM-IV* criteria and offers questions for use by clinicians in eliciting information from patients about their symptoms. While the PRISM, to date, has been used primarily in research settings, clinicians should be encouraged to obtain the instrument and practice with it as a way of learning the *DSM-IV* diagnostic criteria and the procedure for conducting an effective psychiatric interview. Table 12-1A includes questions from the PRISM for aiding diagnosis of anorexia nervosa, and Table 12-1B includes questions from the PRISM for aiding diagnosis of bulimia nervosa.

The Structured Clinical Interview for DSM-IV-TR Axis I Disorders (SCID-I; First et al., 2002) also provides questions to aid diagnosis of anorexia nervosa and bulimia nervosa, as well as binge-eating disorder. Suggested questions from the SCID-I for use in eliciting information from patients about their symptoms of binge-eating disorder are listed in Table 12-1C. Unlike the EDE, the SCID-I and the PRISM do not operationalize types of binge episodes.

ASSOCIATED DISORDERS

Patients with eating disorders commonly have co-occurring conditions, including other mental disorders (in addition to substance use disorders), as well as a variety of medical conditions, some benign and some potentially dangerous or even life-threatening. Table 12-4 provides a brief list of some of the most common co-occurring disorders in patients with eating disorders.

Psychiatric Disorders

Both substance use disorders and eating disorders commonly co-occur with mood, anxiety, and personality disorders. Lifetime histories of major depressive disorder are commonly found in treatment-seeking individuals with eating disorders (Cooper, 1995; Edelstein & Yager, 1992; Hudson, Pope, Jr., Jonas, & Yurgelun-Todd, 1983). Lifetime histories of anxiety disorders are also common in patients seeking treatment for eating disorders. In patients with anorexia nervosa, social anxiety disorder and OCD are the most prevalent of the anxiety disorders (American Psychiatric Association Work Group on Eating Disorders, 2000). Patients with bulimia nervosa exhibit a high lifetime prevalence rate of simple phobias, social anxiety disorder, and OCD. There is limited information on the prevalence of PTSD in patients with eating disorders, but one national survey reported that the lifetime prevalence rate of PTSD was approximately 37 percent among women diagnosed with bulimia nervosa (Dansky et al., 2000). There is considerable variability in the research literature in the prevalence rates of personality disorders in those with eating disorders, but one set of studies suggests that Cluster C personality disorders are more prevalent in individuals with anorexia nervosa than in the general population, while Cluster B disorders are more prevalent in patients with bulimia nervosa than in the general population (Bulik, Sullivan, Joyce, & Carter 1995; Herzog, Keller, Lavori, Kenny, & Sacks, 1992).

Medical Disorders

In patients with anorexia nervosa, medical complications are related to extreme weight loss and its consequences. As a woman begins to lose weight, she may cease menstruating (amenorrhea). Low calorie intake leads to reduced metabolic rate, which can lead to reduced body temperature (hypothermia); in places where other people are comfortable, patients feel cold and need to wear extra clothing. Low blood pressure (hypotension) may also occur. These are all signs that the weight loss is becoming medically serious. With chronic low weight or poor nutritional intake, patients may develop signs and symptoms of malnutrition such as loss of calcium and weakening of the bones (osteoporosis), anemia, and growth of lanugo.

When low food intake and weight loss become extreme (generally when the patient reaches less than 75 percent of ideal body weight), dangerous acute conditions may occur including abnormalities in blood electrolyte levels, which, in turn, may lead to impaired cognition or confusion, epileptic seizures, cardiac arythmias, and death. This is a medical emergency indicating that the patient needs to be hospitalized, stabilized medically, and force fed (if necessary) to bring the patient's body weight into the normal range. Patients who are extremely thin and who begin to experience episodic symptoms, such as episodes of amnesia or confusion, fainting spells, or seizures, should be hospitalized immediately for medical intervention.

Patients with bulimia usually remain closer to their ideal body weight and usually do not experience the medical effects of extreme weight loss described above and listed in

Table 12-4
Disorders Associated With Eating Disorders

Anxiety Disorders
   Social Phobia
   Obsessive compulsive disorder
   Specific phobia
   Posttraumatic stress disorder

Mood Disorders
   Major depressive disorder
   Dysthymic disorder

Other substance use disorders
   Alcohol abuse or dependence
   Stimulant abuse or dependence

Personality disorders
   Borderline personality disorder
   Avoidant personality disorder
   Obsessive compulsive personality disorder
   Antisocial personality disorder
   Histrionic personality disorder

Medical disorders associated with anorexia
   Amenorrhea
   Emaciation
   Hypotension
   Normochromic normocytic anemia
   Hypothermia
   Lanugo
   Osteoporosis
   Serum electrolyte disturbances
   Seizures
   Confusion
   Stupor, coma, and death

Medical disorders associated with bulimia and binge-eating disorder
   Gastroesophagitis
   Demineralization of teeth
   Damage to colon from laxative overuse
   Damage to musculo-skeletal system from excessive exercise
   Medical consequences of obesity

Table 12-4. However, binging and purging may cause damage to the esophagus, throat, or teeth that results from exposure to excessive acid during repeated vomiting over a long period of time. Similarly regular use of strong laxatives can damage the colon. Excessive exercise can lead to musculoskeletal problems including stress fractures and arthritis. Patients with binge-eating disorder who are overweight may experience the adverse medical consequences of obesity including risk of cardiovascular problems. Patients should be referred for evaluation and treatment of these medical conditions. A substance abuse treatment counselor can have an important role in encouraging patients to follow up with medical care and follow the medical treatment plan. Medical problems may motivate patients to change eating and substance use habits.

TREATMENT PLANNING

Treatments for Eating Disorders

Cognitive Behavioral Therapy. Cognitive Behavioral Therapy (CBT) is a short-term (approximately twenty weeks) structured behavioral therapy. It is designed to help patients identify and modify dysfunctional thoughts and behaviors in order to reduce psychiatric symptoms. CBT was developed as an extension of behavioral therapy in the 1960s and 1970s, when it became apparent that behavioral therapies could be improved by adding a focus on the important role of cognition in sustaining behavior.

A large body of research has found that CBT is an effective treatment strategy for a number of psychiatric disorders, including depression and anxiety. Marlatt and Gordon's (1985) work on relapse prevention is based on CBT principles. CBT has been used successfully with a wide variety of patients, including adults, adolescents, children, and the severely mentally ill. It has been adapted for use in individual, group, and family treatment settings. CBT also is an effective treatment for bulimia and appears to improve functioning for individuals with binge-eating disorder. It has not been shown to be effective for reduction of anorexic symptoms. This discussion of CBT for eating disorders will focus on bulimia and binge-eating disorder.

CBT treatment for eating disorders is problem-oriented and addresses current behaviors and cognitions. It focuses on the processes that maintain binge-eating and purging behaviors and aims to disrupt these processes and foster the development of more positive cognitions and healthier eating habits. Treatment is based on an additive model: new techniques are added to previous ones in order to broaden the patient's repertoire of coping skills and range of healthy cognitions. In accordance with CBT practice, a key element of the treatment is a respectful collaborative working relationship between therapist and patient. The role of the therapist is to provide information, guidance, support, and encouragement, while the patient holds the responsibility for change.

Treatment generally moves from initial psychoeducation about CBT and replacement of binge eating with a stable pattern of food consumption to an emphasis on identification and modification of cognitive schemas. For more than twenty years, Fairburn, Marcus, and Wilson's (1993) manual for the CBT treatment of binge eating and bulimia has guided clinicians. Although the manual focuses on an individual treatment approach, techniques in the manual can be adapted for a group therapy format. The first stage of treatment primarily uses behavioral techniques (e.g., monitoring eating habits, weighing patients weekly, restricting patients' food intake to preplanned meals and snacks, replacing binge eating with alternative pleasant behaviors, and using stimulus control techniques to restrict eating). The second stage of treatment continues the behavioral emphasis on establishing stable eating habits and introduces cognitive restructuring focused on the thoughts, beliefs, and values (e.g., body image and weight) that maintain symptomatic behaviors. Problem-solving skills also are targeted and improved. At the end of treatment, therapists and patients focus on maintenance of newly developed cognitions and behaviors following treatment completion. Unrealistic expectations about never engaging in binge eating or purging behaviors are addressed through relapse prevention interventions that predict a "lapse" and introduce interventions to prevent a "relapse."

CBT is the most extensively researched psychological intervention for binge eating and bulimia, and many clinical trials have utilized a version of Fairburn, Marcus, and Wilson's

(1993) manual. Evaluations of its effectiveness for bulimia show that purging and dietary restraint behaviors and depression decrease as a result of treatment, and positive attitudes toward body shape, self-esteem, and social functioning increase. Less research has been conducted on CBT for binge-eating disorder, and results suggest that CBT works better than no treatment, but it may not be more effective than alternative therapies such as Interpersonal Psychotherapy (IPT). Weight seems to decrease in patients with binge-eating disorder who abstain from binge eating, although the long-term effects of weight loss vary.

Although CBT is an effective treatment for bulimia, only 50 percent of individuals in CBT treatment completely cease their binge and purge behaviors (Wilson, 1996). Food consumption behaviors are more likely to change than underlying attitudes about weight or cognitions concerning body image. During the twenty years of research on the treatment of bulimia with CBT, there have been no clinical trials that focus exclusively on an important subpopulation of patients: women with co-occurring bulimia or binge-eating and substance use disorders. The few clinical trials of CBT for bulimia that have included women with substance use disorders have yielded mixed results. Thus, although there is strong evidence supporting the use of CBT for the treatment of bulimia or binge eating, CBT cannot be considered a panacea. However, limited evidence suggests that CBT may be a useful treatment for patients with substance use disorders, especially if CBT is combined with addiction treatment.

In order to integrate the treatment of substance use with the treatment of eating disorders, traditional CBT treatment could be modified to include an initial focus on increasing the motivation of patients with substance use disorders to address their eating disorder behaviors. Treatment could also focus on increasing patients' awareness of the interconnections between the eating disorder and substance abuse; for example, in self-monitoring exercises, patients could be asked to record food intake, substance use, and compensatory behaviors such as vomiting or laxative abuse. Education concerning the differences between addiction and eating disorders also may increase patients' understanding of the rationale for abstaining from substances of abuse while consuming food in moderation. Behavioral interventions designed to reduce stress and improve coping and problem-solving skills might help to relieve substance-related stress and cravings.

Interpersonal Psychotherapy. IPT is a structured, short-term (usually fifteen to twenty sessions) psychotherapy designed to help patients identify and address problems in social functioning. IPT makes no assumptions about the cause of a psychiatric disorder; instead, symptoms are examined and addressed within an interpersonal context. IPT focuses on current relationships that lead to, exacerbate, and/or perpetuate psychological symptoms with the goal of helping patients to develop greater mastery in interpersonal situations and, in turn, bring about symptom change.

IPT was originally developed for the treatment of depression (Klerman, Weissman, Rounsaville, & Chevron, 1984) but has been expanded for use in treatment of other populations and disorders, including eating disorders (Klerman & Weissman, 1993). The rationale for applying the IPT model to eating disorders is the interrelationship between interpersonal functioning, low self-esteem, negative mood, traumatic life events, and eating behavior (Fairburn, Jones, Peveler, Hope, & O'Connor, 1993). Both patients who present with eating disorders and their clinicians often identify interpersonal relationships as a major area of difficulty and agree on the need to make it a focus during treatment.

In constructing a treatment plan, the IPT therapist should address problem areas within four social domains: (1) grief, (2) interpersonal disputes (e.g., conflicts with spouse, lover, children, other family members, friends, or co-workers), (3) role transitions (marked changes in life such as divorce, economic changes or family changes, leaving home, a new job or relocation, going away to school), and (4) interpersonal deficits (e.g., loneliness and social isolation). The treatment has three stages. The initial phase involves examination of a patient's interpersonal history in order to identify the interpersonal problem areas associated with eating disorder onset and maintenance; a plan is provided for the patient to work on specified problem areas. During the intermediate phase of treatment, strategies are implemented to help patients make changes in identified problem areas. In the termination phase, patients evaluate and consolidate gains, create plans for maintaining improvements, and outline remaining work.

IPT was applied to patients with bulimia nervosa by Fairburn et al. (1991); in eating disorders treatment studies, it was initially intended as a credible comparison to CBT, which was often considered the leading treatment for bulimia. Results of a large-scale treatment trial showed that IPT was as effective as CBT, although IPT took longer to produce effects. Patients in both treatment conditions improved substantially; changes were maintained over a twelve-month treatment-free follow-up period, and both treatments were superior to behavioral therapy for bulimia (Fairburn, 1995; Fairburn, Jones et al., 1993). These findings were initially surprising consideringthat, unlike CBT, IPT does not directly address dietary issues or attitudes towards shape and weight. The researchers concluded that bulimia can be successfully treated without focusing upon the individual's eating habits and cognitions concerning shape and weight.

A group version of IPT has been used by Wilfley et al. (1993) to treat obese patients who binge eat. Findings from a large-scale controlled treatment trial comparing group IPT to group CBT yielded results that were similar to results for bulimia (Wilfley et al., 2002). Both therapies demonstrated initial and long-term efficacy for the treatment of core symptoms and related symptoms of binge-eating disorder, thereby indicating that group IPT is a viable alternative to group CBT for the treatment of overweight patients with binge-eating disorder.

In summary, IPT continues to gain recognition in the field of eating disorders and is considered an effective treatment for bulimia nervosa and binge-eating disorder. To date, there is no empirical evidence supporting its role in the treatment of anorexia, and research on applying IPT to adolescents with bulimia is in the early stages, although initial work looks promising (Robin, Gilroy, & Dennis, 1998).

Pharmacotherapy. A number of medications are used in the treatment of eating disorders, especially bulimia nervosa. In particular, antidepressant medications have proven effective (American Psychiatric Association Work Group on Eating Disorders, 2000; Wilson, 1996; Wilson & Fairburn, 2002). A number of clinical studies have demonstrated that antidepressant medications are effective in reducing both binge eating and purging symptoms in patients with bulimia nervosa compared with placebo (Alger, Schwalberg, Bigaoutte, Michalek, & Howard, 1991; American Psychiatric Association Work Group on Eating Disorders, 2000; Fichter, Kruger, Rief, Holland, & Dohne, 1996; Fichter et al., 1991; Fluoxetine Bulimia Nervosa Collaborative Study Group, 1992; Goldstein, Wilson, Thompson, Potvin, & Rampey, 1995; Pope, Keck, McElroy, & Hudson, 1989; Rothschild et al., 1994; Wilson, 1996; Wilson & Fairburn, 2002). In particular, selective serotonin reuptake inhibitors (SSRIs), such as fluoxetine, have been helpful medication treatments for these symptoms. Researchers have speculated about the most likely mechanism for the utility of SSRIs: eating disorders are characterized by alterations in serotonin activities in the brain, and these changes are modified by active medication. Across studies, the effectiveness of SSRIs in reducing binge eating and vomiting ranges from 50 to 75 percent reduction in these behaviors. In addition to reducing symptoms of binging and purging, SSRIs can reduce co-occurring symptoms of depression and anxiety that are common both in patients with eating disorders and in patients with substance use disorders. Randomized controlled trials of antidepressant agents that have been effective for treatment of bulimia nervosa include tricyclic antidepressants (Agras, Dorian, & Kirkley, 1987; Barlow, Blouin, Blouin, & Perez, 1988; Blouin et al., 1988; Pope, Hudson, Jonas, & Yurgelun-Todd, 1983; Walsh, Hadigan, Devlin, Gladis, & Roose, 1991), fluoxetine (Fluoxetine Bulimia Nervosa Collaborative Study Group, 1992; Goldstein et al., 1995), monoamine oxidase inhibitors (Kennedy et al., 1988; Walsh, Stewart, Roose, Gladis, & Glassman, 1984), and trazodone (Pope et al., 1989). The effort to find medications to treat anorexia nervosa has been less successful. Pharmacotherapy may be helpful in the treatment of patients with anorexia as one component of treatment following acute treatment to restore weight and may be especially helpful in treating patients with other co-occurring psychiatric disorders (e.g., depression or anxiety). Studies have shown that SSRIs help alleviate depression and promote weight maintenance (American Psychiatric Association Work Group on Eating Disorders, 2000; Kaye, Weltzin, Hsu, & Bulik, 1991).

Combination Treatments. Patients with eating disorders usually are treated using a combination of treatments that are tailored to the specific clinical need of the patient. These treatments include cognitive, behavioral, psychological, nutritional, and pharmacological treatments. Nutritional rehabilitation is an important element of treatment to help patients establish a regular pattern of eating. Psychosocial treatments include individual therapy (e.g., CBT, IPT), along with family and group therapies. A number of studies have examined the efficacy of combining medication and individual psychotherapy in the treatment of bulimia nervosa (American Psychiatric Association Work Group on Eating Disorders, 2000). One study found that combining CBT and active medication was more effective than either intervention alone in reducing eating disorder behaviors (Walsh et al., 1997), but other studies have not found the same results (American Psychiatric Association Work Group on Eating Disorders, 2000; Kaye et al., 1991).

In eating disorders treatment, twelve-step model support groups that stress abstinence from the behavior but do not attend to nutritional considerations or behavioral effects arc not recommended for the treatment of bulimia nervosa in its initial stages (American Psychiatric Association Work Group on Eating Disorders, 2000). When integrating eating disorder treatment with substance abuse treatment, clinicians should remember that substance abuse treatment emphasizes abstinence from alcohol and drugs, whereas eating disorder treatment emphasizes moderation and regularity in eating behaviors. Each of these goals is disorder specific. It is sometimes difficult for patients to work simultaneously on both sets of goals when they are trying to recover from both an eating disorder and a substance use disorder. After learning principles of moderation during treatment of eating disorders, some patients will find it difficult to realize that abstinence, not moderation, is the goal in treatment of alcohol or drug abuse. Clinicians can play a key role in helping patients understand the appropriateness of each of these goals for treatment of the specific disorder.

Determining Level of Care for Treatment

For patients with co-occurring eating and substance use disorders, the determination of the appropriate level of care is critical (American Psychiatric Association Work Group on Eating Disorders, 2000). Patients with acute intoxication or withdrawal syndromes that require medical management may need inpatient treatment. In addition, patients with co-occurring psychiatric disorders who experience psychosis, mania, severe depression, or suicidal ideation may require inpatient care. Patients who do not need inpatient treatment but who are at high risk of relapse or who have a substance use disorder that is complicated by symptoms of other co-occurring psychiatric disorders may require partial hospitalization or residential care. Many patients benefit from outpatient substance abuse treatment that combines individual and/or group therapy, relapse prevention, pharmacotherapy, family treatment, and self-help treatments.

Guidelines established in 2000 for the treatment of eating disorders (American Psychiatric Association Work Group on Eating Disorders, 2000) include a number of domains of evaluation to determine the appropriate level of care. For example, medical stability is one important consideration. Adults with unstable vital signs, electrolyte imbalance, low glucose or potassium, low temperature, dehydration, or hepatic, cardiovascular, or renal compromise require acute inpatient treatment and medical stabilization. For those patients who do not require intravenous fluids, nasogastric tube feedings, or multiple daily laboratory tests, lower levels of care can be considered. The need for residential treatment, partial hospitalization, intensive outpatient treatment, or less-intensive outpatient care is determined by a number of other clinical factors. For example, body weight is one important factor especially in children and adolescents. Motivation for recovery, suicidal ideation, co-occurring psychiatric disorders, need for structured treatment, impairment in self-care, co-occurring substance use disorders, degree and severity of purging behaviors and laxative abuse, environmental stress, and treatment availability and living situations should be considered in determining the appropriate level of care.

Organization of Treatment Services

Stages of change are similar for patients with substance use disorders and eating disorders. Patients must first be motivated to make a significant change in their behavior. Patients with substance use disorders must be motivated to stop using alcohol and drugs. Patients with eating disorders must be motivated to stop the cycles of binging and purging or to give up food restriction or use of laxatives or exercise as a means of controlling weight. Both disorders may require acute care in the initial phase of treatment or following significant relapses. After initial treatment, patients with substance use disorders transition from active use of substances to abstinence, and patients with eating disorders transition from active engagement in eating disorder behaviors to management of these behaviors. The next phase of treatment for eating disorders and substance use disorders is often called "recovery and relapse prevention." Recovery and relapse prevention is the phase of treatment in which clinicians help patients to avoid relapsing to previously unhealthy behaviors (e.g., using alcohol and drugs, binging and purging) and to learn strategies that help patients to manage daily life without these unhealthy behaviors by avoiding situations that trigger urges and cravings, by learning new strategies of coping with environmental stressors or mood, by obtaining treatment for other medical and psychiatric disorders, by resolving interpersonal conflicts, and by making other necessary lifestyle changes.

Currently, there are no accepted guidelines regarding the sequencing or integration of treatments for co-occurring eating disorders and substance use disorders. Strategies for treatment of co-occurring substance use disorders and other psychiatric disorders have been described as *sequential, parallel,* and *integrated* (Busch, Weiss, & Najavits, 2005; Mueser, Noordsy, Drake, & Fox, 2003). *Sequential* treatment means that patients first obtain treatment for one disorder (e.g., the eating disorder) and then are transferred to another program for subsequent treatment of the other disorder (e.g., the substance use disorder). *Parallel* treatment means that patients receive treatment for both disorders simultaneously, but treatment is offered in two separate settings or with two separate clinicians who each specialize in treatment of one of the disorders. *Integrated* treatment means that treatment of both disorders is delivered at the same time by the same clinician or within the same treatment program. *Integrated* treatments and *integrated* treatment programs are generally uncommon for treatment of substance use disorders and many co-occurring psychiatric disorders. *Sequential* treatment and *parallel* treatment are the more common treatment approaches.

While many patients with co-occurring substance use and eating disorders would benefit from *integrated* treatment of their disorders, systems that provide this type of treatment do not currently exist (Sinha & O'Malley, 2000). One approach that may be helpful in treatment planning is to utilize *sequential* treatment for acute and subacute care for co-occurring eating and substance use disorders and then to use *parallel* or *integrated* treatment for outpatient care.

The following case example illustrates a treatment approach in which a patient receives *sequential* treatment for an eating disorder and alcohol dependence in acute and subacute care settings, followed by either *parallel* treatment or *integrated* treatment (i.e., relapse prevention and recovery support) in an outpatient setting.

> ***Example:*** A patient who requires inpatient stabilization of the severe consequences of an eating disorder may be transferred to a partial hospital program for treatment of the eating disorder. There she may receive CBT, nutritional therapy, pharmacotherapy, or other treatments focused on her eating disorder. If such a patient also had alcohol dependence upon entry into treatment, she may receive medical detoxification in an inpatient setting, after which she may not receive any additional treatment directed specifically toward recovery from alcohol dependence. At this juncture, treatment providers may recommend that the patient be transferred from the partial hospital program for eating disorders to a program specifically focused on recovery from alcohol dependence. A partial hospital, intensive outpatient, or outpatient program may be clinically indicated.

After receiving such acute and subacute *sequential* treatment, the patient is ready for relapse prevention and recovery support, which is most often delivered in outpatient or intensive outpatient settings. Depending on the availability of services, the patient may receive *parallel* treatment or *integrated* treatment. *Parallel* treatment might be accomplished by encouraging the patient to see a CBT therapist for management of eating disorder symptoms and eating disorder relapse prevention and to attend group therapy for relapse prevention of alcohol dependence (e.g., early recovery group). The patient may also attend a self-help group for alcohol dependence (e.g., Alcoholics Anonymous or Self-Management and Recovery Training (SMART), a nationwide nonprofit organization that offers support groups to individuals who are working to recover from addictive behaviors). The patient's CBT therapist and alcohol recovery group may or may not be in the same clinical treatment program, and these treatments are said to be occurring simultaneously or in "parallel." In an *integrated* treatment approach, the patient might see a CBT therapist who is familiar with relapse prevention for both eating disorders and substance abuse and who targets both sets of symptoms within the same treatment. While *integrated* treatment seems to be most effective, clinicians with expertise in treating both disorders are rare (National Center on Addiction and Substance Abuse at Columbia University (CASA), 2003). In addition, there is no current research comparing *integrated* versus *parallel* treatment approaches for co-occurring eating and substance use disorders. Alternatively, the patient may receive *integrated* treatment from a psychiatrist who may prescribe medication to treat the eating disorder and a mood disorder (e.g., fluoxetine) and offer anticraving and relapse prevention pharmacotherapy for alcohol dependence (e.g., acamprosate or naltrexone). It is important that the *parallel* treatment for the eating disorder and substance use disorder take place simultaneously. If multiple clinicians are involved in providing care, it is important that they have permission from the patient to communicate with each other and with the patient about treatment goals, progress in reaching these goals, cravings or triggers to relapse, and relapse prevention strategies.

One other important consideration in determining the appropriate organization of services and treatment plan for a patient with co-occuring eating disorder and substance use disorder is the severity and phase (e.g., acute, remission) of each disorder. For example, a patient may have severe alcohol dependence and a history of bulimia in long-term remission. This patient may require intensive treatment for alcohol dependence. The patient may not require any specific treatment for active bulimia at this time (bulimia is in long-term remission); however, relapse prevention treatment for bulimia may be important because the risk for relapse increases with abstinence from alcohol. Similarly, a patient may have met criteria for alcohol dependence in the past and may have not used alcohol for many years while actively binging and purging. This patient may enter treatment for the eating disorder and may successfully stop these unhealthy behaviors. While the patient would not require treatment for active alcohol dependence, treatment targeted at alcohol relapse prevention would be useful; for patients with co-occurring disorders, there is an increased risk of relapse to drinking when these patients are recovering from bulimia.

Treatment Planning for the Case Example

TG (see "Case Presentation") sought treatment because of the concern of her friends and negative consequences of alcohol abuse. She was somewhat motivated to learn more about her problematic use of substances, but she did not appear ready to address symptoms of bulimia. Since the medical examination did not indicate that TG needed inpatient care for the negative consequences of laxative abuse, the therapist began treatment with a focus on increased awareness of her substance abuse and motivation to decrease substance use. If the therapist had attempted to address TG's laxative abuse too early in treatment, TG may have terminated treatment. Thus, initial treatment goals were focused on substance abuse, such as identifying negative consequences of use, increasing commitment to a period of abstinence from substances, and learning skills to maintain abstinence.

The therapist did not neglect TG's ongoing laxative abuse and helped the patient to identify links between substance abuse and laxative abuse. As TG reduced her use of substances, there was a risk that she might increase her reliance on laxatives for emotional relief. She also may not have been able to abstain from substances successfully while she was actively purging. Once TG identified the interconnections between substance abuse and bulimia, she became motivated to address her laxative abuse (in order to decrease the likelihood of a relapse to substance abuse).

Then the therapist, skilled in the treatment of substance use and eating disorders, initiated treatment that focused on learning and maintaining skills to promote abstinence from laxatives. A team approach is recommended for the treatment of eating disorders. TG required a medically monitored detoxification from laxatives. She also was referred to a nutritionist, who monitored food intake. Behavioral therapeutic goals included an examination of body image concerns and development of methods to manage emotions without the use of substances, food, or laxatives.

SUMMARY

The goal of this chapter was to provide an introduction to the assessment, diagnosis, and treatment of patients with co-occurring eating disorders and substance use disorders. The main points of this chapter can be summarized as follows:

1. Eating disorders and substance use disorders commonly co-occur.

2. The most prevalent co-occurrence is between bulimia nervosa and alcohol and drug use disorders, and the highest prevalence occurs in women.

3. Patients with co-occurring eating disorders and substance use disorders commonly have mood and anxiety disorders.

4. In spite of the high rates of co-occurring eating disorders and substance use disorders, it is common for one disorder to be undetected, undiagnosed, and often untreated.

5. Clinicians who are trained to treat either eating disorders or substance use disorders should fully assess their patients for the presence of symptoms of both disorders.

6. With practice, any clinician or clinical program can become competent at eliciting a psychiatric history and making the diagnosis.

7. Both eating disorders and substance use disorders respond to treatment, but the disorders must be diagnosed for appropriate treatment planning to be implemented.

Good fundamental treatment for both eating disorders and substance use disorders is essential. Clinicians need to assess the severity of each disorder, the stage of illness (e.g., active, early remission, long-term remission), and other patient-specific and clinical characteristics (e.g., motivation for change, presence of other co-occurring psychiatric disorders, need for structure) in order to develop the most effective treatment plan for their patients with co-occurring eating and substance use disorders. Future research should seek to determine the comparative effectiveness of *parallel* treatment versus *integrated* treatment approaches for these prevalent co-occurring disorders.

Suggestions for Further Reading

For readers who wish to study further in this area, we recommend:

☐ **Prevalence and Prognostic Effects of Eating Disorders**

- Grilo, C. M., Sinha, R., & O'Malley, S. S. (2002). Eating disorders and alcohol use disorders. *Alcohol Research & Health, 26,* 151-160.

- Holderness, C. C., Brooks-Gunn, J., & Warren, M. P. (1994). Co-morbidity of eating disorders and substance abuse review of the literature. *International Journal of Eating Disorders, 16,* 1-34.

- Wilson, G. T. (1993). Binge eating and addictive disorders. In C. F. Fairburn & G. T. Wilson (Eds.), *Binge eating: Nature, assessment, and treatment,* pp. 97-120. New York: Guilford Press.

☐ *DSM-IV* **Criteria for Eating Disorders and Case Examples**

- Daniels, E. S., Masheb, R. M., Berman, R. M., Mickley, D., & Grilo, C. M. (1999). Bulimia nervosa and alcohol dependence: A case report of a patient enrolled in a randomized controlled clinical trial. *Journal of Substance Abuse Treatment, 17,* 1-2.

- Spitzer, R. L., Gibbon, M., Skodol, A. E., Williams, J .B. W., & First, M. B. (1994). *DSM-IV casebook: A learning companion to the Diagnostic and Statistical Manual of Mental Disorders* (4th ed.). Washington DC: American Psychiatric Association.

☐ **More on Eating Disorders**

- Fallon, P., Katzman, M. A., & Wooley, S. C. (Eds.). (1994). *Feminist perspectives on eating disorders.* New York: Guilford Press.

- Siegel, M., Brisman, J., & Weinshel, M. (1988). *Surviving an eating disorder: Strategies for family and friends.* New York: Harper & Row.

☐ **Diagnostic Methods and Approach to Treatment Planning**

- American Psychiatric Association Work Group on Eating Disorders. (2000). Practice guideline for the treatment of patients with eating disorders (revision). *American Journal of Psychiatry, 157*(1 Suppl.), 1-39.

- Anderson, D. A., & Maloney, K. C. (2001). The efficacy of cognitive-behavioral therapy on the core symptoms of bulimia nervosa. *Clinical Psychology Review, 21,* 971-988.

- Chen, E., Touzy, S. W., Beumont, P. J. V., Fairburn, C. G., Griffiths, R., Butlow, P., et al. (2003). Comparison of group and individual cognitive-behavioral therapy for patients with bulimia nervosa. *International Journal of Eating Disorders, 33,* 241-254.

- Fairburn, C. G., Marcus, M. D., & Wilson, G. T. (1993). Cognitive-behavioral therapy for binge eating and bulimia nervosa: A comprehensive treatment manual. In C. F. Fairburn & G. T. Wilson (Eds.), *Binge eating: Nature, assessment, and treatment*, pp. 361-404. New York: Guilford Press.

- Hornyak, L. M., & Baker, E. K. (Eds.). (1989). *Experiential therapies for eating disorders.* New York: Guilford Press.

- Kinoy, B. P. (Ed.). (1994). *Eating disorders: New directions in treatment and recovery.* New York: Columbia University Press.

- Lewandowski, L. M., Gebing, T. A., Anthony, J. L., & O'Brien, W. H. (1997). Meta-analysis of cognitive-behavioral treatment studies for bulimia. *Clinical Psychology Review, 17,* 703-718.

- Lundgren, J. D., Danoff-Burg, S., & Anderson, D. A. (2004). Cognitive-behavioral therapy for bulimia nervosa: An empirical analysis of clinical significance. *International Journal of Eating Disorders, 35,* 262-274.

- Schneider, J. A., & Agras, W. S. (1985). A cognitive behavioural group treatment of bulimia. *British Journal of Psychiatry, 146,* 66-69.

- Wilson, G. T. (1996). Treatment of bulimia nervosa: When CBT fails. *Behavior Research Therapy 34,* 197-212.

- Wilson, G. T., Loeb, K. L., Walsh, B. T., Labouvie, E., Petrova, E., Liu, X., et al. (1999). Psychological versus pharmacological treatments of bulimia nervosa: Predictors and processes of change. *Journal of Consulting and Clinical Psychology, 67,* 451-459.

☐ **Popular Press Books**

- Fairburn, C. G. (1995). *Overcoming binge eating.* New York: Guilford.

- Knapp, C. (1996). *Drinking: A love story.* London: Quartet Books.

- Zerbe, K. J. (1995). *The body betrayed: A deeper understanding of women, eating disorders and treatment.* New York: Gurze Books.

Authors' Note

The research in this chapter was supported in part by grants DA 19855 (Dr. Greenfield) and DA 15434 (Dr. Greenfield) from the National Institute on Drug Abuse (NIDA). This publication was also supported by a series of grants from NIDA as part of the Cooperative Agreement on the National Drug Abuse Treatment Clinical Trials Network (CTN): Northern New England Node/Harvard University—U10 DA15831 (Dr. Greenfield), Long Island Node/Columbia University—U10 DA13035 (Dr. Cohen), and Delaware Valley Node/University of Pennsylvania—U10 DA13043 (Dr. Gordon). The contents of this chapter are solely the responsibility of the authors and do not necessarily represent the official views of NIDA.

References

Agras, W., Dorian, B., & Kirkley, B. (1987). Imipramine in the treatment of bulimia: A double-blind controlled study. *International Journal of Eating Disorders, 6,* 29-38.

Alger, S. A., Schwalberg, M. D., Bigaouette, J. M., Michalek, A. V., & Howard, L. J. (1991). Effect of a tricyclic antidepressant and opiate antagonist on binge-eating behavior in normoweight bulimic and obese, binge-eating subjects. *American Journal of Clinical Nutrition, 53,* 865-871.

American Psychiatric Association. (1994). *Diagnostic and statistical manual of mental disorders* (4th ed.).Washington, DC: Author.

American Psychiatric Association. (2000). *Diagnostic and statistical manual of mental disorders* (4th ed., text rev.).Washington, DC: Author.

American Psychiatric Association Work Group on Eating Disorders. (2000). Practice guideline for the treatment of patients with eating disorders (revision). *American Journal of Psychiatry, 157,* 1-39.

Barlow, J., Blouin, J. H., Blouin, A., & Perez, E. (1988). Treatment of bulimia with desipramine: A double-blind crossover study. *Canadian Journal of Psychiatry, 33,* 129-133.

Beary, M., Lacey, J., & Merry, J. (1986). Alcoholism and eating disorders in women of fertile age. *British Journal of Addiction, 81,* 685-689.

Black, C., & Wilson, G. T. (1996). Assessment of eating disorders: Interview versus questionnaire. *International Journal of Eating Disorders, 20,* 43-50.

Blouin, A. G., Blouin, J. H., Perez, E. L., Bushnik, T., Zuro, C., & Mulder, E. (1988). Treatment of bulimia with fenfluramine and desipramine. *Journal of Clinical Psychopharmacology, 8,* 261-269.

Brady, K. T., Killeen, T. K., Brewerton, T., & Lucerini, S. (2000). Comorbidity of psychiatric disorders and posttraumatic stress disorder. *Journal of Clinical Psychiatry, 61,* 22-32.

Bulik, C. M. (1987). Drug and alcohol abuse by bulimic women and their families. *American Journal of Psychiatry, 144,* 1604-1606.

Bulik, C. M., Sullivan, P. F., Joyce, P. R., & Carter, F. A. (1995). Temperament, character, and personality disorder in bulimia nervosa. *Journal of Nervous and Mental Disease, 83,* 593-598.

Busch, A., Weiss, R., & Najavits, L. (2005). Co-occurring substance use disorders and other psychiatric disorders. In R. Frances, S. Miller, & A. Mack (Eds.), *Clinical textbook of addictive disorders* (3rd ed., pp. 271-302). New York: Guilford Press.

Carroll, M. E., France, C. P., & Meisch, R. A. (1979). Food deprivation increases oral and intravenous drug intake in rats. *Science, 205,* 319-321.

Cooper, P. J. (1995). Eating disorders and their relationship to mood and anxiety disorders. In K. D. Brownwell & C. J. Fairburn (Eds.), *Eating disorders and obesity: A comprehensive handbook* (pp. 159-164). New York: Guilford Press.

Dansky, B. S., Brewerton, T. D., & Kilpatrick, D. G. (2000). Comorbidity of bulimia nervosa and alcohol use disorders: Results from the National Women's Study. *International Journal of Eating Disorders 27,* 180-190.

Deep, A. L., Lilenfeld, L. R., Plotnicov, K. H., Pollice, C., & Kaye, W. H., (1999). Sexual abuse in eating disorder subtypes and control women: The role of comorbid substance dependence in bulimia nervosa. *International Journal of Eating Disorders, 25,* 1-10.

Deep, A. L., Nagy, L. M., Weltzin, T. E., Rao, R., & Kaye, W. H. (1995). Premorbid onset of psychopathology in long-term recovered anorexia nervosa. *International Journal of Eating Disorders, 17,* 291-297.

Edelstein, C., & Yager, J. (1992). Eating disorders and affective disorders. In J. Yager, H. E. Gwirtsman, & C. K. Edelstein (Eds.), *Special problems in managing eating disorders* (pp. 15-50). Washington, DC: American Psychiatric Publishing.

Fairburn, C. G. (1995). *Overcoming binge eating.* New York: Guilford Press.

Fairburn, C. G., & Beglin, S. J. (1994). Assessment of eating disorders: Interview or self-report questionnaire. *International Journal of Eating Disorders, 16,* 363-370.

Fairburn, C. G., & Cooper, Z. (1993). The eating disorder examination. In C. G. Fairburn & G. T. Wilson (Eds.), *Binge eating: Nature, assessment and treatment* (12th ed., pp. 317-360). New York: Guilford Press.

Fairburn, C. G., Jones, R., Peveler, R. C., Carr, S. J., Solomon, R. A., O'Connor, M. E., et al. (1991). Three psychological treatments for bulimia nervosa: A comparative trial. *Archives of General Psychiatry, 48,* 463-469.

Fairburn, C. G., Jones, R., Peveler, R. C., Hope, R. A., & O'Connor, M. (1993). Psychotherapy and bulimia nervosa: The longer term effects of interpersonal psychotherapy, behavior therapy and cognitive behavior therapy. *Archives of General Psychiatry, 50,* 419-428.

Fairburn, C. G., Marcus, M. D., & Wilson, G. T. (1993). Cognitive-behavioral therapy for binge eating and bulimia nervosa: A comprehensive treatment manual. In C. G. Fairburn & G. T. Wilson (Eds.), *Binge eating: Nature, assessment and treatment* (pp. 361-404). New York: Guilford Press.

Fichter, M. M., Kruger, R., Rief, W., Holland, R., & Dohne, J. (1996). Fluvoxamine in prevention of relapse in bulimia nervosa: Effects on eating-specific psychopathology. *Journal of Clinical Psychopharmacology, 16,* 9-18.

Fichter, M. M., Leibl, K., Rief, W., Brunner, E., Schmidt-Auberger, S., & Engel, R. R. (1991). Fluoxetine versus placebo: A double-blind study with bulimic inpatients undergoing intensive psychotherapy. *Pharmacopsychiatry, 24,* 1-7.

First, M. B., Spitzer, R. L., Gibbon, M., & Williams, J. B. W. (2002, November). Structured Clinical Interview for DSM-IV-TR Axis I Disorders, Patient Edition (SCID-I/P). New York: Biometrics Research Department, New York State Psychiatric Institute.

Fluoxetine Bulimia Nervosa Collaborative Study Group (1992). Fluoxetine in the treatment of bulimia nervosa: A multicenter, placebo-controlled, double-blind trial. *Archives of General Psychiatry, 49,* 139-147.

Garner, D. M., & Garfinkel, P. E. (1979). The Eating Attitudes Test: An index of the symptoms of anorexia nervosa. *Psychological Medicine, 9,* 273-279.

Garner, D. M., Olmstead, M. P., Bohr, Y., & Garfinkel, P. E. (1982). The Eating Attitudes Tests: Psychometric features ands clinical correlates. *Psychological Medicine, 12,* 871-878.

Goldbloom, D. S., Naranjo, C. A., Bremner, K. E., & Hicks, L. K. (1992). Eating disorders and alcohol abuse in women. *British Journal of Addiction, 87,* 913-919.

Goldstein, D. J., Wilson, M. G., Thompson, V. L., Potvin, J. H., & Rampey, A. H., Jr. (1995). Long-term fluoxetine treatment of bulimia nervosa. *British Journal of Psychiatry, 166,* 660-666.

Grilo, C. M., Levy, K .N., Becker, D. F., Edell, W. S., & McGlashan, T. H. (1995). Eating disorders in female inpatients with versus without substance use disorders. *Addictive Behaviors, 20,* 255-260.

Grilo, C. M., Sinha, R., & O'Malley, S. S. (2002). Eating disorders and alcohol use disorders. *Alcohol Research & Health, 26,* 151-160.

Hasin, D. S., Samet, S., Nunes, E., Meydan, J., Matseoane, K., & Waxman, R. (2006). Diagnosis of comorbid disorders in substance users: Psychiatric Research Interview for Substance and Mental Disorders (PRISM-IV). *American Journal of Psychiatry, 163,* 689-696.

Herzog, D. B., Keller, M. B., Lavori, P. W., Kenny, G. M., & Sacks, N. R. (1992). The prevalence of personality disorders in 210 women with eating disorders. *Journal of Clinical Psychiatry, 53,* 147-152.

Holderness, C.C., Brooks-Gunn, J., & Warren, M.P. (1994). Co-morbidity of eating disorders and substance abuse review of the literature. *International Journal of Eating Disorders, 16,* 1-34.

Hudson, J. I., Pope, H. G., Jr., Jonas, J. M., & Yurgelun-Todd, D. (1983). Phenomenologic relationship of eating disorders to major affective disorder. *Psychiatry Research, 9,* 345-354.

Kaye, W. H. (1999). The new biology of anorexia and bulimia nervosa: Implications for advances in treatment. *European Eating Disorders Review, 7,* 157-161.

Kaye, W. H., Weltzin, T. E., Hsu, L. K., & Bulik, C. M. (1991). An open trial of fluoxetine in patients with anorexia nervosa. *Journal of Clinical Psychiatry, 52,* 464-471.

Kendler, K. S., MacLean, C., Neale, M., Kessler, R., Heath, A. C., & Eaves, L. J. (1991). The genetic epidemiology of bulimia nervosa. *American Journal of Psychiatry, 148,* 1627-1637.

Kennedy, S. H., Piran, N., Warsh, J. J., Prendergast, P., Mainprize, E., Whynot, C., et al. (1998). A trial of isocarboxazid in the treatment of bulimia nervosa. *Journal of Clinical Psychopharmacology, 8,* 391-396.

Klerman, G., & Weissman, M. M. (1993). *New applications of interpersonal psychotherapy.* Washington, DC: American Psychiatric Publishing.

Klerman, G., Weissman, M. M., Rounsaville, B., & Chevron, E. S. (1984). *Interpersonal psychotherapy of depression.* New York: Basic Books.

Marlatt, G. A., & Gordon, J. R. (1985). *Relapse prevention: Maintenance strategies in the treatment of addictive behaviors.* New York: Guilford Press.

Mueser, K., Noordsy, D. L., Drake, R. E., & Fox, L. (Eds.) (2003). *Integrated treatment for dual disorders: A guide to effective practice.* New York: Guilford Press.

National Center on Addiction and Substance Abuse at Columbia University (CASA). (2003). *The formative years: Pathways to substance abuse among girls and young women ages 8-22.* Retrieved August 30, 2009, from http://www.casacolumbia.org

Pearlstein, T. (2002). Eating disorders and comorbidity. *Archives of Women's Mental Health, 4,* 67-78.

Pope, H. G., Hudson, J. I., Jonas, J. M., & Yurgelun-Todd, D. (1983). Bulimia treated with imipramine: A placebo-controlled, double-blind study. *American Journal of Psychiatry, 140,* 554-558.

Pope, H. G., Keck, P. E., Jr., McElroy, S. L., & Hudson, J. L. (1989). A placebo-controlled study of trazodone in bulimia nervosa. *Journal of Clinical Psychopharmacology, 9,* 254-259.

Robin, A. L., Gilroy, M., & Dennis, A. B. (1998). Treatment of eating disorders in children and adolescents. *Clinical Psychological Review, 18,* 421-446.

Rothschild, R., Quitkin, H. M., Quitkin, F. M., Stewart, J. W., Ocepek-Welikson, K., McGrath, P. J., et al. (1994). A double-blind placebo-controlled comparison of phenelzine and imipramine in the treatment of bulimia in atypical depressives. *International Journal of Eating Disorders, 15,* 1-9.

Sansone, R. A., Fine, M. A., & Nunn, J. L. (1994). A comparison of borderline personality symptomatology and self-destructive behavior in women with eating, substance abuse, and both eating and substance abuse disorders. *Journal of Personality Disorders, 8,* 219-228.

Sinha, R., & O'Malley, S. S. (2000). Alcohol and eating disorders: Implications for alcohol treatment and health services research. *Alcoholism: Clinical and Experimental Research, 24,* 1312-1319.

Smith, D. E., Marcus, M. D., & Eldredge, K. L. (1994). Binge eating syndromes: A review of assessment and treatment with an emphasis on clinical application. *Behavior Therapy, 25,* 635-658.

Spitzer, R. L., Yanovski, S. Z, Marcus, M. D. (1993). The Questionnaire of Eating and Weight Patterns-Revised (QEWP-R). New York: New York State Psychiatric Institute.

Spitzer, R. L., Gibbon, M., Skodol, A. E., Williams, J. B. W., & First, M B. (1994). *DSM-IV casebook: A learning companion to the Diagnostic and Statistical Manual of Mental Disorders* (4th ed.). Washington DC: American Psychiatric Association.

Thelen, M. H., Farmer, J., Wonderlich, S., & Smith, M. (1991). A revision of the Bulimia Test: The BULIT-R. Psychological Assessment. *Journal of Consulting and Clinical Psychology, 3,* 119-124.

Wade, T., Martin, N. G., & Tiggemann, M. (1998). Genetic and environmental risk factors for the weight and shape concerns characteristic of bulimia nervosa. *Psychological Medicine, 28,* 761-771.

Wade, T. D., Bulik, C. M., Sullivan, P. F., Neale, M., & Kendler, K. S. (2000). Anorexia nervosa and major depression: Shared genetic and environmental risk factors. *American Journal of Psychiatry, 157*, 469-471.

Walsh, B. T., Stewart, J. W., Roose, S. P., Gladis, M., & Glassman, A. H. (1984). Treatment of bulimia with phenelzine: A double-blind, placebo-controlled study. *Archives of General Psychiatry, 41,* 1105-1109.

Walsh, B. T., Hadigan, C. M., Devlin, M. J., Gladis, M., & Roose, S. P. (1991). Long-term outcome of antidepressant treatment for bulimia nervosa. *American Journal of Psychiatry, 148,* 1206-1212.

Walsh, B. T., Wilson, G. T., Loeb, K. L., Devlin, M. J., Pike, K. M., Roose, S. P., et al. (1997). Medication and psychotherapy in the treatment of bulimia nervosa. *American Journal of Psychiatry, 154*, 523-531.

Wilfley, D. E., Agras, W. S., Telch, C. F., Rossiter, E. M., Schneider, J. A., Cole, A. G., et al. (1993). Group cognitive-behavioral therapy and group interpersonal psychotherapy for the nonpurging bulimic individual: A controlled comparison. *Journal of Consulting and Clinical Psychology, 61,* 296-305.

Wilfley, D. E., Schwartz, M. B., Spurrell, E. B., & Fairburn, C. G. (1997). Assessing the specific psychopathology of binge eating disorder: Interview or self-report? *Behaviour Research and Therapy, 35,* 1151-1159.

Wilfley, D. E., Welch, R. R., Stein, R. I., Spurrell, E. B., Cohen, L. R., Saelens, B. E., et al. (2002). A randomized comparison of group cognitive-behavioral therapy and group interpersonal psychotherapy for the treatment of overweight individuals with binge-eating disorder. *Archives of General Psychiatry, 59,* 713-721.

Williamson, D. A., Anderson, D. A., Jackman, L. P., & Jackson, S. R. (1995). Assessment of eating disordered thoughts, feelings, and behaviors. In D. B. Allison (Ed.), *Handbook of assessment measures for eating behaviors and weight-related problems: Measures, theory, and research* (pp. 347-386). Thousand Oaks, CA: Sage Publications.

Wilson, G. T. (1996). Treatment of bulimia nervosa: When CBT fails. *Behavior Research Therapy, 34,* 197-212.

Wilson, G. T., & Fairburn, C. G. (2002). Treatments for eating disorders. In P. E. Nathan & J. M. Gorman (Eds.), *A guide to treatments that work* (2nd ed., pp. 559-592). New York: Oxford University Press.

Wolfe, W. L., & Maisto, S. A. (2000). The relationship between eating disorders and substance use: Moving beyond co-prevalence research. *Clinical Psychological Review, 20,* 617-631.

Zaider, T. I., Johnson, J. G., & Cockrell, S. J. (2002). Psychiatric disorders associated with the onset and persistence of bulimia nervosa and binge eating disorder during adolescence. *Journal of Youth and Adolescence, 31,* 319-329.

Part 6

Special Issues

Part 6 covers a series of problems that are commonly encountered in the treatment of substance-dependent patients. For example, despite the well-known adverse health effects of cigarette smoking and the availability of easily implemented effective treatments for nicotine dependence, drug and alcohol treatment programs often do not address nicotine dependence (a substance use disorder). In addition, clinicians who work in substance abuse treatment programs often neither identify medical problems that are common in substance-dependent patients nor refer them to appropriate care. Chronic pain, which is common in substance-dependent patients (particularly patients in treatment for opioid dependence), can be difficult to treat; by effectively treating patients with pain and substance abuse problems or helping these patients to access specialized care, clinicians in substance abuse treatment programs can improve treatment outcome. Since substance-dependent patients are at risk for suicide (the presence of other psychiatric disorders, such as schizophrenia, increases risk of suicide), substance abuse treatment providers must address patients' suicidal ideation and should learn to evaluate suicide risk and refer patients to appropriate psychiatric care. Part 6 also discusses issues that are relevant to adolescents with substance use disorders and children at risk for development of substance use disorders. Treatment of substance use disorders and co-occurring psychiatric disorders in adolescents often is based on guidelines for treatment of adults, and research is needed in order to develop and refine guidelines for treatment of children and adolescents. Finally, clinicians should be wary of possible interactions between medications that are commonly used to treat substance use disorders and co-occurring psychiatric disorders and medications to treat medical problems (e.g., human immunodeficiency virus (HIV)); certain medications can retard or accelerate metabolism of other medications, thereby affecting medication blood levels and therapeutic effectiveness and causing toxic side effects.

Chapter 13

Cigarette Smoking Among Patients With Substance Use Disorders

by Eric Schindler, Ph.D., Patricia Penn, Ph.D., and
Malcolm S. Reid, Ph.D.

INTRODUCTION

Cigarette smoking (and other forms of nicotine use/abuse) is probably the most common co-occurring condition in America in patients with other substance use problems, and smoking is more common in persons with other Axis I diagnoses, such as mood disorders, anxiety disorders, and schizophrenia. A substantial body of epidemiological literature confirms the high prevalence of smoking among individuals with alcohol and drug problems. Smoking-related diseases are a leading cause of premature death among substance users and in the general population. Preliminary evidence suggests that attempts to quit smoking do not adversely impact treatment for other types of substance dependence or abuse. Nevertheless, few substance abuse treatment programs routinely view nicotine use as a drug problem that should be treated. In fact, few cessation programs screen for use of nicotine and rarely view nicotine use/abuse in the same way as they view use/abuse of alcohol and other substances, and funding is more likely obtained for programs to treat the latter.

Importance of Addressing Nicotine Dependence in the Context of Other Drug Treatment

Substance abusers not only are more likely to smoke cigarettes in comparison to the general population but also are more heavily dependent on them (i.e., smoking in greater frequency and inhaling more deeply). In fact, smokers receiving treatment for alcohol and other drugs of abuse are more likely to die from tobacco-related illnesses than from complications associated with drug abuse (Hurt et al., 1996).

Prevalence of Smoking in Substance Abusing Populations and in the General Population

Currently, about 23 percent of Americans smoke cigarettes. Slightly more men than women smoke, and adult prevalence is decreasing. However, among the substance abusing populations, rates of smoking vary from two to three times rates found in the general population, with some studies showing that nearly every other cigarette smoked in the United States is smoked by someone with a *Diagnostic and Statistical Manual of Mental Disorders*, 4th edition (*DSM-IV*; American Psychiatric Association, 1994) psychiatric diagnosis. Roughly 90 percent of adult patients presenting for treatment of alcoholism or drug dependence (e.g., opiates) smoke (Grant, Hasin, Chou, Stinson & Dawson, 2004; Kalman, Morissette, & George, 2005; Lasser et al., 2000).

Consequences of Tobacco Use

The widespread and deleterious health consequences of nicotine use and abuse are well known to most Americans. In addition to health problems, which result in approximately 430,000 preventable deaths a year, use of cigarettes leads to decreased quality of life. Smokers are at significantly higher risk for a myriad of illnesses, such as cancer, cardiac diseases, and pulmonary diseases, as well as other negative health consequences, such as decreased physical strength, premature aging, and loss of taste and smell. In addition, there are significant economic costs of tobacco use and abuse. A pack-a-day smoker, depending on where he/she lives, may spend as much as $2,000 to $3,000 per year on cigarettes. For patients who are treated in public sector systems of care for substance abuse disorders and who are living on Social Security disability payments of $9,000 per year, potentially 30 percent of their income may be used to buy cigarettes. According to 1993 data, the direct medical cost of smoking is estimated to be about $73 billion per year—about 12 percent of all health care costs in the United States (Miller, Zhang, Rice, & Max, 1998). Smokers are 40 percent more likely than nonsmokers to suffer injuries from on-the-job accidents (Ryan, Zwerling, & Orav, 1992), and they have considerably more absenteeism, physician visits, and poor performance on the job. According to a recent study, up to $2,500 a year is lost per smoking employee in comparison to nonsmoking employees (Centers for Disease Control and Prevention (CDC), 2002). The cost from loss of productivity due to smoking is estimated to be as much as $80 billion per year (CDC, 2002). In addition, use of nicotine interferes with other medications that patients may be taking for treatment of substance use disorders or other psychiatric conditions.

Importance and Feasibility of Treating Tobacco Use

Clinicians working in substance abuse treatment programs often already have the necessary skills required for providing treatment for nicotine dependence and for incorporating this treatment into the substance abuse treatment program. These professionals are often recovery-oriented and holistic.

A myth persists that patients who are drug and alcohol dependent and who smoke cigarettes do not want to quit smoking. In fact, up to 80 percent of cigarette smokers who have substance abuse problems have indicated an interest in cutting back or quitting smoking (Clarke, Stein, McGarry, & Gogineni, 2001). This finding was recently confirmed in a large multisite study of smoking cessation treatment in the National Institute on Drug Abuse (NIDA) Clinical Trials Network; surveys filled out by patients at a number of methadone clinics and drug-free outpatient treatment programs across the United States indicated a high level of interest in attempting to quit smoking (Reid et al., 2007). Regardless of other psychiatric disorders or substance use disorders, persons who are addicted to cigarettes want to quit smoking and often find quitting difficult.

CASE PRESENTATIONS

This section presents two cases of patients who smoke and who are in substance abuse treatment. Suggestions for treatment are presented in "Treatment Options."

Case 1

SF, a 46-year-old Hispanic male and a heavy substance user, has used primarily alcohol but also has used most substances subject to abuse. He has had occasions of sobriety. He has had several bouts of major depression and has been prescribed antidepressants, which he takes intermittently. A writer, he supports himself on a Social Security disability income. He lives alone in an apartment. He has an intimate relationship with a girlfriend that is characterized by periodic breakups. He has had several years of treatment in twelve-step treatment programs and often uses twelve-step language. People in his twelve-step meetings have advised him that if he stops smoking cigarettes, he might jeopardize his recovery. In the past, he has not wanted to stop smoking, which he views as "one of the few pleasures that [he] still [has]." He is interested in concrete strategies for quitting and believes that quitting ultimately "boils down to motivation." He is concerned about the health consequences of smoking; his father died of a heart attack. Certain triggers seem to increase his smoking. For example, when he recently visited his sister, who is a smoker, his smoking increased but then decreased when he returned home. Finally, about a year ago, he likely suffered from a mild head injury (which likely occurred while he was under the influence of alcohol), and he displays subtle deficits in impulse control, executive functioning, and memory that are associated with substance dependence disorders.

Case 2

JS, a 62-year-old female, has smoked for forty years. She has a diagnosis of paranoid schizophrenia and subsists on a Social Security disability income. She lives in an assisted living center and engages in episodes of binge drinking that meet *DSM-IV* criteria for alcohol abuse. She has poor oral health due to smoking and borderline hypertension. With no family or support system she relies on behavioral health care providers. She has a dependent personality. Her case manager believes that she should continue smoking because quitting might be too stressful for her. As a result of her mental illness, she sometimes hears voices (auditory hallucinations), which take the form of treatment staff making unreasonable suggestions or comments. She has some religious delusions related to her schizophrenia: she feels that Jesus tells her to quit smoking and that it is immoral to smoke. However, when she stops smoking, she develops a delusional belief that "bad things will happen to [her] body if [she] does not smoke."

DIAGNOSTIC CRITERIA

Like caffeine, nicotine is unique among addictive substances: it is a legal drug that does not cause noticeable social or physical impairment during intoxication. Nicotine use causes mild intoxication, and the effects of nicotine use may be helpful to patients with some substance use disorders and psychiatric disorders. For example, with mild stimulant properties nicotine may improve deficits in attention or executive functioning in patients with attention deficit hyperactivity disorder (ADHD), may alleviate the negative (deficit state) symptoms of schizophrenia, and may function as an antidepressant for depressed patients. Impairment due to nicotine dependence is chronic and long term, including serious health consequences (e.g., heart and lung disease and cancer) and economic consequences, particularly for patients who are living on limited incomes. Social stigma is increasing, as more states or municipalities adopt policies that prohibit smoking in public places.

Ask About Smoking

The diagnosis of nicotine dependence is easy to make. Cigarette smokers usually do not feel any need to hide their use since the drug is legal, and there are fewer stigmas attached to nicotine in comparison to other drugs (e.g., heroin, cocaine, alcohol). A clinician can expect to obtain accurate information from patients with little obfuscation. In addition, most individuals who use nicotine regularly are dependent. Thus, the simple questions "Do you smoke cigarettes?" and "How many packs per day?" can be used to screen for nicotine dependence and can be easily incorporated into a standard admitting evaluation or periodic follow-up visits. The developers of the Psychiatric Research Interview for Substance and Mental Disorders (PRISM; Hasin et al., 2006), a semistructured interview that aids clinicians in making current and past major Axis I *DSM-IV* diagnoses of alcohol, drug, and psychiatric disorders, are designing a computer-assisted version of the PRISM that includes questions to assess nicotine dependence and withdrawal (Hasin, Samet, Aivadyan, Geier, & Przybylinski, in preparation; see Tables 13-1 and 13-2). Although semistructured diagnostic instruments like the PRISM are generally used in research studies, clinicians are encouraged to try out such instruments in their clinical practices.

The same *DSM* criteria for diagnosing dependence on alcohol and other drugs are applied for diagnosis of nicotine dependence (see Table 13-1). It is important, while interviewing a regular smoker, to review the *DSM-IV* criteria to confirm that a dependence syndrome is operating. Typically, regular smokers will display withdrawal symptoms if they attempt to quit (Criterion (2), Table 13-1), have a persistent desire and/or unsuccessful attempts to quit (Criterion (4), Table 13-1), spend a significant amount of time in smoking-related behavior (Criterion (5), Table 13-1), and exhibit continued use despite knowledge of physical problems and risks caused by smoking (Criterion (7), Table 13-1). It is also important to be familiar with the symptoms of nicotine withdrawal (see Table 13-2). Nicotine withdrawal includes a number of symptoms that resemble symptoms of mood or anxiety disorders and that need to be distinguished from symptoms of co-occurring psychiatric disorders. Further, emergence of withdrawal symptoms often drives smoking behavior in patients; recognition of this phenomenon is helpful in counseling patients in order to maximize their chances of quitting.

Table 13-1
DSM-IV Criteria for Nicotine Dependence

Symptoms	DSM-IV Criteria[a, b]	PRISM Questions to Aid Diagnosis[c, d]
Core Symptoms	A maladaptive pattern of nicotine use, leading to clinically significant impairment or distress, as manifested by three (or more) of the following, occurring at any time in the same 12-month period:	
	(1) tolerance, as defined by either of the following:	
	(a) a need for markedly increased amounts of nicotine to achieve intoxication or desired effect	Did you ever find that after a while you needed to smoke more to get the same effect?
	(b) markedly diminished effect with continued use of the same amount of nicotine	Did you ever find that after a while … the same amount of cigarettes had much less effect than it used to?
	(2) withdrawal, as manifested by either of the following:	
	(a) the characteristic withdrawal syndrome for nicotine (refer to Criteria A and B of the criteria sets for withdrawal from nicotine (see Table 13-2))	
	(b) nicotine (or a closely related substance) is taken to relieve or avoid withdrawal symptoms	
	(3) nicotine is often taken in larger amounts or over a longer period than was intended	Did you ever end up smoking more than you meant to or for longer than you planned to? For example, did you end up smoking 10 cigarettes or more when you tried to limit yourself to only 1 or 2?
	(4) there is a persistent desire or unsuccessful efforts to cut down or control nicotine use	Did you often feel you should stop or cut down on smoking? Did you try to cut down on smoking and were unable, or did you make rules for yourself about smoking and were unable to keep them?

(Continued)

Symptoms	DSM-IV Criteria[a, b]	PRISM Questions to Aid Diagnosis[c, d]
	(5) a great deal of time is spent in activities necessary to obtain nicotine (e.g., driving long distances), use nicotine (e.g., chain-smoking), or recover from its effects	
	(6) important social, occupational, or recreational activities are given up or reduced because of nicotine use	Did you ever cut down on any kinds of activities because you would not be able to smoke?
	(7) nicotine use is continued despite knowledge of having a persistent or recurrent physical or psychological problem that is likely to have been caused or exacerbated by nicotine (e.g., current nicotine use despite recognition that asthma was made worse by nicotine use)	Did you often have any emotional or physical problems related to smoking? For example, feeling nervous or anxious, problems with your heart or blood pressure, lung trouble, asthma, bronchitis, coughing or another medical condition. Did you continue to smoke cigarettes anyway?

[a] Derived from *DSM-IV* criteria for substance dependence (American Psychiatric Association, 1994).
[b] Reprinted with permission from the *Diagnostic and Statistical Manual of Mental Disorders*, Fourth Edition (Copyright 1994). American Psychiatric Association.
[c] Hasin, Samet, Aivadyan, Geier, & Przybylinski (in preparation).
[d] Reprinted with permission from computer-assisted PRISM (in preparation).

Table 13-2
***DSM-IV* Criteria for Nicotine Withdrawal**

Symptoms	*DSM-IV* Criteria[a, b]	PRISM Questions to Aid Diagnosis[c,d]
Core Symptoms	A. Daily use of nicotine for at least several weeks.	
	B. Abrupt cessation of nicotine use, or reduction in the amount of nicotine used, followed within 24 hours by four (or more) of the following signs:	Many people experience problems on occasions when they stop or cut down on smoking … Did at least four of … [the following] experiences happen in the first 24 hours after you stopped or cut down on smoking?
		When you stopped smoking or smoked less than usual, did you ever …
	(1) dysphoric or depressed mood	… feel down or depressed?
	(2) insomnia	… have trouble sleeping?
	(3) irritability, frustration, or anger	… feel irritable or frustrated?
	(4) anxiety	… feel nervous or anxious?
	(5) difficulty concentrating	… have trouble concentrating?
	(6) restlessness	… feel restless or like you couldn't sit still?
	(7) decreased heart rate	… feel like your heart slowed down?
	(8) increased appetite or weight gain.	… gain weight or have an increased appetite?
	C. The symptoms in Criterion B cause clinically significant distress or impairment in social, occupational, or other important areas of functioning.	You just mentioned that you experienced some bad after-effects of stopping smoking or smoking less than usual. Were any of these bad after-effects uncomfortable or upsetting to you, or did they cause problems in your life—like at work or school or with family or friends?
Other Criteria	D. The symptoms are not due to a general medical condition and are not better accounted for by another mental disorder.	

[a] American Psychiatric Association (1994).
[b] Reprinted with permission from the *Diagnostic and Statistical Manual of Mental Disorders,* Fourth Edition (Copyright 1994). American Psychiatric Association.
[c] Hasin, Samet, Aivadyan, Geier, & Przybylinski (in preparation).
[d] Reprinted with permission from computer-assisted PRISM (in preparation).

Other Forms of Nicotine Delivery

In addition to cigarettes, nicotine is taken through chewing tobacco and snuff. It is important for clinicians to ask patients about nicotine delivery through all routes of administration. Chewing tobacco is particularly popular among teenagers, since cigarettes are generally illegal in that age group, and chewing tobacco is easily concealed at school and in other public settings. Nicotine absorbed through chewing tobacco is as addictive as smoked tobacco, and it carries most of the same health risks, including oral and esophageal cancer.

Nicotine Dependence: Often Overlooked or Misunderstood

Assessment and diagnosis of nicotine dependence is not done routinely in most substance abuse treatment programs, perhaps because clinicians and program directors do not view nicotine as a drug in the same sense as alcohol or other drugs of abuse (Hurt, Crogan, Offord, Eberman, & Morse, 1995). Although not supported by the literature, a belief persists that quitting smoking impairs treatment for other drugs of abuse and that quitting smoking will jeopardize patients already in recovery. Clinicians also fear that smoking cessation treatment will result in greater program dropout and reduced referral rates for new patients (Williams et al., 2005). Furthermore, in many treatment settings, cigarette smoking is common among staff members. The staff members in substance use treatment settings smoke at twice the national average—40 to 50 percent. The high rate of smoking among clinicians in substance use treatment programs leads to some cognitive dissonance when thinking about tobacco as another drug of abuse and a drug worthy of assessing, diagnosing, and treating (Gill & Bennett, 2000). Another impediment to accurate diagnosis and treatment is the perception that conducting an assessment obligates the treatment provider to offer smoking cessation treatment services. Many programs do not receive funding for smoking cessation treatment, thereby discouraging the treatment provider from conducting the assessment.

Nevertheless, to provide state-of-the-art treatment to substance abusers, clinicians should consider the following recommendations. Tobacco use should be assessed at the time of intake, along with a concurrent assessment of the patient's level of motivation to change and interest in smoking cessation treatment. Use of tobacco should be documented in the treatment record, and the treatment plan should address tobacco use. Simple interventions, including advice to quit, brief motivational interventions, and referral to self-help materials and nicotine patch (available over the counter), can be effective. Thus, evaluation and basic intervention for smoking can be integrated into standard counseling services with little extra expenditure of time or money.

NATURAL HISTORY AND ETIOLOGY

Genetic and Environmental Determinants of Nicotine Dependence

Twin studies provide estimates of the extent to which a particular trait or disorder is determined by inherited, genetic factors versus environmental factors (recall that identical twins share 100 percent of the same genes, and fraternal twins, like other siblings, share 50 percent of the same genes). Twin studies that have focused on alcohol and other drug use disorders have shown that addictions are determined by both genetic and environmental factors. Similarly, twin studies that have focused on smoking behavior and nicotine dependence have revealed both genetic and environmental factors determining risk. Further, some of the genetic risk for smoking appears to overlap with the genetic risk for major depressive disorder (Johnson, Rhee, Chase, & Breslau, 2004). Specific genes conveying risk have not been identified yet. However, it seems unlikely that there are just one or a few "smoking genes." As with other complex behavioral traits and disorders, it seems likely that risk for smoking is conveyed by a number of genes, each contributing a small amount to overall risk. Individuals vary in their likelihood of becoming dependent on nicotine if they try tobacco products. Thus, some individuals may smoke cigarettes but give them up easily, while other individuals will become dependent and have difficulty quitting.

Environmental risk factors for smoking resemble environmental risk factors for other addictions and include availability of cigarettes or other tobacco products, peer pressure, social attitudes, degree of acceptance versus stigma, and stress. Individuals may be influenced by the example set by family members who smoke. In school, peers may smoke, and there can be peer influence to smoke. For example, some patients learn how to smoke while in jail or in residential treatment settings. In these residential settings, both residents and staff members may smoke. Stress increases susceptibility to substance abuse, particularly to nicotine abuse. Smokers often say that they smoke to reduce stress, although studies have refuted the belief that nicotine reduces stress (Parrott, 1995). The feeling of stress that smokers hope to alleviate with a cigarette may be symptoms of nicotine withdrawal; self-reports of stress levels are correlated with degree of physiological withdrawal.

Cigarettes as a Gateway Drug

Cigarette smoking or use of other tobacco products tends to begin in the early teenage years. Along with alcohol and marijuana, cigarettes and tobacco products are among the first substances to which teenagers are exposed. Widespread availability of cigarettes and chewing tobacco, peer pressure to smoke, and common expectations about smoking contribute to teenage smoking. Common perceptions about smoking among teenagers include that smoking is "cool," that smoking feels good, and that smoking promotes weight loss (a belief often held by girls). Thus, it is important for parents and other adults to combat these messages by discouraging experimentation with tobacco products. Teenagers need to understand that once they begin smoking, they may be unable to stop.

The early onset of smoking has led to the notion of nicotine as a "gateway drug." Teenagers who initiate smoking at an early age are at increased risk for development of dependence on alcohol and other drugs. It is not clear whether early smoking *causes* increased risk for later drug problems (perhaps by inducing adaptations in the brain that increase sensitivity to addictive drugs) *or* simply serves as a signal for the emergence of a general susceptability to addiction. It is important that clinicians view smoking as a danger signal, work to encourage teenagers to avoid smoking, and aggressively address smoking once a teenager starts.

The majority of regular smokers quit on their own without any formal treatment or assistance other than self-help materials. For a smaller proportion of regular smokers, the habit becomes chronic and difficult to break and is characterized by multiple efforts to quit followed by relapse; these individuals likely have greater genetic susceptibility and may be exposed to more environmental risk factors, such as smoking at home or in the workplace or chronic stress.

INSTRUMENTS AND METHODS FOR SCREENING AND DIAGNOSIS

All treatment providers should ask about tobacco use. Most smokers have little to gain by minimizing or denying tobacco use (unlike use of illegal or less socially acceptable drugs) and tend to give honest estimates of use.

Biological Markers of Nicotine Use

Carbon monoxide breath monitors are the most common and inexpensive form of biological markers of nicotine use. An assessment of cotinine in urine or saliva is commonly used but is more expensive than carbon monoxide breath monitors. Cotinine is a byproduct of nicotine metabolism in the body.

Self-Report Instruments and Clinician-Administered Assessments

There also are many self-report instruments for assessing nicotine use, including the Fagerstrom Test for Nicotine Dependence (Heatherton, Kozlowski, Frecker, & Fagerstrom, 1991), the most commonly used brief screening questionnaire. There are many instruments to assess smoking history and past use patterns, including diaries. Smoking assessment is similar to assessment of other drug use, and tools used to assess other substance use can be adapted for smoking assessment. An important part of assessment is to ask patients about previous attempts to quit, experiences related to attempts to quit, smoking cessation techniques that have worked well, and barriers to quitting that have emerged in the past; this information will inform counseling strategies and treatment planning.

The PRISM (Hasin et al., 2006)—a semistructured interview that requires approximately 120 minutes to administer—was designed for use among substance-dependent patients and permits clinicians to evaluate each psychiatric symptom separarely in terms of its relationship to substance abuse. Although the paper version of the PRISM includes modules for substance use disorder screening and diagnosis, this version currently does not include questions to assess nicotine dependence and withdrawal. Tables 13-1 and 13-2 provide questions from a computer-assisted version of the PRISM (currently under development by Hasin, Samet, Aivadyan, Geier, & Przybylinski) for aiding diagnosis of nicotine dependence and withdrawal. While the PRISM, to date, has been used primarily in research settings, clinicians who use it in clinical practice will become familiar with *DSM-IV* diagnostic criteria and the procedure for conducting an effective psychiatric interview.

CO-OCCURRING SUBSTANCE ABUSE AND PSYCHIATRIC DISORDERS

Nicotine use and dependence is highly prevalent in individuals with other psychiatric disorders. Lasser et al. (2000) found that 44 percent of all the cigarettes that are smoked in the United States are smoked by persons with a *DSM-IV* diagnosis. Studies have shown that approximately 50 percent of smokers have had a major depressive episode at some point during their lifetime; 60 percent of patients with bipolar illness smoke; and 35 percent of patients with anxiety disorders smoke (Grant et al., 2004; Kalman et al., 2005; Lasser et al., 2000). Seventy percent of patients with psychotic disorders (e.g., schizophrenia) and posttraumatic stress disorder (PTSD) smoke. Substance users remain the population with the highest rate of smoking: 90 percent of people who abuse alcohol or other drugs report being smokers. Furthermore, 20 percent or more of patients seeking smoking cession treatment may have a history of alcohol abuse or dependence (Grant et al., 2004).

Depression is one of the most common co-occurring disorders among tobacco users, and a history of major depression predicts greater difficulty quitting smoking and higher relapse rates (Glassman et al., 1990). Persons with histories of major depression or anxiety disorders tend to report more severe nicotine withdrawal (Breslau, Kilbey, & Andreski, 1992). Nicotine withdrawal symptoms include a number of symptoms that are similar to symptoms of depressive and anxiety disorders. Further, depression sometimes emerges after a patient quits smoking, as if the nicotine had been functioning as an antidepressant. It has been shown that components of cigarette smoke, other than nicotine, inhibit an enzyme in the brain called monoamine oxidase (MAO), which is responsible for metabolizing neurotransmitters, like dopamine, that are involved in mood regulation. Drugs that inhibit MAO (known as MAOIs), including phenelzine, tranlycypromine, selegeline, marplan, and meclobemide, are effective treatments for depression. The antidepressant medications bupropion (Zyban, Wellbutrin) and nortriptyline have also been shown to help patients quit smoking (Hall et al., 1998; Hurt et al., 1997). The effectiveness of these antidepressants does not appear to depend on the presence of a major depression syndrome at the time of the attempt to quit, but there is some evidence that these medications may improve the chances of quitting and reduce the risk of relapse by lessening depressive and anxiety symptoms that may emerge during nicotine withdrawal.

Cigarette smoking is almost universal among persons with schizophrenia. Patients with schizophrenia score higher on ratings of nicotine dependence, smoke more cigarettes, and inhale more deeply in comparison to other nicotine-dependent populations. In addition, patients with schizophrenia are at high risk for chronic health effects of smoking, such as heart and lung disease (Ziedonis, Kosten, Glazer, & Frances, 1994). Schizophrenia is characterized by both delusions and hallucinations (known as the positive symptoms) and symptoms of apathy, flat affect, anhedonia, and social withdrawal (known as the negative symptoms). The stimulant-like effects of nicotine may temporarily counteract some of the negative symptoms, which in part may explain the strong relationship between smoking and schizophrenia. Nicotine also reverses deficits in sensory gating and attention in schizophrenic patients (Adler, Hoffer, Wiser, & Freedman, 1993; Sacco et al., 2005). Finally, the neuroleptic medications used to treat schizophrenia block dopamine receptors and can produce side effects of sedation and anhedonia, which may be partly counteracted by nicotine.

Since cigarette smoke induces higher activity in metabolic enzymes (P450 1A2) in the liver that are responsible for metabolizing a number of drugs, including caffeine, clozapine, haloperidol, imipramine, and olanzapine (see Chapter 18 of this volume), discontinuation of tobacco use may require adjustments to doses of medications that are used to treat mood disorders and schizophrenia. Thus, when someone stops smoking, activity of these enzymes declines, and the blood levels of these drugs or medications may go up, causing side effects to emerge. Further, patients who are regular smokers may require higher than normal doses of some of these medications to achieve therapeutic benefits.

TREATMENT OPTIONS

Even though tobacco use presents a significant health threat, few clinicians consistently assess or treat nicotine dependence. Although many effective interventions for nicotine dependence have been studied in rigorous controlled trials, few studies have been conducted in patients who are also alcohol-dependent or drug-dependent. Several studies offer preliminary evidence that treatment methods for nicotine dependence remain effective in patients with other dependencies. Further, these studies do not support the common notion that an attempt to quit smoking will worsen the outcome of alcohol or other drug dependencies. Rather, levels of nicotine and other substance abuse appear to be correlated, suggesting that addictions can be, and perhaps should be, treated simultaneously (Frosch, Stein, & Shoptaw, 2002). Treatment methods developed for nicotine dependence in the general population can be applied to substance-dependent patients. Clinicians who work with nicotine-dependent patients should familiarize themselves with these techniques. Behavioral health care programs and substance abuse treatment programs are ideal settings for nicotine intervention for several reasons:

1. They build on rapport (an important ingredient in treatment success) that has already been established between clinician and patient;

2. They allow clinicians to further promote the healthy living principles emphasized during treatment; and

3. They serve as a convenient option for patients to receive treatment (patients can receive treatment for multiple problems in one setting). Indeed, patients are more likely to take advantage of nicotine treatment if it is convenient for them.

In what follows, we discuss some general principles of treatment for nicotine dependence, followed by specific descriptions of pharmacological and behavioral approaches.

Context of Counseling and Approach to Patient

Research has shown that even very brief interventions by health care providers, such as counselors, nurses, physicians, psychologists, and health educators, are effective at increasing quit rates. The Public Health Service (PHS) guideline outlines brief interventions of three to ten minutes in length, and patients should be encouraged to obtain, read, and follow the available self-help materials (U.S. Department of Health and Human Services (USDHHS), 2000). Useful basic principles for counseling patients about nicotine dependence and cessation include the "five A's" and the "five R's."

The Five A's. The five A's include: ask (i.e., identifying use of tobacco); advise (i.e., motivating clients to consider reducing or quitting their use of tobacco by informing them of the risks); assess (i.e., determining if the patient is ready to quit); assist (i.e., aiding a client's quitting attempt); and arrange follow-up. This treatment model is based on basic principles of motivational enhancement treatment.

1. *Ask.* The clinician inquires about, and adequately assesses, the patient's relationship with nicotine by using accepted instruments and good clinical interviewing skills in order to determine the level of nicotine dependence.

2. *Advise.* For advice to be more readily accepted, especially by substance abusing patients, clinicians should offer advice in a nonconfrontational, helpful, friendly, and nondemanding fashion. Avoid various attempts to scare or preach. Advice should be clear, strong, and personalized. For example, the treatment provider might say, "I think that it is important that you quit smoking now, and I will help you. Cutting down just while you are ill is not enough." The

treatment provider also might say, "I need you to know that quitting smoking is the most important thing that you can do to protect your current and future health." The treatment provider might tie smoking to a personal situation, such as the impact of second-hand smoke on the patient's children or on others in the household.

3. *Assess.* Use and familiarity with readiness-to-change principles can aid assessment of the patient's readiness to quit. If the patient answers that he/she is not ready to quit, then it is the precontemplation stage. If the patient answers that he/she is thinking about quitting, then it is the contemplation stage. If the patient says that he/she is ready to quit, it is the ready-for-action stage.

4. *Assist.* For patients who are not willing to attempt to quit, it is important not to argue or debate. Rather, the treatment provider should accept this decision for the time being and should advise the patient that the treatment provider will continue to provide information and to engage in dialogue with the patient concerning the patient's use of the drug. If the patient is willing to quit smoking, the treatment provider should assist the patient in developing a quit plan. Set a quit date. Encourage the patient to seek social and clinical support. Help the patient to identify what form of treatment (e.g., Nicotine Replacement Therapy (NRT)) he/she may wish to use. Help the patient to identify specific and unique challenges that are likely to lead to relapses. Treatment for nicotine dependence is consistent with treatment for dependence on other types of drugs. Offer community resources and provide literature to both patients who are ready to quit and patients who are not ready to quit.

5. *Arrange for follow-up.* Schedule follow-up contact, preferably within the first week.

The Five R's. A second paradigm, known as the five R's, follows on the five A's as a methodology for increasing motivation for patients who are in the precontemplation or contemplation stage. The five R's include the following.

Relevance. Clinicians should make information that they provide relevant to the patient's current situation. Patients who complain that they have bills and no money might be impacted by learning that they may be spending up to $2,000 to $3,000 a year on cigarettes. Smokers who complain that their children have frequent ear infections may not realize that their use of tobacco may impact on children's health.

Risks. Short-term risks of tobacco use include stained teeth, halitosis, exacerbation of asthma, impotence, and infertility. There are a host of long-term risks, including cardiovascular conditions and cancers.

Rewards. Make sure that patients recognize the full range of rewards that can occur when tobacco is eliminated. Patients may experience, in addition to improved health, that food tastes better; a person's sense of smell improves; patients often experience improved self-esteem; home, car, and breath smell better; and there are other benefits that are individually determined. It is important to inform patients that the body can heal and, within short periods of time, lung capacity begins to recover. Following four years of smoking abstinence, risk of heart attack is almost equivalent to that of a nonsmoker.

Roadblocks. Identify those barriers to quitting that are particularly powerful for each patient. Common forms of roadblocks include fear of failure, fear of weight gain, lack of support, inability to tolerate withdrawal symptoms, and depression.

Repetition. This last R is the most commonly overlooked. It is vital that treatment providers inform patients that they will continue to encourage patients to address tobacco use and to help them to understand the full repercussions of their use of this drug. Competent substance treatment abuse clinicians continue to bring up the problems associated with cocaine and methamphetamine use or abuse even if the patient feels that it is not important to address the use of these products, and the same can be done for nicotine.

During the quitting phase, it is important to educate the patient on potential withdrawal symptoms (see Table 13-2) and to develop some concrete plans on how to address these symptoms. Medication options should be a topic for exploration, since medications often help with some withdrawal symptoms. Nutrition and exercise are helpful and often overlooked. The treatment provider should provide the patient with some ideas about proper nutrition. Outcome of substance abuse treatment is greatly influenced (positively and negatively) by family and friends, who can either support or sabotage treatment. Discuss ways to avoid individuals who are sabotaging treatment and ways to seek out supportive people.

Setting a Quit Date

Setting a quit date is a fundamental principle of medication approaches to smoking cessation and most behavioral approaches. At the time that a clinician initiates a discussion on quitting smoking, regular smoking is accepted, and the patient is encouraged to pick a target day in the near future when he/she will attempt to quit. Preparations for the quit date are discussed, including removing all cigarettes and paraphernalia (matches, lighters, ashtrays, other triggers to smoke) from the home and workplace, anticipating what quitting will feel like, making contingency plans for avoiding people and places associated with smoking, coping with withdrawal symptoms and urges to smoke, and informing significant others about the quit date and enlisting their help.

Effects of Nicotine Withdrawal and Importance of Monitoring for Emergence of Depression

Nicotine blood levels drop rapidly after nicotine intake ceases. Thus, within twenty-four hours of quitting smoking, withdrawal symptoms are likely to develop (see Table 13-2). There are temporary increases of anger, anxiety, impatience, irritability, and sleep problems associated with nicotine withdrawal. Sometimes withdrawal symptoms mimic side effects from other medications, and temporary withdrawal-induced depression occurs more commonly in persons with preexisting histories of depression. Similarly, sleep problems during nicotine withdrawal occur more commonly among patients with a history of sleep disorders. In rare instances, a more severe and persistent syndrome of depression, consistent with major depression (see Chapter 1 of this volume), emerges. Thus, it is important to monitor patients' moods and overall sense of well-being during smoking cessation, both to help patients cope with routine symptoms that are typical of nicotine abstinence and to identify serious depression and refer patients to psychiatrists for further evaluation.

Multiple Attempts to Quit

Statistics on smoking treatment outcome show that the probability that any one attempt to quit will succeed in establishing sustained abstinence from smoking is low (i.e., in the 10 to 30 percent range), but patients who continue to try to quit are highly likely to succeed. Thus, it is important that the treatment provider not become discouraged if the first attempt to quit fails, and, instead, praise the patient for his/her willingness to try and encourage the patient to try again (repeatedly, if necessary). It may be worthwhile to try different interventions if the first efforts fail. For example, if a patient fails to quit with self-help materials and nicotine patches, treatment providers might prescribe one of the antidepressant medications that have been shown to be effective (bupropion or nortriptyline), along with more intensive counseling or behavioral interventions.

Pharmacotherapies

Nicotine Replacement. The most well-researched and common form of treatment for smoking is NRT. A variety of methods of delivery of nicotine replacement have been approved based on clinical trials that demonstrate that nicotine replacement increases the likelihood that patients will succeed in quitting in comparison to placebo plus counseling alone. The most common method of NRT is the nicotine patch, which is now available over the counter in different dosage strengths. Nicotine replacement delivered through lozenges, gum, inhalers, and nasal sprays are less commonly used methods. One-year abstinence rates using NRT in research studies are typically between 10 percent and 30 percent (nicotine gum (15 percent), nicotine patch (20 to 25 percent), nasal spray (20 to 25 percent), and inhaler (25 to 30 percent)). While quit rates for a particular attempt to quit are relatively low, many patients who attempt repeatedly to quit eventually are successful.

Since nicotine replacement products can be bought over the counter at pharmacies without a prescription, patients can obtain and use them without medical supervision, and clinicians at drug treatment programs should encourage their patients who smoke to try nicotine replacement products. Patients should be instructed to read the material that accompanies the product, which includes instructions on use and precautions. Clinicians may wish to read these materials with patients to ensure that patients understand how to use the products. Patients should consult their physician if they have any concerns. In particular, patients with significant cardiovascular disease should consult their physician before using nicotine replacement products.

Treatment providers should instruct patients to set a quit date, make preparations in the preceding days, and on the morning of the quit date apply a nicotine patch and refrain from smoking. The patch comes in 21 mg, 14 mg, and 7 mg doses, but 21 mg is the usual starting dose. The patch provides a steady blood level of nicotine in the system and should relieve withdrawal discomfort. Cravings may still occur, perhaps in part because cigarette smoking produces surges in nicotine blood levels. Cravings can be managed with nicotine gum, which can be used in addition to the patch. Treatment providers might instruct patients to carry nicotine gum and to chew a piece when they experience significant cravings. It is generally not recommended that patients smoke cigarettes while wearing a nicotine patch, which may result in higher than usual blood levels of nicotine and greater potential for toxic effects (e.g., placing greater strain on the cardiovascular system). If the attempt to quit fails and a patient begins to smoke again, instruct the patient to remove the patch and encourage him/her to set another quit date in the near future. If the attempt to quit succeeds, then the patch dose can be tapered and discontinued after eight to twelve weeks. Treatment providers should monitor patients for relapse, which remains likely even after several months of abstinence on patches.

Antidepressant Medications. Antidepressant medications have been shown to be effective for the treatment of nicotine dependence. These medications require a prescription and evaluation and monitoring by a physician but should be considered for patients with a history of failed attempts to quit with nicotine patches, self-help materials, and/or counseling and behavioral methods. Bupropion, known by either of two brand names, Zyban or Wellbutrin SR (slow release), was the first antidepressant to be tested for smoking cessation and has been found to be effective (Hurt et al., 1997). Zyban is the brand name marketed for smoking cessation, while Wellbutrin is the brand name marketed for treatment of depression, but they are interchangeable. One trial showed that buproprion was more effective than the nicotine patch (Jorenby et al., 1999). The tricyclic antidepressant nortriptyline has been shown to be effective in promoting smoking cessation, apparently by relieving mood symptoms that emerge during attempts to quit (Hall et al., 1998). Both bupropion and nortriptyline work by affecting the norepinephrine system and, to a lesser extent, dopamine system in the brain; bupropion can be stimulant-like. Neither medication has abuse potential, but each medication is associated with risks that are rare but that need to be considered during the evaluation session. Bupropion can increase the risk of epileptic seizures in susceptible individuals (e.g., patients with seizure disorders or patients who are susceptible to seizures due to heavy alcohol or sedative use and discontinuation). Nortriptyline, like other tricyclic antidepressants, can cause cardiac arrhythmias in susceptible individuals, although it is easy to screen for this risk with a routine electrocardiogram.

Serotonin reuptake inhibitors (SRIs; e.g., fluoxetine)—antidepressant medications that act mainly on the serotonin system—have also been studied in nicotine-dependent patients in large, carefully controlled trials; the evidence for their effectiveness is less clear (Niaura et al., 2002; Saules et al., 2004). Mimicking findings for nortriptyline (Hall et al., 1998), evidence suggests that SRIs relieve mood symptoms surrounding attempts to quit smoking (Blondal et al., 1999; Cook et al., 2004). Thus, SRIs should be considered in patients who cannot tolerate, or have failed to respond to, bupropion or nortriptyline.

Unlike treatment with nicotine patches, where the medication is begun on the quit date, antidepressant medications should be started ten to fourteen days before the quit date and titrated upwards to the effective dose before the patient attempts to quit. This recommendation is based on the knowledge that antidepressants, when used to treat depressive or anxiety disorders, generally take at least one to two weeks to begin to work, presumably because they are causing gradual changes in brain chemistry and function that require several weeks to fully develop. For bupropion (Zyban or Wellbutrin SR) the target dose is 300 mg, and it is usually wise to titrate the dose upwards to 300 mg gradually over the first week to two weeks. Bupropion is stimulant-like, so it should be taken in the morning; possible side effects include restlessness and headache, among others, but it is generally well tolerated. Doses of up to 450 mg per day are indicated for treatment of depression and could be tried in smoking cessation if the 300 mg per day dose fails. For nortriptyline, the effective dose is usually in the 50 mg to 100 mg per day range. Nortriptyline is usually mildly sedating and best given at bedtime, although some patients find it activating, in which case it should be taken in the morning. Other common side effects include dry mouth and constipation, which are usually mild and can be managed with regular fluid intake and stool softeners.

Varenicline (Brand Name Chantix). Varenicline (known by its brand name Chantix), a nicotine receptor partial agonist, is a newly approved alternative to NRT and antidepressant medications. Clinical trials suggest that this medication is more effective than NRT in promoting abstinence and possibly more effective than antidepressants (Gonzalez et al., 2006; Nides et al., 2006). This medication, a high-affinity partial agonist, tightly binds to nicotine receptors but only partially activates them; it substitutes for the effects of nicotine and suppresses withdrawal. At the same time, this medication blocks the effects of self-administered nicotine, because nicotine does not easily displace it from the receptors. When a patient smokes cigarettes while taking varenicline, the reinforcing effects of nicotine are blocked. Patients may continue to take varenicline while actively smoking, and the blockade should help to extinguish smoking behavior over time. Experience in using this medication in the field is limited, but initial feedback from practitioners seems positive. Unfortunately, this medication tends to be expensive. Clinicians should consider this promising medication as a first-line treatment or as a treatment for patients who have not responded to behavioral treatments or medication treatments for smoking cessation.

Psychosocial Interventions

Behavioral and psychosocial interventions for smoking cessation have been extensively tested. These interventions range from brief interventions (like the five A's and five R's, outlined above (see "Context of Counseling and Approach to Patient")) and self-help interventions to more formal psychotherapeutic techniques, including motivational interviewing (MI), Cognitive Behavioral Therapy (CBT), and contingency management with voucher incentives. The literature is less clear on the effectiveness of alternative interventions, such as hypnosis and acupuncture, but some patients appear to find such interventions helpful.

Self-Help Programs

Organizations, such as the American Lung Association and various state health agencies, have developed treatment programs that focus on peer support, psychosocial education, and self-help interventions. Many people elect to treat their smoking through the use of self-help books and manuals, which are available on the Web, for purchase in bookstores, or through telephone help lines. Help lines, which are run by many states, local, and regional health entities, and commercial health plans, can provide good information and support, including strategies for quitting smoking.

Motivational Interviewing

MI is a nonconfrontational, yet subtly directive style of interviewing that seeks to help patients to resolve their ambivalence about changing behaviors or making a commitment to change (Miller & Rollnick, 2002). This interview method has been applied to a variety of problems, including nicotine dependence, as well as alcohol and other substance dependence. In fact, MI is a basic interviewing skill that increases the effectiveness of all clinicians who work with substance-dependent or dually diagnosed patients. MI is a brief intervention that can be applied in a single visit, as well as during an ongoing therapeutic relationship. MI is not trivial to learn. Clinicians can begin to familiarize themselves with the MI method by reading Miller and Rollnick's (2002) text and attending a workshop given by a certified trainer. However, evidence suggests that ongoing supervision and feedback from an expert in MI is needed in order to become proficient in using the MI method (Miller & Mount, 2001).

Cognitive Behavioral Therapy and Relapse Prevention

CBT and its variants (many of these variants are referred to as relapse prevention (RP)) seek to teach patients skills that they can use to manage thoughts, feelings, and behaviors that may arise during efforts to quit drugs and that may interfere with achieving abstinence or that may increase risk of relapse after abstinence has been established. Slips are viewed as opportunities to learn what caused the slip, how to avoid the slip, and how to apply the skills to avoid slips and reduce relapse risk in the future. When patients slip, it is important that the patient and clinician analyze when, where, and what happened. Like MI, CBT has been applied to a variety of drug and alcohol problems. A specific version of CBT has been developed for treatment of smoking and has been demonstrated in controlled trials to be effective (Hall et al., 1998). Studies that were performed at therapeutic community and residential treatment programs with substance abusers who smoke have shown that it is feasible to provide effective smoking cessation treatment for substance abusers and that CBT is an important component of the intervention (Bobo, McIlvain, Lando, Walker, & Leed-Kelly, 1998; Burling, Burling, & Latini, 2001; Burling, Marshall, & Seidner, 1991; Kalman, 1998). However, overall quit rates among substance-dependent patients are generally lower than rates seen in the general population, suggesting that more intensive treatment may be needed in order to produce a significant reduction in smoking in substance-dependent patients (Joseph, Willenbring, Nugent, & Nelson, 2004; Joseph et al., 2004).

Contingency Management

Contingency management (CM) with voucher incentives is a method based on behavioral theory in which vouchers, exchangeable for appropriate goods or services, are offered as reinforcers contingent upon a target behavior reflective of abstinence. CM has been studied most intensively in cocaine-dependent patients (Higgins et al., 1994) and opioid-dependent patients (Silverman et al., 1996; Stitzer, Iguchi, & Felch, 1992), with whom it has been found to be a powerful intervention. Recently low-cost vouchers have been shown to be effective across a wide range of community-based substance abuse treatment programs in a controlled trial carried out in the NIDA Clinical Trials Network (Petry et al., 2005; Peirce et al., 2006). CM has also shown promise for smoking cessation (Higgins et al., 2004; Robles et al., 2005). Voucher incentive approaches have sometimes been criticized as unrealistic in community-based care due to costs of supplying incentives and negative feelings about the notion of "paying patients to abstain." However, the findings of the Clinical Trials Network trials (Petry et al., 2005; Peirce et al., 2006), as well as subsequent projects disseminating low-cost vouchers into community-based treatment (Kellogg et al., 2005), suggest that these interventions are well received by community-based practitioners and treatment programs. Interestingly, a recent smoking cessation study in methadone clinics found that smoking abstinence rates in groups receiving CM treatment were superior to groups receiving CBT (Shoptaw et al., 2002). More research on CM for smoking cessation in community-based drug treatment is needed.

Organizational or Systems-Level Interventions

It is important to note that an evolving literature on treatment for tobacco dependence looks at the organizational level, not the individual level. Organizations and cultures develop attitudes toward the use of nicotine that indirectly lead to reductions in individual's use of tobacco. For example, as cities pass laws that restrict smoking to certain areas, reductions in smoking occur. More progressive smoking treatment agencies have emulated these organizational change strategies and have moved from initial strategies of prohibiting staff from smoking near patients to requiring that all smoking occurs outside the building (Williams et al., 2005). More progressive organizations have adopted policies prohibiting tobacco use at work. For example, some personnel policies treat the use of tobacco similarly to the use of other legal drugs, such as alcohol; staff members are not allowed to use these drugs during work hours.

Treatment Planning for the Case Examples

Case 1. Since SF was already aware of the negative consequences of smoking, the clinician discussed these consequences with him in more detail as a way of building motivation for quitting smoking. The clinician also talked with the patient about self-efficacy and built up his sense of personal control by pointing out that SF could stop smoking in certain situations (e.g., if he was going to take a breathalyzer). Contingent reinforcements proved to be especially helpful; he participated in a study that provided $5 to $20 for each time that he remained abstinent during periodic study follow-up visits. SF never stopped smoking 100 percent; he slips occasionally, but he has greatly reduced his smoking. His smoking frequency gradually increased after the study ended.

Case 2. To build rapport and treatment alliance with JS, who has paranoid schizophrenia, the counselor encouraged her to talk freely about her life and to disclose information. The counselor learned from her that she usually smoked during hours of isolation and boredom. They focused on activities that might serve as alternatives to smoking. Over time, they were able to identify an activity that she liked—bingo. The counselor encouraged her to attend the bingo events at her assisted living facility and to buy a small hand-held bingo game to play during times that she had an urge to smoke. They tried several strategies that did not work, including counting and eliminating the number of cigarettes she smoked and using contingent reinforcement (e.g., money or little rewards). JS did not try nicotine patches because she was afraid of the health consequences and was paranoid that they may kill her. The counselor's support and expression of concern proved to be the most important motivator to help JS to cut down from thirty cigarettes per day to approximately six per day.

These cases illustrate the application of the five A's and five R's (see "Context of Counseling and Approach to Patient"); the counselors assessed the patients' level of motivation and readiness to quit and evaluated the potential effectiveness of counseling and behavioral interventions—skills within the range of most clinicians working in addiction treatment programs. Neither patient in the case studies achieved complete abstinence. It has been found that cigarette smokers tend to compensate for using fewer cigarettes by inhaling more deeply, resulting in breath carbon monoxide and nicotine blood levels similar to patients who smoke more cigarettes but inhale less deeply. Moreover, individuals who continue to smoke at low levels (i.e., without fully quitting) have a greater probability of relapsing and returning to their pretreatment smoking frequency. For the patients in the case examples, trials of nicotine patch or an antidepressant should be considered in an effort to achieve complete abstinence. Case 2 illustrates reluctance to consider medication treatment, which is not uncommon; fear of taking medication may be amplified if program staff members are uncomfortable with medication treatments. Education (of both patients and staff) is helpful to address this issue and to help patients make fully informed choices. Case 2 is also a complicated dually diagnosed patient with schizophrenia and nicotine dependence. While clinicians may apply to more complex cases the principles of smoking cessation treatment that have been developed and tested in routine samples of smokers, clinicians should apply these principles to such complex cases with caution, since research on smoking cessation in patients with mental disorders or other substance use disorders or multiple diagnoses is limited.

SUMMARY

Tobacco use is extremely common among substance-dependent patients and represents a serious health threat. Effective interventions are documented in the literature. While there is no panacea or uniquely effective treatment strategy for nicotine dependence, success rates in treatment of nicotine dependence are equivalent to success rates seen in treatment of other substance use problems. However, clinicians rarely routinely document and treat nicotine dependence in the same way that they document and treat dependence on other substances subject to abuse.

The following conclusions regarding nicotine dependence and interventions are supported by evidence:

1. Nicotine interventions do not interfere with the completion of other substance abuse treatments (e.g., do not cause patients to leave treatment early for other drug problems).

2. Nicotine interventions do not increase the rate of relapse to alcohol and other drugs.

3. More research is needed to establish the optimal time to incorporate smoking cessation treatment into treatment for other types of substance abuse. Interestingly, similar attention has not been paid to the sequencing of treatments in patients who abuse both alcohol and cocaine. There may be no compelling reason not to introduce nicotine treatment concurrent with the initiation of other interventions, such as those for alcohol and cocaine abuse.

4. Tobacco treatment can be successfully integrated into addiction treatment.

5. Most patients want to address their tobacco dependence, and the greatest resistance to treatment of tobacco addiction often comes from staff members, not patients.

6. Organizational change interventions, such as tobacco-free facilities, are felt to be the most challenging aspects of tobacco interventions for patients; enforcement of policies and laws is important.

7. Medications, including NRT, antidepressant medications (bupropion and nortriptyline), and varenicline, are a helpful treatment component for many patients and should be more widely applied in substance abuse treatment programs.

8. Evaluation and treatment for nicotine addiction follows principles of treatment for addiction to other substances subject to abuse. Clinicians and programs should be encouraged to implement screening and smoking cessation interventions for their patients.

Suggestions for Further Reading

For readers who wish to study further in this area, we recommend:

- Abrams, D. B., Niaura, R., Brown, R. A., Emmons, K. M., Goldstein, M. G., Monti, P.M., et al. (2003). *The tobacco dependence treatment handbook: A guide to best practices.* New York: Guilford Press.

- American Psychiatric Association. (1996). Practice guideline for the treatment of patients with nicotine dependence. *American Journal of Psychiatry*, *153*(Suppl. 10), 1-31.

- Burling, T. A., Ramsey, T. G., Seidner, A. L., & Kondo, C.S. (1997). Issues related to smoking treatment for substance abusers. *Journal of Substance Abuse, 9*, 27-40.

- Hall, S. M. (1999). Psychological interventions: State of the art. *Nicotine and Tobacco Research*, 1(Suppl. 2), S169-S173, discussion S207-S210.

- Kalman, D. (1998). Smoking cessation treatment for substance misusers in early recovery: A review of the literature and recommendations for practice. *Substance Use and Misuse, 33*, 2021-2047.

- Rustin, T. A. (1994). *Quit and stay quit: A personal program to stop smoking.* Center City, MN: Hazeldon.

- Tobacco Dependence Program. (2006). *Drug-free is nicotine-free: A manual for chemical dependency treatment programs.* New Brunswick, NJ: University of Medicine and Dentistry of New Jersey (UMDNJ) School of Public Health, from http://www.tobaccoprogram.org.

- U.S. Department of Health and Human Services (USDHHS). (2000). *Treating tobacco use and dependence: Clinical practice guideline.* Rockville, MD: USDHHS Public Health Service.

Authors' Note

The research in this chapter was supported in part by cooperative agreements U10 DA15815 (Dr. Sorensen) and U10 DA13046 (Dr. Rotrosen) the California-Arizona and New York Clinical Trials Network Nodes, from NIH/NIDA and grant ID No. 7-039 (Dr. Penn) from the Arizona Biomedical Research Commission.

References

Adler, L. E., Hoffer, L. D., Wiser, A., & Freedman, R. (1993). Normalization of auditory physiology by cigarette smoking in schizophrenic patients. *American Journal of Psychiatry, 150*, 1856-1861.

American Psychiatric Association. (1994). *Diagnostic and statistical manual of mental disorders* (4th ed.). Washington, DC: Author.

Blondal, T., Gudmundsson, L. J., Tomasson, K., Jonsdottir, D., Hilmarsdottir, H., Kristjannson, F., et al. (1999). The effects of fluoxetine combined with nicotine inhalers in smoking cessation—A randomized trial. *Addiction, 94*, 1007-1015.

Bobo, J. K., McIlvain, H. E., Lando, H. A., Walker, R. D., & Leed-Kelly, A. (1998). Effect of smoking cessation counseling on recovery from alcoholism: Findings from a randomized community intervention trial. *Addiction, 93,* 877-887.

Breslau, N., Kilbey, M. M., & Andreski, P. (1992). Nicotine withdrawal symptoms and psychiatric disorders: Findings from an epidemiologic study of young adults. *American Journal of Psychiatry, 149,* 464-469.

Burling, T. A., Burling, A. S., & Latini, D. (2001). A controlled smoking cessation trial for substance-dependent patients. *Journal of Consulting and Clinical Psychology, 69,* 295-304.

Burling, T. A., Marshall, G. D., & Seidner, A. L. (1991). Smoking cessation for substance abuse inpatients. *Journal of Substance Abuse, 3,* 269-276.

Centers for Disease Control and Prevention (CDC). (2002). Annual smoking-attributable mortality, years of potential life lost, and economic costs—United States, 1995-1999. *MMWR Morbidity and Mortality Weekly Report, 51,* 300-303.

Clarke, J. G., Stein, M. D., McGarry, K. A, & Gogineni, A. (2001). Interest in smoking cessation among injection drug users. *American Journal on Addictions, 10,* 159-166.

Cook, J. W., Spring, B., McChargue, D. E., Borrelli, B., Hitsman, B., Niaura, R., et al. (2004). Influence of fluoxetine on positive and negative affect in a clinic-based smoking cessation trial. *Psychopharmacology (Berl), 173,* 153-159.

Frosch, D. L., Stein, J. A., & Shoptaw, S. (2002). Using latent-variable models to analyze smoking cessation clinical trial data: An example among the methadone maintained. *Experimental and Clinical Psychopharmacology, 10,* 258-267.

Gill, B. S., & Bennett, D. L. (2000). Addiction professionals: Attitudes regarding treatment of nicotine dependence [letter to the editor]. *Journal of Substance Abuse Treatment, 19,* 317-318.

Glassman, A. H., Helzer, J. E., Covey, L. S., Cottler, L. B., Stetner, F., Tipp, J. E., et al. (1990). Smoking, smoking cessation, and major depression. *Journal of the American Medical Association, 264,* 1583-1584.

Gonzalez, D., Rennard, S. I., Nides, M., Oncken, C., Azoulay, S., Billing, C. B., et al. (2006). Varenicline, an alpha4beta2 nicotine acetylcholine receptor partial agonist, vs sustained release bupropion and placebo for smoking cessation: A randomized trial. *Journal of the American Medical Association, 296,* 47-55.

Grant, B. F., Hasin, D. S., Chou, P., Stinson, F. S., & Dawson, D. A. (2004). Nicotine dependence and psychiatric disorders in the United States: Results from the National Epidemiologic Survey on Alcohol and Related Conditions. *Archives of General Psychiatry, 61,* 1107-1115.

Hall, S. M., Reus, V. I., Munoz, R. F., Sees, K. L., Humfleet, G., Hartz, D. T., et al. (1998). Nortriptyline and cognitive-behavioral therapy in the treatment of cigarette smoking. *Archives of General Psychiatry, 55,* 683-690.

Hasin, D. S., Samet, S., Aivadyan, C., Geier, T., & Przybylinski. E. Psychiatric Research Interview for Substance and Mental Disorders (PRISM), Computer-Assisted Version (In preparation).

Hasin, D. S., Samet, S., Nunes, E., Meydan, J., Matseoane, K., & Waxman, R. (2006). Diagnosis of comorbid disorders in substance users: Psychiatric Research Interview for Substance and Mental Disorders (PRISM-IV). *American Journal of Psychiatry, 163,* 689-696.

Heatherton, T. F., Kozlowski, L. T., Frecker, R. C., & Fagerstrom, K. O. (1991). The Fagerstrom Test for Nicotine Dependence: A revision of the Fagerstrom Tolerance Questionnaire. *British Journal of Addictions, 86,* 19-27.

Higgins, S. T., Budney, A. J., Bickel, W. K., Foerg, F. E., Donham, R., & Badger, G. J. (1994). Incentives improve outcome in outpatient behavioral treatment of cocaine dependence. *Archives of General Psychiatry, 51,* 568-576.

Higgins, S. T., Heil, S. H., Solomon, L. J., Bernstein, I. M., Lussier, J. P., Abel, R. L., et al. (2004). A pilot study on voucher-based incentives to promote abstinence from cigarette smoking during pregnancy and postpartum. *Nicotine and Tobacco Research, 6,* 1015-1020.

Hurt, R. D., Crogan, I. T., Offord, K. P., Eberman, K. M., & Morse, R. M. (1995). Attitudes toward nicotine dependence among chemical dependency unit staff—Before and after a smoking cessation trial. *Journal of Substance Abuse Treatment, 12*, 247-252.

Hurt, R. D., Offord, K. P., Crogan, I. T., Gomez-Dahl, L., Kottke, T. E., Morse, R. M., et al. (1996). Mortality following inpatient addictions treatment: Role of tobacco use in a community-based cohort. *Journal of the American Medical Association, 275*, 1097-1103.

Hurt, S. D., Sachs, D. P., Glover, E. D., Offord, K. P., Johnston, J. A., Dale, L. C., et al. (1997). A comparison of sustained-release bupropion and placebo for smoking cessation. *New England Journal of Medicine, 337*, 1195-1202.

Johnson, E. O., Rhee, S. H., Chase, G. A., & Breslau, N. (2004). Comorbidity of depression with levels of smoking: An exploration of the shared familial risk hypothesis. *Nicotine and Tobacco Research, 6*, 1029-1038.

Jorenby, D. E., Leischow, S. J., Nides, M. A., Rennard, S. I., Johnston, J. A., Hughes, A. R., et al. (1999). A controlled trial of sustained-release bupropion, a nicotine patch, or both for smoking cessation. *New England Journal of Medicine, 340*, 685-691.

Joseph, A. M., Arikian, N. J., An, L. C., Nugent, S. N., Sloan, R. J., Pieper, C.F., et al. (2004). Results of a randomized controlled trial of intervention to implement smoking guidelines in Veterans Affairs medical centers: Increased use of medications without cessation benefit. *Medical Care, 42*, 1100-1110.

Joseph, A. M., Willenbring, M. L., Nugent, S. M., & Nelson, D. B. (2004). A randomized trial of concurrent versus delayed smoking intervention for patients in alcohol dependence. *Journal of Studies on Alcohol, 65*, 681-691.

Kalman, D. (1998). Smoking cessation treatment for substance misusers in early recovery: A review of the literature and recommendations for practice. *Substance Use and Misuse, 33*, 2021-2047.

Kalman, D., Morissette, S. B., & George, T. P. (2005). Co-morbidity of smoking in patients with psychiatric and substance use disorders. *American Journal on Addictions, 14*, 106-123.

Kellogg, S. H., Burns, M., Coleman, P., Stitzer, M., Wale, J. B., & Kreek, M. J. (2005). Something of value: The introduction of contingency management interventions into the New York City Health and Hospital Addiction Treatment Service. *Journal of Substance Abuse Treatment, 28*, 57-65.

Lasser, K., Boyd, J. W., Woolhandler, S., Himmelstein, D. U., McCormick, D., & Bor, D. H. (2000). Smoking and mental illness: A population-based prevalence study. *Journal of the American Medical Association, 284*, 2606-2610.

Miller, W. R., & Mount, K. A. (2001). A small study of training in motivational interviewing: Does one workshop change clinician and client behavior? *Behavioral and Cognitive Psychotherapy, 29*, 457-471.

Miller, W. R., & Rollnick, S. (2002). *Motivational interviewing: Preparing people for change* (2nd ed.). New York: Guilford Press.

Miller, L. S., Zhang, X., Rice, D. P., & Max, W. (1998). State estimates of total medical expenditures attributable to cigarette smoking, 1993. *Public Health Reports, 113*, 447-458.

Niaura, R., Spring, B., Borrelli, B., Hedeker, D., Goldstein, M.G., Keuthen, N., et al. (2002). Multicenter trial of fluoxetine as an adjunct to behavioral smoking cessation treatment. *Journal of Consulting and Clinical Psychology, 70*, 887-896.

Nides, M., Oncken, C., Gonzales, D., Rennard, S., Watsky, E. J., Anziano, R., et al. (2006). Smoking cessation with varenicline, a selective alpha4beta2 nicotinic receptor partial agonist: Results from a 7-week, randomized, placebo- and bupropion-controlled trial with 1-year follow-up. *Archives of Internal Medicine, 166*, 1561-1568.

Parrott, A. C. (1995). Stress modulation over the day in cigarette smokers. *Addiction, 90*, 233-244.

Peirce, J. M., Petry, N. M., Stitzer, M. L., Blaine, J., Kellogg, S., Satterfield, F., et al. (2006). Effects of lower-cost incentives on stimulant abstinence in methadone maintenance treatment: A National Drug Abuse Treatment Clinical Trials Network study. *Archives of General Psychiatry, 63*, 201-208.

Petry, N. M., Peirce, J. M., Stitzer, M. L., Blaine, J., Roll, J. M., Cohen, A., et al. (2005). Effect of prize-based incentives on outcomes in stimulant abusers in outpatient psychosocial treatment programs: A national drug abuse treatment clinical trials network study. *Archives of General Psychiatry, 62*, 1148-1156.

Reid, M. S., Fallon, B., Sonne, S., Nunes, N., Lima, J., Jiang, H., et al. (2007). Implementation of a smoking cessation treatment study at substance abuse rehabilitation programs: Smoking behavior and treatment feasibility across varied community-based outpatient programs. *Journal of Addiction Medicine, 1,* 154-160.

Robles, E., Crone, C. C., Whiteside-Mansell, L., Conners, N. A., Bokony, P.A., Worley, L. L., et al. (2005). Voucher-based incentives for cigarette smoking reduction in a women's residential treatment program. *Nicotine and Tobacco Research, 7*, 111-117.

Ryan, J., Zwerling, C., & Orav, E. J. (1992). Occupational risks associated with cigarette smoking: A prospective study. *American Journal of Public Health, 82*, 29-32.

Sacco, K. A., Termine, A., Seyal, A., Dudas, M. M., Vessicchio, J. C., Krishnan-Sarin, S., et al. (2005). Effects of cigarette smoking on spatial working memory and attentional deficits in schizophrenia: Involvement of nicotinic receptor mechanisms. *Archives of General Psychiatry, 62*, 649-659.

Saules, K. K., Schuh, L. M., Arfken, C. L., Reed, K., Kilbey, M. M., & Schuster, C.R. (2004). Double-blind placebo-controlled trial of fluoxetine in smoking cessation treatment including nicotine patch and cognitive-behavioral group therapy. *American Journal on Addictions, 13*, 438-446.

Shoptaw, S., Rotheram-Fuller, E., Yang, X., Frosch, D., Nahom, D., Jarvik, M. E., et al. (2002). Smoking cessation in methadone maintenance. *Addiction, 97*, 1217-1228, discussion 1325.

Silverman, K., Wong, C. J., Higgins, S. T., Brooner, R. K., Montoya, I. D., Contoreggi, C., et al. (1996). Increasing opiate abstinence through voucher-based reinforcement therapy. *Drug and Alcohol Dependence, 41*, 157-165.

Stitzer, M., Iguchi, M., & Felch, L. (1992). Contingent take-home incentive: Effects on drug use of methadone maintenance patients. *Journal of Consulting and Clinical Psychology, 60*, 927-934.

U.S. Department of Health and Human Services (USDHHS). (2000). *Treating Tobacco Use and Dependence: Clinical Practice Guideline.* Rockville, MD: USDHHS Public Health Service.

Williams, J. M., Foulds, J., Dwyer, M., Order-Connors, B., Springer, M., Gadde, P., et al. (2005). The integration of tobacco dependence treatment and tobacco-free standards into residential addictions treatment in New Jersey. *Journal of Substance Abuse Treatment, 28*, 331-340.

Ziedonis, D. M., Kosten, T. R., Glazer, W. M., & Frances, R.J. (1994). Nicotine dependence and schizophrenia. *Hospital and Community Psychiatry, 45,* 204-206.

Chapter 14

Common Medical Illnesses in Patients With Substance Use and Psychiatric Disorders

by Jeanne Manubay, M.D., and Terry Horton, M.D.

INTRODUCTION

Dually diagnosed patients are at a high risk for medical problems. Both psychiatric and substance-related issues can contribute to poor health. There are five principal factors that can impact patients' health:

1. Common medical problems occur in dually diagnosed patients.

2. Most substances of abuse have direct toxicities that are responsible for a host of medical sequelae.

3. Certain factors related to lifestyle, such as injection drug use and homelessness, place patients at risk for health problems (e.g., risk for endocarditis, poor living conditions).

4. Patients who have psychiatric disorders or who prioritize drug seeking over health maintenance may not seek medical attention for health problems.

5. Medications, especially psychiatric medications, may have adverse side effects such as weight gain.

Obstacles Faced by Substance Abusers in Obtaining Medical Care

A breakdown in three critical areas of our health care system poses additional obstacles for substance abusers. These areas include problems with comprehensiveness of care, coordination of care, and continuity of care. Many primary care physicians have had poor training in addiction medicine and may not ask patients about substance abuse problems. Primary care physicians focus on identification and treatment of more common health conditions, such as diabetes mellitus, hypertension, and obesity. As a result, substance use and other relevant issues, such as sexually transmitted diseases (STDs), may be ignored. Access to care is another impediment; many drug abusers may not have health insurance. Substance abusers seek medical attention in one of three settings: the emergency room (ER), a psychiatric setting, or a generalist's office. Patients who frequent the ER for medical problems are often lost to follow-up. Their issues can never be fully addressed or understood, and appropriate care cannot be coordinated. In addition, treatment of medical, psychiatric, and substance-related issues is provided by different doctors in separate settings, and patients receive fragmented care. When there is poor communication between treatment services and when patients frequently miss appointments, continuity of care is impossible. Substance abusers often maintain chaotic lifestyles characterized by violence, rape, and exchange of sex for drugs.

Significant Morbidity and Mortality Related to Substance Abuse

Addiction is a chronic brain disease that has significant negative impact on the overall health of victims. Morbidity related to drug use is compounded by the presence of co-occurring medical problems. The National Vital Statistics Reports for 2002 reported 26,018 deaths in the United States from drug-induced causes and 19,928 deaths from alcohol-related causes (Kochanek, Murphy, Anderson, & Scott, 2004). These statistics include deaths of both individuals with drug dependence and individuals without drug dependence, deaths caused by legal drugs and illegal drugs, deaths caused by alcohol, and deaths caused by poisonings from any drug and alcohol. Cigarette smoking alone accounts for more than 440,000 deaths a year (Fellows, Trosclair, Adams, & Rivera, 2002); this statistic highlights the need for smoking cessation advocacy. There is a high prevalence of smoking among both substance abusers and patients with psychiatric disorders. Approximately 50 to 90 percent of patients with schizophrenia smoke regularly (Ziedonis, Kosten, Glazer, & Frances, 1994). Nicotine may be particularly attractive to patients with schizophrenia. Patients report improvement in cognition and negative symptoms, and nicotine may counteract sedating side effects of neuroleptic medications that are used to treat the disorder. Statistics imply that there is much greater mortality from cigarette smoking than alcohol and illegal drug use combined (Centers for Disease Control and Prevention (CDC), 2007). This statistic should prompt clinicians to educate patients about smoking cessation, particularly patients with psychiatric disorders and substance use disorders.

Another agency that collects information about drug-related mortality is the Drug Abuse Warning Network (DAWN; Substance Abuse and Mental Health Services Administration, Office of Applied Studies (SAMHSA), 2002). Participation in DAWN is voluntary, and about one third of the U.S. population (mostly in major urban areas) participate in DAWN. DAWN mortality data indicate that multiple drugs (an average of 2.7 drugs per case) are involved in drug-related deaths. Opiates, including heroin and prescription pain relievers, were most frequently implicated; opiates suppress respiration, causing patients to fall asleep and stop breathing. In comparison to the general population, heroin users are at a substantially greater risk for premature death; mortality rates in heroin users are between six and twenty times higher than the general population (Darke & Zador, 1996). Other common drugs reported in deaths caused by drug misuse include antidepressants and benzodiazepines. Illicit drug use was identified in less than 20 percent of drug-related suicides. In DAWN, amitriptyline, a tricyclic antidepressant (TCA), is one of the most frequently mentioned prescription drugs used for suicide; TCAs are toxic to the heart when taken in excessive doses. The newer generation of antidepressant medications are safer in regard to overdose. Nonprescription drugs (aspirin and acetaminophen (Tylenol) overdose) are frequently reported in suicide attempts.

Mortality rates for drug and alcohol abuse are compelling. Clinicians must confront drug abuse and intervene. Surprisingly, the majority of people with a drug or alcohol problem who need treatment do not see their drug use as a contributor to their medical and psychiatric problems. Many drug users ignore health problems. Treatment providers must recognize critical symptoms, address medical problems, and provide help and referrals. Clinicians should also be aware of the development of potentially dangerous symptoms, such as delirium tremens (DTs) in patients who suddenly give up drinking after years of heavy alcohol dependence or seizures in patients experiencing benzodiazepine withdrawal. It is also safest to assume that active drug users are noncompliant with medications, may underreport symptoms, may minimize symptoms, and may hide symptoms. Since denial by patients of drug use is common, clinicians should routinely conduct urine testing in addiction treatment settings.

Need for Coordination of Care

Improvement in the medical care of substance abusers requires drastic changes in our health care system that are not foreseeable in the near future. Without communication and coordination of care, the health care burden of substance abuse will only escalate. Integration of services is necessary. Communication between personnel from medical clinics, psychiatric treatment programs, and substance abuse treatment services is essential for effective treatment and permits treatment providers to address noncompliance, missed appointments, and diversion of medication. All clinicians, including substance abuse treatment counselors and staff with minimal medical training, can improve medical care of patients with psychiatric disorders and substance use disorders by facilitating communication between health care providers.

Chapter Overview

This chapter encourages clinicians, including clinicians with little or no training in diagnosis and treatment of medical issues, to learn about medical problems of substance-dependent patients and to take an active role in helping patients gain access to the specialized medical care they need. The chapter should serve as a useful review for psychiatrists, internists, and other medical personnel (e.g., nurses, physician assistants) who care for patients with substance use disorders. The chapter will help elucidate some of the more common presentations of medical disorders and less common presentations by patients with psychiatric disorders and substance use disorders. The literature lacks studies on epidemiology of medical disorders in these dually diagnosed patients. Thus, much of the information presented in this chapter comes from case reports and clinical experience of substance abuse treatment experts.

Medical problems frequently seen in patients with psychiatric disorders will be discussed separately from medical problems frequently seen in patients with substance use disorders. The medical consequences of specific drugs of abuse and different routes of drug administration will be discussed. This chapter offers recommendations for collecting an accurate medical history and conducting a physical examination and discusses common laboratory abnormalities and special medical issues in patients with psychiatric disorders and substance use disorders, including tuberculosis (TB), hepatitis B and C, human immunodeficiency virus (HIV), and pain. Acute and chronic pain are also discussed in Chapter 16 of this volume. This chapter will not discuss the care of pregnant substance abusers, especially opiate-dependent women, who are often referred to high-risk pregnancy clinics.

HEALTH ISSUES IN PATIENTS WITH PSYCHIATRIC DISORDERS

The presence of a psychiatric illness increases a person's risk of developing a number of medical conditions (Karasu, Waltzman, Lindenmayer, & Buckley, 1980). Psychiatric disorders predispose patients to a variety of medical problems in four ways:

1. There can be direct medical complications from psychiatric disorders (e.g., dental erosion from repetitive self-induced vomiting in patients with bulimia nervosa).

2. Dangerous behaviors resulting from psychiatric disorders put an individual's health at risk (e.g., delusional beliefs leading to accidents).

3. Medical problems can be caused by the treatment of psychiatric disorders (e.g., weight gain from many psychiatric medications can lead to diabetes mellitus).

4. Obstacles in obtaining appropriate medical treatment exist, and patients with psychiatric disorders often receive fragmented care (e.g., lack of integration of medical and psychiatric services).

Poor utilization of health care services characterizes patients with psychiatric disorders. Studies have found poor self-care among patients with schizophrenia, who lack physical exercise, have poor diets, smoke, and lack control of alcohol intake (Holmberg & Kane, 1999). Women with serious psychiatric disorders, who often have histories of abuse, are less likely than the general population to receive preventative medical care (e.g., routine physicals, pap smears, mammograms) (Steiner, Hoff, Moffett, Reynolds, Mitchell, & Rosenheck, 1998). One study found that patients with psychiatric disorders use the medical system less efficiently and are more likely to utilize ambulance and emergency department services than outpatient medical services (Berren, Santiago, Zent, & Carbone, 1999). Many treatment providers hold stigmatized attitudes against patients with psychiatric disorders (Hayward & Bright, 1997).

The lack of integration of medical and psychiatric services and poor continuity of care places patients with psychiatric disorders at risk for drug-drug interactions (see also Chapter 18 of this volume). Many commonly used medications can interfere with the metabolism of psychiatric medications, and vice versa, causing increased or decreased drug levels (e.g., erythromycin inhibits the CYP3A4 enzyme system and increases buspirone levels; ritonavir (a protease inhibitor) can increase the potency of selective serotonin reuptake inhibitors (SSRIs) including paroxetine and fluvoxamine; amitriptyline and fluvoxamine can make methadone more potent). In addition, several psychotropic medications used alone can have adverse side effects. Many SSRIs, TCAs, and mood stabilizers cause weight gain that can lead to hypertension and diabetes mellitus. Certain psychotropic medications (i.e., antipsychotic medications, especially phenothiazine derivatives) have been associated with a reversible side effect, extrapyramidal symptoms (EPS). Symptoms include tremors, muscular rigidity, drooling, shuffling gait, restlessness, dystonia (involuntary movements) and dyskinesias (stereotyped and exaggerated movements of the mouth, jaw, and tongue).

Tardive dyskinesia, which is a persistent movement disorder, is a syndrome that can be caused by neuroleptic drugs. It is characterized by repetitive, involuntary, purposeless movements, such as lip smacking, grimacing, and the rapid movement of arms and legs. There is no standard treatment for this disorder, but some symptoms may improve with cessation of the neuroleptic and with time. Neuroleptic malignant syndrome, which is one of the most serious and potentially fatal reactions to neuroleptics, usually develops shortly after initial exposure to the drug but can also be seen months later. This syndrome is rare (0.5 to 1 percent of patients exposed to neuroleptics are diagnosed with this syndrome) and has mostly been seen in patients taking haloperidol and trifluperazine (also clozapine and metoclopramide). The combination of haloperidol and lithium increases the risk of developing this syndrome. There is a classic triad of symptoms, including EPS, autonomic instability (fluctuating heart rate and blood pressure), and cognitive changes. Patients always develop fever; additional symptoms may include tremor, rigidity, sweating, drowsiness, labile blood pressure, confusion, stupor, coma, seizures, and cardiac arrhythmias. There can be elevations in the enzymes, creatine phosphokinase (CPK), lactate dehydrogenase (LDH), and white blood cell (WBC) count. Treatment consists of early recognition, discontinuation of the neuroleptic, cooling, hydration, supportive therapy, and medications (dantrolene and bromocriptine).

When physicians prescribe some psychotropic medications, they may need to request routine lab work in order to look for any hormonal or blood abnormalities (e.g., complete blood count (CBC) to look for agranulocytosis with clozapine). Antipsychotics can induce hyperprolactinemia (elevated levels of prolactin in the blood), which can cause profound sexual and reproductive side effects in men and women, including decreased libido, erectile dysfunction, infertility, amenorrhea (cessation of menses), and galactorrhea (abnormal milk production). Prolactin levels up to 100 ng/ml are usually medication-related, and dose reductions or changes to other antipsychotics are unnecessary if the individual has no adverse clinical symptoms.

Electrocardiograms (EKGs) and drug levels for many psychotropic medications need to be monitored regularly; changes in EKGs or elevations in drug levels may have serious health consequences. A baseline EKG should be obtained. High doses of lithium, tricyclic antidepressants, mellaril, or Geodon (ziprasidone) can cause QRS or QT prolongation, abnormalities in the EKG that can lead to arrhythmias. Lithium levels should be carefully monitored as there is a narrow therapeutic window (toxic levels are very close to levels within the therapeutic range). Physicians should also test for kidney and thyroid function prior to initiation of pharmacotherapy, since lithium has been associated with hypothyroidism and kidney disease (nephrogenic diabetes insipidus, renal tubular acidosis, nephritic syndrome, and chronic interstitial nephritis). Clinicians should be aware that patients taking lithium often report increased thirst and urination and frequently gain weight within the first year. Early signs and symptoms of lithium toxicity include abdominal pain, vomiting, diarrhea, drowsiness, slurred speech, muscle weakness, lack of coordination, and tremors. An individual can later develop blurred vision, tinnitus (ringing in the ear), and an elevated WBC count.

Health care providers frequently encounter medication noncompliance. Patients with psychiatric disorders often have poor adherence to treatment regimens, which may be related to impaired cognition or communication, mistrust of the health care system, or poor understanding of their illnesses. Noncompliance can result in the abrupt cessation of medications. Many classes of medications are associated with withdrawal syndromes when they are abruptly discontinued including SSRIs, TCAs, and serotonin-norepinephrine reuptake inhibitors (SNRIs). Symptoms that emerge when patients abruptly discontinue medication likely are related to that discontinuation. The SSRI withdrawal syndrome results from a sudden discontinuation of an SSRI; patients commonly present with dizziness, nausea, lethargy, and headache. Other symptoms reported include anxiety, tremor, sweating, confusion, insomnia, irritability, anorexia, and memory impairments. Some patients may report sensory disturbances, such as numbness, parethesias (a sensation of prickling, tingling, or numbness of a person's skin), or problems with balance. Symptoms are more prominent in patients who discontinue SSRIs with shorter half-lives, such as paroxetine, and in patients who have been taking SSRIs for more than two months. Symptoms can appear in days to weeks of cessation, depending on the half-life of the SSRI. Discontinuation of TCAs and SNRIs can result in flu-like syndromes. Patients stop taking medications for many reasons (e.g., perception of ineffectiveness, insistence on not depending on an antidepressant, cost). It is important to ask patients if they are taking their prescribed medications as directed.

Some medical conditions have a higher rate of psychiatric comorbidity. Irritable bowel syndrome has been frequently associated with anxiety and mood disorders. Individuals with fibromyalgia and multiple sclerosis have higher rates of major depression and anxiety disorders. Hepatitis C is associated with mood disorders, and interferon-alpha, an antiviral medication commonly used for treatment of hepatitis C, can cause depression and fatigue. Other conditions can even cause or mimic depression. Hypothyroidism (low levels of thyroid hormone) is common and can produce fatigue, low energy, and depressed mood. It is treatable with thyroid hormone and can be easily detected (by obtaining thyroid stimulating hormone (TSH) blood levels).

Some psychiatric conditions have a higher rate of medical comorbidity. There are higher rates of diabetes mellitus in both patients with depression and patients with bipolar disorder. There may be shared genetic predispositions for these illnesses, or there may be long-term effects from hypercortisolism seen with mood disturbances (Cassidy, Ahearn, & Carroll, 1999). Many psychiatric medications may cause glucose intolerance, a precursor to diabetes mellitus and weight gain. The prevalence of HIV has increased in psychiatric populations and has been studied extensively (Peretta et al., 1998). Patients with severe mental illness often engage in unhealthy behaviors (e.g., multiple sexual partners, intravenous (IV) drug use) that put them at increased risk for HIV. Both neuropsychiatric complications and side effects from HIV treatments can make treatment of psychiatric disorders more difficult.

Health professionals have long known that patients with psychiatric disorders have reduced life expectancy. Within this population, there is a significantly higher frequency of deaths from accidental and intentional injury, including deaths caused by adverse effects of psychotropic medications.

MEDICAL PROBLEMS IN PATIENTS WITH SUBSTANCE USE DISORDERS

Medical Problems Related to Drugs of Abuse

Medical consequences of drug and alcohol use may be related to drug-specific effects, route of administration, and contaminants. This section will address medical problems associated with each major drug of abuse and route of administration.

Alcohol. Alcohol affects almost every organ system in the body. This section discusses the effects of alcohol intoxication and withdrawal on the body and adverse consequences from chronic alcohol consumption (see Table 14-1) on each major organ system.

Alcohol Intoxication. As blood alcohol concentration (BAC) rises, its clinical effects become more serious. A BAC between 20 and 99 mg% causes impaired coordination and changes in mood and behavior. When BAC is 100 to 199 mg%, there is increasing neurologic (brain) impairment including slow reaction time, ataxia (difficulty walking straight) and mental impairment. When BAC is between 200 and 299 mg%, there is usually marked intoxication, and nausea and vomiting may occur. When BAC is greater than 300 mg%, there can be hypothermia (low body temperature). When BAC is above 400 mg%, patients experience alcoholic coma. A BAC of above 600 and 800 mg% is often fatal. Higher BAC levels may be better tolerated by patients with increased tolerance from chronic alcohol intake. As patients become more intoxicated, they experience progressive obtundation (decreased consciousness) and a decrease in respiration (breathing), blood pressure, and body temperature. Death can occur if breathing stops from a loss of airway protective reflexes (inability to keep airway open), pulmonary (lung) aspiration of stomach contents or respiratory arrest from central nervous system (CNS) depression (the brain center that controls breathing stops working).

Management of alcohol intoxication is primarily supportive, and protection of the airway (providing oxygen, oropharyngeal airway (mouthpiece) and intubation (in some)) is of utmost importance so that a person can continue breathing. Ethanol can cause low glucose (sugar) levels in the blood, which may cause coma, and most patients with impaired consciousness are given IV glucose and thiamine. Since alcohol is rapidly absorbed, induction of vomiting is usually not indicated unless a patient has

Table 14-1
Medical Problems Related to Chronic Alcohol Use

Organ/System	Medical Problems
Brain	Hepatic encephalopathy, short-term and long-term memory loss, Wernicke-Korsakoff disease, increased risk of stroke, peripheral neuropathy
Heart	High blood pressure, enlarged heart, irregular heart rhythm, heart failure
Digestive Tract	Irritation of the esophagus and stomach, stomach and intestinal ulcers, acute and chronic pancreatitis, esophageal varices
Liver	Fatty liver, alcoholic hepatitis, portal hypertension and varices, cirrhosis
Metabolic/Endocrine	Low glucose, sodium, potassium, magnesium, calcium, and phosphorus possibly causing weakness, vomiting, irregular heart rhythms
Blood	Increased susceptibility to infections, prolonged bleeding
Other	Gout, increased risk of many cancers, including cancer of the mouth, lip, esophagus, stomach, breast, liver, bile duct, and colon.

ingested a substantial amount within thirty to sixty minutes, or the patient has ingested other drugs. There are no antidotes for alcohol intoxication, and patients are best managed without medications and with support and reassurance. If a patient becomes severely agitated, a short-acting benzodiazepine (e.g., lorazepam) or a neuroleptic agent (e.g., haloperidol) may be used.

It is widely known that alcohol use is associated with behaviors leading to accidents or trauma. Impairments in judgment and consciousness can lead to injuries and death (e.g., burns from cigarettes not properly extinguished, car accidents from driving under the influence (DUI)). Intoxication increases risk for rape and victimization (perhaps related to impaired judgment, and perpetrators may be more likely to commit an offense because of decreased inhibition from alcohol intoxication).

Alcohol Withdrawal. Withdrawal symptoms can begin six to twenty-four hours after the last drink. Early symptoms include anxiety, nausea, headache, sweating, and sleep disturbances. There can be elevations in heart rate, blood pressure, and temperature. Tremors may be present and are best seen in the tongue or with arms extended. Seizures often occur within forty-eight hours of cessation. DTs, which can begin forty-eight to seventy-two hours after the last drink, are associated with a mortality rate of 1 to 5 percent and require hospitalization and intensive medical treatment. Patients may experience visual, auditory, or tactile hallucinations. Treatment of alcohol withdrawal requires a comprehensive workup, maintenance of fluid balance, and supportive care. Long-acting benzodiazepines are routinely used to reduce the signs and symptoms of withdrawal and to protect against the risk of seizures; long-acting benzodiazepines are usually given in fixed amounts at scheduled times over a period of five to seven days. Additional agents such as beta-blockers and centrally acting alpha-adrenergic agonists (clonidine) have been used for treatment of mild to moderate withdrawal.

Neurological Problems. The chronic effects of alcohol use may cause short-term and long-term memory loss, mild to severe cognitive deficits, and problems with activities of daily living. Patients with Wernicke-Korsakoff disease, which results from thiamine (Vitamin B$_1$) deficiency, often as a consequence of chronic alcohol use, can present with confusion, unsteady gait, and nystagmus (rhythmic jerking movements of the eyes). Later manifestations of this disease can lead to Korsakoff's syndrome, a form of dementia characterized by memory impairment and confabulation (nonsense talk to fill in memory gaps of which a person is unaware). A nonspecific dementia similar to Alzheimer's disease is also a possible complication from chronic alcohol use. Heavy drinkers have a higher risk of stroke and often have other comorbid conditions. Peripheral neuropathies (symptoms of numbness, burning on hands and feet that result from vitamin deficiencies, pressure on nerves from passing out in awkward positions, or ethanol toxicity) are common.

Cardiac Problems. Hypertension, electrical disturbances in the heart causing "holiday heart" (palpitations), and chronic cardiomyopathy (poor contraction of an enlarged heart) are among the common cardiac consequences of chronic alcohol use. Although some studies suggest that moderate alcohol intake may be protective to the heart, the risks of other alcohol-related problems outweigh any benefits. Heavy alcohol use may lead to congestive heart failure and even sudden cardiac death.

Gastrointestinal Problems. Frequent complaints of heartburn, nausea, vomiting, and diarrhea may signal more serious pathology. Alcohol has direct toxicity to cells and can cause disease in the esophagus, stomach, small bowel, liver, and pancreas. Diseases include gastroesophageal reflux (GERD or acid reflux), gastritis, chronic esophagitis, Mallory-Weiss tears (tears in the stomach from violent vomiting), peptic ulcer disease, fatty liver, alcoholic hepatitis, cirrhosis, and acute and chronic pancreatitis. Any symptoms of weight loss, hematemesis (vomiting with blood or with a coffee-ground appearance), difficulty or pain in swallowing, yellow eyes (may indicate jaundice), and protuberant abdomen (may indicate ascites (fluid in the abdomen from liver failure)) indicate severe medical problems and may warrant immediate medical attention.

Metabolic/Endocrine Problems. Fluid and electrolyte abnormalities are common in alcoholics who present for medical care. Vomiting can cause severe dehydration, which can lead to coma after significant volume depletion. Chronic alcohol use can deplete the body's stores of potassium, magnesium, calcium, and phosphorus. Osteoporosis (which can lead to bone fracture), menstrual problems, infertility, and early menopause have been associated with alcohol abuse. Toxic effects to the thyroid and adrenal glands have been reported.

Hematopoietic Problems. Prolonged bleeding may be a sign of the liver's inability to synthesize clotting factors (from liver damage). There may be a reduction in platelets, which is associated with a tendency to bruise easily. Alcohol exerts a toxic effect on cells of the immune system, which can ultimately lead to poor immune function, thereby making an individual more susceptible to infections.

Malignancy. Alcohol increases the risk for many cancers, including cancer of the lip, oral cavity, larynx, esophagus, stomach, breast, liver, bile duct, and colon. Smoking further increases this risk.

Other Problems. Alcohol intoxication can lead to aspiration and even respiratory depression (impaired breathing) and can increase the risk for pneumonia. Patients with gout, which is more common in alcoholics, may present with a painful, enlarged great toe or other joint pain. There is a higher prevalence for dental disease in alcohol-dependent patients.

Cocaine. Patients who abuse cocaine and other stimulants have a unique set of comorbid medical problems related to intoxication, withdrawal, and chronic use (see Table 14-2).

Cocaine Intoxication. The degree and duration of subjective effects of cocaine depend on dose and route of administration. Injected or smoked cocaine has faster absorption and more immediate effects than cocaine inhaled through the nose. Effects of cocaine and stimulants include increased energy, alertness, and sociability, elation, euphoria, increased perception of a rapid heart rate, irritability, and restlessness. Higher doses may lead to elevated body temperature, emotional lability, paranoia, psychosis, violent behavior, generalized seizures, and multiorgan failure. Hyperthermia and grand mal seizures may occur as a result of other stimulant toxicity. Treatment of stimulant intoxication usually requires supportive measures. Agitation may be controlled with benzodiazepines, and psychosis may be controlled with neuroleptic medications such as haloperidol.

Cocaine Withdrawal. Withdrawal from stimulants is associated with depression, anxiety, fatigue, poor concentration, hypersomnia, and apathy, which are often mild and transient. Hospitalization is rarely indicated, although when patients experience significant suicidal thinking, which occasionally occurs, they should be hospitalized.

Neurological Problems. Cocaine use has been linked to multiple neurological symptoms including severe headaches, tremors, vertigo, dizziness, fainting, blurred vision, ataxia, seizures, transient ischemic attacks (TIAs), and stroke. One rare condition called the "crack dance" manifests as choreiform movements of the arms (involuntary writhing) related to crack use. The incidence of stroke, particularly of the hemorrhagic (bleeding) type, is especially high in individuals aged 17 to 44 (Kaku & Lowenstein, 1990; Klonoff, Andrews, & Obana, 1989).

Cardiac Problems. It is well known that cocaine use can cause myocardial infarction (or heart attack). One study found that regular cocaine use was associated with about one of every four nonfatal myocardial infarctions in persons aged 18 to 45 (Qureshi, Suri, Guterman, & Hopkins, 2001). The link between cocaine use and myocardial infarction may be explained by increased workload of the heart following cocaine use and spasms of the coronary arteries. Other cardiovascular problems include hypertension, tachycardia (increased heart rate), and palpitations. More serious consequences include cardiac arrhythmias (electrical conduction disturbances leading to irregular heart beats), cardiomyopathy (disease of the heart muscle), aortic dissection (a life-threatening tear in one of the major arteries), and sudden death.

Gastrointestinal Problems. Stimulants may cause nausea and vomiting. Severe abdominal pain may indicate intestinal ischemia (blockage of blood flow to bowel) or perforation of the bowel, which is rare but serious. Liver toxicity has also been reported.

Other Problems. Stimulants may induce acute kidney failure, which may be accompanied by altered mental status. Rhabdomyolysis is a condition of muscle breakdown

Table 14-2
Medical Problems Related to Stimulant (i.e., Cocaine,
Methamphetamine) Use

Organ/System	Medical Problems
Brain	Severe headache, dizziness, tremor, vertigo, ataxia, fainting, seizures, stroke, psychosis (delirium), hypersomnia
Heart	Heart attack, elevated heart rate and blood pressure, palpitations, irregular heart rhythms, aortic dissection
Digestive Tract	Intestinal ischemia, perforation of the bowel, liver damage
Other	Kidney failure, shortness of breath, wheezing

that may be related to the direct effect of stimulants or excessive muscle activity, which may lead to kidney failure. Stimulants can also cause shortness of breath, hyperventilation, wheezing, chest pain, and pulmonary edema (fluid buildup in the lungs).

Methamphetamine. Methamphetamine abuse is becoming a serious and growing problem (SAMHSA, 2003). Also known as "speed," "ice," "crystal," and "chalk," methamphetamine can be taken orally, intranasally (snorting), or through inhaled (smoking) or IV routes. The effects of methamphetamine last about ten hours. Although many of the consequences of methamphetamine use are similar to those of cocaine use (see Table 14-2), some unique conditions specific to methamphetamine abuse exist.

Methamphetamine Intoxication. Death from methamphetamine overdose can result from heart failure, cerebral hemorrhage, seizures, or elevated body temperature. Chronic use may result in "amphetamine psychosis," which is characterized by the development of delusions and paranoia. Some individuals have displayed repetitive stereotyped behaviors, such as dismantling and reassembling gadgets.

Methamphetamine Withdrawal. After a binge, a person may feel depressed, agitated, anxious, and anhedonic (loss of interest in things), have decreased energy, and experience intense drug cravings.

Cardiovascular Problems. Methamphetamine can increase heart rate and cause heart attack and arrhythmias that can result in sudden death.

Pulmonary Problems. There have been reports of acute lung congestion, chronic bronchitis, and emphysema from methamphetamine abuse.

Neurological Problems. In addition to acute and chronic psychosis, strokes and seizures have been known to occur.

Other Problems. There have been cases of kidney and liver failure reported in association with methamphetamine use. "Speed bumps," a unique skin condition associated with amphetamine abuse, may result from a higher acidity in the skin. Formication, an abnormal sensation of insects running over or into the skin, is associated with cocaine or amphetamine intoxication.

Opioids. Opioids include heroin and various prescription narcotic painkillers (e.g., methadone, oxycodone, fentanyl, and morphine). Unlike alcohol use and cocaine use, opioid use is not commonly associated with medical problems with one major exception: higher does of opioids can cause respiratory arrest (breathing stops) and death. Death from opioid overdose is not uncommon, particularly in newer users, who have not yet developed high tolerance, and chronic addicts after they have been detoxified or have been abstinent from opioids for a period of time (and lack tolerance). Problems with opioids are mainly associated with acute intoxication, withdrawal, and issues related to smoking or injection drug use. Needle tracks and pinpoint pupils can indicate opioid use.

Opioid Intoxication. At high doses, usually from accidental or intentional overdose, opioids can cause lethargy, respiratory depression, coma, and death. Naloxone, an antidote, may be used to reverse symptoms. Management of overdose includes supporting ventilation and airway, while replacing fluids.

Opioid Withdrawal. Opioid withdrawal is not life-threatening but is often very uncomfortable. Opioid withdrawal is relatively easy to treat with a tapering schedule of a long-acting opioid such as methadone or buprenorphine. However, the risk of relapse to opioid use after detoxification is high. Symptomatic treatment with nonnarcotic medications can be given as needed for vomiting, diarrhea, muscle and joint pains, anxiety, and insomnia. The antihypertensive medication clonidine is moderately effective at reducing many of these symptoms. General supportive measures should also be provided.

Medical Problems. Heroin has been associated in a few rare cases with hypotension (low blood pressure), seizures, and kidney diseases (e.g., glomerulonephritis, amyloidosis, and rhabdomyolysis-induced kidney failure, all sequelae of IV drug abuse) (see Table 14-3). Smoking heroin may cause leukoencephalopathy, a condition that resembles symptoms of infection of the brain. In low doses, opioids do not cause medical problems other than nausea, vomiting, constipation, and sedation. Most of the medical problems associated with opioid use (heroin specifically) are related to injection drug (see "Injection Drug Use").

Tobacco. Cigarette smoking remains the leading preventable cause of death in the United States. There are twice as many deaths from cigarette smoking as from HIV and acquired immune deficiency syndrome (AIDS), alcohol abuse, illicit drug use, motor vehicle accidents, and suicides combined. In addition, improperly extinguished cigarettes can cause fires, which can lead to smoke inhalation and death. Cigarette smoking can cause other unwanted side effects including stained teeth and fingers.

Nicotine Withdrawal. Withdrawal from nicotine may cause symptoms of restlessness and agitation, which are unpleasant but not life-threatening. Pharmacologic and behavioral therapies can help a smoker become abstinent. The antidepressant bupropion (Wellbutrin, Zyban) has been used successfully to reduce withdrawal symptoms and increase the likelihood that patients quit smoking. Nicotine replacement therapy (nicotine patch, inhaler, lozenges) also prevents withdrawal symptoms and has been used successfully for smoking cessation. The nicotine receptor partial agonist varenicline is a newly approved medication that has been shown to help cigarette smokers quit;

Table 14-3
Medical Problems Related to Opioid Use

Organ/System	Medical Problems
Brain	Seizures, spongiform leukoencephalopathy, coma
Other	Hypotension, bronchospasm, pulmonary edema, constipation, ileus, kidney disease (glomerulonephritis, amyloidosis, rhabdomyolysis-induced kidney disease)

Note: See Table 14-5 for consequences of injection drug use.

varenicline is a high-affinity partial agonist that binds to nicotine receptors tightly but only partially activates them, in theory alleviating nicotine withdrawal while, at the same time, blocking the effects of nicotine.

The long-term effects of tobacco use are discussed below and summarized in Table 14-4.

Neurological Problems. Cigarette smokers are at an increased risk for stroke. Tobacco use contributes to atherosclerosis (plaque build up in the arteries) leading to coronary vascular disease (heart attacks) and peripheral vascular disease, which can lead to the loss of limbs.

Cardiac Problems. Cigarette smokers are at a higher risk for heart disease, especially patients with other medical problems including diabetes and hypercholesterolemia.

Pulmonary Problems. Cigarette smoking is the leading cause of lung cancer and chronic obstructive pulmonary disease (COPD), which consists of chronic bronchitis and emphysema. Other lung conditions resulting from tobacco use include pulmonary hypertension, interstitial lung disease, and pneumothorax. Cigarette smokers have more frequent upper-respiratory infections and are at increased risk for bronchitis and pneumonia.

Malignancy. In addition to lung cancer, the following cancers have been associated with tobacco use: cancer of the oral cavity, larynx, esophagus, bladder, kidney, pancreas, stomach, and cervix.

Kidney Problems. Atherosclerosis in the renal arteries can cause hypertension from narrowing of arteries (renal artery stenosis) or kidney failure (from ischemia).

Hematologic Problems. Cigarette smoking is a risk factor for deep vein thrombosis (deep clots in veins of legs) by causing hypercoaguability (thickening of blood and tendency to clot, causing blockages).

Endocrine Problems. Nicotine can contribute to insulin resistance (risk for diabetes). Cigarette smoking is associated with osteoporosis and fractures.

Marijuana. In most states, marijuana is considered a Schedule I drug (high potential for abuse and no currently accepted medical uses). However, Marinol, an oral form and a synthetic tetrahydrocannabinol (THC), is approved for treatment of nausea and

Table 14-4
Medical Problems Related to Tobacco Use

Organ/System	Medical Problems
Brain	Stroke, peripheral vascular disease
Heart	Heart disease, heart attack
Lung	Reactive airways, chronic bronchitis, emphysema, lung cancer, frequent lung infections, pulmonary hypertension, interstitial lung disease, pneumothorax, cor pulmonale
Cancer	Oral cavity, larynx, esophagus, bladder, kidney, pancreas, stomach, cervix
Kidney	Kidney failure, hypertension from renal artery stenosis
Blood	Risk for deep vein thrombosis (clots in deep veins of legs)
Other	Osteoporosis, fractures, risk for diabetes, peptic ulcers, gastroesophageal reflux disease

vomiting in patients undergoing chemotherapy and for treatment of weight loss in patients with AIDS (stimulates appetite).

Marijuana Intoxication. The physical and psychological effects of marijuana vary depending on the amount smoked, the setting, and the psychological make up of the smoker. A first-time user may initially become anxious but later feel settled among supportive friends. Patients who use marijuana frequently report a feeling of calmness, mild euphoria, a sensation that time passes more slowly, increased acuity of the senses, elation, hilarity, and rapidity and clarity of thoughts. At high doses, a person may experience hallucinogenic effects and sedation. Attention and coordination may become impaired, and slowed reaction time can put a person at increased risk for injury. A few cases of psychosis related to cannabis use have been reported. The ingestion of high doses of cannabis can result in confusion, restlessness, a clouding of consciousness, disorientation, fear, illusions, and hallucinations. Panic reactions or acute feelings of anxiety are frequent complaints, are often short-lived, and are best treated with reassurance from a clinician that the feelings are temporary. An elevation of heart rate and reddening of the eyes (conjunctiva) are common physiologic reactions. There have been no reports of marijuana overdose or death.

Marijuana Withdrawal. Chronic smokers of marijuana may experience a withdrawal syndrome after cessation that is characterized by symptoms of anxiety, insomnia, irritability, anorexia, and flu-like symptoms. These symptoms are usually mild and last a day or two, although the syndrome can be more severe with marked irritability.

Cardiac Problems. An elevated heart rate with subsequent orthostatic hypotension (a drop in blood pressure when standing) has been reported in marijuana users but is rare. A rapid heart rate can exacerbate heart conditions and worsen high blood pressure.

Pulmonary Problems. The most common adverse consequence of marijuana use is lung injury caused by contaminants and carcinogens (similar to damage caused by tobacco smoke). There is greater risk of lung cancer and lung damage with concomitant tobacco use. Marijuana smoking may lead to poor pulmonary function, and much of the damage is irreversible even with abstinence.

Immunologic Problems. Studies in mice have shown that THC administration is associated with impaired resistance to infections (Buckley et al., 2000). Results of studies on the immunologic effects of marijunan in humans have been equivocal (Polen, Sidney, Tekawa, Sadler, & Friedman, 1993).

Reproductive Problems. Marijuana use has been associated with alterations in hormone levels, including growth hormone, luteinizing hormone, and prolactin. The female reproductive system may be adversely affected by marijuana, and some female patients may experience galactorrhea (unnatural breast milk discharge). Low birth weight has been reported in infants of women who smoke marijuana while pregnant. Experiments in male animals have shown that high doses of THC can lead to decreased testosterone and sperm production, but similar findings have not been found in humans (Mendelson & Mello, 1984).

Sedative-Hypnotics. Use of benzodiazepines and other sedative medications, which are prescribed for anxiety and insomnia may lead to abuse and dependence in some individuals. Some newer sleep medications, such as Ambien (zolpidem) and Sonata (zaleplon), are believed to have less abuse potential; however, physicians should use caution when prescribing these medications since abuse or dependence is possible. This chapter does not discuss barbiturates, which are not commonly prescribed.

Benzodiazepines. Benzodiazepines are prescribed for treatment of anxiety, insomnia, seizure disorders, and alcohol withdrawal. Benzodiazepines (e.g., clonazepam) are frequently prescribed to prevent withdrawal symptoms in patients who are dependent on heroin, alcohol, and other drugs, and to alleviate anxiety and agitation from cocaine or methamphetamine abuse. Benzodiazepines may be abused to enhance effects of other drugs including methadone, cocaine, methamphetamine, and alcohol. Benzodiazepine abuse is particularly common in methadone-maintained patients. There have been a few deaths linked to IV benzodiazepine use in combination with IV buprenorphine (Reynaud, Petit, Potard, & Courty, 1998).

Benzodiazepine Intoxication. Benzodiazepines are rarely used alone to induce intoxication. The effects of high doses of benzodiazepines are similar to the effects of alcohol intoxication: feelings of "drunkenness," disinhibition, amnesia, and sedation. Overdose of benzodiazepines can result in death. The abuse of alprazolam (Xanax) has been associated with hostility, rebound insomnia, depression, amnesia, and violent behavior. The benzodiazepine antagonist flumazenil can reverse the effects of benzodiazepine overdose. The combination of benzodiazepines and alcohol or drugs can lead to respiratory depression, coma, and death.

Benzodiazepine Withdrawal. Withdrawal from benzodiazepines, like withdrawal from alcohol, can result in medical complications and in death. The severity and duration of withdrawal depends on the dose and half-life of the drug. Patients may experience anxiety, nausea, vomiting, tremors, insomnia, nightmares, postural hypotension, delirium, seizures, and elevated body temperature. Chronic benzodiadepine use or abuse requires a gradual tapering to prevent withdrawal symptoms.

Neurologic Problems. Anterograde amnesia (inability to recall new information) and an increased incidence of falls have been associated with high doses of benzodiazepines.

Pulmonary Problems. Benzodiazepine use can increase the risk for lung aspiration and respiratory depression in neurologically impaired patients.

Zolpidem (Ambien). Zolpidem (Ambien) is similar pharmacologically to benzodiazepines: its sedative effects are reversed by flumazenil. It is commonly prescribed for insomnia. Although the abuse potential of zolpidem may be less than the abuse potential of regular benzodiazepines, physicians should avoid prescribing zolpidem to patients with substance abuse problems.

Zaleplon (Sonata). Prescribed for insomnia, zaleplon (Sonata) is chemically different from benzodiazepines but binds to a benzodiazepine receptor. Use of this drug is associated with less cognitive impairment. Although the abuse potential of zaleplon may be less than the abuse potential of regular benzodiazepines, physicians should avoid prescribing zaleplon to patients with substance abuse problems.

Desyrel (Trazodone). Trazodone is frequently prescribed at low doses (e.g., 50 to 100 mg) for insomnia in patients with drug or alcohol dependence; it is an antidepressant medication that is sedating but does not have potential for abuse. The most common side effect is daytime sedation. A rare but serious side effect is priapism, a painful, persistent erection of the penis that requires medical attention.

Tricyclic Antidepressants. TCAs are among the first classes of medications developed for the treatment of depression. Several medications in this class of drugs, mainly amitriptyline (Elavil), doxepin (Sinequan), and imipramine (Tofranil), are sedating and are sometimes prescribed at low doses for insomnia. Low doses of TCAs can be helpful in treatment of chronic pain. A few cases of abuse have been reported (presumably patients abused these drugs for their sedating effects). Overdose of TCAs can cause prolongation of cardiac conduction, resulting in cardiac arrest and death.

Other Sedating Medications. Other types of medications have sedating properties, including diphenhydramine (Benadryl), which is present in many over-the-counter cold and allergy medications, dextromethorphan, which is present in over-the-counter cough medicines, and neuroleptics, which are used to treat psychosis and bipolar illness (e.g., Zyprexa, Seroquel). Although these medications are rarely abused, clinicians should take a complete history of patients' medications and should monitor patients' use of sedating medication.

Ecstasy (Methylenedioxymethamphetamine). Ecstasy (methylenedioxymethamphetamine (MDMA)) has become increasingly popular, especially among young users who desire its psychoactive effects (SAMHSA, 2003). Users report "feelings of closeness," empathy, and greater insight. MDMA can increase heart rate and produce effects similar to the effects of amphetamines, including anxiety, restlessness, bruxism (teeth grinding), and decreased appetite.

Methylenedioxymethamphetamine Intoxication. MDMA overdose can result in death. Fatalities have been associated with cardiovascular and respiratory collapse, but most deaths have occurred in individuals with preexisting cardiac and lung disease. It is possible that concurrent use of alcohol and other drugs may have contributed to death following MDMA use. A few rare cases of severe stroke and liver damage linked to MDMA use have been reported. A dangerous elevation in body temperature leading to rhabdomyolysis (muscle damage), kidney and liver failure, seizures, and death has been reported in patients who have engaged in extended periods of exercise (e.g., dancing at rave parties following MDMA use) and who have become dehydrated. MDMA use has been associated with life-threatening and fatal complications from hyponatremia (a decrease in sodium levels in the blood) resulting from excessive fluid ingestion and involving inappropriate secretion of antidiuretic hormone. Impure Ecstasy may contain contaminants, including aspirin, cocaine, phencyclidine (PCP), and ketamine, which have toxic effects.

Neurological Problems. The long-term effects of MDMA use are not known. Evidence that links MDMA use to damage to serotonin neurons in laboratory animals suggests that depression or dementia might emerge after long-term use of MDMA (Ricaurte, Yuan, & McCann, 2000; Ricaurte, Yuan, Hatzidimitriou, Cord, & McCann, 2003). However, it is unclear how this depletion of serotonin manifests: animals function and behave normally. Human studies have been criticized for methodological problems.

Gamma Hydroxybutyrate. Gamma hydroxybutyrate (GHB), which has been used as an anesthetic and as a treatment for narcolepsy, produces effects similar to alcohol and induces euphoria and disinhibition. Its street name, "liquid ecstasy," is misleading since its chemical structure is completely different from Ecstasy.

Gamma Hydroxybutyrate Intoxication. Adverse effects of GHB use include nausea, vomiting, dizziness, respiratory depression, and coma. GHB has a short half-life of approximately twenty minutes; users have been known to awaken suddenly after being in a comatose state.

Gamma Hydroxybutyrate Withdrawal. Withdrawal symptoms can range from mild anxiety and/or insomnia to agitation, delirium, and psychosis. Symptoms can occur within six hours of use and can last up to two weeks; effects peak within twenty-four hours of use. High doses of benzodiazepines have been used to treat GHB withdrawal symptoms.

Hallucinogens. Effects of hallucinogens such as lysergic acid diethylamide (LSD), mescaline, peyote, and psilocybin (mushrooms) vary in rate of onset, duration, and intensity. LSD is one of the most potent hallucinogens and can produce dramatic effects ranging from dizziness, tremor, paresthesias, and altered visual and auditory perceptions to depersonalization, and dream-like states. Hallucinogens can cause impairments in attention and concentration and induce emotional lability, panic attacks, and paranoia. LSD can elevate heart rate, blood pressure, and body temperature and cause pupillary dilation and tremor. Nausea and vomiting are common effects of peyote and mescaline.

Lysergic Acid Diethylamide Overdose. The dose at which LSD is lethal in humans has not been established, and deaths related to LSD use have been secondary to accidental deaths from distorted perceptions (e.g., jumping out of a window to "fly"). Anxiety should be monitored and can be treated with benzodiazepines such as lorazepam (Ativan). Long-term adverse effects from hallucinogens include psychoses, depression, flashbacks, and visual trails. It is unclear whether psychoses or depression develop in individuals with predispositions to these effects.

Lysergic Acid Diethylamide Withdrawal. There are no withdrawal symptoms from chronic hallucinogen use.

Disorders Related to Route of Drug Administration

Injection Drug Use. Injection drug use is associated with many important medical comorbidities (see Table 14-5). The introduction of contaminants and infectious agents can result from nonsterile injections, use of shared needles and other injection paraphernalia, and poor personal hygiene. Contaminants from a needle or skin flora can cause local infection. Skin and soft tissue lesions can lead to cellulitis (infection of the skin), skin abscesses, and several serious skin, soft tissue, and venous infections including septic thrombophlebitis (clotting and inflammation within veins), necrotizing fasciitis (a very painful and potentially life-threatening infection deep in the skin that spreads rapidly), gas gangrene, and lymphedema (retention of lymphatic fluid that causes swelling, most often in the arms and legs). In prisons and close living quarters, there have been outbreaks of community-acquired methicillin-resistant Staphylococcus aureus (MRSA), a persistent and difficult-to-treat skin infection (CDC, 2003a) that may initially resemble a rash and can be easily misdiagnosed as an insect bite. Most skin infections respond to antibiotic treatment, but some abscesses require surgical drainage.

Many active IV drug users have "track marks" on their arms and other parts of their body as a result of long-term IV drug use, which can lead to scarred veins that are usually purplish in color. The most common micro-organism responsible for skin and vascular infections is a bacterium called Staphylococcus aureus. Other bacterial agents include streptococci, Pseudomonas, and anaerobic cocci and bacilli. These micro-organisms can travel through the bloodstream and cause endocarditis (infection of a heart valve). A person with endocarditis may present with fever, fatigue, and a cardiac murmur. The tricuspid valve is one of the primary sites of infection in the heart. Septic pulmonary emboli (infected clots) may break off, travel through the bloodstream, and cause damage to the lungs and other organs. Blood cultures usually identify the micro-organism and aid antibiotic choice. Echocardiogram (ultrasound of the heart) usually reveals vegetations (clots) on the affected heart valve.

Other organs can be affected as well. Bacterial infections that result from injection drug use can lead to bacteremia (bacteria in the bloodstream), causing pneumonia (infection in the lung), osteomyelitis (infection of the bone causing localized bone pain), meningitis (infection of the brain lining causing headache and mental status change), septic arthritis (infection of a joint causing pain, swelling, and redness), and spinal abscess.

Injection drug use has been associated with many viral illnesses, including hepatitis (A, B, C, and delta) and HIV. Hygienic injection techniques, such as the use of alcohol and clean needles, can prevent infection.

An injection drug user may unknowingly inject insoluble products such as talc, which may cause complications including chronic granulomatous inflammation of the lung (inflammation of the lung characterized by the formation of nodules) and angiothrombosis (blood vessel damage). "Skin-popping," a subcutaneous or intramuscular drug injection technique, is a risk factor for skin and soft tissue infections (abscesses). This technique is often used by chronic drug users who are unable to (or are reluctant to) inject the drug intravenously or are frantic for a dose of drug.

Table 14-5
Medical Problems Related to Injection Drug Use

Organ/System	Medical Problems
Skin	Cellulitis, abscess, necrotizing fasciitis, MRSA skin infection
Heart	Endocarditis, heart attack (cocaine)
Lung	Infection, bronchospasm
Liver	Hepatitis B, hepatitis C
Kidney	Focal glomerular sclerosis, amyloidosis, chronic renal failure, nephrotic syndrome
Other	HIV, septic thrombophlebitis, osteomyelitis, meningitis, septic arthritis, spinal abscess

Inhaled Drug Use. Drugs may be inhaled by "snorting," smoking, and "shebanging" (mixing cocaine and water or heroin and an acidic liquid, and squirting the mixture up the nose). Snorting, a popular route of drug administration for several drugs, including, but not limited to, cocaine, heroin, and methamphetamine, can cause epistaxis (nosebleeds) and nasal symptoms that mimic allergic or vasomotor rhinitis. Repeated "snorting" may result in the erosion of the nasal septum and cause perforation, especially in cocaine users.

There are numerous medical complications that result from smoking drugs (Table 14-6). Smoking "crack" can cause chest pain (and heart attack), shortness of breath, cough, sputum production, and hemoptysis (coughing up blood). Other serious lung conditions can result from the inhalation of cocaine, including atelectasis (collapse of lung tissue), alveolar hemorrhage (bleeding in the alveoli, tiny air sacs in the lung), pneumothorax (collapsed lung), pneumomediastinum (condition in which air is present in the mediastinum, space between the two lungs), bronchiolitis obliterans (rare form of obstructive lung disease), pulmonary infarction (death of lung tissue caused by obstruction of the arterial blood supply), pulmonary talc granulomatosis (pulmonary disease due to talc), and pulmonary edema (rapid fluid build up in the lungs causing shortness of breath that is life-threatening). The use of matches and lighters can cause burns.

Drug users may inhale heroin using a technique called "chasing the dragon," in which drug users inhale vapor from heroin that is heated on tin foil with a lighter. A rare medical condition called spongiform leukoencephalopathy (mimicking an infection of the brain) has been associated with use of this technique and has a mortality rate of 25 percent. Symptoms of this condition include cognitive impairment, ataxia, and motor restlessness.

The inhalation of heroin and marijuana has been linked to asthma (Tashkin, 2001; Taylor, Poulton, Moffitt, Ramankutty, & Sears, 2000). In addition, marijuana contains many carcinogens that are found in tobacco and that can lead to lung cancer. Many drug users are heavy smokers and are at increased risk for lung cancer. Contaminants of marijuana may lead to a fungal infection of the lung called pulmonary aspergillosis.

Table 14-6
Medical Problems Related to Inhaled Drug Use

Organ/System	Medical Problems
Brain	Spongiform leukoencephalopathy (heroin)
Nose	Nosebleeds, stuffy nose, nasal septum perforation
Heart	Heart attack (cocaine)
Lung	Asthma, reactive airways, airway burns, bronchospasm, pulmonary hypertension, infection, atelectasis, hemoptysis, alveolar hemorrhage, pneumothorax, pulmonary edema, lung cancer

COMMON MEDICAL CONDITIONS IN THE DUAL DIAGNOSIS POPULATION

Alcohol and drug use can cause or exacerbate medical problems in the dual diagnosis population, and polysubstance abuse is prevalent in this population. Medical conditions, some of which are unique to patients with psychiatric disorders, are organized alphabetically in this section. HIV, hepatitis, and TB are discussed in a subsequent section (see "Special Issues"). Table 14-7 lists symptoms of medical problems commonly seen in substance abusers. Some of these symptoms result from drug intoxication or withdrawal.

Acute Bronchitis

Bronchitis, an inflammation of the airways of the lung, can be caused by the irritating effects of cigarette smoke and is characterized by persistent cough, sometimes with production of sputum. Bronchitis is common in patient populations with a high prevalence of smoking including substance-dependent patients and patients with psychiatric disorders. Smoking damages cellular mechanisms for clearing particles and infections from airways, thereby predisposing patients to various respiratory infections. Poor living conditions and overcrowding can increase exposure to respiratory infections.

Asthma

Asthma refers to spasm of the small airways of the lung and is characterized by wheezing and shortness of breath. An acute asthma attack that leads to respiratory arrest can be life-threatening. Smoking worsens asthma, and second-hand smoke can exacerbate asthma, especially in children.

Back Pain

Trauma, accidents, and violence, frequently associated with drug abuse, can lead to injuries that result in chronic back pain. IV drug users are at particularly high risk for the development of rare spinal abscess located along the spinal cord. Symptoms

Table 14-7
Symptoms of Medical Problems Commonly Seen in
Substance-Dependent Patients

Symptom	Possible Medical Problems
Weight gain	Psychiatric medications, diabetes, thyroid problem
Weight loss	Poor nutrition, chronic illness, diabetes, thyroid problem, cancer, depression
Weakness on one side of body[a]	Stroke, migraine
Fever	Infection (e.g., sinus, lung, bladder, brain), inflammation (inflammatory bowel disease)
Night sweats	Tuberculosis, hepatitis
Headache	Tension, migraine, brain aneurysm, high blood pressure
Cough	Irritants, infection (sinus, lung), chronic bronchitis, asthma, gastroesophageal reflux disease
Runny nose	Allergy, infection (sinus, nose)
Nausea, vomiting	Early pregnancy, infection (e.g., gastrointestinal, appendix, kidney), food poisoning, gastrointestinal obstruction (blockage)
Vomiting blood[a]	Ruptured vessels or tears in esophagus, stomach
Diarrhea	Infection (gastrointestinal), food poisoning, inflammation (inflammatory bowel disease), irritable bowel syndrome
Shortness of breath[a]	Asthma, chronic bronchitis, emphysema, heart failure, pneumothorax, pulmonary edema, pulmonary embolus, panic attack
Wheezing[a]	Infection (small airways, lung), asthma, chronic bronchitis, emphysema, congestive heart failure, aspiration, pulmonary embolus
Chest pain[a]	Heart attack, muscle pain (from coughing), gastroesophageal reflux disease (heartburn), aortic dissection/aneurysm, infection (pericarditis, pneumonia), pulmonary embolus
Palpitations[a]	Arrhythmias (irregular heart beat), thyroid problem, panic attacks
Abdominal pain[a]	Inflammation (inflammatory bowel disease), infection (gastritis, hepatitis, pancreatitis, appendicitis), peptic ulcer disease, gas, gallstones, bowel obstruction, ischemic bowel disease, pelvic inflammatory disease
Pelvic pain[a]	Ectopic pregnancy, sexually transmitted disease, endometriosis, pelvic inflammatory disease, ovarian cyst
Black stools, blood in stools[a]	Bleeding from intestines, hemorrhoids
Dark urine	Dehydration, liver disease
Seizures[a]	Epilepsy, mineral imbalance (sodium, glucose), intoxication or withdrawal from drugs, hypoxia, infection (brain), fever, trauma, brain tumor, toxins (lead, mercury)
Tingling in feet	Diabetes, HIV
Memory loss	Delirium, dementia, depression
Back pain	Injury, lumbar disk herniation (slipped disc), spinal abscess[a] (severe), arthritis

[a] These symptoms can be life-threatening and may warrant immediate medical attention.

include back pain, fever, chills, weakness, paresthesias, bladder or bowel incontinence, and acute paraplegia, and require prompt referral to the emergency room.

Cancer

Almost any organ system of the body is at risk for cancer from substances of abuse (e.g., alcohol use is associated with stomach and breast cancer; smoking is associated with cervical cancer and lung cancer). Female drug addicts often engage in risky sexual practices, which place them at greater risk for human papillomavirus (HPV), a risk factor for the development of cervical cancer in women. Annual gynecological examinations should be encouraged in all females.

Chronic Bronchitis and Emphysema

Cigarette smoking is a major cause of COPD, which is a chronic, irreversible breakdown of lung tissue and is the fourth leading cause of death (Kochanek et al., 2004). Symptoms of COPD, like chronic bronchitis and emphysema, include wheezing and difficulty breathing. Patients with chronic bronchitis have a chronic cough with sputum production.

Diabetes Mellitus

Many psychiatric medications, including antidepressants and antipsychotics, cause weight gain that can lead to, or exacerbate, adult-onset diabetes mellitus. Patients with diabetes mellitus commonly experience symptoms of increased thirst and urination. Since some patients may be asymptomatic, screening is important in patients who are overweight, have a family history of diabetes mellitus, or are African American, Hispanic, or Native American. Complaints of recurrent infections (e.g., yeast infections in women), visual problems, and unexplained peripheral neuropathy (tingling or decreased sensation in hands or feet) should prompt screening. Early detection and treatment of diabetes mellitus can prevent long-term complications that affect the eyes, nerves, kidneys, blood vessels, and feet and can reduce the risk for heart disease.

Heart Disease

Cardiomyopathy (enlarged heart with poor contraction) can result from excessive alcohol use. Drug abusers, especially crack addicts, suffer heart attacks at an early age (often in their 20s) (Roldan, Aliabadi, & Crawford, 2001). Patients with complaints of chest pain when using drugs or during exertion should see a doctor. Risk factors for heart disease include high blood pressure, high cholesterol, diabetes mellitus, male gender, and a family history of heart disease at an early age (i.e., 40s, 50s).

Hypertension

Poor diet, sedentary lifestyle with lack of exercise, or psychiatric medications can cause obesity, which increases the risk for developing hypertension. Drugs that can cause hypertension include alcohol, amphetamines, Ecstasy, and cocaine. Continued use of drugs and alcohol may make control of hypertension difficult. Clinicians should suspect substance abuse in patients with blood pressure that remains high following multiple failed antihypertensive medication therapies.

Nutritional Deficiencies

Drug users and alcoholics often have poor diets and nutritional deficiencies, which can result in anemia (e.g., anemia can result from deficiencies in vitamin B_{12} or folic acid in patients with alcoholism or from iron deficiency from chronic bleeding caused by injury to the digestive tract), poor healing of wounds, and neurological impairments (e.g., ataxia with vitamin E deficiency, dementia with vitamin B_{12} deficiency).

Obesity

Weight gain is associated with high calorie diet, sedentary lifestyle, and lack of exercise, as well as with many antidepressants (venlafaxine, mirtazapine, fluoxetine, paroxetine, sertraline, citalopram) and mood stabilizers (lithium, valproate, olanzapine). During substance abuse treatment, aftercare, or treatment of psychiatric disorders, patients often gain weight quickly and are at greater risk for glucose intolerance, diabetes mellitus, and hypertension. Clinicians should encourage patients to maintain a balanced diet.

Seizures

Cocaine overdose, amphetamine overdose, and withdrawal from alcohol and sedative-hypnotics (benzodiazepines) can cause seizures. New onset seizures in early adulthood or middle age should prompt drug and alcohol screening.

Serotonin Syndrome

Serotonin syndrome, caused by excessive stimulation of serotonin receptors from various mechanisms, has been seen with intoxication and overdoses with amphetamines, Ecstasy, cocaine, and SSRIs (usually with two or more of these drugs in combination). Classic symptoms include cognitive/behavioral changes, autonomic instability, and neuromuscular abnormalities. Individuals can present with confusion, agitation, delirium, low-grade fever, tachycardia, nausea, vomiting, diarrhea, hypertension, myoclonus, tremor, rigidity, and even coma. Laboratory findings may include elevated CPK, liver enzymes, WBC count, and serum bicarbonate. More serious symptoms include rhabdomyolysis (breakdown of muscle fibers resulting in release of muscle fiber contents into the bloodstream), kidney failure, disseminated intravascular coagulation, and death. Treatment requires cessation of all serotinergic drugs, supportive care, IV hydration, and symptomatic relief.

Sexually Transmitted Diseases

Risky sexual behavior places drug addicts at high risk for STDs. Individuals with these diseases, especially chlamydia, may be asymptomatic. Treatment of the patient's partner is necessary to prevent reinfection and spread of disease.

Skin Infections

Abscesses and cellulitis are common in intravenous drug users. The lifestyle of some drug addicts can predispose them to develop scabies and lice infestations. Fungal infections and athlete's foot are common complaints among drug users. MRSA is a common infection in prisons and drug treatment settings.

Sleep Disorders

Chronic use of sedative-hypnotics often confounds normal sleep-wake cycles. Drugs, alcohol, and caffeine can disturb sleep patterns. Alcohol can cause initial sleepiness after ingestion but can disturb sleep several hours later (a phenomenon known as rebound insomnia). Alcohol can also exacerbate breathing-related sleep disorders (e.g., sleep apnea; Herzog & Riemann, 2004). Amphetamines and cocaine can cause insomnia during drug use and hypersomnia during drug withdrawal. Opioids can cause initial sleepiness after use but patients who develop tolerance to opioids can experience insomnia.

Stroke

Crack use has been associated with stroke at a younger age compared to nondrug users (Petitti, Sidney, Quesenberry, & Bernstein, 1998).

REASONABLE ROUTINE MEDICAL EXAMINATION FOR DRUG USERS

When patients present for treatment at drug treatment centers, clinicians should carefully assess patients' health and immediately address health problems that require urgent attention by either providing appropriate treatment or referring patients for care (e.g., to a psychiatric hospital for suicidal ideation or to a hospital for serious withdrawal symptoms from alcohol). A carefully collected medical history and physical examination can reveal the extent of damage that drug use has caused. The examination provides an opportunity for a clinician to identify acute and chronic health problems and needs for vaccination, dental care, and eye care.

A routine medical examination of a patient with a substance use disorder should comply with recommendations outlined by the U.S. Preventive Services Task Force (USPSTF; 1996). Clinicians must differentiate symptoms of drug use from symptoms of comorbid medical and psychiatric conditions; drug abuse may exacerbate preexisting conditions. Assessment of risk for withdrawal is imperative. A complete medical history, a physical examination, and a complete psychiatric history (including drug use history) are necessary for accurate assessment of a drug addict's health and for the selection of appropriate treatment and referrals.

Medical History and Physical Examination

All medical examinations should include a thorough history of drug and alcohol use and consequences of use (e.g., DUI, seizures from alcohol withdrawal). An understanding of a patient's drug practices (e.g., injection drug techniques) is helpful in determining risk and severity of drug use. It is important to ask about living conditions (e.g., homelessness), sexual practices and condom use, diet, physical activity, and dental care. Given the high prevalence of comorbid psychiatric disorders in patients with substance use problems, clinicians should screen patients for depression and anxiety. Clinicians should ask patients about medications, allergies, hospitalizations, surgeries, immunization history, travel, receipt of any blood products, and family history of disease. Clinicians should perform a thorough physical examination with a special focus on any system about which the patient complains. Height, weight, heart rate, respiratory rate, temperature, and blood pressure should be measured. The overall appearance of a patient can offer clues about diet and personal hygiene. Patients may exhibit symptoms of intoxication, have slurred speech, have an unsteady gait, have an odor of alcohol on their breath, wear clothing that smells of cigarettes or marijuana. An examination of patients' skin may reveal rashes, bruises, needle marks, abscesses, jaundice, cirrhosis, or palmar erythema (red palms, which can be seen in patients with alcoholism). Patients may have burns on their hands, between fingers, or around the mouth. Patients' eyes can reveal conjunctival irritation or injection (redness in the white part of eyes). Examination of the oral cavity can reveal gum disease, gingivitis, poor dentition with caries (progressive destruction of bone or teeth) or abscesses, or suspicious lesions that may require medical attention. Clinicians should examine patients' noses for septal perforations and inflamed nasal mucosa. Since lymphadenopathy (enlargement of lymph nodes) can be indicative of TB, HIV, syphilis, and a number of other conditions, clinicians should examine lymph nodes throughout the body. A heart examination may reveal tachycardia, arrhythmias (abnormal heart rhythms), or murmurs. An examination of the lungs can indicate wheezing, rales, and rhonchi (abnormal sounds). Tenderness or enlargement of the liver, which can be detected during an examination of the abdomen, may warrant further evaluation. Women should be asked about pelvic discomfort, menses, and unusual vaginal discharge, and men should be asked about testicular atrophy (shrinking of testes), penile discharge, and gynecomastia (breast enlargement). Calves should be examined for edema (swelling, tenderness). Neurological assessment can reveal sensory, motor, cognitive, and memory impairments, as well as neuropathy, tremor, and ataxia.

Questions that may be used to collect a medical history and that provide a guideline for routine care are presented in Table 14-8. Components of the physical examination and common abnormal findings are presented in Table 14-9.

Basic Laboratory Workup

1. CBC, glucose, creatinine, liver function tests (LFTs).

2. Total cholesterol and triglycerides (TGs).

3. RPR (rapid plasma reagin), TSH.

4. Urine dipstick test.

5. Hepatitis A, B, C antibodies, hepatitis B antigen.

6. Tuberculin skin test (purified protein derivative (PPD) test).

7. HIV, STD tests.

Table 14-8
Sample Questions to Aid Collection of a Medical History

Questions to Ask
Do you have any chronic medical conditions (e.g., diabetes, hypertension, asthma)?
Are you taking any medications on a regular basis?
Are you taking any vitamins, supplements, or alternative medicines (e.g., St. John's Wort)?
Do you have any medication allergies?
Have you had any hospitalizations or surgeries?
Have you ever been diagnosed with any psychiatric conditions? Do you suffer from depression or anxiety? Have you had any psychiatric hospitalizations or suicide attempts?
Are your immunizations up to date (e.g., tetanus shot every 10 years)?
Have you been tested for hepatitis and HIV? When?
Have you had a test for tuberculosis (PPD)?
Ask about diet, physical activity, living situation, occupation, criminal record, sexual practices, contraception/condom use, travel, receipt of any blood products, contact with someone with active tuberculosis, dental care, and vision.
Ask women about menstrual problems, unusual vaginal discharge, and history of abnormal pap smears.
Ask men about any rashes or lumps in the groin area and testes, and abnormal discharge from the penis.
Do you have a family history of any medical problems?
Obtain a detailed history of substance use and consequences of use (e.g., seizures from alcohol withdrawal). Ask about age of first use of each drug, route of administration (smoked vs. IV routes), maximum amount taken, periods of abstinence, history of drug treatment, and therapy. What treatments have you had success with in the past (e.g., Alcoholics' Anonymous)? Ask about smoking habits and prior attempts to quit.

Complete Blood Count. A CBC can detect anemia (low red blood cell count), which has many causes. Anemias often resolve spontaneously, so a CBC should be monitored regularly. However, if anemia persists, the cause should be investigated. Anemia may indicate iron deficiency, chronic bleeding, or a hemoglobinopathy (alpha or beta thalassemia, sickle cell disease). An elevated mean corpuscular volume (MCV) or size of red blood cells (RBCs)) can result from B_{12} or folate deficiency from alcoholism. In some cases, a low WBC count may warrant HIV testing. Persistent thrombocytopenia (low platelet count) may be early signs of HIV or hepatitis infection.

Liver Function Tests. LFTs, especially alanine aminotransferase (ALT), may be elevated from chronic alcohol use and will usually decrease with abstinence. A ratio of greater than 2/1 for AST/ALT (aspartate aminotransferase/alanine aminotransferase) is highly suggestive of alcoholic liver disease. Gamma-glutamyl transferase (GGT), another enzyme produced by the liver, is the most sensitive laboratory test for alcoholism. Elevations in GGT also are seen in patients taking phenobarbital and in patients

Table 14-9
Components of Physical Examination, Common Abnormal Findings,
and Their Indications

Components of Physical Examination	Common Abnormal Findings and Their Indications
– Height, weight, body mass index (BMI) – General appearance	Disheveled appearance: indicative of poor self-care Overweight: indicative of sedentary lifestyle, excess calories in diet Cachexia (severe underweight): indicative of malnutrition or chronic disease (e.g., AIDS)
– Vital signs (heart rate, blood pressure, respiratory rate, temperature)	Increased pulse (> 100 beats/min) or blood pressure (>140/90): indicative of intoxication or withdrawal Chronic high blood pressure common
– Gait	Abnormalities in gait: indicative of neurological problems (e.g., prior stroke) or a history of trauma with damage to back, hips, or legs
– Skin	Track marks, rashes, jaundice (yellowing of skin from liver disease)
– Head & face – Ears – Eyes – Nose	Weakness or drooping on one side of the face: indicative of prior stroke Pupillary constriction or dilation: indicative of drug intoxication or withdrawal Nasal septum perforations from chronic inhalation of drugs (i.e., cocaine)
– Vision – Hearing	Impairments in vision or hearing (corrections (e.g., proper eyeglasses) may improve functioning)
– Mouth, throat, teeth	Lesions: indicative of infection Lack of dental care and poor oral hygiene common
– Neck – Lymph nodes	Enlarged lump in the neck: indicative of goiter (thyroid problem) Lymph nodes in the neck, axilla (armpits), supraclavicular (above collarbone): provide clues to diagnosis of infection, TB, HIV, lung cancer
– Breast exam	Breast cancer in women (screen for breast cancer and encourage women to learn breast self-exam) Enlarged breasts in men: indicative of liver disease
– Chest – Heart	Wheezing in the lungs or other abnormal breath sounds (rales, rhonchi): indicative of infection, asthma, heart failure Heart murmurs: indicative of bacterial endocarditis, valve problems
– Abdomen	Tender and enlarged liver or small and hard liver: indicative of liver disease
– Genital exam	Lesions or discharge: indicative of sexually transmitted disease
– Extremities (i.e., arms, legs, hands, feet)	Arthritis, history of trauma, peripheral vascular disease
– Neurological, mental status exam	History of stroke Peripheral neuropathy (numbness or muscle weakness related to nerve damage); may be metabolic (e.g., diabetes) or traumatic Deficits in orientation, concentration, memory: indicative of intoxication, delirium, or dementia (see Chapter 6 of this volume)

with liver disease. Carbohydrate-deficient transferrin (CDT) can be used to screen for alcohol abuse. Hepatitis can cause elevations in LFTs. LFTs that remain high despite abstinence and a negative hepatitis panel might indicate steatosis (fatty liver).

Glucose. Glucose monitoring can detect glucose intolerance or diabetes mellitus (increased blood glucose).

Creatinine. Increased creatinine indicates poor kidney function.

Triglycerides. Uric acid and TGs may be elevated in patients with alcoholism.

Cholesterol. Total cholesterol should be below 200, and an elevation of TGs is a risk factor for pancreatitis.

Rapid Plasma Reagin. A RPR will test for syphilis (beware of false positives). A positive RPR should be followed by FTA-ABS (fluorescent treponemal antibody-absorption) testing.

Urinalysis. The presence of many WBCs in urine may indicate an STD, a urinary tract infection, or chronic prostatitis in older men.

Thyroid Stimulating Hormone. Since thyroid disorders can cause mood disturbances, patients with anxiety or depression should have their TSH measured. Elevated TSH is indicative of low thyroid function.

Tuberculosis. TB is prevalent among drug users, and PPD skin tests are easy to administer.

Hepatitis, Human Immunodeficiency Virus, and Sexually Transmitted Diseases. Clinicians should consider offering testing for hepatitis, HIV, and STDs. Pretest and posttest counseling should be available in clinics that offer HIV testing.

Additional Medical Assessments

Clinicians should ask about gynecological care, most recent pap smear, mammography, sigmoidoscopy, or colonoscopy. Clinicians should keep in patients' charts an EKG against which future EKGs may be compared (TCAs may cause changes in the EKG). Clinicians should ask about dental care, vision, and orthopedic problems. Dental problems that often result from poor personal hygiene, including missing teeth, retained root tips, caries, periodontal disease, and oral abscesses, are common and frequently ignored. Patients with substance use disorders often have poor vision and lose their glasses. Orthopedic problems, including lower back pain, knee injuries, ligament damage, meniscal tears, joint swelling and pain, and foot problems, should be addressed. Trauma from falls and injuries from gunshot and stab wounds are common among patients with substance use disorders.

Clinicians should encourage patients to quit smoking. Tobacco use is the leading cause of preventable death; more patients die as a result of tobacco use than all other drugs combined. Finally, abberant behaviors and treatment noncompliance (detected with random urine drug screening and pill counting) should be addressed.

SPECIAL ISSUES

Tuberculosis

TB is a bacterial infection (mycobacterium TB) that infects primarily the lungs but can invade almost any organ system during advanced disease. TB is transmitted through inhalation of infected droplets produced by the coughing of an infected individual. Poor living conditions, overcrowding, malnutrition, and impaired immune system functioning (common in patients with HIV) increase susceptibility to the disease. These factors, which are often seen in drug users, may account for the reemergence of the disease among crack cocaine users, IV drug users, patients who have been incarcerated, and persons with HIV. TB can be detected with a simple skin test, in which a small amount of antigen related to TB (PPD) is injected into the skin. If a patient has ever been infected with TB, the patient's immune system recognizes the antigens and causes a delayed-type hypersensitivity reaction, which occurs within twenty-four to forty-eight hours and manifests as induration or a raised red lesion around the point of injection. Most cases of TB are "latent" (i.e., the patient was infected, but the immune system successfully fought off the infection, which now lies dormant). The prevalence of latent TB (asymptomatic) may be as high as 15 to 25 percent among chronic drug users (Salomon, Perlman, Friedmann, Ziluck, & Des Jarlais, 2000; Howard, Klein, Schoenbaum, & Gourevitch, 2002). Malnutrition and alcohol-induced immune dysfunction may account for the association between alcoholism and reactivation of latent TB. Weakened immune systems in patients with HIV may cause them to have a reduced response to the PPD skin test. All substance abusers should be screened for TB annually.

Latent TB is diagnosed when a PPD test is positive but a patient is without active disease (i.e., has a normal chest x-ray and negative sputum cultures). Patients with latent TB should be offered prophylactic treatment: isoniazid (INH) for nine months or INH for six months, rifampin and pyrazinamide for two months. Since HIV increases risk for progression from latency to active disease, patients with a positive PPD test and HIV should be treated immediately. Since rifampin is a potent inducer of methadone metabolism and can precipitate narcotic withdrawal symptoms, clinicians should manage methadone maintenance carefully (e.g., splitting doses to twice daily doses and cautiously managing methadone increases).

Active TB is diagnosed by a positive PPD test and an abnormal chest x-ray, a positive sputum culture (grows the TB bacteria), or symptoms seen in other organs. While acute TB may have a variable presentation, patients with pulmonary TB frequently exhibit symptoms of chronic cough, fever, night sweats, and weight loss. Medication regimen and duration of treatment varies by level of drug resistance and differs across the country. Substance users frequently have poor treatment compliance. To ensure that patients take their TB medications regularly (to prevent TB organisms in their body from developing resistance to standard antibiotics), clinicians might insist that patients in methadone maintenance programs or residential drug treatment programs take their TB medications under the observation of the clinician.

Hepatitis

Viral hepatitis (hepatitis A, B, and C) is commonly seen in substance abusers, especially IV drug users. Symptoms of acute hepatitis can include fever, headache, nausea, vomiting, fatigue, and anorexia, and patients often notice dark urine, light-colored stools, and jaundice. Patients suffering from chronic hepatitis may be asymptomatic, have more nonspecific symptoms, or have symptoms of advanced liver disease.

Hepatitis A is commonly transmitted through oral contact with fecal matter (i.e., through ingesting contaminated water or food), and less commonly through blood and needle sharing. Low socioeconomic status and lifestyle factors may account for the increased prevalence of hepatitis A in drug users. The diagnosis of acute hepatitis A is made through a blood test that detects anti-hepatitis-A antibodies. Hepatitis A usually lasts from six to nine months. There is no chronic course (i.e., the immune system eventually eradicates the virus). IgM anti-hepatitis-A antibodies can be detected two weeks to six months after exposure. IgG anti-hepatitis-A antibodies, which can be detected five weeks after exposure (and can persist for decades), indicate lifelong protection against hepatitis A. If serology is negative, the patient should be offered hepatitis A vaccination.

Hepatitis B is primarily transmitted though sexual contact and injection drug use. There are more than 300,000 new hepatitis B infections in the United States every year, and 20 percent of those cases occur among drug users (Lemberg & Shaw-Stiffel, 2002; Seal & Edlin, 2000). Hepatitis B has a chronic course and can lead to cirrhosis (damage and scarring of the liver, leading eventually to liver failure) and hepatocellular carcinoma (liver cancer). Hepatitis B antibodies are present in 50 to 80 percent of injection drug users in the United States, and transmission usually occurs in the early years of patients' injection drug use (Thiede, Hagan, & Murrill, 2000; Garfein, Vlahov, Galai, Doherty, & Nelson, 1996). About 40 percent of individuals infected with hepatitis B develop symptoms of acute hepatitis. Infection can be diagnosed early with the detection of hepatitis B surface antigens (HbsAg), the presence of which is followed by an elevation in hepatitis B e antigen (HbeAg) and transaminases (liver enzmyes), followed by the appearance of antibodies to the hepatitis B core antigen (which indicates infection within the past few years). Antibodies to HbeAg correlate with decreased infectivitiy, and the appearance of anti-Hbs indicates immunity to hepatitis B. Five to 10 percent of patients with acute hepatitis B will develop chronic infection and will remain positive for HbsAg. These patients are at higher risk for cirrhosis (replacement of functioning liver tissue by scar tissue) and liver failure. Hepatitis D can only occur in individuals infected with hepatitis B. The risk factors for acquiring hepatitis D are the same for hepatitis B. Although hepatitis D is the least common form of chronic viral hepatitis, patients with hepatitis D are more likely to develop cirrhosis.

Drug users should be screened for hepatitis B. If serology is negative, vaccination against hepatitis B should be offered; vaccination, which consists of three intramuscular injections at zero, three, and six months, offers protection to more than 90 percent of healthy adults who complete the course of injections. Since drug users often have poor treatment compliance, clinicians should consider administering the vaccinations at drug treatment programs.

Hepatitis C is the most common chronic blood-borne infection and the most common cause of chronic liver disease in the United States. Most patients with acute hepatitis C are asymptomatic, but up to 80 percent of patients with hepatitis C will become chronically infected. Injection drug use is the primary route of hepatitis C transmission in the United States; sexual transmission of hepatitis C is less common. After one year of IV drug use, about 80 percent of drug users will contract hepatitis C (Garfein, Vlahov, Galai, Doherty, & Nelson, 1996). There is no vaccination for hepatitis C. Since the co-occurrence of hepatitis A or hepatitis B with hepatitis C is common and can accelerate progression to advanced liver disease, it is important to offer hepatitis A and hepatitis B vaccinations to all drug users, especially IV drug users. Vaccinations against pneumococcus, influenza, and tetanus should also be offered. A diagnosis of hepatitis C is confirmed with the presence of anti-hepatitis-C antibodies. Since alcoholism may accelerate the progression of liver disease in patients with hepatitis C, clinicians should encourage abstinence from alcohol. Cirrhosis develops in 10 to 20 percent of patients with chronic hepatitis C infection; hepatocellular carcinoma (liver cancer) develops in 1 to 5 percent of patients with chronic hepatitis (CDC, 2005).

Hepatitis B and hepatitis C can be treated with antiviral medications, but the treatments often are only partially effective and have side effects. Interferon, which has been shown to be effective in treating hepatitis C, may worsen psychiatric symptoms (e.g., depression). Clinicians should screen for depression before initiating treatment. Ribavirin, another medication used for treatment of hepatitis C, may cause anemia and neutropenia (low WBCs). The most common indication for live transplantation in the United States is end-stage liver disease related to hepatitis C.

Human Immunodeficiency Virus

HIV, the retrovirus that causes AIDS, can be transmitted through dirty needles and unprotected sex and from mother to child during pregnancy or breast feeding. Although effective medications are available for treatment of HIV, there is no cure, and resistance to HIV medications is a problem. Infectivity of HIV is higher two to three months following initial infection, and clinical symptoms may not develop until long after infection. Drug users may spread the disease to other people before diagnosis is made.

Research on HIV, especially studies of HIV and injection drug use, has prompted many public health initiatives. In the United States, IV drug use is associated with about one third of AIDS cases, and IV drug use accounts for more than half of heterosexual transmission. The drop in HIV seroprevalence rates among IV drug users from 2000 through 2003 (CDC, 2003b) may be attributed to increased awareness of HIV and safer injection techniques and increased availability of sterile equipment. The most effective prevention programs include needle exchanges, community/street outreach efforts, education, and widespread HIV counseling and testing. Treatment of substance abuse problems and availability of methadone and buprenorphine, which have reduced IV drug use, have contributed to the decreased prevalence of HIV.

A screening test for HIV antibodies, called enzyme-linked immunoabsorbent assay, is the first step in HIV testing. If the result of this test is positive, a western blot, a confirmatory test, is used.

The CDC has developed a clinical staging system for HIV infection and disease with three categories that each include a variety of specific medical conditions and that are defined by a specific CD4$^+$ T-lymphocyte count (CDC, 1992). AIDS is diagnosed when a patient has a CD4$^+$ T-lymphocyte count of less than 200/mm^3 or conditions indicative of AIDS.

The standard treatment for HIV is a regimen of drugs called Highly Active Antiretroviral Therapy (HAART). This combination therapy is composed of different anti-HIV drugs, usually one nucleoside analog, one protease inhibitor, and either a second nucleoside analog or a nonnucleoside reverse transcriptase inhibitor (NNRTI). Often these medications are started before a patient's CD4[+] T-lymphocyte count falls below 350 cells/ml and before the onset of any AIDS symptoms. Patients must take these medications exactly as prescribed, since missed doses can lead to drug resistance. Noncompliance may engender medication-resistant strains that can be difficult to treat with currently available drugs.

Immune dysfunction from HIV/AIDS increases susceptibility of patients to a spectrum of diseases. Pneumocystis carinii pneumonia is the most common AIDS-defining opportunistic infection in the United States (CDC, 1986). Drug users are particularly prone to bacterial infections, especially pneumonia, endocarditis, and bacterial sepsis. HIV-infected individuals who smoke illicit drugs may be at increased risk for the development of bacterial pneumonia. High rates of pneumonia among HIV-infected individuals have led to recommendations for preventive interventions. Current guidelines from the CDC recommend pneumococcal vaccination (against streptococcus pneumonia, one of the most common causative agents for bacterial pneumonia; USPHS/ISDA, 2000) for all HIV-positive individuals with CD4[+] T-lymphocyte counts of 200 cells/mm^3 or more. Trimethoprim-sulfamethoxazole, dapsone, or pentamidine should be given to prevent pneumocystis carinii pneumonia in patients with CD4[+] T-lymphocyte counts less than 200 cells/mm^3. Azithromycin, clarithromycin, or rifabutin should be given to prevent mycobacterium avium complex pneumonia in patients with CD4[+] T-lymphocyte counts less than 50 cells/mm^3. Patients with HIV/AIDS should receive yearly influenza vaccinations and vaccinations for hepatitis A and hepatitis B after confirmation of negative serologies.

Rates of TB in patients with HIV are rising, especially among injection drug users in the United States. HIV is considered the greatest risk factor for the progression of latent TB to active disease. The presence of mycobacterium TB (the bacterium causing TB) also accelerates the progression of HIV disease. Therefore, yearly PPD tests should be offered to patients with HIV. Following a positive PPD test, INH or alternative therapy should be given. Patients with HIV who are in close contact with persons with active TB should receive INH prophylaxis regardless of PPD test results.

Pain

Among drug users, there is a high prevalence of problems with pain resulting from a variety of medical conditions (see Chapter 16 of this volume). Common causes of pain include trauma (resulting in musculoskeletal pain), infection, liver disease, HIV-related conditions, and peripheral neuropathies. Chronic opioid therapy (e.g., methadone maintenance) may increase analgesic tolerance.

Fear of regulatory sanctions and fear of manipulation by potential "drug-seekers" cause physicians to undertreat pain in drug users. Clinicians should carefully monitor the effect of pain medication on functioning (improvements in pain or strength and ability to work). Lack of improvement in pain or functioning may indicate misuse of medications or inadequate treatment of pain, thereby indicating a need for further workup. Pain patients with "pseudoaddiction" exhibit drug-seeking behaviors that disappear once pain is adequately treated.

Pain management guidelines help physicians to choose appropriate treatments for pain. The Federation of State Medical Boards (FSMB) of the United States has developed treatment guidelines for good medical practices for treating pain with controlled substances (American Pain Society, 1999; Health and Public Policy Committee, American College of Physicians, 1983). The FSMB recommends that physicians who treat pain in patients with substance use disorders consult addiction medicine specialists, carefully monitor prescription drug use, and clearly define treatment goals.

Some recommendations for treating pain in drug users include use of long-acting opioids with limited supply of rescue does, use of pain medications that are less euphorigenic and have low street value, and use of transdermal patches. Medications should be provided on a scheduled regimen rather than as needed. Physicians should warn patients who require indwelling venous catheters, percutaneous infusion pumps, and patient-controlled analgesia that any signs of abuse will lead to discontinuation. Analgesic tolerance in opioid addicts may require physicians to prescribe them higher doses of opioids at more frequent intervals.

Clinicians can minimize abuse of pain medications by outpatients by writing prescriptions for small quantities of medications, requiring frequent clinic visits, asking patients to sign contracts that outline expectations, treatment goals, and consequences of misue of prescriptions, giving random urine tests, enforcing rules in substance abuse treatment, and encouraging the family members of patients to become involved in patients' treatment. Finally, a variety of nonopioid medications may be helpful in treating chronic pain and may reduce or eliminate the need for narcotic analgesics: analgesics such as acetaminophen (Tylenol), aspirin or nonsteroidal anti-inflammatory drugs (NSAIDS; e.g., ibuprofen (Motrin)), antidepressant medications (e.g., duloxetine (Cymbalta), tricyclics such as amitriptyline (Elavil)), and anticonvulsants (e.g., gabapentin (Neurontin)).

SUMMARY

The medical problems of dually diagnosed patients can be complex and influenced by multiple factors. Lifestyle choices, drug toxicities, and treatment noncompliance can exacerbate existing medical problems. Addicts' tendency to deny their drug problems and the fragmentation of health care and social services prevent drug addicts from obtaining medical care and psychiatric care. Dually diagnosed patients are an underserved population burdened by health problems. There is a lack of literature on medical conditions in patients with psychiatric disorders and substance use disorders, and further research is needed.

This chapter serves as a pragmatic guide to help clinicians in addiction treatment programs and mental health care settings to recognize common medical problems and facilitate communication between patients and health care providers about patients' medical problems. A thorough assessment of a patient's medical problems, substance abuse problems, and psychiatric problems will help clinicians to design appropriate treatment plans. Clinicians should refer patients with serious symptoms (e.g., poor balance, tremor, nystagmus) to appropriate medical services. Patients with active suicidal ideation should be assessed by a physician. Clinicians should ensure the safety of intoxicated patients. Clinicians should be familiar with services available within their communities in order to make appropriate referrals. To determine the level of care required for a patient with a substance use disorder, clinicians should refer to the American Society of Addiction Medicine Patient Placement Criteria (Mee-Lee, Shulman, Fishman, & Gastfriend, 2001).

Suggestions for Further Reading

For readers who wish to study further in this area, we recommend:

☐ **Books and Journal Articles**

- Cherubin, C. E., & Sapira, J. D. (1993). The medical complications of drug addiction and the medical assessment of the intravenous drug user: 25 years later. *Annals of Internal Medicine, 119,* 1017-1028.

- Ciraulo, D. A., Shader, R. I., Greenblatt, D. J., & Creelman, W. (Eds.) (1995). *Drug interactions in psychiatry* (2nd ed.). Baltimore: Williams & Wilkins.

- Enoch, M. A., & Goldman, D. (2002). Problem drinking and alcoholism: Diagnosis and treatment. *American Family Physician, 65,* 449.

- Finkelstein, R., & Ramos, S. E. (Eds.). (2002). *Manual for primary care providers: Effectively caring for active substance abusers.* New York: New York Academy of Medicine.

- Friedmann, P. D., Saitz, R., & Samet, J. H. (1998). Management of adults recovering from alcohol or other drug problems: Relapse prevention in primary care. *JAMA, 279,* 1227-1231.

- Galanter, M., & Kleber, H. D. (1999). *Textbook of substance abuse treatment.* (2nd ed.). Washington, DC: American Psychiatric Press.

- Graham, A. W., Schultz, T. K., Mayo-Smith, M. F., Ries, R. K., & Wilford, B. B. (2003). *Principles of addiction medicine* (3rd ed.). Chevy Chase, MD: American Society of Addiction Medicine.

- Kane, J. M., & Lieberman, J. A. (1992). *Adverse effects of psychotropic drugs.* New York: Guilford Press.

- Kranzler, H. R., & Rounsaville, B. J. (Eds.). (1998). *Dual diagnosis and treatment: Substance abuse and co-morbid medical and psychiatric disorders.* New York: Michael Dekker.

- Laine, C., Hauck, W. W., Gourevitch, M. N., Rothman, J., Cohen, A., & Turner, B. J. (2001). Regular outpatient medical and drug abuse care and subsequent hospitalization of persons who use illicit drugs. *JAMA, 285,* 2355-2362.

- Lowinson, J. H., Ruiz, P., Millman, R. B., & Langrod, J. G. (2005). *Substance abuse: A comprehensive textbook* (4th ed.). Baltimore: Williams & Wilkins.

- Mallin, R., & Tumblin, M. (February 2000). Addiction treatment in family medicine. *Home Study Self-Assessment Program. Monograph, Edition No. 249.* American Academy of Family Physicians.

- McLellan, T., Lewis, D. C., O'Brien, C. P., & Kleber, H. D. (2000). Drug dependence, a chronic medical illness: Implications for treatment, insurance, and outcome evaluation. *JAMA, 284,* 1689-1695.

- Seymour, R. B., & Smith, D. E. (1987). *Physician's guide to psychoactive drugs.* Binghamton, NY: Haworth Press.

- Shuckit, M. A. (1990). *Drug and alcohol abuse: A clinical guide to diagnosis and treatment* (3rd ed.).New York: Plenum Medical Books.

- Smith, D. E., & Seymour, R. B. (2001). *Clinician's guide to substance abuse.* New York: McGraw-Hill.

□ **Internet Resources for Clinicians and Patients**

- Centers for Disease Control and Prevention: http://www.cdc.gov.

- eMedicineHealth, Inc. (owned and operated by WebMD): http://www.e MedicineHealth.com.

- Family Practice Notebook, LLC: http://www.fpnotebook.com.

- Mayo Clinic: http://www.mayoclinic.com.

- MedicineNet, Inc.: http://www.medicinenet.com.

- National Institutes of Health (NIH) Health Information: http://health.nih.gov/.

- Office of Disease Prevention and Health Promotion of the U.S. Department of Health and Human Services: http://www.healthfinder.gov.

- WebMD, Inc: http://www.webmd.com.

References

American Pain Society. (1999). *Principles of analgesic use in the treatment of acute pain and cancer pain*. Skokie, IL: American Pain Society.

Berren, M. R., Santiago, J. M., Zent, M. R., & Carbone, C. P. (1999). Health care utilization by persons with severe and persistent mental illness. *Psychiatric Services, 50,* 559-561.

Buckley, N. E., McCoy, K. L., Mezey, E., Bonner, T., Zimmer, A., Felder, C. C., et al. (2000). Immunomodulation by cannabinoids is absent in mice deficient for the cannabinoid CB(2) receptor. *European Journal of Pharmacology, 396,* 141-149.

Cassidy, F., Ahearn, E., & Carroll, B. J. (1999). Elevated frequency of diabetes mellitus in hospitalized manic-depressive patients. *American Journal of Psychiatry, 156,* 1417-1420.

Centers for Disease Control and Prevention (CDC). (1986). Update: Acquired immunodeficiency syndrome-United States. *MMWR Morbidity Mortality Weekly Report, 35,* 17-21.

Centers for Disease Control and Prevention (CDC). (1992). 1993 revised classification system for HIV infection and expanded surveillance case definition for AIDS among adolescents and adults. *MMWR Morbidity Mortality Weekly Report, 41,* 1-19.

Centers for Disease Control and Prevention (CDC). (2003a). Outbreaks of community-associated methicillin-resistant staphylococcus aureus skin infections—Los Angeles County, CA, 2002-2003. *MMWR Morbidity Mortality Weekly Report, 52,* 88.

Centers for Disease Control and Prevention (CDC). (2003b). *HIV/AIDS surveillance report*. Atlanta, GA.: U.S. Department of Health and Human Services, Public Health Service, Centers for Disease Control and Prevention.

Centers for Disease Control and Prevention (CDC). (2005). *Hepatitis surveillance report No. 60*. Atlanta, GA: U.S. Department Of Health and Human Services, Public Health Service, Centers for Disease Control and Prevention.

Centers for Disease Control and Prevention (CDC). (2007). Smoking and Tobacco Use—Fact Sheet: Tobacco-Related Mortality. Retrieved September 3, 2008, from http://www.cdc.gov/ tobacco/data_statistics/fact_sheets/health_effects/tobacco_related_mortality.htm

Darke, S. & Zador, D. (1996). Fatal heroin "overdose": A review. *Addiction, 91,* 1765-1772.

Fellows, J. L., Trosclair, A., Adams, E. K., & Rivera, C. C. (2002). Annual smoking-attributable mortality. Years of potential life lost, and economic costs—United States, 1995. *MMWR Morbidity Mortality Weekly Report, 51,* 300-303.

Garfein, R. S., Vlahov, D., Galai, N., Doherty, M. C., & Nelson, K. E. (1996). Viral infections in short-term injection drug users: The prevalence of the hepatitis C, hepatitis B, human immunodeficiency, and human T-lymphotropic viruses. *American Journal of Public Health, 86,* 655-661.

Hayward, P., & Bright, J. (1997) Stigma and mental illness: A review and critique. *Journal of Mental Health, 6,* 345-354.

Health and Public Policy Committee, American College of Physicians. (1983). Drug therapy for severe chronic pain in terminal illness. *Annals of Internal Medicine, 99,* 870-873.

Herzog, M., & Riemann, R. (2004). Alcohol ingestion influences the nocturnal cardio-respiratory activity in snoring and non-snoring males. *European Archives of Oto-Rhino-Laryngology, 261,* 459-462.

Holmberg, S. K., & Kane, C. (1999). Health and self-care practices of persons with schizophrenia. *Psychiatric Services, 50,* 827-829.

Howard, A. A., Klein, R. S., Schoenbaum, E. E., & Gourevitch, M. N. (2002). Crack cocaine use and other risk factors for tuberculin positivity in drug users. *Clinical Infectious Diseases, 35,* 1183-1190.

Kaku, D. A., & Lowenstein, D. H. (1990). Emergence of recreational drug abuse as a major risk factor for stroke in young adults. *Annals of Internal Medicine, 113,* 821-827.

Karasu, T. B., Waltzman, S. A., Lindenmayer, J. P., & Buckley, P. J. (1980). The medical care of patients with psychiatric illnesses. *Hospital Community Psychiatry, 31,* 463-472.

Klonoff, D. C., Andrews, B. T., & Obana, W. G. (1989). Stroke associated with cocaine use. *Archives of Neurology, 46,* 989-993.

Kochanek, K. D., Murphy, S. L., Anderson, R. N., & Scott, C. (2004). *Deaths: Final data for 2002.* National Vital Statistics Reports; col. 53 no. 5. Hyattsville, MD: National Center for Health Statistics. Retrieved September 3, 2008, from http://www.cdc.gov/nchs/data/nvsr/nvsr53/nvsr53_05.pdf

Lemberg, B. D., & Shaw-Stiffel, T. A. (2002). Hepatic disease in injection drug users. *Infectious Disease Clinics of North America, 16,* 667-679.

Mee-Lee, D., Shulman, G., Fishman, M., & Gastfriend, D. (Eds.). (2001). *ASAM patient placement criteria for the treatment of substance-related disorders* (2nd ed. rev.). Chevy Chase, MD: American Society of Addiction Medicine.

Mendelson, J. H., & Mello, N. K. (1984). Effects of marijuana on neuroendocrine hormones in human males and females. *Effect of Marijuana on Pregnancy and Fetal Development in the Human, NIDA Research Monograph 44* (pp. 97-114). Rockville, MD: National Institute on Drug Abuse.

Peretta, P., Akiskal, H. S., Nisita, C., Lorenzetti, C., Zaccagnini, E., Della Santa, M., et al. (1998). The high prevalence of bipolar II and associated cyclothymic and hyperthymic temperaments in HIV patients. *Journal of Affective Disorders, 50,* 215-224.

Petitti, D. B., Sidney, S., Quesenberry, C., & Bernstein, A. (1998). Stroke and cocaine or amphetamine use. *Epidemiology, 9,* 596-600.

Polen, M. R., Sidney, S., Tekawa, I. S., Sadler, M., & Friedman, G. D. (1993). Health care use by frequent marijuana smokers who do not smoke tobacco. *Western Journal of Medicine, 158,* 596-601.

Qureshi, A. I., Suri, M. F., Guterman, L. R., & Hopkins, L. N. (2001). Cocaine use and the likelihood of nonfatal myocardial infarction and stroke: Data from the Third National Health and Nutrition Examination Survey. *Circulation, 103,* 502-506.

Reynaud, M., Petit, G., Potard, D., & Courty, P. (1998). Six deaths linked to concomitant use of buprenorphine and benzodiazepines. *Addiction, 93,* 1385-1392.

Ricaurte, G. A., Yuan, J., & McCann, U. D. (2000). (+/-)3,4-Methylenedioxymethamphetamine ("Ecstasy")-induced serotonin neurotoxicity: Studies in animals. *Neuropsychobiology, 42,* 5-10.

Ricaurte, G. A., Yuan, J., Hatzidimitriou, G., Cord, B. J., & McCann, U. D. (2002). Severe dopaminergic neurotoxicity in primates after a common recreational dose regimen of MDMA ("ecstasy"). *Science, 297,* 2260-2263. [Retraction in Ricaurte, G. A., Yuan, J., Hatzidimitriou, G., Cord, B. J., & McCann, U. D. (2003). *Science, 301,* 1479; PMID: 12970544].

Roldan, C. A., Aliabadi, D., & Crawford, M. H. (2001). Prevalence of heart disease in asymptomatic chronic cocaine users. *Cardiology, 95,* 25-30.

Salomon, N., Perlman, D. C., Friedmann, P., Ziluck, V., & Des Jarlais, D.C. (2000). Prevalence and risk factors for positive tuberculin skin tests among active drug users at a syringe exchange program. *International Journal of Tuberculosis and Lung Disease, 4,* 47-54.

Seal, K. H., & Edlin, B. R. (2000). Risk of hepatitis B infection among young injection drug users in San Francisco: Opportunities for intervention. *Western Journal of Medicine, 172,* 16-20.

Steiner, J. L., Hoff, R. A., Moffett, C., Reynolds, H., Mitchell, M., & Rosenheck, R. (1998). Preventative health care for mentally ill women. *Psychiatric Services, 49,* 696-698.

Substance Abuse and Mental Health Services Administration, Office of Applied Studies. (2002). *Mortality data from the Drug Abuse Warning Network* (DHHS Publication No. (SMA) 02–3633). Rockville, MD: U.S. Government Printing Office.

Substance Abuse and Mental Health Services Administration, Office of Applied Studies. (2003). *Emergency department trends from Drug Abuse Warning Network final estimates 1995-2002* (DHHS) Publication No. SMA 03-3780, DAWN Series D-24). Rockville, MD: U.S. Government Printing Office.

Tashkin, D. P. (2001). Airway effects of marijuana, cocaine, and other inhaled illicit agents. *Current Opinion in Pulmonary Medicine, 7,* 43-61.

Taylor, D. R., Poulton, R., Moffitt, T. E., Ramankutty, P., & Sears, M. R. (2000). The respiratory effects of cannabis dependence in young adults. *Addiction, 95,* 1669-1677.

Thiede, H., Hagan, H., & Murrill, C. S. (2000). Methadone treatment and HIV and hepatitis B and C risk reduction among injectors in the Seattle area. *Journal Urban Health, 77,* 331-345.

USPHS/ISDA Prevention of Opportunistic Infections Working Group. (2000). 1999 USPHS/IDSA guidelines for the prevention of opportunistic infections in persons infected with human immunodeficiency virus. *Clinical Infectious Diseases, 30,* S29-S65.

U.S. Preventive Services Task Force (USPSTF). (1996). *Guide to clinical preventive services,* (2nd ed). Alexandria, VA: International Medical Publishing.

Ziedonis, D. M., Kosten, T. R., Glazer, W. M., & Frances, R. J. (1994). Nicotine dependence and schizophrenia. *Hospital Community Psychiatry, 45,* 204-206.

Chapter 15

Substance Abuse During Adolescence

by Jeffrey J. Wilson, M.D.

INTRODUCTION

Adolescence is a tumultuous developmental stage during which most individuals will be exposed to nicotine, alcohol, or other drugs. Many individuals will use these drugs with some regularity, and some will develop substance use disorders. Early onset substance use disorder (i.e., during the teenage years) is associated with greater comorbidity with other psychiatric disorders and has a worse prognosis than adult onset substance use disorder. At the same time, many teenagers may use substances intermittently, even heavily, for a period of time, but then "age out" and never develop a chronic course of substance dependence.

This chapter on substance abuse during adolescence has two aims. The first aim is to discuss evaluation and treatment of substance use disorders in adolescent patients. The second aim is to examine how adolescence affects the assessment and treatment of co-occurring psychiatric disorders and substance use disorders.

Adolescence is the period when psychiatric disorders that commonly co-occur with substance use disorders (mood disorders, anxiety disorders, and schizophrenia) begin to occur. Adult diagnostic criteria are applied to adolescents for most psychiatric disorders (except attention deficit hyperactivity disorder (ADHD)), and most of the research on co-occurring psychiatric and substance use disorders has examined adult samples. This chapter will draw from the limited existing data from studies with adolescents, as well as clinical experience with adolescents, to examine how adolescence influences the symptoms, course of common disorders, and treatment of co-occurring psychiatric and substance use disorders.

This chapter should help readers to understand how diagnostic criteria and treatment recommendations described in other chapters can be applied to teenagers. The chapter should help readers to understand the roots of adult psychiatric and substance use disorders and should guide clinicians in advising their adult patients about how to monitor and intervene early if psychiatric and substance use problems begin to emerge in their children.

CASE PRESENTATION

SP's father arranged an appointment for his daughter, who urgently needed treatment because she was suicidal. SP came alone to her first appointment. She was a 16-year-old junior in high school who reported telling her parents she was suicidal three weeks before the appointment. Three weeks prior to her appointment, while her family was getting ready to go to church, she had an argument with her sister over a hair dryer. Frustrated, she went to her room and cut her wrist with a razor blade. She denied any plan or intent to kill herself. SP felt she was irritable because she was hung over from a party that they had had at her home the night before. She and her sister had invited several friends to their home; both SP and her sister had had only a few hours of sleep and had been drinking vodka and smoking "blunts." SP said that she and her sister often had parties and that her parents generally did not interrupt them unless they were too noisy. SP said she had been smoking marijuana several times daily over the past year, but she was not sure how much she spent on it because she often shared it with her friends. SP also consumed three or four alcoholic drinks two or three times a week, usually on the weekend. She said she has not felt suicidal since the fight with her sister.

SP felt that her real problem was her depression, which began after her grandmother died eight months before the appointment. She also blamed much of her depression on her mother, who was depressed and an alcoholic. She felt closer to her father, but he was often working and unavailable. She hated feeling sad and tried to appear happy. She was a B student, worked part time in a retail store, and was on the basketball team. Nonetheless, she often felt sad, enjoyed activities less and less, had trouble sleeping, and felt fatigued. After her grandmother died, she began to feel depressed and to use marijuana daily to "help [her] deal with the pain." She found herself increasingly unable to cope with life without marijuana, and she used it throughout the day. She began stealing clothing from the store where she worked and used the money her parents gave her for clothes to buy marijuana. She also began taking money out of the cash register in the retail store. She was afraid she would get in trouble but was also afraid to stop. She missed more and more days at school. Sometimes she stayed out all night to go to parties, but she told her parents she was sleeping at a friend's house.

DIAGNOSTIC CRITERIA

Alcohol and drug use by children and adolescents is clearly discouraged, but, nonetheless, most adolescents try alcohol, marijuana, or nicotine before graduating high school. Using these substances has become a normative part of adolescent development. When does use become a problem (i.e., abuse)? For a drug treatment provider, differentiation between substance use and substance abuse is an important aspect of a diagnostic assessment. However, since adolescents are minors, their use of legal drugs is illegal. For many parents and professionals, any substance use is unacceptable. There is a difference between use, which is less often associated with life-course-persistent problems with drugs or alcohol, and abuse, which is more often associated with these problems. Most youths use (or "experiment") with drugs; fewer youths develop substance-related problems, and even fewer develop chronic substance use disorders. While 80 percent of adolescents experiment with alcohol by the end of high school, fewer teens (about 7 percent) develop a substance use disorder.

NATURAL HISTORY AND ETIOLOGY

Substance Use

The Monitoring the Future Study has been following substance use in community samples of eighth, tenth, and twelfth graders in the United States since 1978 (Johnston, O'Malley, & Bachman, 1999). This study involves samples of over 100 schools across the country, and each cohort contains over 15,000 boys and girls. Critics suggest that since it is school based, it may actually underestimate substance use among older adolescents (the study does not include high school dropouts). Any lifetime substance use, use in the past thirty days, and daily use are reported. Rates are reported for legal and illegal substances. While rates vary across years, the relative patterns of use between substances differ little. Among eighth graders in 2002, one fifth had used alcohol in their lifetime, one fifth had used marijuana in their lifetime, and one third had used tobacco. By twelfth grade, four fifths of students had used alcohol in their lifetime, one half had used marijuana, and one half had used tobacco (Johnston, O'Malley, Bachman, & Schulenberg, 2004).

Gender and Ethnic Differences

There is little difference in frequency of substance use between boys and girls during adolescence. In the Substance Abuse and Mental Health Services Administration (SAMHSA; 2001) household survey, 9.8 percent of boys (12-17 years) versus 9.5 percent of girls had used an illicit substance in the past thirty days (all frequencies in the remainder of this paragraph are reported for the past thirty days). However, young men (18-25 years) have a higher degree of substance use than young women (19.0 percent versus 12.7 percent in 2000). Men over the age of 26 also tend to use more substances than women of similar age (5.4 percent versus 3.1 percent). There are some racial differences in substance use among adolescents. The substance use frequency rate is highest among Native Americans (20 percent) and lowest among Asian Americans (5.8 percent). Caucasian Americans have the next highest substance use frequency rate (10.1 percent report use in the past thirty days), followed by Hispanic Americans (9.5 percent) and Black Americans (8.4 percent). Ethnic differences change somewhat with increasing age, although most of the general patterns remain the same.

Substance Use Disorders

In a recent survey of 401 children and adolescents (14-17 years old), 6.2 percent had a substance use disorder (Kandel et al., 1999). While alcohol and marijuana are the most commonly abused substances among adolescents, it is relatively uncommon to find marijuana use disorders without the presence of other drug or alcohol use disorders. Urine drug screens easily identify marijuana use, but they may not be very sensitive to alcohol or some other drug use. The presence of marijuana in an adolescent's urine increases the chance that the adolescent may be experimenting with other substances of abuse that may be more difficult to identify with urine screens. In clinically referred patient populations (e.g., patients in child/adolescent mental health clinics, delinquent patient samples), the incidence of early onset substance use disorder is considerably higher.

Availability of Substances

Perhaps the most important correlate of adolescent substance use is availability of substances (Luthar, Cushing, & McMahon, 1997). Factors that influence availability of drugs include peer groups, parental monitoring, and familial drug use (particularly siblings but also parents and other family members). Individual risk factors for substance use include temperamental traits such as novelty seeking, disruptive behaviors, and positive expectations about alcohol or drug use. Substance use is a risk factor for the development of a substance use disorder. Given the high frequency of substance use in the adolescent and young adult population, substance use alone cannot be considered a specific marker of disorder.

Gateway Drugs

Experimentation by children and adolescents and abuse often begin with use of alcohol, tobacco, and marijuana. These substances have been called "gateway" substances. The gateway hypothesis states that the use of these substances contributes to increased risk for further experimentation and tendency toward dependence (Galanter & Kleber, 1999). For example, youths commonly first experiment with cigarettes, then alcohol, and then marijuana. Marijuana is commonly considered the gateway drug that encourages use of illicit drugs. Once a person has experimented with marijuana, he/she is at increased risk for use of other substances. However, these associations are often based on naturalistic studies that do not control for individual variables that may also contribute to further substance use. While exposure to marijuana is one explanation for increased risk for experimentation with other more dangerous substances, there are other explanations for this association. For example, youths who use marijuana may be more likely to experiment with other drugs because of positive expectations of use, because they have conduct disorder, or because they have other risk factors associated with substance use and dependence. Differences in prevalence and age of onset appear to account for this stage-like progression; this observation may be exaggerated because of groups of adolescents who are more or less likely to use any substances. Hence, it is possible that the so-called gateway phenomenon is an artifact of individual liabilities toward substance dependence (Miller, 1994.)

Family Factors and Development of Substance Use Disorders

There is little question that family factors (genetic, environmental, or both) contribute to the development of a substance use disorder. Children of parents with substance use problems are at risk for a variety of health problems, both medical and psychiatric. Many of these problems may be related to neglect caused by their parents' addictions. For example, in comparison to children with parents who do not abuse drugs or alcohol, children with parents who abuse drugs and alcohol are nearly three times more likely to be physically or sexually assaulted and over four times more likely to be neglected (National Center on Addiction and Substance Abuse at Columbia University (CASA), 1999). Children of parents with drug addictions have an eight-fold increase in risk of developing a substance use disorder (Merrikangas et al., 1998). Tsuang et al. (1996) reported concordance rates for drug abuse of 26.2 percent (monozygotic) versus 16.5 percent (dizygotic) in a large nonclinical sample of over 3,000 twin pairs. Genetic factors accounted for 34 percent of the variance in drug abuse, while shared environmental factors accounted for 28 percent of the variance; nonshared factors accounted for 38 percent of the variance. It should be noted that both genetic factors (e.g., child temperament may "select" for certain parenting styles) and environmental factors (e.g., certain parenting styles may be more or less compatible with certain child temperaments) may contribute to a child's unique, or nonshared, experience of common, or shared, environmental factors.

Psychological Factors

Lack of behavior control, emotional distress, and individual beliefs about alcohol use are associated with the transition from substance use to substance abuse (Colder and Chassin, 1999). In addition, a lack of psychosocial protective factors, such as prosocial activity, intolerance of deviance, and conventional peer models of behavior, lead to problematic use of alcohol. In studies of youths at high risk for alcoholism, preadolescent conduct disorder is a strong predictor of early adolescent marijuana abuse. Conduct disorder has been implicated in the relationship between ADHD and substance use disorders (Clark, Parker, & Lynch, 1999). Deficits in behavioral regulation may lead to ADHD and/or conduct disorder, which may in turn increase the risk for development of a substance use disorder (Wilson & Levin, 2005). Studies of adolescents have linked deficits in behavioral regulation (e.g., high novelty seeking) to the development of alcohol use. These traits appear in a group of alcohol abusers with an earlier onset of alcohol abuse (Galanter & Kleber, 1999). Thus, identifying these traits may be important for the prevention and treatment of adolescent substance use disorders.

Antisocial Behavior

The development of early onset substance use disorder is closely linked to antisocial behavior. Tarter et al. (1999) provide a developmental model to explain this relationship. They suggest that drug abuse and addiction are closely tied to environmental factors (e.g., parental substance use or levels of parental monitoring). More specifically, they suggest that interactions between genes and environment may produce biobehavioral phenotypes that are associated with increased risk for substance use disorders. Children with developmental delays in behavioral and emotional regulation are at high risk for developing substance use disorders. Although having a parent who is an alcoholic seems to increase risk for the development of alcohol use disorders, most of these children do not actually develop alcohol use disorders (Lieberman, 2000). The presence of disruptive behavior disorders, particularly conduct disorder, mediates the development of a substance use disorder, even in this high risk group (Clark et al., 1999).

SPECIAL ISSUES IN DIAGNOSIS OF SUBSTANCE ABUSE IN ADOLESCENTS

Early Onset Versus Late Onset of Substance Use Disorders

Many factors interfere with diagnosis of a substance use disorder in adolescents. It is rare for adolescents to spontaneously seek treatment. Usually, they are referred by parents, teachers, counselors, probation officers, or other adults, often because of behavior problems. They are usually referred after they have been caught using drugs or alcohol, and many times they resist receiving a psychiatric evaluation. Problem behaviors are present in the overwhelming majority of youths who are referred for adolescent substance abuse treatment (Hendren, 1999). Early onset substance use disorder differs from later onset substance use disorder in a few important ways. Early onset substance use disorder is associated with antisocial behavior, high novelty seeking, and low reward dependence. Later onset substance use disorder appears to be associated with less antisocial behavior (e.g., fewer arrests, disruptive behavior disorder diagnoses) and different temperamental characteristics (low novelty seeking and high reward dependence; Cloninger, Sigvardsson, & Bohman, 1988).

Diagnostic Orphans

Since adolescents' patterns of substance use frequently differ from adults' for a variety of reasons (e.g., availability, freedom, supervision), the validity of the diagnostic criteria for substance use disorders for young people has been questioned. Some clinicians are puzzled by "diagnostic orphans" (i.e., adolescents who meet one or two criteria for substance dependence but do not meet criteria for substance abuse). Almost one third of youths who use alcohol regularly but do not meet criteria for any substance use disorder may exhibit this "subclinical" pattern of problem use. This observation has implications for the definition of early onset substance use disorder. In some cases, the progression of substance use disorders proceeds from use through abuse to dependence (e.g., by definition, dependence is an exclusion criterion for abuse). However, evidence suggests that the progression also can begin with the appearance of one or two of the symptoms of dependence, short of the minimum of three or more required symptoms for a diagnosis of dependence according to the *Diagnostic and Statistical Manual of Mental Illness*, 4th edition, text revision (*DSM-IV-TR;* American Psychiatric Association, 2000). These "diagnostic orphans" appear similar to youths with substance abuse diagnoses but have symptoms of dependence before symptoms of abuse. Further, many of these "diagnostic orphans" appear to have a level of impairment that is similar to youths with substance abuse diagnoses. While conduting a psychiatric evaluation, clinicians should ask about symptoms of dependence and should not rely exclusively on substance abuse criteria to rule out impairment due to substance use (Pollock & Martin, 1999). Researchers continue to work to better define early onset substance use disorder.

Alcohol Use Disorders During Adolescence

After nicotine, alcohol is the most commonly abused substance in adolescents and adults. The natural course of alcohol use disorders from adolescence into young adulthood has been evaluated by Rohde, Lewinsohn, Kahler, Seeley, and Brown (2001). In this study, 944 subjects (ages 14-18) were recruited from a community sample in the western United States and were followed up at age 24. Adolescents were classified as having: (1) an alcohol use disorder (according to *DSM-IV-TR* criteria), (2) a drinking problem (i.e., symptoms of an alcohol use disorder without diagnoses of abuse or dependence), or (3) nonproblematic use. Findings at follow-up showed that about half of adolescents with alcohol use disorders develop a persistent substance use disorder by early adulthood. A little more than a third who have drinking problems develop a persistent substance use disorder, and about a fifth of children without drinking problems develop a substance use disorder during early adulthood. Thus, while there is clear prognostic significance to the diagnosis of substance use disorder or problem drinking during adolescence, substance use problems may remit spontaneously in many youths.

Risk Factors for Persistent Substance Use Disorders

Identification of risk factors associated with persistence of alcohol use disorder or other substance use disorders may help to inform individual treatment recommendations. Conduct/oppositional defiant disorders and daily smoking, which have been linked to persistence of alcohol use disorder, should be seen as risk factors and should be treated when possible. Patients with drug-related criminal charges, charges of drug-related theft, and charges of driving under the influence should strongly be encouraged to work toward lifelong abstinence.

Consequences of Improper Diagnosis

Experimentation with alcohol, tobacco, and even marijuana can be normal for older adolescents and young adults. An improper diagnosis of a substance use disorder can be harmful in many ways. Such a diagnosis carries a stigma that may destroy trust and negatively affect family relationships or have legal consequences. It may even prohibit an adolescent from receiving some types of care (e.g., foster care placement or placement in other residential settings).

Adaptive Impairment

Many clinically referred adolescent substance abusers continue to have substance-related problems in early adulthood. Adolescents with substance-related problems have a higher degree of psychiatric comorbidity and dysfunction in social and academic areas. For many of these youths, active substance use clearly worsens psychiatric comorbidity, limits response to treatment, and impairs overall functioning. Early exposure to addictive substances may prevent normal development of behavioral and emotional regulatory mechanisms. Hence, it is important that mental health professionals conduct careful psychiatric evaluation of children and adolescents in order to avoid misdiagnosis. More research is needed to improve identification of early onset substance use disorders.

Abstinence

The highest prevalence of alcohol or substance use disorders across all age groups is found among adolescents and young adults. The prevalence of substance use disorders declines following adolescence, perhaps the result of a natural developmental decline in substance use disorders. Although many treatment providers in the United

Table 15-1
Domains of Assessment of Adolescent Substance Abuse

Substance use type, quantity, and frequency
Substance-related problem severity
Psychiatric comorbidity
Acute risks (e.g., suicidality, overdose)
Family environment
Delinquency/criminal record
Peer environment
Academic functioning
Physical/sexual abuse
Sexual behavior
Areas of competence
Leisure activities

States argue that abstinence is necessary in all substance abuse cases, the scientific evidence supporting this claim is limited. Clearly, abstinence is the safest approach for minimizing problems associated with substance dependence or abuse. Over 99 percent of treatment programs in the United States recommend abstinence for all patients with substance use disorders. These programs are based on a twelve-step treatment program that has limited scientific support, yet is widely accepted by clinicians. Indeed, abstinence may be necessary to break the cycle of abuse and withdrawal in some cases. Millions of substance-dependent individuals have benefited from twelve-step programs and methods of community support. However, if a patient does not maintain abstinence, should treatment be deemed a failure? Most scientific studies use a measure of reduced substance use as the primary outcome measure. Moreover, there are reasons why abstinence may be particularly difficult for adolescents to accept (e.g., "hitting bottom," acceptance of a higher power; see Deas & Thomas, 2001).

INSTRUMENTS AND METHODS FOR SCREENING AND DIAGNOSIS

Table 15-1 describes areas of assessment of adolescent substance abuse. All evaluations should include an assessment of the safety of the child. Adolescents are at elevated risk for a wide variety of negative outcomes, and adolescents with a substance use disorder are at higher risk for suicide, homicide, assault, rape, motor vehicle accidents, and overdose (Wu et al., 2004). Once relative safety is established, clinicians should evaluate all areas of adolescent functioning. Since youths may deny the use of alcohol or drugs, clinicians should be wary of an unexplained decline in academic functioning, which is often an indicator of a drug use problem.

Standardized Instruments

A variety of standardized instruments can be informative for clinical practice. Types of structured instruments that can be used to assess substance use disorders include screening instruments and more comprehensive structured interviews. The most sensitive screening instruments ask not only about substance use but also about substance-related problems. For example, the Substance Abuse Subtle Screening Inventory (SASSI) is a self-report assessment tool that concentrates on substance-related problems (i.e., the adaptive significance of substance use symptoms; Miller, 1988). Additional examples include the Personal Experience Inventory (Winters & Henly, 1989; Winters, Stinchfield, & Henly, 1993), the Problem Oriented Screening Instrument for Teenagers (Latimer, Winters, & Stinchfield, 1997; Rahdert, 1991), and the Rutgers Alcohol Problem Index (White & Labouvie, 1989); these assessment tools and others are reviewed by Winters, Estroff, & Anderson (2003). Two examples of well-designed structured interviews that comprehensively assess the relationship between substance use and other domains of functioning include the Comprehensive Addiction Severity Index (CASI; Meyers, McLellan, Jaeger, & Pettinati, 1995) and the Global Assessment of Individual Needs (GAIN; Dennis et al., 2004). Both of these give *DSM-IV-TR* diagnoses of substance abuse and assess a variety of domains of functioning, including substance use, substance-related problems, family relationships, peer relationships, delinquency, psychiatric problems, and leisure activities.

The recently developed childhood disorders form of the Structured Clinical Interview for DSM-IV Axis I Disorders (SCID; First, Spitzer, Gibbon, & Williams, 1996), called the KID-SCID (Matzner, Silva, Silvan, Chowdhury, & Nastasi, 1997), is a semistructured diagnostic interview that includes questions for assessment of childhood disorders (e.g., disruptive behavior disorders) and questions for assessment of mood disorders, anxiety disorders, psychosis, and substance abuse (questions found in the SCID). The KID-SCID, used primarily in research studies rather than in clinical practice, requires approximately two hours to administer. Although the vast majority of studies that have used the SCID and the Structured Clinical Interview for DSM-IV Axis II Personality Disorders (SCID-II; First, Spitzer, Gibbon, & Williams, 1997) have examined adult patients, some investigators have successfully administered the SCID and SCID-II to adolescents (e.g., Chanen et al., 2004).

Therapeutic Environment and Confidentiality

The creation of a therapeutic environment in which an adolescent is able to talk freely about alcohol or drug use is essential to assessment. While clinicians should collect information about an adolescent's condition from multiple sources (e.g., parents, screening instruments), an adolescent's self-report of substance-related problems is extremely important for accurate diagnosis and treatment. The creation of a safe therapeutic environment requires establishment of therapeutic boundaries, particularly the bounds of confidentiality. The usual agreement of confidentiality includes a safety exclusion (i.e., a parent or guardian will be told about information that indicates that an adolescent is a danger to him/herself or others). Although some clinicians believe substance use should be excluded from the scope of the confidentiality agreement between the adolescent patient and the clinician, these clinicians risk discouraging their patients from discussing drug use. The author feels that clinicians should recognize the developing autonomy of an adolescent and should avoid divulging to caretakers normative substance experimentation. However, parental involvement is needed when substance use places a youth in dangerous situations (e.g., driving under the influence) or when a youth meets criteria for a substance use disorder diagnosis or other serious impairment. Clinicians must consider each case individually and the level of risk for harm to the patient before speaking with parents about the patient's substance use. For example, parental involvement is needed if an adolescent is using inhalants a couple times weekly (there is potential for neurotoxicity) but may not be needed if an adolescent is smoking marijuana a couple of times weekly. Inhalant use is more commonly associated with irreversible cognitive deficits, and urine toxicology cannot monitor the levels of exposure (as tetrahydrocannabinol (THC) levels can). In short, there is a risk-benefit ratio related to where a clinician and an adolescent define the bounds of confidentiality for substance use. Each case needs to be individually decided based on the particular risks involved.

Urine Toxicology

Urine drug screens are commonly available, but safeguards must be used to maintain the validity of these measures. Supervised urines are the gold standard in substance abuse treatment but are not easy to implement in clinical practice, particularly with adolescents. There are alternatives. Plastic thermometers on the specimen bottles can be used to monitor temperature and can help guard against altered or substituted urine samples. Urine creatinine levels can be used to monitor watering down or diuretic use. Urine specimens obtained without use of at least these two safeguards are suspect and highly unreliable. Saliva tests are becoming more widely available.

Urine toxicology is not highly sensitive for many substances of abuse, with the exception of marijuana. The length of time that drugs can be detected in a urine sample depends upon the frequency of use and can vary from three days to almost a month after last use. THC levels can help to monitor abstinence from marijuana as well as to estimate exposure levels. By giving youths who claim that their use is sporadic seven days' notice prior to a urine drug screen, clinicians can gauge severity of marijuana use. If use is sporadic, their urine test should be negative. A positive result indicates a greater level of use. Most other drugs do not remain in the urine for very long, and most drugs require testing within two days of use (e.g., amphetamines, cocaine, heroin). Hence, weekly drug screens, especially those given on the same day every week, may not detect ongoing substance use. Specialized tests are available for lysergic acid diethylamide (LSD), methylenedioxymethamphetamine (MDMA), Ketamine, and phencyclidine (PCP), but these tests are not part of routine urine drug screens. Routine urine drug tests screen for use of marijuana, cocaine, heroin and other opiates, and benzodiazepines. Specialized tests for LSD, MDMA, Ketamine, and PCP usually need to be ordered and are expensive. In the United States, a MDMA test is approximately $250.

In summary, early onset substance use disorder is best assessed using multiple informants, but the adolescent's self-report (obtained in a safe therapeutic environment) is the cornerstone of assessment. Clinicians should compare an adolescent's report to reports from multiple sources (e.g., parent reports, school reports, urine drug screens). Collection of information about the patient from multiple sources helps clinicians to accurately evaluate a patient's substance use disorder.

DIFFERENTIAL DIAGNOSIS AND COMORBIDITY

Application of Diagnostic Criteria to Case Example

In the case example (see "Case Presentation"), SP clearly meets criteria for marijuana dependence. Her depressive symptoms seem significant, although it is unclear if they represent a primary depression or a substance-induced depression. Her symptoms meet criteria for "depression not otherwise specified." She also exhibits symptoms of conduct disorder. Depression is common among adolescent girls who have substance abuse problems; these two disorders often occur together with disruptive behavior problems such as conduct disorder or oppositional defiant disorder. SP felt unhappy and guilty much of the time but refused to view marijuana use as a problem; instead she viewed marijuana use as a symptom of her depression. If SP is able to view her marijuana abuse as a problem, she is likely to benefit from Cognitive Behavioral Group Therapy or similar therapies, but, given the family problems, she should receive therapy in the context of family treatment. Finally, the relationship between depression and substance use is not easy to determine, since her symptoms developed simultaneously (after her grandmother's death). Marijuana use may contribute to depressive symptomatology and may result in dependence (Bovasso, 2001). Marijuana withdrawal may worsen mood; some antidepressants may worsen mood during marijuana withdrawal (Haney et al., 2001).

Challenges in Differential Diagnosis

Adolescence can be a turbulent period of development, as adolescent children try to fit into adult roles. An adolescent's search for autonomy can contribute to a variety of family conflicts and may not necessarily indicate the presence of a psychiatric disorder. As children emerge into adults during adolescence, developmental delays contribute to the development of psychiatric disorders that are linked to the development of substance abuse (e.g., conduct disorder, ADHD). Moreover, one psychiatric disorder can be associated with more than one comorbidity (e.g., ADHD can be associated with conduct disorder, bipolar disorder, and anxiety disorders). Psychiatric symptoms in adolescence tend to be nonspecific. For example, irritability, a common symptom in adolescents, could indicate depression, bipolar illness, ADHD, conduct disorder, borderline character disorder, or substance abuse withdrawal, or may be a normal response to the stresses of adolescent development. Substances of abuse can also cause psychiatric symptoms such as inattention, mood dysregulation, and anxiety. Readers are encouraged to consult chapters on depression (Chapter 1 of this volume), bipolar disorder (Chapter 2 of this volume), ADHD (Chapter 5 of this volume), and antisocial personality disorder (Chapter 8 of this volume). Finally, it is important to remain nimble as a diagnostician; as patients' symptoms change and remit over time, clinicians should be willing to modify their diagnoses.

Negative Affectivity

Adolescent substance abusers often have affective and behavioral dysregulation. Both externalizing disorders (e.g., ADHD, conduct disorder) and internalizing disorders (depressive or anxiety disorders) may contribute to the development of a substance use disorder, and there may be different developmental pathways to a substance use disorder. Many studies of adult early onset substance use disorders have examined the self-medication hypothesis (the theory that patients choose certain psychoactive substances to alleviate negative affective states). While the most common pathway to early onset substance use disorder appears to be mediated by severe deficits in behavioral regulation, emotional dysregulation also may play a role in the development of a substance use disorder in youths with disruptive and nondisruptive disorders. For example, youths may attempt to manage overwhelming aggression, depression, or anxiety with substance use. According to the self-medication hypothesis, anxious youths may attempt to self-medicate with sedative-hypnotic substances, while depressed youths may attempt to self-medicate with stimulants. There is little scientific support for the self-medication hypothesis. The presence of a psychiatric disorder may make these youths more vulnerable to the development of a substance use disorder (Khantzian, 1999).

Substance-Induced Symptoms

The relationship between psychiatric and substance use disorders is not always easy to determine. Only through a comprehensive psychiatric assessment can this relationship be accurately evaluated. A developmental timeline that includes onset of substance use, the development of substance abuse-related problems, the development of psychiatric symptoms and their relationship to onset of substance use, intoxication, withdrawal, and abstinence can be beneficial. While, in most cases, it appears that disruptive behavior disorders seem to occur before the development of a substance use disorder, symptoms of substance use disorders may be considered when making diagnoses of disruptive behavior disorders, including ADHD, oppositional defiant disorder, and conduct disorder. For example, symptoms of inattentiveness, distractibility, temper outbursts, and stealing or lying to obtain substances can occur because of intoxication or withdrawal from various substances of abuse (Steiner & Wilson, 1999). Learning disabilities may also contribute to the development of substance use disorders. Conversely, inhalant abuse ("huffing") is associated with significant cognitive deficits that may mimic learning disabilities. Children with learning impairments face failure in school. Failing as a result of learning disability, ADHD, or disruptive behavior and/or substance abuse limits positive social rewards. If adolescents excel in few areas (e.g., sports, arts, church) and do not receive positive reinforcement (an important factor in achievement motivation), these adolescents may be drawn to drugs and alcohol and deviant peer groups.

Mood and Anxiety Disorders

Mood and anxiety disorders may contribute to the development of substance use disorders, but they may also result from substance abuse or associated problems. Psychotic disorders may result from intoxication by stimulants (methamphetamine, cocaine), psychotomimetics (phencyclidine (PCP) or ketamine ("Special K")), hallucinogens (LSD, mescaline, psilocybin ("magic mushrooms")), and even marijuana. Prolonged psychotic states following use of these substances have also been reported, although it is generally thought that extended psychoses are unmasked rather than precipitated *de novo*. Conversely, patients may attempt to self-medicate the frightening symptoms of psychotic disorders. Mood, anxiety, and psychotic disorders thought to be secondary to substance abuse can be coded as a substance-induced disorder. The relationship between substance use and psychopathology may be unclear. When clinicians are unsure whether a psychiatric disorder is independent of substance use, diagnosis of the disorder as "not otherwise specified" is most accurate. Time in treatment and information from multiple informants clarify the relationship between psychiatric disorder and substance use.

Psychiatric Comorbidity

In community samples and samples of patients in treatment, adolescents with substance use disorders have a high level of psychiatric comorbidity. In one well-designed community study of 14- to 17-year-old boys and girls, 76 percent of children with a diagnosis of a substance use disorder had a mood, anxiety, or disruptive behavior/antisocial personality disorder diagnosis (compared to 24.5 percent of youths without a substance use disorder diagnosis). The most common comorbid disorders were disruptive behavior disorder and antisocial personality disorder, and over two thirds (68.0 percent) of the youths who were evaluated met criteria for one of these disorders (compared to only 10.1 percent of youths without a substance use disorder diagnosis). Almost one third (32.0 percent) of youths with a substance use disorder had a mood disorder, but only 11.2 percent of children without a substance use disorder had a mood disorder. However, when disruptive behavior/antisocial personality disorders were controlled for, the association between substance use disorders and mood disorder became nonsignificant. While more anxiety disorders were found in the group of patients with substance use disorders than in the group of patients without substance use disorders, this difference was nonsignificant (20.0 versus 15.7 percent; Kandel et al., 1999). Anxiety disorders may become more relevant to the pathogenesis of substance use disorders with age (e.g., Type 1 Alcoholics; see Galanter & Kleber 1999). Use of illicit substances to alleviate symptoms of anxiety and antisocial behavior may lead to substance use disorders (Wilson & Steiner, 2002). Clinicians must consider the developmental context in which a patient uses drugs and should try to determine possible causes of the patient's symptoms (e.g., anxiety) and compensatory behaviors (e.g., marijuana use).

TREATMENT OPTIONS

Treatment of Case Example

SP (see "Case Presentation"), like many adolescents, was not motivated to stop smoking marijuana. SP identified depression as her main problem. The therapist focused on the patient's motivation for coming to treatment (i.e., treatment for depression). SP was able to view her mood as a problem and, in time, set a goal to feel better. Discrepancies between her personal goals (e.g., self-improvement) and her behaviors (stealing, smoking marijuana) motivated her to stop her marijuana use. The therapist supported SP's choice to stop use of marijuana, alcohol, and other drugs. Over time, SP began to see the negative role that marijuana played in her life and chose abstinence as an important goal.

Motivational Interviewing

Adolescents often enter treatment with a different understanding of problems than their family members or other authorities have. Lack of motivation to change is often an obstacle in the treatment of adolescents. Adults (e.g., parents and teachers) can be frustrated by an adolescent's refusal to recognize substance use as a problem, and it is not always possible for families or schools to force a patient into treatment. Promoting willingness to change is preferable to coercion (although some amount of coercion is often necessary in order to get adolescents into treatment). Motivational interviewing (MI) may prove to be ideal for use with adolescents because it emphasizes autonomy and collaboration with the patient and encourages "change talk" reflecting the patient's own motives for change. Some clinicians are beginning to utilize this approach with adolescents in order to help them develop their own reasons for seeking treatment (Miller & Rollnick, 2002).

Adolescent Substance Abuse Research

There are an increasing number of controlled studies of substance abuse treatment for adolescents. Differences between outcome measures in various studies make comparisons between studies complicated, and some authors have questioned the validity of the methods used. Evidence-based treatments for substance use disorders include family therapy, multisystemic therapy, behavioral therapy, Cognitive Behavioral Therapy, and (to a more limited extent) twelve-step facilitation therapies. There is little support for psychopharmacological approaches to reduce adolescent substance abuse in the absence of psychiatric comorbidity (Deas & Thomas, 2001).

It is not uncommon to find that parents of adolescent patients may be inaccessible for a variety of reasons (e.g., depression, drug use, work). Lack of parental involvement can contribute to the development of adolescent substance abuse and hinder recovery. In the case example (see "Case Presentation"), the patient's parents were inaccessible—her mother had active alcohol dependence, and her father was often working and unavailable.

Family Therapies

Family therapies that include adolescents have the greatest scientific support. These therapeutic methods attempt to reduce familial contributions to the development and/or maintenance of adolescent substance abuse behaviors. Examples of empirically validated family therapies include functional family therapy (which includes positive relabeling, consistently clear communication, and the development of a supportive recovery environment) and family system therapy. Brief strategic family therapy, which focuses on the correction of maladaptive family interaction patterns, is an empirically validated therapy for use with adolescent substance abusers (Szapocznick & Williams, 2000). Parental psychoeducation may be part of these family therapy approaches but is not in itself sufficient. Family therapy has been reported to be more effective in reducing adolescent drug use than family psychoeducation, peer group therapy, and individual therapy (Stanton & Shadish, 1997). Self-reports of reduced substance use and increased levels of abstinence (supported by random urine drug screens) have been reported.

Family participation is an essential component of outpatient adolescent substance abuse treatment. If familial factors maintain substance use behaviors (e.g., alcohol use or use of other drugs in the home, poor parental supervision, high levels of conflict), effecting behavioral change (even with fairly robust treatments) can be very difficult. Moreover, clinicians should request reports from parents and teachers about the patient's ability to function in social settings. It is often difficult for substance-dependent individuals, who may fear legal and social consequences of their drug use, to admit the extent of their impairment and/or substance use. Factors outside the home (e.g., peers who use substances and availability of drugs in schools) may contribute to the persistence of addiction and should be addressed in the plan for treatment of a substance use disorder. Families who are able to monitor factors that may contribute to relapse can be critical to the success of a treatment effort. Similarly, treatment of co-occurring disruptive behaviors is a critical aspect of most forms of family-based substance abuse treatment.

Cognitive Behavioral Methods

Cognitive behavioral methods that concentrate on building coping skills to avoid relapse appear to be particularly effective for individual therapy. Behavioral therapy (e.g., role playing, response rehearsal, homework assignments, and diary keeping) has been shown to be effective in reducing substance use (measured by urine drug screen, adolescent self-reports, and reports from parents or significant others), when compared to supportive therapy. Cognitive behavioral group approaches have been shown to effect both short- and long-term change in adolescents with substance use disorders. Differences between various group therapy modalities are minimal. Some evidence also exists for the efficacy of interactional group therapy and twelve-step facilitation therapy. Clinicians must carefully monitor group sessions with adolescents to prevent negative group dynamics that may cause negative outcomes (e.g., encouragement of deviant behavior; Dishion, Capaldi, Spracklen, & Li, 1995).

Multisystemic Therapy

Multisystemic Therapy (MST) is an evidence-based, multicomponent treatment for conduct disorder. This type of therapy combines individual and family therapy, intensive case management, and treatment for co-occurring psychiatric disorders; a major advantage of such an integrated treatment is that it can address many problems that youths with serious behavior problems often have. MST has empirical support within criminally mandated substance abusing populations (Deas & Thomas 2001; Henggeler, Pickrel, & Brondino, 1999). Reductions in drug-related arrests and self-reports of reduced alcohol and drug use have been reported with the use of MST, when compared to individual therapy. An intensive combination of treatments (like MST) is often required for severely impaired youths and may prevent inpatient detoxification and/or rehabilitation. This intensive intervention may facilitate community reintegration of severely impaired youths after inpatient or residential treatment.

Inpatient/Residential Treatments

Sometimes even the most supportive families and the best possible use of outpatient treatment resources fail to produce abstinence or a reduction in substance use. Inpatient detoxification can be helpful in stopping substance abuse, particularly when the discomfort associated with withdrawal from opiates or alcohol (or to a lesser extent marijuana) discourages patients from seeking abstinence. Long-term residential treatment can range from a few weeks to a year or more (e.g., the traditional therapeutic community) and can help patients to identify positive alternatives to substance use that may generalize to the outpatient setting. Adolescents who remain in therapeutic communities demonstrate long-term benefits, including adaptive functioning and reductions in substance use and criminal recidivism. However, there are high levels of attrition (30 to 40 percent within the first month and up to 80 percent within the first year). Criminal justice mandates to treatment (alternatives to incarceration that reduce sentences if treatment is completed) may improve retention; however, even in such cases, the majority of residents leave prior to completing a year in the program (Wilson et al., 2001). Nonetheless, there appears to be a direct relationship between length of treatment and outcome; improved self-regulation is evident to both residents and treatment providers in such settings (Galanter & Kleber, 1999). Substance abuse treatment can be effective even when mandated. Mandated community support groups may be effective in reducing criminal recidivism among incarcerated delinquents who have committed drug-related crimes (Wilson et al., 2001).

Treating Psychiatric Comorbidity

Psychiatric comorbidity among adolescents with substance use disorders is as high as among adults with substance use disorders. An understanding of whether such comorbid disorders are primary (independent of substance use disorders) or substance-induced can aid treatment planning. Even substance-induced psychiatric disorders do not necessarily remit within the first thirty days of treatment (Hendren, 1999). Psychiatric comorbidity can contribute to the persistence of substance use disorders. In such cases, the risks of psychiatric treatment (even in the presence of active substance use) must be weighed against the potential benefits of psychiatric treatment. Medications need to be carefully monitored to ensure that they are taken as directed, that the dose is adjusted to achieve the desired benefits, and that adverse side effects do not emerge. Some family community support groups and treatment facilities discourage the use of medication in treatment of adolescents.

There are few studies of treatment for adolescents with co-occurring psychiatric disorders and substance abuse. There is some evidence that treatments of comorbid mood disorders (e.g., treatment of explosive temper with the anticonvulsant valproate (Donovan et al., 2000), treatment of bipolar disorder with lithium (Geller, Cooper, Watts, Cosby, & Fox, 1992; Geller et al., 1998), and treatment of depression with the selective serotonin reuptake inhibitor fluoxetine (Riggs et al., 2007)) may reduce adolescent substance abuse. Mood disorders may cause persistence of substance use disorders (e.g., depression is frequently associated with conduct disorder and substance use disorders among adolescent girls). Because of the lack of empirically based research in this area, treatment of most psychiatric disorders is determined on a case-by-case basis. In all cases, it is preferable to stabilize active substance use and acute psychiatric symptoms first; and any psychiatric treatment of comorbid disorders should occur in the context of evidence-based substance abuse treatment. Clinicians should rule out psychiatric symptoms caused by intoxicqtion or withdrawal.

ADHD commonly co-occurs with substance use disorders (with or without conduct disorder). There is some evidence that treatment of ADHD with nonstimulants is effective in adolescent substance abusers, although published studies on the safety and efficacy of stimulant treatments are lacking (Riggs, Hall, Mikulich-Gilbertson, Lohman, & Kayser, 2004; Riggs, Leon, Mikulich, & Pottle, 1998). Nonstimulant treatments may not be as effective as stimulant treatments for some youths. A clinician may need to consider prescribing a stimulant agent for ADHD. Reductions in the incidence of substance use disorders have been reported with stimulant treatment of ADHD, although there is some debate about the effects of stimulants on the onset of substance use (Faraone & Wilens, 2003; Loney, Kramer, & Salisbury, 2002). Stabilization of active substance use or acute psychiatric symptoms is necessary before developing a long-term treatment plan. Careful monitoring and use of less readily abusable agents (e.g., bupropion, once-daily preparations of methylphenidate) may help to prevent abuse of these medications. A parent/guardian might dispense medication to ensure compliance and prevent diversion or misuse (see Wilson & Levin, 2005).

SUMMARY

While alcohol and drug use among teenagers is discouraged in our society, the majority of youths use alcohol, marijuana, or nicotine at least once during high school, and many will use these substances with some regularity. Early onset use, use of less commonly used substances (i.e., substances other than nicotine, alcohol, or marijuana) at an early age, and/or conduct problems increase the risk for development of a substance use disorder. Most youths who use substances during mid- to late adolescence do not develop serious substance use disorders. Many youths who have substance use disorders develop life-course-persistent substance abuse problems, although some youths may remit spontaneously. Youths who develop substance use disorders are at high risk for psychiatric comorbidity that may contribute to the development and persistence of a substance use disorder. Accurate psychiatric diagnosis in adolescents may be difficult: psychiatric symptoms may change with age, and symptoms of a substance use disorder or psychiatric disorder can be difficult to distinguish from variants of normal development. Research on adult substance abuse diagnosis and treatment may inform the development of treatments for adolescents, but treatments for adolescents need to be tested on adolescents. Evidence-based treatments (i.e., treatments that have been determined to be effective based on controlled clinical trials) are available for adolescents (e.g., family therapy approaches). More work is needed to make such treatments widely accessible to patients (e.g., training of clinicians and other dissemination effort).

Suggestions for Further Reading

For readers who wish to study further in this area, we recommend:

☐ **Books and Journal Articles**

- Deas, D., & Thomas, S. E. (2001). An overview of controlled studies of adolescent substance abuse treatment. *The American Journal on the Addictions, 10*, 78-189.

- Miller, W. R., & Rollnick, S. (2002). *Motivational interviewing: Preparing people for change* (2nd ed.). New York: Guilford.

- Wilson, J. J., & Levin, F. R. (2005). ADHD and early-onset substance use disorders. *Journal of Child and Adolescent Psychopharmacology, 15*, 751-763.

- Winters, K. C., Latimer, W. W., & Stinchfield, R. (2002). Clinical issues in the assessment of adolescent alcohol and other drug use. *Behavior Research and Therapy, 40*, 1443-1456.

☐ **Web Sites for Adolescents, Parents, and Clinicians**

- National Institute on Drug Abuse for Teens (The Science Behind Drugs): http://teens.drugabuse.gov/.

- National Institute on Drug Abuse for Teens (Parents and Teachers): http://teens.drugabuse.gov/parents/index.php.

- National Institute on Drug Abuse (NIDA InfoFacts: High School and Youth Trends): http://www.nida.nih.gov/Infofacts/HSYouthtrends.html.

Author's Note

The research in this chapter was supported in part by grant K23 DA14572 (Dr. Wilson) from the National Institutes of Health.

References

American Psychiatric Association (2000). *Diagnostic and statistical manual of mental disorders* (4th ed., text rev.). Washington, DC: Author.

Bovasso, G. B. (2001). Cannabis abuse as a risk factor for depressive symptoms. *American Journal of Psychiatry, 158*, 2033-2037.

Chanen, A. M., Jackson, H. J., McGorry, P. D., Allot, K. A., Clarkson, V., & Yuen, H. P. (2004). Two-year stability of personality disorder in older adolescent outpatients. *Journal of Personality Disorders, 18,* 526-541.

Clark, D. B., Parker, A. M., & Lynch, K. G. (1999). Psychopathology and substance-related problems during early adolescence: a survival analysis. *Journal of Clinical Child Psychology, 28*, 333-341.

Cloninger, C. R., Sigvardsson, S., & Bohman, M. (1988). Childhood personality predicts alcohol abuse in young adults. *Alcoholism, Clinical and Experimental Research, 12*, 494-505.

Colder, C. R., & Chassin, L. (1999). The psychosocial characteristics of alcohol users versus problem users: Data from a study of adolescents at risk. *Development and Psychopathology, 11*, 321-348.

Deas, D., & Thomas, S. E. (2001). An overview of controlled studies of adolescent substance abuse treatment. *American Journal on Addictions, 10*, 178-189.

Dennis, M., Godley, S. H., Diamond, G., Tims, F. M., Babor, T., Donaldson, J., et al. (2004). The Cannabis Youth Treatment (CYT) Study: Main findings from two randomized trials. *Journal of Substance Abuse Treatment, 27*, 197-213.

Dishion, T. J., Capaldi, D., Spracklen, K. M., & Li, F. (1995). Peer ecology of male adolescent drug use. *Development and Psychopathology, 7*, 803-824.

Donovan, S. J., Stewart, J. W., Nunes, E. V., Quitkin, F. M., Parides, M., Daniel, W., et al. (2000). Divalproex treatment for youth with explosive temper and mood lability: A double-blind, placebo-controlled crossover design. *American Journal of Psychiatry, 157*, 818-820.

Faraone, S. V., & Wilens, T. (2003). Does stimulant treatment lead to substance use disorders? *Journal of Clinical Psychiatry, 64*(Suppl. 11), 9-13.

First, M. B., Spitzer, R. L., Gibbon, M., & Williams, J. B. W. (1996). Structured Clinical Interview for DSM-IV Axis I Disorders (SCID). Washington, DC: American Psychiatric Press.

First, M. B., Spitzer, R. L., Gibbon, M., & Williams, J. B. W. (1997). Structured Clinical Interview for DSM-IV Axis II Personality Disorders (SCID-II). Washington, DC: American Psychiatric Publishing.

Galanter, M., & Kleber, H. D. (1999). *Textbook of substance abuse treatment* (2nd ed.). Washington, DC: American Psychiatric Press.

Geller, B., Copper, T. B., Sun, K., Zimerman, B., Frazier, J., Williams, M., et al. (1998). Double-blind and placebo-controlled study of lithium for adolescent bipolar disorders with secondary substance dependency. *Journal of the American Academy of Child and Adolescent Psychiatry, 37,* 171-178.

Geller, B., Cooper, T. B., Watts, H. E., Cosby, C. M., & Fox, L. W. (1992). Early findings from a pharmacokinetically designed double-blind and placebo-controlled study of lithium for adolescents comorbid with bipolar and substance dependency disorders. *Progress in Neuro-Psychopharmacology & Biological Psychiatry, 16,* 281-299.

Haney, M., Ward, A. S., Comer, S. D., Hart, C. L., Foltin, R. W., & Fischman, M. W. (2001). Bupropion SR worsens mood during marijuana withdrawal in humans. *Psychopharmacology, 155,* 171-179.

Hendren, R. L. (1999). Oppositional defiant disorder. In R. L. Hendren (Ed.), *Disruptive behavior disorders in children and adolescents* (Vol. 18, pp. 99-132). Washington, DC: American Psychiatric Publishing.

Henggeler, S. W., Pickrel, S. G., & Brondino, M. J. (1999). Mulitsystemic treatment of substance-abusing and dependent delinquents: Outcomes, treatment fidelity, and transportability. *Mental Health Services Research, 1,* 171-184.

Johnston, L. D., O'Malley, P. M., & Bachman, J. G. (1999). *National survey results on drug use from the Monitoring the Future Study, 1975-1998* (Vol. 1: Secondary School Students) (NIH Publication 99-4660). Bethesda, MD: National Institute on Drug Abuse.

Johnston, L. D., O'Malley, P. M., Bachman, J. G., & Schulenberg, J. E. (2004). *Monitoring the future national results on adolescent drug use: Overview of key findings, 2003* (NIH Publication No. 04-5506). Bethesda, MD: National Institute on Drug Abuse.

Kandel, D. B., Johnson, J. G., Bird, H. R., Weissman, M. M., Goodman, S. H., Lahey, B. B., et al. (1999). Psychiatric comobidity among adolescents with substance use disorders: Findings from the MECA study. *Journal of the American Academy of Child and Adolescent Psychiatry, 38,* 693-699.

Khantzian, E. J. (1999). *Treating addiction as a human process.* Northvale, NJ: Jason Aronson, Inc.

Latimer, W. W., Winters, K. C., & Stinchfield, R. D. (1997). Screening for drug abuse among adolescents in clinical and correctional settings using the Problem-Oriented Screening Instrument for Teenagers. *American Journal of Drug and Alcohol Abuse, 23,* 79-98.

Lieberman, D. Z. (2000). Children of alcoholics: An update. *Current Opinion in Pediatrics, 12,* 336-340.

Loney, J., Kramer, J. R., & Salisbury, H. (2002). Medicated versus unmedicated ADHD children: Adult involvement with legal and illegal drugs. In P. S. Jensen & J. R. Cooper (Eds.), *Attention deficit hyperactivity disorder: State of the science; best practices* (pp. 1-16). Kingston, NJ: Civic Research Institute.

Luthar, S. S., Cushing, G., McMahon, T. J. (1997). Interdisciplinary interface: Developmental principles brought to substance abuse research. In S. S. Luther, J. A. Burack, D. Cicchetti, & J. R. Weisz (Eds.), *Developmental psychopathology: Perspectives on adjustment, risk and disorder* (pp. 437-465). New York: Cambridge University Press.

Matzner, F., Silva, R., Silvan, M., Chowdhury, M., & Nastasi, L. (1997, May). *Preliminary test-retest reliability of the KID-SCID* (pp. 172-173). Presented at the 150th meeting of the American Psychiatric Association, New Research Program and Abstract, San Diego, CA.

Merikangas, K. R., Stolar, M., Stevens, D. E., Goulet, J., Preisig, M. A., Fenton, B., et al. (1998). Familial transmission of substance use disorders. *Archives of General Psychiatry, 55*, 973-979.

Meyers, K., McLellan, A. T., Jaeger, J. L., & Pettinati, H. M. (1995). The development of the Comprehensive Addiction Severity Index for Adolescents (CASI-A): An interview for assessing multiple problems of adolescents. *Journal of Substance Abuse Treatment, 12*, 181-193.

Miller, G. (1988). *The Substance Abuse Subtle Screening Inventory manual.* Spencer, IN: Spencer World Publishing.

Miller, T. Q. (1994). A test of alternative explanations for the stage-like progression of adolescents substance use in four national samples. *Addictive Behaviors, 19*, 287-293.

Miller, W. R., & Rollnick, S. (2002). *Motivational interviewing: Preparing people for change* (2nd ed.). New York: Guilford.

National Center on Addiction and Substance Abuse at Columbia University (CASA). (1999). *No safe haven: Children of substance-abusing parents.* New York: Author.

Pollock, N. K., & Martin, C. S. (1999). Diagnostic orphans: Adolescents with alcohol symptoms who do not qualify for DSM-IV abuse or dependence diagnoses. *American Journal of Psychiatry, 156*, 897-901.

Rahdert, E. R. (1991). *The adolescent assessment/referral system manual* (DHHS Publication No. ADM91-1735). Rockville, MD: National Institute on Drug Abuse.

Riggs, P. D., Hall, S. K., Mikulich-Gilbertson, S. K., Lohman, M., & Kayser, A. (2004). A randomized controlled trial of pemoline for attention-deficit/hyperactivity disorder in substance-abusing adolescents. *Journal of the American Academy of Child and Adolescent Psychiatry, 43*, 420-429.

Riggs, P. D., Leon, S. L., Mikulich, S. K., & Pottle, L. C. (1998). An open trial of bupropion for ADHD in adolescents with substance use disorders and conduct disorder. *Journal of the American Academy of Child and Adolescent Psychiatry, 37*, 1271-1278.

Riggs, P. D., Mikulich-Gilbertson, S. K., Davies, R. D., Lohman, M., Klein, C., & Stover, S. K. (2007) A randomized controlled trial of fluoxetine and cognitive behavioral therapy in adolescents with major depression, behavior problems, and substance use disorders. *Archives of Pediatric and Adolescent Medicine, 161*, 1026-1034.

Rohde, P., Lewinsohn, P. M., Kahler, C. W., Seeley, J. R., & Brown, R. A. (2001). Natural course of alcohol use disorders from adolescence to young adulthood. *Journal of the American Academy of Child and Adolescent Psychiatry, 40*, 83-90.

Stanton, M. D., & Shadish, W. R. (1997). Outcome, attrition, and family—Couples treatment for drug abuse: A meta-analysis and review of the controlled, comparative studies. *Psychological Bulletin, 122*, 170-191.

Steiner, H., & Wilson, J. J. (1999). Conduct disorder. In R. L. Hendren (Ed.), *Disruptive behavior disorders in children and adolescents* (Vol. 18, pp. 47-98). Washington, DC: American Psychiatric Publishing.

Substance Abuse and Mental Health Services Administration, Department of Health and Human Services (2001). *Summary of findings from the 2000 National Household Survey of Drug Abuse.* Rockville, MD: National Clearinghouse for Alcohol and Drug Information.

Szapocznik, J., & Williams, R. A. (2000). Brief strategic family therapy: Twenty-five years of interplay among theory, research and practice in adolescent behavior problems and drug abuse. *Clinical Child and Family Psychology Review, 3*, 117-34.

Tarter, R., Vanyukov, M., Giancoila, P., Dawes, M., Blackson, T., Mezzich, A., et al. (1999). Etiology of early age onset substance use disorder: A maturational perspective. *Development and Psychopathology, 11*, 657-683.

Tsuang, M. T., Lyons, M. J., Eisen, S. A., Goldberg, J., True, W., Lin, N., et al. (1996). Genetic influences on DSM-III-R drug abuse and dependence: A study of 3,372 twin pairs. *American Journal of Medical Genetics, 67*, 473-477.

White, H. R., & Labouvie, E. W. (1989). Towards the assessment of adolescent problem drinking. *Journal of Studies on Alcohol, 50,* 30-37.

Wilson, J. J., & Levin, F. R. (2005). Attention-deficit/hyperactivity disorder and early-onset substance use disorders. *Journal of Child and Adolescent Psychopharmacology, 15*, 751-763.

Wilson, J. J., Rojas, N., Haapanen, R., Duxbury, E., & Steiner, H. (2001). Substance abuse and criminal recidivism: A prospective study of adolescents. *Child Psychiatry and Human Development, 31*, 297-312.

Wilson, J., & Steiner, H. (2002). Conduct problems, substance use and social anxiety: A developmental study of recovery and adaptation. *Clinical Child Psychology and Psychiatry, 7*, 235-247.

Winters, K. C., Estroff, T. W., & Anderson, M. (2003). Adolescent assessment strategies and instruments. In A. W. Graham, T. K. Schultz, M. F. Mayo-Smith, R. K. Ries, & B. B. Wilford (Eds.) *Principles of addiction medicine* (3rd ed., pp. 1535-1546). Chevy Chase, MD: American Society of Addiction Medicine.

Winters, K. C., & Henly, G. A. (1989). *The Personal Experience Inventory manual.* Los Angeles, Western Psychological Services.

Winters, K. C., Stinchfield, R. D., & Henly, G. A. (1993). Further validation of new scales measuring adolescent alcohol and other drug abuse. *Journal of Studies on Alcohol, 54,* 534-541.

Wu, P., Hoven, C. W., Lui, X., Cohen, P., Fuller, C. J., & Shaffer, D. (2004). Substance use, suicidal ideation and attempts in children and adolescents. *Suicide and Life Threatening Behavior, 34*, 408-420.

Chapter 16

Pain in Patients With Substance Use Disorders

**by Deborah L. Haller, Ph.D., A.B.P.P., and
Sidney H. Schnoll, M.D., Ph.D.**

INTRODUCTION

Pain is the number one reason people go to doctors (Haddox et al., 1997). Twenty percent of Americans suffer from chronic pain; fifty million Americans are partially or totally disabled by pain (Turk, 1996). Among substance abusers, pain prevalence rates are even higher, although appropriate medical care often is lacking (Rosenblum et al., 2003). Untreated (or poorly treated) pain can lead to increased drug-seeking behavior and relapse among patients in substance abuse recovery (Savage, 1996). Other consequences of inadequate pain management include excessive medical costs, lost workplace productivity, and suffering. By identifying pain problems and assisting patients in obtaining appropriate treatment, substance abuse treatment counselors can manage problems of substance abuse and pain.

Pain is an enigma. Specialists from many disciplines (e.g., neurologists, surgeons, anesthesiologists, physiatrists, psychiatrists, and psychologists) treat pain, and their views of what it is and how it should be addressed vary considerably. The International Association for the Study of Pain (IASP) defines pain as "an unpleasant sensory and emotional experience associated with actual or potential tissue damage or described in terms of such damage" (Merskey & Bogduk, 1994).

This definition highlights the complex nature of pain. Pain is a subjective experience (i.e., it is experienced (and expressed) differently by different people and is "filtered" through their past experiences with injury and tissue damage). A person's cultural background and psychological makeup also influence how pain is experienced. For example, stoic people may tolerate the unpleasantness associated with pain better than depressed people.

Many health care providers underestimate the importance of emotions, cognitions (beliefs), and behavior to the overall experience of pain and have difficulty understanding how these components of pain interact with the physical sensation to produce the experience of pain. Furthermore, clinicians' biases and lack of understanding cause them to respond differently towards patients who have a strong emotional experience of pain. Patients with very similar injuries may experience pain in dramatically different ways. One patient may continue to function relatively normally, while another patient may become disabled. Success of treatment may depend, at least in part, on where treatment is sought and what treatment approach is taken. Because of the complex nature of pain, many patients with moderate-severe and chronic pain are referred to multidisciplinary pain management programs where staff from different disciplines work together as a team to address patients' needs. In order to treat a patient's pain effectively, a clinician must understand the causes of the patient's pain and must provide treatment that is consistent with the patient's needs.

FOUR COMPONENTS OF PAIN

Pain is a complex phenomenon that is comprised of the following four components:

1. Physical (pain sensation);

2. Emotional;

3. Cognitive (beliefs); and

4. Behavioral (pain behavior and functional status).

The relative contribution of these components varies from person to person. Pain is an unpleasant physical sensation, and sensations that are not deemed to be unpleasant should not be referred to as pain. When pain is reported in the absence of identifiable damage to the body, pain *may be* psychologically driven, although it still is pain. According to the Taxonomy Committee of the IASP (Merskey & Bogduk, 1994), "if people regard their experience as pain and . . . if they report it in the same ways as pain caused by tissue damage, it should be accepted as pain."

Physical Component

Physical pain usually is divided into two types: (1) nociceptive pain and (2) neuropathic pain. Nociceptive pain results from damage to the body from an injury or disease. The damage that occurs can be located and often treated, resulting in a diminution of the pain. Examples of nociceptive pain include broken bones, burns, and tumors. In contrast, neuropathic pain is not always associated with a specific injury and is more difficult to treat because of the lack of specific pain generator. Examples of neuropathic pain include diabetic neuropathy and complex regional pain syndrome, formerly known as reflex sympathetic dystrophy (RSD).

Another way of describing pain is typical versus atypical (see Figure 16-1). Typical pain is similar to nociceptive pain. It is protective because it identifies an injury; pain can be acute or prolonged. When the pain occurs, there is a normal protective action, such as withdrawing a hand from a hot stove or placing the body in a protective position. Chronic typical pain occurs with diseases like rheumatoid arthritis. Atypical pain is similar to neuropathic pain. It is not protective and is usually prolonged. The origin of the pain can be from peripheral nerves or can be central, secondary to a stroke or other brain injury. This type of pain is very difficult to diagnose and treat. Patients with atypical or neuropathic pain often are denied treatment because there is no identifiable cause for the pain, and, therefore, doctors may doubt its validity.

Pain Perception. There are four basic processes that are involved in the perception of pain. It is important to recognize that pain has an adaptive function: it alerts the organism that an injury has occurred and that care should be taken not to exacerbate the situation.

Transduction. This process involves the transformation of a mechanical signal (the injury) to a chemical and then to an electrical signal.

Transmission. Once the sensation is transformed to an electrical signal, it is sent along the peripheral nerves to the spinal chord and finally to the brain.

Perception. Once the impulse reaches the brain, the type and nature of the pain is identified by the brain. For instance, the pain may be perceived as burning, sharp, or dull.

Modulation. The brain sends information back down the spinal chord that may alter the perception of the pain (based on the emotional or physical state of the person at the time of the painful impulse).

Aspects of Physical Pain. There are many aspects of physical pain.

Pain Generator. It is important to try to identify a "pain generator." Pain generators include both injuries and diseases. Examples of pain generators include a herniated disk, a cancerous tumor, or a broken bone. Identification of the pain generator helps clinicians determine how to treat the patient. Some patients have vague complaints or controversial diagnoses (e.g., fibromyalgia) that are difficult to pinpoint on examination. Patients with such complaints often are misdiagnosed and treated as psychiatric cases.

Duration of Pain. Pain that exceeds three months' duration is termed chronic (as opposed to acute). The expectations for recovery from chronic pain differ from those for acute pain; patients must learn to adjust to living with pain on a longer-term basis. Unfortunately, when acute pain is ignored or undertreated, it can become chronic pain.

Intermittent Versus Persistent Pain. Pain may be intermittent (comes and goes) or persistent (always there). Both acute and chronic pain conditions may be intermittent or

Figure 16-1
Types of Pain

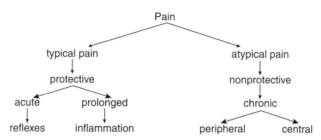

persistent. One of the problems with persistent pain is that the patient is never able to achieve a period of relief. Therefore, persistent pain conditions may be associated with great emotional, cognitive, and behavioral complaints. Patients with persistent pain often feel that they have little or no control over their situation and, over time, display significant pain behavior. While patients with constant pain often are placed on longer-acting opioids "round-the-clock," patients with intermittent pain may be advised to take shorter-acting opioids only when the pain is bothersome. Pain management in patients who have sporadic, very intense pain (such as with sickle cell disease), can be particularly difficult.

Malignant Versus Nonmalignant Pain. A distinction often is made between malignant pain (i.e., cancer-related pain) and nonmalignant pain (sometimes referred to as "benign" pain). Patients with cancer tend to be treated differently than patients without cancer. Patients' cancer-related impairment and need for potent opioid analgesics often are forgiven. There often is less shame associated with having pain from cancer as opposed to back pain or headaches with unclear origins. Although treatment providers may be more likely to prescribe pain medication and at higher doses to patients with malignant pain than to patients with nonmalignant pain, the pain experienced by some patients with cancer may be undertreated.

Variability of Pain Intensity. Pain often is variable in its intensity (i.e., it is worse at some times). Patients often report that pain is worse in the morning, when medication has worn off, or in the evening following a day's activities. As it is rare for patients to experience pain at a constant intensity, such constant pain may indicate a stronger psychological/emotional component.

Quality of Pain. Patients describe their pain in different ways, usually using adjectives that capture the acuteness of the pain (e.g., sharp, dull, aching, stabbing, burning, cramping, or nagging). Some of these descriptors are helpful in making a diagnosis. For example, burning or shooting pain is most often related to neuropathic pain.

Severity of Pain. Since pain is a subjective experience, it is difficult to measure. The most frequently used instrument to assess pain severity is the Visual Analogue Scale (VAS), which asks patients to rate their pain on a scale from 1 to 10, on which 1 reflects "no pain" and 10 reflects "the worst pain imaginable." This scale is used to rate each of the following types of pain: (1) worst pain, (2) least pain, (3) usual pain, and (4) tolerable pain (which is often the goal of treatment). By repeatedly assessing pain during the course of treatment, the practitioner can gauge the effectiveness of a treatment. For instance, if adequate doses of opioid analgesics are given, but the pain remains the same or worsens, this type of treatment may not be appropriate for the patient, and another treatment should be considered.

Factors That Exacerbate or Reduce Pain. It can be helpful to ask the patient what factors make the pain worse and which ones abate it. This information provides some clues about functional limitations and possible interventions. For instance, patients who experience severe "flare ups" of pain after mowing the lawn may need to limit such activities. It is important to encourage individuals who tend to overexert themselves and experience worsening pain to pace themselves. At the same time, it is important for individuals with pain not to avoid all activities with the potential to induce pain; avoidance of all activities may result in dysfunction and disability.

Emotional/Affective Component

A patient's personality and coping style influences the interpretation of, and response to, pain. Strong negative affect (depression, anxiety, or irritability/anger) tends to increase pain complaints. As a result, patients with a strong emotional component to pain may be viewed as difficult to manage, weak, or crazy. Additionally, some pain syndromes are predominantly psychological in nature, even though they are described in physical terms. Patients with this type of presentation (e.g., patients with somatoform pain disorder) dismiss psychological interpretations and resist evaluation and/or treatment by mental health treatment providers. Such patients can be difficult to treat, and conventional pain management methods may prove insufficient.

It is important to recognize the contribution of emotions to pain. Emotions can play a role in the provocation, exacerbation, and maintenance of chronic pain syndromes. Pain generally is not physical or psychological, but rather some unique contribution of the two components. Unfortunately, the myth that pain is either real (i.e., physical) or not real (i.e., psychological) persists, despite the definitions proposed by the IASP and pain clinicians' experiences in treating patients.

Personality Style. Personality is the characteristic way that someone behaves in relation to others and the world. One's personality "style" may be either adaptive or nonadaptive. However, when certain personality traits become extreme (i.e., characteristics of personality disorders), they can complicate pain management efforts. For instance, patients who are histrionic may demand excessive attention and exaggerate their pain symptoms in order to remain the center of attention. In a busy pain treatment practice, these patients are difficult to tolerate and may frustrate the staff.

Emotional Distress. Patients with significant pain complaints often experience emotional distress that ranges from mild to severe. Symptoms of depression, anxiety, and irritability are especially common. Patients also may experience low self-esteem, guilt, and shame. Because of shifting responsibilities/roles in the family that may occur when someone becomes disabled, family and marital conflicts also can arise. Patients may feel diminished or dependent and may experience fear of abandonment and/or lack of social support. Comprehensive pain management programs frequently work with a psychologist, who may conduct formal evaluations in order to determine how patients are coping with pain. There are a number of standardized instruments that may be used to assess psychological functioning, distress, and patients' concerns about pain: (1) West-Haven Yale Multidimensional Pain Inventory (Kerns, Turk, & Rudy, 1985); (2) Millon Behavioral Medicine Diagnostic (Millon, Antoni, Millon, Meagher, & Grossman, 2001); (3) Minnesota Multiphasic Personality Inventory (Hathaway & McKinley, 1943); and (4) SCL-90 or Brief Symptom Inventory (Derogatis & Melisaratos, 1983).

Psychiatric Comorbidity. Patients with pain may tell clinicians that their doctor, family, or friends do not believe that their pain is "real" (i.e., their pain symptoms are attributed to psychological problems rather than to a physical condition). In fact, the interplay between somatic pain and psychologically induced pain is complex. Pain often has a strong emotional component; comorbid psychiatric disorders, including depression, anxiety, sleep disorders, and sexual disorders, and psychological factors that affect patients' physical condition are commonly seen in the pain population. There are several psychiatric disorders for which pain is a primary symptom in the absence of an identifiable pain generator. These "somatoform" disorders include somatization disorder (Table 16-1A), hypochondriasis (Table 16-1B on page 16-10), and pain disorder (Table 16-1C on page 16-12).

The Structured Clinical Interview for DSM-IV-TR Axis I Disorders (SCID-I; First, Spitzer, Gibbon, & Williams, 2002) is a semistructured interview that offers guidance in asking about symptoms of various psychiatric disorders, including somatization disorder, hypochondriasis, and pain disorder, and in determining if *Diagnostic and Statistical Manual of Mental Disorders*, 4th edition, text revision (*DSM-IV-TR;* American Psychiatric Association, 2000) criteria for the disorders have been met. Experience using the SCID-I will improve clinicians' ability to elicit a psychiatric history. Although the SCID-I typically is used in research studies, treatment providers are encouraged to use it in clinical practice (see Tables 16-1A, 16-1B, and 16-1C for examples of questions from the SCID-I).

Somatization Disorder. Somatization disorder (see Table 16-1A) is characterized by multiple physical complaints that are sufficiently severe to cause impairment or lead the patient to seek treatment. A pattern of physical complaints must be present before age 30 and for several years (Criterion A). The following criteria also must be met: (1) four pain symptoms, (2) two GI symptoms, (3) one sexual symptom, and (4) one pseudoneurological symptom (Criterion B). Complaints cannot be accounted for by a general medical condition or the direct effects of a substance; if symptoms occur along with a general medical condition, the symptoms must be in excess of the symptoms that are expected (Criterion C). Finally, the symptoms must not be intentionally produced or feigned (Criterion D).

Hypochondriasis. Hypochondriasis (see Table 16-1B) is characterized by fear of having a serious disease (or the belief that one already has a serious disease) based on misinterpretation of body sensations (Criterion A). Doctors are unable to find a medical condition that explains the fear/belief; symptoms persist despite reassurance (Criterion B). The fear/belief is neither delusional, nor is it limited to concern about appearance as in Body Dysmorphic Disorder (Criterion C). The preoccupation with symptoms causes distress and/or impairs functioning (Criterion D), lasts at least six months (Criterion E), and is not better explained by another mental disorder (Criterion F).

Table 16-1A
DSM-IV Criteria for Somatization Disorder

Symptoms	DSM-IV Criteria[a, b]	SCID-I Questions to Aid Diagnosis[d, e]
Core Symptom	A. A history of many physical complaints beginning before age 30 years that occur over a period of several years and result in treatment being sought or significant impairment in social, occupational, or other important areas of functioning.	Have you been sick a lot over the years? ... How old were you when you first started to have a lot of physical problems or illnesses?
Associated Symptoms	B. Each of the following criteria must have been met, with individual symptoms occurring at any time during the course of the disturbance:	
	(1) four pain symptoms: a history of pain related to at least four different sites or functions (e.g., head, abdomen, back, joints, extremities, chest, rectum, during menstruation, during sexual intercourse, or during urination)	Have you ever had .... a lot of trouble with headaches? ... a lot of trouble with abdominal or stomach pain? ... a lot of trouble with back pain? ... pain in your joints? ... pain in your arms or legs other than in the joints? ... chest pain? ... pain in your rectum? FOR WOMEN: Other than during your first year of menstruation, have you had very painful periods? ... Has having sex often been physically painful for you? Have you ever had pain during urination? [Have you ever had] pain anywhere else?
	(2) two gastrointestinal symptoms: a history of at least two gastrointestinal symptoms other than pain (e.g., nausea, bloating, vomiting other than during pregnancy, diarrhea, or intolerance of several different foods)	Have you had a lot of trouble with ... ... nausea? ... excessive gas or bloating of your stomach or abdomen? ... vomiting (when you weren't pregnant)? ... loose bowels or diarrhea? Have there been any foods that you couldn't eat because they made you sick? What are they?
	(3) one sexual symptom: a history of at least one sexual or reproductive symptom other than pain (e.g., sexual indifference, erectile or ejaculatory dysfunction, irregular menses, excessive menstrual bleeding, vomiting throughout pregnancy)	Would you say that your sex life has been important to you or could you have gotten along as well without it? FOR MEN: Have you often had any sexual problem, like not being able to get an erection? FOR WOMEN: Other than during your first year of menstruation (or during menopause), have you had irregular periods? ... What about an unusual amount of bleeding during your periods? ... Did you vomit throughout any pregnancy?

(Continued)

Symptoms	DSM-IV Criteria[a, b]	SCID-I Questions to Aid Diagnosis[d, e]
	(4) one pseudoneurological symptom: a history of at least one symptom or deficit suggesting a neurological condition not limited to pain (conversion symptoms such as impaired coordination or balance, paralysis or localized weakness, difficulty swallowing or lump in throat, aphonia, urinary retention, hallucinations, loss of touch or pain sensation, double vision, blindness, deafness, seizures, dissociative symptoms such as amnesia; or loss of consciousness other than fainting).	Have you ever… … had trouble walking? … been paralyzed or had periods of weakness when you couldn't lift or move things that you could normally? … had trouble swallowing or felt a "lump" in your throat? … lost your voice for more than a few minutes? … been completely unable to urinate for a whole day (other than after childbirth or surgery)? … felt numbness or "pins and needles" in parts of your body? … had double vision? … had "visions" or seen things that weren't really there? … been completely blind for more than a few seconds? … been completely deaf for more than a few seconds? … had a seizure or convulsion? … had a period of amnesia? … had a time when you "blacked out"?
Other Criteria	C. Either (1) or (2):	
	(1) after appropriate investigation, each of the symptoms in Criterion B cannot be fully explained by a known general medical condition or the direct effects of a substance (e.g., a drug of abuse, a medication)	Did you see a doctor about [symptom]? What was the diagnosis? … Was anything abnormal found on tests or x-rays? … Were you taking any medication, drugs, or alcohol around the time you were having [symptom]?
	(2) when there is a related general medical condition, the physical complaints or resulting social or occupational impairment are in excess of what would be expected from the history, physical examination, or laboratory findings	Did [symptom] interfere with your life a lot? Did [symptom] make it hard for you to do your work or be with friends?
	D. The symptoms are not intentionally produced or feigned (as in factitious disorder or malingering).[c]	

[a] American Psychiatric Association (1994).
[b] Reprinted with permission from the *Diagnostic and Statistical Manual of Mental Disorders*, Fourth Edition (Copyright 1994). American Psychiatric Association.
[c] Consult *DSM-IV* criteria (American Psychiatric Association, 1994) for factitious disorder and malingering.
[d] First et al. (2002).
[e] Reprinted with permission.

Table 16-1B
DSM-IV Criteria for Hypochondriasis

Symptoms	DSM-IV Criteria[a, b]	SCID-I Questions to Aid Diagnosis[d, e]
Core Symptom	A. Preoccupation with fears of having, or the idea that one has, a serious disease based on the person's misinterpretation of bodily symptoms.	Do you worry a lot that you have a serious disease that the doctors have not been able to diagnose? What makes you think so? What do you think you have?
Other Criteria	B. The preoccupation persists despite appropriate medical evaluation and reassurance.	What have your doctors told you?
	C. The belief in Criterion A is not of delusional intensity (as in delusional disorder, somatic type) and is not restricted to a circumscribed concern about appearance (as in body dysmorphic disorder).[c]	
	D. The preoccupation causes clinically significant distress or impairment in social, occupational, or other important areas of functioning.	How much have [symptoms] interfered with your life? Has it made it hard for you to do your work or be with friends?
	E. The duration of the disturbance is at least 6 months.	When did all this begin?
	F. The preoccupation is not better accounted for by generalized anxiety disorder, obsessive-compulsive disorder, panic disorder, a major depressive episode, separation anxiety, or another somatoform disorder.[d]	

(a) American Psychiatric Association (1994).
(b) Reprinted with permission from the *Diagnostic and Statistical Manual of Mental Disorders*, Fourth Edition (Copyright 1994). American Psychiatric Association.
(c) Consult *DSM-IV* criteria (American Psychiatric Association, 1994) for delusional disorder and body dysmorphic disorder.
(d) Consult *DSM-IV* criteria (American Psychiatric Association, 1994) for generalized anxiety disorder, obsessive-compulsive disorder, panic disorder, major depressive episode, separation anxiety, and somatoform disorders.
(e) First et al. (2002).
(f) Reprinted with permission.

The range of complaints is quite broad, including vague symptoms and minor abnormalities. The symptoms are attributed to the imagined disease, and the person is very concerned about their cause, meaning, and authenticity. The complaints may involve multiple body systems; alternatively, they may be limited to a single system or organ. Repeated medical examinations and tests are insufficient to quell the patient's anxiety.

Pain Disorder. The most prominent feature of pain disorder (see Table 16-1C) is pain that is severe enough to warrant medical attention (Criterion A) and causes emotional distress and functional impairment (Criterion B). Psychological factors are judged to play a significant role in the onset, exacerbation, severity, and maintenance of pain (Criterion C), either alone or in combination with physical factors. The pain is neither intentionally produced (as in factitious disorder) nor feigned (as in malingering) in order to assume the sick role or for purposes of secondary gain. Pain disorder is not diagnosed if symptoms can be accounted for by another mental disorder such as depression (Criterion E). There are several subtypes of pain disorder that reflect the duration of pain and extent to which symptoms are accounted for by psychological factors. The *DSM-IV-TR* diagnosis of pain disorder associated with a general medical condition is not considered a mental disorder since psychological factors (if present) do not play a major role in onset, exacerbation, or maintenance of pain. In contrast, the *DSM-IV-TR* diagnosis of pain associated with psychological factors and a general medical condition requires the presence of psychological factors and a general medical condition. Finally, the *DSM-IV-TR* diagnosis of pain disorder associated with psychological factors requires the presence of psychological factors that play a major role in the development of the disorder. Patients with pain disorder commonly experience, in addition to symptoms that are specific to the pain site, negative/distorted cognitions, inactivity, increased pain requiring intervention, insomnia/fatigue, depression/anxiety, and impaired interpersonal relations.

Cognitive Component

The cognitive component of pain, which includes patients' beliefs and perceptions about pain, perceived ability ot control it, and ability to overcome it, is frequently overlooked (and/or trivialized). Patients who believe that they are helpless, that they have no control over their situation, and that their condition will not improve are less likely to put effort into rehabilitation and are more likely to give up in comparison to patients who believe that their situation can and will improve. Some patients with pain develop a somatic preoccupation (i.e., excessive attention to bodily discomfort and sensations), which can lead to heightened sensitivity and attention to small, often insignificant, bodily sensations. For instance, patients with strong disease convictions (e.g., "I must have cancer") often continue to display symptoms of the disease even after their functional and emotional status and pain behavior have improved. Clinicians can address the cognitive component of pain through the use of cognitive restructuring, such as Cognitive Behavioral Therapy (CBT).

Behavioral Component

"Pain behavior" consists of signals that alert an observer that an individual is experiencing pain (e.g., audible complaints of pain), use of supportive devices (e.g., canes, braces, wheelchair), use of medication despite lack of efficacy, shifting position, moaning/groaning, wincing, and limping. Patients with pain often will resist functional

Table 16-1C
DSM-IV Criteria for Pain Disorder

Symptoms	DSM-IV Criteria[a, b]	SCID-I Questions to Aid Diagnosis[e, f]
Core Symptom	A. Pain in one or more anatomical sites is the predominant focus of the clinical presentation and is of sufficient severity to warrant clinical attention.	Have you been to see a doctor because of physical pain?
Other Criteria	B. The pain causes clinically significant distress or impairment in social, occupational, or other important areas of functioning.	How much does the pain interfere with your life? Has it made it hard to do your work or be with friends?
	C. Psychological factors are judged to have an important role in onset, severity, exacerbation, or maintenance of the pain.[c]	What was going on in your life when this pain began? Have the doctors told you that your pain is more than you should be having?
	D. The symptom or deficit is not intentionally produced or feigned (as in factitious disorder or malingering).[c]	
	E. The pain is not better accounted for by a mood, anxiety, or psychotic disorder and does not meet criteria for dyspareunia.[d]	

(a) American Psychiatric Association (1994).
(b) Reprinted with permission from the *Diagnostic and Statistical Manual of Mental Disorders*, Fourth Edition (Copyright 1994). American Psychiatric Association.
(c) Consult *DSM-IV* criteria (American Psychiatric Association, 1994) for factitious disorder and malingering.
(d) Consult *DSM-IV* criteria (American Psychiatric Association, 1994) for mood disorders, anxiety disorders, psychotic disorders, and dyspareunia.
(e) First et al. (2002).
(f) Reprinted with permission.

improvements (e.g., walking) because they fear that increased activity will make the pain worse. However, continued poor functioning leads to increased disability. Some patients engage in pain behavior for secondary gain. For example, when someone is disabled, family members may assume his/her responsibilities or treat him/her in a more caring way. Disability benefits (e.g., Social Security Disability Insurance (SSDI), Workers' Compensation) can be powerful incentives that inadvertently act to maintain dysfunctional behavior. Patients who receive disability benefits for long periods of time are less likely to return to work.

Pain behavior is assessed via direct observation. Clinicians should observe patients' aberrant behavior when patients are unaware that they are being watched in order to determine if patients continue to display these behaviors. Clinicians may also instruct patients to maintain a pain diary. Pain diaries require patients to keep track of their daily activities, rate the severity of their pain while engaging in various tasks, and record use of pain medication (to allow clinicians to determine patterns of medication use). Self-monitoring allows patients to become more aware of their behavioral patterns and can be a useful treatment strategy, even in the absence of a more formal behavioral treatment program. Awareness of medication-taking behavior can influence medication taking, just as calorie counting influences eating behavior.

Patients with pain can consume a large amount of medical resources (e.g., frequent emergency room visits, expensive laboratory tests, multiple surgeries, specialized treatments). For instance, it is not uncommon for someone with back pain to undergo multiple surgical procedures, often with increasingly negative results (referred to as "failed back surgery syndrome"). One goal of pain management is to help contain costs associated with unnecessary medical procedures.

CHRONIC PAIN SYNDROME

Chronic Pain Syndrome (CPS) is a severe variant of chronic pain that is characterized by a constellation of significant physical, emotional, cognitive, and behavioral symptoms (see "Four Components of Pain"). CPS is difficult to treat and requires management with a multidisciplinary approach (i.e., with medical, rehabilitation, mental health, and addiction experts). According to both the Commission on the Evaluation of Pain (1986) and Commission on Accreditation of Rehabilitation Facilities (1984-1995), for patients to be diagnosed with CPS, their symptoms must meet three of the following criteria (one of which must be the first criterion): (1) report persistent pain (at least three months), which may be consistent with, or out of proportion to, physical findings; (2) demonstrate progressive deterioration in ability to function at home, socially, and at work; (3) show a progressive increase in requests for, and usage of, medications and invasive medical procedures; (4) demonstrate mood disturbance; and (5) exhibit significant anger and hostility. Because of their complex symptom picture, patients with CPS, especially patients with comorbid addictive disease, often represent treatment failures.

PAIN AND SUBSTANCE ABUSE: ISSUES IN EVALUATION AND TREATMENT

Substance abuse and dependence can complicate the evaluation and treatment of pain. Drugs of abuse may interact with other medications that are prescribed to treat pain and its sequellae. Medication that is prescribed to treat pain may be abused. The following section discusses ways in which substance abuse may be manifested by patients with pain and the implications for evaluation and treatment.

Overuse

Overuse occurs when patients take more pain medication than prescribed by their treating physician (i.e., take larger amounts of a drug at one time and/or take the drug more frequently than prescribed). Patients who take more medication than prescribed will run out of pain mecication before they can refill the prescription and may have insufficient medication to control pain. In patients with opioid tolerance, abrupt cessation will lead to increased pain and may also produce a characteristic opioid withdrawal syndrome that is identical to the syndrome seen among users of illicit opioids like heroin and will likely prompt drug-seeking behavior.

Drug Seeking

Drug seeking occurs when patients with pain are chronically undertreated (not receiving adequate medication to treat pain), as well as when they run out of opioid medication as a result of overuse. Drug-seeking behaviors include: (1) increased demands for more medication, (2) "doctor shopping" to obtain multiple prescriptions, (3) attempts to get the pharmacist to refill prescriptions early, (4) visits to the emergency room to obtain opioids, (5) requests to borrow medications from others, (6) purchase of supplemental prescription medications on the street, and (7) illicit drug use (e.g., heroin).

Use for Wrong Reasons

Although opioid analgesics are prescribed to treat pain, some patients use them for other reasons, including sleep problems and anxiety. Some patients with both pain and addiction problems may use prescribed analgesics to get "high."

Concurrent Abuse of Nonopioid Substances

Some patients with pain abuse other drugs such as alcohol, cannabis, and benzodiazepines. Although the use of cocaine or other stimulants may exacerbate pain when they are used alone, their use in combination with opioids may increase analgesia while decreasing the sedating effects of opioids. In fact, adding stimulants to opioids in certain situations is an accepted, well-studied approach. Other drugs, when taken in combination with opioids, increase the intoxicating and analgesic effects. Patients' practice of polypharmacy can be problematic and can make it difficult to determine the efficacy of the therapeutic agent (i.e., the prescribed opioid). Patients who supplement their prescribed opioid with illicit or prescribed opioids from other sources are at risk of overdose. Furthermore, the combination of mixed agonist-antagonist drugs or partial agonists (buprenorphine) and full agonist drugs (e.g., morphine) may precipitate opioid withdrawal symptoms. Providers who maintain patients on opioids for pain are advised to conduct periodic drug screens to determine whether the patient is using other substances that could interfere with the treatment regimen.

The use of cannabis by patients with pain raises additional issues. Some patients report that marijuana has analgesic properties when used in combination with opioids;

in fact, the animal literature (Welch & Stevens, 992) supports these patients' claims. Limited research has been conducted in humans, and findings have been inconsistent (Campbell et al., 2001). More studies are needed to determine whether cannabis is a feasible adjunct treatment for pain management.

A history of nonopioid substance abuse may indicate a worse prognosis. In a recent study of a treatment protocol designed to address pain and concurrent opioid analgesic abuse, a lifetime history of nonopioid substance use disorders was associated with poorer outcome in terms of pain, adherence to opioid regimen, other substance use, and psychosocial functioning (Bethea, Acosta, & Haller, 2008).

Reactivated or New Onset Drug Use Disorders

While a few patients may develop new onset (i.e., iatrogenic) drug use disorders secondary to opioid therapy, development of these disorders is rare in patients without a history of substance abuse (Portenoy & Foley, 1986). Clinicians should be concerned about reactivating addiction problems in patients with a past history of substance abuse. It is not advisable for pain providers to undertake opioid maintenance therapy in patients with remitted or partially remitted opioid use disorder before obtaining training in addiction medicine and/or the assistance of a substance abuse treatment program or professional. Physicians who treat opioid abusers with pain will need to modify their office procedures to include safeguards such as more frequent office visits, urine drug screens, and medication contracts (Weaver & Schnoll, 2002).

Diversion

While established drug abusers occasionally infiltrate pain treatment programs in order to procure drugs to use or sell for nontherapeutic reasons (i.e., to divert or abuse), these patients' schemes usually are discovered quickly, particularly in the absence of a legitimate pain complaint.

Similarly, while it is possible for drugs that are obtained from legitimate sources (i.e., doctors and clinics) for legitimate pain problems to end up on the street, patients with valid pain complaints are unlikely to share prescribed analgesics. Rather, they tend to hoard any medications that they do not use.

Undertreatment and "Pseudo-Addiction"

Undertreatment occurs when a patient is given insufficient medication to treat his/her pain and results in suffering. While some patients who are undertreated suffer in silence, other patients engage in drug-seeking behavior in an attempt to obtain more medication. This behavior frequently is interpreted as a sign of addiction. Pseudo-addiction is a term used to describe behaviors that occur when a patient's pain is undertreated and that resemble the behaviors of drug addicts.

Clinicians may distinguish pseudo-addiction from addiction by providing an adequate dose of opioid medication: symptoms should resolve in a nondrug abuser. Unfortunately, many providers fail to take this step, since it seems counterintuitive to give more drugs to a patient who may be an addict. Instead, they may do the opposite— withhold medication, withdraw the patient from opioids for noncompliance, and/or terminate treatment. Any of these steps may cause a therapeutic rupture; the patient will feel that he/she has been treated like an addict, and the provider will feel manipulated and duped. Once the patient has been labeled a "drug seeker," this label may prevent the patient from obtaining appropriate treatment, even in the absence of an addiction problem.

Reasons That Doctors Undertreat Pain

There are a number of reasons why doctors undertreat pain. Many doctors lack knowledge of modern pain treatment techniques and strategies or have a poor understanding of chronic disease management. Some treatment providers feel that it is inappropriate to prescribe potent medications. Doctors also are concerned that, in the absence of clear physical findings, patients who are maintained on opioid analgesics may develop tolerance, hyperalgesia, dependence, or addiction, may divert drugs or relapse, or may overdose on medication (American Society of Anesthesiologists Task Force on Pain Management, 1997). Unfortunately, doctors often confuse tolerance, physical dependence, and addiction. The following myths influence prescribing practices.

Myth #1: Tolerance Leads to Continual Increases in Doses. When patients begin opioid therapy for pain, the treatment provider "titrates" (adjusts) the dose based on feedback from the patient on how well the medication is working (without side effects) and how much functioning has improved. It is not uncommon for doctors to more than double the starting dose before the patient reports receiving adequate relief. While doctors often express concern about the size of the dose, the size of the does is not as important as the effects of the dose. Once the patient has "stabilized," the doctor likely will not need to raise the dose. It is possible that the doctor will need to adjust the dose if the patient's disease progresses or if other medications added to the patient's regimen render the pain medication less effective (e.g., initiation of antiretroviral therapy for human immunodeficiency virus (HIV)). The dose of opioid medication that is needed to treat pain may be much higher than the amount that is needed to address addiction. The dose needed for effective treatment of pain varies by individual and is not an indication of severity of addiction.

Myth #2: Tolerance Is Synonymous With Addiction. Treatment providers may confuse tolerance and addiction. Tolerance occurs as cells adapt to the presence of a drug. When a patient becomes tolerant to a medication, more of a drug is needed to achieve the same effect that previously was obtained at a lower dose. Tolerance is common among patients maintained on opioids to treat pain. As tolerance develops, the amount of opioid needed to relieve pain increases. Addiction is a behavioral disorder characterized by loss of control over drug use and craving (among other criteria). Although tolerance is not necessary for a diagnosis of addiction to be made, most opioid abusers will display tolerance. However, the majority of pain patients who are maintained on opioids and who are tolerant do not have an addiction.

Myth #3: Physical Dependence Is Synonymous With Addiction. Physical dependence is a physiological phenomenon that occurs as cells adapt to the presence of a drug such that, when the drug is abruptly taken away, a characteristic drug-class-specific withdrawal syndrome occurs. When opioid-dependent patients stop taking opioids, they experience a flu-like syndrome that is uncomfortable but not fatal.

Physical dependence is one of the criteria considered when making a diagnosis of addiction; however, by itself, it is insufficient to make this diagnosis.

Common Prescribing Practices That May Interfere With Effective Management of Pain

Many treatment providers have difficulty addressing the psychological, cognitive, and behavioral aspects of pain. They are overly concerned about being manipulated by their patients and/or monitored by state regulatory boards. Some treatment providers hold cultural values/beliefs about opioids that influence their prescribing patterns. For instance, they may believe that opioids are inherently bad or that their use is a sign of personal weakness. Providers may engage in the following prescribing practices that, unfortunately, may cause increased drug-seeking behavior in their patients.

Using Short-Acting Analgesic Medications. Since short-acting medications have a more rapid onset and offset than long-acting drugs, they are more likely to produce euphoria that is reinforcing and may lead to increased self-administration to "get high." Short-acting opioid analgesics may cause "mini-withdrawals" that also encourage increased self-administration. Thus, longer-acting opioid analgesics such as MS Contin (morphine), Oxycontin (oxycodone), Duragesic Patch (fentanyl), and methadone are preferable when treating substance abusers with chronic pain with or without a co-occurring addictive disorder. Treatment providers should carefully monitor use of long-acting analgesics by patients with substance use disorders, in order to prevent these patients from altering the delivery matrix of the medication to take a large dose of medication all at once (methadone does not have this problem).

Using *Pro Re Nata* (as Needed) Analgesic Medication. Some clinicians believe that patients will use less medication if they take it only when their pain is severe. In fact, they may use more medication, since it is more difficult to treat pain when it is severe. It is preferable to maintain patients with chronic pain on scheduled medications that are taken "round the clock" (regardless of pain level) in order to maintain pain at a more tolerable level. However, clinicians should provide patients with "breakthrough" (as needed) medication for times when patients cannot control the pain with the scheduled dose.

Giving Pain Medication at Longest Possible Interval to Prevent Addiction. When medication dosing intervals are spaced too far apart, patients experience increased pain and may engage in drug-seeking behavior in order to address this problem. This drug-seeking behavior is exhibited by both substance abusers and nonabusers.

Patients with opioid use disorders who are maintained on methadone or buprenorphine for addiction are more likely to be undertreated than other patients with pain for three reasons. First, treatment providers may not consider the patient's level of opioid tolerance when they establish the dosage of pain medication. Second, the treatment provider may falsely assume that the patient's medication for addiction will also cover pain. Third, the treatment provider may be reticent to provide a known drug abuser with medications that can be abused and may cite concerns about possible overdose, diversion, or other illegal activity. Undertreatment of pain in opioid-dependent individuals may lead to increased drug-seeking behavior (as patients search for medication to control pain) and may result in relapse (Savage et al., 2001).

TREATMENT FOR PAIN

Pain treatments fall into three categories: (1) somatic/physical, (2) pharmacological, and (3) psychosocial. The type of intervention that is provided may vary based on where the patient seeks treatment and the provider's area of expertise. For instance, when a patient with back pain consults an orthopedic surgeon or neurosurgeon, it is likely that surgery will be recommended; an anesthesiologist might suggest nerve blocks and analgesic medication. In other instances, a more conservative approach (e.g., physical therapy and psychological counseling) might be recommended. Psychiatrists, psychologists, and other mental health professionals, who may be the "point of entry" for pain treatment, should refer the patient for a diagnostic workup that assesses physical causes of pain and determines what (if any) treatments might be appropriate. It is inappropriate for a psychiatrist to start a patient with pain on opioids without a full understanding of the problem. Treatment providers who are initiating "first line" treatment should choose the least invasive interventions (e.g., physical therapy) and should recommend more invasive procedures (e.g., surgery) only after less invasive interventions have failed. Exceptions to this approach include patients whose functioning is severely compromised (e.g., paralysis, lack of bladder control). Patients with chronic pain often seek cure-all treatments and often opt for invasive procedures over other interventions that take longer, require a greater commitment, or are perceived as having less dramatic outcomes. Patients' optimism for finding a cure-all treatment for chronic pain frequently persists for a year or more following diagnosis of pain before patients begin to adjust to having a chronic disorder. Clinicians can help patients to adjust to living with chronic pain by providing them with information on pain and treatment options.

Table 16-2 lists common interventions for pain. Patients often receive multiple types of treatment, either sequentially or concurrently. Some interventions (e.g., physical therapy, surgery) may be repeated multiple times, despite lack of a therapeutic response. Outcomes associated with each intervention can vary according to patients' emotional, cognitive, and behavioral nature. No single intervention is appropriate or effective 100 percent of the time for any given pain problem or patient. Rather, treatment often is initiated on a "trial and error" basis. This strategy can be frustrating for patients, who continue to suffer and lose hope of experiencing relief from pain.

Pharmacotherapy

Individuals with pain use many medications that can be abused, including opioids (pain medication), anxiolytics (benzodiazepines), hypnotics (sleeping pills), cannabis, stimulants, and alcohol. Approximately 45 percent of patients in a large pain management program used one to three of these medications, 21 percent used four to six of these medications, and 29 percent used seven or more of these medications (Deardorff, Rubin, & Scott, 1991). Unfortunately, these rates were based on self-report and thus may be underestimates of actual medication use (Katon, Egan, & Miller, 1985; Ready, Sarkis, & Turner, 1982). Haller, Ingersoll, Dawson, Poklis, and Rafii (1994) investigated the prevalence of prescription, over-the-counter, and illicit drug use among 291 consecutive admissions to a multidisciplinary pain program using both self-report and urine toxicology (UT). Seventeen percent of patients denied taking any medications for pain, while 49 percent reported taking opioids, 32 percent reported taking nonsteroidal antiinflammatory drugs (NSAIDS), 22 percent

Table 16-2
Interventions for Pain

Intervention	Symptoms Targeted	Treatment Provider
physical therapy, massage therapy, aquatherapy	muscular pain, joint pain	physical therapist
surgery (including placement of hardware, stimulators, and pumps to deliver medications)	orthopedic pain, nerve pain	surgeon (orthopedist, neurosurgeon, anesthesiologist)
nerve blocks, trigger point injections, acupuncture	localized pain syndromes	anesthesiologist or other pain specialist
medications	pain and sequallae	physician, physician assistant, nurse practitioner
counseling, biofeedback, hypnosis	emotional distress	psychologist, psychiatrist, social worker

reported taking tricyclic antidepressants (TCAs), 19 percent reported taking benzo-diazepines, 11 percent reported taking muscle relaxants, 6 percent reported taking anticonvulsants, 5 percent reported taking barbiturates, and 20 percent reported taking over-the-counter analgesics. UT revealed that 32 percent of patients had recently used one or more prescription drugs with abuse liability (24 percent used opioids, 16 percent used benzodiazepines, 5 percent used barbiturates); additionally, 15 percent of patients had used illicit drugs (14 percent used marijuana, 4 percent used cocaine). The investigators examined drug use patterns to determine the odds that patients were recreational or prescription drug users based on selected demographic characteristics. The percentage of "drug-free" patients was stable across gender, age, and ethnic groups; half of the sample used no addictive drugs. Interestingly, patients with active law suits that were related to injuries and/or treatment were five times less likely to use medications with abuse potential. Additionally, younger patients, male patients, patients who smoked, and unmarried patients were more likely to use illicit drugs. These data indicate that a substantial proportion of patients with chronic pain use medications with abuse potential while a minority of patients use illicit drugs that they do not report.

While patients with pain problems usually request treatment from their primary care physician, most family doctors have minimal training in pain management, particularly management of chronic pain. Since primary care physicians may have little or no access to nonpharmacological treatment modalities for pain (see Table 16-2), and since patients often demand immediate relief from pain with medication, most primary care physicians use pharmacotherapy for pain management. A variety of medications in different drug classes are used to treat pain and sequallae. Table 16-3 provides a list of commonly prescribed medications and includes symptoms targeted by each class of medication.

The use of opioid analgesics to treat pain remains controversial, especially in treatment of noncancer pain. At the same time, opioid therapy is a common intervention that is used by many medical specialties to treat pain. Writing a prescription is easy. Patients may request (or demand) opioids to obtain immediate relief. Some physicians believe that opioids should be provided when they show efficacy or after other treatments have failed; other treatment providers claim that opioid maintenance increases dysfunction and should not be prescribed except for brief "flare ups."

When a treatment provider decides to begin opioid therapy, he/she may choose from a variety of drugs. Patients with acute or intermittent pain may be prescribed short-acting opioids such as Vicodin (hydrocodone) or Percocet (oxycodone); patients with chronic pain may be prescribed longer-acting opioids such as MS Contin (morphone), Oxycontin (oxycodone), Duagesic Patch (fentanyl), or methadone. Longer-acting medication allows patients to obtain relief for an extended period of time with one dose of medication, thereby preventing patients from "clock watching" (a common phenomenon in patients who take short-acting opioids for pain, which often wear off before the next dose can be taken). In comparison to short-acting opioids, longer-acting opioids produce less euphoria ("high" feeling) because their onset and offset of action is less rapid. Although the pharmacokinetic properties of longer-acting opioids should make them less attractive to individuals who are seeking a "high" feeling, drug abusers often alter longer-acting opioids in order to make them more like immediate-release drugs. For example, they may extract the fentanyl from Duragesic Patches and then inject it or crush an Oxycontin tablet in order to snort it. While individuals who use these drug-taking methods are usually drug abusers seeking a "high" (not patients with pain problems), this small number of drug abusers discourages doctors from prescribing opioids at adequate doses to patients with legitimate pain complaints.

Prescribing Practices for Patients With Opioid Dependence and Pain. Patients who have pain and an opioid use disorder may be at increased risk for misusing pain medication. However, experts in pain medicine and addiction medicine concur that these patients can be successfully maintained on prescribed opioids for pain as long as the provider adheres to certain safeguards (Weaver & Schnoll, 2002). When treating patients with pain and opioid use disorder, treatment providers should make the following modifications to office procedures:

1. See patients more frequently;

2. Write prescriptions for smaller amounts of medication;

3. Ask patients to sign an opioid "contract" that describes expectations of the patient in treatment and the procedure for addressing violations of treatment guidelines;

4. Educate patients about use of opioids;

5. Conduct surveillance (e.g., UT) to determine if patients are using other substances, including nonprescribed opioids;

6. Require patients to enroll in substance abuse treatment concurrent with treatment for pain;

7. Maintain contact with patients' family members and significant others, who may provide information about behaviors that patients do not report; and

8. Require patients to submit to unscheduled medication checks in order to determine if patients are taking medication as prescribed.

Table 16-3
Drugs Used in Treatment of Pain

Drug Class	Examples	Symptoms Targeted
nonsteroidal anti-inflammatory drugs (NSAIDS)	ibuprofen (Motrin), naproxen sodium (Aleve), celecoxib (Celebrex), ketorolac tromethamine (Torradlo), diclofenac sodium (Voltaren), rofecoxib (Vioxx), ketoprofen (Orudis), indomethacin (Indocin), naproxen sodium (Anaprox), sulindac (Clinoril), piroxicam (Feldene), etodolac (Lodine), aspirin	pain inflammation
anticonvulsants	gabapentin (Neurontin), carbamazepine (Tegretol), phenytoin (Dilantin), valproic acid (Depakote), topiramate (Topimax)	nerve pain
antidepressants	tricyclic antidepressants (TCAs) such as amitriptyline (Elavil) and imipramine (Tofranil); selective serotonin reuptake inhibitors (SSRIs) such as fluoxetine (Prozac), sertraline (Zoloft); other antidepressants such as venlafaxine (Effexor), bupropion (Wellbutrin)	pain sleep disturbance depression
sedative-hypnotics	diazepam (Valium), chlordiazepoxide (Librium), alprazolam (Xanax), zolpidem tartrate (Ambien), clonazepam (Klonopin), lorazepam (Ativan)	anxiety sleep disturbance
muscle relaxants	methocarbamol (Robaxin), diazepam (Valium), cyclobenzaprine (Flexeril), metaxalone (Skelaxin), carisoprodol (Soma)	spasms
opioids	propoxyphene (Darvon), acetaminophen plus codeine (Tylenol #3), oxycodone with acetaminophen (Percocet), meperidine (Demerol), hydromorphone hydrochloride (Dilaudid), hydrocodone bitartrate and acetaminophen (Vicodin), hydrocodone bitartrate plus acetaminophen (Lorcet), morphine immediate release (MS IR), morphine (MS Contin), oxycodone (Oxycontin); methadone, fentanyl transdermal (Duragesic Patch), buprenorphine (Buprenex)	pain
local anesthetics	lidocaine, novacaine	localized pain
capsaicin	capsaicin (Zacin Cream)	localized pain

Selecting Opioid Analgesics for Pain Treatment. Treatment providers should select with care an opioid for a patient with a history of substance abuse (particularly opioid abuse). Injectable drugs should not be used to treat patients with substance use disorders. Longer-acting opioids produce less euphoria and minimize drug self-administration (short-acting opioids are taken every few hours). When treatment providers decide to prescribe methadone for treatment of pain to patients receiving methadone for treatment of addiction, treatment providers may need to increase the dose of methadone. Methadone should be provided multiple (i.e., three to four) times per day to control pain, instead of once per day to control addiction (Gourlay, Cherry, & Cousins, 1986). Methadone does not have to be prescribed for pain to an opioid abuser in a licensed methadone maintenance program. Methadone that is used for pain treatment may be given via prescription to patients with pain, including patients who are opioid-dependent and who are maintained on methadone for treatment of addiction. Treatment providers who prescribe methadone for pain to opioid abusers outside a methadone maintenance treatment program should be knowledgeable about addiction medicine and should consult with a substance abuse treatment program or provider.

The efficacy of buprenorphine for concurrent treatment of pain and addiction is unknown. While buprenorphine is an effective treatment for opioid dependence, it may or may not be an effective analgesic. Because buprenorphine is a partial agonist, the antagonist effects of this drug at higher doses result in a "ceiling effect" that limits its usefulness in patients who may require more pain medication than equivalent to 80 mgs of methadone. Thus, patients who require much higher doses of analgesic medication may not receive adequate relief from buprenorphine, even after adjustment of the dosing schedule. Buprenorphine, which is relatively long acting, may be helpful to patients who do not need high doses of opioids to control pain. No special license other than Drug Enforcement Administration (DEA) registration is needed to prescribe buprenorphine or methadone for pain.

Table 16-4 provides a list of opioid analgesics routinely used to treat pain; the table includes generic (chemical) names, brand names, and information on duration of action, route of administration, relative potency, and detectability with routine opioid screening tests. This information may help clinicians to select the most appropriate analgesic for patients with pain and a substance use disorder. In general, it is preferable to prescribe a longer-acting medication that is taken orally for the treatment of chronic pain. Some opioid medications cannot be detected in urine using standard drug-testing strategies, thereby preventing treatment providers from determining if patients are taking the prescribed medication (or hoarding or diverting it). Use of certain nonprescribed substances could easily go undetected. Unfortunately, many of the most commonly prescribed synthetic opioid analgesics (including hyrocodone and oxycodone) are not detected with standard UT tests or are detected only at very high doses. Treatment providers should check with the laboratory running the tests in order to determine which substances can be detected and at what levels.

Behavioral Interventions

Role of Mental Health Professionals in Evaluation Process. Although pain, which is considered the "fifth vital sign," is evaluated during routine medical visits, the quality of pain assessments varies considerably, and there is no guarantee that appropriate treatment will be provided when a patient complains of pain. Pain is difficult to assess because it is a subjective experience. There are no tests for pain; instead clinicians assess the "unpleasantness" of pain. To fully evaluate a pain complaint, a clinician must conduct a comprehensive evaluation (i.e., a history and physical exam, laboratory testing, and a mental health/substance use evaluation), which is rarely completed outside

Table 16-4
Opioid Analgesics Used in Treatment of Pain

Generic Name	Brand Name	Duration of Action	Route of Administration	Equianalgesic Oral Dose	Detected via Routine Opioid Screens
morphine	MS IR MS Contin Kadian Avinza	3-4 hours 12 hours 24 hours 24 hours	IV, oral oral oral oral	30 mg	yes
oxycodone	Percocet Oxycontin	3-4 hours 8-12 hours	oral oral	20 mg	no
hydrocodone	Vicodin Lortab Lorcet	3-4 hours	oral	30 mg	no
codeine	Tylenol #3 and #4	3-4 hours	oral	130 mg	yes
fentanyl	Duragesic Sublimaze Actiq Fentora	72 hours 1-2 hours 1-2 hours 1-2 hours	transdermal IV transmucosal transmucosal	not available not available not available not available	no
methadone	Dolophine	6-8 hours	oral	20 mg	yes (separate assay)
hydromorphone	Dilaudid	3-4 hours	oral	7.5 mg	no
meperidine	Demerol	2-3 hours	oral	300 mg	no
propoxyphene	Darvon	3-4 hours	oral	not available	no
buprenorphine	Suboxone Subutex	6-8 hours	oral	not available	no
pentazocine	Talwin NX	3-4 hours	oral	150 mg	no
levorphanol	Levodromoran	6-8 hours	oral	4 mg	no

of multidisciplinary pain management programs. Usually, diagnosis and treatment of pain are addressed by a doctor who works out of his/her office and cares for the patient alone. Only patients who manifest severe pain behavior or psychological symptoms and/or who are abusing medications are referred to a mental health/substance abuse professional. Often pain patients who display psychological symptoms or behaviors indicative of substance abuse are discharged from care for being "noncompliant."

Given the prominence of emotional, cognitive, and behavioral symptoms in patients with pain, mental health and substance abuse professionals should be involved in diagnosis and treatment of patients with pain problems. A mental health evaluation may be needed when physical findings are insufficient to explain pain. A diagnosis of somatoform disorder or factitious disorder needs to be ruled out (or confirmed) before treatment proceeds. A psychosocial evaluation is needed when a patient displays significant emotional distress or psychopathology. For instance, patients with pain often experience depression, anxiety, sleep disturbances, and sexual dysfunctions (among other symptoms), and these conditions need to be considered when developing a treatment plan for pain. Input from a mental health professional should be sought when developing a treatment plan for patients with substance abuse problems. Although treatment providers are concerned about misuse of pain medication, the prevalence of opioid use disorders in the pain population is only 3 to 19 percent (Fishbain, Goldberg, Meagher, Steel, & Rosomoff, 1986); in contrast, between 20 to 40 percent of pain patients have alcohol-use disorders (Katon et al., 1985; Ready et al., 1982). Although illicit drug use (e.g., cocaine, cannabis) can have a negative impact on pain rehabilitation efforts, it is unclear what percentage of patients with pain are illicit drug users; approximately 15 percent are users of illegal drugs (Haller et al., 1994). Finally, a mental health evaluation may be required when a patient's functioning is poorer than expected based on physical findings alone. For example, patients with minor pain problems who are profoundly disabled require further assessment. Mental health and substance abuse professionals should be viewed as integral members of the pain management team. If routine psychosocial evaluation is not feasible, treatment providers in pain treatment services should identify consultants who can conduct psychiatric evaluations on an as-needed basis.

Role of Substance Abuse Treatment Clinician in Treatment of Patients With Pain and Substance Use Disorders. The Institute of Medicine (Rettig & Yarmolinsky, 1995) has recommended that patients with chronic pain should be treated in medical settings, and patients with opioid addiction should be treated in methadone maintenance treatment programs. Unfortunately, no suggestions were given for patients with both disorders. Patients with chronic pain and substance use disorders tend to be poorly managed. Pain patients who abuse prescribed analgesics may be denied access to opioids and/or may be terminated from treatment, since few pain treatment providers have the knowledge, interest, or energy to modify their clinical practices in order to accommodate substance abusers. Methadone treatment programs often do not offer services to evaluate and treat pain, even though failure to do so can result in increased drug-seeking behavior, unsanctioned opioid use, and relapse (Savage, 1996). Patients with pain and a substance use disorder who receive simultaneous care with multiple opioids from a pain treatment provider and a substance use treatment program may be engaged in prescription opioid abuse (Portenoy, 1990). At the same time, it is inappropriate to insist that patients with pain who do not have addictive disorders should receive treatment for pain from a methadone treatment program, since once daily dosing with methadone will not provide adequate analgesia. Successful simultaneous treatment of pain and addiction requires treatment providers to modify standard treatment procedures according to answers to the following questions: (1) What is the patient's primary problem? (2) What substances is the patient taking (e.g., prescribed medications, illicit drugs)? (3) What is the goal of treatment (abstinence versus maintenance)?

Treatment of Patients Who View Pain as Primary Problem. Patients who identify pain (not substance abuse) as their primary problem present differently to treatment and have different treatment needs than patients who identify substance abuse (not pain) as their primary problem. Pain patients view themselves as sick; they view use of medication as justifiable, and, in instances of addiction, they view their addiction problems as "iatrogenic" (i.e., side effect of pain treatment). These patients may or may not drink alcohol or use nonprescribed drugs. In comparison to other substance abusers, pain patients who misuse prescribed drugs tend to be older, more psycho-socially stable, and married, and fewer of these patients are in trouble with the law. When treating pain patients who abuse prescribed analgesics, substance abuse treatment counselors may need to modify the approach that they typically use to treat patients who abuse street drugs. For instance, if a substance abuse treatment counselor focuses on addiction to the exclusion of pain, is too confrontational, demands abstinence, or labels the patient as an addict, the substance abuse treatment counselor may damage the therapeutic alliance and discourage the patient from speaking openly about drug abuse. Instead, when a patient identifies pain (not substance abuse) as the primary problem, the counselor should recognize the difficulties that patients with chronic pain face, address medication misuse as a treatment adherence problem, and establish treatment goals that are consistent with the patient's medical status and treatment needs.

The treatment parameters of pain treatment programs are different from the treatment parameters of drug treatment programs, particularly methadone maintenance programs. Patients in pain management programs have different expectations about their care than patients in drug treatment programs. They are used to receiving large amounts of pain medications at one time (usually thirty days' worth or more) and usually come to the clinic once a month. Pain patients receive treatment for a legitimate medical problem, and treatment, including analgesic medications, is usually covered by insurance. They may or may not be asked to provide urine samples and/or sign a medication contract (strategies that drug treatment programs frequently implement in order to make discharge of "noncompliant" (i.e., drug seeking) patients easier). Psychosocial treatment is rarely required in order to participate in pain treatment programs. It is important that substance abuse treatment counselors establish good working relationships with the staff of pain treatment services that provide care for their patients in order to focus on consistency in treatment goals. For instance, if a pain treatment provider believes a patient must be maintained on opioids, then the substance abuse treatment counselor should not establish abstinence as the treatment goal. Two-way releases that allow open exchange of information (e.g., prescribed medications, results of urine drug screens) are essential to coordinate care.

Treatment of Patients Who View Addiction as Primary Problem. Some substance abusers have long-standing pain complaints that have never been diagnosed or treated, while other substance abusers with pain problems may have sought help for pain but were refused treatment (because of substance use). A substance abuse treatment counselor may be the first person to recognize problems with pain in a substance abuser.

Expression of empathy is important. Several studies have shown that pain problems are more prevalent among individuals in drug treatment than among the general population. Among 248 methadone maintenance patients in three Massachusetts clinics, 61 percent reported having moderate-severe chronic pain (Jamison, Kauffman, & Katz, 2000). Patients with pain had more health problems and psychiatric problems, used more prescribed and nonprescribed medication, and were more likely to express the belief that they were "undertreated." Nearly half of these patients (44 percent) expressed the belief that opioids that had been prescribed for pain had contributed to their addiction problems. These patients were less likely to be employed and more likely to receive disability benefits in comparison to patients without pain. These patients had been in methadone maintenance treatment longer (ninety-one months versus sixty-four months) and their daily dose was substantially higher (82 mgs versus 66 mgs), perhaps because methadone was being used (surreptitiously) to treat pain and addiction. Rosenblum et al. (2003) evaluated 390 methadone maintenance patients in two New York City clinics. Thirty-two percent reported chronic, severe pain; two thirds of these patients reported significant functional impairments. Age, chronic illness, lifetime psychiatric illness, current psychiatric distress, and time in treatment correlated with pain. Forty-seven percent of patients with moderate-severe pain had received prescriptions for opioids to treat pain during the preceding three months; the most frequently prescribed drugs were codeine, extra methadone, hydrocodone, and oxycodone. Findings from a study by Karasz et al. (2004) that employed qualitative research methods to describe the experiences of twelve methadone maintenance patients with chronic pain suggest that pain and associated dysfunction are prevalent in patients receiving methadone maintenance treatment and are underrecognized. The study identified several themes in participants' reports of their experiences, including relationships between pain and illicit drug use, social isolation, and role failure. Participants commonly complained that providers lacked concern and an ability to listen. Although most participants were receiving treatment for pain, none felt that their pain was adequately addressed. The investigators identified several barriers to effective pain management including insurance/financial problems, fear of addiction to pain medication, and past negative experiences with pain treatment providers. Some participants admitted that personality characteristics and inability to assume responsibility may have contributed to poor outcome.

Because untreated (or undertreated) pain can lead to drug-seeking behavior and relapse, counselors should inquire about pain during the patient's initial psychosocial evaluation. Pain should be viewed as another comorbid condition (like depression or HIV) that has the capacity to interfere with substance abuse treatment outcomes and that should be addressed in treatment. While a substance abuse treatment counselor is not qualified to diagnose or treat pain, the counselor can encourage patients to discuss their problems with pain and relationships between pain and drug use or abuse. In addition, the counselor can refer the patient for treatment of pain. After the patient begins treatment with a pain treatment provider, the counselor should continue to inquire regularly about pain, medication management, and associated functioning, thereby demonstrating empathy and interest in the patient's recovery and capitalizing on an opportunity to gather information about the patient that may aid the addiction recovery process.

Substance abuse treatment counselors must tailor their treatment approaches to the nature and severity of patients' pain and substance abuse problems and must collaborate closely with pain treatment providers in order to help patients meet their treatment goals. For patients with pain and addiction problems who must be maintained on opioids (in spite of past difficulties with opioid abuse), substance abuse treatment counselors should work with pain treatment providers to identify and address instances of medication mismanagement (medication nonadherence) and to provide ongoing support for recovery. For patients who experience less severe pain and/or who are responsive to nonopioid interventions (for whom a drug-free approach may be preferable), substance abuse treatment counselors can assist patients during the process of withdrawal from opioid analgesics and can encourage patients during the addiction recovery process.

Assessing Pain

Although substance abuse treatment counselors are generally not qualified to diagnose and treat pain, they can help to identify and monitor pain problems. Substance abuse treatment counselors may wish to use the following list of questions to formulate an impression of a patient's problems with pain. If the answer to the gateway question is "no," the assessment is complete, and the clinician can conclude that the patient is not currently experiencing pain.

Gateway Question: "Do you have an ongoing problem with pain"?

If the patient answers "yes," then the clinician should observe and document pain behavior (e.g., limping, moaning, groaning, verbal complaints of pain) and should ask the following questions:

1. For how long have you had pain? (Pain that lasts longer than six months is considered chronic pain.)

2. What is the cause of your pain (e.g., disease, motor vehicle accident)?

3. Where is your pain located? (Clinicians should ask patients to point to the location of their pain and should record all sites mentioned.)

4. Is the pain always present or does it come and go?
   - If the pain comes and goes, how frequently does it come and go?
   - Is the pain worse during a certain time of day?
   - What causes the pain and what makes it worse?
   - What lessens the pain?

5. What words best describe your pain (e.g., burning, sharp, dull, stabbing, throbbing)?

6. On a scale from 0 to 10, on which 0 reflects "no pain" and 10 reflects "worst pain imaginable," how bad is your pain?
   - When it is at its worst?
   - When it is at its lowest?
   - On average, how bad is your pain?
   - What level of pain can you tolerate (i.e., are you able to live with it)?

7. On a scale from 1 to 10, on which 1 indicates "not at all" and 10 indicates "completely," how much does pain affect your functioning in the following areas?
   - Activity level
   - Work ability
   - Walking
   - Mood

- Relationships
- Sleep
- Appetite
- Cognitive functioning (e.g., thinking, memory).

8. What treatment(s) are you currently receiving for pain? What treatments have you received in the past for pain? How effective have these treatments been: effective, somewhat effective, not effective?

9. Do you expect your pain to be cured? Do you expect to take pain medicine on an ongoing basis? (Clinicians should fully assess patients' goals and expectations for treatment.)

10. Have you noticed a relationship between your pain and drug use? If yes, please describe this relationship.

Clinicians should ask question 10 to elicit information from the patient about prescribed and illicit substances to treat pain. Some patients may use more heroin or supplement their daily methadone dose with prescribed opioids when they experience severe pain. Patients with pain often drink alcohol and/or use nonopioid medications with abuse potential (e.g., benzodiazepines) to cope with pain. Some patients believe that marijuana helps them tolerate pain. Substance abuse treatment counselors should determine the relationship between patients' pain and substance abuse.

Selecting a Behavioral Treatment

Many psychosocial interventions that are used to treat patients with chronic pain are also used to treat patients with addictions (although others will be unfamiliar to substance abuse treatment clinicians). CBT is useful in addressing the cognitive aspects of pain (e.g., that pain is uncontrollable), analyzing episodes of medication misuse, and targeting symptoms of depression. Although motivational interviewing (MI) is not routinely employed in pain treatment settings, this patient-centered approach likely would appeal to patients who have had many negative experiences with doctors. Psychoeducation is helpful in increasing problem awareness. Behavioral approaches such as therapeutic contracting and self-monitoring (e.g., diaries in which patients record pain severity, medication taking, and physical activity) encourage patients with comorbid pain and substance use disorders to be active participants in their treatment. Recently completed research by Acosta and Haller (2006) has yielded promising results that suggest that a combination of common drug treatment approaches and adequate doses of analgesic medication can be helpful in addressing opioid abuse in patients with pain: in a small controlled trial of several interventions that combined MI, CBT, and behavioral techniques with methadone (every six hours), 78 percent of treatment completers had a good outcome and were able to be maintained on opioids for pain. Although patients with depression/anxiety were harder to retain in treatment, those patients with depression/anxiety who remained in the study did just as well as those patients without psychiatric problems. While patients with alcohol and other substance use disorders had lower success rates compared to patients with opioid abuse only, most patients with alcohol and other substance use disorders did well.

Since pain and associated dysfunction often cause patients to decrease their involvement in social activities and become isolated (with social interactions often limited to visits with medical providers), participation in group therapy can help patients connect with other people and to receive support. Group sessions that include other patients with pain are helpful (although not essential as long as the group leader is sensitive to the issues faced by patients with pain and is knowledgeable about pain). Although self-help groups like Alcoholics Anonymous and Narcotics Anonymous can be helpful to patients with pain and substance use problems, many patients resist attending these meetings because they do not view themselves as addicts, have physical conditions that limit mobility, and/or fear criticism of their use of opioids for treatment of pain. Finally, treatment providers might encourage patients to learn about their medical disorders on the Internet and to participate in online discussions about pain (see "Suggestions for Further Reading").

Coordination of Care

In order to provide high quality care to substance abusers with pain, a substance abuse treatment counselor must work collaboratively with the physician who is treating a patient's pain. The establishment of a collaboration between a substance abuse treatment counselor and a physician can be challenging for several reasons: (1) in order to manipulate their treatment providers, patients with pain and addictions may not allow their treatment providers to have access to all information about their care; (2) restrictions implemented by the Health Insurance Portability and Accountability Act (HIPAA) make sharing information among clinicians more difficult than before HIPAA's enactment; and (3) treatment providers must adhere to federal regulations that protect the confidentiality of patients in drug treatment. The consequences of failure to coordinate care are considerable: (1) the patient is unlikely to receive effective treatment; (2) the relationship between doctor and patient likely will be poor; and (3) potentially dangerous medical errors may occur (e.g., a patient may receive multiple prescriptions for the same drug or for drugs that interact with one another). It is essential for clinicians to obtain permission from patients to communicate with all care providers. Clinicians should explain to patients who refuse to sign a release form that their refusal compromises their care and may be an indication of a desire to continue abuse of drugs.

The alliance between a substance abuse treatment counselor and a pain treatment provider is critical. In a recent study of a treatment protocol designed to address pain and concurrent opioid analgesic abuse, treatment alliance with the primary counselor was lower for patients who did not make progress and were treatment failures (Bethea et al., 2008). This association shows that the treatment alliance can be an important indicator of prognosis and should be monitored during treatment. It could indicate a tendency for clinicians to become frustrated and withdraw from opioid-abusing pain patients who do not improve. Some substance abuse treatment counselors have more expertise in substance abuse treatment than many physicians, who often lack training in addiction medicine. Substance abuse treatment counselors may be more knowledgeable about treatment of illicit drug abuse than prescription drug abuse in pain patients. The physician may not be a pain specialist and may have limited training in pain management. Since neither treatment provider likely will have expertise in both pain treatment and addiction treatment, they should monitor the patient closely, discuss all treatment options with the patient before initiating treatment, communicate with each other frequently by phone, and work together to implement a treatment plan that includes a medication contract (if opioids are prescribed), counseling, and frequent urine drug screening.

When treatment providers prescribe opioids, it is important that they indicate whether they are for addiction or for pain. Agonist therapy for addiction is not pain treatment. Maintenance agonist therapy for addiction (i.e., methadone or buprenorphine) does not cover pain: in most instances, the dose will be too low, the medication may not be the most effective agent to treat the patient's pain, and the schedule of dosing for addiction (once a day or less) is inappropriate for management of pain. When treatment providers decide to prescribe methadone for treatment of pain, it typically is given three to four times per day. Patients with pain may require "breakthrough" medication in addition to their regularly scheduled dose. Patients should use breakthrough medication with discretion and are responsible for determining if additional medication is needed. Breakthrough medication is not taken on a regular basis; it is available for those times when a patient cannot control pain with the usual dose. When patients require breakthrough medication routinely, physicians should consider raising the patient's regular dose of pain medication. Most importantly, patients with both pain and addictions should receive treatment for both conditions.

Suggestions for Further Reading

For readers who wish to study further in this area, we recommend:

☐   **Books and Journal Articles**

- Gatchel, R. J., & Turk, D. C. (Eds.). (2002). *Psychological approaches to pain management: A practitioner's handbook*. New York: Guilford Press.

- Loeser, J. D., Butler, S. H., Chapman, C. R., & Turk, D. C. (Eds.). (2001). *Bonica's management of pain* (3rd ed.). Philadelphia: Lippincott Williams and Wilkins.

- Pridmore, S. (2002). *Managing chronic pain: A biopsychosocial approach*. London: Taylor & Francis, Inc.

- Tollison, C. D., Satterthwaite, J. R., & Tollison, J. W. (Eds.). (2002). *Practical pain management* (3rd ed.). Philadelphia: Lippincott Williams and Wilkins.

☐   **Web Sites**

- American Chronic Pain Association: http://www.theacpa.org.

- American Pain Foundation: http://www.painfoundation.org.

- Emerging Solutions in Pain: http://www.emergingsolutionsinpain.com.

- National Fibromyalgia Association: http://www.fmaware.org.

- Partners Against Pain: http://www.partnersagainstpain.com.

Authors' Note

The research in this chapter was supported in part by grant R01 DA13169 (Dr. Haller) from the National Institutes of Health/National Institute on Drug Abuse.

References

Acosta, M., & Haller, D. L. (2006). *Psyciatric and substance abuse comorbidity influences treatment outcomes in opioid-abusing pain patients.* Presented at the annual meeting of the College on Problems of Drug Dependence, Scottsdale, AZ.

American Psychiatric Association. (1994). *Diagnostic and statistical manual of mental disorders* (4th ed.). Washington, DC: Author.

American Psychiatric Association. (2000). *Diagnostic and statistical manual of mental disorders* (4th ed., text rev.). Washington, DC: Author.

American Society of Anesthesiologists Task Force on Pain Management. (1997). Practice guidelines for chronic pain management. *Anesthesiology, 86*, 995-1004.

Bethea, A. R., Acosta, M. C., Haller, D. L. (2008). Patient versus therapist alliance. Whose perception matters? *Journal of Substance Abuse Treatment, 35*, 174-183.

Campbell, F. A., Tramer, M. R., Carroll, D., Reynolds, D. J. M., Moore, R. A., & McQuay, H. J. (2001). Are cannabinoids an effective and safe treatment option in the management of pain? A qualitative, systematic review. *British Medical Journal, 323*, 13-16.

Commission on Accreditation of Rehabilitation Facilities (1984-1995). *CARF: Standards manual for organizations serving people with disabilities.* Tucson, AZ: Author.

Commission on the Evaluation of Pain (1986). *Report of the commission on the evaluation of pain.* Washington, DC: U.S. Department of Health and Human Services.

Deardorff, W. W., Rubin, H. S., & Scott, D. W. (1991). Comprehensive multidisciplinary treatment of chronic pain: A follow-up study of treated and non-treated groups. *Pain, 45*, 35-43.

Derogatis L. R., & Melisaratos N. (1983). The Brief Symptom Inventory: An introductory report. *Psychological Medicine, 13,* 595-605.

First, M. B., Spitzer, R. L., Gibbon, M., & Williams, J. B. W. (2002, November). Structured Clinical Interview for DSM-IV-TR Axis I Disorders, Patient Edition (SCID-I/P). New York: Biometrics Research Department, New York State Psychiatric Institute.

Fishbain, D. A., Goldberg, M., Meagher, B. R., Steel, R., & Rosomoff, H. (1986). Male and female chronic pain patients categorized by DSM-III psychiatric diagnostic criteria. *Pain, 26*, 181-197.

Gourlay, G. K., Cherry, D. A., & Cousins, M. J. (1986). A comparative study of the efficacy and pharmacokinetics of oral methadone and morphine in the treatment of severe pain in patients with cancer. *Pain, 25*, 297-312.

Haddox, J. D., Joranson, D., Angarola, R. T., Brady, A., Carr, D. B., Blonsky, R., et al. (1997). The use of opioids for the treatment of chronic pain: A consensus statement from the American Academy of Pain Medicine and the American Pain Society. *Clinical Journal of Pain, 13*, 6-8.

Haller, D. L., Ingersoll, K. S., Dawson, K. S., Poklis, A., & Rafii, A. (1994, July). Factors associated with prescription and recreational drug use in out-patient chronic pain patients. Paper presented at the NIDA Technical Review on the Treatment of Pain in Addicts. Sponsored by the National Institute of Drug Abuse (NIDA), Bethesda, MD.

Hathaway, S. R., & McKinley, J. C. (1943). *The Minnesota Multiphasic Personality Inventory* (Rev. ed.) Minneapolis: University of Minnesota Press.

Jamison, R. N., Kauffman, J., & Katz, N. P. (2000). Characteristics of methadone maintenance patients with chronic pain. *Journal of Pain and Symptom Management, 19*, 53-62.

Karasz, A., Zallman, L., Berg, K., Gourevitch, M., Selwyn, P., & Arnsten, J. H. (2004). The experience of chronic severe pain in patients undergoing methadone maintenance treatment. *Journal of Pain and Symptom Management, 28*, 517-525.

Katon, W. K., Egan, K., & Miller, D. (1985). Chronic pain: Lifetime psychiatric diagnoses and family history. *American Journal of Psychiatry, 142,* 1156-1160.

Kerns, R. D., Turk, D. C., & Rudy, T. E. (1985). The West Haven-Yale Multidimensional Pain Inventory (WHYMPI). *Pain, 4,* 345-56.

Millon, T., Antoni, M., Millon, C., Meagher, S., & Grossman, S. (2001). *Millon Behavioral Medicine Diagnostic.* Minneapolis, MN: NCS Assessments.

Merskey, H., & Bogduk, N. (Eds.) (1994). *Classification of chronic pain: Descriptions of chronic pain syndromes and definitions of pain terms* (2nd ed.). Report by the International Association for the Study of Pain Task Force on Taxonomy. Seattle, WA: IASP Press.

Portenoy, R. K. (1990). Chronic opioid therapy in non-malignant pain. *Journal of Pain and Symptom Management, 5,* 46-61.

Portenoy, R. K., & Foley, K. M. (1986). Chronic use of opioid analgesics in non-malignant pain: Report of 38 cases. *Pain, 25,* 171-186.

Ready, L. B., Sarkis, E., & Turner, J. A (1982). Self-reported versus actual use of medications in chronic pain patients. *Pain, 12,* 285-294.

Rettig, R. A., & Yarmolinsky, A. (Eds.). (1995). *Federal regulation of methadone treatment: The committee report on federation regulation of methadone treatment.* Institute of Medicine, Division of Biobehavioral Science and Mental Disorders, Washington DC: National Academy Press.

Rosenblum, A., Joseph, H., Fong, C., Kipnis, S., Cleland, C., & Portenoys, R. K. (2003). Prevalence and characteristics of chronic pain among chemically dependent patients in methadone maintenance and residential treatment facilities. *Journal of the American Medical Association, 289,* 2370-2378.

Savage, S. R. (1996). Long-term opioid therapy: Assessment of consequences and risks. *Journal of Pain and Symptom Management, 11,* 274-286.

Savage, S., Covington, E. C., Heit, H. A., Hunt, J., Joranson, D., & Schnoll, S. H. (2001). Definitions related to the use of opioids for the treatment of pain. A consensus document from the American Academy of Pain Medicine, the American Pain Society, and the American Society of Addiction Medicine. *WMJ: Official Publication of the State Medical Society of Wisconsin, 100,* 28-29.

Turk, D. C. (1996). Clinicians' attitudes about prolonged use of opioids and the issue of patient heterogeneity. *Journal of Pain and Symptom Management, 11,* 218-230.

Weaver, M. F., & Schnoll, S. H. (2002). Opioid treatment of chronic pain in patients with addiction. *Journal of Pain and Palliative Care Pharmacotherapy, 16,* 5-26.

Welch, S. P., & Stevens, D. L. (1992). Antinociceptive activity of intrathecally administered cannabinoids alone, and in combination with morphine, in mice. *Journal of Pharmacology and Experimental Therapeutics, 262,* 10-18.

Chapter 17

Suicide and Substance Abuse

by Richard K. Ries, M.D.

INTRODUCTION

Suicide Is a Common Cause of Death in Adolescents and Adults

Suicide is the third leading cause of death in people between the ages of 15 and 24 and is the third to fourth leading cause of death in those up to 40 years old in the United States. More people die from suicide in these age groups than from cancer,

AIDS, heart disease, and lung disease combined (Institute of Medicine, 2002; National Center for Injury Prevention and Control, 2002; United States Department of Health and Human Services (USDHHS), 2001). Given that these age ranges overlap the age ranges of those patients seen by addiction treatment agencies and personnel, it is not surprising that suicide is an issue that may emerge as part of treatment of addiction or may be a part of its presentation. The use of drugs or alcohol results in significant changes in mood and cognition, heightened impulsiveness, and endangerment to others and to self. Research studies show that addiction is one of the disorders most frequently associated with suicide attempts and completed suicide (Institute of Medicine, 2002; National Center for Injury Prevention and Control, 2002; National Institute of Mental Health (NIMH), 2003, 2008; USDHHS, 2001).

Clinicians Who Treat Patients With Substance Use Disorders Need to Know About Suicide

Although most clinicians think of suicide as being related to depression, and suicidal thinking is one of the symptom criteria for major depression (see Chapter 1 of this volume), suicide is just as likely caused by the use of drugs or alcohol as by mood disorders. In fact, a review of mortality in suicide performed by Inskip, Harris, and Barraclough (1998) found that death by suicide occurred in approximately 7 percent of those who qualified as substance-dependent patients, as opposed to 6 percent in patients with affective disorders and 4 percent in patients with schizophrenia. Thus, at least one large, carefully done study found that, of the major psychiatric disorders, addiction disorders are at or near the top of the list in terms of risk of suicide. Why do we always refer suicidal patients to the emergency room or to psychiatric units instead of treating them in addiction treatment agencies? This is a good question. In fact, one of the purposes of this chapter is to suggest that addiction treatment staff need to know more about suicide, its differential diagnosis, and its interventions, while recognizing the potential limitations that they may have.

The purpose of this chapter is to provide an overview of the causes and risk factors for suicide in general and more specifically among those with addiction disorders. In addition, this chapter provides addiction treatment agencies and their personnel with a model to better deal with the kinds of suicidal patients they will likely encounter. Some of the risk factors that have been determined to be associated with suicide are discussed in the next section.

SUICIDE RISK FACTORS

There are somewhat different risk factors related to nonlethal suicide attempts than to completed suicides (lethal attempts).

Gender

Females make more nonlethal suicide attempts (attempts that do not end in death) than males; males make fewer suicide attempts than females but make more lethal suicide attempts (i.e., males are more likely to succeed in killing themselves). In fact, males make about four times as many lethal attempts than do females and are much more likely to use a firearm.

Guns and Other Lethal Means

The means of suicide that a patient is thinking about using is related to lethality. In general, violent means (e.g., firearms, jumping from a high place, hanging, crashing a car) represent greater risk than less violent means, such a taking a pill overdose, although overdose can also be deadly. Firearms are involved in a minority of suicide attempts, but they are involved in 60 percent of successful suicide attempts. Access to lethal means is also an important risk factor. Does the patient own or have access to a gun, own or have access to a car, or have knowledge of, and access to, other dangerous machinery? In general, when asking patients about what they are thinking of doing to harm themselves, it is important to assess their access to the means by which they intend to commit suicide.

Age and Ethnicity

While the majority of suicide attempts are made by younger people, rates of suicide increase with age (i.e., highest among the elderly). White males account for 79 percent of completed suicides, and suicide rates are higher in Native Americans but lower in African Americans (although rates are increasing in younger African Americans).

Substance Use and Other Psychiatric Disorders

Alcohol dependence alone increases the risk of suicide attempts by approximately 700 percent, as demonstrated in a carefully designed study by Preuss et al. (2002), which followed matched samples with or without alcohol dependence over five years. In the alcohol-dependent population, factors associated with increased risk included (highest first) past history of attempts, more severe dependence, being separated or divorced, panic attacks, and substance induced mood disorder. Among patients with psychiatric disorders alone, patients with panic disorder, bipolar depression, borderline personality disorder, and major depression are among those patients most at risk of suicide, as well as patients with schizophrenia or other seriously disabling psychiatric illnesses (USDHHS, 2001). Conduct disorder in adolescents is often accompanied by internalizing, depressive symptoms and is also associated with increased risk of suicide. Since many of these patients may have co-occurring substance use disorders, there is often additive risk for suicide attempts and completed suicide. Patients with bipolar depression and borderline personality disorder are at greatest risk for making the most suicide attempts and successful suicide attempts, and both of these disorders have high co-occurrence with addictions (e.g., bipolar women have seven times the rate of substance use disorders than women without any psychiatric disorder).

Past History and Family History of Suicide Attempts

It is important to ask patients whether they have made a suicide attempt(s) in the past. Past behavior is a predictor of future behavior. It is also important to get a good description of the attempt(s) and the surrounding circumstances and to evaluate risk factors and the extent to which each attempt was higher or lower in terms of risk of death. Was the patient using substances at the time? Which ones? Was the patient suffering from depression or another psychiatric disorder? Had the patient sustained a recent loss?

What was the plan and the risk of death? For example, a woman who made superficial cuts to her wrist after an argument with a boyfriend in the past represents a lower risk scenario, while a man who several years ago got drunk and ran his car into a tree, or aimed a gun at himself but missed or misfired, represents a serious risk. Family history is also important. Evidence suggests that the risk of suicide has a genetic or inherited component. Patients may also model the behavior of other family members.

Neurobiology and Tendency Toward Impulsive Aggression

Tendency toward violent suicide and violence in general has been associated with reduced functioning of the brain's serotonin neurotransmitter system. This is indicated, for example, by reduced levels of serotonin in the brains (measured at autopsy) of individuals who have committed suicide by violent means and reduced levels of serotonin metabolites in the cerebral spinal fluid (CSF) of patients who have made serious, violent suicide attempts, as well as in the CSF of prisoners incarcerated for murder. These and other biological measures are only research tools at this point, and there are no biological measures of suicide risk currently available for clinical use. It is important that clinicians ask patients about impulsive aggression (e.g., history of fights, arguments, degree of harm done to others, arrests for assault) and the circumstances under which such aggression occurred. A tendency toward impulsive aggression should increase concern about the risk of suicide.

Assessing Risk for Assault or Homicide

Assessment of risk for assault or homicide is often neglected. Given the relationship between risk of suicide and risk of violence, an assessment of suicide risk should include at least a brief assessment of risk for assault or homicide. Antisocial personality disorder is a risk factor for development of addiction, and many patients with antisocial personality disorder have trouble with aggression. The disinhibiting effects of drugs and alcohol can reduce inhibitions to violence just as they reduce inhibitions to suicide. Many of the basic principles for assessment of risk of violence are similar to those for assessment of suicide risk. Clinicians should ask about history of violence, about the circumstances under which it occurred, and about whether the patient is currently thinking about harming anyone.

Other Risk Factors and Combinations of Risk Factors

Other risk factors include lack of, or recent loss of, meaningful social support systems (e.g., divorce, living alone, few social contacts, friends, or family members to assist with problems or lend emotional support, job loss), co-occurring medical illness, especially lethal illnesses, such as cancer, and illnesses involving unrelenting pain, history of childhood physical or sexual abuse, or ongoing abuse (see Table 17-1). It is unclear to what degree combinations of risk factors add together to increase risk, but it is clear that they are cumulative (i.e., the more risk factors that are present, the greater the risk of suicide attempt and of death by suicide). For example, a person who is old, lives alone, is medically ill with access to a firearm, and has both depression and alcohol dependence would be at extremely high risk.

Table 17-1
Risk Factors for Suicide Attempts in Populations
With Substance Use Disorders

	Risk Factors
1	Current suicidal thoughts or plans, past history of suicide attempts, family history of suicide
2	Recent, severe substance dependence (especially stimulants)
3	Acute loss of meaningful relationship(s) or other serious loss (e.g., job, housing)
4	Co-occurring psychiatric disorder, especially bipolar depression, borderline personality disorder, substance-induced mood disorder, panic/agitation, acute posttraumatic stress disorder symptoms
5	Physical or sexual abuse during childhood

Roles of Specific Substances in Suicides and Accidents

In terms of the individual substances of abuse, research indicates that risk of suicide attempt is probably highest among persons using amphetamines, methamphetamines, and cocaine (Zweben et al., 2004). Since alcohol dependence is much more common, more alcohol-related suicide attempts are reported. It is hard to determine which substances may be most suicide inducing, since often many substances are used together, and it is difficult to determine which substance might be primary. Further, it is difficult to determine whether many injuries, accidents, and deaths that involve substances are accidents or suicides. For example, if an alcohol-dependent farmer who has been having trouble with finances, family matters, and health is found dead in his car, which hit a tree on a rural road, in a single-vehicle accident (his blood alcohol concentration (BAC) is 250 at the time of the accident), should his death be considered an accident or a suicide? Since insurance coverage for death benefits can be significantly different for accidents than for suicide, interpretations of events with ambiguous causes tend to be more conservative (i.e., the farmer's death was due to an accident caused by inadvertent alcohol overdose rather than a planned suicide attempt). Similarly, if a heroin addict is found alone and dead from an overdose of heroin, should his death be ruled a suicide or an accident due to inadvertent heroin overdose? It is likely that substance-related suicides are significantly underreported, as are suicides in general; thus, the 1.7 to 1 ratio of death by suicide to death by homicide is conservative. Death by suicide is probably twice as common as death by homicide.

Summary

Table 17-2 summarizes some of the main factors that indicate increased suicide risk and, among individuals at risk, factors associated with greater risk of death by suicide. The table can be used during assessment of patients in any treatment setting (e.g., addiction, psychiatric, or medical). In addition, the following differences exist between substance-related suicide attempts and nonsubstance-related suicide attempts:

Table 17-2
Factors Increasing Risk of Suicide and Risk of Death by Suicide

Risk of Suicide Attempt	Risk of Death by Suicide
Previous suicide attempt	Male (Four times as many men as women die by suicide)
Family history of suicide	Firearms (this method accounted for 57% of all suicides in 2000)
Psychiatric disorder	Older adult (older than age 70)
Alcohol/drug disorder	Alone
Alcohol/drug intoxication	Alcohol
Loss (e.g., recent death, divorce, job loss)	Loss of social support
Hopelessness ("at the end of my rope")	Serious illness
History of violence, impulsive aggression	Medical disorder, psychiatric disorder

Note: Statistics in Table 17-2 were compiled from the following reports: Institute of Medicine (2002); National Center for Injury Prevention and Control (2002); NIMH (2008); NIMH (2003); USDHHS (2001).

1. Substance-related suicide attempts are more likely to be impulsive, with planning occurring in minutes to hours, versus days to months in nonsubstance-related suicidal acts.

2. Substance-related suicide attempts are more likely to occur following relationship loss or during stress.

3. Substance-related suicide attempts are more likely to involve lethal means (may be related to greater prevalence of substance abuse among men; Institute of Medicine, 2002).

PREPAREDNESS FOR DEALING WITH PATIENTS' SUICIDAL THOUGHTS AND PLANS

How prepared are clinicians to deal with a patient's suicidal thoughts and plans? As mentioned in the introduction, suicide is a serious concern in the general population and is about seven times more common in patients in treatment for addictive disorders, whether these patients have comorbid psychiatric disorders or not. Most suicidal patients are referred out of addiction treatment agencies to emergency rooms or mental health agencies because it is often erroneously assumed that patients who are suicidal must have a primary psychiatric disorder. Most addiction treatment personnel and agencies have not considered themselves capable of dealing with suicidal patients. However, since modern research has indicated that addiction is one of the top factors for risk of suicide, the addiction treatment system and its personnel need to reconsider their capacity for dealing with suicidal patients. If all suicidal patients are referred out of the addiction treatment system into the mental health system, patients become at risk for the misdiagnosis of substance-induced suicidal thoughts as symptoms of a primary psychiatric disorder. They are then at risk for mistreatment or undertreatment of their addiction. A treatment plan that is developed by a mental health agency likely will focus on treatment of depression, anxiety, or other psychiatric disorders, with less focus on what may be the patient's primary problem (i.e., addiction).

Readers should note that the typical addiction treatment agency or addiction treatment counselor may not be prepared to treat certain cases of suicidality. For example, an extremely suicidal, impulsive patient will likely need the safeguards of a locked unit that has been designed and staffed to decrease the odds of impulsive suicidal acts, and such units are virtually always psychiatrically based. Addiction inpatient residential units and outpatient units are not designed or staffed to deal with this type of acute case. However, the bulk of patients at risk for suicide in the addiction population do not fall into this category, and the adage "an ounce of prevention is worth a pound of care" applies. Counselors and agencies can follow several steps in order to become more capable of recognizing potential risk of suicide, assessing potentially suicidal patients, and intervening.

Step 1: Identify Suicide as an Issue That Addiction Treatment Personnel and Agencies Need to Address: The rationale for recognizing suicide as an issue that addiction treatment personnel and agencies need to deal with is outlined in the above sections. The addiction treatment system needs to stop ignoring its responsibility to help these patients.

Step 2: Identify Current Capabilities, Practices, and Referrals: Readers who work in addiction treatment agencies should evaluate the effectiveness of their current policies, procedures, and resources for dealing with suicidal patients, in order to develop a personal and agency-wide quality improvement plan for managing suicidal patients. Readers might consider the following questions.

1. Are all admitted patients to the addiction treatment program screened for suicide with a standardized questionnaire or evaluation?

2. If suicidal history or current thoughts and plans are identified, what is the current practice of the agency or personnel in terms of further assessment, consultation with other providers, referrals, and involuntary civil detention in an emergency?

3. What training do the clinicians have in terms of suicide recognition, screening, assessment, intervention, and referral?

4. What are the local resources that may be used in a crisis (e.g., emergency rooms, psychiatric units, units to treat co-occurring disorders, involuntary treatment professionals, and the police)?

In fact, the first part of an evaluation of an agency's attitude toward care of suicidal patients and the feasibility of a quality improvement plan for management of suicidal patients might be to assess readiness to change using the Stages of Change model (Prochaska, DiClemente, & Norcross, 1992). The below-listed statements about treating suicidal patients in addiction treatment clinics represent attitudes that characterize each stage in the Stages of Change model.

1. *Precontemplation* (e.g., "Suicide is a problem for mental health practitioners not for an addiction treatment agency.").

2. *Contemplation* (e.g., "I understand that our patients with addictions are at risk for suicide, but I am not sure how we should deal with it.").

3. *Action* (e.g., "I am convinced that suicide can be a problem for our patients with addictions, and we have developed a plan to improve our agency's ability to treat suicidal patients.").

4. *Relapse Prevention* (e.g., "We have some policies and procedures for treating suicidal patients, but we have not reviewed them recently, and we have not had any training in this area recently; we need to review our policies and plan for an inservice.").

Clinicians should match the type of intervention to the stage of change. For example, in an agency where staff members' attitudes are representative of the precontemplation stage (e.g., staff members are not convinced that suicidal patients should be treated in an addiction treatment clinic), staff members should be encouraged to share their concerns about treating suicidal patients and should be offered a basic education about suicide (perhaps staff members might read this chapter). Staff members with attitudes that are representative of the precontemplation stage likely will be unwilling to participate in intensive workshops that teach suicide intervention skills.

Step 3: Work on Specific Screening and Intervention Skills: After completing an assessment of the counselors' and agency's ability to manage suicidal patients, staff members can begin to work on specific screening and intervention skills.

HOW TO SCREEN PATIENTS FOR SUICIDE RISK

Many agencies use standard screening forms as part of admission. Clinicians should evaluate the screening form that is used in their agency and should determine if questions on suicide are included. Simple questions include "Have you ever been suicidal?" and "Have you ever made a suicide attempt?" These questions should be followed with questioning on when the suicidal thoughts and attempts occurred, what happened, and whether the patient is experiencing suicidal impulses now or has any current suicide plans. A basic question or two on suicide are included in the Addiction Severity Index (ASI; McLellan et al., 1992). Reports by patients of suicidal ideation or suicide attempts require follow-up, as described below.

Alternatively, many clinicians may use a free-form clinical interview and then later chart the patient's responses in an evaluation note. Either way, in patients with substance use disorders, suicidality always needs at least basic screening. In an open clinical interview, suicidality may come up in the clinical history. The clinician should follow up on the question "Have you ever been in the hospital for medical problems, psychiatric problems, or addiction problems?" by asking the patient if he/she has ever experienced any of the following symptoms associated with the hospitalizations: depression, losing touch with reality, and being suicidal or making a suicide attempt. The clinician should determine when the attempt occurred, the circumstances under which the attempt occurred, other attempts, and risk of death, as well as how the patient feels at present and, if the patient feels better, how the patient improved.

Clinicians may ask about passive suicidal thoughts by using questions like "Do you ever wish you could go to sleep and never wake up?" or "Have you wished that you stopped living or died from a medical problem or accident?" Questions on more active suicidal thinking include questions like "Have you had thoughts of ending it all?" or "Have you considered suicide or had thoughts about harming yourself?" or "Has suicide become an option for you now or in the past?" When inquiring about a patient's drug and alcohol use and suicide thoughts or attempts, a clinician might ask "Are there ever times, when you are drinking or not, that you have become self-destructive (e.g., become suicidal or made a suicide attempt)?" or "Do you see any relationship between using drugs or alcohol and feeling dangerous to yourself or others?" Do not ask the question "You are not thinking of killing yourself, are you?" This question indicates to the patient that you do not wish to hear about the patient's suicide plans. Experience in asking these questions results in clinical competence and comfort in assessing suicidal thinking.

A model for suicide assessment and intervention is provided by the QPR Institute (Quinnett, 2007), an organization dedicated to assessment of suicide risk and intervention. The QPR model includes three steps:

1. *Question:* Question the patient about suicide through screening and more detailed assessment.

2. *Persuade:* The clinician should persuade the patient to get help or to accept the clinician's help.

3. *Refer:* Refer the patient if the clinician cannot provide the level of care that the patient requires.

Clinicians should consider the six "W" questions (detailed below) when assessing patients' suicidal thoughts, impulses, plans, or past attempts. We will examine the use of the six "W" questions in eliciting information from patients in the following four case studies:

Case 1: A 32-year-old male arrives at an addiction treatment agency with problems of combined alcohol and cocaine dependence. He recently lost his job, developed financial problems, and was arrested. He has a history of a suicide attempt three years ago and has admitted that the only thing that he has left is the dedication of his girlfriend; if she left him, he would probably kill himself (he is not sure how). He says that he is not currently suicidal.

Case 2: A 28-year-old woman with methamphetamine dependence and numerous losses in her life has just found out that she has hepatitis C. She reports that her mother killed herself when she was 28 years old on a wintry day in December. The current month is October, and the patient describes her hatred for the holidays and the month of December, which reminds her of her mother's death. The patient wonders how she will "get through it" this year. She has made two suicide attempts in the past around the date of her mother's death; on both occasions she stored up the medications that she had been receiving from her primary care doctor and took an overdose.

Case 3: A 52-year-old African American male is mandated to intensive outpatient addiction treatment through the courts as a result of a domestic violence charge. He and his wife are in the process of separation and divorce. He has lost a significant number of friends and some relatives around the split of the marriage. He is currently homeless. When discussing his circumstances, he comments that if his wife hates him so much, she should be happy if he dies. He has a friend with a handgun and knows where it is.

Case 4: A 25-year-old Latino is admitted for alcohol dependence after a DUI. He says that his father killed himself. Although he is depressed about his DUI and ashamed that he must come for treatment, he says he would never kill himself. He goes to church regularly, but he feels that he has failed both his family and his priest.

In each of these cases there is a significant suicide risk.

1. *What* is wrong? This question should be answered from the patient's perspective; the clinician's feedback comes later. In Case 3, if the patient reports that his main problem is his wife, then she is in danger (this is a scenario for a murder or a murder/suicide). The clinician should encourage him to call his friend (in front of the clinician) in order to tell him to never give him the gun and to hide it from him.

2. *Why* now? The question "Why now?" elicits from the patient the precipitating events, crises, or problems, thereby allowing the clinician to evaluate if there is a current crisis, whether the patient has been hopeless for a long time, what the magnitude is of change events, and whether the patient has any support. The clinician should try to assess if the patient has a "hair-trigger" condition, if the person has just experienced "the final straw," or if the patient expects to experience "the final straw" at any minute. In Case 1, the patient has lost his job, developed financial problems, and was arrested recently. A breakup with his girlfriend might be the "final straw."

3. *With what?* This question elicits the methods of suicide under consideration. In Case 1, the clinician might ask "If your girlfriend left, would you consider suicide?" If the patient answers "yes," the clinician should ask "With what?" or "How have you considered doing it?" In order to determine how concrete the patient's plans are, to assess how dangerous the suicidal crisis is, and to elicit ideas for intervention, the clinician should ask if the patient has access to lethal means (e.g., a gun) and if the patient has developed a plan. If the patient in Case 1 owns a loaded gun, and if he considers his life to be dependent upon the preservation of an already stressed relationship with his girlfriend, then this patient is likely to be on the edge of a suicidal cliff. Dealing with the lethal means and getting the girlfriend involved would be indicated. Likewise, in Case 3, it is important to insure that the patient does not have access to a gun. In Case 2, talking about medication hoarding is indicated.

4. *Where* and *when?* These questions elicit possible location and timing of a suicide attempt. The clinician should assess what type of lethal planning has occurred and how soon the patient is planning to commit suicide (e.g., immediately, next week, or on an anniversary date). Since one of the best predictors of future suicide attempts is past attempts, and since future attempts often mimic past attempts, it is important to discuss with patients where they made suicide attempts in the past and with what. In Case 2, the patient has made two suicide attempts, both of which occurred with overdoses and around the date of her mother's death. In order to determine the amount of planning that the patient in Case 2 has completed and to assess relative risk, the clinician should ask the patient if she is starting to store up medications now. While overdose on pills can kill a person, most overdoses do not (more lethal means include jumping from a bridge or building, using a firearm, or crashing one's vehicle into an overpass). Since the holidays are often hard for patients in recovery, programs (e.g., Alcholics Anonymous or Narcotics Anonymous) often have extra meetings, dinners, and other activities that provide support to patients during the holidays. This person also needs one-on-one work to address grief and loss issues (many addiction treatment professionals are quite skilled in this area).

5. *Who* is involved? Since suicide often relates to interpersonal issues, clinicians should find out who is involved and what is going on in these relationships. Suicide is often misplaced aggression toward another person that is aimed at oneself. Especially in domestic violence cases, murder and suicide often occur together. More than half of these cases are drug or alcohol related. Clinicians should ask "Who is important to you?" and "Who knows that you are in this much pain?" Clinicians might also ask "Who do you rely on for support, and who can help you right now?" and "Who would be most affected by your suicide?" Clinicians should try to determine whether a patient's suicidality is related to the patient's conflict with another person. In Case 3, the clinician will have to look for potential sources of support and help the patient to find reasons for living. In Case 4, the clinician should mobilize this patient's family and clergy members.

6. *Why not* now? This question is designed to elicit protective factors or reasons for living (e.g., religious or spiritual prohibitions, as in Case 4; important relationships with children, relatives, and pets). During a discussion of a past suicide attempt, the clinician might mention that the patient must have lived through the prior attempt for a higher purpose and might encourage the patient to identify that purpose. As a way to dispel the patient's "end my pain" fantasies, the clinician might discuss in detail the patient's caregiving responsibilities to children, pets, or neighbors. The clinician might also encourage the patient to list reasons for living.

HOW TO ASSESS PATIENTS' RISK OF SUICIDAL DANGER

Using a patient's answers to the six "W" questions (see "How to Screen Patients for Suicide Risk"), the clinician should determine if the patient is at mild, moderate, or severe risk for immediate suicidal danger. Patients at mild risk have vague thoughts without plans or access to lethal means, passive death fantasies, or characteristics that do not fit typical high-risk profiles (e.g., a younger person with a fully intact support system with no medical illnesses and no lethal means). Indicators of moderate risk include actual plans and potential access to lethal means, loss of relationship or other psychosocial support, important upcoming anniversaries or events for which expectations may not be met, and a history of suicide attempts. Moderate-risk and high-risk patients are more likely to have comorbid medical problems or psychiatric disorders in addition to their addiction problems. Patients who are at severe risk have a definite plan, access to lethal means, seem "at the end of their rope," feel that they do not have much or any support, and see no other alternatives. A patient at severe risk of suicide needs an immediate crisis response that involves personnel who are trained and equipped to ensure the safety of such a person (e.g., an emergency room, crisis outreach team, or involuntary commitment). Persons at severe risk should not be permitted to drive alone to an emergency room. Action is needed immediately.

PERSUADING SOMEONE TO GET HELP

Clinicians who encounter patients at mild to moderate risk should proceed, following screening, to the second step in the QPR model (Quinnett, 2007): persuade (i.e., persuade the patient to get help). With many patients at mild to moderate suicidal risk, a clinician's active listening and questioning may significantly defuse the situation. Discussion of a patient's problems likely will allow a patient at mild to moderate risk to form some potential solutions to the problems. The clinician may also point out solutions by asking questions or by responding to obvious issues and should ask the patient if his/her ideations or plans have changed since the start of the discussion. If the patient's feelings have not changed and moderate risk remains, then the clinician should persuade the patient to see a more highly trained staff member in the agency or to seek help outside the agency. If suicidal impulses appear even more serious than they originally seemed, or if the patient refuses to see the treatment providers who the clinician has recommended, the patient may be at greater risk. The clinician may need to treat this person like a more severely suicidal person (see "How to Assess Patients' Risk of Suicidal Danger").

REFERRAL

After reviewing the agency's resources and policies for managing suicidal patients, the clinician is prepared to deal with a suicidal patient and to choose resources that will address that patients's problems and needs. In order to effectively work with suicidal patients, clinicians must be familiar with community resources for suicidal patients to which clinicians may refer their patients. Some suicidal persons may believe that they are in spiritual crisis and have nothing to live for and may feel that they have lost their way with their religion. A pastoral counselor or chaplain who is experienced in working with suicidal patients may be a perfect match for such a patient. For a patient who has bipolar disorder and alcohol dependence, has experienced a severe bipolar depression while making past suicidal attempts, denies having bipolar diorder, and has stopped taking all medications recently, the obvious referral would be to a prescribing mental health practitioner who treats patients with combined alcholism and bipolar disorder and who could prescribe appropriate medication and assess suicide risk. The acuity of such a patient's illnesses might dictate whether an admission to a co-occurring disorders inpatient unit is more appropriate than treatment in an intensive, outpatient addiction treatment program with regular visits to a prescribing psychiatrist. A young patient who has experienced two traumatic rapes while intoxicated during the three months prior to entering treatment, who has had suicidal thoughts but no plan, and who has become discouraged with her treatment at a combined men's/women's intensive outpatient program, might benefit from an all women's addiction treatment group and a female case manager or therapist.

Clinicians must be able to make appropriate referrals that match the symptoms and issues that suicidal patients have described during their evaluation. Hopelessness predicts an eventual suicide attempt. Providing direction, hope, and an avenue towards solutions will increase patients' hope.

GROUP THERAPY WITH SUICIDAL PATIENTS

About 20 to 30 percent of patients in addiction treatment have made suicide attempts in the past. Discussion of recovery following suicide attempts by these patients during group therapy sessions can engender hope in patients and may act as a suicide preventative. It is important to ensure that group therapy sessions include participants with positive suicide recovery histories, who can serve as role models.

Just as positive stories can move the focus of group therapy sessions toward suicide prevention, negative affect and hopelessness can foster further hopelessness. Many therapeutic interventions for grief and for patients who have made multiple suicide attempts are group based.

CONCLUSION

This brief overview has provided addiction treatment counselors and agencies with a rationale for why suicide should be addressed by clinicians in addiction treatment clinics and has offered both agencies and individual practitioners a method for self-evaluation of attitudes and competencies.

This chapter offered an introduction to suicide screening, methods for persuading patients to get help, and referral. Further reading and training in these areas are recommended. Independent practitioners and clinicians and program directors in addiction treatment agencies should evaluate their current policies for managing suicidal patients and implement appropriate changes to improve quality of care of suicidal patients.

Suggestions for Further Reading

For readers who wish to study further in this area, we recommend:

- American Association of Suicidology: http://www.suicidology.org.

- American Foundation for Suicide Prevention: http://www.afsp.org.

- Institute of Medicine. (2002). *Reducing suicide: A national imperative.* Washington, DC: The National Academies Press.

- National Center for Injury Prevention and Control: http://www.cdc.gov/ncipc/dvp/suicide.

- National Strategy for Suicide Prevention: http://www.mentalhealth.org/suicideprevention/.

- QPR Institute: http://www.qprinstitute.com.

- Substance Abuse and Mental Health Services Administration: http://www.samhsa.gov.

- Suicide Prevention Action Network U.S.A. (SPAN USA): http://www.spanusa.org.

References

Inskip, H. M., Harris, E. C., & Barraclough, B. (1998). Lifetime risk of suicide for affective disorder, alcoholism and schizophrenia. *British Journal of Psychiatry, 172,* 35-37.

Institute of Medicine. (2002). *Reducing suicide: A national imperative.* Washington, DC: National Academies Press.

McLellan, A. T., Kushner, H., Metzger, D., Peters, R., Smith, I., Grissom, G., et al. (1992). The fifth edition of the Addiction Severity Index. *Journal of Substance Abuse Treatment, 9,* 199-213.

National Center for Injury Prevention and Control. (2002). *Suicide in the United States*. Atlanta, GA: Centers for Disease Control and Prevention.

National Institute of Mental Health (NIMH). (2003). *In harm's way: Suicide in America*. NIH Publication No. 03-4594. Bethesda, MD: Author.

National Institute of Mental Health (NIMH). (2008). *Suicide in the U.S.: Statistics and prevention*. NIH Publication No. 06-4594. Bethesda, MD: Author. Retrieved July 23, 2008, from http://www.nimh.nih.gov/health/publications/suicide-in-the-us-statistics-and preven- tion.shtml

Preuss, U., Schuckit, M., Smith, T., Danko, G., Buckman, K., Bierut, L., et al. (2002). Comparison of 3190 alcohol-dependent individuals with and without suicide attempts. *Alcoholism: Clinical and Experimental Research*, *26*, 471-477.

Prochaska, J., DiClemente, C. C., & Norcross, J. C. (1992). In search of how people change: Applications to address addictive behaviors. *American Psychologist, 47,* 1102-1104.

Quinnett, P. R. (2007). *QPR gatekeeper training for suicide prevention: The model, ratio- nale, and theory.* Spokane, WA: QPR Institute. Retrieved July 23, 2008, from http://www. qprinstitute.com

United States Department of Health and Human Serivces (USDHHS). (2001). *National strat- egy for suicide prevention: Goals and objectives for action.* Document No. SMA-01-3517. Rockville, MD: Author. Retrieved July 23, 2008, from http://mentalhealth.samhsa.gov/ publications/allpubs/SMA01-3517

Zweben, J. E., Cohen, J. B., Christian, D., Galloway, G. P., Salinardi, M., Parent, D., et al., (2004). Psychiatric symptoms in methamphetamine users. *American Journal on Addictions*, *13*, 181-190.

Chapter 18

Drug Interactions in the Pharmacological Treatment of Substance Use Disorders

by Elinore F. McCance-Katz, M.D., Ph.D.

INTRODUCTION

Drug interactions can significantly impact the treatment of patients with comorbid medical or mental disorders who require treatment with several medications. Drug interactions can be associated with a variety of toxicities that can result in adverse events in patients and lead to poor clinical outcomes. Drug users may abuse more than one illicit drug and/or alcohol, as well as prescription drugs. In addition, doctors may prescribe multiple medications for medical problems and/or mental illnesses in these patients. Clinicians must be aware of the potential for drugs to interact and negatively affect patients. This chapter will discuss interactions between opioid therapies and human immunodeficiency virus (HIV) medications and the clinical problems that can arise as a result of drug interactions. Clinicians may use the methods described in this chapter for preventing and detecting interactions between HIV medications and opioid therapies as a model for clinical care for dual-diagnosis patients. Opioid therapies are the most studied medications for substance-dependent patients, and the most information on drug interactions is available for these drugs. The mechanisms for the drug interactions that are described in this chapter might apply to other medications and illicit substances that are used in combination (although, to date, these have not been systematically studied). This chapter provides a foundation on interactions between opioid therapies and HIV medications for clinicians and should encourage clinicians to think about clinical situations that may result from adverse drug interactions in dual-diagnosis patients.

The prevalence of opioid dependence as a result of the abuse of heroin or prescription opioids is rising in the United States (Substance Abuse and Mental Health Services Administration (SAMHSA), 2003). There are several substance abuse treatment options available to opioid-dependent individuals including medical withdrawal, antagonist therapy, and opioid therapy. Medical withdrawal is associated with high relapse rates, and antagonist therapy is often not acceptable to opioid-dependent patients. Opioid therapies have been the treatment of choice, particularly for opioid-dependent patients who have previously failed medical withdrawal or antagonist treatment. Opioid-assisted therapies that have been approved by the U.S. Food and Drug Administration (FDA) include methadone, levo-alpha-acetylmethadol (LAAM) (although LAAM is not currently produced in the United States), and buprenorphine. These agents prevent opiate withdrawal by replacing short-acting opioids (e.g., heroin, hydrocodone) with long-acting agents that can be given once a day (methadone and buprenorphine) or once every two to three days (LAAM). Long-acting opioids can produce tolerance to short-acting opioids like heroin so that illicit drug use can be discontinued. Methadone and LAAM must be administered to patients with addictions through specialized treatment programs that are regulated and overseen by the government. Buprenorphine can be given by prescription from a doctor with special qualifications and a waiver from the Center for Substance Abuse Treatment (CSAT) to prescribe. These medications, when given in the context of ongoing psychosocial therapy and urine drug screening, have been shown to be effective pharmacotherapies for opioid dependence (McCance-Katz & Kosten, 2005).

MEDICATION LEVELS AND DRUG INTERACTIONS

Drugs and medications exert their effects when they reach certain concentrations (or "levels" as they are commonly referred to) in blood and target tissues (mainly the central nervous system for illicit substances and their medication treatments). Levels that are too low render the medication ineffective; levels that are too high make the medication toxic. The level in the system is determined by dosage or intake and rate of elimination or metabolism (also known as the pharmacokinetics of the drug). The most important factors that determine the levels of drugs in the blood and tissues are prescribed dosage (or nonadherence to the prescribed dosage (i.e., missed doses or excess doses)) and rate of metabolism.

Nonadherence

Nonadherence to the prescribed dosage is extremely common in medical treatment. When clinicians work with patients who are taking medications, clinicians should always ask their patients about adherence in an open and nonjudgmental fashion. Don't ask "You're taking your two pills in the morning, right?" This question likely will elicit the answer that the patient thinks the clinician wants to hear rather than an accurate one. Instead, clinicians should ask "How's it going with the medication?"; "How much of the medication are you taking?"; "What's your routine for taking the medication?"; "How often do you miss taking the medication?"; "Do you take extra medication sometimes?" Often, these types of questions will reveal that the patient is forgetful or disorganized, in which case the clinician can help the patient to identify strategies that encourage the patient to take his/her medication. Side effects or worry over potential adverse events may discourage patients from taking the medication. The case presented below (see "Case Presentation") describes a patient who fails to take HIV medication after experiencing unpleasant effects of an interaction between her HIV medication and an opioid therapy (methadone). Every clinician should ask about medication adherence. Counselors and other nonmedical personnel are often the primary therapists for substance-dependent patients and often form strong treatment alliances with their patients that should allow them to ask about and address problems with medication adherence.

Drug Metabolism and Elimination by the Liver or Kidneys

The levels of a drug or medication in the body are determined mainly by the rate of metabolism (if a constant dosage of medication is given). When determining medication levels and potential interactions, clinicians must know if a medication is eliminated by the liver or kidneys and how well these organs are functioning. Most drugs are metabolized by the liver, and a few drugs are eliminated by the kidneys.

A family of enzymes in the liver called the cytochrome P450 system (CYP), of which the CYP 450 3A family of enzymes, CYP 450 2D6, and CYP 450 2B6 are the most important, metabolize most drugs in the liver. These enzymes catalyze the chemical reactions that break down medications into metabolites (some active and some inactive) that are then excreted from the body either through the bloodstream and the kidneys or through the bile ducts into the gastrointestinal (GI) tract. The functioning of these enzymes is determined by many factors, including the health of the liver or degree of liver damage that a patient may have. The most common cause of liver damage in substance-dependent patients is viral hepatitis (mainly hepatitis B and hepatitis C). The liver has a large functional reserve and can sustain a great deal of damage before its ability to metabolize drugs and medications is impaired. However, chronic alcoholism and hepatitis B and hepatitis C (after many years of chronic infection) can cause cirrhosis or scarring of the liver (healthy liver cells are replaced by inert scar tissue), ultimately leading to liver failure. At a certain point, impaired metabolism will cause medication blood levels to increase or accumulate.

A few drugs are eliminated by the kidneys, including lithium and gabapentin (Neurontin). The levels of these drugs may go up if kidney function deteriorates either acutely (e.g., severy dehydration or acute kidney failure) or chronically.

Drug Interactions: Substrates, Inhibitors, and Inducers

Drug interactions occur when one drug or medication alters the metabolism of another drug or medication (i.e., slowed or accelerated metabolism), leading to a change in the blood level of the latter drug or medication. Drugs that are metabolized by a particular CYP 450 enzyme are called substrates for that enzyme. Drugs that reduce the functioning of a particular CYP 450 enzyme are called inhibitors. A drug that is a substrate for a particular CYP 450 enzyme will be metabolized more slowly, leading to increased blood levels, in the presence of a drug that is an inhibitor of that CYP 450 enzyme. When two drugs that are both substrates for the same CYP 450 enzyme are given together, an interaction may occur in which the metabolism of one drug is slowed down. A drug is an inducer if it increases the functioning of a particular CYP 450 enzyme, usually by inducing the liver to synthesize more of the enzyme; inducers will lead to increased rates of metabolism of substrate drugs, thereby reducing their blood levels.

Table 18-1 categorizes common medications and drugs as substrates, inhibitors, or inducers for several CYP 450 enzymes. For ease of reference, the lists of substrates for each enzyme are subdivided into psychotropics, including substances of abuse and medications that are used to treat psychiatric and substance use problems. The table is not exhaustive but is useful as a reference. The *Physicians' Desk Reference* (PDR; http://www.pdr.net) provides more detailed information about the metabolism of medications and interactions that have been studied. Unfortunately, the PDR does not list all common medications, and often entries on older medications that are no longer patented are removed from the PDR. Another excellent source of information about drug interactions is the Web site http://medicine.iupui.edu/flockhart/clinlist.htm. This Web site provides a regularly updated detailed table of substrates, inhibitors, and inducers that are subdivided by drug class.

Clinical Significance of Drug Interactions

Table 18-1 or the detailed table of substrates, inhibitors, and inducers found at http://medicine.iupui.edu/flockhart/clinlist.htm provides a guideline for the reactions that may occur when two or more drugs are administered together, but the determinants of the actual clinical outcome are more complex. For example, many drugs are metabolized and eliminated by more than one pathway and/or more than one CYP 450 enzyme, and these additional pathways may be able to compensate for alterations in the main metabolic pathway. Further, small changes in drug levels may not have much effect. For example, a small increase of 10 or 20 percent in methadone blood levels over a period of days may be experienced like gradual dose increases (i.e., with development of tolerance rather than emergence of toxic effects). Careful studies of drug interactions are needed in order to determine the impact of the addition of one drug on the blood levels of another drug. Tables 18-2A, 18-2B, and 18-2C summarize interactions between opioid therapies and illicit drugs and alcohol, medications for HIV, psychotropics, and other medications for disorders that commonly co-occur with substance use disorders. As the case example below illustrates (see "Case Presentation"), clinicians need to look for clinical signs and symptoms of potential drug interactions, even if they might not be expected. Assays for the most commonly prescribed medications, including methadone, as well as most psychotropics and antivirals, are available through commercial laboratories. Medication level determinations may be expensive. When clinically indicated, a patient's trough blood level of methadone (blood is drawn just prior to the next scheduled dose to capture the lowest point, or trough, in the blood level) can be measured to determine if the methadone level is too low ($\leq$ 200ng/ml) or too high ($\geq$ 400ng/ml). It is often not feasible to get blood concentrations of other medications, and it can be difficult to determine the significance of those values.

Table 18-1
CYP 450 Metabolism of Common Drugs and Medications

P450 Enzyme	Substrates	Inhibitors[a]	Inducers
1A2	**Psychotropics:** Caffeine[b], clozapine, haloperidol[b], imipramine[b], olanzapine **Other Drugs:** Phenacetin, tacrine, theophylline[b], verapamil[b], warfarin[b]	Fluoroquinolones (ciprofloxacin, norfloxacin), fluvoxamine, cimetidine	Charcoal-broiled beef, cigarette smoke, cruciferous vegetables, marijuana smoke, omeprazole
2A6	**Psychotropics:** Nicotine **Other Drugs:** Coumarin	Tranylcypromine	Barbiturates
2B6	**Psychotropics:** Bupropion, nicotine, diazepam[b], methadone[b] **Other Drugs:** Cyclophosphamide, tamoxifen		Phenobarbital, cyclophosphamide (in vitro)
2C9	**Psychotropics:** Amitriptyline[b], tetrahydrocannabinol[b], **Other Drugs:** Diclofenac, metoclopramide, phenytoin, propranolol[b], tolbutamide, warfarin[b]	Fluvoxamine, D-propoxyphene, disulfiram, fluconazole, sulfaphenazole	Rifampin, phenytoin, secobarbital
2C19	**Psychotropics:** Amitriptyline[b], clomipramine[b], desmethyldiazepam[b], diazepam[b], imipramine[b], moclobemide **Other Drugs:** Ibuprofen, naproxen, omeprazole[b], S-mephenytoin, piroxicam, tenoxicam	Omeprazole	Rifampin
2D6	**Psychotropics:** Amitriptyline[b], aripiprazole, codeine[b], desipramine, duloxetine, haloperidol[b], imipramine[b], methadone, nortriptyline, oxycodone[b], paroxetine, pindolol, propafenone, risperidone, thioidazine, venlafaxine[b], codeine, hydrocodone[b] **Other Drugs:** Debrisoquin, dextromethorphan, metoclopramide, metoprolol, mexiletine, ondansetron[b], orphenadrine, propranolol[b], sparteine, timolol	Duloxetine, fluoxetine, methadone, paroxetine, quinidine, sertraline	None

(Continued)

P450 Enzyme	Substrates	Inhibitors[a]	Inducers
2E1	**Psychotropics:** Caffeine[b], ethanol **Other Drugs:** Dapsone[b]	Disulfiram	Ethanol
3A4	**Psychotropics:** Alprazolam, amitriptyline[b], bupropion, caffeine[b], carbamazepine, clonazepam, codeine[b], cortisol, desmethyldiazepam[b], diazepam[b], fluoxetine, haloperidol[b], imipramine[b], midazolam, nefazodone, sertraline, trazodone, triazolam, venlafaxine[b], zolpidem, ziprasidone, oxycodone[b], hydrocodone[b] **Other Drugs:** Amiodarone, astemizole, cisapride, clarithromycin, cyclosporin, dapsone[b], diltiazem, erythromycin, estradiol, ethinylestradiol, lidocaine, loratadine, lovastatin, nicardipine, nifedipine, omeprazole[b], ondansetron, orphenadrine, progesterone, quinidine, rifampin, tamoxifen, terfenadine, testosterone, verapamil[b]	Fluoxetine, fluvoxamine, ketoconazole, naringenin, nefazodone, cimetidine, erythromycin, indinavir, ritonavir, saquinavir, sertraline (weak), atazanavir, delavirdine	Barbiturates, carbamazepine, dexamethasone, phenytoin, rifampin, St. John's wort, efavirenz, nevirapine

Note: Information in Table 18-1 excerpted primarily from DeVane (2004), as well as from http://medicine.iupui.edu/flockhart/table.htm and Pies (2005); excerpt from DeVane (2004) reprinted with permission from the *Textbook of Psychopharmacology* (Copyright 2004). American Psychiatric Publishing, Inc.

[a] Inhibition potency varies greatly.

[b] More than one P450 enzyme is known to be involved in the metabolism of these drugs.

Table 18-2A
Drug Interactions Between Opioid Therapies and Psychotropics and Other Medications for Commonly Co-Occurring Disorders

Psychotropic Medications	Interaction With Methadone	Interaction With Buprenorphine (BUP) or LAAM
Fluvoxamine (Antidepressant)	↑ Methadone levels reported	Not studied
Alprazolam (Anxiolytic)	Not studied	Severe adverse events including death when injected in combination with BUP
Desipramine	None	Not studied
Fluoxetine (Antidepressant)	↓ Methadone levels reported in preclinical studies (Iribarne et al., 1998)	Not studied
Sertraline (Antidepressant)	↑ Methadone levels by 26%; no reported adverse events	Not studied
St. John's Wort (Herbal antidepressant)	Not studied	Not studied
Valproic acid (Anticonvulsant)	None reported	Not studied
Carbamazepine (Anticonvulsant)	↓ Methadone levels; opiate withdrawal reported; methadone dose increases may be required	Not studied
Other Medications		
Rifampin (Tuberculosis medication)	↓ Methadone levels; opiate withdrawal; methadone dose increases required	Not studied
Rifabutin (Tuberculosis medication)	No change in methadone levels Mild narcotic withdrawal symptoms have been reported	Not studied
Fluconazole (Antifungal medication)	↑ Methadone levels by ≈35%; clinical significance unknown	Not studied
Phenytoin (Anticonvulsant)	↓ Methadone levels; opiate withdrawal may occur, and methadone dose increases may be required	Not studied
Phenobarbital (Anticonvulsant)	↓ Methadone levels; opiate withdrawal may occur, and methadone dose increases may be required	Not studied
Ciprofloxacin (Antibiotic)	Opiate toxicity reported	Not studied

Note: Some interactions are reported in a review article by Leavitt (2005); for further information on CYP 450 metabolism of drugs, see http://medicine.iupui.edu.

Table 18-2B
Drug Interactions Between Opioid Therapies and Medications for HIV

	Interaction With Methadone	Interaction With Buprenorphine (BUP) or LAAM
Nucleoside Reverse Transcriptase Inhibitors (NRTI)		
Zidovudine (AZT)	↑ AZT AUC by 40%; no effect on methadone levels	Nonclinically significant ↓ AZT concentrations with buprenorphine and LAAM
Didanosine (ddI) tablet	↓ ddI AUC by 63%; no effect on methadone levels[a]	Not studied
Didanosine (ddI) enteric-coated	No significant effect of methadone on ddI in this formulation	Not studied
Zalcitabine (ddC)	None	Not studied
Lamivudine (3TC)	None	Not studied
Lamivudine/zidovudine (Combivir)	None	
Stavudine (d4T)	↓ d4T AUC by 25%	Not studied
Abacavir (ABC)	↑ Methadone clearance but no withdrawal; no clinically significant effect on ABC	Not studied
Tenofovir	No significant interaction	Not studied
Nonnucleoside Reverse Transcriptase Inhibitors (NNRTI)		
Nevirapine	Withdrawal symptoms; need for increased methadone dose	Not studied
Delavirdine (DLV)	↑ Methadone levels; no effect on DLV	↑ BUP and LAAM concentrations; no effect on DLV

(Continued)

	Interaction With Methadone	Interaction With Buprenorphine (BUP) or LAAM
Efavirenz (EFV)	↓ Methadone levels; withdrawal symptoms; ↑ methadone dose necessary	↓ BUP levels; no withdrawal; no dose change needed; no effect on EFV levels[b]
Protease Inhibitors (PI)		
Nelfinavir (NLF)	↓ Methadone levels but no withdrawal symptoms observed; increased NLF; decreased M8 metabolite; no clinically significant change in NLF exposure	NLF: no effect on BUP; increase in LAAM levels; no significant effect of BUP or LAAM on NLF[c]
Indinavir	Not studied	Not studied
Ritonavir	↑ Methadone levels reported but not clinically significant	↑ BUP levels, not clinically significant; no effect of BUP on RTV[c]
Saquinavir	↓ Methadone levels (S entantiomer); no withdrawal	Not studied
Amprenavir	↓ methadone levels; no withdrawal	Not studied
Lopinavir/ritonavir (L/R)	↓ methadone levels; withdrawal may occur; methadone may need to be increased	No significant effect on BUP; LAAM not studied; no effect of BUP on L/R[c]
Atazanavir		↑ BUP levels; case report of sedation, cognitive impairment[d]

Note: Some interactions are reported in a review article by Leavitt (2005); for further information on CYP 450 metabolism of drugs, see http://medicine.iupui.edu; for further information on interactions between medications and HIV therapeutics, see http://www.hiv-druginteractions.org.
[a] Rainey et al. (2000).
[b] McCance-Katz et al. (2006a).
[c] McCance-Katz et al. (2006b).
[d] McCance-Katz et al. (2007).

Table 18-2C
Drug Interactions Between Opioid Therapies and Illicit Drugs and Alcohol

Illicit Drug or Alcohol	Interaction With Methadone	Interaction With Buprenorphine (BUP) or LAAM
Heroin	Not reported, but opioid tolerance in patients withdrawn from methadone treatment may be reduced with possible toxicity if heroin use is resumed	BUP: opiate withdrawal possible if opioid-dependent individual uses heroin around the time of buprenorphine use; LAAM: Not reported, but opioid tolerance in patients withdrawn from LAAM treatment may be reduced with possible toxicity if heroin use is resumed
Alcohol	Not studied but metabolized by alcohol dehydrogenases and CYP 450 2E1; no pharmacokinetic interaction likely; synergistic depressant effects possible	Not studied but no pharmacokinetic interaction likely; synergistic depressant effects possible
Cannabis	Not studied	Not studied
Cocaine	Not studied but commonly abused by methadone maintained individuals without associated adverse events; cocaine primarily metabolized by esterases, which are not known to be affected by opioids	Not studied but commonly abused by BUP-maintained individuals without reported adverse events
Amphetamines	Not studied but metabolized by CYP 450 2D6, so interaction with methadone is possible	Not studied
Methyl-3,4-methyle-nedioxyamphetamine (MDMA)	Not studied but metabolized by CYP 450 2D6, so interaction with methadone possible	Not studied

Note: Some interactions are reported in a review article by Leavitt (2005); for further information on CYP 450 metabolism of drugs, see http://medicine.iupui.edu.

Genetic Influence on Drug Metabolism

Pharmacogenetics is an emerging field that studies the contribution of inherited factors to drug response. Different genetic forms of the major enzymes that metabolize drugs may have altered function due to genetic differences in activity level, resulting in patients who are "slow metabolizers" of certain drugs. For example, a common poorly functional variant of CYP 450 2D6 can result in unusually high blood levels of tricyclic antidepressants (amitriptyline, nortriptyline, imipramine, desipramine), which may result in toxicity. A poorly functional variant of CYP 450 2C19 can result in unusually high levels of diazepam. When clinicians prescribe new medications or when they adjust medication doses, they should monitor patients carefully for side effects. Emergence of side effects may indicate that the patient is a relatively slow metabolizer of the drug. In patients who are taking standard clinical doses of a drug and who are slow metabolizers, blood levels may be too high.

DRUG INTERACTIONS BETWEEN OPIOIDS AND MEDICATIONS USED TO TREAT CONCOMITANT ILLNESS

Patients with substance use disorders often have comorbid medical illnesses and conditions and/or mental illnesses that require treatment with medication (in addition to medications for opioid dependence). Drug interactions can occur in patients taking medications that are substrates of, or alter the function of, enzymes that are responsible for metabolism of drugs (cytochrome P450 enzymes) including opioids that are used as therapies for opioid dependence. The opioid therapies methadone, LAAM, and buprenorphine are principally metabolized by CYP 450 3A4; other cytochrome P450 enzymes are involved in opioid metabolism to a lesser extent. Drug interactions can result in reduction of medication effectiveness, side effects, and toxicities related to increased concentrations of medication.

Methadone is the most studied drug of the opioid therapies. Methadone withdrawal symptoms can occur when other medications cause induction (or production) of greater amounts of the liver enzymes that metabolize methadone, thereby lowering plasma methadone concentrations. Methadone toxicity, markedly increased sedation, decreased respiration, and mental status changes, might occur if a concomitant medication inhibits methadone metabolism. Similar toxic effects may occur with LAAM and buprenorphine. For example, a study that examined the effect of a combination protease-inhibitor drug (lopinavir/ritonavir) on methadone plasma concentrations found that methadone concentrations were reduced significantly, and some participants experienced opiate withdrawal (McCance-Katz, Rainey, Friedland, & Jatlow, 2003). A study that examined the interaction of buprenorphine with lopinavir/ritonavir found that buprenorphine plasma concentrations were not significantly altered, and no opiate withdrawal was observed (McCance-Katz et al., 2006b). It is also possible for opioid therapies to impact plasma concentrations of antiretroviral medications. However, the effect of one opioid on an antiretroviral medication may not be indicative of the interaction that might occur between that antiretroviral medication and other opioid therapies. For example, the combination of methadone and zidovudine, a nucleoside reverse transcriptase inhibitor (NRTI) used in the treatment of HIV disease, results in increased zidovudine concentrations that can be associated with zidovudine toxicity (McCance-Katz, Rainey, Jatlow, & Friedland, 1998). In contrast, in a study by McCance-Katz et al. (2001), LAAM and buprenorphine treatment was associated with lower zidovudine concentrations. Research is ongoing to define drug interactions between many commonly prescribed medications and methadone and buprenorphine. Available information on drug interactions between methadone, LAAM, and buprenorphine and psychotropic and other medications (Table 18-2A), HIV medications (Table 18-2B), and illicit drugs and alcohol (Table 18-2C) is provided in the tables in this chapter.

CONSEQUENCES OF UNDETECTED DRUG INTERACTIONS

Case Presentation

KW a 31-year-old woman with a ten-year history of injection drug use, was admitted to a methadone maintenance program one year ago. This is her first treatment for addiction to heroin. The doctor at the clinic has had difficulty stabilizing her on methadone; during the first eight months of treatment, she continued to use injected heroin and cocaine intermittently. For the past three months, she has been able to discontinue heroin and cocaine use, and her dose of methadone has been stable at 100 mg daily over this time period. Her annual HIV test has come back positive, and her T-cell CD4 count is 150 cells/mm³ with viral load of 5 logs. Her physician recommends Highly Active Antiretroviral Therapy (HAART), which is the current standard of care for HIV disease and consists of at least three antiretroviral medications (either one protease inhibitor or nonnucleoside reverse transciptase inhibitor (NNRTI) and two NRTIs). Her doctor selects a regimen consisting of efavirenz, tenofovir, and emtricitabine. Within a week of taking these medications, KW begins to experience muscle and joint pain, anxiety, restlessness, insomnia, and nausea. She tells the staff at the methadone maintenance program that she thinks she is in withdrawal. Her dose is increased to 110 mg/day. Three days later, she returns to the methadone maintenance program to report that her withdrawal symptoms are worse, and she asks for another dose increase. Her request is refused, and the doctor at the clinic tells her that she needs time to adjust to the dose increase recently given. Her withdrawal symptoms worsen, and two days later, she returns to the clinic to report that she continues to feel sick all of the time and to ask again for a dose increase. She is told that her request will be discussed in the next team meeting. KW suspects that the HAART is causing her sickness, so she stops her medications. Within a few days she is feeling much better and no longer complains of withdrawal. Her dose is held at 110 mg/day. She tells her doctor who is treating her HIV that she is having no trouble with the prescribed HAART. Her next viral load has increased to 6 logs. Six months later, KW is hospitalized for pneumonia. Her treatment team reviews her medications and concludes that efavirenz probably caused induction of CYP 450 3A4 with increased methadone metabolism, which led to subtherapeutic methadone concentrations and a severe withdrawal syndrome. The team is concerned that KW stated that she resumed injected heroin use when she experienced the withdrawal symptoms and that she shared needles on several occasions during that time. An elevated HIV viral load may have increased risk of transmission of the virus to her drug-using partners.

Consequences of Drug Interactions Between Opioids and Antiretroviral Therapies

The treatment of injection drug users (IDU) who receive opioid substitution therapy (specifically methadone maintenance treatment) with HAART can be challenging. Studies have identified significant and serious adverse drug interactions between methadone and antiretroviral therapies. Opioids (methadone, LAAM, and buprenorphine) and some of the currently available antiretroviral therapies are metabolized by hepatic cytochrome P450 (CYP 450) enzymes, especially CYP 450 3A4. In vitro studies have shown that certain antiretroviral therapeutics have significant effects on CYP 450 3A4 function, particularly inhibition of enzyme activity (Iribarne et al., 1998). Other antiretroviral agents have been shown to induce (increase) CYP 450 enzyme function. Inhibition of enzyme(s) responsible for opioid metabolism could potentially lead to accumulation of the opioid medication with excessive plasma concentrations and toxicity. Symptoms of opioid toxicity, which include sedation, decreased respiration, and impaired thinking, can be life threatening. Conversely, drugs that induce hepatic enzyme activity cause increased metabolism of opioids that can lead to an opioid abstinence syndrome in which the patient experiences opioid withdrawal symptoms. This problem is common in treating HIV-infected patients who receive opioid substitution therapy. The effects of some antiretroviral agents on CYP 450 enzyme function might lead to antiretroviral toxicity that requires clinical attention.

Nonadherence to HAART by patients who have HIV disease and who are opioid dependent has serious consequences. These include development of viral resistance to HIV medications and lack of efficacy of HIV therapies. Opioid-dependent injection drug users who experience adverse drug effects frequently try to alleviate their symptoms by using illicit drugs (e.g., patients may continue to abuse heroin when they experience withdrawal symptoms). Unrecognized drug interactions lead to poor clinical outcomes for treatment of drug abuse and HIV disease.

SUMMARY

There is a growing body of literature on the significance of interactions between medications for illnesses that occur frequently in opioid-dependent individuals and medications for opioid dependence. While many drug interaction studies focus on interactions between methadone and antiretroviral agents for HIV disease, it is clear that other medications can interact with methadone, as well as with buprenorphine or LAAM. Some interactions between methadone and various medications may not occur with other opioid therapies. For example, the adverse drug interactions between methadone and efavirenz have not been seen with buprenorphine (McCance-Katz, 2005). Future research should determine the likelihood of clinically significant drug interactions between opiates and HIV medications. Knowledge of these drug interactions will aid clinicians in selecting opioid therapies and medications to treat medical and mental illnesses in opioid-dependent individuals.

Studies that examine interactions of illicit substances (other than opioids) with commonly prescribed medications have not been completed. The enzymes that are important in the metabolism of opioids may be associated with other drug-drug interactions (namely, medications used to treat common psychiatric disorders, including antidepressant medications, antianxiety medications, mood stabilizers (often used to treat bipolar illness), and antipsychotic medications). Clinicians should carefully evaluate patients who report adverse symptoms immediately after they begin treatment with a new medication or after use of illicit drugs; clinicians may uncover a dangerous drug interaction. Clinicians should be wary of possible drug interactions when prescribing medications. Prevention or elimination of adverse drug interactions can improve clinical outcomes in patients who receive opioid substitution therapy and who have co-occurring illnesses.

Suggestions for Further Reading

For readers who wish to study further in this area, we recommend:

☐ **CYP 450 Metabolism of Drugs**

- Cytochrome P450 Drug-Interaction Table [Indiana University School of Medicine Division of Clinical Pharmacology Web Site]: http://medicine.iupui.edu/flockhart/clinlist.htm.

- DeVane, C. L. (2004). Principles of pharmacokinetics and pharmacodynamics. In A. F. Schatzberg & C. B. Nemeroff (Eds.), *Textbook of psychopharmacology* (3rd ed., pp. 129-145). Washington, DC: American Psychiatric Publishing, Inc.

- Rendic, S., & Di Carlos, F. J. (1997). Human cytochrome P450 enzymes: A status report summarizing their reactions, substrates, inducers and inhibitors. *Drug Metabolism Review, 29*, 413-550.

☐   **Interactions Between Medications and HIV Therapeutics**

- Physician's Desk Reference Website: http://www.pdr.net.

- University of Liverpool. HIV-Drug Interactions: http://www.hiv-druginteractions.org.

Author's Note

The research in this chapter was supported in part by grants R01 DA13004 (Dr. McCance-Katz), K02 DA00478 (Dr. McCance-Katz), and K24 023359 (Dr. McCance-Katz) from the National Institutes of Health/National Institute on Drug Abuse.

References

Cytochrome P450 Drug-Interaction Table [Indiana University School of Medicine Division of Clinical Pharmacology Web site]. (2006, March 3). Retrieved April 17, 2006, from http://medicine.iupui.edu/flockhart/clinlist.htm

DeVane, C. L. (2004). Principles of pharmacokinetics and pharmacodynamics. In A. F. Schatzberg & C. B. Nemeroff (Eds.). *Textbook of psychopharmacology* (3rd ed., pp. 129-145). Washington, DC: American Psychiatric Publishing.

HIV-Drug Interactions Web Site [University of Liverpool Web site]. Retrieved April 13, 2006, from http://www.hiv-druginteractions.org

Iribarne, C., Berthou, F., Carlhant, D., Dreano, Y., Picart, D., Lohezic, F., et al. (1998). Inhibition of methadone and buprenorphine n-dealkylations by three HIV-1 protease inhibitors. *Drug Metabolism and Disposition, 26*, 257-260.

Leavitt, S. B. (2005, November). *Methadone-drug interactions* (3rd ed.). Addiction Treatment Forum. Mundelein, IL: Clinco Communications. Retrieved August 1, 2008, from http://www.atforum.com/SiteRoot/pages/addiction_resources/Drug_Interactions.pdf

McCance-Katz, E. F. (2005). Treatment of opioid dependence and HIV/HCV co-infection in opioid dependent patients: The importance of drug interactions between opioids and antiretroviral medications. *Clinical Infectious Diseases, 41*, S89-S95.

McCance-Katz, E. F., & Kosten, T. R. (2005). Psychopharmacological treatments. In S. Miller & R. Frances (Eds.), *Clinical textbook of addictive disorders* (3rd ed., pp. 588-614). Guilford Press: New York.

McCance-Katz, E. F., Moody, D. E., Morse, G D., Ma, Q., DiFrancesco, R., Friedland, G. et al. (2007). Interaction between buprenorphine and atazanavir or atazanavir/ritonavir. *Drug and Alcohol Dependence, 91*, 269-278.

McCance-Katz, E. F., Moody, D. E., Morse, G. D., Friedland, G., Pade, P., Baker, J. et al. (2006a). Interactions between buprenorphine and antiretrovirals. I. The nonnecleoside reverse-transcriptase inhibitors efavirenz and delavirdine. *Clinical Infectious Diseases, 43*(Suppl. 4), S224-S234.

McCance-Katz, E. F., Moody, D. E, Smith, P. F., Morse, G. D., Friedland, G., Pade, P., et al. (2006b). Interactions between buprenorphine and antiretrovirals. II. The protease inhibitors nelfinavir, lopinavir/ritonavir, and ritonavir. *Clinical Infectious Diseases, 43*(Suppl. 4), S235-S246.

McCance-Katz, E. F., Rainey, P., Friedland, G., & Jatlow, P. (2003). The protease inhibitor lopinavir/ritonavir may produce opiate withdrawal in methadone-maintained patients. *Clinical Infectious Diseases, 37,* 476-482.

McCance-Katz, E. F., Rainey, P. M., Friedland, G., Kosten, T. R., & Jatlow, P. (2001). Effect of opioid dependence pharmacotherapies on zidovudine disposition. *American Journal of Addictions, 10,* 296-307.

McCance, E. F., Rainey, P. M., Jatlow, P., & Friedland, G. (1998). Methadone effects on zidovudine disposition (AIDS Clinical Trials Group 262). *Journal of Acquired Immune Deficiency Syndromes and Human Retrovirology, 18,* 435-443.

Pies, R. W. (2005). Introduction to pharmacodynamics and pharmacokinetics. In D. P. Rogers (Ed.), *Handbook of essential psychopharmacology* (2nd ed., pp. 1-17). Washington, DC: American Psychiatric Publishing.

Rainey, P. M., Friedland, G., McCance-Katz, E. F., Andrews, L., Mitchell, S. M., Charles, C., et al. (2000). Interaction of methadone with didanosine and stavudine. *Journal of Acquired Immune Deficiency Syndromes, 24,* 241-248.

Substance Abuse and Mental Health Services Administration. (2003). *Overview of findings from the 2002 National Survey on Drug Use and Health* (Office of Applied Studies, NHSDA Series H-21, DHHS Publication No. SMA 03–3774). Rockville, MD: U.S. Government Printing Office.

Part 7
Future Directions

The crisis in the organization of the health care system in the United States requires a solution that will control escalating health care costs and ensure that patients receive high quality treatment. Since private third-party payers often limit coverage of treatment for substance abuse and psychiatric disorders, the financial burden falls on the pubic sector. As medical care improves and medical treatments become increasingly more sophisticated, costs of care rise. Future research must determine if improved diagnosis and treatment of substance use disorders and psychiatric disorders and increased referrals to specialists improves treatment outcome and offsets higher short-term treatment costs. The chapters in Part 7 highlight issues in organization of care and areas of research that must be addressed in order to improve treatments for substance use disorders and psychiatric disorders. In order to improve quality of care for patients with substance use disorders and psychiatric disorders, the stigma attached to substance use disorders and psychiatric disorders must be shattered, and these disorders must receive more public attention and research funding (equivalent, at least, to the attention and funding given to other medical disorders, such as cancer and heart disease).

Chapter 19

Choosing Treatment Services and Levels of Care: American Society of Addiction Medicine Patient Placement Criteria

by Gustavo Angarita, M.D., Sang Lee, B.S., and David R. Gastfriend, M.D.

INTRODUCTION

The treatment of co-occurring psychiatric disorders among substance-dependent patients must occur in the context of a particular treatment program and a larger treatment plan. So far, this book has concentrated on the identification of particular psychiatric disorders among substance-dependent patients and on specific treatment techniques (behavioral therapies and medications). This chapter now directs our attention to the larger question of how to choose a treatment program with the right level of intensity of services to best serve patients with co-occurring disorders. The chapter focuses on the American Society of Addiction Medicine (ASAM) Patient Placement Criteria (PPC). The PPC were designed to address this question and are increasingly being adopted in the field by both treatment systems and third-party payers.

CASE PRESENTATION

A 53-year-old divorced white female teacher who lived alone arrived at the intake office asking for an admission to "rehab." Diagnosed with chronic anxious depression, she also had twenty-five years of intermittent periods of drinking to intoxication and benzodiazepine overuse. For the past six months, she had persistent frequent episodes of intoxication despite regularly seeking help from a psychopharmacologist for anti-depressant and antianxiety medication, a social worker for outpatient insight-oriented psychotherapy, and Alcoholics Anonymous (AA) meetings, which she attended several times a week with her sponsor. She was judged to have a risk of mild-to-moderate alcohol withdrawal, had lost track of how many pills she was taking each day, reported suicidal thoughts without any plan, and lived alone. Following evaluation of the patient at a residential detoxification and rehabilitation program, insurance authorization was initially denied on the grounds that she had not yet failed partial hospital level of care. An appeal of this decision was also denied. The admitting physician then directly contacted the medical director of the patient's health insurance plan and notified him that the state endorsed the ASAM PPC, and that, according to the PPC, the patient was recommended for Level III.7 residential detoxification and acute rehabilitation. The admission was then granted, and the patient stabilized over an extended treatment, which included transfer to a halfway house and then a sober house.

AMERICAN SOCIETY OF ADDICTION MEDICINE CRITERIA

Background and Rationale for Patient Placement Criteria

A dilemma exists for comorbid patients, in that they have multidimensional problems, and yet the addiction and the mental health treatment systems generally address only one type of disorder only or one disorder at a time (Minkoff, Zweben, Rosenthal, & Ries, 2003). In addition, until recently, managed care systems have had no standards of care for treating co-occurring disorders (Minkoff, 2001). In the case described above (see "Case Presentation"), successive levels of behavioral managed care review employed only substance abuse placement guidelines (and overly restrictive ones, at that), without considering the interactions between suicidal ideation, withdrawal symptoms, and continued access to substances due to an environment lacking in evening supervision. The presence of both a substance use disorder and another mental disorder strongly predicts that, with less than adequate treatment, this patient will have difficulty engaging in definitive treatment and a poor outcome (Rubin & Gastfriend, 2001).

The ASAM PPC are consensus decision rules designed to help clinicians and payers use levels of care in a rational and individualized way that hews to no single ideology but is instead clinically driven and outcome oriented and built on a continuum of care. The PPC (in its second edition, revised (PPC-2R); Mee-Lee, Shulman, Fishman, Gastfriend, & Griffith, 2001) requires caregivers to first conduct a multidimensional needs assessment of the patient (see Table 19-1) and then follow an intricate sequence of decision rules to arrive at a recommendation of the level of care that is most likely to be effective and least restrictive.

Levels of Care (From Most Intensive to Least Intensive)

Level IV: Medically Managed Intensive Inpatient Treatment. This service is appropriate for patients who have acute and severe problems with intoxication (e.g., frank psychosis or violent behavior) or withdrawal (e.g., delirium tremens), biomedical problems (e.g., acute pancreatitis), emotional problems, behavioral problems, or cognitive problems (e.g., acute suicidality) that require primary medical and nursing care. Treatment is provided twenty-four hours a day in a permanent facility with inpatient beds (Mee-Lee et al., 2001).

Level III: Residential/Inpatient Treatment. These programs provide care in a twenty-four-hour residential setting but do not include on-site, round-the-clock medical attention. They serve individuals who, because of specific functional deficits, need safe and stable living environments in order to develop their recovery skills.

Level III encompasses four types of programs: clinically managed low-intensity residential treatment (Level III.1), clinically managed medium-intensity residential treatment (Level III.3), clinically managed high-intensity residential treatment (Level III.5), and medically monitored inpatient treatment (Level III.7). These sublevels exist on a continuum ranging from the least intensive residential services to the most intensive medically monitored intensive inpatient services.

Table 19-1
ASAM PPC-2R Dimensions of Assessment

Dimension	Title
1	Acute Intoxication and/or Withdrawal Potential
2	Biomedical Conditions and Complications
3	Emotional, Behavioral or Cognitive Conditions and Complications
4	Readiness to Change
5	Relapse, Continued Use or Continued Problem Potential
6	Recovery/Living Environment

Note: For description of the ASAM PPC-2R Assessment Dimensions, see Mee-Lee et al. (2001).

Level III programs that treat individuals with co-occurring mental and substance-related disorders are generally more flexible, more individualized, and less confrontational than the typical Level III program.

Level II: Intensive Outpatient Treatment/Partial Hospitalization. This level involves treatment that may be delivered during the day, in the evening, or on a weekend, but treatment is nonresidential. These programs provide treatment while allowing patients to apply their newly acquired skills in "real world" environments. Within Level II, there are two treatment levels: intensive outpatient treatment (Level II.1) and partial hospitalization programs (Level II.5). They differ in the intensity of clinical services that are directly available. Specifically, most Level II.1 intensive outpatient programs have less capacity to treat patients who have substantial unstable medical and psychiatric problems than do Level II.5 partial hospitalization programs.

Level I: Outpatient Treatment. Outpatient services are provided in regularly scheduled sessions with the goal of helping the individual achieve permanent changes in his/her alcohol and drug use behavior and mental functioning. Level I is appropriate for individuals who have been evaluated as having only mild or no severity in the six dimensions (see Table 19-1), or conditions that can be stabilized with available outpatient resources (e.g., chronic major depression that is well-controlled with outpatient pharmacotherapy).

Level 0.5: Early Intervention. Level 0.5 was developed for individuals who are at risk of developing substance-related problems or for those for whom there is not yet sufficient information to document a substance use disorder. One example of a Level 0.5 patient might be the individual who has been convicted of driving while intoxicated (DWI).

Dual Diagnosis Capacity of Program

The PPC-2R requires programs at each level of care to determine whether they offer dual diagnosis enhanced (DDE) services (e.g., with readily available psychiatric medical and nursing services), dual diagnosis capable (DDC) services (e.g., with consulting psychiatric care and ability to manage some co-occurring psychiatric conditions), or addiction only services (AOS), which is a discouraged status, given the growing complexity of the patient population. These designations are to be appended after the level of care decimal terminology, and detailed decision rules are provided for choosing which sublevel is recommended for a given patient's needs.

VALIDITY OF AMERICAN SOCIETY OF ADDICTION MEDICINE CRITERIA

Early evaluations of the ASAM PPC first edition found that its use was associated with treatment engagement and services development. In the Boston Target Cities Project, PPC use was associated with 38 percent greater likelihood to engage in continuing treatment within thirty days after detoxification (odds ratio = 1.55, $p < .05$) and significantly less readmission to detoxification within ninety days (odds ratio = .57, $p < .05$) compared to conventional direct admission without criteria (Plough et al., 1996). An evaluation of Oregon's statewide formal PPC-1 training and implementation reported increased individualization of length of stay and significant expansion of the innovative day treatment services compared to a more modest introduction in Washington State (Deck, Gabriel, Knudsen, & Grams, 2003). These findings were promising, especially since the version of the PPC used in these evaluations was little more than a paper and pencil short form. While a rudimentary PPC-oriented guide might demonstrate improvements in these large population studies, critics pointed out that the complexity of the PPC books would make it difficult to reliably use the intricate PPC rules on a patient-by-patient basis. Clearly, there was a need for a common method of implementing the PPC, with a common language, an organized and comprehensive question sequence, precise ratings, and an accurate scoring process to calculate the optimal level of care.

Standard Implementation: American Society of Addiction Medicine PPC-2R Assessment Software

Over the period of 1990-2000, the ASAM PPC became recommended by over twenty states, by the U.S. Veterans Administration Hospitals, and by the U.S. Department of Defense. In a nationally representative survey of 400 private U.S. treatment centers in 1996, 70 percent already reported having adopted the PPC. One of the significant determinants of adoption was comorbidity: programs that served comorbid patients and needed to distinguish between patients they could treat versus those who would need referral were substantially more likely to be using the PPC (Johnson & Gastfriend, 2005).

With this growth in use, it became essential to ensure that counselors would be able to evaluate patients and obtain consistent, precise (i.e., reliable), and clinically meaningful (i.e., valid) level of care recommendations (Baker & Gastfriend, 2003). Work at the Massachusetts General Hospital and Harvard Medical School was funded by the National Institute on Drug Abuse to create a computerized version that would help counselors to ask the necessary questions, to correctly interpret and rate patients' answers, and to quickly calculate the best level of care recommendation. A series of studies demonstrated the feasibility, reliability, and validity of an initial PPC-1 version, and validity has been reported on the PPC-2R version (Gastfriend, 2003). Evaluation with the PPC-2R computerized version also showed its value as a needs assessment tool. A Russian translation in Bukhara, Uzbekistan, demonstrated that nearly half of forty-five patients receiving the mandated long-term residential treatment available in that system would have been recommended instead for other levels of care, with 20 percent needing

Level IV hospital care due to their acute psychiatric and/or physical disorders (Boltaev, Bakhtiyor, Gromov, Lefebvre, & Gastfriend, 2004). Question items for the ASAM PPC-2R assessment software (CMHC Systems, Inc., Dublin Ohio, and other vendors) were selected on the basis of their known validity and reliability. The following is a short description of these interview items that comprise the assessment protocol.

Clinical Institute Withdrawal Assessment-Alcohol/Revised and Clinical Institute Narcotic Assessment. Dimension 1 (see Table 19-1) requires a careful, objective assessment of withdrawal risk. Since clinicians vary in their expertise in assessing withdrawal, these instruments help by providing a clinical quantification of the severity of the alcohol or drug withdrawal syndrome (Fudala, Berkow, Fralich, & Johnson, 1991; Peachey & Lei, 1988; Sullivan, Sykora, Schneiderman, Naranjo, & Sellers, 1989). With training, non-medical personnel such as detoxification unit workers and research assistants can reliably use these scales (Saitz et al., 1994; Wartenberg et al., 1990; Wasilewski et al., 1996).

Addiction Severity Index. Developed by McLellan et al. (1992), the Addiction Severity Index (ASI) is the most widely used addiction behaviors assessment in the world. It is organized in a clinically logical sequence; the ASI is designed to ask pragmatic questions about a patient's substance use and functional consequences in the following areas (see Table 19-1): medical status (useful for assessing Dimension 2), employment/support status (Dimension 6), drug and alcohol use (Dimension 5), legal status (Dimension 6), family history (Dimension 6), family/social relationships (Dimension 6), and psychiatric status (Dimension 3). Its validity and reliability are good in a wide range of patient populations (McLellan et al., 1985). The ASAM PPC-2R assessment software implements the complete ASI fifth edition question sequence and calculates composite scores for each ASI subscale.

Other Question Categories. Dimensions 1, 2, and 3 (see Table 19-1) require supplementation because the ASI (see "Addiction Severity Index") assesses problems in a cross-sectional fashion (i.e., "in the moment" or during the past thirty days), whereas much of clinical judgment depends on how a patient's problems have evolved over time and how they have responded in the past to any treatment efforts. Therefore, a number of questions are included to enhance the ASI in a longitudinal perspective. There are additional questions for the medical review of systems to provide a broad, basic medical problems screening, as well as a sequence for the review of psychiatric problems. Problems like depressed mood may have multiple important components that require assessment, such as mood, guilt, impact on work status, psychomotor retardation, anxiety, and somatic symptoms (Bech et al., 1981; Hamilton, 1960; O'Sullivan, Fava, Agustin, Baer, & Rosenbaum, 1997). The software also includes a set of questions for basic cognitive function screening and the details of suicidal ideation and plan. This is provided in a structured format because, in spite of its routine use in psychiatric assessment, not all addiction counselors are acquainted with this assessment.

Dimension 4 requires an assessment of the patient's awareness of problems, agreement with the need for treatment, understanding of his/her responsibility in changing behavior, and degree of active versus passive behaviors toward recovery. These parameters have been studied and validated as reliable and useful predictors (Gastfriend, Filstead, Reif, Najavits, & Parrella, 1995). Questions addressing each of these areas are incorporated in a manner that is structured and quantified.

Research Findings on Matching to Level of Care With American Society of Addiction Medicine Patient Placement Criteria

Studies of the ASAM PPC computerized assessment approach have demonstrated that this method yields good agreement with well-accepted research instruments (Turner, Turner, Reif, Gutowski, & Gastfriend, 1999) and good interrater reliability (Baker & Gastfriend, 2003). Research on the PPC in the United States and abroad has shown that if a patient is placed in a level of care that is recommended by the PPC (or more intensive treatment; i.e., "matched" or "overmatched" care), better outcomes will result compared to an assignment to a level of care less intense than the recommended level ("undermatched"). Problems with undermatching include higher acute no-show rates to treatment (Kang, Sharon, Gastfriend, & Pirard, 2004; Lefebvre, Sharon, Kang, & Pirard, 2003), worse global clinical ratings at one month after treatment (Reggers et al., 2004), more frequent drinking at ninety days after treatment (Magura et al., 2003), and higher rates of hospital bed utilization in the year following undermatched treatment (Sharon et al., 2003).

Research Findings on Comorbidity and Related Problems and American Society of Addiction Medicine Patient Placement Criteria

The ASAM PPC have also been used to assess problems that contribute to psychiatric comorbidity. Using the original computerized algorithm, counselors questioned 700 public-sector uninsured and Medicaid-insured patients who were seeking treatment for alcohol or drug problems about their lifetime history of sexual or physical abuse. At baseline, patients who acknowledged an abuse history had significantly worse clinical impairment on psychiatric status scores than subjects without this history. Patients with an abuse history also had more prior utilization of various psychiatric services. Approximately half of these patients entered intensive substance abuse treatment (either Level II day treatment or partial hospital or Level III residential care). Over a one-year follow-up after treatment, the group with abuse histories had worse psychiatric status, more psychiatric hospitalizations, and more outpatient treatment than the nonabused group (Pirard, Sharon, Kang, Angarita, & Gastfriend, 2005). This finding shows that, with the help of a structured assessment, it is feasible to determine abuse history at intake and that it is important to plan for potential comorbid symptoms and treatment needs during these patients' recovery.

Matching patients with co-occurring psychiatric disorders to treatment appears to be more complex than for patients without psychiatric comorbidity. In the same cohort of 700 patients, no-show rates were examined for 204 patients with substance use disorders who also had other psychiatric problems (Angarita et al., 2007). All patients were assessed using the PPC-1 computerized assessment. The computer then blindly randomized each patient to be assigned to either Level II (intensive outpatient/partial hospitalization treatment) or Level III (residential rehabilitation). This created four groups: undermatched (recommended for Level III but assigned to Level II); overmatched (recommended for Level II but assigned to Level III); matched to Level II (recommended for and assigned to Level II); and matched to Level III (recommended for and assigned to Level III). Results showed that, overall, under-matching was associated with far more no-shows than matching. Among patients with co-occurring psychiatric disorders, however, overmatching resulted in significantly more no-shows than in patients without co-occuring psychiatric disorders (54 percent versus 28 percent, $p < 0.01$). Thus, patients with co-occurring psychiatric disorders appear to be more sensitive to mismatching—in both directions (up and down)—and the PPC appear to help improve no-show rates in this population.

COMPREHENSIVE CONTINUOUS INTEGRATED SYSTEM OF CARE

Individuals with dual diagnoses cannot be adequately served with only a few specialized programs; rather, the expectation of comorbidity must be addressed throughout the system of care. The Comprehensive Continuous Integrated System of Care (CCISC) is a model for system design, which permits any system to address this problem in an organized manner within the context of existing resources (Minkoff, 2005). The basic premise of this model is that all programs become dual diagnosis programs, meeting minimal standards for dual diagnosis competency. This restructuring began with expert consensus panels focused on standards of care for specific populations. In 1998, a report from one of these panels described the basic standards for best practices in diagnosis and treatment of patients with dual diagnoses: the system must be welcoming, accessible, continuous, and comprehensive (Minkoff, 2001). These standards answer the question "If I were an individual with co-occurring disorders, how would I want the system of care to be organized to best meet my needs?" and address the following principles.

Dual Diagnosis: Expectation, Not Exception

Any psychiatric patient requiring diagnostic or psychopharmacologic evaluation may also have a substance use disorder. Psychiatrists and counselors in addictions treatment need to incorporate this expectation into every clinical contact, beginning with assessment and continuing throughout the treatment process. This principle contributed to the need for replacement of the PPC-2 by the PPC-2R, which added the expectation that the level of care assessment process should assume that co-occurring disorders are often present (Minkoff et al., 2003).

Importance of Empathic, Hopeful, Integrated, and Continuing Relationship in Treatment

Successful treatment of psychiatric disorders, be it psychopharmacological or behavioral, is not an absolute science governed by the application of rigid rules. Rather, it is best performed in the context of an empathic, hopeful relationship, which integrates ongoing attention to both psychiatric and substance use issues. Emphasis needs to be placed on an initial integrated evaluation of both mental health and substance use and continuous reevaluation of diagnoses and treatment response.

Importance of Individualized Treatment With Structured Approach

The "four quadrant" model for categorizing individuals with co-occurring disorders (see Table 19-2) can be a first step in organizing treatment matching. This model divides patients throughout a service system into four quadrants based on high and low severity of each disorder. Therapeutic strategies may need to be adjusted based on type and level of severity of each illness. Individuals with high severity substance use disorders generally are those with active substance dependence (addiction), as opposed to those with lower severity disorders, such as substance abuse, or substance dependence of low severity. Pharmacological treatment strategies for either mental illness or substance use disorder may vary depending on the severity of the mental illness and the diagnosis of dependence versus abuse.

Case Management

Case management (which assists with supportive advocacy, follow-up, and living resources for individuals who cannot provide for themselves) and clinical care must be properly balanced with empathic detachment, opportunities for empowerment and choice, contracting, and contingent learning. As patients cannot prescribe their own medication (with the exception of over-the-counter medications such as nicotine replacement products or herbal and nutritional supplements such as St. John's Wort), the ability to receive medication for the treatment of dual diagnoses is a vital aspect of the integrated treatment relationship. Given that treatment involves learning, the psychopharmacologic treatment relationship needs to balance ongoing necessary continuity of care with opportunities for contingent learning (negotiation of type, quantity, and duration of treatment with any medication) without threat of loss of the treatment relationship. This contingent learning may require a "trial and error" process and several attempts before success is achieved. Contingency plans (e.g., "let's talk about what might happen if … and how you might cope with that") are most effective in the context of a good therapeutic alliance.

Chicken and Egg Conundrum: Mental Illness and Substance Use

When two disorders coexist, each disorder is "primary," requiring integrated, properly matched, diagnosis-specific treatment of adequate intensity. Thus, in general, psychopharmacological or behavioral interventions are designed to maximize the outcome of two primary disorders as follows:

1. For a psychiatric illness, the patient receives the most clinically effective psychopharmacological treatment available, regardless of the status of the comorbid substance disorder (special considerations apply for utilization of addictive or potentially addictive medications that may have psychiatric indications, such as benzodiazepines and stimulants).

2. For substance disorders, appropriate psychopharmacologic treatments (e.g., disulfiram, naltrexone, opiate maintenance) are used as ancillary

Table 19-2
**"Four Quadrant" Model for Categorizing Patients With Co-Occurring
Psychiatric and Substance Use Disorders for Treatment Planning**

		Severity of Psychiatric Disorder	
		Low	*High*
Severity of Substance Use Disorder	Low	Both psychiatric and substance use disorders are low severity	Psychiatric disorder is high severity, substance use disorder is low severity
	High	Substance use disorder is high severity, psychiatric disorder is low severity	Both psychiatric and substance use disorders are high severity

Note: Adapted from Minkoff (2005); reprinted with permission

treatments to support a comprehensive psychosocial program of recovery, regardless of the status of the comorbid psychiatric disorder (although clinicians should take into account the individual's cognitive capacity and disability).

Within the application of the above rules, some evidence for improvement in certain addictive disorders has been reported with several medications that also have common psychiatric indications (e.g., selective serotonin reuptake inhibitors (SSRIs), buproprion, and topiramate). When choosing medication for a psychiatric disorder, a clinician may wish to consider the possible effect of the medication on a co-occurring substance use disorders.

Temporal Factors: Context of "Disease and Recovery" Model

Treatment for each condition must be matched to its own phase of recovery. Acute stabilization of a substance use disorder requires engagement, for which motivational enhancement may be needed. In the active treatment phase, long-term stabilization issues need to be addressed in the realm of rehabilitation and recovery approaches. The stages of change (precontemplation, contemplation, preparation, action, maintenance) are important for each type of disorder and may be different for each disorder in a given patient.

Psychopharmacologic practice may vary depending on whether the patient is requires acute stabilization (e.g., detoxification) versus relapse prevention or rehabilitation. In addition, within the psychopharmacologic relationship, individuals may be engaged in active treatment or prolonged stabilization of one disorder (usually mental illness), which may provide an opportunity for the prescriber to participate in provision of motivational strategies regarding other comorbid conditions.

No One-Size-Fits-All Approach

For each patient, clinical intervention must be matched according to the current need for engagement in an integrated relationship, level of impairment or severity, specific diagnoses, phase of recovery, and stage of change. This is the underlying principle for ASAM PPC treatment matching.

Clinical Outcomes Must Be Individualized

Just as clinicians must individualize treatment interventions, clinicians must also to individualize the goals of treatment. Outcome expectations such as abstinence from all substances and full recovery from mental illness are usually long-term goals, but short-term clinical outcomes must be individualized. Goals for a nicotine-dependent depressed patient might include gradual reduction in cigarettes per day plus induction of an antidepressant and stabilization of suicidal ideation. Goals may include reduction in symptoms or use of certain substances or routes of administration (e.g., elimination of needle sharing), increases in level of functioning, increases in disease management skills, movement through stages of change, reduction in harm exposure (passive or active), reduction in service use, or movement to a lower level of care.

MULTIDIMENSIONAL PATIENT PLACEMENT CRITERIA ISSUES IN COMORBID PATIENTS: APPLICATIONS TO CASE PRESENTATION

These principles demonstrate how substance use problems interact with other psychiatric problems and why optimal care requires decision rules for more than just the single dimension of emotional/behavioral/cognitive assessment.

Manifestation of Clinical Issues in American Society of Addiction Medicine Patient Placement Criteria Dimensions

In the case presented at the beginning of this chapter (see "Case Presentation"), the patient manifests important clinical issues in five of the six ASAM PPC dimensions (see Table 19-1):

- *Dimension 1*: Possible mild-moderate withdrawal from a combination of alcohol and benzodiazepines.
- *Dimension 2*: No acute biomedical conditions or complications.
- *Dimension 3*: Anxious depression, chronic, with passive suicidal ideation.
- *Dimension 4*: Motivation to pursue various treatments, with recent active attendance at AA meetings and a sponsor relationship and willingness to seek inpatient rehabilitation now.
- *Dimension 5*: Virtually certain likelihood of continued use of substances without a change in current circumstances that isolates the patient from access to alcohol and medicines.
- *Dimension 6*: Unsupportive environment for recovery needs; the patient lives alone, has much free time during evenings, weekends, and summers, and lacks a supportive network other than her sponsor.

Interactions Across Dimensions

In addition to the concerns in each dimension, several dimensions (see Table 19-1) interact with one another. The patient's withdrawal (Dimension 1), although perhaps medically mild to moderate, might exacerbate her anxiety beyond her ability to cope

(Dimension 3), even with partial hospital care during the daytime. If the patient's depression worsens, it is possible that her motivation to pursue recovery efforts may diminish (Dimension 5). She is losing track of how many tranquilizer pills she is taking, and if this is due to mild cognitive impairment (Dimension 3), this may cause her to lose her job (Dimension 6), and her suicidal ideation may turn to suicidal intent and gesture. These interactions must be calculated to determine a risk-benefit ratio for the candidate levels of care.

Proper Placement of Patient in Case Presentation

Data presented earlier in the research discussion indicates that the comorbid conditions are complex, and both undermatching and overmatching could be counterproductive. Clearly, there is no "cookie cutter" standard treatment for this patient. Since outpatient care has failed to stabilize the patient, the possible levels of care include Level II.5 (partial hospitalization), Level III (residential treatment), or Level IV (hospital care). Since she does not show imminent severe withdrawal, acute suicidal intent, or psychotic depression, Level IV would be overly restrictive at this time. Her combination of problems and the multiple interactions between dimensions strongly suggest that she would not be safely treated in Level II. The best recommendation is Level III. The program should be DDC, at least, and may need to be DDE, particularly initially, to permit stabilization of the patient's acute anxiety. Indeed, as the case evolved, this placement did prove effective for her.

CONCLUSION

The goal of dual diagnosis interventions is recovery from two serious illnesses (psychiatric and substance use disorders), in which the patient learns to manage both illnesses so that he/she can grow in health and pursue meaningful life goals.

Successful implementation of dual diagnoses services within mental health systems depends on changes at several levels: clear policy directives with consistent organizational and financial supports, program changes to implement the mission of addressing co-occurring substance abuse, supports for the acquisition of expertise at the clinical level, and availability of accurate information to consumers and family members (Drake et al., 2001).

Like other forms of managed care, managed behavioral health care attempts to control the costs of treatment. One prominent approach to cost control is achieved through limiting the utilization of services. Utilization is limited by imposing a variety of restrictions and financial incentives with respect to which services are covered and which practitioners may be selected. Managed care procedures have contained costs of health care. The unintended consequences of the managed care revolution have been decreased substance abuse treatment benefits, decreased availability of appropriate care, and decreased autonomy of clinicians to make treatment decisions for their patients. Given the overwhelming cost that inadequately treated substance abuse imposes on society, it is vital that these trends be reversed (Galanter, Keller, Dermatis, Egelko, & ASAM, 2001).

In creating the PPC, ASAM intended to serve the needs of dual diagnosis patients with a paradigm for multidimensional service intensity assessment. Although the PPC have apparently achieved an important degree of success, judging by their high rate of adoption by dual diagnosis capable treatment programs (Johnson & Gastfriend, 2005), they still needs ongoing research to inform future refinements (Gastfriend, 2003).

Suggestions for Further Reading

For readers who wish to study further in this area, we recommend:

- Gastfriend, D. R. (Ed.). (2003). Addiction treatment matching: Research foundations of the American Society of Addiction Medicine (ASAM) criteria. Binghamton, NY: Haworth Press, Inc.

- American Society of Addiction Medicine patient placement criteria: Background and instruction for placing order: http://www.asam.org/PatientPlacementCriteria.html.

References

Angarita, G. A., Reif, S., Pirard, S., Lee, S., Sharon, E., & Gastfriend, D. R. (2007). No-show for treatment in substance abuse patients with comorbid symptomatology: Validity results from controlled trial of the ASAM patient placement criteria. *Journal of Addiction Medicine, 1*, 79-87.

Baker, S. L., & Gastfriend, D. R. (2003). Reliability of multidimensional substance abuse treatment matching: Implementing the ASAM patient placement criteria. *Journal of Addictive Disease, 22*(Suppl. 1), 45-60.

Bech, P., Allerup, P., Gram, L. F., Reisby, N., Rosenberg, R., Jacobsen, O., et al. (1981). The Hamilton depression scale. *Acta Psychiatrica Scandinavica, 63*, 290-299.

Boltaev, A., Bakhtiyor, S., Gromov, I., Lefebvre, R., & Gastfriend, D. R. (2004). *Initial results of utilization of ASAM PPC-2R software in Bukhara.* Presented at the National Institute on Drug Abuse International Forum, San Juan, Puerto Rico.

Deck, D., Gabriel, R., Knudsen, J., & Grams, G. (2003). Impact of patient placement criteria on substance abuse treatment under the Oregon Health Plan. *Journal of Addictive Disease, 22*(Suppl. 1), 27-44.

Drake, R. E., Essock, S. M., Shaner, A., Carey, K. B., Minkoff, K., Kola, L., et al. (2001). Implementing dual diagnosis services for clients with severe mental illness. *Psychiatric Services, 52*, 469-476.

Fudala, P. J., Berkow, L. C., Fralich, J. L., & Johnson, R. E. (1991). Use of naloxone in the assessment of opiate dependence. *Life Sciences, 49*, 1809-1814.

Galanter, M., Keller, D. S., Dermatis, H., Egelko, S., & American Society of Addiction Medicine. (2001). The impact of managed care on substance abuse treatment: A problem in need of a solution. A report of the American Society of Addiction Medicine. *Recent Developments in Alcoholism, 15*, 419-436.

Gastfriend, D. R., Filstead, W. J., Reif, S., Najavits, L. M., & Parrella, D. (1995). Validity of assessing treatment readiness in patients with substance use disorders. *American Journal on Addictions, 4*, 254-260.

Gastfriend, D. R. (Ed.) (2003). *Addiction treatment matching: Research foundations of the American Society of Addiction Medicine (ASAM) criteria.* Binghamton, NY: Haworth Press.

Hamilton, M. (1960). A rating scale for depression. *Journal of Neurology, Neurosurgery, and Psychiatry, 23*, 56-62.

Johnson, A., & Gastfriend, D. R. (2005). *Use of ASAM PPC: Data from a national sample of addiction treatment programs.* Presented at the American Society of Addiction Medicine Annual Medical-Scientific Conference, Dallas, TX.

Kang, S. K., Sharon, E., Gastfriend, D. R., & Pirard, S. (2004). *Preference for residential rehabilitation in high frequency cocaine dependence: Validation of the American Society of Addiction Medicine (ASAM) criteria.* Presented at the World Forum on Drugs and Dependencies, Montreal, Canada.

Lefebvre, R., Sharon, E., Kang, S., & Pirard, S. (2003). *Concurrent validity of the ASAM criteria in heroin users.* Presented at the 14th Annual Meeting of the American Academy of Addicion Psychiatry, New Orleans, LA.

Magura, S., Staines G, Kosanke, N., Rosenblum, A., Foote, J., Deluca, A., et al. (2003). Predictive validity of the ASAM patient placement criteria for naturalistically matched versus mismatched alcoholism patients. *American Journal on Addictions, 12,* 386-397.

McLellan, A. T., Kushner, H., Metzger, D., Peters, R., Smith, I., Grissom, G., et al. (1992). The fifth edition of the Addiction Severity Index. *Journal of Substance Abuse Treatment, 9,* 199-213.

McLellan, A. T., Luborsky, L., Cacciola, J., Griffith, J., Evans, F., Barr, H. L., et al. (1985). New data from the Addiction Severity Index: Reliability and validity in three centers. *Journal of Nervous and Mental Disease, 173,* 412-423.

Mee-Lee, D., Shulman, G. D., Fishman, M., Gastfriend, D. R., & Griffith, J. H. (Eds.). (2001). *ASAM patient placement criteria for the treatment of substance-related disorders* (2nd ed.-rev.). Chevy Chase, MD: American Society of Addiction Medicine.

Minkoff, K. J., Zweben, J., Rosenthal, R., & Ries, R. (2003). Development of service intensity criteria and program categories for individuals with co-occurring disorders. *Journal of Addictive Disease, 22*(Suppl. 1), 113-129.

Minkoff, K. (2001). Developing standards of care for individuals with co-occurring psychiatric and substance use disorders. *Psychiatric Services, 52,* 597-599.

Minkoff, K. (2005). *Comprehensive Continuous Integrated System of Care (CCISC): Psychopharmacology practice guidelines for individuals with Co-Occurring Psychiatric and Substance Use Disorders (COD).* Retrieved April 3, 2008, from http://www.kenminkoff. com/article1.html

O'Sullivan, R., Fava, M., Agustin, C., Baer, L., & Rosenbaum, J. F. (1997). Sensitivity of the six-item Hamilton depression rating scale. *Acta Psychiatrica Scandinavica, 95,* 379-384.

Peachey, J., & Lei, H. (1988). Assessment of opioid dependence with naloxone. *British Journal of Addiction, 83,* 193-201.

Pirard, S., Sharon, E., Kang, S. K., Angarita, G. A., & Gastfriend, D. R. (2005). Prevalence of physical and sexual abuse among substance abuse patients and impact on treatment outcomes. *Drug and Alcohol Dependence, 78,* 57-64.

Plough, A., Shirley, L., Zaremba, N., Baker, G., Schwartz, M., & Mulvey, K. (1996). *CSAT target cities demonstration final evaluation report.* Boston: Office for Treatment Improvement.

Reggers, J., Ansseau, M., Gustin, F., Pirard, S., VanDenn, P., Seghers, A., et al. (2004). *Adaptation and validation of the ASAM PPC-2R criteria in Belgian drug-addicts.* Presented at the International Society of Addiction Medicine Annual Meeting, Helsinki, Finland.

Rubin, A., & Gastfriend, D. R. (2001). Patient placement criteria and their relation to access to appropriate level of care and engagement in alchoholism treatment. *Recent Developments in Alcoholism, 15,* 157-176.

Saitz, R., Mayo-Smith, M. F., Roberts, M. S., Redmond, H. A., Bernard, D. R., & Calkins, D. R. (1994). Individualized treatment for alcohol withdrawal: A randomized double-blind controlled trial. *Journal of the American Medical Association, 272,* 519-523.

Sharon, E., Krebs, C., Turner, W., Desai, N., Binus, G., Penk, W., et al. (2003). Predictive validity of the ASAM patient placement criteria for hospital utilization. *Journal of Addictive Diseases, 22*(Suppl. 1), 79-93.

Sullivan, J. T., Sykora, K., Schneiderman, J., Naranjo, C. A., & Sellers, E. M. (1989). Assessment of alcohol withdrawal: The revised Clinical Institute Withdrawal Assessment for Alcohol Scale (CIWA-Ar). *British Journal of Addiction, 84,* 1353-1357.

Turner, W. M., Turner, K. H., Reif, S., Gutowski, W. E., & Gastfriend, D. R. (1999). Feasibility of multidimensional substance abuse treatment matching: Automating the ASAM patient placement criteria. *Drug and Alcohol Dependence, 55,* 35-43.

Wartenberg, A. A., Nirenberg, T. D., Liepman, M. R., Silvia, L. Y., Begin, A. M., & Monti, P. M. (1990). Detoxification of alcoholics: Improving care by symptom-triggered sedation. *Alcoholism: Clinical and Experimental Research, 14,* 71-75.

Wasilewski, D., Matsumoto, H., Kur, E., Dziklińska, A., Woźny, E., Stencka, K., et al. (1996). Assessment of diazepam loading dose therapy of delirium tremens. *Alcohol and Alcoholism, 31,* 273-278.

Chapter 20

Directions for Future Research on Treating Co-Occurring Substance Use and Psychiatric Disorders

by Jennifer P. Wisdom, Ph.D., M.P.H., Christiane Farentinos, M.D., M.P.H., C.A.D.C.-II, N.C.D.C.-II, Tim Hartnett, M.S.W., M.H.A., Lucy Zammarelli, M.A., N.C.A.C.-II, and Dennis McCarty, Ph.D.

INTRODUCTION

Co-occurring psychiatric and addiction disorders in patients challenge practitioners with complex symptom presentations and require creative treatment planning and increased services. Research on treatment for co-occurring disorders challenges investigators to recognize the complexity of diagnosis and to craft innovative studies. Efforts to improve care for patients with co-occurring alcohol, drug, and mental health problems demand multidimensional and creative research designs reflecting the needs of special populations, integration of multiple care providers, and acknowledgment of the constraints of available resources in the field.

This chapter outlines a research agenda that responds to the variability and complexity of the patients and the clinical environments. We draw on our experience as clinicians, directors, and payers for treatment services, and we illustrate the research possibilities with case examples from the patients in our care. The chapter begins with suggestions for improvements in quality of care through research on system change and integration strategies. Opportunities to test training and workforce development methods are identified, research on recovery models is examined, and studies of specific treatments and combinations of disorders are reviewed.

IMPROVING SYSTEMS OF CARE

Adolescent Case Study Involving Multiple Stakeholders

MT is 15 years of age. She smokes marijuana, drinks alcohol, and uses methamphetamine. She has a diagnosis of bipolar disorder and has had prior outpatient treatment for alcohol and drug use. Her county juvenile probation officer requested residential treatment for MT because she was continuing to use drugs and was at high risk for increased criminal involvement. MT was referred to an adolescent treatment program (grant-funded bed). Despite her parents' skepticism of drug treatment, their reluctance to allow their daughter to enter residential care, and their resistance to involvement with social services, her mother, father, grandparents, and aunt signed permission forms and release of information forms. Since MT was able to receive free treatment, her family was more amenable to the placement and became more cooperative with treatment staff. Her school eventually released records and authorized the treatment program to assume responsibility for the individualized education plan during the teen's stay. The outpatient treatment program where MT received prior treatment was contacted for clinical records. The admissions coordinator at the residential program spoke with the psychiatrist from the juvenile detention facility who had prescribed psychiatric medications and with physicians at the facility who had written orders for additional medications. MT was enrolled in the Children's Medical Fund (the state children's health insurance program) so that she had access to medical care while in treatment. Medical appointments were scheduled with a nurse and physician at the county health center. The scheduling of these medical appointments required the execution of a power of attorney (so that the treatment program had the authority to act on behalf of the patient). Subsequent treatment planning and coordination required contacts with Services for Children and Families (the state child protection agency), County Mental Health, Planned Parenthood, County Parks and Recreation, Sexual Assault Support Services, Catholic Charities and other faith-based support groups, and the local school district. The drug court for teens required regular reports on the patient's progress. Since MT did not have children, she was not required to take parenting classes and did not receive referrals to Women, Infants, and Children (WIC), an early childhood specialist, a pediatrician, Court Appointed Special Advocates, foster care, or housing.

Integration of Services

The patient in the above example (see "Adolescent Case Study Involving Multiple Stakeholders") illustrates the multifaceted nature of the treatment environment and the variety of roles a treatment provider must assume in order to provide residential care for adolescents. Co-occurring disorders provide a unique opportunity for studies of how treatment systems facilitate and inhibit treatment access, retention, and recovery. Adolescents with co-occurring disorders who require drug abuse treatment have many needs and generally must obtain services from multiple venues, including drug treatment, mental health treatment, child welfare, juvenile justice, and school-based programs. Each of these services is typically funded through different sources and requires separate consents and releases, leading to challenges in obtaining and integrating care. The integration of care and case management that assists in the use of multiple service venues appears to enhance outcomes for patients (e.g., Friesen & Winters, 2003; New Freedom Commission on Mental Health, 2003; Simpson, 2004) but may not occur in part due to the complexities and costs of the interventions. Research should focus on expanding and integrating systems of mental health and substance abuse treatment for adolescents with co-occurring disorders, as well as other patient populations, such as homeless individuals, pregnant women and single mothers, older adults, lesbians, gays, and trans-sexuals, or individuals involved in the justice system. Studies exploring the spiritual components of recovery for women and men with co-occurring disorders are also needed (e.g., Cook, 2004); many former patients refer to spiritual encounters as the impetus to change their substance abuse behavior, yet little research has been conducted to explore the use of spiritual interventions. While integration of services is often endorsed, little research has been conducted on the organization and financing of such services (Drake et al., 2001).

Need for Evaluation and Modification of Mental Health and Drug Treatment Systems

An evaluation of mental health and drug treatment systems should determine existing infrastructure, staffing and training budgets, and areas of responsibility, particularly regarding patients with co-occurring mental health and substance use disorders. Mental health systems typically draw from multiple professions including psychiatry, psychology, nursing, social work, and vocational rehabilitation and have greater access to medical support than the alcohol and drug treatment systems. Alcohol and drug treatment systems tend to have little if any medical support; their budgets do not support staffing of treatment professionals from multiple disciplines or case managers who can handle a more demanding and complex caseload. Alcohol and drug treatment facilities are often in poor condition and in stigmatized settings. These differences in systems' infrastructure have the biggest impact on patients with co-occurring mental health and addiction problems. States may need to delineate clearly each system's responsibility for individuals with co-occurring mental health and addiction disorders, determine appropriate placement criteria, and provide support for infrastructure development in order to ensure quality treatment. If mental health systems take primary responsibility for the drug treatment needs of individuals with severe and persistent mental illness and of children and adolescents with severe emotional disturbance, they will need to retrain staff and modify current programming. When alcohol and drug treatment programs provide care for people who have addictions and co-occurring severe mental illness, staff members require training, and the infrastructure must be changed in order to manage the complex medical needs of these patients.

Need for Coordination of Systems

The present stage of mental health and drug treatment systems must be assessed separately, and ways in which the systems might be coordinated should be considered. The ability of multiple systems to collaborate to provide care often can affect treatment outcomes (Bickman, 1997). Gains in measures of treatment process, such as service intensity and duration of treatment, are associated with improved outcomes (Hser, Evans, Huang, & Anglin, 2004). In a study of individuals in treatment for both addiction and depression, researchers found that integrating psychiatric case management increased the patients' engagement in treatment and their likelihood of obtaining psychiatric referrals (Womack et al., 2004). Other systems, such as child welfare and criminal justice, may need to be integrated into mental health and drug treatment services. Research challenges include identifying models that aid cross-institutional policy development and developing methods to find or create contrasting systems of care. New systems must be constructed or existing service delivery formats must be modified in order to create environments where research questions can be tested. For example, while many states aim to integrate drug treatment and addiction services, institutions and local agencies may resist participating in statewide collaborations.

Network for the Improvement of Addiction Treatment

The cost of research often limits the size of studies and research projects, thereby limiting the generalizability of findings. One current project, however, suggests that small changes in how services are organized can enhance care for patients and may provide a model for determining ways to improve care. The Network for the Improvement of Addiction Treatment (NIATx) includes thirty-nine drug abuse treatment programs and five states and uses process improvement techniques to facilitate organizational changes that reduce days to admission and improve retention in care. The Center for Substance Abuse Treatment and the Robert Wood Johnson Foundation support the project to assess the feasibility of making and sustaining incremental improvement in patient care. Participating programs have restructured admission processes and reduced wait time substantially. Improvements in scheduling and staff skills are leading to better retention (see the project Web site for more information: http://www.niatx.org). Application of these system improvement techniques to systems of care for treatment of co-occurring disorders is a future research opportunity.

TRAINING AND WORKFORCE DEVELOPMENT

Agency Efforts to Implement Evidence-Based Practice

Agencies with the goal to enhance the capability for delivering evidence-based interventions may have different training and workforce development strategies. ChangePoint, an alcohol and drug treatment agency in Portland, Oregon, invested considerable resources in training and supervising clinicians to use motivational interviewing (MI), a nonconfrontational counseling method that encourages behavior change by helping patients to identify and resolve ambivalence to change (Miller & Rollnick, 2002). In 1998, the agency established a six-month study group for clinicians to review articles and chapters about MI. In 2000, ChangePoint joined the National Institute on Drug Abuse's Clinical Trials Network and was selected to be part of the "Motivational Interviewing to Improve Treatment Engagement and Outcome in Subjects Seeking Treatment for Substance Abuse" protocol, which introduced the rigors of research-driven supervision and quality assurance, including the use of fidelity measures (e.g., recording and coding of MI sessions to ensure protocol adherence). Through weekly small group supervision sessions that were dedicated to MI skill building, taping and coding of individual group sessions, and role playing, ChangePoint staff members improved their proficiency in MI. Implementation of evidence-based practices requires patience, creativity, and perseverance.

CODA, Inc., another alcohol and drug treatment agency in Portland, Oregon, has also created a workforce development infrastructure. In partnership with the Northwest Frontier Addiction Technology Transfer Center, CODA adopted a multisite clinical supervision model to support and monitor the implementation of evidence-based practice. The model relies on the frequent supervision of clinical work by supervisors with direct feedback. CODA's executive director contracted with several universities to provide ongoing clinical skills training through coursework that lasts three to four months and long-term consultation on the mechanics of creating a full continuum of care that moves individuals seamlessly from more intensive to less intensive services (e.g., detoxification, residential, intensive outpatient, outpatient, aftercare). CODA also hired a senior manager to oversee these efforts and to orient new program staff to CODA's clinical model. In addition, the agency's executive director works with state, university, and community college officials to address the ongoing challenge of recruiting and training future workers.

Staffing Issues

Training and staffing issues are at the forefront of improving systems of care for patients with co-occurring disorders. High annual staff turnover (rates of 18 to 25 percent are reported among counselors working in alcohol and drug treatment) disrupts patient engagement and retention in care; these rates are much higher than in other related fields (Knudsen, Johnson, & Roman, 2003; Gallon, Gabriel, & Knudsen, 2003). Training for mental health and addiction therapists in co-occurring disorders and cross-disciplinary techniques is inadequate (Harwood, Kowalski, & Ameen, 2004; Substance Abuse and Mental Health Services Administration (SAMHSA), 2004), and there is some evidence that professionals may have negative attitudes toward patients with co-occurring mental health and addiction disorders (e.g., Richmond & Foster, 2003). Because of high turnover rates, minimal training, and stigma, addiction treatment programs must invest substantial resources in staff development. Counselors are expected to do too much with too few resources. They regularly assess and address physical, mental, and behavioral problems, family and relationship issues, low education levels, criminal and legal involvement, trauma histories, patient alienation from medical/mental health fields, domestic violence, and poverty.

Stress among counselors increases with high-needs patients. Patients with dual diagnoses may display violent behavior, emotional outbursts, and poor patient compliance; medication management is often sporadic. Medication compliance can be difficult to assess in patients who lack daily structure and commitment to treatment.

Vicarious traumatization (Jenkins & Baird, 2002) is also an issue for counselors, who may listen to numerous horrific stories from patients every week. The salaries of substance abuse counselors usually fall on the lower end of the health care pay scale, and many counselors struggle financially to meet the needs of their families. The workforce has shifted toward a greater percentage of female staff members (Roget, Storti, Albers, Horvatich, & Skinstad, 2005), many of whom are mothers and must juggle child care, housekeeping tasks, and their careers. In addition, benefits are often quite limited, leaving family members of counselors without adequate health insurance and staff without retirement benefits.

Research to Address Staffing Issues

Research that investigates variability in education and salary levels of counselors and the impact of counselors' backgrounds and working conditions on patient outcomes is needed. Research also can assess a range of strategies to reduce turnover: increase the autonomy and accountability of "front-line" employees; support staff creativity and knowledge ownership of new ideas; link rewards to performance; and provide continuing education, direct supervision, and in-service training (Gallon et al., 2003; Knudsen et al., 2003).

Research must be conducted to evaluate efforts to improve staff skills; the most effective methods for improving staff skills in evidence-based practices are unknown. The adoption of new practices is a complicated process (Miller & Mount, 2001; Miller, Yahne, Moyers, Martinez, & Pirritano, 2004), and strategies for training can be tested and compared. For example, Miller et al. (2004) compared five training conditions for MI education: two-day clinical workshop, workshop plus feedback, workshop plus coaching, workshop plus feedback and coaching, and a self-study control group. The addition of feedback and/or coaching improved the retention of proficiency after the workshop, and the participants in the self-study group did not show any significant improvement in proficiency. The workshop-only condition yielded modest gains, and participants' skills returned to baseline after four months. This study suggests the need for structured supervision and coaching. A study by Peters et al. (2005) found that counselors with access to trained opinion leaders were more likely to use the evidence-based treatment manual. Future research should focus on how much counselor education actually affects patient outcome.

Need for Evaluation and Modification of Training and Licensing Requirements

An evaluation of state training and licensing requirements for professionals who provide care to individuals with either mental health disorders or addiction disorders, or both, might help to improve training for treatment of co-occurring disorders. Licensing and certification standards vary substantially between the substance abuse and mental health fields. Research is needed to assess the impacts of different standards on the quality and effectiveness of services. SAMHSA (2004) recommends that state licensure requirements should support a "whole person" model that offers respect for the individual within his/her environment. State licensure bodies can implement similar ideas and training requirements to reflect each state's perspective on recovery. In addition, policy research is necessary to determine the impact of state measures that tie funding to adoption of evidence-based practices and the impact of laws requiring parity between funding for mental health and substance abuse treatment. Research can also examine whether the inclusion of consumer advocates on advisory boards results in a more holistic perspective of practitioner/patient relationships (SAMHSA, 2004). The primary objectives of staff development, training, and certification are to promote quality of care and the use of evidence-based practices. The goal is to train practitioners who can provide a holistic system of care for the treatment of the disease of addiction from detoxification through continuing care.

IMPLEMENTATION OF EVIDENCE-BASED PRACTICES

Adult Case Study With Domestic Violence and Family Issues

When confronted with choices between drug use and their roles as parents, employees, students, and citizens, those using drugs and alcohol sometimes make poor decisions that complicate their lives. SD, for example, is 24 years of age, is dependent on methamphetamine, and has three children under the age of five. Although she describes herself as a good mother, her children are all in foster care because of neglect and exposure to violence. Her current partner has a history of violence and has been court-ordered to attend an intervention program for batterers. SD has been court-ordered to go to a residential drug treatment facility; she is participating in the "Seeking Safety" program, a manualized treatment program for patients who have posttraumatic stress disorder (PTSD) and are at risk for further abuse (Najavits, 2001). The program helps SD to focus on her personal safety while also addressing her substance abuse problems. SD is receiving parenting classes, and plans are in place for reunification with her children. To help SD and her children remain safe, her treatment program tracks her partner's treatment progress and assesses potential risk for SD and her children. A restraining order prevents him from visiting the treatment center or contacting SD and the children. However, SD secretly arranged a meeting with him while out of the facility on a pass. She insists she did not know that seeing her partner would compromise her plans for reunion with her children.

Treatment and Practice Guidelines

Treatment and practice guidelines offer suggestions for addressing challenging symptoms and assisting patients in recovery. Many of these guidelines would benefit from more examination, including use of rigorous assessments, manuals, and fidelity measures ((Drake et al., 2001). For example, symptoms of co-occurring depression and substance abuse are often difficult to distinguish; care is needed during evaluation of the patient, which should include observations during an abstinence period prior to diagnosis or, if possible, a careful evaluation of the patient's depression history (Nunes & Levin, 2004). A method for determining which patients are most likely to benefit from early medication management might improve outcomes.

Need for Targeted Interventions for Special Populations

Manualized assessments such as "Seeking Safety" (Najavits, 2001) for co-occurring PTSD and substance abuse have demonstrated efficacy. There is much need for research that investigates the active treatment elements and real-world application of manualized interventions. Individuals with co-occurring disorders are frequently excluded from large-scale studies, and the focus of investigations is often on the intervention rather than on the individuals' process of recovery (SAMHSA, 2004). Increased attention in the development of manualized treatments for patients with co-occurring substance abuse and depression, attention deficit hyperactivity disorder (ADHD), chronic pain, and conduct disorder is needed.

Targeting interventions to specific subpopulations has demonstrated efficacy in health behavior interventions (e.g., Strecher, Wang, Derry, Wildenhaus, & Johnson, 2002). A demonstrated need for gender-targeted interventions has led to increased research on differences between women and men in their needs for treatment and experiences in treatment. Adolescent boys with co-occurring ADHD and substance abuse problems are likely to be incarcerated and to meet criteria for conduct disorder (Rosler et al., 2004). They would likely benefit from targeted treatment. Therapies for these patient groups have not been widely tested and must be improved.

A focus on randomized trials (advocated by the research community) may reduce the study of certain groups if these proposals are given funding priority. Researchers should include children and older adults, people with eating disorders, incarcerated individuals, and gender and sexual minorities in their studies (SAMHSA, 2004). Generalization from clinical trials to specific patient populations is often risky. Large-scale trials with heterogeneous patient populations may provide more guidance to practitioners. The focus also needs to broaden and include a long-term perspective on recovery.

Treatment for Adult Case Example With Domestic Violence and Family Issues

The counselor of the patient in the above case example (see "Adult Case Study With Domestic Violence and Family Issues") recognized the complexity of the patient's problems and sought guidance from the treatment literature. "Seeking Safety" helped SD understand how some of her actions were not in her best interests, and she began to make better choices that supported her family reunification. In addition, working from a comprehensive case management approach, the counselor requested that the patient sign a "Release of Information" form so that contact could be initiated between the treatment agency and the intervention program for batterers. The patient's partner took accountability for his role in breaking the restraining order; eventually he became more supportive of her treatment goals and her reunification with her children. Although it took several weeks of collaborative counseling work, SD was able to focus on herself, her children, and her own recovery.

RECOVERY PROCESSES

Adult Case Study With Homeless Individual

WS arrived from the state hospital after serving time following a "guilty but insane" plea. He reported years of homelessness before being convicted. He did not have personal identity papers such as a driver's license or birth certificate. Patients without valid identification face challenges—they cannot get a job without a driver's license, and they cannot get a driver's license without a birth certificate and Social Security number. Counselors helped WS to contact the Department of Motor Vehicles and the Department of Health (in another state, of course) in order to request copies of records and to begin the often slow process of reestablishing an identity. Slowly, he gained confidence, found a job, and began putting his life back together while maintaining sobriety. He now lives in subsidized housing and cares for his two teen-age daughters and a grandchild. His apartment is beautifully decorated and showcases his skill and talent at interior design. His landlord has agreed to make more apartment units available to graduates of the treatment program. A case manager checks in on WS weekly and more frequently on other patients in order to help them remain in their jobs and apartments.

Need for Further Study of Factors That Impact Recovery

Recovery models (e.g., Anthony, 1993; Green, 2004) address consumer-driven approaches that recognize the impact of interactions between patients and providers on recovery. The models stress the importance of patients' subjective experiences and need for autonomy during recovery, which can sometimes conflict with the standard medical or evidence-based practice models (Frese, Stanley, Kress, & Vogel-Scibilia, 2001). Preliminary studies indicate that aspects of health services like the patient-provider relationship, treatment continuity, and family involvement in treatment are important factors in individuals' recovery from mental illness or addiction; these aspects have yet to be studied rigorously in individuals with co-occurring disorders.

Self-directed care and consumer participation in treatment decisions have the potential to redefine treatment (New Freedom Commission on Mental Health, 2003; SAMHSA, 2005). It is important to consider how these developments impact the integration of a recovery model and the medical/evidence-based treatment model in order to ensure that services are appropriately redesigned, that stakeholders have a voice in changes to treatment systems, and that clinicians are prepared for these changes.

Positive changes in service delivery and in the perspective of providers will likely reduce the stigma of addictions and mental disorders, thereby encouraging more individuals to obtain treatment. Lehman, Greener, and Simpson (2002) examined how findings on organizational assessment can be used to identify barriers and issues that need to be addressed before new clinical methods can be adopted. Lehman, Greener, and Simpson's assessment of organizational functioning and readiness for change focuses on the importance of motivation and personality attributes of program leaders and staff members, institutional resources, and organizational climate in the introduction of new technologies into a program. Research is needed on factors that influence changes in organizational culture and the adoption of new technology.

A stigma of mental disorders and addictions remains; removal of this stigma would improve treatment experiences, increase potential social support for recovery, and reduce the shame and fear associated with treatment (SAMHSA, 2004). The role of families in patients' recovery is underexplored; a family history of trauma, violence, substance abuse, and mental illness, family treatment experiences, and family views on professional treatment and medication can have enormous impact on a person's decision to seek treatment (SAMHSA, 2004) The term "family" should be redefined to include all those whom the patient views as influencing his/her recovery (rather than just biological relatives and spouses/partners), thereby increasing a patient's social support. Adolescents and young adults are likely to have destroyed fewer family relationships than older addicts. Many youths report that parental substance use and mental illness impacts their own conditions. Support from extended family may contribute greatly to positive long-term outcomes.

SUMMARY AND DIRECTIONS FOR FUTURE RESEARCH

Given that there are plenty of areas in which to conduct research and only limited resources, priorities must be established. Research could focus on treatment for patients who have the most needs and fewest resources, such as patients with co-occurring schizophrenia and substance use and incarcerated individuals. Another option is to address those areas that are most amenable to change or those areas in which the most promising preliminary work has been completed. SAMHSA (Power & DeMartino, 2004) encourages evaluation of treatment capacity and treatment effectiveness, despite the numerous barriers to conducting these evaluations.

A primary barrier to research is the quality of data available from many drug treatment agencies. Many agencies collect data principally for state or federal requirements (McLellan, Carise, & Kleber, 2003). There is a need for a thorough examination of the quantity and quality of data across all areas of the drug treatment system, including caseloads, sources of funding, treatment system infrastructure, and state and federal funding and policies. Recent initiatives have educated agencies on the value of data and the use of data-driven decisions (e.g., NIATx); with technical assistance and a focus on the value of data, substantial changes can be made in the use and interpretation of data.

In addition, research should be conducted and outcomes should be reported in ways that ensure widespread application of findings (collection of data and distribution of findings should not be limited to academics). Treatment agencies would benefit from opportunities to collaborate on projects that address common problems and to consult on common issues that require attention. Several models of research-to-practice partnerships, such as the National Institute on Drug Abuse (NIDA) Clinical Trials Network and SAMHSA's Addiction Technology Transfer Centers and Practice Improvement Collaboratives (Cotter, Bowler, Mulkern, & McCarty, 2005), focus on collaborations between academic research institutions and community drug treatment centers.

Like many young fields, the substance abuse treatment field is largely based on nonscientific theories and unresearched interventions. Treatment approaches vary widely between agencies and across the country, and treatment in private practice is generally very different from treatment in community-based clinics. Twelve-step models may guide recovery-based programs, while a focus on medications may prevail in medical facilities. The quality of psychological counseling varies from inadequate to excellent. Basic health care is not available to many individuals. Little is known about unique needs of special populations, and specific interventions for specific substance use disorders are just beginning to be accepted. Although research on evidence-based practices has received a great deal of funding, the adoption of these practices by professionals in the field is slow.

The blending of the mental health field and addictions field has resulted in fewer specialists and fewer specialty practices; patients may try numerous medications in a "guinea pig" model. Limited resources in substance abuse treatment programs are inadequate for dual diagnosed patients. The two fields make uncomfortable partners; the pay scales and education levels of their employees vary widely.

Research opportunities abound. Better care results in better outcomes, and better outcomes will facilitate the integration of substance abuse treatment into the health care system. Most importantly, the quality of life for patients will improve.

Suggestions for Further Reading

For readers who wish to study further in this area, we recommend:

- Cotter, F., Bowler, S., Mulkern, V., & McCarty, D. (2005). Practice improvement collaboratives: An overview. *Journal of Addictive Diseases, 24*(Suppl. 1), 1-14.

- Institute for Healthcare Improvement: http://www.ihi.org/ihi.

- Institute of Medicine. (2001). *Crossing the quality chasm: A new health system for the 21st century*. Washington, DC: National Academy Press.

- Institute of Medicine. (2006). *Improving the quality of health care for mental and substance use conditions*. Washington, DC: National Academy Press.

- McCarty, D., Edmundsom, E., & Hartnett, T. (2006). Charting a path between research and practice in alcoholism treatment. *Alcohol Research and Health, 29*, 5-10.

- Network for the Improvement of Addiction Treatment: http://www.niatx.net.

- New Freedom Commission on Mental Health (2003). *Achieving the promise: Transforming mental health care in America* (Final Report; DHHS Publication No. SMA-03-3832). Rockville, MD: U.S. Government Printing Office.

Authors' Note

The research in this chapter was supported in part by grants U10 DA013036 (Dr. McCarty), K23 DA020487 (Dr. Wisdom), and R01 DA018282 (Dr. McCarty) from the National Institute on Drug Abuse, and grants 46876 and 50165 (Dr. McCarty) from the Robert Wood Johnson Foundation.

References

Anthony, W. (1993). Recovery from mental illness: The guiding vision of the mental health service system in the 1990s. *Psychosocial Rehabilitation Journal, 16*, 11-23.

Bickman, L. (1997). Resolving issues raised by the Fort Bragg Evaluation: New directions for mental health services research. *American Psychologist, 52*, 562-565.

Cook, C. C. (2004). Addiction and spirituality. *Addiction, 99*, 539-551.

Cotter, F., Bowler, S., Mulkern, V., & McCarty, D. (2005). Practice improvement collaboratives: An overview. *Journal of Addictive Diseases, 24*(Suppl. 1), 1-14.

Drake, R. E., Essock, S. M., Shaner, A., Carey, K. B., Minkoff, K., Kola, L., et al. (2001). Implementing dual diagnosis services for clients with severe mental illness. *Psychiatric Services, 52*, 469-476.

Frese, F. J., III, Stanley, J., Kress, K., & Vogel-Scibilia, S. (2001). Integrating evidence-based practices and the recovery model. *Psychiatric Services, 52*, 1462-1468.

Friesen, B. J., & Winters, N. C. (2003). The role of outcomes in systems of care: Quality improvement and program evaluation. In A. J. Pumariega & N. C. Winters (Eds.), *The handbook of child and adolescent systems of care: The new community psychiatry* (pp. 459-486). San Francisco: John Wiley & Sons.

Gallon, S. L., Gabriel, R. M., & Knudsen, J. R. W. (2003). The toughest job you'll ever love: A Pacific Northwest Treatment Workforce Study. *Journal of Substance Abuse Treatment, 24*, 183-196.

Green, C. (2004). A synthesis and model for fostering recovery from life-transforming mental health disorders. *Social Theory and Health, 2*, 293-314.

Hardwood, H.J ., Kowalski, J., & Ameen, A. (2004). The need for substance abuse training among mental health professionals. *Administration and Policy in Mental Health, 32*, 189-205.

Hser, Y., Evans, E., Huang, D., & Anglin, D. M. (2004). Relationship between drug treatment services, retention, and outcomes. *Psychiatric Services, 55*, 767-774.

Jenkins, S. R., & Baird, S. (2002). Secondary traumatic stress and vicarious trauma: A validational study. *Journal of Traumatic Stress, 15*, 423-432.

Knudsen, H. K., Johnson, J. A., & Roman, P. M. (2003). Retaining counseling staff at substance abuse treatment centers: Effects of management practices. *Journal of Substance Abuse Treatment, 24*, 129-135.

Lehman, W. E. K., Greener, J. M., & Simpson, D. D. (2002). Assessing organizational readiness for change. *Journal of Substance Abuse Treatment, 22*, 197-209.

McLellan, A. T., Carise, D., & Kleber, H. D. (2003). Can the national addiction treatment infrastructure support the public's demand for quality care? *Journal of Substance Abuse Treatment, 25*, 117-121.

Miller, W. R., & Mount, K. (2001). A small study of training in motivational interviewing: Does one workshop change clinician and client behavior? *Behavioural and Cognitive Psychotherapy, 29,* 457-471.

Miller W. R., & Rollnick, S. (2002). *Motivational interviewing: Preparing people for change,* (2nd ed.). New York: Guilford Press.

Miller, W. R., Yahne, C. E., Moyers T. B., Martinez, J., & Pirritano, M. (2004). A randomized trial of methods to help clinicians learn motivational interviewing. *Journal of Consulting and Clinical Psychology, 72,* 1050-1062.

Najavits, L. M. (2001). *Seeking safety: A treatment manual for PTSD and substance abuse.* New York: Guilford Press.

New Freedom Commission on Mental Health (2003). *Achieving the promise: Transforming mental health care in America* (Final Report; DHHS Publication No. SMA-03-3832). Rockville, MD: U.S. Government Printing Office.

Nunes, E. V., & Levin, F. R. (2004). Treatment of depression in patients with alcohol or other drug dependence: A meta-analysis. *Journal of the American Medical Association, 291*, 1887-1896.

Peters, R. H., Moore, K. A., Hills, H. A., Young, M. S., LeVasseur, J. B., Rich, A. R., et al. (2005). Use of opinion leaders and intensive training to implement evidence-based co-occurring disorders treatment in the community. *Journal of Addictive Diseases, 24*(Suppl. 1), 53-74.

Power, K., & DeMartino, R. (2004). Co-occurring disorders and achieving recovery: The Substance Abuse and Mental Health Services Administration perspective. *Biological Psychiatry, 56*, 721-722.

Richmond, I. C., & Foster, J. H. (2003). Negative attitudes towards people with co-morbid mental health and substance misuse problems: An investigation of mental health professionals. *Journal of Mental Health, 12*(4), 393-403.

Roget, N. A., Storti, S. A., Albers, E. C., Horvatich, P. K., & Skinstad, A. H. (2005). *Gender and the substance abuse treatment workforce: Implications for the field.* Presented at the annual meeting of the College on Problems of Drug Dependence, Orlando, FL.

Rosler, M., Retz, W., Retz-Junginger, P., Hengesch, G., Schneider, M., Supprian, T., et al. (2004). Prevalence of attention deficit-/hyperactivity disorder (ADHD) and comorbid disorders in young male prison inmates. *European Archives of Psychiatry and Clinical Neuroscience, 254*, 365-371.

Simpson, D. D. (2004). A conceptual framework for drug treatment process and outcomes. *Journal of Substance Abuse Treatment, 27*, 99-121.

Strecher, V., Wang, C., Derry, H., Wildenhaus, K., & Johnson, C. (2002). Tailored interventions for multiple risk behaviors. *Health Education Research, 17,* 619-626.

Substance Abuse and Mental Health Services Administration. (2004). *Building bridges: Co-occurring mental illness and addiction: Consumers and service providers, policymakers, and researchers in dialogue* (DHHS Publication No. (SMA) 04-3892). Rockville, MD: U.S. Government Printing Office.

Substance Abuse and Mental Health Services Administration. (2005). *Free to choose: Transforming behavioral health care to self-direction* (DHHS Publication No. (SMA) 05-3982). Rockville, MD: U.S. Government Printing Office.

Womack, S., Compton, W. M., Dennis, M., McCormick, S., Fraser, J., Horton, J. C., et al. (2004). Improving treatment services for substance abusers with comorbid depression. *American Journal on Addictions, 13*, 295-304.

Appendix A

Continuing Education and Clinical Skills Examination

by Bachaar Arnaout, M.D., and Petros Levounis, M.D., M.A.

INSTRUCTIONS

This examination consists of sixty multiple-choice questions (three multiple-choice questions for each chapter) about information presented in the book. Read carefully all four options before selecting the best answer. Assume that all substances that are mentioned in this examination are in their pure form (not mixed with other substances, which is often the case in real life). Please write your answers neatly on the answer sheet (found in the back of this book at page AS-1, after the Index).

After finishing the examination, you may obtain the answer key, a certificate of completion, and information about continuing education credits by mailing your answer sheet to The Addiction Institute of New York (note that only an original answer sheet can be accepted):

The Addiction Institute of New York
St. Luke's and Roosevelt Hospitals
Attention: CECSE
1000 Tenth Avenue
New York, New York 10019

For further information about obtaining continuing education credits, visit the Web site of The Addiction Institute of New York at http://www.AddictionInstituteNY.org/CECSE. If you are interested in obtaining the answer key without receiving continuing education credits, please e-mail The Addiction Institute of New York at CECSE@AddictionInstituteNY.org. Good luck!

The examination questions begin on the next page.

Chapter 1
Depression in Patients With Substance Use Disorders

1   A 62-year-old teacher with a long history of alcohol dependence, but no other psychiatric history, is admitted to the hospital for severe alcohol withdrawal. At the time of admission, she complains of depressed mood. The most appropriate intervention at this time is:
a   prescribing a mood stabilizer.
b   prescribing an antidepressant.
c   prescribing a benzodiazepine.
d   holding all medications.

2   The vegetative symptoms of depression include:
a   depressed or irritable mood.
b   appetite change and sleep disturbance.
c   feelings of worthlessness or excessive guilt.
d   poor concentration and difficulty making decisions.

3   Which one of the following statements most accurately describes the relationship of depression and substance use disorders?
a   Abstinence from alcohol usually results in exacerbation of depressive symptoms.
b   Chronic but moderate cocaine use improves depressive symptoms.
c   For most patients, treatment of depression alone results in the resolution of a substance use disorder.
d   Substance use disorders and depression should be considered as separate but related disorders that require simultaneous treatment.

Chapter 2
Bipolar Disorder in Patients With Substance Use Disorders

4   A 25-year-old plumber presents for outpatient treatment for cocaine dependence. Her mood is irritable, and her speech is pressured. She also indicates that she has not slept for five days (since her last use of cocaine). Urine toxicology is negative. Her symptoms are most likely due to:
a   cocaine intoxication.
b   cocaine withdrawal.
c   attention deficit hyperactivity disorder (ADHD).
d   manic episode.

5   Which of the following is a relapse prevention treatment for patients with bipolar disorder and substance use disorders that addresses both disorders simultaneously using cognitive behavioral strategies?
a   Psychoeducation.
b   Integrated Group Therapy (IGT).
c   Interpersonal Social Rhythm Therapy (IPSRT).
d   Family-Focused Therapy (FFT).

6   The federally established policy of "No Wrong Door" refers to the responsibility of all addiction treatment programs to:
    a   assist dually diagnosed patients by either providing treatment services or referring patients to appropriate treatment services.
    b   provide comprehensive "addiction only" services.
    c   gather information from family members about patients' substance use and mental health issues.
    d   implement rules regulating patient participation in treatment activities.

Chapter 3
Posttraumatic Stress Disorder in Patients With Substance Use Disorders

7   Symptoms of posttraumatic stress disorder (PTSD) are organized into which of the following three hallmark clusters?
    a   alterations in self-perception, alterations in relations with others, and alterations in systems of meaning.
    b   reexperience, avoidance, and hyperarousal.
    c   inattention, hyperactivity, and impulsivity.
    d   dissociation, somatization, and anxiety.

8   Which of the following disorders most commonly co-occur with PTSD?
    a   panic disorder and agoraphobia.
    b   dysthymic disorder.
    c   major depressive disorder and substance use disorders.
    d   generalized anxiety disorder (GAD).

9   A 51-year-old bartender with a history of alcohol dependence is seen for individual counseling on an inpatient rehabilitation unit. He reveals to his counselor that he is a survivor of a domestic violence assault that nearly killed him. He endorses symptoms of PTSD, including feeling numb and trying to avoid thoughts relating to the traumatic event. The most appropriate intervention at this time is to:
    a   refer the patient to an exposure-based therapy because he needs to intensively process his trauma-related experiences.
    b   avoid asking the patient about suicidal ideation because evaluation of suicidality during the early stages of the treatment process exacerbates symptoms of PTSD.
    c   address trauma only after a year of treatment for alcohol dependence because treatment of PTSD during the early stages of recovery typically worsens the course of substance dependence.
    d   request a psychiatric consultation because the patient may benefit from pharmacotherapy.

Chapter 4
Other Anxiety Disorders in Patients With Substance Use Disorders:
Panic Disorder, Agoraphobia, Social Anxiety Disorder, and Generalized Anxiety Disorder

10 Substance-induced anxiety disorder typically results in:
    a   apprehension about being in crowded stores and traffic jams.
    b   fear of appearing at social events.

c   generalized uneasiness and irritability.
d   dread of speaking in mutual help groups.

11 Cognitive Behavioral Therapy (CBT) teaches patients that panic attacks:
a   feel empowering but are dangerous.
b   feel terrible and are dangerous.
c   feel terrible but are not dangerous.
d   feel empowering and are not dangerous.

12 A 75-year-old retired farmer has attended Alcoholics Anonymous (AA) regularly since she successfully stopped drinking alcohol thirty years ago. While she is interested in the topics of discussion during the meetings, she has always felt uncomfortable in AA and other social groups in which she is expected to talk. What is an appropriate recommendation?
a   Continue going to AA and consider taking an antidepressant (e.g. escitalopram).
b   Continue going to AA and consider taking a benzodiazepine (e.g. alprazolam).
c   Continue going to AA but do not talk during the meetings.
d   Stop going to AA; thirty years is long enough.

Chapter 5
Adult Attention Deficit Hyperactivity Disorder in Patients With Substance Use Disorders

13 The *DSM-IV-TR* diagnosis of attention deficit hyperactivity disorder (ADHD) requires:
a   all of the *DSM-IV-TR* symptoms of inattention and hyperactivity-impulsivity.
b   impairment prior to age of 5.
c   impairment in two or more work settings.
d   clinically significant impairment in social, academic, or occupational functioning.

14 Which of the following statements about evaluating ADHD in adult patients is most accurate?
a   The presence of symptoms of inattention or hyperactivity should be evaluated in all patients with substance use disorders, unless a patient is abusing a stimulant.
b   The gold standard for diagnosing ADHD is the Conners' Adult ADHD Diagnostic Interview for DSM-IV (CAADID).
c   School report cards and information from family members can be helpful in determining whether a patient's symptoms caused significant impairment during childhood.
d   All of the above.

15 A 23-year-old college student attends an outpatient program for cocaine abuse and has been abstinent for three weeks. During a counseling session, she complains of lifelong inability to focus on school tasks, which frustrates her and leads to low self-esteem. A psychiatric consultation is obtained, and, following a comprehensive evaluation, she is diagnosed with moderate to severe ADHD. Which of the following interventions is most likely to be effective for the patient's ADHD symptoms?
a   prescribing a stimulant, such as methylphenidate.
b   prescribing a sedative, such as lorazepam.

c   prescribing an antidepressant, such as citalopram.
d   recommending continued abstinence from cocaine.

Chapter 6
Delirium, Dementia, and Other Cognitive Disorders in Patients With Substance Use Disorders

16 A 34-year-old repairman who suffers from chronic alcohol dependence is brought to the emergency room complaining of ill-defined cognitive "fogging," poor memory, and visual hallucinations. His wife tells you that the patient has not had any alcohol since his back surgery (three days ago). The most likely diagnosis is:
a   alcohol intoxication delirium.
b   alcohol withdrawal delirium.
c   alcohol-induced persisting dementia.
d   cognitive impairment not otherwise specified.

17 Asking the patient to count backwards by 7 starting at 100 primarily tests:
a   short-term memory.
b   intermediate-term memory.
c   comprehension.
d   attention.

18 Which one of the following counseling techniques is most appropriate for patients with attention deficits?
a   Arrange for short and frequent therapy sessions.
b   List all the topics of concern at the beginning of each session.
c   If the session dialogue derails, "go with the flow" and allow patients to discuss irrelevant topics.
d   At the end of each session, provide comprehensive psychoeducation about cognitive impairments.

Chapter 7
Schizophrenia and Schizoaffective Illness in Patients With Substance Use Disorders

19 Which of the following symptoms of schizophrenia are most likely to respond to treatment with antipsychotic medications?
a   cognitive symptoms, such as impairment in memory, attention, problem solving, and abstract thinking.
b   negative symptoms, such as social withdrawal, low motivation, and apathy.
c   positive symptoms, such as hallucinations, delusions, and disorganized speech and behavior.
d   all symptoms respond equally.

20 Intoxication with which of the following substances is most likely to mimic schizophrenia?
a   haloperidol and aripiprazole.
b   alcohol and phenobarbital.
c   morphine and buprenorphine.
d   phencyclidine (PCP) and methamphetamine.

21 A 54-year-old cook with a history of schizophrenia and polysubstance dependence attends an outpatient "double trouble" group. She listens carefully but rarely speaks. She also leaves every session at least once, saying she needs to use the bathroom. The most appropriate intervention at this point is:
a   inquire about the patient's experience, while providing support and praise.
b   confront the patient on her ambivalence.
c   tell the patient that she is in denial of her diagnoses.
d   urge the patient to sign a treatment contract.

Chapter 8
Antisocial Personality Disorder in Patients With Substance Use Disorders

22 The *DSM-IV* diagnosis of antisocial personality disorder requires:
a   evidence of conduct disorder with onset before age 10.
b   occurrence of antisocial behavior exclusively during periods of abstinence from substance use.
c   a pervasive pattern of disregard for, and violation of, the rights or others occurring since age 15.
d   a documented history of incarceration.

23 Which of the following statements about patients with antisocial personality disorder is most accurate?
a   They are likely to attempt, but unlikely to commit, suicide.
b   They are likely to be dependent on multiple substances.
c   They are unlikely to have co-occurring anxiety or mood disorders.
d   They are unlikely to sustain relationships and, therefore, are impossible to treat.

24 A 64-year-old photographer with antisocial personality disorder attends methadone maintenance therapy. After the patient has attended sessions regularly and has provided a series of negative urine samples, the treatment team discusses the possibility of offering the patient take-home doses of methadone. This suggestion is:
a   unethical because long-term methadone maintenance therapy causes osteoporosis.
b   useful because a subsequent positive urine sample will be grounds for administrative discharge from the clinic.
c   futile because patients with antisocial personality disorder respond best to limit setting and confrontation.
d   reasonable because contingency management has been shown to be effective for patients with antisocial personality disorder.

Chapter 9
Borderline Personality Disorder in Patients With Substance Use Disorders

25 *DSM-IV* diagnostic criteria for borderline personality disorder include:
a   polysubstance dependence.
b   chronic feelings of emptiness.
c   a pattern of interpersonal rigidity.
d   a history of trauma.

26 The primary dialectic in Dialectical Behavior Therapy (DBT) centers around which of the following two poles?
   a   insight and judgment.
   b   exploration and support.
   c   confrontation and motivation.
   d   acceptance and change.

27 A 40-year-old cashier with borderline personality disorder has been seeing a psychiatrist for the past two years. Despite biweekly outpatient visits and trials of several different medications, he continues to have chaotic relationships. His cocaine use is escalating. He often wishes he "would just not wake up one morning" but does not intend to commit suicide. The most appropriate intervention at this time is to:
   a   refer the patient to an inpatient psychiatric unit.
   b   refer the patient for cocaine detoxification.
   c   refer the patient to a program that provides Dialectical Behavior Therapy (DBT) for substance use disorders.
   d   recommend that the patient signs a recovery contract.

Chapter 10
Pathological Gambling Among Patients With Substance Use Disorders

28 The World Health Organization and the American Psychiatric Association currently consider pathological gambling:
   a   an addiction.
   b   an impulse control disorder.
   c   a variant of obsessive-compulsive disorder.
   d   a mood disorder.

29 A 45-year-old social worker comes to counseling accompanied by his wife. She explains that her husband has demonstrated "self-defeating behaviors": he has spent all their savings in the last six months. The patient calmly explains that he is a "professional poker player" and has quit his day job in order to focus on his poker career. There is no history of sleep disturbance. The most likely diagnosis is:
   a   pathological gambling.
   b   professional gambling.
   c   social gambling.
   d   gambling in the context of a manic episode.

30 Which of the following statements best describes treatment options for pathological gambling?
   a   Gamblers Anonymous (GA), a treatment model inspired by Alcoholics Anonymous (AA), has been proven to be highly effective in clinical trials but is rarely utilized by pathological gamblers.
   b   In Cognitive Behavioral Therapy (CBT), a functional analysis allows the patient to recognize triggers and precipitants of gambling and evaluate the positive and negative consequences of gambling.
   c   Opioid antagonists typically augment the "thrill" that gambling provokes in the central nervous system.
   d   Although seldom affordable, psychoanalysis continues to be the most effective treatment for pathological gambling.

Chapter 11
Intermittent Explosive Disorder and Impulsive Aggression in Patients With Substance Use Disorders

31 The *DSM-IV* diagnosis of intermittent explosive disorder requires:
  a   deliberate and purposeful fire setting on more than one occasion.
  b   lack of empathy, as indicated by an unwillingness to recognize or identify with the feelings and needs of others.
  c   several discrete episodes of failure to resist aggressive impulses that result in serious assaultive acts or destruction of property.
  d   lack of remorse, as indicated by indifference to (or rationalization of) instances of hurting or mistreating people or stealing.

32 Intoxication with which of the following substances is most likely to promote aggression?
  a   cannabis.
  b   cocaine.
  c   fluoxetine.
  d   heroin.

33 A 58-year-old physician attends an intensive outpatient program. After one month of sobriety, she continues to feel depressed and irritable and tells her counselor that she recently punched her best friend after a heated argument. The most appropriate intervention at this time is to:
  a   ask the patient firmly and calmly to stop talking about punching people because she needs to focus on her sobriety.
  b   discharge the patient because there is no treatment for cold, predatory aggression.
  c   confront the patient on her anger because any sign of "giving in" will reinforce aggression.
  d   consider a psychiatric consultation because the patient may benefit from an antidepressant.

Chapter 12
Eating Disorders in Patients With Substance Use Disorders: Bulimia, Anorexia, Overeating Disorder, and Obesity

34 Which of the following questions is most likely to elicit an accurate answer when assessing a patient for anorexia nervosa?
  a   "Are you on a diet?"
  b   "Have you ever weighed much less than people thought you should weigh?"
  c   "How often do you binge?"
  d   "You are skinny and probably suffer from anorexia. What are your thoughts about that?"

35 Which of the following challenges are clinicians likely to encounter when treating patients with co-occurring substance use disorders and eating disorders?
  a   Treatment of one disorder can lead to the exacerbation of symptoms of the other disorder.
  b   Substance abuse treatment emphasizes abstinence, whereas eating disorder treatment focuses on moderation.

   c   Integrated treatment programs for both disorders are rare.

   d   All of the above.

36 A 43-year-old policeman attends Alcoholics Anonymous (AA) regularly and has been abstinent from alcohol and alprazolam for ten years. At the insistence of his wife, he reluctantly seeks treatment for his binging and purging behaviors. Which of the following statements best describes treatment options at this time?

   a   Interpersonal Psychotherapy (IPT) might be beneficial but only if the patient has social anxiety disorder (formerly called social phobia) or poor social supports.

   b   Relapse prevention for substance use would be inappropriate because Alcoholics Anonymous (AA) seems to work well.

   c   Cognitive Behavioral Therapy (CBT) might be beneficial and is the most extensively researched psychological intervention for bulimia nervosa.

   d   Prescription of a selective serotonin reuptake inhibitor (SSRI), such as fluoxetine, would be inappropriate unless the patient suffers from a mood or anxiety disorder.

Chapter 13
Cigarette Smoking Among Patients With Substance Use Disorders

37 Which of the following statements about integrating nicotine interventions into addiction treatment is most accurate?

   a   Nicotine interventions usually encourage drop-out from substance abuse treatment programs.

   b   Brief interventions by health care providers are effective at increasing nicotine cessation rates.

   c   Attempts to quit smoking during early stages of recovery from alcohol dependence usually cause relapse to alcohol use.

   d   Most patients with alcohol dependence do not wish to address their nicotine dependence.

38 Symptoms of nicotine withdrawal include:

   a   muscle aches.

   b   dysphoria.

   c   seizures.

   d   anorexia.

39 A 70-year-old retired nurse attempts to quit smoking for the fifth time. In the past, he has tried the nicotine patch, behavioral counseling, and self-help materials. The most appropriate intervention at this time is:

   a   Refer the patient to a physician for possible treatment with bupropion or varenicline.

   b   Praise the patient and provide more extensive self-help materials, including Internet resources.

   c   Ask the patient to come back for help when he is more motivated to quit.

   d   Advise the patient to continue using the nicotine patch.

Chapter 14
Common Medical Illnesses in Patients With Substance Use and Psychiatric Disorders

40 Which of the following conditions is most likely to result in seizures?
a   alcohol intoxication.
b   opioid withdrawal.
c   cocaine intoxication.
d   methylenedioxymethamphetamine (Ecstasy) withdrawal.

41 A 77-year-old prison inmate presents with a left forearm skin rash that he attributes to an insect bite. There is marked reddening and swelling. Five other inmates have similar rashes. The condition is deemed serious, and a physician is contacted. The most likely diagnosis is:
a   an increased response to a purified protein derivative (PPD) test.
b   a skin infection related to injection drug use.
c   "speed bumps" related to "angel dust" use.
d   gout related to alcohol abuse.

42 Drug users who do not already have the antibodies should be offered vaccination against which of the following diseases?
a   hepatitis A and B.
b   hepatitis C and D.
c   methicillin-resistant Staphylococcus aureus (MRSA).
d   tuberculosis (TB).

Chapter 15
Substance Abuse During Adolescence

43 Which of the following challenges are clinicians likely to encounter when diagnosing adolescents with substance use disorders?
a   Most adolescents "experiment" with substances of abuse, but few adolescents later develop a substance use disorder.
b   Some adolescents do not meet criteria for any substance use disorder but exhibit a subclinical pattern of problem use.
c   A diagnosis of substance use disorder may prevent an adolescent from receiving some types of services, such as foster care placement.
d   All of the above.

44 In comparison to later onset substance use disorder, earlier onset substance use disorder is associated with:
a   fewer arrests.
b   less likely disruptive behavior disorder diagnoses.
c   lower novelty seeking.
d   lower reward dependence.

45 A 15-year-old high school sophomore with conduct disorder has been arrested for driving while intoxicated with alcohol for the second time in four months. Her

father recently died from liver cirrhosis, and her mother is struggling with depression. The most appropriate treatment at this time is:
a   pharmacologic management with disulfiram.
b   Multisystemic Therapy (MST).
c   individual counseling.
d   parental education.

Chapter 16
Pain in Patients With Substance Use Disorders

46   Patients with which one of the following conditions intentionally feign pain in order to assume the sick role?
a   malingering.
b   hypochondriasis.
c   factitious disorder.
d   somatization disorder.

47   Which one of the following statements most accurately describes the appropriate prescription of methadone to patients with chronic pain and an opioid use disorder?
a   Methadone should be avoided because it will worsen the patient's addiction problem.
b   Methadone can be prescribed in a physician's office and may need to be taken multiple times per day.
c   Methadone should only be given once daily at a methadone maintenance treatment program.
d   Methadone can be prescribed after shorter-acting substances, such as hydrocodone, have failed.

48   A 68-year-old real estate broker with a history of chronic pain, depression, and opioid dependence is referred by her physician to an addiction treatment program. During intake the patient insists on full confidentiality protection for psychiatric, substance abuse, and medical information, and she refuses to sign a release allowing free communication between care providers. The most appropriate approach at this time is:
a   contact her physician anyway on the basis of "therapeutic privilege."
b   explain to the patient that her refusal to allow communication between care providers compromises care.
c   agree that "too many cooks spoil the broth," document the patient's refusal, and proceed with treatment as usual.
d   acknowledge that asking the patient to sign a release was a mistake and a violation of the Health Insurance Portability and Accountability Act (HIPAA).

Chapter 17
Suicide and Substance Abuse

49   Which of the following statements about risk factors for suicide is most accurate?
a   Suicide risk increases following recent loss of meaningful social support systems.
b   Rates of completed suicide decrease with age.
c   Females make more lethal suicide attempts than males.
d   Patients with a history of suicide attempts are less likely to attempt suicide again.

50 Which of the following statements best describes treatment options for suicidal patients?
   a   The current addiction treatment system is not able to assess or manage suicidal patients.
   b   Almost all patients experiencing serious suicidal thoughts suffer from major depressive disorder and should be referred to the mental health system.
   c   Patients with suicidal thoughts that are substance induced are at risk for under-treatment of their addiction in the mental health system.
   d   The current addiction treatment system is prepared to treat almost all cases of substance-induced suicidality.

51 A 29-year-old carpenter attends addiction treatment at a halfway house. He has stopped snorting heroin but continues to use cocaine and alcohol. After spending his paycheck on a cocaine binge, he appears despondent and informs his physician that he wishes he could go to sleep and never wake up. The most appropriate intervention at this time is to:
   a   ask the patient to drive to the nearest emergency room.
   b   apply the QPD model for suicide assessment and intervention, which includes the following three steps: question, prescribe, discharge.
   c   apply a commonly used cognitive behavioral intervention by asking: "You are not thinking of killing yourself, are you?"
   d   assess the patient's suicidality by asking the six "W" questions: "What is wrong?"; "Why now?"; "With what?"; "Where and when?"; "Who is involved?"; "Why not now?"

Chapter 18
Drug Interactions in the Pharmacological Treatment of Substance Use Disorders

52 Which of the following questions about medication adherence is most likely to elicit an accurate answer?
   a   "How often do you miss taking medication?"
   b   "You're taking two pills in the morning, right?"
   c   "You would tell me if you were not taking your medication, wouldn't you?"
   d   "I hope you have been taking your medication since our talk last week. Have you missed any doses?"

53 Which one of the following statements about cytochrome P450 drug metabolism is most accurate?
   a   Most drugs are metabolized by the kidney.
   b   Substrates are drugs that either inhibit or induce (stimulate) the functioning of a particular enzyme.
   c   Inhibitors lead to reduced rates of metabolism of substrate drugs, thereby leading to reduced blood levels.
   d   Inducers lead to increased rates of metabolism of substrate drugs, thereby leading to reduced blood levels.

54 A 30-year-old businesswoman with a history of injection heroin use has been in methadone maintenance treatment for six months. She was recently diagnosed with human immunodeficiency virus (HIV) disease and has been motivated to obtain regular medical care. One week after initiating Highly Active Antiretroviral

Therapy (HAART), her urine toxicology examination is positive for opioids (the first time in four months). The most likely reason for the patient's opioid use is:
a   treatment fatigue and decreased motivation to address her addiction.
b   lower level of methadone resulting in symptoms of opioid withdrawal.
c   cytochrome P450 enzyme inhibition.
d   nonadherence to HAART regimen.

Chapter 19
Choosing Treatment Services and Levels of Care: The American Society of Addiction Medicine Patient Placement Criteria

55   A 38-year-old homemaker has been convicted of driving while intoxicated. He has no prior history of substance-related problems and does not meet criteria for a psychiatric disorder or substance use disorder. According to the Patient Placement Criteria (PPC) of the American Society of Addiction Medicine (ASAM), the most appropriate level of care at this time is:
a   Level IV: medically managed intensive inpatient treatment.
b   Level III.1: clinically managed low-intensity residential treatment.
c   Level II.5: partial hospitalization program.
d   Level 0.5: early intervention.

56   Which of the following statements best guides treatment matching in patients with co-occurring psychiatric disorders?
a   Undermatching is recommended for patients with co-occurring disorders because it is less confrontational.
b   Overmatching is recommended because comorbidity requires the most intensive treatment available.
c   Both undermatching and overmatching may result in poorer attendance at treatment sessions by patients with co-occurring disorders.
d   The Patient Placement Criteria (PPC) of the American Society of Addiction Medicine (ASAM) are of limited use in patients with co-occurring disorders.

57   The implementation of the Comprehensive Continuous Integrated System of Care (CCISC) model is guided by which of the following principles?
a   Dual diagnosis is an expectation, not an exception.
b   Treatment must be based on confrontational, not supportive, relationships.
c   Clinical outcomes must be structured, not individualized.
d   All of the above.

Chapter 20
Directions for Future Research on Treating Co-Occurring Substance Use and Psychiatric Disorders

58   Which of the following statements about research on treating co-occurring disorders is true?
a   Cost often limits research to small projects.
b   Findings from large-scale trials with heterogeneous patient populations are usually misguiding.
c   Federal and state agencies are not interested in funding research.
d   Attempts to train and supervise clinicians in evidence-based interventions have failed.

59 Research direction(s) that aim to explore the active elements of treatments and real-world applications of interventions may involve:
   a   including individuals with co-occurring disorders in large-scale studies.
   b   focusing investigations not only on the intervention but also on the individual's process of recovery.
   c   investigating differences in treatment experiences and treatment needs of women and men.
   d   all of the above.

60 The Network for the Improvement of Addiction Treatment (NIATx) is an organization that primarily works with:
   a   computer engineers to develop on-line addiction treatment protocols.
   b   fundraising professionals to lobby for better addiction treatment.
   c   addiction health care providers to improve treatment access and retention.
   d   social interest groups to liaise with academia, the Clinical Trials Network (CTN), and managed care organizations.

Appendix B

Table of Abbreviations and Acronyms

AA	Alcoholics Anonymous
ACT	assertive community treatment
ADATP	Alcohol and Drug Abuse Treatment Program
ADHD	attention deficit hyperactivity disorder
AIDS	acquired immune deficiency syndrome
ALT	alanine aminotransferase
AOS	addiction only services
ASAM	American Society of Addiction Medicine
ASD	acute stress disorder
ASI	Addiction Severity Index
ASPD	antisocial personality disorder
AST	aspartate aminotransferase
BAC	blood alcohol concentration
BDI	Beck Depression Inventory
BSL	Borderline Symptom List
BULIT-R	Bulimia Test-Revised
BUP	buprenorphine
CAADID	Conners Adult ADHD Diagnostic Interview for DSM-IV
CAMH	Centre for Addiction and Mental Health
CASA	National Center on Addiction and Substance Abuse at Columbia University
CBC	complete blood count
CBT	Cognitive Behavioral Therapy
CCISC	Comprehensive Continuous Integrated System of Care
CD	conduct disorder
CDT	carbohydrate-deficient transferrin
CECSE	Continuing Education and Clinical Skills Examination
CIDI	Composite International Diagnostic Interview
CM	contingency management
COPD	chronic obstructive pulmonary disease
CPI	California Personality Inventory
CPK	creatine phosphokinase
CPS	Chronic Pain Syndrome
CPT	continuous performance test
CSAT	Center for Substance Abuse Treatment
CSF	cerebral spinal fluid
CT	Computed Tomography

CTN	Clinical Trials Network
CVT-12S	Comprehensive Validation Treatment With 12 Step
CYP	cytochrome P450 system
DALI	Dartmouth Assessment of Lifestyle Instrument
DATOS	Drug Abuse Treatment Outcome Study
DBT	Dialectical Behavior Therapy
DBT-SUD	Dialectical Behavior Therapy for Substance Use Disorders
DDC	dual diagnosis capable
DDE	dual diagnosis enhanced
DEA	Drug Enforcement Administration
DESNOS	disorders of extreme stress not otherwise specialized
DIGS	Diagnostic Interview for Gambling Severity
DIS	Diagnostic Interview Schedule
DSM-III	*Diagnostic and Statistical Manual of Mental Disorders,* 3rd edition
DSM-III-R	*Diagnostic and Statistical Manual of Mental Disorders,* 3rd edition, revised
DSM-IV	*Diagnostic and Statistical Manual of Mental Disorders,* 4th edition
DSM-IV-TR	*Diagnostic and Statistical Manual of Mental Disorders,* 4th edition, text revision
DTs	delirium tremens
DUI	driving under the influence
DWI	driving while intoxicated
EAT-26	Eating Attitudes Test (twenty-six questions)
ECA	Epidemiologic Catchment Area
EDE	Eating Disorder Examination
EDE-Q	Eating Disorder Examination Questionnaire
EKG	electrocardiogram
EOP	endogenous opioid peptide
EPS	extrapyramidal symptoms
ER	emergency room
FFT	Family-Focused Therapy
FSMB	Federation of State Medical Boards
FTA-ABS	fluorescent treponemal antibody-absorption
GA	Gamblers Anonymous
GABA	gamma-aminobutyric acid
GAD	generalized anxiety disorder
GAM-IV	Gambling Assessment Module (GAM-IV)
GBI	Gambling Behavior Interview
GED	general educational development (test); general equivalency diploma
GGT	gamma-glutamyl transferase
GHB	gamma hydroxybutyrate
GI	gastrointestinal
HAART	Highly Active Antiretroviral Therapy
HAM-D or HDS	Hamilton Depression Scale
HbeAg	hepatitis B e antigen
HbsAg	hepatitis B surface antigen

HIPAA	Health Insurance Portability and Accountability Act
HITS	Hurt-Insult-Threaten-Scream
HIV	human immunodeficiency virus
HPA	hypothalamic-pituitary-adrenal
HPV	human papillomavirus infection
IASP	International Association for the Study of Pain
ICD	impulse control disorder
IDU	injection drug user
IED	intermittent explosive disorder
IGT	Integrated Group Therapy
INH	isoniazid
IPDE	International Personality Disorder Examination
IPSRT	Interpersonal Social Rhythm Therapy
IPT	Interpersonal Psychotherapy
IV	intravenous
LAAM	levo-alpha-acetylmethadol
LDH	lactate dehydrogenase
LFTs	liver function tests
LSD	lysergic acid diethylamide
MAO	monoamine oxidase
MAOIs	monoamine oxidase inhibitors
MCV	mean corpuscular volume
MDMA	methylenedioxymethamphetamine (Ecstasy)
MDQ	Mood Disorder Questionnaire
MI	motivational interviewing
MICA	mentally ill, chemically addicted
MINI	Mini International Neuropsychiatric Interview
MMPI	Minnesota Multiphasic Personality Inventory
MMSE	Mini Mental State Examination
MRI	Magnetic Resonance Imaging
MRSA	methicillin-resistant Staphylococcus aureus
MS	multiple sclerosis
MST	Multisystemic Therapy
NA	Narcotics Anonymous
NIATx	Network for the Improvement of Addiction Treatment
NIDA	National Institute on Drug Abuse
NIMH	National Institute of Mental Health
NNRTI	nonnucleoside reverse transcriptase inhibitor
NOS	not otherwise specified
NRT	Nicotine Replacement Therapy
NRTI	nucleoside reverse transcriptase inhibitor
NSAIDS	nonsteroidal anti-inflammatory drugs
OAS	Overt Aggression Scale
OCD	obsessive compulsive disorder
OTB	off-track betting
PAI	Personality Assessment Inventory
PCOS	polycystic ovary syndrome
PCP	phencyclidine
PDR	Physicians' Desk Reference

PG	pathological gambling
PHQ	Patient Health Questionnaire
PHS	Public Health Service
PI	protease inhibitor
PORT	Schizophrenia Patient Outcomes Research Team
PPC	Patient Placement Criteria
PPD	purified protein derivative
PRIME-MD	Primary Care Evaluation of Mental Disorders
PRISM	Psychiatric Research Interview for Substance and Mental Disorders
PSST	Problem Solving Skills Training
PTSD	posttraumatic stress disorder
QEWP-R	Questionnaire on Eating and Weight Patterns-Revised
RBC	red blood cell
RP	relapse prevention
RPR	rapid plasma reagin
RSD	reflex sympathetic dystrophy
SAD	social anxiety disorder
SAMHSA	Substance Abuse and Mental Health Services Administration
SCID-I	Structured Clinical Interview for DSM-IV-TR Axis I Disorders
SCID-II	Structured Clinical Interview for DSM-IV Axis II Personality Disorders
SERT	serotonin transporter
SIADH	syndrome of inappropriate antidiuretic hormone
SMART	Self-Management and Recovery Training
SNRI	serotonin-norepinephrine reuptake inhibitor
SOGS	South Oaks Gambling Screen
SRI	serotonin reuptake inhibitor
SSDI	Social Security Disability Insurance
SSI	Supplemental Security Income
SSRI	selective serotonin reuptake inhibitor
STD	sexually transmitted disease
TARGET	Trauma Adaptive Recovery Group Education and Therapy
TB	tuberculosis
TCA	tricyclic antidepressant
TGs	triglycerides
THC	tetrahydrocannabinol
TIA	transient ischemic attack
TIPs	SAMHSA's Treatment Improvement Protocols
TREM	Trauma Recovery and Empowerment Model
TSH	thyroid stimulating hormone
UT	urine toxicology
VAS	Visual Analogue Scale
WBC	white blood cell
WCDVS	Women, Co-Occurring Disorders, and Violence Study
WIC	Women, Infants, and Children

Index

[References are to pages.]

Continuing Education and Clinical Skills Examination Answer Sheet

Name: _____ Date: _____

Address: _____

Substance Dependence and Co-Occurring Psychiatric Disorders: Best Practices for Diagnosis and Clinical Treatment

Continuing Education and Clinical Skills Examination

ANSWER SHEET

Chapter 1
1. ____
2. ____
3. ____

Chapter 2
4. ____
5. ____
6. ____

Chapter 3
7. ____
8. ____
9. ____

Chapter 4
10. ____
11. ____
12. ____

Chapter 5
13. ____
14. ____
15. ____

Chapter 6
16. ____
17. ____
18. ____

Chapter 7
19. ____
20. ____
21. ____

Chapter 8
22. ____
23. ____
24. ____

Chapter 9
25. ____
26. ____
27. ____

Chapter 10
28. ____
29. ____
30. ____

Chapter 11
31. ____
32. ____
33. ____

Chapter 12
34. ____
35. ____
36. ____

Chapter 13
37. ____
38. ____
39. ____

Chapter 14
40. ____
41. ____
42. ____

Chapter 15
43. ____
44. ____
45. ____

Chapter 16
46. ____
47. ____
48. ____

Chapter 17
49. ____
50. ____
51. ____

Chapter 18
52. ____
53. ____
54. ____

Chapter 19
55. ____
56. ____
57. ____

Chapter 20
58. ____
59. ____
60. ____

Mail the answer sheet to the following address:
The Addiction Institute of New York
St. Luke's and Roosevelt Hospitals
Attention: CECSE
1000 Tenth Avenue
New York, New York 10019

CUT HERE